WEYERHAEUSER ENVIRONMENTAL BOOKS

WILLIAM CRONON, EDITOR

Weyerhaeuser Environmental Books explore human relationships with natural environments in all their variety and complexity. They seek to cast new light on the ways that natural systems affect human communities, the ways that people affect the environments of which they are a part, and the ways that different cultural conceptions of nature profoundly shape our sense of the world around us. A complete listing of the books in the series appears at the end of this book.

Marsha Weisiger's work on *Dreaming of Sheep in Navajo Country* has benefited from the support and intellectual community of the William P. Clements Center for Southwest Studies, Southern Methodist University.

Dreaming of Sheep

MARSHA WEISIGER

UNIVERSITY OF WASHINGTON PRESS

in Navajo Country

FOREWORD BY WILLIAM CRONON

SEATTLE AND LONDON

Dreaming of Sheep in Navajo Country is published with the assistance of a grant from the Weyerhaeuser Environmental Books Endowment, established by the Weyerhaeuser Company Foundation, members of the Weyerhaeuser family, and Janet and Jack Creighton.

Additional support was received from the William P. Clements Center for Southwest Studies, Southern Methodist University.

© 2009 by the University of Washington Press
Printed in the United States of America
Designed by Pamela Canell
Maps by Barry Levely
12 11 10 09   5 4 3 2 1

All rights reserved. No part of this publication may be reproduced or transmitted in any form or by any means, electronic or mechanical, including photocopy, recording, or any information storage or retrieval system, without permission in writing from the publisher.

University of Washington Press
P.O. Box 50096, Seattle, WA 98145 U.S.A.
www.washington.edu/uwpress

Library of Congress Cataloging-in-Publication Data
Weisiger, Marsha.
Dreaming of sheep in Navajo country / Marsha Weisiger. — 1st ed.
p. cm. — (Weyerhaeuser environmental books)
Includes bibliographical references and index.
ISBN 978-0-295-98881-8 (hardback : alk. paper)
1. Navajo Indians—Land tenure.
2. Navajo Indians—Domestic animals.
3. Land use—Navajo Indian Reservation—History.
4. Navajo Indian Reservation—History. I. Title.
E99.N3W437 2009   979.1004'9726—dc22   2008050290

The paper used in this publication is acid-free and 90 percent recycled from at least 50 percent post-consumer waste. It meets the minimum requirements of American National Standard for Information Sciences—Permanence of Paper for Printed Library Materials, ANSI Z39.48-1984. ∞ ♻

Chapter 5 appeared in somewhat different form in *Journal of the Southwest* 46 (2004): 253–82. © 2004 by the Arizona Board of Regents

Chapter 9 appeared in somewhat different form in *Western Historical Quarterly* 38 (2007): 431–49. © 2007 by Western History Association

To Tim

When I go to sleep I dream about herding the sheep. I know as I get older I'll do what others have done. I'll start imagining all of that in my mind even during the day. People do that when they get real old. They talk about the sheep day and night, all the time. It's like they forget everything else except the sheep. That's because that's all we were raised with, that's all we did—take care of the sheep.

—'Asdzą́ą́ Tsosie *(Slim Woman) (quoted in Mitchell 2001)*

CONTENTS

FOREWORD · Sheep Are Good to Think With, by William Cronon ix

Preface xv

Acknowledgments xxi

PROLOGUE · A View from Sheep Springs 3

PART 1 · FAULT LINES 15

1 · Counting Sheep 17

2 · Range Wars 31

PART 2 · BEDROCK 61

3 · With Our Sheep We Were Created 63

4 · A Woman's Place 79

PART 3 · TERRA FIRMA 103

5 · Herding Sheep 105

6 · Hoofed Locusts 128

PART 4 · EROSION 153

7 · Mourning Livestock 155

8 · Drawing Lines on a Map 181

9 · Making Memories 202

EPILOGUE · A View from the Defiance Plateau 228

Notes 245

Glossary 337

Plants 339

Bibliography 341

Index 377

FOREWORD

Sheep Are Good to Think With

BY WILLIAM CRONON

In 1962, the French anthropologist Claude Lévi-Strauss introduced the notion that all manner of plants, animals, objects, and things are *"bonnes à penser"* (good to think with). This phrase has since become among the most suggestive and celebrated ideas in modern social science. Its core insight is that human beings interact with the world around them, not as a vast collection of individual material objects but instead as a complex, multilayered, endlessly rich web of symbolic meanings that exist only in relationship with each other. For us, a rock is never just a rock, a tree a tree, a cow a cow. Instead, we label these things with words whose denotations and connotations of similarity and difference become the raw materials from which we create the metaphors and narratives we use to construct our identities and cultures—and thereby navigate our lives. And because different people in different times and places have thought so differently about things like rocks or trees or cows, environmental histories of these things must also be cultural histories of the changing ideas and relationships human beings have woven around them.

In her brilliant new book *Dreaming of Sheep in Navajo Country*, Marsha Weisiger takes a notorious episode in twentieth-century American Indian history and demonstrates the value of using sheep to rethink its many meanings. The broad outlines of the story are familiar enough. In the

1930s, New Deal scientists and managers became persuaded that a drought was amplifying the effects of severe overgrazing on the lands of the Navajo Reservation to produce what they viewed as an environmental catastrophe. Navajo sheep and goats, the New Dealers believed, had stripped grass and other vegetation from lands that now lacked the root systems that had formerly held loose desert soils in place. Catastrophic erosion in a growing network of gullies was the seemingly inevitable result, so that immense quantities of soil and sand were being swept downstream into the Colorado River. There—to the alarm of government engineers—they threatened the long-term viability of the new Boulder Dam, then under construction south of Las Vegas. To save the dam and the soon-to-be-named Lake Mead that would be created behind it—and just as important, the New Dealers thought, to save the Navajos from themselves—the Bureau of Indian Affairs ordered a "livestock reduction" that ultimately slaughtered hundreds of thousands of sheep, goats, and cattle that were the mainstays of the Navajo economy and of Navajo cultural life. More than half the herd was destroyed as a result. Using elaborate quota systems to allocate grazing rights on the reservation, government managers put into effect regulatory arrangements for fitting herds to the "carrying capacity" of the land that remain in place to this day.

By one reading, this is a heroic tale of progressive conservation at its best: enlightened managers, relying on insights derived from modern science, tried to solve a severe environmental problem using governmental power to create more sustainable relationships among people and land, animals and grazing resources. But by another reading—a reading shared by many of the Diné, as the Navajos call themselves—this is among the great tragedies of American Indian history. Arrogant bureaucrats, with supreme confidence that they knew better than the Diné themselves how to manage the herds and resources of the tribe's homeland, wreaked havoc on a people's economy, ecosystems, and culture.

Stated so starkly, these would seem to be two irreconcilable narratives. Indeed, much of the writing about this episode leans strongly toward one or the other interpretation in explaining the events that unfolded on the Navajo Reservation in the 1930s. Yet history is rarely so simple. Marsha Weisiger's remarkable achievement in this book, over and over again, is to refuse to make obvious choices between competing narratives. This is partly because she works so hard to understand the world views of the chief actors in this drama in an effort to understand what motivated them to act as they did. Even more importantly, though, she seeks to put into practice the Lévi-Straussian insight that "sheep are good to think with"—for, in fact, New Deal bureaucrats and Diné grazers thought about sheep in radically different ways.

To take an obvious example, one might say of the Diné that there are few indigenous peoples in the western hemisphere who have more thoroughly embraced a non-native species to radically reinvent their own culture. Perhaps only the adoption of the horse by Plains Indian peoples comes close. Environmental historians and scientists "know" that sheep were brought to the Americas by Spanish and Portuguese explorers and that the eventual adoption of sheep by the Diné in the sixteenth, seventeenth, and eighteenth centuries left almost no part of Navajo culture untouched or untransformed. Imagine the Diné today without woolen blankets or mutton or the pastoral grazing traditions that have been at the core of Diné family and tribal life. Yet Weisiger is far from content to let the story stand there, for the Diné's own creation narratives—including the famed Blessingway—offer starkly contrasting accounts of that people's emergence amid the four sacred mountains that still mark the boundaries of their homeland. In the Blessingway, sheep and other livestock were created right here, on this land, at the same moment that the Diné were emerging as a people. By this telling, sheep and goats and cattle are not Eurasian species brought by invading conquistadors, but products of the same sacred narrative that gave birth to the Diné and their homeland. From the moment of their emergence, this is where these people and their animals have always been.

Readers of the preceding paragraph will have their own biases about which of these two stories is most likely to be "true." One will seem factual; the other, more likely, a fairy tale. Difficult though it may be to accept, not everyone will make the same choice about which is which. Still, this is not Weisiger's main reason for asking readers to consider the two sets of stories together. For her, these different views of land, people, and animals offer vital keys to the misunderstandings that explain why the events of the 1930s unfolded as they did. Because New Deal scientists and managers failed to ask themselves what sheep meant to the Diné—to their families, their economy, their culture, their way of life—they made choices that had devastating consequences for Navajo families.

That these consequences were unanticipated and came as a surprise to the New Dealers—who genuinely thought they were doing good by bringing progress and modern range management to an unenlightened people—demonstrates that it never occurred to them to "think with sheep." For these managers, sheep were just unwitting biological agents of the ecological destruction of desert grasslands. They never recognized the extent to which Navajos and sheep were part of an integrated cultural universe in which the destruction of one could hardly help but have tragic consequences for the other. Had they paid more attention to the Blessingway and recognized that the Diné and the sheep had been created together—as in a profoundly true sense they had been, no matter which history one might prefer for how their lives came to be so deeply commingled—these government managers might have been more cautious about the policies they so confidently put into place in the name of progressive conservation.

But Marsha Weisiger's arguments go far deeper than asking us to take seriously the sacred creation narratives of the Diné. Among the most innovative contributions of this book is its insistence that we cannot understand the impact of Navajo livestock reduction without recognizing the radically different relationships to animals of Diné women compared with Diné men. Most documents about the herd reductions, whether created by the New Dealers or by the Navajo Tribal Council, were written by and about men. And yet it was Navajo women who owned most of the sheep—and, strikingly, virtually *all* of the goats, an organism whose significance doesn't become fully visible until one starts seeing the Diné landscape through the eyes of women. It was Navajo women who did the weaving that produced Navajo rugs for sale in commercial markets, and it was Navajo women who to a considerable degree controlled access to Navajo grazing land. Weisiger's close attention to facts like these, and to the environmental and cultural relationships they imply, makes this book one of the most important contributions any scholar has yet made to the full integration of questions about gender into a work of environmental history.

In an effort to forge a multigendered, multicultural understanding of a tragic environmental episode, Marsha Weisiger rethinks that episode through the lenses of Enlightenment science, progressive optimism, Diné culture, the gendered experiences of women and men, and—not least—the changing web of material and symbolic relationships within which animals and people occupy their shared landscapes. *Dreaming of Sheep in*

Navajo Country points in myriad exciting ways toward what we can expect from the next generation of environmental historical scholarship. By showing so vividly the understandings we gain if only we remember how good it is to think with sheep—along with all the other creatures and objects and places and peoples that constitute this shared world of ours—it reveals deep truths not just about sheep, but about ourselves as well.

PREFACE

For a time, I used to travel each year from my home near Phoenix to the San Juan River in southern Utah, a journey that took me through the western part of the Navajo Reservation. Framed by my car window, windswept moonscapes layered in pink, salmon, and gray, volcanic pinnacles, and sandstone spires broke the monotony of the vermillion tablelands, speckled with gray-green shrubs. As I gazed across the breathtaking yet bleak landscape, I sometimes wondered what part the Navajos had played, if any, in creating such desolation. *Dreaming of Sheep in Navajo Country* seeks to answer that question. An environmental history, this book explores the dynamic relationship between livestock grazing, environmental change, cultural identity, gender, and memory during the New Deal era of the 1930s and its aftermath. I argue that although Navajos indeed ravaged the range by allowing their livestock to overgraze, federal officials made matters worse. Soil conservationists and policymakers with the Bureau of Indian Affairs, led by Commissioner John Collier, ignored the deeper cultural meanings of livestock and failed to treat Navajos, especially women, as real partners in developing and implementing a workable conservation program. The result has been a collective memory of trauma, a long-lasting rejection of range conservation policies, and a chronic wasteland.

When I began this research, my initial questions went to the heart of the conservation program: Did Diné (their name for themselves) overgraze the range, or was the problem actually drought, as many Diné maintained? With some notable exceptions, most scholars have *assumed* that overgrazing desiccated the land, based both on the word of New Deal scientists and on the scholars' own observations of the current landscape. So I began with the contrary assumption that the Diné were right and searched for evidence that might prove or disprove that claim. After a good deal of digging, I concluded that the issue was more complicated than some have thought. A brutal combination of climatic change, which began in the late nineteenth century, and overgrazing by Diné livestock led to the accelerated erosion that prompted the New Deal program.[1] At the same time, I came to realize that the New Deal scientists and policymakers, as well as the Diné, bore responsibility for current conditions. The New Dealers gave insufficient attention to the cultural, economic, and ecological implications of their conservation program and dismissed those Navajos who tried to help them create a more culturally coherent approach. In consequence, they exacerbated the crisis. New Dealers and Diné, thus, shared complicity and culpability for an increasingly depleted land.[2]

I had been curious at the outset about what Diné women had thought about the conservation program. As a former anthropology student, I was vaguely aware that Navajos had historically lived within a matricentered web of relationships. And yet the scholarship on the New Deal program focused largely on the response of the Navajo Tribal Council and other male political leaders. So I wondered: How did New Deal range policies impinge on women? Did women figure significantly in the rebellion against the New Deal program? I discovered that livestock reduction threatened women's economic autonomy by nearly eradicating their flocks of goats, destroying their means to support their families with their sheep, and restricting their use of traditional grazing areas. And so women, like men, fought back against Collier's conservation program and helped shape the memories that continue to cloud modern efforts to manage the range.

A number of historians have already narrated the story of livestock reduction on the Navajo Reservation. Donald Parman, in *The Navajos and the New Deal*, argued that stock reduction, though necessary, brought excessive trauma to the Navajos largely because of poor planning and because Collier was only dimly aware of just how attached the Navajos were to their sheep, goats, and horses. An excellent administrative history written in the 1970s during the early emergence of ethnohistory, his book gave uncommon attention to the Navajo perspective. Yet it left the impression that opposition to the conservation program emerged primarily because a handful of Navajo men fanned the flames while acting out their political and personal rivalries.³ Even more mindful of Navajo culture and ideas was Richard White's masterful book, *The Roots of Dependency*, which persuasively argued that stock reduction transformed the once self-supporting Navajos into an impoverished "colonial appendage." That decline was all the more reprehensible, White wrote, because a concern for Boulder Dam, rather than the Navajos themselves, had given the program its urgency. Fearing that silt from the eroding Navajo Reservation might destroy the dam's ability to power the Los Angeles economy, the government had sacrificed the Navajos' way of life.⁴

The Diné have their own interpretation of these events, perhaps best articulated in Ruth Roessel and Broderick Johnson's provocatively titled *Navajo Livestock Reduction: A National Disgrace*. Although this compilation of oral histories offers no formal thesis, the Diné who were interviewed argue, collectively, that the federal program was not only unjust, but also unnecessary, indeed incomprehensible. According to their recollections, the land had been laden with lush vegetation until the conservationists arrived. And that was not mere coincidence, they insisted. The chronically droughty and degraded land was the product of stock reduction itself, for the cruel and cavalier slaughter of sheep and goats had angered the Diyin Dine'é, the Holy People who controlled the rain.⁵ We could simply dismiss these recollections as faulty, nostalgic, angry, or self-serving. But if we really want to uncover the truth about this pivotal era, we must pay careful attention to what Diné have to tell us. Their recollections suggest a far more complicated story than it would seem at first glance. This painful chapter in Diné history was not a simple matter of factional politics, ecological naïveté, or resistance to economic dependency.

If we really want to understand the complexities of this revealing episode, we must also pay attention to the central part that women played in this story. In her provocative essay, "Man and Nature! Sex Secrets of Environmental History," the historian Virginia Scharff challenges us to consider that environmental history will never quite explain relationships between humans and nature until we "take seriously ... and understand women's lives and attitudes and work and the environmental consequences of what women do."⁶ *Dreaming of Sheep in Navajo Country* takes up Scharff's challenge by examining the ways in which Diné women stood at the center of ecological transformations on the Colorado Plateau. In so doing, I join a small but growing group of environmental historians who have placed women at the center of their stories.⁷

At the same time, by putting women with men on center stage, this book attempts to rethink Navajo history. The historian Peter Iverson wrote in *The Navajo Nation* that to understand Navajo history one first must develop that history as Navajos perceived it.⁸ Such an insight should have led to a fundamental reconception of the Navajo experience, a new angle of vision examining the ways in which Euro-American conquest collided with the matricentered structure of Navajo society. And yet, with a few recent exceptions, including the work of historians Jennifer Nez Denetdale and Colleen O'Neill and anthropologist Kathy M'Closkey, women remain largely absent from historical pictures of Navajo life.⁹ This neglect of women has several causes. Men struck the most public poses, as warriors, raiders, and intercultural mediators. And men at Spanish missions, military forts, and federal agencies—that is, those who created much of the historical record—looked through a lens shaped by their own world, dominated by men. Historians using the same viewfinder have yet to incorporate fully into their analysis the fact that women exercised a good measure of control over the means of production by owning major portions of the family sheep herds and all of the goats, weaving for commercial markets, and controlling access to grazing land. As it turns out, when we refocus our attention to include women, the picture of this most tumultuous time becomes more richly textured, more reflective of the lived experience.

This story also expands our understanding of "environmental justice" by illustrating how well-meaning efforts to conserve Navajo land and natural resources led to social and economic devastation. We tend to use the term "environmental justice" to refer to the recent political movement to fight for poor and marginalized racial and ethnic communities that bear the burden of our society's toxic wastes and other environmental hazards.¹⁰ But noxious neighborhoods are not the only sites of environmental injustice. Today the indigenous peoples of the American West and Nuevo Mexicanos define their struggles with the federal agencies that dispossessed them from their lands and livelihoods, often in the name of conservation, as battles for environmental justice.¹¹ This story of the Navajos and the New Dealers seeks to complicate our understanding of those struggles. It exemplifies, moreover, a fundamental tenet of the environmental justice movement: that human societies are intrinsic parts of ecosystems and that, in the words of sociologist Dorceta Taylor, "the health of one depends on the health of the other."[12]

The environmental justice movement tends to define race, class, and, to some extent, ethnicity and gender as its focus. But notions of race and ethnicity are also intricately interwoven with culture. And so this story attempts to rethink environmental and Navajo history by taking culture seriously. By "culture," I mean the ideas a people share that give order and meaning to their world and shape their behavior, social relationships, technology, and material lives. Cultures and their environments are interactive and reciprocal; each shapes the other. Diné viewed themselves and nature through a very different lens than we *bilagáana*, or Anglo-Americans, do. And while I do not fully explain those differences in all their complexity, I try to give a sense of how cultural understandings of the world shaped Diné responses to the New Deal conservation program.

I have organized the book to foreground cultural and ecological issues. After introductory chapters that lay out my argument and foreshadow the story, I contrast the cultural differences between Diné and New Deal conservationists. Next, I explain two foundations of Diné culture in the 1930s: their pastoral ethnic identity, as articulated in their traditional stories, and the significance of women within their society. I then step back in time to trace the rise of Diné pastoralism in the eighteenth and nineteenth centuries and the ecological effects of burgeoning numbers of sheep, goats, and horses, owned not only by Diné but also by the Anglo and Hispano ranchers with whom they competed for land. I spend the rest of the book describing the implementation of the conservation program, the resistance it engendered, and the implications of that resistance for Navajo land and life.

The struggles over the Navajo range echo in conflicts that continue throughout the American West, where some 70 percent of the land is used for livestock grazing.[13] At their essence, these battles reflect two conflicting ways of thinking about the land. Environmentalists conceive it as an ecological system that can best be understood through and sustained by science and technology. Ranchers view it as the substance of their families' livelihoods and the place of their dreams. Both ranchers and environmentalists like myself must strive for sustainable ways of managing the range. To do that, we must find ways to treat each other with respect as partners in creating ecologically, economically, and culturally coherent approaches to conservation. The fate of the land depends on it.

ACKNOWLEDGMENTS

Historians often maintain a fiction that their work is a solitary endeavor, but truth be told, almost all histories are collaborative to some degree. This one is perhaps more of a group effort than most. It began life as a doctoral dissertation, and I remain deeply indebted to those who guided me in that work and set a high standard by their own scholarly and ethical examples. I am especially grateful to Bill Cronon, an extraordinary mentor, teacher, and scholar. He gave me the freedom to follow my own path but wisely pulled me back when I seemed in danger of wandering off cliffs. I thank him for guiding me through thickets of thorny sources and clarifying my often muddy thinking. His wisdom, humanity, and commitment to helping me fulfill my own goals leave me with debts I can never fully repay. Linda Gordon proved to be the tough critic that I hoped she would be and helped to sharpen my analysis. Her model of intellectual honesty never ceases to astonish me, and I am richer for having worked with her. Art McEvoy offered useful advice, guidance, thoughtful insights, and theoretical grounding at key points in the project. I am especially grateful to him for pointing out the importance of collective memory to my story. Nancy Langston and Matt Turner helped me avoid egregious errors in my discussions of range ecology and pastoralism. Earlene Parr, my high school anthropology and history teacher, first sparked my interest in culture, and to the extent that this work brings together my twin passions for history and anthropology, it owes much to her example.

This history, moreover, could not have been written without a wealth of information created through the hard work of a multitude of scholars, and it seems appropriate to acknowledge them beyond the standard practice of citing their work in footnotes. J. Lee Correll made my initial immersion into early Navajo history less daunting with his compendium of early documents, published in multiple volumes under the title *Through White Men's Eyes: A Contribution to Navajo History*, and Peter Iverson's *Diné: A History of the Navajos* offered a perceptive and much-needed historical overview just in time for me to profit from it. I owe a huge debt, especially, to the work of Richard White, Donald Parman, Ruth Roessel, and Broderick Johnson, all of whom stimulated my initial thoughts about Navajo environmental history.

I would be terribly remiss if I did not also acknowledge my debt to the generosity of those Diné who shared their stories with ethnographers and oral historians or wrote them down themselves. Profound thanks goes particularly to Kay Bennett (Kaibah), Curly Tó Aheedlíinii (River Junction Curly), Hataałii Nez (Tall Chanter), Left Handed, Slim Curly, Tall Woman (Rose Mitchell), and Frank Mitchell. I hope that I have not done violence to the meanings they intended to impart.

A number of ethnographers and archaeologists, moreover, have unearthed information that informed my grasp of the larger context within which these events transpired. Patrick Hogan, Michael Marshall, and Ron Towner led the way among archaeologists in rethinking early Navajo history, and others working on the lengthy archaeological projects on Gallegos and Black mesas contributed measurably to my understanding of the Navajo past. David Aberle, David Brugge, Charlotte Frisbie, Berard Haile, Louise Lamphere, Gladys Reichard, Mary Shepardson, and Gary Witherspoon have devoted their lives to studying and writing about Navajo life and thought; they often focused on women when others ignored them, and my interpretation of events would not have been possible without their insights.

Several archaeologists also helped me to see the lay of the land and the ways in which Navajos have used it by taking me on incredible tours of Dinétah, Canyon del Muerto, and Chaco Canyon. Jim Copeland with the federal Bureau of Land Management, Doug Dykeman and Jeff Wharton with the Farmington office of the Navajo Nation Archaeology Department, Scott Travis at Canyon de Chelly National Monument, and G. B.

Cornucopia at Chaco Culture National Historic Park were remarkably generous in giving me full days of their time to show me some truly special places. I will never forget the thrill of looking out over the landscape through the loophole of an eighteenth-century fortress, nor the spectacle of the summer solstice from a Diné sun marker in Chaco Canyon. Aside from the sheer exhilaration of those experiences, however, they offered important perspectives about Diné land use and history that archaeological reports alone could never convey. Larry Vogler and Kris Langenfeld with the Navajo Nation Archaeology Department, Tara Travis with Canyon de Chelly National Monument, and Patrick Hogan offered valuable insights regarding Navajo archaeology and land use.

I must express my gratitude especially to a number of range managers, ecologists, and other wise people who took time to help me better understand Navajo land use issues and the ecology of the Colorado Plateau. Thomas Swetnam, director of the Laboratory of Tree-Ring Research at the University of Arizona, helped me to understand and interpret the climate data recorded in tree rings (published on the website of the National Oceanic and Atmospheric Administration), thereby clarifying my picture of landscape change. Rick Tafoya, formerly with the Natural Resources Conservation Service at St. Michaels, was especially generous in teaching this novice the basics of range ecology, taking me out on a mock plant inventory, and inviting me to accompany him to a range-management workshop at Crownpoint. Jerry Thompson, also once with the NRCS at St. Michaels, taught me important lessons on reading the land during a tour that included the historic Mexican Springs Demonstration Area, and Ralph Goh of that agency offered valuable observations about the history of Diné relations with their environment. Geno Bahe took me and others on an awe-inspiring trip through Navajoland, including Monument Valley and the Rainbow Plateau. Casey Begay, formerly with the Navajo Nation Department of Agriculture; Jon Martin and Steve Wangemann, both with the Bureau of Indian Affairs, Department of Natural Resources in Gallup; and Virginia Yazzie-Ashley of the United States Forest Service provided me with information and shared their perspectives on past and current range issues. Nelson Roanhorse, of the BIA's Department of Natural Resources in Fort Defiance, read a portion of the manuscript and discussed current range issues with me at length. Tom Shirley, Wallace Tsosie, and other members of the Fort Defiance Soil and Water Conservation District allowed me to observe a meeting and discussed their concerns and viewpoints with me. Reldon Beck of New Mexico State University; Kris Havstad with the Jornada Experimental Range; Nathan Sayre, now at the University of California, Berkeley; Joe Truett, biologist for the Ted Turner ranches in New Mexico; Bill deBuys, creator of the Valle Grande Grassbank; Mac Donaldson of the Empire Ranch; and Jim Sachse helped me to understand some of the complexities of range ecology and range management. I also thank the students in my Southwest Environmental History class for enthusiastically traveling with me across New Mexico to gain a better understanding of grasslands ecosystems.

Many other people helped me in crafting this work. Most importantly, I want to thank my former colleagues at the University of Wisconsin–Madison. Milford Muskett helped me conceive this project and offered encouragement and insight. Lynne Heasley, Jared Orsi, Bill Philpott, Louise Publos, and Greg Summers read most of the first draft and gave me perceptive criticism, editorial advice, moral support, and friendship over cups of coffee and tea and pints of ale. Katie Benton-Cohen, Ned Blackhawk, Jeanne Boydston, Flannery Burke, Joe Hall, Zoltan Grossman, Abby Markwyn, and Cindy Poe all read portions of the work and provided helpful criticism and encouragement. Thomas Andrews, Sarah Fatherly, Cynthia Milton, Hannah Nyala West, Bethel Saler, Lisa Tetrault, and Jules Unsel helped shape my analysis. Jarno Arnovich, Barb and Neil Howells, and Gene Mitchell offered unflagging support. No one could ask for a better group of friends and colleagues.

A number of other scholars helped me, as well, with generous gifts of their time and expertise. Tom Hagen initiated this odyssey by introducing me to the history of the Navajo New Deal, and he kindly gave me a copy of an important congressional hearing. Louise Lamphere was generous with her research files. Peter Iverson encouraged and steered me toward important sources at the National Archives and Records Administration center in Laguna Niguel. Rick Hendricks generously read most of the Spanish and Mexican documents cited in this book, corrected or verified the English translations I relied on, and helped rectify misinterpretations that appeared in an earlier published version of chapter 5. Marc Simmons provided me an early Spanish document I could not have seen otherwise. I also thank Tom Dunlap, Gunlög Fur, Joan Jensen, Margaret Jacobs, Colleen O'Neill, Jacki Rand, Mary Rothschild, Gingy Scharff, Elba Serrano, Chris Wobbe, Don Wolff, and my fellows with the Environmental Leadership Program, all of whom gave me support, insight, and sage advice at critical points in the development of this book.

A number of scholars read drafts of my manuscript and helped me shape the analysis and narration. Phil Deloria and Bill deBuys both read portions of my work during an early stage of research, and their comments helped me struggle with troublesome issues. Bill especially offered sharp criticism, pointed me toward important sources, and shaped my analysis and narration; though he may continue to disagree with my interpretation, I am grateful for his help. Of particular importance was an extraordinary workshop sponsored by the Clements Center for Southwest Research at Southern Methodist University, where Bill deBuys, Edward Countryman, David Edmunds, Peter Iverson, Sherry Smith, and Richard White offered valuable critiques that helped sharpen my interpretation. David Brugge read a draft with meticulous care and offered numerous corrections and suggestions for greater precision. Clarinda Begay, Jennifer Nez Denetdale, Bill Eamon, Peter Edward, Liz Horodowich, Margaret Malamud, Harley Shaw, and Louis Warren also generously helped hone the narrative. Ronald Maldonado, with the Navajo Nation Historic Preservation Department, read the manuscript as well. My editor, Marianne Keddington-Lang, provided uncommonly careful attention to my prose, and I thank my copyeditor, Amanda Gibson, for her excellent work. I, alone, of course, bear responsibility for any errors of fact or judgment.

Staff members at various archives and libraries contributed importantly to my research effort. Ann Massmann and Nancy Brown at the Center for Southwest Research, University of New Mexico, offered able assistance and patience with my voluminous photocopying requests. Karen Underhill and Brad Cole, with Special Collections at Northern Arizona University; the staff at the Rio Grande Historical Collections and Interlibrary Loan Services, both at New Mexico State University; and Todd Ellison with the Center of Southwest Studies at Ft. Lewis College offered exemplary research service. Diane Bird, Lou Haecker, Willow Powers, and Tim Seaman provided assistance at the New Mexico Laboratory of Anthropology, as did Roger Meyers at Special Collections, University of Arizona. I thank the staff at the National Archives headquarters in Washington, D.C., and College Park, but special mention for exceptional service goes to Lisa Gezelter, formerly at the archives' regional branch in Laguna Niguel, and Marene Baker at the regional branch in Denver. Thanks, too, go to the capable staff members who helped me at the Navajo Nation Records Management Center; the New Mexico State Records Center and Archives; the Arizona Department of Library, Archives, and Public Records; the Arizona Collections, Arizona State

University; the Arizona Historical Society Library in Tucson; the Arizona State Museum Archives; the Museum of Northern Arizona; and Fort Sumner State Monument. I am also grateful to Alexander Leighton and Evon Vogt for giving me permission to look at ethnographic records at Northern Arizona University and the New Mexico Laboratory of Anthropology.

None of my work at these archives would have been possible without generous financial support. Travel funds came from the Western History Association's Rundell Award, the Coordinating Council for Women in History's Berkshire Award, the American Philosophical Society, the University of Wisconsin–Madison history department, the Charles Redd Center for Western Studies at Brigham Young University, and both the College of Arts and Sciences and the Southwest and Border Cultures Institute at New Mexico State University. Jeff Dean, formerly of the Wisconsin Historical Society, employed me when I arrived in Madison, making it possible to begin my doctoral work. An American Fellowship from the American Association of University Women and a Star Grant from the Environmental Protection Agency supported me while I wrote the dissertation. The Carl B. and Florence E. King Fellowship in Southwest History at the Clements Center for Southwest Research, Southern Methodist University, gave me the opportunity to begin reshaping and expanding the manuscript into its present form. A fellowship from the National Endowment for the Humanities and support from the NMSU College of Arts and Sciences provided me with a one-year release from teaching, which made it possible, at long last, to complete the book.

Others subsidized my work with their hospitality. My greatest thanks, as usual, go to Peggy and John Dole and John and Jan Hays, who made being on the road feel more like coming home. Wade (and Amy Rose) Albrecht, Lisa and David Arnhart, Jon and Julie Swedenburg, Trish Ruppé, Marcy Roberts, and Sarah Weisiger all offered shelter and friendship. Gingy Scharff rescued me from a broken-down vehicle, and Sandra and Gary Haug showed me just how easy it is to turn strangers into good friends. Indeed throughout my travels, the generosity of people I'd only just met never ceased to amaze me. I especially thank Lorenda Joe, Dedra McDonald, Ben and Lil Pubols, Chrissey and George Sokol, and Virginia Yazzie-Ashley for opening their homes to me.

Last of all, I thank the love of my life, Timothy Cockrum—research assistant and travel partner—for turning dreams into reality. Tim, this book is for you.

DREAMING OF SHEEP IN NAVAJO COUNTRY

PROLOGUE

A View from Sheep Springs

In the summer of 1996, I drove my rusty Isuzu Trooper from Wisconsin to the Navajo Reservation, an arid yet awesome landscape of luminous red rock mesas and canyons, dried-up sagebrush and snakeweed, and vast expanses of naked sand.[1] Enclosing some 25,000 square miles of the Colorado Plateau, the reservation lies mainly in northeastern Arizona and spills over into northwestern New Mexico and southeastern Utah. Beyond those boundaries lies a mixed-use territory in which Navajo, federal, state, and privately owned lands form a patchwork nicknamed "the Checkerboard." Together the reservation and the Checkerboard form Diné Bikéyah, Navajo Country.

Like most *bilagáana*, or Anglos, when I thought of Navajo Country, I imagined the iconic spires of Monument Valley and Canyon de Chelly, the otherworldly badlands of the Bisti Wilderness and the Painted Desert, or the somnolent stretches of road through the shrub grasslands. I soon discovered that this land, with elevations ranging from 5,000 to 10,000 feet above sea level, is remarkably diverse.[2] A short drive across Narbona Pass through the heart of Navajo Country took me from the ponderosa pine forests, iris-dotted meadows, and lakes of the mountain highlands, through the piñon-juniper woodlands of the foothills, and on down to the shrub-grasslands of the San Juan basin. By "shrub grasslands," I mean the vegetation communities that geographers and ecologists variously call "desert grassland," "shrub-steppe," or "Great Basin scrub." Some are dominated by grasses, others by sagebrush, four-wing saltbush, shadscale, or greasewood, depending on soils, drainage, elevation, and other factors.[3] Historically, most Diné have used this ecological diversity to support a pastoral life, often in combination with dry-land farming, but there were also those who were primarily farmers, especially in the well-watered canyons de Chelly and del Muerto and on terraces of the San Juan River. I marveled at the farmers, who produce abundance in a stingy landscape. And yet my interests lay with the pastoralists.

I came here to study the infamous livestock reduction program of the 1930s, when the Bureau of Indian Affairs and the Soil Conservation Service slashed Navajo herds by half in an ultimately unsuccessful effort to conserve severely overgrazed rangelands.[4] Tragically, the livestock reduction program—no matter how well-intentioned—took a self-sufficient people, who had supported themselves for at least two centuries with pastoralism and agriculture, and turned them into dependents, who came to rely largely on welfare and what little wage labor they could find.[5]

As I checked into the Navajo Nation Inn that June evening, I was flabbergasted by the headline on that week's *Navajo Times* newspaper, which read: "Council Asking for Livestock Adjustment."[6] It seemed like déjà vu. That summer, the paper proclaimed, portions of Diné Bikéyah were experiencing the worst drought since the 1930s. Although that claim was hyperbole, extremely dry conditions led the Navajo Nation Council to declare a state of emergency and call on the Diné, as they refer to themselves, to reduce their numbers of cattle and sheep and thereby protect the land from further damage.[7]

Indeed, the land was in terrible shape. Driving along the highway, I saw a small flock of sheep by the road looking for all the world as though they were eating dirt. There wasn't a blade of grass anywhere, and the brush had shriveled. I came laden with vegetation field guides, hoping to study plant identification so that I might learn to "read the landscape" and thereby illuminate my understanding of environmental change. But the brush was so parched that it proved difficult to distinguish between woody plants such as sagebrush and greasewood.

Later, as I drove over Narbona Pass to the eastern edge of the Chuska Range, I looked out over Sheep Springs, once a favored winter grazing range. The view was deceptive. From a distance, the earth's pastel colors appeared postcard-pretty. But up close, the land looked as though it had been seared, the largely bare ground dotted with dried-up weeds and clumps of dormant bunch grasses. This was dry, desolate country.

Drought scorched the earth, but at the root of this barren landscape lay decades of overgrazing. Casey Begay, then head of the Navajos' grazing management office, pointed out that "you can tell when you come to reservation land because of the dust storms[,] and likewise, you can tell [w]hen you leave reservation land because you see grass."[8] Similarly, in a horseback tour of the Navajo range a month earlier, Albert Hale, president of the Navajo Nation, expressed shock at finding that overgrazing and drought had left some areas of the reservation completely denuded, dotted with dead and dying livestock. Rick Tafoya, a range specialist with the Natural Resources Conservation Service, observed that although there were still good grazing lands at higher elevations, the worst areas had deteriorated to a point that no one living today would ever see them healthy again.[9]

Navajo Nation officials characterized the situation as dire, which made the newspaper story about selling off livestock all the more interesting. In the first place, it emphasized that the council blamed drought, not overgrazing, for denuded lands. The original wording of the council's declaration referred to "depletion of range forage" as the cause of the emergency, but after a four-hour debate, council members changed the official rationale to read "drought conditions . . . caused by a lack of moisture." In the second place, instead of calling for "livestock reduction," government officials chose the euphemism "livestock *adjustment*," which bore a more ambiguous meaning. As I would later discover, New Deal policymakers, too, employed that euphemism in the latter years of its controversial conservation program. "Adjustment," by the way, said President Hale, merely meant that the Diné should comply with their grazing permits, and he emphasized that compliance would be voluntary.[10]

Complying with grazing permits was a step forward, and Diné stockowners lined up to sell thousands of animals in the largest reduction of livestock since the 1930s. But it seemed obvious to me that this land could no longer sustain the equivalent of 295,000 sheep, the number that range managers tallied. And I wasn't alone. A growing chorus of Diné environmentalists and officials charged that overgrazing was ruining the land without regard for future generations.[11] Ivan Joe, a Diné range specialist then working with the grassroots environmental group Diné CARE, told a reporter with the regional *High Country News* that it was time to address overgrazing. "Regardless of whether it's right or wrong politically," he said, "it's the right thing environmentally. Someone has to make a stand."[12]

But the Navajo council members—knowing well that enforcing grazing regulations could be "political suicide"—were skittish, and they weren't the only ones. When the council called on the BIA to oversee the so-called adjustment program, the agency balked. While the bureau was pleased to see tribal officials addressing range conditions, the last thing the agency wanted was to "be the 'bad guys' in the latest scenario to force the Navajos to reduce their livestock."[13]

A political cartoon in the *Navajo Times* captured the situation exquisitely. It depicted three men on horseback visiting a Navajo rancher. One wearing a traditional turquoise necklace and a hat marked "Prez" passed the buck, saying: "I can't tell him, you tell him!" The next man, whose hat bore the initials of the Navajo Nation Council, responded: "We can't tell him, you tell him!" Finally, an Anglo man with "BIA" on his hat gave in: "Well, alright, I'll tell him. . . . We want you to *adjust* your livestock." To this, the Navajo rancher protested: "You mean Livestock Reduction!!! No way, this is all I have!!" A corner of the cartoon featured two small stock-figures offering pointed commentary. One, a *hataałii*, or medicine man, prayed: "Lord! Help us get the evil out of government. . . ." The other, a coyote, exclaimed: "John Collie Days!"[14]

Clearly this new effort to reduce livestock herds on the reservation struck a nerve, sparking recollections of the 1930s and early 1940s, when John Collier, the commissioner of Indian affairs, embodied all that went wrong with the program to bring the numbers of goats, horses, and sheep into balance with the land's so-called carrying capacity. That New Deal program managed to cut the numbers of livestock in half, but it failed to stem the progress of desertification. Sixty years later, the memories of that era remained bitter, complicating ongoing efforts to conserve the land for future generations.

Collier and his men had felt compelled to decrease herds drastically because Diné had allowed their animals to overgraze the land, which, especially when coupled with climate change beginning in the late nineteenth century, acutely accelerated erosion. As early as the first decades of the 1900s, in fact, increasingly crowded flocks on the reservation—amplified by wealthy stockowners—and competition from Anglo-American and Hispanic ranchers on the reservation's fringes depleted forage, restructured plant communities, and allowed greasewood, snakeweed, and other unpalatable and sometimes toxic weeds to flourish. Some Diné discerned this

Jack Ahasteen's cartoon perceptively portrayed public sentiment when the Navajo Nation Council called for "stock adjustment" in June 1996. Courtesy *Navajo Times*.

degradation and called for the exclusion of competitors from the mixed-use Checkerboard and for expansion into new areas, much as ranchers have done throughout the history of the American West. Some called for the development of stock water so that poorly watered areas could be used for grazing. Others placed faith in their belief that the ceremonies that reenacted the creation of the earth could reestablish order in the natural world and restore *hózhǫ́*, or balance. Still more remained largely unaware of the altered landscape, in part because ecological change often occurs incrementally, escaping notice. Nonetheless, by the 1930s, the damage triggered by overgrazing and climate change could no longer be ignored.

Yet in their haste to respond to an environmental crisis, federal administrators and conservationists unwittingly made matters worse, both ecologically and culturally. With missionary zeal, they imposed on the Navajos an experimental program based on the emerging sciences of ecology and soil conservation, while disparaging local knowledge and ignoring the importance of long-established cultural patterns.[15] They refused to listen to Navajos' advice in implementing the livestock reduction program, restricted traditional seasonal movements of flocks across the land in a misguided effort to tie specific numbers of livestock to particular ranges, and developed new water sources, thereby opening relatively untouched tracts to grazing. Underlying these mistakes was the flawed concept of "carrying capacity," which conservationists treated as a fixed number, despite variable conditions.

Most significantly, the conservationists disregarded cultural issues. They dismissed Diné cultural understandings of nature, ignored the importance of pastoralism to Diné identity, overlooked the centrality of goat and sheep ownership to the autonomy of Diné women, and generally failed to include women in the decision-making. In slashing flocks, the New Dealers destroyed the local economy and pried at women's hold on their communal grazing lands. It comes as no surprise that Diné rejected the conservation program. Worse yet, the trauma of stock reduction etched deeply into the collective memory of Diné, so that even today, many view range-conservation programs with hostility or suspicion.

Elderly Diné still bitterly remember the wholesale slaughter of their animals during the New Deal era, so the reticence of political leaders to impose stock reduction in 1996 was understandable.[16] To be sure, in the 1930s, Diné experienced the New Deal program in different ways, depending on where they lived, their degree of geographical isolation, their social position, their wealth, their gender, their education, and so forth, and their *personal* memories reflect those differences. For some, livestock reduction had been an assault that "came suddenly, like a wind that rises with no warning."[17] They tended to recall the New Deal program as a bewildering reign of terror, one in which government butchers destroyed all that the Diné held dear. Thousands experienced the event as cataclysmic, a calamity from which they never recovered. Others recognized the need to decrease the size of herds; some even worked as range riders or interpreters for the Navajo Service, helped round up stock, and faced the opprobrium of their neighbors.[18] Different people told different stories about the stock reduction era. But the heavy-handedness with which the federal government carried out this program helped produce an overpowering *collective* memory of terror, betrayal, loss, and grief.[19]

The killing of goats and horses, especially, has colored memories of livestock reduction. The landscape itself offers grisly evidence of the program to halve the number of goats in 1934, with piles of bones in some locales adding veracity to the stories of mass slaughter. Pete Sheen, a Diné stockowner, recalled the scene in Kayenta, where range riders rounded up 3,000 goats and sheep into a corral and shot them. "I myself saw it happen right in the corral," he told a visitor in the 1970s. "Some of the bones still remain today, all piled up; and you still can see dried blood on a cliff" where they drove the animals and killed them.[20] Horse reduction, too, brought vivid memories. During the 1930s, some Diné in northern areas of the reservation refused to eliminate excess horses and openly rebelled against the distribution of grazing permits. Today these documents, which stockowners must still retain, stoke a collective memory of the years when men and women defiantly burned their permits and went to jail for exceeding their legal livestock limits.[21]

Navajo oral histories of this period, as historian Robert McPherson has pointed out, tend to emphasize certain narrative tropes. Rich vegetation carpets the earth until malicious range riders arrive and wantonly kill helpless animals in cold blood. Women weep, and their animals run around "crying for their mothers." Men feel powerless against the violence. And families are left destitute.[22] These stories have created a particular social memory of livestock reduction that elides the ecological crisis that the New Deal program hoped to address and continues to complicate government efforts to manage the range.[23] Ironically, then, one unfortunate consequence of the New Dealers' cultural blinders has been a chronically degraded landscape.

In the summers of 2002 and 2003, when I returned to the Navajo Nation, drought once again seared the land. On these trips, I chartered a small aircraft to take a birds-eye view of the reservation, just as the New Deal conservationists had done in some of the government's earliest use of aerial photography. I had been skeptical of this survey technique, since the photographs themselves seemed to capture only generalizations. But as I flew over Sheep Springs, the Chuskas, Black Mesa, Polacca Wash, and Navajo Mountain, I gained a landscape perspective that no one driving along the road or walking across the ground ever sees.

The view was sobering. Immense stretches of bare soil, studded here and there with clumps of vegetation, much of it snakeweed and other noxious plants, brought to mind the mystery that I try to solve in this book: Considering that New Deal conservationists managed to cut livestock numbers to well below the scientifically determined carrying capacity of the land, why is the reservation still in such bad shape? By 1945, only 477,200 sheep and their equivalent numbers of horses and cattle remained in Navajo Country, less than half the size of the herd at the beginning of Collier's campaign and a number that the conservationists thought the range could sustain, although overstocking continued to persist in a few areas.[24] Yet fifty years later, the available forage on the Navajo Nation seemed, if anything, in worse condition. What went wrong?

In part, it was because grazing eventually breached an ecological threshold, the point at which an ecosystem becomes irreversibly changed. As heavy grazing and periodic drought depleted grasses and opened bare spaces to wind and water erosion, the spread of woody plants and annual forbs (herbs other than grass) and the invasion of exotic vegetation forever altered the structure of plant communities. These alterations, along with a drop in the water table, a decrease in soil nutrients, and changes in the biological and chemical properties of the soils, brought a spiraling decline in the ability of the soils to produce their historical forage. By the late 1950s, after a decade of severe drought, much of the range had deteriorated to the point of no return.[25]

In part, it was because Diné population increase and the phenomenal growth of their herds collided against Euro-American expansion. The sustainability of pastoralism had depended on the periodic movement of the largest flocks across long distances, taking in a good deal of the southern Colorado Plateau. Encroaching Anglo and Hispanic ranchers refused to acknowledge the Navajos' prior claims to the land. And Diné shepherds, most of whom kept barely enough sheep and goats to feed their families, were unable and unwilling to adjust their herds to the crowding presence of those interlopers. By the early twentieth century, Diné pastoralism had become unsustainable.

In part, it was because of hubris. Both the New Dealers and the Diné had approached nature with utter certainty. One saw nature through the lens of science, the other through the metaphysical lens of their spiritual world and ceremonies. One had faith that science and engineering could revive Navajo grasslands. The other insisted that maladies other than livestock lay at the root of their problems and that ceremony and rain would restore hózhǫ́.[26] Neither understood nature completely, nor do we today. But ecologists now believe that nature does not conform to the static mechanical models that guided the New Deal conservationists, nor, for that matter, the spiritual models that informed the Diné. Nature, careful observation tells us, is characterized by change, contingency, complexity, and uncertainty.[27] And yet after more than four generations of research into the dynamics of rangeland ecosystems, the only thing that seems certain is that we are uncertain. Given the instability of our own knowledge, perhaps one of the lessons we can draw from this story is that we should approach the earth with humility.

In part, it was because of power. The New Dealers had the power to impose their views on the Navajos, and the Diné, as it turned out, had the power to resist. This story offers a cautionary tale about what can go wrong when those of us who care about the environment devise top-down, authoritative solutions without listening to those who are most affected and live in intimate contact with the land.[28] It is unclear whether a different approach with Diné men and women as full-fledged participants in the decision-making would have buffered the economic repercussions of livestock reduction, deep cuts that were after all necessary, or the erosive effects of the loss of herds on Diné lives. Probably not. But it is worth noting that both the Diné and the New Dealers believed in the so-called balance of nature, which one called hózhǫ́ and the other called equilibrium. Both believed that humans possessed the power to shape nature, for better or worse. Looking back on the political whirlwinds that arose during the drought of 1996, I wonder whether a truly collaborative approach might have produced a different set of memories, ones in which Diné and New Deal conservationists crafted a land ethic that embraced the mutual, though problematic, concept of balance.

One thing is certain: conserving the range was not simply an ecological problem; it was a cultural one, too. By the 1930s, livestock and pastoralism had become so intertwined with Diné life that the New Dealers could not unravel them neatly. And so, in cutting herds and restricting shepherds' movements across the land, conservationists unintentionally rent the fabric of Diné society, with profound consequences that would last more than a generation. In their myopic focus on restoring the land, New Deal conservationists lost sight of the fact that a truly sustainable relationship with the natural world requires an ethical relationship with the land, with those who people it, and with the cultures that give them meaning.

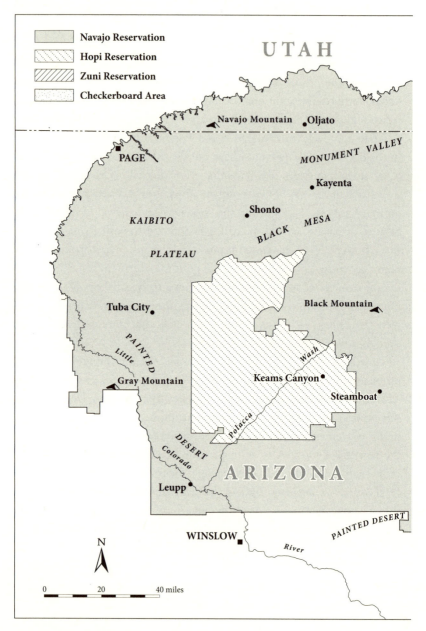

MAP 1 Navajo Country

PART 1 · *Fault Lines*

In 1932, on the eve of stock reduction, photographer Laura Gilpin captured the symbolic relationships between Diné mothers, children, and livestock. Courtesy Amon Carter Museum, Fort Worth, Tex., P1979.95.90.

1 · COUNTING SHEEP

It was a terrible sight where the slaughtering took place.... Near what is now the Trading Post was a ditch where sheep intestines were dumped, and these were scattered all over. The womenfolks were crying, mourning over such a tragic scene." Nearly four decades had passed since the 1930s, but still Howard Gorman could not erase the mental images of the calamitous period of Diné history known simply as "livestock reduction." A handsome, educated man and eloquent orator whose short dark hair and suits suggested a business executive, Gorman served as vice chairman of the Navajo Tribal Council from 1938 until 1942 and represented Ganado on the council for another three decades. More than most Diné, he had gained a broad perspective of the New Deal conservation program, for he often acted as a liaison between the Bureau of Indian Affairs and the Diné during that era, in part as assistant and interpreter for General Superintendent E. Reeseman Fryer, with whom he traveled across the reservation to explain the government's policies. Still, he recalled the era with anger and profound sadness. The butchery he witnessed at the Hubbell Trading Post near his home outside Ganado seared his memory.[1]

Billy Bryant bitterly remembered that time, too. At first, stock reduction had largely escaped his notice. The BIA launched the program in 1933, but it did not affect Bryant right away. He and his wife, who lived near the western boundary of the Hopi Reservation, went about their daily lives as they always had, herding their livestock, eating goat meat and mutton, and occasionally butchering a fat lamb for a feast with their relatives and friends. Then one day in October or November 1934, all that changed. Perhaps on that day Bryant saw a cloud of dust on the horizon announcing a visitor, who arrived to round up his wife's goats.[2] The government at first shipped herds of confiscated goats to various slaughterhouses, where the meat was canned for distribution to Navajo schools, but canneries quickly reached capacity, among other problems. So federal agents simply killed the goats while their owners looked on.[3]

Bryant would never forgive the cruelty and waste he witnessed on that terrible day in 1934, nor the powerlessness and indignity he felt at the hands of federal authorities. "Our goats . . . were put into a large corral where they were all shot down. Then the government men piled the corpses in a big heap, poured oil or gasoline on them and set fire to them. This happened just below Coal Mine Mesa at a place called Covered Spring. One still can see the white bones piled there. . . . Not only the goats, but the sheep, too, were slaughtered right before the owners. Those men took our meat off our tables and left us hungry and heartbroken."[4]

Sarah Begay recalled those nightmarish days, too. Out of the blue, some men rode up to her place in Narrow Canyon, near Kayenta, and killed her goats. "They did it right before my eyes. I was there with my husband. They took so many." Some were actually her mother's, and some belonged to her older sister. "'That is enough; it is enough,' I tried to say." But the men ignored her; they herded the goats to a place behind a bluff, where they beat them with clubs and shot them. "Some of the women were really crying," she remembered. "That is why we don't sleep well sometimes. All we think about is that."[5]

Like Begay and Bryant, hundreds of Diné women and men watched helplessly while federal agents destroyed their means of subsistence, their years of labor invested in building herds, their legacy to their children. But those scenes proved singularly traumatic for deeper, spiritual reasons, too. As Howard Gorman explained, "Some people consider livestock as sacred because it is life's necessity. They think of livestock as their mother."[6]

Livestock had long nurtured the Diné, and as their animals lay dying on the parched, naked ground, the Diné felt an overpowering sense of foreboding. Horses and sheep had been a gift, a life-sustaining blessing from the Diyin Dine'é, the spirits who manifested themselves as wind, thunder, rain, and sun.[7] The ruthless destruction of that gift was savage

Not all goats were slaughtered. Here Diné girls pose with their goats in Monument Valley, probably in the 1950s. Images such as this helped promote Arizona as an exotic land for tourists. Postcard by Petley Studios Inc. Author's collection, with permission of Vickie Petley.

and wasteful, but more than that, it showed profound disrespect for the Diyin Diné'é. Many felt, too, that such an act would disrupt the environmental balance articulated in the spiritual concept of hózhǫ́. It would bring disorder. There would be no more rain and the earth would wither.[8] And so, as soil conservationists introduced one plan after another to slash Navajo herds, the Diné became increasingly defiant. At stake, after all, was the land itself. Today, looking back on the 1930s, many Diné view the shriveled plants and the desiccated and often denuded landscape of Diné Bikéyah as a logical consequence of the federal stock reduction program.

And they are right.

One needn't even accept Diné causality to conclude that stock reduction laid waste the land. The government's wanton slaughter of livestock, without regard to how culturally and economically important sheep, goats, and horses were to Diné, hindered efforts to encourage Diné to manage their herds with an eye toward long-term stewardship of the range. As Howard Gorman observed, "The cruel way our stock was handled is something that should never have happened. The result has left the condition of the land and stock the way it is today. What John Collier did in stock reduction is something the people will never forget. They still consider him a No. 1 enemy of the Navajo people."⁹

John Collier never intended to become the enemy of the Navajos. First as a leading advocate for the Puebloan people of New Mexico and then as executive secretary of the American Indian Defense Association, he had championed the right of native people to self-determination, particularly their right to practice cultural traditions like pastoralism. He fought for religious freedom at Zuni and Taos pueblos and helped defeat efforts to alienate lands from all the New Mexico pueblos. While his battles on behalf of Puebloan people are better known, Collier also fought for Navajo land rights during the 1920s. Since 1871, when Congress abolished the practice of negotiating treaties with Indian tribes, presidents had created new reservations or expanded existing ones by executive order, and the legal title of those lands remained precarious, subject to congressional challenge. Collier lobbied for Navajo rights to royalties from oil and gas leases on their executive-order reservation lands and, in the process, helped confirm tribal title to them.[10]

Collier's commitment to native peoples grew out of his work as a social reformer. Born into a prominent family in Atlanta, Georgia, Collier knew privilege and tragedy. His mother died when he was only thirteen, and his father, a Progressive community leader, perished from a gunshot wound—perhaps an accident, perhaps suicide—less than three years later. Reeling from his father's death, Collier hiked through the southern Appalachians, where he found solace in nature and, as if by revelation, a calling to a life of social reform. At Columbia University, he read widely in philosophy, biology, sociology, and psychology, then traveled to Europe, where he met his first wife, Lucy Wood (whom he would divorce thirty-seven years later to marry the anthropologist Laura Thompson), and became captivated by the emerging collectivist movements.

Like many of his generation, Collier's misgivings about modernity—its industrialism, rationalism, and materialism and its gender and class hierarchies—drew him to other cultures in search of a more authentic existence. Upon returning to New York, he joined the staff of the People's Institute, where he developed youth programs to preserve immigrant traditions and foster a sense of multicultural community. At the same time, he became a regular visitor at Mabel Dodge's famous Greenwich Village salon, a forum for bohemian artists, socialists, feminists, and radical intellectuals. It was Dodge who introduced Collier to the world of native peoples, when she invited him and his family to her new home near Taos Pueblo. In the pueblos, he felt he finally found the cultural persistence and communalism he had been seeking among New York's immigrants. He subsequently moved to Taos to work for the General Federation of Women's Clubs in its mission to investigate and reform federal Indian policy.

Throughout the 1920s, Collier challenged the policy of cultural assimilation that had governed Indian affairs since the late nineteenth century. That policy had defined Indian tribes as "domestic dependent nations," whose relationship to the federal government, wrote Chief Justice John Marshall, was like "that of a ward to his guardian."[11] Guided by that paternalistic notion, the BIA endeavored in the decades after the Civil War to remake Indians into patriarchal families of Christian farmers, first on segregated reservations and later on individually allotted farms. Although this plan had grown out of a humanitarian reform movement to put an end to genocidal Indian wars, in hindsight the program was racist, even cruel. Many children, who became the focus of assimilation, were wrenched from their families and sent to often-distant boarding schools, where they were indoctrinated with Christianity; trained in agriculture, homemaking, and the mechanical arts; instructed in the English language; and punished for speaking their native tongue. Back home, their parents faced persecution for engaging in traditional ceremonial dances and other religious practices. In essence, advocates of assimilation pledged to eliminate what they called the "Indian Problem" through cultural genocide. As Senator John Logan of Illinois tellingly articulated it, the goal was to make them "as white men."[12]

The mishandling of tribal resources accompanied the assimilation program. Under the Dawes Severalty Act of 1887, the BIA broke up reservations into individual farms throughout much of the United States, with relatively little effort to prevent the loss of those allotted lands to predacious Euro-American settlers. Oftentimes, too, Indian agents misappropriated tribal funds earned through oil leases and land and timber sales instead of investing in the equipment and infrastructure that might have fostered economic self-sufficiency. Pervasive poverty thus plagued Indian Country.[13]

For the Diné, the worst had come in the years between 1863 and 1868 with their incarceration at the place they named Hwéeldi. Better known among Euro-Americans as the Bosque Redondo, Hwéeldi was established to punish Navajos for raiding New Mexican stockmen and to secure the western frontier during the Civil War. The nightmare began with a series of forced marches over hundreds of miles to Fort Sumner, which guarded a flat, almost treeless plain along the Pecos River in east-central New Mexico. The Long Walk, as it came to be called, was miserable for everyone, but all the more so for pregnant women, the sick, the elderly, and the very young. At Hwéeldi, the Diné, who were farmers as well as shepherds, found it impossible to cultivate the alkaline soil and combat the swarms of insects that consumed what little corn they managed to grow. Government rations were scanty and often spoiled, and the water was undrinkable. Many Diné died of starvation, exposure, disease, and heartache. Finally, in 1868, the Diné signed a treaty that allowed them to return to their homeland and take up stockraising and farming again. But they would never forget the trauma of those years, nor the power of the United States government.[14]

In the decades after their return from Hwéeldi, the Diné remained remarkably independent of the government, with which most had little contact. To be sure, they were not totally unaffected. Until the 1930s, the BIA divided Navajo Country into six jurisdictions, each with its own federal agent. Some of these men were conscientious custodians who guarded Navajos' interests, others were neglectful. All of them promoted the rapid development of livestock herds for economic self-sufficiency and assimilation into the larger capitalist society. By the end of the nineteenth century, Diné women wove blankets for a commercial market, and families bartered wool, pelts, and blankets for goods at trading posts. Nonetheless most Diné continued to live in traditional matrilocal communities of extended families, maintained age-old spiritual practices, and evaded efforts to educate their children or adopt market-oriented livestock husbandry, with little interference from the government. The far-flung pattern of rural residences across a rugged, largely roadless terrain made it impossible for agents to keep a tight rein.

Collier was particularly mindful of the Navajos' independence when in 1933 President Franklin Delano Roosevelt appointed him commissioner of Indian affairs and endorsed his agenda to replace paternalistic control and assimilationist goals with self-rule and cultural revival. Collier believed that native communities somehow captured a purer, more essential way of life. Native cultures, particularly that of the Navajos, he thought, retained an admirable authenticity. In the 1920s, he had written that the Navajos were paragons of self-sufficiency and cultural integrity, a beacon

Diné women who could afford them began purchasing sewing machines by the 1920s. Photographer Laura Gilpin snapped this hogan interior in Cove, Arizona, in 1954. Courtesy Amon Carter Museum, P1979.128.150.

for the larger society to follow. They had "preserved intact their religion, their ancient morality, their social forms and their appreciation of beauty." Despite major changes to their economy since their return from the Bosque Redondo, "their tribal, family and rich inner life remains unaltered," he acclaimed, "an island of aboriginal culture in the monotonous sea of machine civilization."[15]

Collier might well have become a hero to the Diné, for he waged a revolution in Indian policy during his administration. With his landmark legislation, the Indian Reorganization Act, he promoted a measure of self-government and economic development, restored to many tribes some of the reservation lands that had been parceled out under the Dawes Act, supplanted boarding schools with community day schools, fostered religious freedom, and laid the institutional groundwork for modern native nationalism.[16] He was no less a paternalist than his predecessors, but he took his custodial role seriously. Upon his appointment as commissioner, he announced: "I strongly believe that the responsibility of the United States, as guardian of the Indians, ought to be continued. . . . But the paramount responsibility is with the Indians themselves. Within the limits of a protecting guardianship, the power should be theirs. The race to be run is their race."[17] Collier would repeatedly assert that his mission was to unleash Indians so that they could realize their full potential. "The essence of the new Indian policy," he wrote, "is to restore the Indians to mental, physical, social, and economic health; and to guide them, in friendly fashion, toward liberating their rich and abundant energies for their own salvation and for their own unique contribution to the civilization of America."[18] With the Indian Reorganization Act as the centerpiece of his new program for Indian self-government and economic development, Collier sought to stage a dramatic reversal of a century of federal policy. In so doing, he cast Navajos in a central role. Navajos, in his view, were model Indians on which to drape his New Deal program.

But first, he felt compelled to stave off a looming environmental disaster: accelerated erosion brought on by decades of overgrazing. Each summer, violent rains washed eroded soils through a network of arroyos, the waters gushing into the San Juan and Little Colorado rivers then dumping their silt load into the turbulent Colorado River. Left unchecked, alluvium from the Navajo Reservation threatened to fill up the reservoir behind Boulder Dam, then under construction. That engineering marvel represented an enormous federal investment in the southwestern economy. The dammed waters promised to irrigate the Imperial Valley, sustain the development of Los Angeles, and provide electricity to the entire region. Silt washing down from the Navajo Reservation would eventually bring all that to a halt.[19]

Nonetheless, in Collier's mind, the threat to Boulder Dam was secondary: overgrazing and accelerated erosion endangered the very lives of the Navajos themselves. If the range continued to deteriorate, sheep and goats would starve, and ultimately, so would Navajos. As he admonished the Navajo Tribal Council, the grasses and soils were important "because if they go everything else goes—everything, including your own human life." Collier felt a strong moral obligation to protect the people of the Navajo Reservation, for legally they were wards of the federal government, and he was their guardian. To hesitate could mean the destruction of the range that sustained them. He felt he had to act quickly to restore the land, for the future of an entire people hung in the balance.[20]

His first move was to scale back the vast herds of Navajo livestock. Soil conservationists agreed that the Navajos had far more sheep, goats, and horses than the range could support, thereby impoverishing and killing vegetation, eroding topsoil, building sand dunes, and carving deep gullies.[21] To bring the number of animals into balance with the available forage, Collier instituted a somewhat disorganized program to reduce the number of livestock, a project that was implemented in two broad phases. The first professed to be largely voluntary and the second mandatory, but in the final analysis both proved coercive.[22]

The initial step took place during the winter of 1933–34. With funds from the Federal Emergency Relief Administration and the Agricultural Adjustment Administration, Collier's agents and local traders purchased more than 86,500 sheep from Navajo stockowners, somewhat fewer than the goal of 100,000 head. They dispatched their task with remarkable speed, and yet federal agents barely made a dent in the massive herd of 1.3 million sheep and goats, in part because Collier encouraged owners to sell their unproductive culls. Once the ewes had all lambed, the total herd rebounded, so that the sheep and goats counted at the dipping vats numbered only 7 percent fewer than the year before.[23] The conservationists were nearly back where they started.

In the face of such resilience, the commissioner redoubled his efforts to reduce the number of livestock. In 1934, he targeted goats, which conservationists argued were particularly destructive to the range and less marketable than sheep.[24] Federal stockmen hoped to purchase 150,000 goats and up to 50,000 sheep, and in fact, they acquired the full quota of sheep and 99 percent of the intended number of goats.[25] So from one perspective, this second effort met with great success.

But from a long-term perspective, the project proved disastrous. Poor planning hindered Collier's men from the outset. The remote locations of many herds made it difficult to drive them to railheads, and officials feared that the goats, already in poor condition, would become too emaciated for sale if trailed over long distances. The cost of getting them to market was higher than their value, and, most problematically, range riders rounded up more goats than the canneries could process. William Zeh, then administrator for the United Navajo Jurisdiction, attempted to resolve these and other problems by allowing Navajos to slaughter their goats themselves and keep the jerked meat for their own families.[26] And yet he also authorized agents to "condemn" animals that were in poor condition and shoot them on the spot. In one notorious incident, Carl Beck, a BIA stockman, purchased 3,500 head of goats and sheep around Navajo Mountain, an utterly remote area on the extreme northwestern edge of the reservation. Before long, Beck realized that the animals would never survive the long trek to the nearest passable road where they could be picked up by truck.[27] So he herded them into a tributary of Jones Canyon, ordered them shot en masse, and left them to the coyotes, buzzards, and crows. "Today," Ernest Nelson observed in the 1970s, "you can still see all those bones scattered about 'Adah'ooldǫ́ni (Canyon Trail)."[28]

Accounts of episodes like this one, mostly in the remote western part of the reservation, resounded across Diné Bikéyah. Diné viewed the mass slaughter of goats not only as brutal and wasteful, but also as a threat to their survival. Many subsistence herds consisted largely of goats, for they were hardier, thrived in brushy areas, and survived snowy winters better than sheep and so were more dependable as food. Families, moreover, could eat goat meat while reserving their sheep to breed or barter at the local trading post.[29] To many Diné, goats measured the difference between feast and famine. The massacre of their goats, then, seemed like an assault on the people themselves, and it tainted all subsequent efforts to cut Navajo herds.

Not surprisingly, when in August 1935 Collier asked the Navajos to reduce their livestock a third time, the people balked. Voluntary sales to traders, including those on the Checkerboard, tallied only about 16,200 sheep and 14,700 goats. After two years of livestock reduction, only some 101,900 fewer mature sheep and goats grazed the reservation and the Checkerboard, leaving more than 785,700, as well as innumerable horses and cattle, to forage the increasingly sparse vegetation on the Navajo range.[30]

Growing resistance to the stock reduction program soon derailed the rest of Collier's New Deal for the Navajos. The commissioner met personally with the all-male Navajo Tribal Council, an elected body that the BIA had first assembled in the 1920s to approve oil and gas leases, in order to promote each component of his program. Almost invariably, he fumbled. First, he made the mistake of presenting his signature piece of legislation, the Indian Reorganization Act, for the council's endorsement just before he announced the goat reduction program. Many Navajos thereafter conflated the two issues and rejected his long-dreamed-of plan to lift "the yoke of government from the necks" of America's Indian tribes, as one supporter would later put it.[31] Second, he made promises he couldn't deliver. In his first meeting with the council in 1933, Collier yoked livestock reduction to a pledge to expand the boundaries of the reservation to take in

Diné throng outside the newly built Navajo Tribal Council Building, 1939. Photograph by Milton Snow. Records of the BIA, RG75, National Archives at College Park, Md., RG75-Nav-104.

Photographer Milton Snow took this rare picture of a Navajo Tribal Council meeting in 1943. The council sat in the front rows, while Diné observers filled the back of the hall. Records of the BIA, RG75, National Archives at College Park, Md., RG75-NG-11-337.

much of the New Mexico Checkerboard, but to his chagrin, congressional adversaries blocked the necessary legislation. That defeat opened the door for Navajo leaders to use stock reduction and Collier's broken promise to rally people into a solid bloc of resistance and thereby further their own political ambitions.[32]

Chief among those leaders was Jacob Morgan, a Diné missionary with the Christian Reformed Church, who campaigned against stock reduction to eventually win the chairmanship of the Navajo Tribal Council. A balding and bespectacled man who favored three-piece suits, Morgan had been educated at Hampton Normal and Agricultural Institute, where he became an accomplished violinist and cornet player. He had opposed Collier's shift away from the old assimilationist goals of the BIA toward cultural pluralism, believing that a turn away from assimilation would handicap the Diné in the modern world. He, moreover, resented Collier's tilt toward the leadership of traditional headmen, instead of those, like himself, who had a boarding-school education.[33] Blindsided by Morgan's attack, Collier himself compounded the political damage by becoming increasingly authoritarian in his dealings with the Navajos.

Frustrated by the Navajos' growing unwillingness to voluntarily reduce the size of their herds, Collier and E. R. Fryer, superintendent of the newly reorganized Navajo Service, took a more forceful approach to stock reduction, marking the program's second phase. Data from a variety of ecological and socioeconomic studies shaped this revitalized effort. Range specialists determined that Navajo Country could support only about 560,000 sheep and goats, and actually much fewer, considering the forage needs of the horses and cattle that the people owned as well. But now it seemed clear that the Navajos would never voluntarily reduce their flocks by at least another 30 percent. It also became apparent that families with small subsistence herds had borne the brunt of livestock reduction. As a result, many Navajo families could no longer support themselves with their dwindling numbers of sheep and goats. The owners of large flocks, however, had survived relatively unscathed. Indeed, Collier and his colleagues believed that the real obstacle to meaningful stock reduction had been this relatively small group of wealthy stockowners. So in 1937, under authority from the secretary of the Interior, the commissioner issued special grazing regulations designed not only to bring the number of animals into balance with the carrying capacity of the range, but also to make the reduction of stock more equitable for the Navajo people.[34] Stock reduction thus became more than a conservation program; it evolved into an experiment in economic leveling and social engineering.

Instead of reducing all herds by a flat percentage, as had occurred in the past, Collier's new plan set a cap on the number of livestock each extended family could own. Grazing permits specified the maximum number of sheep and goats, or their equivalent in horses and cattle, that a registered stockowner could keep. This renewed effort to cut the size of herds also targeted horses, since soil conservationists believed that the Navajos owned far more horses than they needed, and many were all but feral. Once the surplus horses were removed, Collier argued, few Navajos would be affected by the new regulations, since most families by now already had very small flocks of sheep and relatively few goats.[35]

If Collier believed that his focus on large-scale stockowners would placate Navajos, he was wrong. Still bitter about the loss of their goats, many Diné openly rebelled against this final move. Some refused to accept their permits or burned them, others petitioned Congress to bring an end to the program, and many more protested by hiding their horses and sheep. A handful even responded by physically attacking range riders and other officials. Still more went to jail for failing to comply. Along with the horrors of goat reduction, this last episode in Collier's program made an indelible mark on the Diné and their memories of the 1930s.[36]

Historians delight in pointing out ironies, and the story of stock reduction is replete with them. As Donald Parman noted, livestock reduction enabled an assimilationist like Jacob Morgan to profit politically from an assault on traditional Diné life and led the people to reject, albeit narrowly, Collier's pièce de résistance, the Indian Reorganization Act.[37] Most grievously, as Richard White observed, Collier had promised the Navajos self-determination and economic vitality; instead he crippled them.[38] And there is one final irony to the story of stock reduction: the program designed to save the soil led to chronic erosion. That became the ultimate environmental legacy of the Navajo New Deal.

In hindsight, so much went wrong that it's hard for us to remember that Collier and the soil conservationists had nothing but the best of intentions when they arrived in Navajo Country in the spring of 1933. More than any of the previous commissioners of Indian affairs over the course of a century, Collier prized cultural pluralism, promoted economic independence, and respected the intelligence of indigenous people. And yet Collier was a romanticist and a rationalist. He valued the Navajos' "ancient morality," while at the same time holding that only modern ecological science could ameliorate a degraded environment. He felt certain that the Navajos, too, whom he knew to be shrewd, practical, and adaptive, would in time accept the truth of the scientific data documenting deteriorating range conditions and voluntarily reduce their herds. How could he have so miscalculated their response?

Collier admired Navajos for their distinctive cultural values, but he did not contemplate the full implications of the differences between that culture and his own. Neither he nor his colleagues pondered the possibility that Navajo understandings of nature were fundamentally at odds with those offered by modern science.[39] Nor did it occur to them that their own linear, rationalist ways of knowing nature were refracted through the prism of their own culture. They looked at the world through a lens tempered by ecological theory, engineering mechanics, and mathematics. The Diné, on the other hand, imagined a profoundly spiritualized universe controlled by ceremony. Each of these divergent views produced a different story, a fundamentally different conception of environmental change. We must come to grips with those two ways of narrating nature, for the struggle between them would have far-reaching implications for the Navajo range.

2 · RANGE WARS

"The talk about grazing conditions was not true," asserted Béésh Biwoo'í, Frank Goldtooth, a Diné hataałii or healer, now quite elderly and largely confined to his bed in Tuba City. "There was plenty of vegetation and water. The ranges and valleys were covered with tall grass and beautiful flowers."[1] In the early 1970s, Goldtooth shared with a visitor his memories of the stock reduction era. During that time, he had represented his area on the Navajo Tribal Council and served as an officer in his chapter, one of the local, federally sponsored councils where rural communities gathered to discuss issues, make decisions, settle disputes, and socialize. But his most powerful memories were of his role as chairman of the local grazing committee, when he helped implement the program to reduce livestock and restrict stockowners to circumscribed areas, all in an effort to protect the range from overgrazing.

Looking back, Goldtooth believed that the government program had been misguided. Federal officials misread the land and the relationship of the Diné to it. The Diné themselves, he told his visitor, long conserved the range by moving in an annual cycle, but government policymakers, disdainful of traditional ways, disrupted those patterns, and in so doing they degraded the land. Before that, he explained, "the people moved with their sheep whenever and wherever they wished with the seasons." It seemed clear to him, in fact, that the Diné knew how to live in harmony with the land. "A homesite," he explained, "is not good when a family lives in the same place too long. The vegetation is tramped on too much, and it never gets a chance to grow again. Long ago, moving with the stock from one place to another was much better than what we do now. It gave the vegetation time to grow again."[2]

But in the 1930s, federal officials portrayed a landscape much different from the one Goldtooth remembered. Rather than reporting lush vegetation, John Provinse, then an anthropologist with the Navajo Service, exclaimed in a radio broadcast that anyone "could look around and see that great barren areas existed on the Reservation, that the grass was short and becoming shorter, that the wind was whipping sand out of dry washes and from barren spots and piling it up into sand dunes, that there were gullies everywhere." Provinse described for his listeners a weary waste of sheet erosion, exotic and unpalatable vegetation, and large areas of grassland, once in excellent condition, but "now so denuded of grass that they will scarcely support a saddle horse."[3]

Each of these narrators told a radically different story about the land, and each presumed an utterly different solution. For Provinse and the conservationists, the earth was eroding before their eyes. Only a drastic cut in the numbers of livestock and a written permit tying each stockowner to a particular piece of land would restore the grasslands and avert disaster. Many Diné disagreed. Like Goldtooth, they maintained that the land remained healthy, that the problem was merely temporary drought. Not only that, they argued, the government's idea of tethering shepherds to land made matters worse. Traditional patterns of transhumance, the seasonal movement of stock from lowlands to highlands and back, were necessary to maintain balance, to maintain hózhǫ́. It was as though Goldtooth and Provinse saw completely different landscapes.

Two sets of "experts," one scientific and one native, offered diametrical descriptions of the land. Each reflected different values and understandings about the way nature works and the relationship of humans to nature. Conservationists employed scientific theories of equilibrium, succession, carrying capacity, and arroyo development to depict the Navajo range as seriously overgrazed. Diné, by contrast, drew on their understandings of cosmology, the mosaic of landscapes on the reservation, and the interrelationships between livestock and land learned through generations of experience grazing sheep on the southern Colorado Plateau, and they concluded that they were witnessing nature's cycle; rain would follow drought, and all would be well again. Neither Diné nor the New Dealers fully grasped the complexities of nature. Each, no doubt, held pieces of the puzzle, but neither could see the value of the other's.[4] One key to understanding what went wrong with the New Deal program to save the soil lies in the disjuncture between these two stories of the land, native and scientific. Each narrator related a conception of the world that the other found incomprehensible. That was not necessarily an unbridgeable divide, for they shared common ground—the desire to maintain some sort of "balance of nature"—although the means to that end certainly differed. The New Dealers, of course, had the power to prescribe their view of nature, but in their unwillingness to consider the Navajos' understandings of the natural world, they proved unsuccessful in actually restoring equilibrium, or hózhǫ́, to the range.

In developing their policies, soil conservationists told themselves tales of a precipitous decline from a formerly luxuriant grassland to a wretched wasteland that positioned them within scientific debates on man's role in changing the face of the western landscape. (And they most certainly thought of the agents of change as masculine.) These scientific storytellers were not unique, of course. We may like to think of science as an objective, nonideological pursuit, and yet all science is socially constructed among communities of scholars, who consciously or unconsciously bring to their work values, experiences, and assumptions that shape their conclusions, even though they may tell themselves otherwise.[5] That does not mean that New Deal scientists fabricated fables, in the sense of purposeful falsehoods. On the contrary, they narrated stories about the land that seemed to them the most plausible, in light of the evidence that they found most persuasive (much as historians do). Nonetheless, the credibility of that evidence depended on their point of view.

The conservationists believed that Navajo rangelands had been overstocked and overgrazed for more than fifty years. As early as 1883, near the end of a five-year drought, Navajo agent Denis Riordan recommended reducing the sheep herd by one-half or two-thirds, a measure he felt would result in "plenty of grass (such as it is) . . . where now there is very scant picking."[6] Riordan was perhaps the first to plant the seed of the idea of stock reduction, a seed that would take half a century to germinate. In the meantime, the Bureau of Indian Affairs had encouraged Navajos to *increase* their herds by restricting sales of breeding stock, a policy whose unfortunate consequences appeared clear to New Deal officials.[7]

Since the 1880s, range conditions seemed to have steadily worsened. By 1930, William Zeh, a forester with the BIA, concluded that erosion was spreading like a cancer across the reservation. "The evil results of erosion are far reaching," he wrote, "and like some insidious disease are [g]nawing at the very vitals of the Navajo people."[8] Zeh argued that the Navajos' 1.3 million sheep and goats exceeded the range's carrying capacity by a factor of two or three. And that shocking figure was a conservative estimate, considering that it excluded the large numbers of Navajo horses, as well as cattle, mules, and other stock. Zeh saw signs of serious overgrazing along washes, around hogans (earthen houses) and popular watering holes, and in woodlands, where goats damaged trees. Even beyond these areas, he was certain that the range was overstocked. Zeh had personally surveyed large tracts of the reservation and concluded that each sheep or goat required twenty to thirty surface acres of land, given the general density of grasses and browse, far more than the nine to ten acres available per animal. In light of such disparities, he wrote, erosion was "inevitable."[9]

Zeh might have added that the rangelands of the entire western United States were in dire straits, victim of the free-for-all that governed the public domain. Since the early 1900s, agronomists, foresters, and other conservationists had issued warnings about the deteriorating condition of western grazing lands.[10] Those voices crescendoed in the 1930s with the passage of the Taylor Grazing Act, which regulated livestock on public lands, and the Department of Agriculture's publication of *The Western Range: A Great but Neglected Natural Resource*, detailing the decline of overstocked ranges since the cattle boom of the post–Civil War era.[11] This broader concern about western lands was a backdrop for the Navajo drama.

The signs of overgrazing that Zeh observed in Navajo Country, moreover, assumed new urgency during the New Deal in light of the widening environmental calamity that would become known as the Dust Bowl. Throughout the "dirty thirties," New Deal agencies—the Soil Conservation Service, the Civilian Conservation Corps, and the Resettlement Administration—hastened to rescue the southern plains from debilitating dust storms and drifting sand dunes by introducing new farming methods and resettling destitute farmers onto communally operated lands.[12] Conservationists feared that excessive soil erosion would destroy the Navajo range, just as it had laid waste to much of the heartland's farmland, leading to economic decline and suffering. If they failed to stop the destruction of the soil, they worried, the reservation would become uninhabitable, forcing the government, as legal guardian, to either relocate Navajos onto new lands or support them on the dole.[13]

Officials acted quickly. In early June 1933, only six weeks after taking office, Commissioner John Collier asked Hugh Hammond Bennett to spearhead a study of erosion on the Navajo Reservation.[14] Bennett soon became head of the newly created Soil Erosion Service, later reorganized as the Soil Conservation Service, and would eventually become known as the "Father of Soil Conservation." A big man who spoke in a folksy manner with a pronounced southern drawl, he had seen firsthand the human impoverishment that accompanied severe soil erosion while growing up on his father's plantation in North Carolina, and now he dedicated his life to spreading the conservation gospel.[15] Conservation, he liked to say, echoing Karl Marx, meant "treating land according to its needs and using it according to its capability."[16]

Bennett's study of the Navajo Reservation consisted of a whirlwind tour lasting less than a week, but everywhere he looked, he saw destruction. Deep gullies etched much of the terrain, and sheet erosion had stripped the topsoil from large portions of the uplands. All in all, he estimated that some 70 percent of the land suffered from serious erosion. Even beyond the denuded areas around hogans and watering holes, ground that once supported blue grama and galleta grasses now yielded mostly snakeweed, a plant that poisoned those sheep that ate its tender young leaves, bringing on miscarriages. Since livestock avoided the pernicious plant as long as other forage was available, snakeweed readily reproduced and spread across land laid bare by excessive grazing. The presence of large fields of the toxin thus told Bennett that the land was overgrazed. In the sagebrush flats used as winter range, Bennett found closely browsed shrubs, juniper trees stripped by goats of their lower bark and branches, and chamiso that had been killed by overbrowsing. Sadly, he predicted, a large part of the range would never fully recover.[17]

The surest remedy, he believed, would be to show Navajos the logic of scientific range management through a demonstration project at Mexican Springs. Encompassing an entire watershed on the eastern edge of the Chuska Mountains, the project would not only model practical procedures for erosion control, revegetation, and range management, but also serve as a sort of mission for conservation. Here small groups of Navajo men, employed for one-month stints by the Emergency Conservation Work program, would be schooled as "Range Conservation Missionaries," evangelists who would spread the gospel and persuade their communities to assume responsibility for erosion and range control.[18]

But Navajos could not tackle the problem alone. The critical condition of the reservation posed problems that Bennett believed only trained professionals could treat. Since the Progressive Era, the movement for conserving and efficiently allocating natural resources had been deeply imbrued with a faith in applied science dispensed by dedicated, college-educated civil servants. Dispassionate and free from the corrupting influence of politics and self-interest, these experts—so the theory went—would use objective scientific principles, systematic methods of recording data, practical experience, and common sense to develop wise policies that would provide, as Gifford Pinchot, the chief of the Forest Service, famously articulated, "the greatest good of the greatest number in the long run."[19] According to this faith, only scientists and technicians had the expertise to make rational decisions about the land.

Soon after Bennett confirmed the seriousness of the erosion problem, Collier decided to implement a conservation program across the entire Navajo Reservation, not just at Mexican Springs. Before long, the Soil Erosion Service, working in cooperation with the BIA and the Biological Survey, sent a legion of experts to the reservation to describe, measure, classify, and analyze the land. Range technicians, soil specialists, engineers, agronomists, and biologists—many of them among the best in the region—swarmed across Navajo Country. They studied the soil, the range, the forests, and all manner of living things. They recorded the topography, drainage patterns, and vegetation. They documented Navajo land use and identified potential dam sites and arable soils. Perhaps most importantly, these troops of trained professionals measured the land, reducing the mesas and canyons, the forests and badlands, the meadows and arroyos, the grasses, forbs, and shrubs to a series of numbers, all in an effort to arrive at a precise, scientific calculation of the range's carrying capacity.[20] These numbers then became the cornerstone of the stock reduction program.

Reduction, however, was already well under way when the first comprehensive studies of the reservation began to roll off the typewriters. Two qualities of these reports are most striking: their focus on riparian areas and their narrative structure. Collectively, these studies told a story that went something like this: In the beginning, the alluvial valleys had been covered by heavy stands of grass. During torrential rains, these grasses had slowed the runoff, allowing the water to spread across the valley floors and trickle

As sheep trailed to arroyos for water, their hooves carved new gullies. Federal conservationists used images like this one to secure congressional support for stock reduction. Photograph by Milton Snow. Records of the BIA, RG75, National Archives, Pacific Region, Laguna Niguel, Calif., 75-08-12.

slowly into the loamy soils. But the Navajos had allowed their sheep to overpopulate the land. Overgrazing had removed the vegetation or reduced its vitality, which led to an invasion of unpalatable and poisonous weeds, exposed the soil to the wind, and encouraged flows of water to cut great gullies, washing the red soil through the watershed of the Colorado River.[21]

This story of a decline from an Edenic pastoral landscape contained a large measure of truth. Grazing does invariably alter the environment, and overgrazing can and did accelerate erosion and bring desertification. When livestock continuously defoliate favored forbs, grasses, and shrubs, they eventually kill the native vegetation they prefer and encourage the invasion and spread of less palatable plants, both native and exotic. As vegetation density decreases, larger areas of soil become exposed to the baking sun, making them more arid. And as the patches of bare ground become wider, the wind begins to carry away the topsoil. Trampling hooves also compact soils, thereby reducing aeration and water infiltration and encouraging runoff and sheet erosion. Overgrazing, then, can indeed destroy the land, just as the soil conservationists narrated it.[22]

And yet, all stories—whether they trace progression toward a better life or tell of decline toward something worse—take their starting point from a set of assumptions and values that consciously foreshadow the conclusion. A story of catastrophically eroding lands necessarily begins with a healthy environment, or one that is at least stable. As any dramatist knows, such a happy beginning is a necessary prelude to a compelling plotline of tragic declension. The New Deal scientists, however, had little actual knowledge of the condition of the land before the Diné began grazing their livestock on it. Instead, as they constructed their stories about Navajo Country, the scientists relied on assumptions about the land's historical condition that they barely acknowledged and never scrutinized.[23]

Following the influential theories of the pioneering ecologist Frederic Clements, the scientists assumed that the stands of shrubs extending across the reservation had invaded a once lush grassland, and they defined those plant communities not dominated by grasses as degraded. An ecologist with the Carnegie Institution of Washington, Clements had studied the desert environment at the Carnegie Desert Botanical Laboratory and the Santa Rita Experimental Range, both near Tucson, Arizona. He is perhaps best known for his "climax theory," which shaped ecological studies for more than a generation. Within each climate, he argued, mature vegetation communities remain stable, or in a state of equilibrium, unless disturbed by something like fire or overgrazing. Following a disturbance, a given vegetation community would redevelop, according to Clements, progressing through a series of stages until it again reached its mature or climax state, and there it would remain until some outside force triggered the succession process once more. Significantly, he also wrote that the sagebrush-dominated lands of the Colorado Plateau—an area he referred to as "sagebrush savanna"—were the product of overgrazing. In its pristine, mature state, he contended, the region was predominantly grassland.[24]

Clements's theories shaped the ways in which soil conservationists thought about Navajo Country, but they were also swayed mightily by mid-nineteenth-century descriptions of the land. In September 1849, for example, Lieutenant James Simpson, a topographer with Colonel John McCrae Washington's command during the U.S.-Mexico War, recorded in his official journal that rich grasses lined the margins of the waters in Canyon de Chelly and other areas. Simpson especially extolled the verdure of Crystal Creek in the Chuska Mountains, writing that "this country . . . is of extraordinary beauty. The soil here is of a very rich quality. The pines are tall and large, the grass luxuriant, and the surface of the ground, which is sweetly undulating, is covered with a profusion of the most beautiful and delicate flowers."[25] Reports like Simpson's had a decided influence on the ways in which soil scientists understood changes in the environment, for they arrived at their conclusions, in part, by comparing conditions in the 1930s to observations by early travelers. Those comparisons persuaded New Deal scientists that the carrying capacity had dropped by one-third to one-half since 1868, when the Navajos returned from the Bosque Redondo.[26]

But such a claim was absurd. The descriptions characterizing the reservation before the 1930s were far too sparse to develop any quantitative picture of past range conditions. Early observers like Simpson, in fact, provided only sketchy impressions of the land, focused on a few well-watered areas. It was the *novelty* of those patches in an otherwise dreary landscape that gave rise to Simpson's pastorals on Navajo meadows. He said so himself when he wrote—revealing his revulsion toward the desert Southwest—that "saving the inconsiderable exceptions which have from time to time been noted in my journal, the country is one extended *naked, barren* waste, sparsely covered with cedar and pine of a scrub growth, and thickly sprinkled with the wild sage, or artemisia, the color . . . suggesting very appropriately the dead, lifeless color of the wild."[27] A close reading of early explorers' accounts suggests that travelers like Simpson generally focused attention on riparian areas and springs—a small fragment of the overall landscape—where they found good forage and water for their horses and mules.[28] The New Dealers' story of an overgrazed range, then, relied at least in part on the misguided notion that a more ideal pastoral landscape once characterized all of Navajo Country.

Certainly the most influential of the nineteenth-century accounts was written by Lieutenant Edward Beale, who in 1857 surveyed a proposed wagon route from Albuquerque to the Colorado River. Unlike Simpson, Beale described Navajo Country as a relatively well-watered pasture of plenty, a vision that had a marked affect on New Dealers' perceptions of the historical landscape.[29] It's worth noting that while Beale traveled during a drier year than Simpson did, he arrived during the monsoon season, when frequent rains (except for a two-week stretch in late August), some lasting most of the day, stimulated the growth of grass. Those rains may help explain how Simpson's "barren waste" turned into Beale's pretty pastures.[30]

The BIA later juxtaposed passages from Beale's journal with images by New Deal photographer Milton Snow and captions by H. Claiborn Lockett

Soil conservationists juxtaposed descriptions of luxuriant landscapes in the mid-nineteenth century with scenes such as this arroyo cutting through an overgrazed pasture of grama grass in the Manuelito Valley. Photograph probably by Milton Snow, 1939. Records of the BIA, RG 75, National Archives at College Park, Md. RG75-FC-Window-10.

Diné contrasted the soil conservationists' dreary landscapes with recollections of verdant meadows such as this, along Bluewater Creek in the Zuni Mountains. Photograph by the author, 1997.

in a booklet designed to counter congressional criticism that the hardships inflicted by stock reduction were unnecessary. These pictures, Lockett wrote, told "a story of wasted rangeland, crumbling walls of mud, and nature thrown out of balance by man's wanton misuse of his resources." As the reader turned the pages of this booklet, Beale's rhapsodic descriptions of verdant meadows, "undulating prairie land, covered with grass," and easily passable rivers contrasted sharply with photographs depicting "giant fingers of erosion," unpalatable snakeweed, and sunken streams "cutting the country like a knife." Consider the comparison at Jacob's Well, once a great sinkhole a third of a mile in circumference, with a depth of 125 feet, located west of Zuni. Beale especially celebrated this "most wonderful place." Its bottom then contained a deep pool of water edged with rushes, willows, and cedars. By the 1930s, however, that resplendent reservoir—so deep in Beale's day that the lieutenant followed a spiraling trail to reach the bottom—had all but disappeared. Snow's photograph exposed this marked transformation: one could barely discern the formerly vast basin amidst the scraggly weeds and naked soil, for silt nearly filled the hole. Lockett contrasted desolate scenes like this one with the verdant vales that still remained in the forests near Flagstaff, Arizona, where the U.S. Forest Service ensured proper management. The differences offered "graphic proof," Lockett made clear, in case the reader missed his point, "that no cycle of drouth, but man's stupid misuse of nature's resources, made the Beale Trail what it is today."[31]

Even now, these images are sobering. Any reader of *Along the Beale Trail* cannot help but be disturbed by the profound differences between the desolate scenes in Snow's photographs and the pastoral landscapes that Beale painted with words. They leave no doubt that over the course of eighty years, the land had markedly deteriorated.

And yet a careful reading of Beale's journal of his trip through Navajo Country reveals that the New Dealers were quite selective in choosing the lieutenant's words to construct a dramatic story of environmental destruction. They omitted those elements of the historic landscape that might have muddied their picture of decline from Eden. Beale found abundant greasewood, as well as grama, indicating a shrub-grasslands, not pure pastures. And while he described most of the terrain as flat or gently rolling, he also encountered deep gullies, primarily on the southwestern edge of the reservation near the Painted Desert. One valley near the scarcely populated westernmost stretch of the Rio Puerco was "intersected in all directions by ravines . . . arroyos, and gullies."³² Such images would have complicated the New Dealers' portraits of an incised landscape caused solely by Navajo overgrazing. At the same time, several of their comparisons were misleading or mistaken. In one glaring instance, the authors erred in matching photograph and description, contrasting Beale's lush meadow at Bluewater, a location at the foot of the Zuni Mountains, with a ruined range several miles distant near Thoreau, New Mexico. Long stretches of Beale's road, moreover, passed through the southern Checkerboard, south of the reservation, which since the turn of the twentieth century had felt the multiple impacts of livestock owned by Diné, Zuni, Anglo-American, and Hispanic stockowners. By carefully choosing which parts of Beale's journal to include or exclude, the New Dealers narrated a simple story of a fall from paradise, unimpeded by the morass of the actual historic landscape.³³

The authors of *Along the Beale Trail* skewed their story in other ways, too. Beale, to be sure, found many good stands of grama, and they far outnumbered those places where he noted sparse or shriveled grass. But his route, like Simpson's, generally followed stream courses, so the good grazing he described was often—though certainly not always—along riparian areas or around springs. Snow's photographs leave no doubt that the grassy meadows along these rivers had vanished by the 1930s, but they also imply that the vast areas of the reservation extending away from these streams were part of the same story.

Yet we know little even now about the historical conditions of that larger mosaic of shrub-grasslands, woodlands, and badlands. One of the few explorers to venture off the riparian trails was Lieutenant Joseph Ives, who during the drought of 1857—a few months before Beale's visit—struck off toward the Hopi villages. Like Beale, Ives described beautiful grasslands along well-watered areas. The valley along the Pueblo Colorado Wash, near present-day Ganado, for instance, offered "a brilliant sheet of verdure dotted with clumps of cedars." There, vast herds of horses and flocks of sheep grazed the plain. Yet a few days earlier, the trail extending north of the Little Colorado River to the Hopi mesas had presented a different picture. "The scene was one of utter desolation," Ives wrote in his journal. "Not a tree nor a shrub broke its monotony." As he trudged onward, conditions grew worse. "There was not a spear of grass, and from the porousness of the soil and rocks it was impossible that there should be a drop of water."³⁴

Neither Ives nor Beale offered a panorama of Navajo Country, but in selecting only Beale's words, the New Dealers cropped the picture, knowingly or not. It would be hard to deny that Snow's powerful photographs documented the desertification of the southern edge of Navajo Country. Nonetheless, his selective viewpoint revealed and reinforced a somewhat distorted understanding of the changes that had taken place since Beale's journey. New Deal soil conservationists surmised that the range had deteriorated progressively, especially since the 1880s, skidding down a continuous slope from the lush pastures of Beale's journal to the denuded lands before their very eyes.[35]

A thorough reading of the annual reports by BIA agents and comparisons with moisture records instead suggest that range conditions fluctuated from year to year, corresponding to rainfall and snow. We can obtain an independent perspective on climatic conditions from the "natural archives" offered by southwestern forests. Ponderosa pines and other trees record the local climate in their annual growth rings because tree growth generally responds to moisture during the growing season; wide rings reflect wet years and narrow rings denote dry. Scientists who study tree rings, dendrochronologists, have painstakingly matched patterns in those rings across the Colorado Plateau, so that they know the exact calendar year of each one. Collecting samples from clusters of trees chosen for particular site and physical characteristics, dendroclimatologists are thus able to construct a continuous record of the region's climate dating as far back as A.D. 1000. Helpfully, one group of climatologists, led by E. R. Cook, compiled a record using a measure known as the Palmer Drought Severity Index, which takes temperature and evaporation into account, so that we can see how much moisture was actually available for vegetation growth. Most of Navajo Country is not forested, of course, and rainfall is highly variable across the reservation, so tree rings offer only approximations. Nonetheless, by comparing various studies using different trees, we can gain a good sense of precipitation patterns on the Colorado Plateau.[36]

These patterns, along with rain gauge and temperature records after 1895, convey a more complicated story than the New Dealers told. Since A.D. 1000, moisture patterns have been remarkably stable, with bouts of drought lasting three to five years, followed by periods of wet years, but with each century circling around the same "normal" average. And yet, from 1899 through 1904, an extreme drought gripped the Colorado Plateau. It was a deeper drought, albeit far less lengthy, than the "megadrought" that seared the Southwest in the 1500s. Then beginning in 1905, just as it seemed all life might shrivel up and die, there came a long glorious period of unusually wet years, lasting more than a decade until roughly 1920. The 1920s brought a drying trend, accompanied by higher temperatures, although it remained wetter than the norm.[37]

During the late nineteenth and early twentieth centuries, the BIA agents' perceptions of the condition of the range tracked these moisture patterns. In seasons of drought or harsh winters, sheep perished due to scarce forage, insufficient water, or snows so deep that they covered the sagebrush favored by flocks in winter.[38] In the drought year of 1893, for example, agent E. H. Plummer reported that "the condition of the Navajo Indians is worse than it has been for a number of years. This is due, partly, to a succession of very dry seasons, which have caused a great scarcity of forage ... [and the] loss of many sheep and ponies from starvation during the winters."[39] But in years of relatively plentiful rain, livestock flourished. In 1903, after an extremely dry year, refreshing rains briefly broke deep drought, prompting agent G. W. Hayzlett to extol the land's fertility and observe that "the grass on the mountains and in the valleys is abundant."[40] We have no clue, of course, whether those stands of grass were as dense or vigorous as they were in the early nineteenth century when Beale passed though; appearances could be deceiving. Nonetheless, judging from the agents' accounts, the vicissitudes of climate affected the quality of the range as much as anything.

Historical observations shaped soil conservationists' perceptions in one more important way: washes and streams that travelers described as shallow in the 1840s and 1850s had become deeply entrenched by the early 1900s, following a boom in the Navajo livestock population. Lieutenant Simpson, for example, had in 1849 described a beautiful pond along an easily traveled route at the bottom of Cañoncito Bonito north of the future Fort Defiance; by 1917, the pond had disappeared and a great gash cut twenty to thirty feet into the earth. This pattern was not novel to Navajo Country. After commercial ranchers introduced enormous numbers of cattle and sheep throughout the West in the last decades of the nineteenth century, gullies laced the entire region, from Oregon to the Mexican border.[41] In both instances, a buildup of herds coincided with the initiation of arroyo-cutting.

The New Dealers assumed that the network of gullies constituted unambiguous evidence of overgrazing. Arroyos posed a serious problem for the reservation. Following violent summer rain storms, roiling waters surged through once-shallow washes, carving away at the upstream heads, undercutting the banks, scouring channels, and thereby lengthening, widening, and deepening trenches. Networks of arroyos extended until they reached major streams like the San Juan and Little Colorado rivers, becoming essentially ephemeral tributaries. As this web of gullies cut ever deeper into the earth, they lowered the water table, which dropped below the reach of the shallow roots of native bunch grasses and encouraged the spread of more xeric plants with long tap roots. Soil scientists blamed the Navajos and their livestock. In report after report, they emphasized that the thousands of miles of arroyos and gullies, from 10 to 100 feet in depth, had spread through accelerated erosion due to human action.[42] This theory that overgrazing had created the gullies became widely accepted by the 1930s, but the only evidence that livestock had *caused* the arroyos was the coincidence in timing.

Conservationists blamed overgrazing, but there was also a competing—though less-popular—theory that southwestern arroyos had been caused primarily by climate change. In 1917, the geologist Herbert Gregory, whose perceptive and thorough studies of Navajo Country in the early twentieth century remain classics, attributed the arroyos to climate change, noting that they appeared to be universal across the Colorado Plateau, even in areas left ungrazed because of the absence of stock water. A decade later, Kirk Bryan, a professor at Harvard University and one of the leading geologists of his day, agreed with Gregory that climate was the principal cause, based on evidence of a previous period of downcutting at Chaco Canyon, beginning around 1100, which led to the abandonment of Pueblo Bonito by the ancient Anasazi. Significantly, that erosive era occurred hundreds of years before the land trembled beneath the hooves of hordes of sheep. Both Bryan and Gregory acknowledged that overgrazing played a role in the modern episode of arroyo-cutting by reducing already impoverished vegetation. But it was only, in Bryan's words, the "trigger pull." Gullying, they argued, would have occurred even without sheep.[43]

New Deal officials rejected this climate theory outright. When Bryan presented his findings at a conference in Flagstaff, Collier's assistant, Walter Woehlke, blasted the geologist's laissez-faire, leave-it-alone attitude toward a problem that seemed to him clearly the result of overstocking.[44] C. Warren Thornthwaite, who headed the SCS's Climatic and Physiographic Research Section, likewise dismissed the climate-change theory. Thornthwaite earned his doctorate at the University of California, Berkeley, under the direction of Carl Sauer, the renowned historical and cultural geographer, and would become a respected authority on applied climatology.[45] He saw no relationship between channel-cutting in the modern era and that which had occurred at Chaco, which he attributed to a "great drought" coupled with a freakish 100- or 500-year rain. Drawing on a study of average rainfall patterns in the Southwest, he found no evidence of a new trend toward drought that would cause the development of gullies in the absence of overgrazing. Bryan, he insisted, confused the proximate and ultimate causes of gullying. Likening channel-cutting to disease, Thornthwaite argued that overstocking, not climate change, had reduced the land's resistance to erosion and made it vulnerable to violent summer storms. These intense rains then acted as "the germ or infection that had touched off the epidemic of accelerated erosion." And yet, he contended, gully washers were nothing new; what *was* new were large herds of livestock. The scientific evidence, Thornthwaite wrote, led to only one conclusion: overgrazing had ruined the Navajo range.[46]

Most importantly, Thornthwaite *wanted to believe* that human agency was responsible. After all, he declared, if one accepted the climate argument, it would then be "questionable whether man can effectively stop the accelerated erosion." Humans had to be placed at the center of his story because only human behavior could be changed readily. Here again, we see how the trajectory of the plotline depended on a well-chosen prelude. If one assumed that overgrazing was responsible, he wrote, it would then be "possible that the land can be improved by improving the use."[47] No one could do anything about the weather, but damage wrought by man could be reversed by man, too. Thornthwaite's emphasis on human destruction reflected, as much as anything, a New Deal faith that human efforts could bring restoration.

Scholars have since concluded that climate change—a long period of intense drought followed by a new pattern of high-energy, convective summer storms—likely initiated the network of arroyos that even now scar the land. According to the tree-ring data, the 1870s and 1880s were extremely dry, although punctuated by years of considerable rain. Then came the severe drought of 1899–1904, with scant snow and rainfall. Some years saw almost none. Not since the 1660s—and before then, the 1250s—had the region suffered such painful drought. With so little moisture, plants weakened, setting the stage for rapid erosion when intense summer downpours brought flash flooding.[48] Such storms came regularly during the prolonged wet period of 1905–1920—the likes of which had not been seen for nearly a century. Compounding the damage, according to some scientists, some of the highly erodible sandstones in the area proved particularly sensitive to these climatic shifts.[49] None of this information on precipitation, in all fairness, was available in the 1930s, but the evidence offered by the esteemed geologists Bryan and Gregory provided clues.

Thornthwaite, however, was absolutely right in one important particular. Navajo Country did not experience deep drought during the 1930s, according to the tree-ring record. True, there were droughty years, especially 1934 and 1936. The ground positively baked during 1934, which registered as the Southwest's warmest year in the twentieth century. In some sections of the eastern reservation and the Checkerboard, moreover, the 1930s continues to hold the record for the least rain during crucial months of the growing season. But generally speaking, the region received average rainfall over the course of the decade. What made it *seem* so dry to Diné and other locals was the marked contrast with the extreme wetness of previous decades. After all, a generation had grown up during an aberrant period when rainfall and snow were well above average. But beginning in 1925, a shift in atmospheric wind patterns brought a steep decline in the availability of moisture, a rate of decline unprecedented since the last millennium.[50] Thornthwaite's observation notwithstanding, climate change transformed the landscape, chiseling arroyos deep into the earth and robbing desert grasses of life-sustaining water. That change, however, began much earlier and reached a critical point not in the drying-out of the 1930s but in a desolating drought two decades later.

No doubt, heavy grazing exacerbated this process by weakening and thinning vegetation. Studies at the Jornada Experimental Range in southern New Mexico have shown that drought in the absence of grazing has roughly the same effect as overgrazing, but together they deliver a double blow.[51] With less vegetation to bind the soil, gullying likely spread more rapidly than it would have in the absence of grazing. But in rejecting the role of climate change, conservationists may well have overstated the part livestock played in shaping the Navajo landscape.

Similarly, as scientists told their declension stories, they downplayed the presence of ancient sand dunes in the desolate western part of the reservation near the Painted Desert. Created thousands of years ago, these dunes, for the most part, form long, narrow ridges pointing in the direction of the prevailing wind. The very existence of these ancient formations suggests that very arid, windy, erosive conditions have been structuring this region for a long, long time. But when a combination of drying conditions, intense winds, and thin vegetation began to revitalize the dunes in the 1930s, New Deal conservationists blamed overgrazing. To them, the thinness of the grasses and the presence of less palatable plants like rabbitbrush (often a sign of overgrazing) seemed to indicate something even more insidious than long-term geological processes.[52]

Other scientists disagreed. John Tilton Hack, a geomorphologist who studied the dunes for an archaeological expedition in the 1930s, believed grazing played a relatively minor role in an age-old drama directed by nature. Active dunes were no different from those of the past, he argued, and the old dunes themselves played a part in the spread of the new. High winds picked up sands from eroding cliffs, ancient alluvial plains, and the dry channels of ephemeral rivers and arroyos. When turbulent winds deflected around the obstacles posed by the existing dunes, they deposited the sand on the leeward side. As the sand piled up, these new drifts, too, became obstacles, and the process continued ever onward. Only a scattering of bunch grass and plants with deep tap roots like rabbitbrush could stake claim to such shifting ground, and the sparseness of these plants encouraged the exposed sands to continue the onward march, a movement that would last as long as dry conditions prevailed.[53] Grazing surely was unsuited to such an environment, but it was not the fundamental cause of the dunes.

New Deal conservationists, then, made a number of problematic and contested assumptions as they constructed their stories about the Navajo range. They postulated that verdant grasslands once characterized the landscape, that the land had degraded steadily since the 1880s, and that climate change played an insignificant role. Most importantly, they *presumed* that overgrazing was the primary cause of the degraded range. That said, overgrazing was significant, and we can't control the weather. So we might ask ourselves: if the only logical course of action was to reduce grazing, do the soil conservationists' assumptions really matter?

Luna Leopold considered that question in the early 1950s and concluded that faulty assumptions profoundly affected the conservationists' imagined landscape and, consequently, their course of action. Son of the celebrated conservationist Aldo Leopold, he served brief stints on the Navajo Reservation and at the SCS headquarters in Albuquerque in the 1930s before studying geology with Kirk Bryan.[54] Eventually, he would become one of the country's most esteemed hydrologists, first at the U.S. Geological Survey, then as a professor at the University of California, Berkeley. After analyzing numerous descriptions of the southwestern environment made by Anglo-American explorers in the nineteenth century, he concluded that his former colleagues wrongly characterized the region as a once-lush grasslands. Conservationists' misconception of those travelers' reports had serious implications, wrote Leopold. The popular "idea of an originally verdant vegetation, deteriorated as a result of man's activities," he reasoned, "has led to overoptimism concerning the possible results of reduced grazing. . . . We may have allowed ourselves to be deluded by hopes of 'restoring' over large areas a level of vegetation density that was originally attained only in selected localities."[55] Those delusions carried social and environmental consequences for the Navajo Reservation. In assuming that overgrazing was solely responsible for the degraded range, New Dealers blamed Navajos for erosion that was, perhaps, a new chapter in a geological saga that had shaped the mesas and valleys of the Colorado Plateau for eons. Most importantly, in so doing, the conservationists distorted their mental pictures of what a healthy landscape might look like.[56]

Nonetheless, in many ways, SCS records reveal a model of the scientific method, a careful study of the ways in which overgrazing at least *accelerated* the course of natural erosion by removing and killing vegetation that might otherwise hold the soil in place. Range technicians documented the land through aerial photographs, color-coded maps, and voluminous reports. They developed various hypotheses for managing the rangelands. And they tested them at demonstration areas scattered across the reservation, proving in a few places, at least, that decreased grazing pressure could revitalize the range, though in most locales, reseeding proved necessary.[57] The conservationists may well have exaggerated the Navajos' role in causing erosion, and yet their studies leave little doubt that overgrazing contributed significantly to the sorry state of the land.

Why, then, did Navajos not see it?

New Deal conservationists seemed baffled by that question, and yet what is striking in their reports is how little the scientists tried to understand the one variable that mattered more than anything: the Navajos themselves. John Collier, it's true, was fairly knowledgeable about Navajo culture and society, and he realized that the conservation program's success depended, in part, on even more knowledge. Writing to Hugh Bennett, he emphasized the need for a sociological study because "soil conservation is not merely a business of mechanical or botanical operations. . . . It is a business of finding out how the land owners . . . can be enabled and persuaded to conserve their soil."[58] Unfortunately, Collier proved unable to secure the appropriations necessary to hire anthropologists until 1935, well after stock reduction began to transform the Diné economy.[59] By the time the research results were in, the conservation program was in its final stages. It was a matter of too little, too late. Still, even if Collier had managed to initiate cultural research far earlier, it seems doubtful that it would have made much difference. His own insistence on "practical" information impeded any effort to understand Navajos on their own terms.

Instead of selecting an anthropologist to oversee the research, Collier chose Eshref Shevky, a Turkish friend with a doctorate in experimental medicine. Shevky had read widely in anthropology, sociology, ecology, and economics and had some experience with southwestern Indians; he conducted a health survey among the Rio Grande Pueblos for Collier's American Indian Defense Association and, later, studied Pueblo land use for the BIA. He would, moreover, eventually become a renowned professor of sociology at the University of California, Los Angeles. And yet he had no background in Navajo ethnography, no formal anthropological training, and no real interest in traditional academic questions about customs, beliefs, myths, or kinship. That kind of information, in his opinion, was useless for developing a workable range management program.[60]

Shevky was skeptical about the value of ethnographic research and insisted on "hard facts." Consequently, the questionnaires he designed for the study—which the Soil Conservation Service called, ironically as it turned out, the "human dependency survey"—asked for quantifiable information about population, economic resources, income distribution, and little else. It read more like a standard census schedule than an instrument for discovering meaningful information about Navajos or their relationships to the land. Only two items on the form referred specifically to Navajo ways of life: clan and "consumption group" (the latter in recognition that more than one family might share economic resources). Otherwise, the form could have been used just as effectively—indeed, even more so—among, say, the residents of Chicago or Boston. Consider the way the survey tracked families. Anthropologists had known for more than half a century that Navajos organized their society around related groups of women, and still Shevky instructed enumerators to describe each member of an extended household in relation to the oldest man, rather than the oldest woman.[61] The results thus precluded any truly realistic understanding of the female networks that grounded Navajo land use.

To his credit, Shevky hired a pair of dedicated anthropologists to head the research effort on the Navajo Reservation: Solon Kimball and John Provinse. Both men received their doctorates from renowned anthropology programs, Kimball from Harvard University, Provinse from the University of Chicago. Both were disciples of A. R. Radcliffe-Brown, who viewed culture through an ecological lens. Every aspect of a cultural system, as they understood it, played a functional, interdependent role in maintaining the whole. As with ecological systems (so Radcliffe-Brown's theory went), cultures thrived or declined depending on their ability to maintain equilibrium among the various interconnected parts. Accordingly, a change in one part of the system could disturb that balance and trigger a succession of changes throughout the cultural organism.[62]

Kimball and Provinse took great pains to try to understand Navajo culture on its own terms by using a more ethnographic approach to their research in one part of the reservation, as a pilot project. They spent time with Navajo families, talking with the men and observing how their families functioned. That effort helped them to recognize what they called the "land-use community," clustered groups of families related through women who shared the same range, worked cooperatively at such tasks as shearing and dipping sheep, and joined together for ritual ceremonies. The two men believed that these land-use communities provided a native mechanism for range management.[63]

Excited to apply their new insights, they negotiated cooperative conservation plans with the leaders of three communities in an area on Black Mesa. Working, for example, with Naat'áanii Sání, Old Leader, head of a group of seven families living along Oraibi Wash, they and their crew of range specialists solicited the old man's advice about the best locations for and types of erosion-control structures, in recognition that he understood the dynamics of flood waters in the area more intimately than they did. Together Old Leader and the New Dealers then developed a range management plan that specified reciprocal obligations between the land use community and the government. The community agreed to graze certain numbers of sheep in particular pastures according to a seasonal schedule, while the government pledged to provide stock water, reseed denuded areas, and build such structures as water-spreaders to help control erosion.[64]

Kimball believed that this approach held the potential for restructuring the relationship between the government and the Navajos from one of "patron-dependent" to a "working partnership of complementary obligations and functions." That hope was perhaps idealistic. Awash in bureaucratic language, the plan gave a federal range specialist, not Old Leader, responsibility for overseeing proper grazing management and carried no mechanism for compelling conservationists to make good on their promises. Still, it was an earnest effort to replace coercion with cooperation. It remains unclear whether this move toward collaboration would have made a real difference. Before Kimball and Provinse could expand their research into other areas of the reservation, or even really see results at Black Mesa, their superiors within the conservation service suspended their work, allegedly over petty turf issues.[65]

Even Kimball and Provinse remained ignorant of many of the most important aspects of Navajo culture, despite their efforts to understand indigenous land use. Kimball would later defend his limited knowledge, arguing that information on Navajo thought and cultural dynamics was either unavailable or irrelevant.[66] The claim that this information was unavailable was disingenuous. A number of the century's shrewdest students of Navajo culture worked on the reservation during the 1930s, people such as Father Berard Haile and Gladys Reichard, both of whom were employed for a time by the BIA. Haile honed a written Navajo vocabulary and grammar, trained interpreters and federal officials to write in the Navajo language, and helped reorganize the Navajo Tribal Council in 1936. Similarly, Reichard briefly taught Navajos to read and write in their own language at a day school near Ganado.[67] Both Reichard and Haile had for some time been delving into Navajo religion, kinship, and social organization, but no one seems to have taken the simple step of asking either of these scholars to share their knowledge.

The apparent dismissal of their work as inadequate and *"irrelevant to the problems of an action program,"* as Kimball put it, probably had as much to do with professional boundaries as anything.[68] Kimball and Provinse both stood on the cutting edge of ethnographic theory and practice, while Reichard's and Haile's research interests seemed old-fashioned and focused on the past. Kimball and Provinse apparently considered Haile's extraordinary work on Navajo origin "myths," in particular, both outmoded and esoteric, for it did not appear likely to yield the "practical" information they sought.[69] Reichard, for her part, had two black marks against her. She was female and, thus, an outsider to the male-dominated academy. Her doctorate from Columbia University made little difference, and her position on the faculty at Barnard College, a women's liberal arts school without graduate students, confirmed her lowly status. Worse yet, she remained a loyal protégée of Franz Boas. His descriptive methods, cultural relativism, and insistence on understanding each culture on its own terms once revolutionized the field of anthropology, but by the 1930s, the functionalist, sociological, cross-cultural theories of Radcliffe-Brown, Provinse's mentor at the University of Chicago, had eclipsed Boas's decidedly non-theoretical approach.[70] Professional provincialism, then, may well have blinded the New Deal anthropologists.

It's certainly possible that they regarded Reichard's techniques as unscientific. She lived with a Navajo family near Ganado for three summers and learned to weave, which allowed her to observe and describe the internal dynamics of family life from the inside. This participant-observer approach—while popular later on—challenged the more distanced, more "objective," and therefore more scientific stance that ethnography took at the time.[71] Reichard's idiosyncratic approach to Navajo studies led anthropologist Clyde Kluckhohn, of Harvard, to question her scientific logic and her ideas of what constituted evidence, and even Haile dismissed her as a dilettante.[72] Only recently have scholars acknowledged her work as trailblazing, so perhaps we should forgive the New Dealers' snub.

Yet attention to Reichard and Haile's work might have made all the difference. Reichard's immersion in the world of Navajo women gave her insight that surely could have helped the New Dealers develop a richer understanding of Navajo life, economy, thought, and gender relations. Moreover, Haile, who had lived among the Navajos for almost thirty years, would have been an obvious person to turn to for information about Navajo thought and customs. He was a respected expert on Navajo spiritual beliefs and had studied Navajo kinship and conceptions of property ownership. In rejecting cultural information on seemingly esoteric matters such as spiritual beliefs and kinship, the New Dealers created an incomplete picture of the Navajos and their relationships with livestock and land.

Importantly, they failed to consider that Navajos might have their own tales to tell about their relationships with nature. Those stories expressed a view of the natural world gained through keen observations of a stingy land that nonetheless nurtured them as hunters, gatherers, farmers, and, later, shepherds for at least four centuries. And yet Diné, too, misread the landscape, often ascribing the desolate condition of the range solely to drought or spiritual disorder. Like the New Dealers, they had an incomplete understanding of the rapidly changing ecological conditions of the first half of the twentieth century. Few were even willing to acknowledge that a more xeric landscape required a different strategy for managing the range. Still, they possessed a local knowledge of the land, an experiential understanding that the soil conservationists largely ignored.[73]

Diné were intimately familiar with their environment, and they expressed it by descriptively naming every clump of trees, every spring and seep, indeed every locale, no matter how minute. These word-pictures mapped the landscape in ways that no line drawing could ever capture. Not surprisingly in this arid landscape, Diné emphasized places where water may be found. Tó Dínéeshzhee', or Kayenta, describes "waters spread out in rivulets, fan-like." Tó Haach'i', or "water is scratched out," describes a sandy creek bed where water can be dug out by hand. And Dibé Bichaan Bii' Tó, meaning "sheep manure spring," locates an apparently popular watering hole.[74] Diné also shrewdly observed the plants on which they depended, and their names for plants both discriminated between species and generalized among allied species in ways that western science echos. Those names told stories about the plants as well, describing not only their physical characteristics but also, for example, their value for healing and for feeding livestock.[75] In naming nature, Diné delineated the richness that they saw in a landscape that outsiders often viewed as impoverished wasteland.

Diné knew nature not only through their connections with the physical environment but also through their ties to the metaphysical world.[76] Blessingway, perhaps the most important of the Diné ceremonies, framed their understanding of the relationship between livestock and land in much the same way that science framed the way that New Deal conservationists comprehended their environment. Blessingway recounts the epic story of creation and chronicles the life of Changing Woman, the most revered of the Diyin Dine'é and, significantly, the being most identified with the earth. According to that saga, Changing Woman first gave life to sheep and goats, and in the process created the plants that cover the ground. As the sheep and goats were born, their amniotic fluid soaked into the soil, and from the moistened earth, vegetation grew.[77] In that way, plants and animals multiplied together.

Like the New Dealers, Diné recognized that plant life had become increasingly desiccated and sparse by the early 1930s, but they had a fundamentally different understanding of the underlying problem and the appropriate solutions. Most believed the problem was temporary drought. Drought had come and gone periodically since the 1870s—and even long before that—and this era, while prolonged, did not seem different. Where soil conservationists saw dead grass and chamizo, the Diné saw dormant vegetation that would revive with rain. And the Diné responded as they always had. When drought caused corn crops to dwindle, Diné traditionally slaughtered more sheep and goats for food, and they bartered animals, wool, and pelts for grain at trading posts.[78] In consuming livestock, Diné decreased their herds and extended webs of reciprocity as stockowners shared their bounty with poorer kin. Diné also typically responded to drought by moving long distances to find better forage. According to oral tradition, for instance, a drought in the early 1820s spurred the Diné leader Narbona to move his family and his flock of some 2,000 sheep and 250 goats more than two hundred miles from their home on the eastern slopes of the Chuskas to Dinnebito Wash on the western edge of the Hopi mesas.[79] Drought brought hardship, but the shepherds always coped somehow.

Many Diné believed that underlying the apparent drought of the 1930s was a more fundamental disorder, hóchx̨ǫ́, or spiritual chaos. Such disorder sprang from imbalances in the social relationships among people, between humans and the Diyin Dine'é, or between humans and the nonhuman world, disequilibriums that only ceremonies could set aright. If hóchx̨ǫ́ was drying up the rain and causing the plants to wither and die, the most important action that they could take was to perform Blessingway and other ceremonies to restore order, or hózhǫ́.

Hózhǫ́ is the central concept of Diné philosophy, but a difficult one to translate. Although often glossed as "beauty," essentially, it refers to the balance or harmony or perfection that surrounds all life, animates the universe, and brings long life and happiness, *są'a naagháii bik'eh hózhǫ́*. Diné do not imagine hózhǫ́ as a static condition; it requires continual maintenance through ritual action. When things become disordered, people restore order or hózhǫ́ by singing Blessingway, which reenacts creation, not figuratively, but literally. This process of re-creation through Blessingway is an important concept that those of us who are not Diné sometimes find difficult to grasp. For Diné who follow the traditional ways, mind and matter are inseparable. Thought, speech, and song *actually create physical reality*.[80]

Traditionally Diné exercised control over their world through thought and speech. In Blessingway, for example, things occur when people think or talk about them, particularly when they repeat a request four times. The spiritual healers known as hataałii, moreover, cure their patients by reenacting creation through song. And even ordinary people in their everyday lives could make things happen, good or bad, through the simple act of thinking or talking about them. Praying for rain would make it rain, and wishing ill on a neighbor would bring disaster. People, for instance, could ensure the health of their horses and sheep or even expand their herds by singing the proper Blessingway songs that reenacted the creation of livestock.[81] Old Man Hat explained the importance of these ritual songs to his son Left Handed in the late 1880s. "If you don't know any songs," he admonished the young man, "you won't have healthy stocks." He added that if Left Handed *did* know some songs, he'd have a good herd. "You'll be raising them year after year and get many lambs. The same with the horses. In the springtime you'll have colts, and they'll be looking fine." And then Old Man Hat warned: "If you don't know any songs you'll soon lose all the stock."[82] This faith in the power of ritual songs persisted through the 1930s and much longer.[83] To the Diné way of thinking, Blessingway songs were—and are—crucial to the well-being of their animals and the land.

Consequently, as drought seemed to grip the reservation and stock began to starve, Diné responded with a flood of ceremonies. This outpouring of ritual struck New Deal scientists as mere superstition; songs could do nothing to increase forage. William McGinnies, director of the reservation's land management program, barely contained his disdain when he observed that "the physical factors of climate and soil determine forage production ... [which] can in no way be increased by prayers or religious fervor."[84] But Diné had a different understanding of the environmental problems they were experiencing. A Diné woman from around Farmington, New Mexico, revealed that one of the Diyin Dine'é, Banded Rock Boy, visited her and explained the reason that the rains no longer came: "We do not live the right way anymore," she reported. "People have forgotten the right way to live and everyone *thinks the wrong thoughts*." And Banded Rock Boy prescribed the solution, as well: "The people should hold ceremonies," he told her. "They must pray for things to be good again."[85] If livestock were a gift of the Diyin Dine'é, then surely the wanton destruction of that gift would bring misery. Importantly, many like the woman from Farmington believed that the people had forgotten the right way to live, had forgotten how to sing the right songs, and so the earth tilted off balance.

Just as New Dealers viewed these ideas as wholly irrational, Diné thought stock reduction itself seemed anything but logical. It flew in the face of everything they understood about their world. Many saw the root of the problem in stock reduction itself. Listen to the story that 'Asdzáá 'Adika'í, Gambler Woman, from near Piñon, narrated:

> Before the reduction period there was a lot of grass, and I think it was the stock reduction that caused our pasture vegetation to be reduced. . . . The Anglos are not telling the truth when they say that the reason for the stock reduction was too much livestock and not enough vegetation to provide for it. There was an abundance of greasewood and other vegetation. During the mid-summers[,] vegetation, like the sunflowers, colored the place. It grew in such abundance that the livestock walked in tunnel-like paths among them. . . . There is very little now for a sheep to take a bite of. All this is due to the lack of precipitation from above. Maybe they reduced that, too.[86]

This story expressed a common conception among the Diné. Like Gambler Woman, many had a completely different sense of the timing of environmental change than the conservationists had. Soil scientists viewed the degraded range as the result of an ecological decline that reached back to the 1880s, but Diné, recalling a recently luxuriant land, believed that desertification began only in the 1930s. Many viewed the land in a light refracted through the prism of memory. Some likely looked back to the particularly wet period between 1905 and 1920, years when Fred Deeshchii'nii had seen grasses "so tall in some areas that all you could see was a horse's back."[87] They remembered patches of land in especially well-watered places at higher elevations and in relatively pristine areas without stock water, for the effects of grazing were unevenly distributed across the landscape. Many saw a correlation between stock reduction and the advent of an extended drought, but they saw them in that order, as cause and effect, transposing the actual course of events. Viewing the landscape through the lens of their spiritual beliefs, they reasoned that, in mercilessly slashing livestock, the New Dealers created hóchxǫ, chaos, and thereby dried up the rain.[88]

Diné blamed drought, disharmony, and the arrival of the conservationists themselves for the decline, while they defended their own stewardship with descriptions of lush vegetation. In doing so, they overlooked environmental changes that had been taking place since the early twentieth century, in part because the incremental scale of those changes eluded day-to-day observations. Many failed especially to acknowledge that growing numbers of people and flocks placed intense pressure on the forage, thereby reshaping the relationships between plants, soils, and water. At the same time, in telling themselves that the problem was temporary drought, they did not recognize that long-term climatic conditions were changing, any more than the New Dealers did. Diné needed to adjust their herds to relatively droughty conditions over the long term. New conditions called for new ways of imagining their world.

Diné had long imagined that world as a mosaic of grasses, forbs, and brush through which they maneuvered with age-old movements that conserved and even created forage, but those seasonal shifts became increasingly difficult by the 1930s. Transhumance probably *had* conserved the range, at least through much of the second half of the nineteenth century, and expansion into new lands had delayed the day of reckoning. After all, if nutritious forage had declined rapidly as they built their herds, the incredible boom in the numbers of livestock could not have occurred, because the land could not have sustained high rates of reproduction. But the efficacy of those strategies began to change in the 1880s and 1890s. Over time, Diné population growth and the encroachment of Anglo and Hispanic ranchers on the periphery began to limit the amount of range available to each family, and seasonal movements became more and more constricted. Between 1868 and 1930, the Diné population itself multiplied fivefold from about 8,000 to perhaps 39,000 people, and their herds increased perhaps fifteenfold.[89] As a consequence, even as early as the drought years of the early 1880s, Diné shepherds found it harder and harder to find new forage. Eventually some began to complain openly that the reservation was overgrazed and demanded an extension of the reservation boundary to give Diné exclusive rights to much of the Checkerboard.[90] But this proposed expansion could not really have solved the population problem, since Diné families and Anglo and Hispanic ranchers already occupied those lands.

Competition for forage was bound to place intense pressure on ecological systems. Many Diné observed the changes, even if they did not fully recognize the cause. Ernest Nelson inadvertently documented the effects of overgrazing when he described the reservation's lush range conditions before government meddlers destroyed everything. "You could see the golden blossoms of sunflowers growing for miles and miles around," he reminisced. There was lots of grass, he recalled, but also "pigweed grass grew thickly everywhere you looked."[91] Without realizing it, Nelson confirmed what the conservationists saw. Overgrazing had encouraged the spread of both native and exotic weeds, like pigweed, which thrives on disturbed, denuded soils. It brought locoweed, which colored the land with beautiful flowers, but poisoned the livestock that ate them.[92]

Diné, of course, were well aware of which plants sickened their stock and avoided those areas where large stands of toxins thrived, but there were also weeds that they welcomed.[93] Diné viewed weeds differently than the soil conservationists did. Many of the plants that thrived on overgrazed ground—native plants such as sunflowers, greasewood, snakeweed, and rabbitbrush—had cultural uses as medicines, food, or dyes. Diné women, for example, prized rabbitbrush for dying blanket wool, as well as for curing headaches and treating colds, and they used snakeweed to treat snake and insect bites, headaches, and cuts.[94] One culture's field of noxious plants was another's pharmacopoeia.

The Diné and the New Dealers looked at the world through cultural lenses that shaped their understandings of the land. Neither group fully understood nature's contingencies and complexities, though they acted as though they were certain they did. Each told themselves a profoundly different story about the earth and the proper way to care for it. Many of us, educated in the catechism of science, are inclined to accept the New Dealers' tale. And yet both narratives, native and scientific, can be used to explain today's poor range conditions. For conservationists, the denuded range itself was proof positive of the damage wrought by overgrazing. But it is interesting that those Diné who believed that stock reduction itself unleashed chaos across the land also pointed to the range as proof.

The New Dealers possessed the power to impose their story on the Navajos, and yet they never quite grasped the symbolic meanings embodied by livestock, meanings that would linger long after sheep no longer meant much economically. Livestock offered long life and happiness, *sq'a naagháii bik'eh hózhǫ́*; they were the substance of Diné thoughts and prayers. The conservationists and even the BIA anthropologists never saw the point of understanding those prayers. They never saw the point of understanding the ceremonies and traditional stories. As far as they were concerned, those stories were merely esoteric "myths" and "legends," with no meaning for conservation. And that was their mistake. Had they listened to those stories, they would have discovered a great deal about the Navajos, their values, their epistemology, their history, and their dreams. For many Diné, livestock formed the warp of the rich tapestry of their identity as a pastoral people, an identity that extended back to their very beginnings, when Changing Woman gave them sheep so that they might prosper.

PART 2 · *Bedrock*

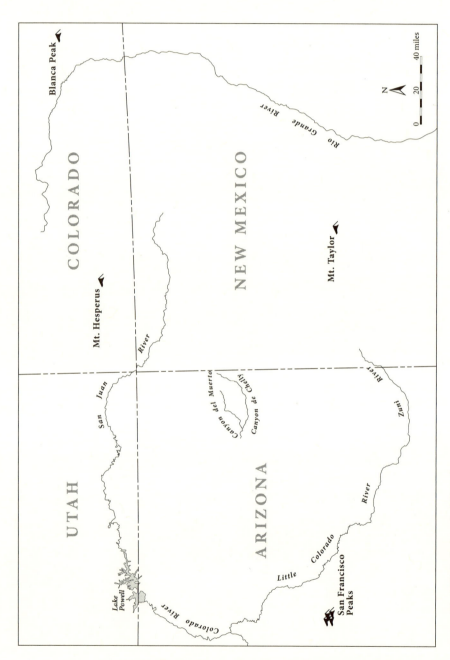

MAP 2 Diné Bikéyah: Land of Creation

3 · WITH OUR SHEEP WE WERE CREATED

In the early 1950s, Hastiin Tó Łtsoii, Mr. Yellow Water, a respected ceremonial singer—a hataałii—living on Black Mesa, tried to explain to a visitor why the Diné cared so much about their sheep. Mr. Yellow Water had lost more than three-fourths of his substantial flock to stock reduction. He had even gone to jail for opposing the program. Now he wanted to make clear just why sheep were so important. "Since time immemorial," he told his listener, "our grandfathers and our grandmothers have lived . . . from their herds of sheep, horses and cattle, for those things originated with the world itself." Sheep, he said, were among "the high-lights of creation. . . . With our sheep we were created."[1] His was not an isolated claim. Howard Gorman, the former vice chairman of the Navajo Tribal Council, likewise maintained that "we always had sheep" from the very beginning.[2]

Some readers may find this story mystifying. After all, Navajos lived within the four sacred mountains for a century or more before the Spanish introduced domesticated livestock to the Southwest.[3] Not until 1598 did don Juan de Oñate bring thousands of sheep, goats, and cattle to the pueblos along the Rio Grande and Rio Chama in northern New Mexico, and another century passed before Spanish soldiers began to report large numbers of domestic sheep grazing the mesas and valleys of Navajo Country. It is tempting, then, to dismiss Mr. Yellow Water's story as a bit of folklore, a quaint tale.

But that would be a grave mistake. In fact, dismissing stories like this one was one of the fundamental errors that New Deal conservationists such as William McGinnies made as they struggled to persuade Navajos to reduce their herds. For by the 1930s, Diné viewed sheep not only as vital to their origins but also as essential to their multilayered identity as a people.

Certainly, a number of other shared traditions and values also shaped that identity, forming the rich cultural tapestry identified as Diné. A web of clans formed networks of kin, creating a remarkable sense of peoplehood among families scattered across vast expanses of land, and a common language and ceremonial practices reinforced those ties. Corn agriculture was also vital; it gave birth to the people and tethered them to the land. Just as important was the land itself. The sacred mountains marking the boundaries of that land mapped the center of the Diné cosmos. In fact, one could argue that Diné Bikéyah itself was the essence of identity, for that land demarcated an imagined community of people long before a political nation arose. Significantly, too, mobility within that landscape, from sagebrush flat to mesa to valley, from one mountaintop to another, distinguished the Diné.[4]

Sheep were, nonetheless, fundamental. It was sheep pastoralism and transhumance—the pattern of movement from winter home to summer pastures—that reinforced the people's sense of themselves as wanderers. Importantly, those migrations reenacted the ritual movements of the Diyin Dine'é from one mountain to the next, the sunwise movements that gave substance to the land in the creation stories. Still, there was more to it than that. Sheep had been a gift from the Diyin Dine'é, a life-sustaining gift. As Mr. Yellow Water maintained, sheep had nurtured Diné lives from the beginning.

Mr. Yellow Water's version of history carried the weight of tradition. Blessingway, the main stalk of Diné philosophy, provided an oral account of creation, including the origins of sheep, and it seems likely that this hataałii drew his understanding of the past from that epic. The story he told his visitor about the origin of sheep echoed the version of Blessingway that another respected hataałii, Curly Tó 'Aheedlíinii (River Junction Curly) of Chinle recounted in the late 1920s or early 1930s. According to that rendition, the Sun, together with his wife, Changing Woman, and a third holy person, Mirage Man, gave life to sheep and horses, but four years passed before Changing Woman became lonely and decided to breathe life into the Earth Surface People.[5] Thus Blessingway holds that the creation of domestic livestock preceded the birth of the Diné themselves. From the beginning, they say, the lives of Diné and sheep have intertwined.[6]

When I began exploring the environmental history of Navajo Country, I vowed not to wander across the treacherous terrain of Diné cosmology and the sacred symbols that explain existence. Diné frown on Anglo-American outsiders like myself—bilagáana—intruding onto sacred ground that we can never fully fathom. More to the point, those Diné who trust in the traditional ways believe that only hataałii—those men (and occasionally women) who have devoted their lives to the study and practice of ceremonies—have the authority to discuss and interpret ceremonial rites and songs. Many native people, not only Diné, rightly take offense when outsiders publish ceremonial knowledge, for oftentimes sacred rituals gain their power from their secrecy. Finally, it initially seemed unclear whether Diné ceremonies would be pertinent to my understanding of the ways in which people related to the twentieth-century material world.

But as I immersed myself in the historical record, I came to realize that I could not write a history of Navajos in a spiritual vacuum, any more than I could understand colonial New England without first grappling with Puritan thought. For in the Diné universe, unlike my own, there was no divide between the sacred and the profane.[7] In fact, it quickly became clear that I would never really understand what happened in the 1930s if I did not come to grips with the ways in which Diné understood the world around them.[8] Much of Diné testimony becomes plain only in the light of Diné cosmology.

It soon became clear, too, that hataałii are not only "medicine men" or healers; they are historians, keepers of the past. Blessingway singers, for example, reestablish harmony in the universe by reenacting creation through song. And in doing so, they tell stories about the past, great mythic stories about the origins of the Diyin Diné'é, the battles that the Hero Twins waged against evil, the creation of Diné Bikéyah, the birth of human beings, and the journey of the Diné to their home within four sacred mountains. No history of this land, surely, could ignore the epic chronicles that Diné themselves tell.[9]

More than that, those mythic stories reveal the cultural creation—the ethnogenesis—of the Diné as a people distinguishable from their Apachean cousins. Embedded within those stories, then, are the roots of Diné

Hataałii reenact creation through ceremonies in which they relate mythic histories of ethnogenesis. These sandpainters demonstrate their ceremonial art at a Navajo tribal fair in the 1930s. Records of the BIA, RG75, National Archives at College Park, Md., RG75-Nav-Y-30.

cultural identity. And because most Diné experienced stock reduction as an assault on that sense of peoplehood, these stories assume great importance. They are one key to understanding why Diné rejected the New Deal program to manage the range.

Cultural groups—be they Americans or Cajuns or Estonians or Diné—tend to define themselves based on a combination of characteristics that together draw a social border between themselves and others. These traits can include language, territory, spiritual beliefs, modes of production, reputation, and even favorite foods. Some of these individual attributes may be held in common with other groups, but, collectively, they distinguish insiders from outsiders. Of course, most cultural groups are not nearly as homogeneous as they may appear to outsiders. But the semblance of a fair measure of homogeneity is in fact one of the functions of cultural identity: groups position themselves in relation to others by emphasizing their commonalities and suppressing differences and contradictions.[10]

Cultural identities and the traditions that reinforce them are by no means static. Shared characteristics change over time as a group integrates new elements, often borrowed from others, into their way of life and as they alter older patterns in the very act of reproducing them. For example, while incarcerated at Hwéeldi in the 1860s, Diné women learned to make fry bread and took note of army wives' fashions to develop the calico and sateen skirts and velveteen blouses that soon came to be seen as traditional.[11] In this way, the notion of "tradition" is continually redefined.

Paradoxically, then, traditions and the identities that flow out of them are at once incrementally changing and yet seemingly static. What are we to make of this paradox? How do we reconcile the apparent timelessness of Diné oral traditions with the actual dynamism of Diné culture? How do we explain the ostensible contradiction between a history that places sheep at the beginning of creation and a historical record suggesting that the Spanish introduced livestock to the Southwest only four centuries ago? For answers, we could turn to either of two broad scholarly approaches, one exploring how oral traditions are reproduced over time, the other examining the purposes that traditions serve.

The folklorist Albert Lord and the ethnohistorian Jan Vansina have argued that this tension between apparent timelessness and change is inherent in the ways in which oral societies reproduce historical memories from one generation to the next.[12] On the one hand, oral narratives tend to be dynamic, both because each performance is adjusted to meet the needs of the particular circumstance in which the story is told and because the stories must absorb new ideas and meanings over time or they become irrelevant to new generations. On the other hand, the process of change is so slow that it can be almost imperceptible, because new elements are incorporated into old patterns. This conservatism is especially true when the stories are told through sacred ceremonies. Ceremonial singers learn the essential ideas, events, phrases, and motifs with a precision necessary for a ritual's success.[13] When the narratives, moreover, are presented in poetic form, as Diné ceremonies are, they tend to change even more slowly because their structure, meter, and repetitions serve as mnemonic devices, making more exact recall possible.

And yet oral traditions *do* change. Over time, as a group embraces new definitions of identity and recognizes the significance of more recent historical events, its oral traditions gradually come to reflect those changes. This is especially true of those narratives that seek to explain how the present world came about. After all, if they did not incorporate new cultural truths, they would no longer be accurate.[14]

Incrementally over time, new narrative layers become enfolded within the old, so that a dynamic form retains the appearance of stability. When, for example, a relatively recent historical event remains fresh in the collective memory, it may first enter the story as a recognizable eyewitness account. Juxtaposed with the rest of the epic, it stands out as an anachronism. And for some time, even as it slowly takes on the patina of myth, the new element may remain anachronistic and thus identifiable. But as the story is told and retold over the course of generations, the new elements fuse with familiar, idealized patterns, and historical actors metamorphose into mythic heroes. In this way, newer cultural elements become integrated within the larger story. Older traditions and identities remain important, however, even as newer ones gain symbolic value. Thus, as time passes and as the newer traditions achieve an antiquity since time out of memory, the old and new appear coeval.[15]

Imagine an exposed rock formation: on its face quite solid but in fact rather fluid. Like ancient geological strata, traditions layer themselves one over the other, and the forces of time may warp and wrinkle and dip and fold, overturning layers back on themselves so that the original stratigraphy becomes convoluted and the more recent layers are cradled in the center of the fold. Newer traditions, then, become deeply embedded within the old. Together these traditions form a kind of cultural bedrock.

A geologist, of course, can visually trace the layers of rock to discover the original order of the strata, and in a similar fashion, we might discern how a relatively recent innovation came to form part of the cultural core. Peeling back these layers is complicated because Diné oral traditions vary from one place to another, reflecting the different histories of Canyon de Chelly, Navajo Mountain, Ganado, Black Mesa, and so on. Variations in Diné oral traditions can reflect the narrators' personal differences, their particular ceremonial traditions and religious philosophies, the men with whom they apprenticed, the regions from which they came, and their clans, even as they convey a shared cosmology. Still, an explication of Blessingway might help explain how Diné livestock could be both ancient and new.

If we were to look at the various narratives of Blessingway, we might first observe that horses and domesticated sheep receive relatively little attention.[16] Corn agriculture, the four sacred mountains, mobility, and the Diyin Dine'é all figure far more prominently, indicating that these elements held cultural meaning over a much longer period of history. And yet, here and there are stanzas and even entire songs praising livestock and explaining their creation. If we were to compare different narrative renditions, we might begin to see how various hataałii and the masters with whom they apprenticed endeavored to account for the introduction of horses and sheep into the Diné economy by interjecting a story at one point or substituting domestic sheep for wild mountain sheep at another. We might conclude that through this gradual process of substitution, livestock appear in the stories of Diné origins not as an afterthought but as an integral part of creation.

But we must be careful: this approach to understanding how sheep became embedded in Diné oral tradition could easily lead us down the wrong trail. In focusing our gaze on the process by which newer cultural elements might have become enmeshed in age-old stories, we could lose our bearings and arrive at the erroneous conclusion that those elements added later are not truly "traditional" or "authentic." The anthropologist W. W. Hill made that mistake during the New Deal. Pastoralism, he believed, was not a truly traditional way of life, because the Navajos adopted it from the Spanish. Instead of helping conservationists understand how sheep, goats, and horses entangled with Navajo culture, he justified the destruction of livestock by reporting that livestock were anomalous to the Navajo economy, that *"sentimentally, religiously,* and practically," agriculture was more important.[17] But in arguing that livestock were sentimentally and religiously (not to mention economically) unimportant, Hill failed to recognize two important things: cultural traditions are dynamic, and relatively new traditions are no less "authentic" than those much older. If we followed Hill's line of thought, many of the traditions bilagáana hold dear—celebrating the Fourth of July, for instance—would not be considered traditional at all. Indeed, the only authentic traditions would be those we could trace directly from Europe or Africa or Asia. Most of us would think that is ludicrous, and rightly so.

Perhaps, though, we should consider the political purposes that cultural traditions often serve. According to historians Eric Hobsbawm and Terence Ranger, imperialist nations consciously *invented* "traditions" to establish a sense of continuity between the colonial present and the indigenous past and thereby legitimate the new social order. Taking up this line of reasoning, some would argue that Diné traditions—like those of European colonizers—assert ancestral claims to a land in which Diné are intruders. Puebloan peoples made their homes on the Colorado Plateau long before Diné arrived, and some scholars maintain that Diné acquired many of the most important themes in their story of origins—along with much of their primary ceremony, Blessingway—from Puebloan traditions. In that light, Diné stories of genesis in the Southwest might seem like little more than the convenient tales that colonial powers often invent to justify their presence. Alternatively, we might argue that Diné oral traditions evolved to make sense of the social and economic transformations that came with increased federal control over their lives, for Hobsbawm and Ranger note that indigenous peoples create neotraditions to maintain group cohesion when rapid social and economic transformations weaken older ways of life.[18]

Just as tracing the development of Diné traditions runs the risk of getting us lost, so too does this analytical path lead us astray.[19] What really matters is this: Diné themselves recognize the ceremonial stories that hataałii tell as the *actual history*, the factual chronicle of their origins. Most important, the people's understanding of that past shaped the ways in which they responded to the events of the 1930s. It's significant, too, that collectively the ceremonial songs do, in fact, convey a complicated narrative of ethnogenesis. They illuminate the cultural identity that forms terra firma. They help to explain why many experienced stock reduction as genocidal.

We must tread cautiously through this landscape, conscious that the traditional texts are indeed sacred. These are not texts in the usual meaning of the word, nor are they truly narratives. These are *oral* traditions, "memories of memories" passed down from one generation to the next, from master to apprentice; only rarely and recently did they become fixed on the written page.[20] In practice, moreover, hataałii never perform any of their highly complex ceremonials in their entirety; they reenact particular segments or episodes in response to specific contexts. So the published "texts" of traditional stories—with their extended, coherent narratives—are, to a certain extent, ethnographic artifacts, the co-creations of the hataałii and the anthropologists who asked them to tell stories.[21] And yet in an important sense, these narratives are quite real, for they provide the mental framework that helps hataałii remember the proper order of the ceremonial chants. They may be ethnographic inventions, but are no less infused with cultural meanings. To understand those meanings, we will explore published accounts of two particular chronicles—the epic story of Diné genesis and Blessingway—both of which have more or less entered the public domain, and avoid the more culturally sensitive sacred rites that take place within ceremonies.[22]

Let's begin with the way in which Hataałii Nez, Tall Chanter, an important Nightway singer, represented Diné history with his origin story. Tall Chanter became in 1884 the first hataałii to permit a bilagáana, ethnographer Washington Matthews, to make a written record of this account of emergence, and his remains the best known epic of Diné origins.[23] The tale opens with a journey undertaken by Insect People, who move up through four lower worlds. The First World, they say, was a land with neither sun, nor moon, nor star, and "to the east extended an ocean, to the south an ocean, to the west an ocean, and to the north an ocean." Before long, a great flood expelled the Insect People through a hole in the sky to the Second World, which was nothing but a vast uninhabited waste, a barren plain. Aside from swallows, there were "no animals of any kind, no trees, no grass, no sage-brush, no mountains, nothing but bare, level ground."[24] The Third World, populated by grasshoppers, appeared similarly stark, yet was marked by a great river that flowed to the east.

And finally, the Insect People entered the Fourth World, a land bounded by four great snow-covered mountains. There were people in this land: Puebloan people, who cultivated fields and taught the wanderers agriculture. Clearly, at this point in the story the travelers have entered Dinétah, the original area of settlement in what is now northwestern New Mexico, although the Fourth World was the inner form of the present world, without its substance. Soon appeared four Mirage People, who laid two ears of white corn and two ears of yellow corn on the ground and covered them with buckskin. When they lifted the buckskin, the ears of corn had disappeared, and in their stead lay First Man and First Woman, who were not mortals, but Diyin Dine'é. After many years of farming, First Man, First Woman, and their descendants, frightened by a flash flood, ascended through hollow reeds up through the center of a lake and emerged onto the surface of the earth.

At last First Man and First Woman entered this, the Fifth World. And it was here that they shaped the four sacred mountains that today bound Diné Bikéyah. To the east they placed Tsisnaajinii (Blanca Peak); to the south, Tsoodził (Mount Taylor); to the west, Dook'o'oosłííd (San Francisco Peaks); and finally, to the north, Dibé Ntsaa (Mount Hesperus in the La Plata Mountains).[25] Within these sacred mountains rises Ch'óol'į́'í (Gobernador Knob), where Talking God and Calling God created Changing Woman.

In the same manner that the Mirage People created First Man and First Woman, the Diyin Dine'é of the Fifth World created Diné. Talking God laid an ear of white corn and an ear of yellow corn on a sacred buckskin on the ground and covered them with another buckskin. He then picked up each ear of corn again and again, laying them in turn in each of the cardinal directions. And for this reason, they say, Diné never abide in one home like the Puebloan people, but move from place to place. Then the Wind entered between the two skins.[26] And after a while, the white ear of corn changed into a man, and the yellow ear of corn became a woman. With the breath of life, the ears of corn transformed into two mortals.[27] As time passed, Diné multiplied and began to form clans, and others joined them: refugees, captives, and intruders from Puebloan villages, Apachean and Ute bands, and neighboring Mexican settlements. These people merged with Diné, forming still more clans, and in this way the population grew.

This story of the Fifth World recounts the ethnogenesis of Diné, based, at least in part, on three key facets of Diné cultural identity: clanship, the dramatic landforms of Diné Bikéyah, and corn agriculture. Diné, it seems, came to believe particularly in the centrality of agriculture to their identity as a people, for it was from ears of corn, they say, that Diné sprang to life. The Diné pantheon includes White Corn Boy, Yellow Corn Girl, Cornbeetle Girl, Cornbeetle Boy, Corn Woman, and Corn Man. Cornmeal and corn pollen remain symbolically important today. Whether they are sprinkling cornmeal to greet the new day, drying themselves with it in rituals, eating it as part of puberty ceremonies and weddings, or using it to create drypaintings, Diné continue to reaffirm that at the dawn of creation, they were made from corn.[28]

Tall Chanter's chronicle also makes clear the importance of the land within the four sacred mountains. In the Fifth World, they say, Changing Woman gave birth to twin boys, who went out to slay the monsters that plagued the earth. As part of their epic journey, the Hero Twins traveled through a hole in the sky to visit the Sun, their father, who had never before laid eyes on them. Uncertain whether they were truly his children, the Sun put the boys through a series of trials. He pierced them with spikes of white shell, then turquoise, then abalone, then jet; he subjected them to a sweatbath so hot it could kill; he passed them a pipe filled with poisonous tobacco. They survived, and yet the Sun remained unconvinced of their true identity. In a fourth test, he at last inquired: "'Where do you belong in the world below? Show me your home.'" Looking down, the boys beheld no familiar landmarks. The ground looked confusingly flat;

wooded mountains appeared merely as dark spots; the lakes gleamed like stars; and the rivers seemed like streaks of lightning. Then the Wind, the source of all thought, whispered to the boys. He pointed out the great streams—the San Juan River and the Rio Grande—along with the sacred mountains that to this day delineate Diné Bikéyah: Blanca Peak, Mount Taylor, the San Francisco Peaks, and Mount Hesperus. Suddenly the land appeared to have form, and the younger of the twins pointed: There lies home! Now the Sun at last recognized the boys. He knew they were indeed his children, so he gave them the weapons they needed to slay the monsters and sent them on their way.[29]

This episode culminates an epic migration that demarcates the Diné homeland. Like an incantation, the holy ones move from one sacred mountaintop to the next, from east to south to west to north, in a pilgrimage that ritually defines the boundaries of the Diné homeland and gives them substance. So it would seem that when the Hero Twins proclaimed that their home lay within those four sacred mountains, they gave renewed significance to those ritual movements from one peak to another. They articulated a congruence between people and place that delineated what it means to be Diné. They drew a map of identity.[30]

Stories like this one bore meaning for Diné that went far beyond allegory. We can hear the echoes of this tale in a speech that Barboncito, the great Diné leader from Canyon de Chelly, made in 1868. Earlier in the 1860s, part of a long period Diné remember as the "Fearing Time," Kit Carson rounded up the Navajos and forced them on the long walk to Hwéeldi, where for four long years the Army incarcerated the Navajos, who suffered from disease, hunger, and above all homesickness. On the eve of their release, Barboncito begged General William Tecumseh Sherman to allow him and his people to return home. "Our grand-fathers," he said through his interpreter, "had no idea of living in any other country except our own and I do not think it right for us to do so[,] as we were never taught to. When the Navajos were first created, four mountains and four rivers were pointed out to us, inside of which we should live[.] [T]hat was to be our country and was given to us by the first woman of the Navajo tribe. It was told to us by our forefathers, that we were never to move east of the Rio Grande ... and I think that our coming here has been the cause of so much death among us and our animals."[31]

Historians have argued that brackish water and poor land led to starvation and despair at the Bosque Redondo.[32] And yet we can see that it was not the quality of the land or the water that Barboncito lamented. The roots of his misery extended far deeper than that. Diné were given a home west of the Rio Grande and admonished never to relocate beyond its boundaries. As Tall Chanter would later explain, Diné Bikéyah was the bedrock of Diné identity.

Curiously, domesticated livestock do not figure prominently in Tall Chanter's chronicle of origins. They appear in only one episode of his lengthy narrative. Known as the tale of the gambler, it interrupts Tall Chanter's history of genesis, forming a story within the story: Long ago, it is said, a gambler descended on the pueblos, and in a series of contests, the stranger enslaved the Puebloan people and took all their property. When a young man—one of the Diyin Dine'é—helped liberate the pueblos by outwitting the gambler and expelling him, the stranger left behind his "pets or domesticated animals." Subsequently, a supernatural being, the Be'gochídí, took pity on the exiled gambler's newly felt poverty and "made for him sheep, asses, horses, swine, goats, and fowls." Some years later, Tall Chanter tells us, the stranger returned to the Rio Grande from the south, where Mexico is today.[33]

This brief episode offers one explanation as to how Diné eventually acquired their herds of sheep, by linking the introduction of livestock to the pueblos and the Spanish-speaking people from the lands to the south. But how does it square with Mr. Yellow Water's story that sheep originated with the world itself?

If Tall Chanter's account fails to answer that question, one important thing to remember about the Diné origin story is that no narrator tells the tale in its entirety. Just as, say, a Protestant minister might emphasize a certain episode of the Gospels while deemphasizing another, so hataałii highlight some details over others without changing the essential epic. Differences in emphasis often reflect the particular ceremonies that the hataałii have been trained to sing, and they also trace the ways in which one hataałii acquired his ceremonial knowledge from another.[34] More than that, much like the Bible, Diné ceremonies express a complex philosophy, and hataałii draw on those portions of their knowledge that best fit a particular circumstance. So in relating the epic chronicle of genesis, one hataałii may elaborate on an episode that another renders elliptically.[35]

In the early 1900s, Tall Chanter's brother, Gishin Biye', Cane Man's Son, related a much more detailed account of origins to Berard Haile, the Franciscan missionary and ethnographer. The story was contemporary to Tall

Chanter's and was likely an extended version of the same tale.[36] According to Cane Man's Son, Changing Woman gave life to Diné and their livestock in a single episode of creation. From her own skin, she formed the people of the first four Diné clans, and then with another bit of skin and the help of Be'gochídí, she created horses, sheep, goats, and other livestock.[37] This story, then, offers one clue for solving the riddle of Mr. Yellow Water's enigmatic words: "With our sheep, we were created."

Later, Cane Man's Son added, as the Hero Twins girded for battle against the earth's monsters, they went to their father in hopes that he would arm them for war. Testing their will to fight, the Sun tempted the boys with gifts. He first showed them his horses and asked if they wanted them, but they said no. They came for weapons. Then he enticed his sons with sheep, deer, elk, and other game, but they did not want them either. They would wait until they had slain the monsters before they would accept an award of livestock.[38] This origin story reveals that at least two generations before the stock reduction era, and probably much earlier, Diné understood that they had possessed sheep and horses since the dawn of creation.

That genesis story continued to resonate through the 1930s, through Blessingway and other ceremonies. Blessingway is particularly valuable for our purpose because Father Haile recorded three renditions between 1928 and 1932, the years just prior to stock reduction.[39] It details the history of the Fifth World, explaining, in part, how the Diyin Dine'é created horses and sheep and gave them to the Diné so that they could live. In that reckoning, sheep predated the creation of mortals, and importantly, they helped to define the landscape of Diné Bikéyah.

River Junction Curley, the Blessingway singer from Chinle, told the story this way: As a prelude to the creation of the Earth Surface People, Monster Slayer, the older of the Hero Twins, had a vision that reveals much about the significance of sheep to Diné identity. Ascending to the top of Wide Belt Mesa (near present-day Cuba, New Mexico), Monster Slayer saw an enormous flock of white sheep to the east. But as he approached them, they turned into chamiso, or four-wing saltbush. Then he saw a large flock of blue sheep, but when he went among them, they were sagebrush. Similarly, a great flock of brown sheep turned out to be Mormon tea, a shrubby plant composed of stems without leaves. And when he approached a huge flock of black sheep, he found nothing but a streak of jet.[40]

This Blessingway account correlates the creation of sheep with the vegetation that dominates much of the range. But more than that, the story links the origins of sheep with the four sacred mountains, for Diné associate each color—white, blue, brown, and black—with one of the peaks.⁴¹ Sheep, it seems, not only signify the mountains that mark the Diné homeland, they also draw Monster Slayer toward each sacred mountain, one after the other, causing him to repeat the patterns of movement that ritually recreate the land. Thus, the story implies, sheep not only created the plants that spread across the earth, they helped form the landscape itself, thereby multiplying their significance.

Blessingway provides the most extensive epic of the creation of the Diné and their livestock. Eventually, Monster Slayer managed to rid the world of various evils and returned to his home. But soon he began worrying that there would not be enough food. Recalling the livestock that he had seen when he visited his father, he approached his mother and asked her four times to tell him where he might find horses and sheep. She denied knowing anything about them. Then he returned to his father, who also declined to give him what he sought. Instead the Sun gave the young man sacred pollen to take home to his mother. And with that pollen and dew, Changing Woman and Mirage Man created sheep and horses. "From now on," the Diyin Dine'é told these animals, "people will live by means of you. As the days go on you will overcome everything. . . . You will overcome hunger, you will overcome poverty." These hardships—the obstacles that livestock would overcome—were among the very enemies that Monster Slayer spared in his battle against evil, for it is in knowing hunger, they say, that Diné avoid gluttony, and it is the specter of poverty that inspires hard work.⁴²

After giving life to sheep and horses, Changing Woman journeyed to her permanent home in the West, on the edge of the earth and sky. And it was there, on an island in the Pacific, that she created the Earth Surface People. This is a second story of Diné genesis contained in Blessingway's complex origin narrative. For four years, Changing Woman lived alone on that island, with only the Sun visiting her each evening. Feeling lonely, she began to think about making human beings to keep her company. While contemplating this, she rubbed her skin, sloughing it off in little balls. Next she covered these fragments of herself with a dark cloud and fog, with darkness and dawn, with daylight and twilight. Then, at last, she breathed life into those pieces of skin, thereby creating two men and two women. As time passed, they multiplied so that they soon overpopulated the island. Fearing that such a burgeoning population would destroy her home, Changing Woman sent the people on a long migration to Diné Bikéyah, to the land within the four sacred mountains. And she sent them home with a gift of livestock, so that they might prosper.[43]

Blessingway, then, forges symbolic bonds between the lives of Changing Woman, the Diné, and their livestock. Changing Woman, to be sure, assumes her position in Diné thought as the most revered of the Diyin Diné'é in part because she gave them this most sacred ceremony. But as the story makes clear, she is beloved for at least one more reason, and an important one at that: it was she, they say, who gave life to the Diné and to the livestock that nurture them.

Blessingway helps us to understand why Mr. Yellow Water proclaimed that the Diné were inextricably bound up with sheep. It was only after giving life to sheep and horses that Changing Woman created the people themselves, and so sheep predated the genesis of the Diné. That order of events was important. But it was even more significant that Changing Woman—the holiest being in Diné cosmology—gave those sheep to the people to sustain them for all time, telling them to care for their stock by singing the proper songs.[44] And remember, too, that livestock did not merely hold hunger and poverty at bay; they shaped the very landscape within the four sacred mountains. Monster Slayer himself saw it happen. When he spied sheep grazing in each of the four cardinal directions, he saw them turn into the sagebrush, saltbush, and other plants that cloak the land. On many levels, the story of Blessingway placed livestock at the core of Diné identity.

To be sure, livestock were but one element of the core, forming only one important layer in the thick stratigraphy of traditions that shaped Diné understandings of themselves as an ethnic people. Those traditions taught that livestock, corn agriculture, clans, ceremonies, mobility, and the great mountains, mesas, and valleys of their homeland, among other things, made Diné distinctive. So given the variegated strata of that identity, why did sheep come to assume such importance in the first decades of the twentieth century?

We might argue that the explanation is simple: livestock long formed the cornerstone of subsistence and systems of exchange, and the decimation of sheep and goats and horses destroyed the people's means of supporting themselves. True enough. But it is also true that the ways in which people choose to sustain themselves reflects something just as fundamental: the beliefs and values they carry in their heads. We might think that beliefs merely reflect modes of production, but it works the other way around, too: modes of production express deeply embedded ideas. They are mutually reinforcing.

There is one more explanation that we should consider. Recall that in 1868, Barboncito focused on land as the key to the vitality of his people. True, he recognized that corn and livestock also lay at the cultural core.[45] And yet in pleading with General Sherman, he emphasized his home between four sacred mountains. It was the *land*, after all, that the United States Army so recently tore from his people. Without it, the Diné would die. In the late 1860s, then, Diné Bikéyah itself was paramount.

The 1930s seemed like déjà vu, with a new twist. Federal officials once again chipped away at the foundations of Diné identity, this time by attacking livestock. Once again, it seemed like cultural genocide. Since time immemorial, the Diné had fashioned their lives around pastoralism; sheep predated the Diné themselves. Life without livestock was, thus, unimaginable. In the turmoil of livestock reduction, Diné understandings of the significance of sheep to their genesis as a people crystallized.

The sacred symbiosis of the Navajos and their livestock completely escaped the attention of the New Deal conservationists, who viewed ceremonies and the origin stories they conveyed as quaint, colorful folklore. The conservationists never comprehended Navajo consciousness, but perhaps more surprising, they never fully comprehended Navajo life. Livestock imbued the daily lives of most Diné with material and social meaning, and this was especially true for women, who owned a substantial share of the family flocks. But to a large degree, the New Dealers ignored Navajo women, and so they never fathomed the fundamental importance of livestock ownership to women's lives, nor the power women wielded within their communities. As it turned out, women really mattered.

4 · A WOMAN'S PLACE

Kaibah looked out over the sagebrush flats near Sheep Springs on the eastern flank of the Chuska Mountains, feeling rich as she watched her herd of sheep spread across the valley. Although she was only a girl of about eleven, for some time her mother had entrusted her with the care of the family flock. In this, her mother, Mary Chischillie, showed good judgment, for by the early 1930s the herd had grown to some six hundred head under her daughter's watchful eye.[1]

Kaibah took good care of the family flock, perhaps because she counted many of the sheep as her very own. That was not at all unusual. Diné children—both boys and girls—commonly acquired their own stock at an early age, as soon as their parents deemed them capable shepherds, and sometimes even earlier. Kaibah, for instance, was just nine years old when her mother gave her thirty lambs, earmarked to distinguish them from those of other family members, and all the offspring remained her property as well.[2]

Livestock ownership gave Kaibah a sense of pride and responsibility, and it also conferred a large measure of economic autonomy. Family members each owned their stock individually and could do with their animals as they saw fit. This independence extended to children, too, even little girls. For example, when Mary Chischillie suggested that her daughter barter her lambs for store-bought food at the local trading post, Kaibah said no, and her mother respected her daughter's decision. Kaibah was just a young girl, and yet she felt free to withhold her lambs from market in order to build her flock, without interference from anyone, even her mother.[3] This autonomy, to be sure, did not mean selfishness, for kinship carried an implicit obligation to share. Still, the very fact that women and even girls had the power to control the products of their own labor gave them an independence that bilagáana often found remarkable.

Women's economic independence was not the only thing that outsiders noticed. From the earliest Anglo-American observations in the mid-nineteenth century through the 1930s and 1940s, ethnographers invariably observed that Navajo families were *matricentered*. Women stood at the center of almost all aspects of Diné life and thought: spiritual beliefs, kinship, residence patterns, land-use traditions, and economy. Diné traced descent exclusively through their mothers, and a newly married couple generally built their hogan near the wife's family. Consequently, closely knit networks of mothers, daughters, and sisters structured families and gave them cohesion.[4]

These bonds between women made their mark on the land, as well. Hogans clustered close to one another, as married daughters remained near their mothers. The range, too, felt the imprint of these spatial patterns, since mothers and daughters generally ran their sheep and goats in common herds on nearby pastures. For generations, probably dating back to the adoption of agriculture as their primary mode of subsistence, Diné had traced their use-rights to much of their land through local matrilineages headed by elder women.[5] Men also had access to these lands, but usually only as long as they remained linked to their communities—linked, that is, through their social relationships to mothers, sisters, and wives. These communities, consisting of scattered homesteads of generally interrelated families, expressed a distinctively matricentered social geography, one that repeated itself all across the Diné landscape.

Within these matricentered communities, Diné women enjoyed a large measure of autonomy and power in the 1930s. The term "power" is often used to suggest notions of authority, dominance, coercion, or even tyranny, but that's not what I mean here. By "power," I mean a person's ability to control *one's own life* and body and to negotiate decisions with others from a position of relative strength, without fear of losing, for example, economic support or custody of children. Since one's power is limited by

A Diné woman returns her small flock of sheep and goats to her corral, 1940. Photograph probably by Milton Snow. Records of the BIA, RG75, National Archives at College Park, Md., RG75-Nav-164.

one's ability to act independently of others, it is necessarily intertwined with the ownership and control of productive resources.[6]

Diné women in the 1930s held power in their communities, where mothers, daughters, and sisters formed strong bonds of interdependence. But women's power did not rest merely on female solidarity. Women were important to economic production, and significantly they also controlled the means of their own production: livestock and land. Women typically owned much of the sheep and generally all of the goats. These herds sustained lives: they provided food for their families, and they also produced the wool that women transformed into blankets, which by the early twentieth century had become valued trade goods. Living in a society that measured wealth and prestige in livestock, those women who owned especially large herds of sheep and goats thereby amplified their autonomy and authority within their rural communities of scattered homesteads. To be sure, many societies depend on women for their sustenance, which does not necessarily translate into any power for women at all, not even over their own lives. But among Diné, autonomous notions of livestock ownership did, indeed, give women a remarkable amount of economic and social independence. Resources, of course, were not usually divided equally between wives and husbands, which could render a woman more or less powerful in familial negotiations, depending on individual circumstances. But women had the same potential to accumulate wealth as their husbands did and thereby acquire economic independence.

We should not confuse this matricentered society with the idea of "matriarchy." In the 1920s, some bilagáana women mistakenly believed that they saw feminist utopias in the American Southwest, where (so they thought) Pueblo and Navajo women enjoyed absolute dominion, or "mother-rule." Their notion of a feminist utopia revealed more about themselves and their desire to reconceive white womanhood than it did about Navajo society, where the issue of "dominance" had little relevance.[7] Nonetheless, it was true that in Navajo society, women mattered.

And yet, somehow, this distinctively matricentered social geography and the economic independence that women exercised escaped the notice of New Deal officials as they developed their program to reduce herds and reshape the relationships between people and land. True, authorities recognized that Navajos reckoned kinship along matrilineal lines and lived in matrilocal homesteads. Nonetheless, they never quite grasped just how much Navajo society orbited women. Only belatedly did they recognize and acknowledge that Navajo women owned the better part of the sheep and goat herds. It certainly didn't occur to them that women enjoyed great influence within their communities. Navajo Service Superintendent E. R. Fryer, for instance, characterized "the Navajo" as "a sheep *man*," and he added that within the family, "authority is definitely crystallized in the male head of the group, who has some of the characteristics of a minor patriarch."[8] Fryer was an active member of the Church of Jesus Christ of Latter Day Saints, and here he seems to have projected his own patriarchal Mormon conception of the world onto Navajo society, for ethnographers working on the reservation in the 1930s and 1940s agreed that Navajo society revolved around women.

Perhaps officials like Fryer were ignorant of the workings of Navajo society because they had relatively little contact with women. Those few Diné who spoke English were generally men, so even on those occasions when government researchers sought out Navajo families, they would most likely have spoken with men. Just as important, if not more so, Diné men had long acted as cultural, political, and interfamilial mediators, a role that may well have grown out of matrilocal residential patterns. Men moved into their wives' communities, but they maintained allegiance to the places where their mothers and sisters lived; in traveling from one locale to the other, they encountered strangers and gained experience with the world outside their own.[9] Men, moreover, formed strong bonds with their uncles and brothers and thus maintained familial networks that extended across the countryside and into the communities where their married kinsmen lived.[10] Perhaps this outward-looking orientation accounted for the fact that, for at least as long as the written record, men had traditionally served as "headmen," or community leaders, and they continued to do so in one capacity or another as members of the federally created all-male Navajo Tribal Council, as elected officers in their local chapters, or as appointed members of grazing committees. Federal authorities thus dealt almost exclusively with men because Diné men were, in fact, political leaders, and the officials assumed that meant these leaders had the authority to make decisions for their communities and the people as a whole.

Federal officials, however, misapprehended the limited power that headmen could actually wield. Headmen gained their authority through their relationships to powerful women or men in their local communities, their own wealth and prestige, their ceremonial knowledge, their proven courage or wisdom, their communication and persuasion skills, and other qualities. They were leaders and spokesmen, and they generally determined the transhumant movements of their family and the related families who "moved together," but their decisions bound no one, and no one felt compelled to follow their lead.[11] In truth, Diné notions of autonomy meant that no individual had the power to make decisions for another, not even their wives or husbands. In the early 1940s, ethnographer Clyde Kluckhohn noted that "by vigorous use of their tongues," Navajo women would "frequently reverse or nullify" decisions that their husbands made.[12] And that observation applied no less to their community leaders. Headmen could make suggestions, coax others, or mediate disputes between groups, but they lacked the means to enforce their will.

Officials like Fryer never acknowledged that women had real autonomy and authority in Navajo society, nor did they comprehend the entangled relationships between Navajo women and their stock. They did not recognize that the various strands of women's lives—their stock ownership, their work as weavers, their secure position within matrilocal communities, and their unmediated access to grazing lands—gave Diné women not only power over their own lives, but also power to affect community decisions.

Like the individual fibers of a braided cord, each of these strands reinforced the other, and Navajo women would not allow them to unravel easily.

The fact that women had autonomy and power does not mean that women were more important than men. Diné conceived of women and men as interdependent partners, each with different but equally valued qualities, each necessary for the holistic harmony embodied in the concept of hózhǫ́. And they developed a way of talking about that interdependence that flowed through their everyday thought. In the Diné cosmos, every living thing and every natural phenomenon exists as a complementary pair, female and male.[13] Of course, animals come in male and female varieties, but so do other things, in ways that are distinctly different from bilagáana notions about nature. Take plants, for example: in the Diné world, white corn is male and yellow corn is female. Similarly, all of the Diné universe is made up of female and male pairs. Thought—which proceeds action—is male. Speech—which actually creates reality—is female. The sun is male, while the earth is female. The San Juan River is male; the Rio Grande is female. In ceremonies like Blessingway, female and male qualities are always invoked in pairs as a condition of ritual success. This male-female dyad may seem like something totally esoteric, unrelated to everyday life, but nothing could be further from the truth, for Diné understand the most common experiences in gendered terms. In midsummer, for instance, when the skies fill with jagged bolts of lightening and torrential downpours rush through arroyos, etching deeper and deeper into the earth, a Diné man or woman describes the event as *níłtsą́ biką'*, male rain. Yet in spring, when gentle, steady showers soak into the ground and awaken vegetation, they call it *níłtsą́ bi'áád*, female rain. Male and female are like two banks on either side of a stream that courses through everyday life, shaping understandings of the actual relationships between women and men.[14]

Diné did not think of gender just in simple binary terms, either. There was a third gender, too, called *nádleeh*, generally men who performed women's work. Diné ascribed them with sacred powers. A number of hataałii were nádleeh, but their cultural meaning becomes most apparent in one of the central episodes of the story of origins. In that story, a conflict arose between women and men, leading the women to move to the other side of a great river. The nádleeh acted as mediator between the two sexes, teaching them that women and men were interdependent, not meant to live in separate worlds. For the Diné, nádleeh embodied both masculine and feminine in a single whole and thus exemplified complementarity.[15]

A Diné woman trades a rug for groceries at Shonto Trading Post, 1932. Women's economic autonomy gave them power within their communities. Courtesy Northern Arizona University, Cline Library, Special Collections and Archives, Philip Johnston Collection, 413.690.

Diné women and men organized their labor along complementary gendered lines, although their roles were by no means rigid. Men generally assumed responsibility for heavy physical labor such as building hogans and corrals, plowing and preparing fields, hunting large game, chopping firewood, hauling water, rounding up horses, and castrating stock. Women worked closer to the hogan, raising children, weaving blankets, grinding corn, milking goats, and preparing meals. They also gathered plants and seeds and managed the care of the flocks, which were often—though certainly not always—herded by girls. Production of livestock for home consumption, particularly outside the agricultural centers of Canyon de Chelly, Canyon del Muerto, and Chaco Canyon, remained of utmost importance even into the 1930s, and here, women's work was crucial. Women were generally the ones who slaughtered, skinned, and butchered livestock. Through their act of killing sheep and goats and spilling their blood, they nurtured kin in ways both tangible and symbolic. Mutton and goat meat (supplemented by goat milk and cheese, and an occasional treat of beef or horseflesh) kept bellies full. Sheep and goat skins, used for bedding, cushions, and so forth, kept families warm and comfortable, as did wool, which women wove into saddle blankets and cloaks. Not all labor was gendered. When a task such as gathering wood, weeding and hoeing fields, or mending clothes needed doing, it fell to whomever was available at the time, male or female. And the entire family participated in shearing and dipping sheep and in planting and harvesting crops.[16] These complementary ways of organizing and valuing work discouraged the creation of a social hierarchy based on gender.

'Asdzą́ą́ Nez, Tall Woman, explained how Diné understood this way of organizing labor. A weaver and midwife from around Chinle, she was a grandmotherly woman, who—in typical fashion—wore strings of turquoise beads over her velveteen blouse and wrapped herself in a Pendleton shawl. Reminiscing about her long life married to Frank Mitchell, a well-known hataałi, she observed: "Both the man and the woman have jobs to do . . . both of them are necessary to make things complete and to raise a family in the right way. That's how things were established by the Holy People at the beginning." Tall Woman, alone, was in charge of the hogan, just as Changing Woman prescribed. She directed the children's chores and controlled her own labor and her share of the flock, all without interference from her husband. Tall Woman had an equal voice in family matters. "We supported and encouraged each other," she said of herself and Frank, "but we didn't decide them for the other one. . . . We didn't try and step ahead of each other, or speak for each other."[17]

The autonomy of which Tall Woman spoke never penetrated the consciousness of the New Deal policymakers. On those rare occasions when they considered Navajo women at all, it was as though they looked into a mirror that reflected their own notions of separate spheres, a universe in which women occupied a subordinate, domestic position that deferred to the worldly wisdom of male authority.[18] The essentially egalitarian, complementary organization of Diné life, in which neither men nor women could speak for each other, eluded the gaze of those in charge of stock reduction. Nor did those men perceive the web of relationships among Diné women that gave them strength.

The Diné world encompassed social relations that simultaneously extended across space and rooted themselves in place, and both positioned women at the center. Diné clans, for example, each trace their origins to a mythological ancestress (whose name is often unknown). Changing Woman herself formed the first four clans. The others arose later, some of them founded by women who initially came to live among the people as captives, wanderers, or refugees.[19] In 1881, Chee Dodge reported some forty-four clans, though there were probably more in areas of Diné Bikéyah with which he was unfamiliar; by the 1920s, Gladys Reichard cataloged sixty-four clans.[20] Membership flowed along matrilineal lines, so that, for instance, a man's own clan was the same as his mother's and her mother's, and so on. Indeed, Diné imagined their own clan as "one woman standing atop those that branch out . . . again and again."[21]

Matrilineal clans shaped Diné understandings of themselves as a people. At least some of these clans probably once signified places where members clustered, although they no longer did by the early twentieth century. The Tó 'Aheedlíinii, or Water-Flows-Together clan, for example, originated at the confluence of the San Juan and Los Pinos rivers. But long ago, perhaps as the early pastoralists migrated across mesas and valleys in search of forage for sheep, clan members had spread out across the countryside. By the 1930s, Diné clans no longer delineated specific residential communities (although some communities were largely composed of members from one or two clans), nor did they provide a structure for organizing communal labor.[22] Still, matrilineal clans remained a focus of group identity in spite of the widespread distribution of their members. Indeed, clans remained important precisely *because* Diné spread out across such expanses. When two Diné strangers encountered one another, they introduced themselves according to their clans, evoking relations of kinship and marriage across Diné Bikéyah. In this way, intricate networks of clans created a sense of peoplehood long before the development of any overarching political identity.

To understand how this worked, we might look at Left Handed's story. In the mid-1930s, when he related his life history, Left Handed was an elderly, hard-bitten man who had lived much of his life at the foot of Black Mountain, near Hopi country. His account shows how matrilineal clans linked families sprawled across vast territories. For example, when he encountered a stranger, he would introduce himself as Bit'ahnii, one of Within-His-Cover People. That was his mother Abaa's clan, the one he was born into, and in speaking the name of his clan, he honored a chain of relationships linked through women. Membership in that group was his primary clan identity, and yet it was not the only one. His father, Old Man Hat, had belonged to the Tł'ízí Łání, the Many Goats clan, and that relationship was important, too. It was the clan Left Handed would say he was "born for," even though he himself was not a member.[23] Consequently, after introducing himself as a member of his own clan, he might also tell the stranger that his father had been Many Goats.[24]

Left Handed and his fellow Diné kept track of these relationships for several important reasons. For one, clans are exogamous, meaning that sex with clan relatives equals incest.[25] The principle of clan exogamy helped to disperse relationships far beyond the limits of a particular community. At the same time, exogamy wove otherwise scattered groups into dense networks, with obligations of sharing, reciprocity, and cooperation. Here, then, was another reason that Diné kept track of clan relationships. If, upon introduction, two strangers discovered they were related, etiquette obligated each of them to share their food and shelter with the other or render aid if needed. For example, when Left Handed was a young boy living with his parents, Abaa' and Old Man Hat, a man and a woman came upon his family's hogan on the way to see one of the man's clan relatives. When it turned out that the woman was a member of Abaa's clan, the travelers stayed overnight, and in the morning Abaa' slaughtered a sheep for them.[26] In similar ways every day, strangers discovered relationships through matrilineal threads that wove individual people into a loose fabric of kinship.

Clans emphasized maternal ties, but clans alone did not place women at the core of Diné society. More important were the bonds women forged within their extended families. When a woman married, she usually brought her husband to live with her, so that her hogan and those of her mother and married sisters clustered near one another, forming the family homestead.[27] "After my older sister was married, she continued to live with us," Tall Woman explained. "My sister and I kept on the way we had been living earlier, before her marriage." Tall Woman's other married sisters lived within her family's homestead, as well, but when her brothers married, they moved with their wives to Black Mesa and elsewhere, for "that is the custom among us," she stated matter-of-factly.[28] That custom had a long history. When he visited the reservation in 1881, Lieutenant John Gregory Bourke observed that this pattern was the general rule. But he added that the rule, "like most rules, is honored just as much in the breach as in the observance."[29]

Not everyone, then, followed the matrilocal ideal. A couple might instead choose to live near the husband's mother for a lot of different reasons. For example, if the husband was an only child or his sisters were unmarried, the couple might establish their home near *his* mother so that she could continue to count on his labor. This was especially common if his mother was widowed or divorced and his mother-in-law already had sons or sons-in-law living near her. The couple might also live near his mother if the wife's mother was dead, if the wife simply did not get along with her own family, or if he could not tolerate his in-laws. And if the wife's mother's grazing range was too crowded, they might move with their livestock to his mother's place. Oftentimes, when both the husband and wife felt the pull of maternal ties (or perhaps the need for better grazing range), they resolved the dilemma by moving seasonally from one mother's winter homestead to the other's summer camp.[30] Even more commonly, as a couple had more children or acquired more sheep and thus needed more range, the pair might break away from the parental group altogether and establish an independent household. And yet, when the couple's own children married, their homestead would typically follow the matrilocal pattern once again.[31] Families, then, took many forms; nonetheless, they almost always revolved around kinswomen.

Change underscored continuity. Matricentered networks among extended families had persevered throughout Diné history in the face of centuries of warfare. Since the seventeenth century, Diné had done battle with Spaniards, Mexicans, Utes, and various Puebloan peoples. Young Diné men raided livestock from Hispanic villages and ranchos and Puebloan flocks; Spaniards and Mexicans retaliated, often assisted by the native enemies of the Diné. All sides captured women and children as slaves. At times, these cycles of raids and reprisals seemed to form a continuous loop. Assaults sparked retaliations, and so on and on.[32] The violence escalated in the late 1840s—part of the long period Diné know as "the Fearing Time"—after the successful conquest of New Mexico by the United States Army. Joined by Ute raiders and New Mexican vigilantes, the army responded to Navajo raids—making no distinction between those who were actually raiders and those who were not—by creating a continual state of terror in the most populous regions of Diné Bikéyah. 'Asdzą́ą́ Tsosie, Slim Woman, granddaughter of the great leader Narbona, who was killed by Colonel Washington's troops when she was a child in 1849, remembered this era well. Time and again, galloping messengers would warn of approaching enemies, and her family would bundle up their possessions and flee to a mountain cave.[33] Such unremitting terror took its toll on Diné families. The sudden loss of fathers, mothers, sisters, and brothers killed or captured in warfare reconfigured domestic life in ways we can only imagine, and few families went wholly untouched.

The Fearing Time climaxed in the 1860s, when Kit Carson's troops, aided by Utes, swooped down on the Diné and incarcerated them at Hwéeldi. In this final assault, families were broken asunder. Ute mercenaries held onto some women captives, and soldiers seized family members who were at home, unwittingly leaving behind those who were, perhaps, off herding sheep or visiting kinsfolk elsewhere. Those who could, fled, taking refuge in the western recesses of Diné Bikéyah—Gray Mountain, the Grand Canyon, Black Mesa, Navajo Mountain, the Kaibito Plateau— forever altering ties to natal lands. Many others died. Navajo men, in particular, lost their lives while struggling to protect their homes, and many more men, women, and children succumbed to starvation or disease while imprisoned, further restructuring families.[34]

Even after the ordeal ended in 1868, families for a time remained in disarray. Carson's troops and the Utes had destroyed the Navajos' crops and slaughtered their livestock, so at first many families camped out around Fort Wingate and later Fort Defiance, where the government distributed rations and, ultimately, sheep. When the Diné finally returned home, some found that those family members who escaped imprisonment had relocated to more secluded western locales, and others discovered strangers in their favorite places. And so the first years after their release were unsettled, both emotionally and physically, as families regrouped, renewed old residential patterns, and established new ones.[35]

Much of what we know about the period, from resettlement in the late 1860s through the 1920s, comes from western outposts—Black Mountain, Navajo Mountain, the Kaibito Plateau—that were founded by refugees, then augmented as kin returned from Hwéeldi. These relatively remote communities attracted ethnographers who flocked to the reservation in the 1920s and 1930s. (According to an oft-told joke, a typical Diné homestead includes two parents, three children, a grandmother, and an anthropologist, and this was perhaps more true in the western part of the reservation than anywhere.) Collectively, these ethnographers tell a history suggesting that incarceration at Hwéeldi opened a chasm in the organization of Diné life: on one side of this imaginary river gorge lay a society structured around networks of related women, and on the other side lay one that followed men.

Consider the Kaibito Plateau, a windswept tableland of swirling slickrock, weathered sandstone formations, brush, and grasslands. During the 1860s, when Kit Carson struck fear across the land, a man named Dághá

Sikaad settled the eastern edge of the plateau, eventually establishing himself as the patriarch of some twenty interrelated families. By the early 1900s, he became a commercial stockowner and solidified his claim to sixty miles of the area's best rangelands and farmlands. And so not only his daughters but also two of his three sons and his grandsons remained there after marriage, bringing their wives to live with them. Their access to good range, the status they acquired from their relationship with Dághá Sikaad, and their desire to concentrate their family's wealth and prestige encouraged them to remain close to their father.[36] Some scholars have thus concluded that the resettlement of Navajo Country in the second half of the nineteenth century created a whole new social geography centered on newly powerful groups of men; patrilocal patterns, so this theory goes, had at least begun to replace matrilocal ways of configuring space.

Perhaps it was the rise of these powerful men in some quarters that gave Fryer the idea that men were "minor patriarchs" in Navajo society. Yet a closer examination reveals that matricentered ideas about organizing society were far too deeply entrenched to be undercut, even by widespread dislocations in the aftermath of warfare and imprisonment. Picture the community living on the Rainbow Plateau at the foot of the sacred Navajo Mountain, which soars to more than ten thousand feet, marking the highest point on the reservation. Bounded on the north and east by the spectacular Glen Canyon, the San Juan River gorge, and Paiute Canyon, this rural settlement is among the most isolated in Diné Bikéyah. By 1890, a man who came to be known as Whiteman Killer appropriated the area from the local Paiutes and made his winter home there with his wife and four daughters.[37] Eventually, at least three of these daughters married Ńdíshchíí', Pine Tree, son of Dághá Sikaad, in a common type of plural marriage that linked one man with a group of sisters, thereby strengthening his claim to grazing land through his wives. At the same time, Pine Tree's marriage allied his father, Dághá Sikaad, with Whiteman Killer, uniting two of the most powerful headmen on the northern frontier. On the surface, then, the Navajo Mountain community looks like a world controlled by men.

And yet, by the 1930s, strong bonds once again linked mothers and daughters in matrilocal homesteads, even though nearly every extended family included one son who elected to remain with his mother or grandmother upon marriage. Take for example the home of Salt Woman, Pine Tree's daughter, who lived in 1938 with her eight unmarried children and two grandchildren (her husband lived nearby with her sister, in a polygamous marriage). Three more hogans clustered to form her maternal homestead. In one lived her married daughter and family; another housed a married son, although each summer he moved with his wife to *her* mother's camp. In the third hogan lived Salt Woman's mother, then nearing seventy years old, who shared her home with her widower son and his two children. In summers, the matricentered geography of this community grew even more pronounced, as many of the married sons living in the Navajo Mountain community joined their wives' families for the season.[38]

More typical than the communities at Navajo Mountain and the Kaibito Plateau was that at Klagetoh, where clusters of hogans shaded by piñon and juniper trees stood on the edge of a shrub-grassland just west of the Defiance Plateau. No one remained on this exposed plain during the 1860s. When families returned from Hwéeldi or from refuges in the mountains to the west, most of them gradually settled into old familiar patterns of life, despite their relative proximity to the railroad, a trading post, and other acculturating forces. By 1938, most of those at Klagetoh lived in matrilocal homesteads (though, again, some sons remained with their mothers) or in polygamous marriages that linked sisters in a single household.[39]

Matrilocal residence fostered female solidarity and authority. Women who remained near their mothers claimed a familiar place for their entire lives, surrounded by sisters and, later, daughters. Husbands, by contrast, entered their wives' households as outsiders, their tenuous standing contingent on the good will of the women around them. In the first years, men remained on the periphery of their marital households. Oftentimes men absented themselves for long periods because their own mothers expected them to return home in order to help with the back-breaking work of building hogans, castrating livestock, and shearing sheep. Others left from time to time to earn wages working on the railroad or freighting for trading posts. These absences could breed distrust, desertion, and divorce. Customs surrounding divorce exemplified the contingent position of men in their wives' communities. A woman could divorce a negligent, lazy, adulterous, or abusive husband at her own discretion, and unless her husband hailed from her community, he would be forced to leave. (She could even sever her relationship with a kind, generous, faithful husband; although men's labor held such high value that a woman's parents would likely try to effect a reconciliation with a good, hard-working man.) A mother also had absolute custody of her children in the event of divorce because her children belonged to her clan, not her husband's.[40] The uncertainties of marriage in its early years, until the couple grew accustomed to each other's company, generally left men more vulnerable than women.[41]

The family sheep herd symbolized this initial uncertainty. Typically, a newly married man took with him only a small number of his sheep, leaving the remainder at his mother's place. He brought only as many as he was willing to risk losing, for it could prove difficult to get them back if he decided to leave (or if his wife made that decision for him). One reason for that difficulty was that a powerful taboo prevented a man from seeing his mother-in-law—on penalty of blindness—and yet it was precisely that woman who often had charge of the family's communal herds. All of his dealings with his mother-in-law had to take place through an intermediary, usually his wife. So unless his wife willingly gave up his stock or he enlisted the help of a sympathetic in-law, he might be forced to leave much poorer than he came. Men were thus initially reluctant to mix their stock in with the wife's family herd. Over the years, as the marriage became more stable, he would gradually bring more and more of his stock into his wife's fold, until eventually all of his sheep ran with hers.[42]

Left Handed's experience back in the late 1880s illustrates that men's wariness was at least sometimes well founded. Shortly after he married, his wife accused him of infidelity, questioning his long absences to visit kin.[43] When he once again prepared to visit relatives, his wife physically assaulted him, and so he determined to leave her. But she kept careful watch on him, making it impossible for him to slip away with his livestock and belongings. "I couldn't do anything then," he explained. "I was trying my best to get away from her, but she wouldn't let me. I tried to think of different ways of getting away, but I didn't know what to do. I had that new saddle and new saddle blanket and new bridle there, and . . . some sheep, and that was holding me back. I didn't know what to do about all those things."[44] Finally, after a particularly violent battle between the two, his wife confessed that her mother and grandmother had encouraged her to pick a fight with him, "because they knew you had horses, cattle, sheep, and property. They knew you had everything, and they wanted to have all of it." Left Handed, indeed, had a good deal to lose, for his mother had given him a small herd of about forty sheep so that he would not have to depend on his wife's family for food. But he had made the mistake (as he saw it now) of putting his livestock in with his wife's family herd, so deserting her meant leaving his sheep and horses behind. Eventually, though, he did manage to leave, joining his mother, Abaa', in the Carrizos.[45]

Matrilocal residence gave women a strong voice in the affairs of their rural communities. Opposition from an alliance of mothers, daughters, and sisters could restrain the most respected headman, whose influence rested primarily on his power to persuade. The ability of these networks of women to reject the unpopular decisions of their political representatives never entered into the calculations of the New Deal conservationists. Nor did they comprehend the connections between women and land.

Matrilocal residence meant that most pastures and springs became associated with particular matrilineages. Certainly Diné did not conceive of land—unlike stock—as something people "owned"; it was communally held, and unused land was available to whoever preempted it.[46] But practically speaking, families tended to graze their livestock in the same general areas year after year, so that over time, they acquired generally recognized, though often overlapping, use-rights to particular areas. And Diné often referred to these customary use areas in terms that evoked their relationships to women. "That's my mother's place" or "that's my grandmother's place," they might say. Men certainly had access to matrilineal lands not only through their wives, but also through their grandmothers, mothers, and sisters. Moreover, by the 1930s, some men who were commercial stockowners had appropriated large areas of land for their herds, challenging others' matrilineal claims, especially in the Checkerboard. Nonetheless, in most places, matrilineal use areas gave women access to forage unmediated by men, thereby securing for them a large measure of economic autonomy.[47]

Access to rangelands would have meant little for women, of course, if they did not also control their own sheep and goats. Unfortunately, it is impossible to say precisely how much livestock women (or men, for that matter) owned. Gladys Reichard observed in the 1920s that women owned substantial numbers of stock, that a woman had "oftentimes more than her husband."[48] In the late 1940s, Deeshchii'nii, then a member of the Navajo Tribal Council, told a congressional committee that "the women folks are the sheep owners, they own most of the sheep."[49] But beyond these general statements, there is little quantitative evidence regarding ownership patterns. The only people who kept written accounts—the kinds of records that historians tend to rely on—were federal agents and Euro-American traders. And that poses a problem for us, because those men (and they were mostly men) recorded their own cultural biases as much as they did sheep and goats.

Take the 1915 census of the Navajo Agency in the central part of the reservation, for example. This was a remarkable project, unusual in its cultural insight. Superintendent Peter Paquette and four Navajo men carefully enumerated the people who lived in the most populous section of the reservation, recording the name and clan of each man, woman, and child. Significantly, Paquette—himself of mixed French and Ho-Chunk heritage—comprehended the differences between Navajo and Euro-American society.[50] His discussion of Navajo clans and naming practices was as ethnographically astute as anything written up to that time, and he paid uncommon attention to the position of Navajo women. The Navajo wife, he observed "in nearly every instance is really the head of the family[,] the women very largely controlling property."[51] Paquette somewhat elevated the position women actually held, for every member of a pastoral family owned stock individually, although they mixed them into common herds, which the women often managed.[52] Still, he seems to have been in touch with the matricentered contours of Diné life.

And yet, in preparing the census, Paquette fell back on prevailing cultural biases. Despite his own perception of the relative importance of women to Navajo households, he designated the husband as the "head" of each family and the owner of the family's herd, according to census custom. And so it appears from the census that relatively few women—all of them widowed or divorced or unmarried—had any livestock at all. For example, the record implies that Jim Blackgoat of Red Lake possessed all of his family's 3,000 sheep. Indeed, that might have been true. Or it may have been that his wife Yaa Diibaa' owned them, though more likely as not, Jim, Yaa Diibaa', and their older daughters and sons each had holdings in the flock.[53] The census masks the truth.

Paquette's census is not the only record that perplexes historians. Federal sheep-dipping counts—the most commonly used stock "censuses"—pose similar problems. By the 1920s, the states of New Mexico and Arizona, the federal Bureau of Animal Industry, and the Bureau of Indian Affairs required all Navajos to dip their sheep and goats in a foul solution of sulphur and nicotine at least once per year and sometimes twice in an effort to eradicate scabies, a highly contagious, mite-borne disease.[54] This operation took place at special vats set up across the reservation, usually near trading posts. At each of these vats, federal officials enumerated the stock, crediting ownership to the manager of each herd. Government agents assumed that the person who drove the stock through the vats actually owned them, and those drovers were overwhelmingly male.[55]

The evidence, then, is ambiguous at best, making it possible to draw two diametrically opposed conclusions. If we were to rely solely on the official counts, we might easily decide that, for the most part, men controlled the chief means of production as the ostensible owners of the livestock herds. But that would mean that Reichard and Paquette—both careful observers—were downright wrong. It would mean that the Diné leader Deeshchii'nii lied. Each, at different times and in different places, reported that Navajo women controlled the flocks that grazed the reservation. If we were to follow *their* lead, we might assume that women owned most of the stock, and that men acted merely as intermediaries with government officials.

In fact, we do know that both women and men held stock within the family flock, even though the proportions remain obscure. Lorenzo Hubbell and his son Roman, two of the largest traders in Navajo Country, kept their accounts under the names of the actual owners, at least when the merchants knew who they were. Their trading post ledgers reveal, for instance, that Slim Judge, his wife, and his daughter each had stock. Likewise, Naakaii Yazzie and his two wives owned their own flocks, as did Black Whiskers, his mother, and his son. We may know only the numbers they chose to sell, not the size of their herds, but we do know that many women, as well as men, were substantial stockowners.[56] The wealthy Chee Dodge, for example, testified that he and his wife Nánibaa' owned equal amounts of their 3,000-head herd. "My wife owns her own property," he emphasized, "and I own mine."[57]

Men and women with enormous herds, like Nánibaa' and Chee Dodge, had wealth and with it social status. Large herds signified prestige and prosperity. They represented an owner's hard work, careful management, and ritual knowledge of the songs that ensured fecundity, and it was these implied qualities, as much as the numbers of animals themselves, that earned respect. For the owner, a large flock meant freedom from hunger and want. It was a form of stored wealth that insured against hard times brought on by drought or deep snow. Yet stockowners gained prestige not merely by accumulating animals for their own consumption, but by sharing their bounty with poorer relatives and sponsoring ceremonial feasts. Inequities in the distribution of wealth within a community could breed resentment, accusations of stinginess, and even charges of witchcraft, so generosity became a necessary condition of prestige.[58]

In an important way, stock embodied the reciprocal obligations, expressed by the Diné as *k'é*, that knitted a far-flung people into a social fabric. K'é is the foundation of Diné social relationships. It refers both to kinship and to the acts of generosity, kindness, cooperation, and respect that sustain others, both physically and emotionally. In sharing a leg of mutton with poorer kinsfolk or with visiting clan relatives, Diné women and men engaged in a communal act that tied them to each other. That communion became most readily apparent in the days surrounding large ceremonies for healing the sick, warding off evil, or restoring hózhǫ́. Sheep served as payment to hataałii for their ritual singing. And all those who attended and participated in the ceremony partook in a great feast of mutton and goat meat. Livestock, then, helped enmesh the Diné in networks of reciprocity that linked spiritual life with family and kin.[59]

Both women and men could earn prestige through their generosity with livestock, yet there were gendered differences in the kinds of stock they owned. As one Navajo man explained to anthropologist Emma Reh in the 1930s, "the woman owns her sheep and the man his cattle."[60] Although trading post ledgers, autobiographies, oral histories, and other records indicate that both men and women had sheep, women tended to own much more, and they owned nearly all the goats. By contrast, men sometimes had cattle and far more horses. Women, to be sure, owned horses, which remained necessary for transportation, herding sheep, hauling water, pulling wagons, and other daily tasks in a land with few graded roads and only a few dozen automobiles or trucks even through the 1930s. 'Asdzą́ą́ Yazzie, Little Woman, who was in 1915 the second-richest stock owner in the central part of the reservation, counted thirty-two horses among her holdings.[61] By contrast, however, men's mustang herds could reach astonishing proportions: back in the 1880s, Slim Man reportedly had at least six hundred head at Black Mountain, and Hashké Neiniih, a particularly wealthy and powerful headman from around Oljato, near Monument Valley, possessed an estimated *one to three thousand* nearly feral horses![62] Perhaps that was hyperbole. But the cold facts suggest that some men had incredible herds. According to Paquette's census of the central reservation in 1915, one man near Chinle owned four hundred horses, and another twenty-one men had one hundred head or more.[63]

Diné men prized horses as marks of masculinity. Photograph by J. R. Willis. Courtesy Museum of New Mexico, Palace of the Governors (MNM/DCA), 98187.

Diné men prized enormous herds of horses as marks of masculinity, prestige, and ceremonial knowledge. Horses held symbolic meanings. They evoked spiritual relationships with the Sun, the deity who first introduced those powerful creatures to the Hero Twins. Moreover, since Diné sang Blessingway songs for their horses so that they would prosper and multiply, large numbers of horses betokened a man's knowledge of powerful songs. Horses represented manliness. Men associated horses with marriage, for a bride's family expected as many as a dozen ponies—a token of his family's wealth—as a wedding gift. But more than that, horses connoted prowess in hunting, raiding, racing, and other scenes of male camaraderie.[64]

In a similar way, sheep and goats signified womanhood, or more specifically, motherhood. Sheep and goats meant sustenance, which the Diné, in their gendered way of thinking, construed as female.[65] This association among women, sustenance, and sheep had roots far deeper than the material world of stock ownership. Changing Woman—the primordial symbol of womanhood—created the Diné and gave them sheep and goats to sustain them for all time. This symbolic relationship between women and their flocks was generally apparent to outsiders, even if they did not fully comprehend its meaning.

Women's ownership of livestock gave them power that clearly impressed many Americans but seems to have eluded New Deal officials. Back in the mid-nineteenth century, Jonathan Letherman, the assistant army surgeon at Fort Defiance, concluded that Navajo women drew authority from their economic autonomy as livestock owners. "The husband," he reported, "has no control over the property of his wife, their herds being kept separate and distinct; from which, doubtless, arises the influence of the women not only in their own peculiar sphere, but also in national matters, which it is well known they oftentimes exert."[66] This authority remained apparent to Gladys Reichard in the 1920s and 1930s. She observed that women not only managed the family flocks of sheep and goats, but also had an equal say, vis-à-vis men, in family and community decision-making. A Navajo woman, she wrote, "has a voice in all family affairs and many times her decision on a matter is final since she may have control of the family purse-strings according to the relative wealth of herself and her husband."[67]

Livestock intertwined with nearly every fiber of women's economic lives, which by the 1930s included not only subsistence pastoralism but also a nascent market economy. With the arrival of the Atlantic and Pacific Railroad (later called the Atchison, Topeka and Santa Fe) in 1881, trading posts proliferated across the reservation and along its boundaries.[68] By World War I, with the growing demand for wool, Diné families came to count on trading posts for some foodstuffs and household goods. Some of the largest stockowners—Chee Dodge, Crooked Finger, Henry Bigman—became commercial ranchers, growing large numbers of livestock primarily for their market value, although subsistence and reciprocal obligations remained important, too.[69] This market economy could have elevated the position of Diné men at the expense of women. After all, in the Euro-American economy, the shift from subsistence to market activities often resulted in a devaluing of women's work.[70] But if anything, the trading posts enhanced women's status as producers.

In the 1890s, falling wool prices and a growing tourist demand for Navajo blankets and, later, rugs prompted Diné women to convert increasing amounts of their raw wool into textiles.[71] This was, in many ways, an expansion of age-old patterns. Women had been bartering blankets since

Diné weaver, 1921. The sale of rugs like this one helped feed families during the long seasons between lamb and wool sales. Photograph by Jesse Nusbaum. Courtesy Denver Public Library, Western History Collection, N-338.

at least the late eighteenth century and had earned a regional reputation as expert weavers.[72] The trader Josiah Gregg, who helped open the Santa Fe market to the United States in the 1820s, wrote that Navajo blankets had such a fine weave that they were "highly prized for protection against the rains." The finest blankets, he observed, "are often sold among the Mexicans as high as fifty or sixty dollars each."[73] But by the 1890s, weaving had become a form of wage labor. The chief beneficiaries of this labor proved to be the trading posts themselves, for they profited handsomely from the sale of Navajo textiles, while paying the producers a pittance. Nonetheless, that pittance contributed considerably to the purchasing power of Diné families.[74]

Weaving meant more than trade. It was a spiritual process—accompanied by sacred songs and stories—that connected Diné women with Spider Woman, who had woven the universe itself on a gigantic loom.[75]

Shiłʼ hózhǫ́,
Shįįʼ hózhǫ́,
Shitsʼ ą́ą́ dóó hózhǫ́.

With me there is beauty,
In me there is beauty,
From me beauty radiates.

And the designs were often sacred, too, even as the weavers responded to the market demands of trading posts. They incorporated symbolic bits of feather, sinew, or plant materials and invoked, in their various patterns, the mythic stories of the Diyin Diné'é, the movement of the sun across the sky, the complementary patterns of male and female.[76]

Even as livestock sales grew during World War I and after, textiles remained important to the emerging market economy. Rugs became the chief currency with which Diné women acquired from trading posts the goods they wanted, such as coffee, flour, canned tomatoes and fruit, fabric, and clothing.[77] Women also continued to barter wool and pelts, just as men did, but they spent increasing amounts of their time weaving for commercial trade. From at least the mid-1910s through the early 1930s, weavers earned perhaps 20 to 30 percent of the income credited at trading posts, which was less than the total earnings from raw wool but still significant.[78] By 1935, traders estimated that weavers' percentage of trading-post income was 30 to 50 percent.[79] And unlike livestock or wool, blankets and rugs were not tied to a seasonal cycle. The textile trade, thus, allowed women to exercise more control over their economic lives. They could choose when to pay off debts or exchange their rugs for goods at the trading post, and because they generally traded their weavings themselves, they could control how those earnings would be spent. Through their work as weavers, women reinforced their economic autonomy and their stature within their domestic circle.

Women mattered in Diné society, which had important implications for the stock reduction program. They formed the warp that gave their social and economic fabric shape and strength. They stood at the center of a web of social relationships, controlled access to matrilineal grazing lands, owned their own livestock, and contributed importantly to their family's subsistence. All of this gave them a powerful voice in community decisions. That voice was evident in 1938, when federal officials brought up the issue of women's suffrage just prior to the first popular election of the Navajo Tribal Council. The right of women to vote was so self-evident that the leadership of the existing, appointed council saw no point in even discussing the issue. Robert Curley pointed out that women had "just as much right as men" to vote; why would it be otherwise? Without another word, the men passed the measure unanimously, in what may well have been their quickest decision on record.[80] Women's opinions counted, but more than that, Diné notions of autonomy mean that no one—not even their community leaders—could rightfully tell them how to dispose of their sheep and goats. Any effort to seize them by force would certainly provoke an outcry.

Livestock connected women and men to the future and the past, and not only the deeply distant past when Changing Woman first gave Diné livestock. Margaret Kee's flock, for instance, were descended from the sheep her grandparents received when they returned from Hwéeldi. The government gave sheep or goats to each couple, she explained to a visitor, and "from there, they have babies." Generations of their offspring, she added, had been passed down through her parents to her, so that "to this day, one of those sheep is still here."[81] Kee hoped to pass her own flock's progeny on to her children and, through them, to her grandchildren, thereby reproducing the generational bonds that dated back to the earliest days when Diné first herded sheep and gave shape to a pastoral society. It was tradition. For more than seven generations, Diné had herded sheep across the canyons, mesas, and mountains of Diné Bikéyah, along trails leading back to the time when they first became shepherds on the Colorado Plateau.

PART 3 · *Terra Firma*

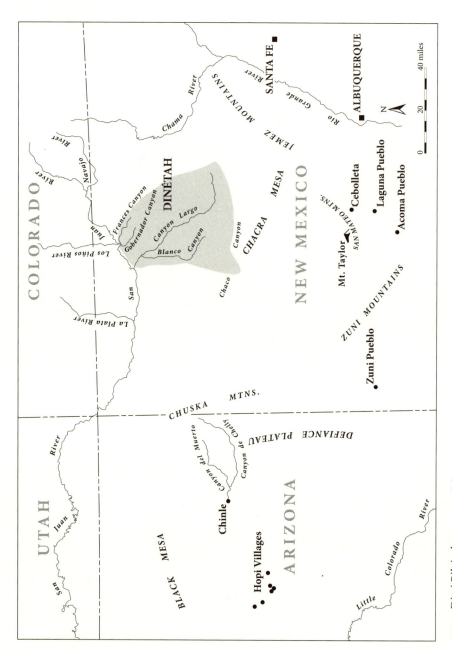

MAP 3 Diné Bikéyah: ca. 1500–1860

5 · HERDING SHEEP

"In my very early days, we never lived in one spot for any length of time; we just roamed about from place to place, and from time to time." Tall Woman, the respected weaver and midwife from Chinle, had spent nearly ninety years herding sheep and goats. "See that Black Mountain range over there?" she asked her visitor, pointing to Black Mesa. "We had relatives living there on one side, and we used to go over and live with them, or near them during the wintertime." Her family did not always go to the same place, however. "There were a number of places we lived in the Black Mountain area; sometimes we spent the winter closer to Salina Springs, or at a place called Salty Water, or in other places." In summer, her family traveled to Fluted Rock, by way of the Chinle Valley. "We moved around like that the whole time I was growing up and even after I became a young woman and started raising my own children."[1]

Tall Woman's migrations had a long history reaching back beyond the beginnings of Diné pastoralism, back into the time before memory, when the people first emerged onto the southern Colorado Plateau. Pastoralism itself arose early in the eighteenth century from the arid canyons of the Diné homeland—Dinétah—where women and men incorporated Spanish livestock herds into their own world and gave them indigenous meanings. Before long, burgeoning flocks spurred families to spread out across the region and promoted the adoption of an ancient pastoral pattern known as transhumance, the seasonal migrations from one ecological zone to another. These movements across the landscape made herding in this arid land possible and reinforced the people's sense of themselves as wanderers.[2]

To trace the history of pastoralism and transhumance in this landscape, we must first step back to what we might call the beginning of Diné time, when the Diné first appeared on the land within the four sacred mountains. This task is trickier than it might seem. Historians increasingly acknowledge that our picture of the past is only partial, and that observation is particularly true of Diné history. Written documents such as diaries, letters, government reports, and the like are the materials that most historians use to create their narratives, but this near fetish for ink on paper presents real problems when we try to uncover the beginnings of Diné pastoralism. Navajos first enter the written record in early Spanish documents, and yet these provide only fleeting glimpses. In fact, much of the earliest record consists of secondhand or thirdhand accounts—rumors, as it were—of settlements of farmers or bands of raiders who lived somewhere to the west beyond the pueblos.

Until the early seventeenth century, Spanish chroniclers wrote only vaguely about those living in the mountains or on the plains outside the familiar realm of the Rio Grande valley, often referring to populations in terms that are unrecognizable today. Names such as "Querechos" or "Cocoyes" probably designated specific groups in some instances; at other times, they signified something more generic like "wild Indians," much as "Chichimecas" came to mean "nomadic barbarians" in northern Mexico.[3] Some historians have speculated that the Querechos or Cocoyes were the same people who later came to be called "Navajo," but we really have no way of knowing whether those terms in fact referred to Diné or to other groups living in or traversing the cultural crossroads of the Colorado Plateau.

Even after the Spaniards clearly recognized the Navajos, fuzzy snapshots emerged from the pages of their reports. Diné moved on the margins of the Spanish empire in a rugged terrain that the Europeans found difficult to penetrate. Encounters were few, unwelcome, and often marked by violence. On those rare occasions before the mid-eighteenth century when the two peoples actually saw each other with their own eyes—particularly on Diné turf—they met, more often than not, in the heat of battle. As Diné fled or fought off Spanish military expeditions and the slave raiders who captured women and children, or as they made their own forays against villages or herds, neither side saw the other quite clearly. The Spanish who recorded these events likely viewed the Navajos during the adrenaline rush of a guerrilla skirmish or glimpsed them from behind as they sped away. They developed blurry impressions of the Navajos in the fury and confusion of some sneak attack.[4]

The violence of these encounters is not the only matter that distorts our early picture of Diné history. Spanish soldiers and missionaries perceived Navajos through viewfinders shaped by their own world. And they manipulated their images—exaggerating this, minimizing that—in ways they hoped would bring approval from their superiors or patrons in Mexico City, not to mention increased military and monetary support. Even if they had tried to represent Navajos accurately, the few opportunities they had to observe them would still leave more questions than answers. It would be like putting together a jigsaw puzzle with only half the pieces.

Archaeologists have tried to fill in parts of this puzzle, but here, too, the evidence remains elusive. By its very nature, archaeology—even more than history—can piece together only fragments of the past. Archaeology is essentially the study of rubbish and ruin, and only certain kinds of physical debris survive the ravages of the weather, sun, water, scavengers, insects, and microorganisms that eventually reduce much of the material world to dust. Even when remnants of the past defy the elements, the odds of an archaeologist stumbling onto them are fairly slim. Making matters worse, until only quite recently most Southwestern archaeologists kept their sights fixed on the prehistoric Anasazi, who abandoned their dramatic cliff dwellings, pueblos, and ceremonial centers by the fifteenth century. Researchers often walked over the radial pattern of logs that marked the ruins of a Diné hogan without knowing or even caring that they did so.[5]

Compounding the problem, the growing numbers of archaeologists who *do* care have found it difficult to identify and interpret the earliest Navajo settlements. Among the many obstacles, the most commonly used techniques for determining *when* people inhabited a particular place, including radiocarbon and tree-ring dating, are not nearly as precise as is popularly supposed. Both of these methods depend largely on wood specimens, and therein lies the snag. Native people in the arid Southwest commonly used and reused old wood that had been dead for many years—sometimes centuries—before they incorporated it into the framework of a dwelling or burned it in a hearth. Deteriorated wood and various forms of contamination can also dramatically skew the apparent age of a log or piece of charcoal.[6] More problematic still, archaeologists have difficulty distinguishing early Navajo sites from the remarkably similar camps inhabited by Utes. Each of these distinct ethnic groups lived in the San Juan River valley, built log-framed dwellings, and manufactured plain pottery, making it awfully hard to tell the two apart in the absence of culturally idiosyncratic evidence.[7] And there is at least one more significant complication: the Diné who migrated to the Southwest as hunters and gatherers likely came with a noticeably different set of cultural markers than we think of as characteristically Navajo. If, for example, they initially lived in less permanent structures than hogans—such as portable tipis—when they moved onto the Colorado Plateau, and if they began manufacturing pottery only after they more or less settled down as farmers, early sites would be difficult to identify.[8] Archaeologists, then, probably continue to walk blindly over the oldest Navajo sites, even as they try their best to find them.

So the fragmentary nature of the evidence, both archaeological and documentary, makes it difficult to know with any certainty just when Diné first entered the Southwest. While Diné oral traditions describe how Changing Woman sent the newly created Earth Surface People from her island home in the Pacific to the land between the four sacred mountains, those stories do not provide any temporal clues to tell us exactly when that migration took place.[9] Turning to the written record, we discover that sightings of Navajos were exceedingly few and far between until the mid-eighteenth century. Accounts of the initial Spanish *entrada* do not mention any people that we can clearly identify as Navajo. Nonetheless, it would be a mistake to assume, as some scholars have, that the omission of Navajos from these early accounts means that Diné were themselves very recent newcomers whose arrival coincided with or followed that of the Spanish.[10] It should come as no surprise at all that the Spanish failed to note the presence of Navajos until fairly late. After the initial *entrada* of 1539–42, nearly two generations passed before any more Spaniards ventured into the area, and more than a half-century had come and gone by the time don Juan de Oñate brought the first European settlers up the Rio Grande. In 1599, soon after he established his headquarters on that stream, Oñate wrote that a large settlement of people dwelled in jacal huts and farmed at the river's source. He may well have been referring to a group of Diné.[11] Or maybe not. Either way, the early historical record tells us nothing concrete about the whereabouts of the Diné before the seventeenth century.

A growing body of archaeological evidence, however, suggests that Diné families lived in the uplands of the San Juan valley at least by the early 1500s, and they continued to make their homes there for another century or more. The remains of their conical hogans lie scattered along the arroyos draining into the La Plata River, north of its confluence with the San Juan. The people who lived here were not yet pastoralists, nor did they farm this area, apparently, although they may have cultivated corn and beans elsewhere, perhaps on the valley floor. They likely moved seasonally through this gently rolling terrain where shrub-grasslands grade into juniper woodlands, harvesting the abundance of wild plants and hunting deer, antelope, rabbit, and an occasional bighorn sheep.[12] Moving from one place to another from one season to the next to exploit the earth's bounty, Diné learned to value mobility in this arid land, a wisdom that would ultimately resonate through transhumance.

Archaeological evidence of their presence may date to the 1500s (or perhaps earlier), but not until 1627 did the Diné make a clear mark on the *written* record. That year, Fray Gerónimo de Zárate Salmerón, missionary to the Jemez, reported secondhand that the "apaches de Nabajú" lived somewhere north of his pueblo, along the Chama River.[13] The name "Nabajú" came from the Tewa word "Návahúú," meaning a large arroyo with cultivated fields. This first definite appearance in the historic record revealed two important things about the ways in which outsiders viewed Navajos. First, the Spaniards recognized that Navajos were a branch of the Apaches (Zuni for "enemies"), all of whom spoke one of the languages that linguists label southern Athabaskan.[14] And second, the Spaniards distinguished Navajos from other Apaches by virtue of their farming. Fray Alonso de Benavides confirmed this characterization three years later when he wrote that although the Navajos were indeed Apaches, they led a quite different way of life. "The Navajos," he wrote, "are very skillful farmers, for the word *navajo* means 'large cultivated fields.'"[15]

According to Benavides, the Navajos' *rancherías* scattered across an area so vast that "one never reaches the end of it," but the heart of their province lay some fifty leagues northwest of the southernmost pueblos, which would place them in the vicinity of the San Juan River. By the 1660s, Diné families had spread throughout the San Juan valley between the La Plata and Navajo rivers, spilling into the rugged canyonlands that came to be called Dinétah.[16] Here the land rises hundreds of feet from the narrow canyon floors in a series of benches, which step up to the mesa tops. Diné continue to remember this place as their ancestral homeland. It was here on Gobernador Knob where Changing Woman herself was born. And it was here, near the place where the Rio de Los Piños crosses the muddy San Juan, where her sons, the Hero Twins, went to live. For centuries (until Navajo Reservoir's waters inundated it in the 1960s), an ancient pictograph of the two young men marked their home, enshrining them in living memory.[17] Dinétah signifies a mythic birthplace, but it is also a literal birthplace, for this region gave rise to the pastoral and farming people who call themselves Diné. It is fitting, then, that when viewed from above, the San Juan River resembles a thick rhizome winding through the earth, below which a series of canyons—La Jara, Frances, Gobernador, Largo, Blanco—extend southward like fibrous roots. From these roots, Diné pastoralism blossomed.

When viewed from the east, however, Dinétah once looked like a formidable stronghold, for a nearly impenetrable ridge—a part of the Continental Divide—shielded the area from the Rio Grande settlements. The Spaniards appropriately named the region beyond this cordillera "Casa Fuerte," meaning "fortified house" or "fortress."[18] The ridge rose up from the plain like a rampart, checking Spanish incursions while emboldening the people who lived behind its barrier. From Casa Fuerte, Diné men launched the raids on villages and pueblos that made them infamous throughout northern New Mexico.

Raiding during this early period was far more complicated than the image conjured up with the phrase "Navajo raiders." Certainly some raids involved small bands of young men bent on acquiring horses or proving their bravery, and nascent stockowners or hungry hunters tempted by the prospect of such docile prey as sheep. But just as often, raiders avenged attacks on their kin and the capture of wives, sisters, and children. Indeed, Diné lives entangled with those of their neighbors in the pueblos in ways that have often perplexed outsiders. From time to time, Diné traded with Puebloan people, established political and military alliances with them, offered refuge to native slaves and servants fleeing Spanish masters, and forged intercultural bonds through marriage. And from time to time, they preyed on the pueblos, stealing livestock and taking captives.[19] If this seems schizophrenic, it is because we imagine Navajos as monolithic. And yet the Diné were never united politically, not until the twentieth century—some might argue not even then. One group of families or several allied groups may have made friends in the pueblos, while another made war. Our mistake is in lumping all Navajos together.[20]

We should remember, too, that contrary to the popular image, raids were only one way in which Diné families acquired Spanish livestock. In the wake of the Pueblo Revolt of 1680, fleeing Spaniards abandoned their stock, leaving behind thousands of animals for the taking. After the soldiers and missionaries returned more than a decade later, refugees from Jemez and other pueblos turned to Diné for shelter, sometimes bringing their stock with them. Moreover, in the years following reconquest, Diné may well have acquired at least some of their horses and sheep through trade.[21] Others may have obtained them through networks of reciprocity. Not all Diné stockowners were raiders.

And yet there is little doubt that by the late seventeenth century, Diné raiders intensified their assaults, enraging the Spanish and the people of the Rio Grande pueblos.[22] In 1669, a raid on Acoma pueblo captured 800 sheep and a herd of cattle, and three years later, raiders "sacked and robbed" the Rio Grande valley, killing or carrying off "all except a few small flocks of sheep, which were saved by the vigilance" of their herders.[23] Fray Francisco de Ayeta identified these raiders only as "hostile Apaches," but the provincial governors in Santa Fe certainly understood them to be Navajos.

Punitive campaigns against the Navajos in retribution for those raids give us our first images of life within Casa Fuerte. In 1675 and 1678, Juan Domínguez de Mendoza led three military invasions of these lands, seizing Navajo horses, taking men, women, and children captive, killing others, and burning their corn fields. Diné lived in a rich agricultural area in the latter half of the seventeenth century. The San Juan River valley offered deep soils for farming maize along its terraces, alluvial fans, and the meanders of sandy washes. That was particularly true at the confluences of its tributary streams, where a high water table provided enough moisture in this land of little rain to allow kernels to germinate.[24] Unfortunately for us, however, Domínguez's report of his assault on Navajo fields did little more than confirm that Navajo farmers lived in the canyonlands of Casa Fuerte. He left little record of his observations.

The first eyewitness account was not penned until 1705, when Antonio Alvarez Castrillón, secretary of war to Roque Madrid, created a detailed journal of a punishing campaign against the Navajos, following a raid on the pueblos of San Juan, Santa Clara, and San Ildefonso. His diary offers our first real picture of Navajos on their own ground, although certainly captured through his cultural viewfinder and filtered through the lens of conquest. *Maestre de campo* Roque Madrid had been among the soldiers who fled the upper Rio Grande during the Pueblo Revolt, and he had the honor of leading the vanguard in the Spanish Reconquest of 1692. Now he penetrated the canyons of Casa Fuerte with as many as sixty presidial soldiers, forty militiamen, and three hundred native auxiliaries from San Juan, Picuris, Tesuque, Taos, and Jemez pueblos, men bent on avenging raids on their villages. This impressive force, accompanied by hundreds of horses, of course, did not take the Diné by surprise. When Madrid's men entered these craggy lands, they found the *rancherías* and *casas* abandoned, for the Navajos had retreated to the mesas and cliffs. Riding though canyons and around isolated pinnacles that he called *peñoles*, Madrid and his men found clusters of *milpas*, or corn fields, which they systematically destroyed. The Navajos clearly farmed these lands, but if they had many sheep, Madrid's secretary did not take notice. The soldiers found and slaughtered only some thirty-two head.[25]

It is tempting to conclude, then, that Diné, by and large, were not yet pastoralists. After all, when they first began acquiring sheep, they likely butchered them right away, much as they did when they hunted deer or bighorn sheep. It took some time before they transformed themselves from hunters to herders.[26] Still, this apparent scarcity of sheep may be misleading. Having been forewarned of impending attack, Diné likely drove their flocks onto the mesas, which the Spaniards themselves could not ascend, by their own account.[27] Madrid's men failed to capture many sheep because the Diné moved their flocks away from danger.

In fact, we have plenty of evidence that Diné maintained at least small flocks by the early 1700s. Antonio de Ulibarrí, a member of Madrid's force, later recalled that he had seen several small herds of sheep during that initial campaign.[28] Similarly, Alfonzo Rael de Aguilar, who took part in an assault on Dinétah in 1713, swore that the Navajos tended flocks on their ranchos; indeed, he and his fellow soldiers had seized three hundred head of stock.[29] These men, it's true, recorded their recollections decades after the event, so we might question their veracity. But consider this: Governor Francisco Cuervo y Valdez, writing in 1706, only one year after Madrid's first campaign, reported that the Navajos raised livestock throughout their province. And he offered one more bit of proof of a nascent pastoral society: Navajo women wove wool from their own sheep.[30] Significantly, then, by the early years of the eighteenth century, Navajo women had already acquired a reputation as herders and weavers.

These women likely had begun to nurture small flocks as a reliable and portable means of feeding and clothing themselves and their families. And yet this gradual shift toward pastoralism proved that security and fear were two sides of the same story. Small herds of sheep and goats allowed families to flee enemies who threatened or burned their fields, and still eat. They were moveable feasts. And yet those same animals must have attracted hungry enemies, unable to resist passive prey.[31] Indeed, the maintenance of flocks may well have bred the nearly half-century of terror that reigned in Dinétah.

Beginning in the early 1710s and continuing through mid-century, a formidable alliance between Ute and Comanche bands pressured Diné to take an increasingly defensive posture. Already, continued Spanish assaults encouraged Diné to begin constructing masonry "pueblitos" in some of the canyons. More importantly, though, Utes and Comanches—both accomplished horsemen—began to swoop down on Diné camps, taking women and children as captives and slaves, seizing livestock, and making off with blankets, pelts, and other valued property. Diné responded by building masonry fortresses designed to secure their families against sneak attack.[32]

For much of the twentieth century, archaeologists surmised that these stone houses were built by a large influx of refugees from the Rio Grande pueblos, who took flight in the early 1690s following the Spanish reconquest of New Mexico.[33] To be sure, Jemez refugees sought protection among the Diné after soldiers besieged their pueblo in 1694.[34] Even today there stand the ruins of a house that was built in the months after the siege, sitting on a mesa high up above Canyon Largo near its confluence with Tapacito Creek. This structure, with four or maybe as many as seven rooms, especially thick stone walls, and a rooftop entry hidden behind a parapet wall, became home, perhaps, to one or two refugee families. The locals must have befriended these escapees from Spanish oppression, for an extended Diné family apparently allowed the new arrivals to build within the bounds of their own homestead.[35] It seems likely that the families already knew each other, that they had struck up a friendship in the course of trading or some other circumstance that we will never know. Indeed, the visitors may well have *become* family, for it appears that they continued to live among the Diné for quite some time. In 1705, Madrid encountered a pair of women, one Jemez, the other Navajo, who hailed from the canyonlands of Casa Fuerte. Who knows? Perhaps these two women lived together on the mesa near Tapacito Creek. It may well be,

Frances Canyon Tower, built incrementally between 1710 and 1743, is the largest of the fortresses that the Diné built in Dinétah to protect themselves from assaults by Spanish soldiers and Ute raiders. Courtesy Library of Congress, Historic American Buildings Survey Collection, NM-155-4.

too, that these Jemez expatriates gave birth to the Coyote Pass clan, which traces its origins to a Jemez woman.[36] In any event, it seems clear that at least a few refugee families—or as historian James Brooks suggests, a few captives—lived in Dinétah, especially considering the obvious Puebloan influence on Diné ceremonies.[37] And yet we have no concrete evidence of a particularly large population of refugees from the pueblos residing in these canyons. What we do know is this: these mesas and valleys were home to many Diné, who girded themselves for a half-century of warfare against horsemen armed with bows and arrows.

Their citadels still stand above canyon mouths, atop gigantic boulders and sandstone knobs, and along the rims of mesas, keeping watch over the approaches to Dinétah's valleys.[38] Among these fortresses, the complex of sandstone buildings positioned on the rim of a tributary of Frances Canyon is surely the most impressive. A four-story, triangular tower at the edge of the cliff kept lookout for those who took shelter within the substantial main structure, whose two-story walls, built incrementally between 1710 and 1743, eventually enclosed upwards of forty rooms. At the other end of the scale: a tiny sandstone room perches atop a house-sized boulder high above Palluche Canyon. Enemies approaching this hideout would have had to look very hard just to see it, so successfully does it blend, in both form and materials, with its natural base. They would have had an even more difficult time gaining entry, for even those who concealed themselves within its walls had to scale the gigantic rock using footholds and handholds carved into its face. On the cliff above this site is a second fortress, built on a rock outcrop a decade earlier in the mid-1720s. Surrounding it, as at most of these defensive structures, are the remains of ordinary hogans, framed by wooden, forked-stick tripods, walled in with smaller poles, and covered with bark and a thick layer of earth. Most people probably lived in these hogans, using the fortified buildings as temporary refuges in the event of attack.[39]

The design and location of these structures were part of an ingenious defensive network, an advance warning system, as it were. When they peered through the loopholes in the upper walls, the people who hid within these rooms took in sweeping vistas of the landscape below, allowing them to anticipate the approach of enemies. Many of these structures offered a clear view of another fortification nearby or across the canyon, so that one family could signal an approaching threat to others.[40]

Remarkably, it was here amidst all this apparent strife that Diné developed a distinctive way of life that would endure for generations. For many that life increasingly revolved around livestock. Certainly the Diné who lived in these canyonlands continued to support themselves with a combination of farming, gathering, and hunting, as well as herding.[41] But as the eighteenth century progressed, the importance of Diné flocks grew. One measure of this importance was the presence of weavers among the women living at Dinétah, who left behind wooden battens, spindle whorls, loom fittings carved into stone, and even hanks of wool. Physical evidence of sheep husbandry, nonetheless, remains extremely sparse, and we may never fully understand this early period in the development of Diné pastoralism. There are plenty of rock shelters and box canyons where Diné shepherds could have created makeshift corrals shut off with branchwork fences, just as they did later on.[42] Still, our picture of Diné pastoralism remains muddy.

If we are uncertain about the details, one thing is clear: by the middle of the eighteenth century, many Diné families herded flocks of sheep and probably goats. Consider the recollections of the Spanish soldiers who traveled through Navajo Country in 1743. Unlike previous forays, this was a peaceful encounter by a military guard on its way home from a misguided search for silver in the La Plata Mountains, so the men had the opportunity to view the people of Casa Fuerte with calm and clarity.[43] When called to testify before New Mexico governor Joachín Codallos y Rabal, who sought information on conditions in Navajo Country, Antonio Montoya reported that "the natives occupy themselves in raising their stocks and cultivating their farms." A second soldier, Juan Tafoya, elaborated that he had seen a flock of some 150 head of sheep, and don Manuel Saenz de Garvisu guessed that he had observed as many as 700 sheep milling about. These numbers, of course, were general impressions, not necessarily reliable accounts of livestock holdings. And yet one thing is absolutely certain. When sworn under oath, one soldier after another described the Navajos as shepherds and weavers.[44]

Within Dinétah, these shepherds likely moved their flocks from one place to another with the changing seasons, making the most of the canyons' meager resources. From the bottomlands, where cottonwoods and willows sometimes shaded seeps and riparian grasses, to the sloping shrub-grasslands, to the piñon-juniper woodlands of the mesa tops, each zone offered fresh forage at different times of the year. Stockowners also made good use of the area's water resources, which were more abundant than they seem at first glance. In some canyons, streams offered perennial sources of water, if not on the surface, then just below. To tap a makeshift well, a shepherd or a farmer had to dig only a foot or so into a streambed or arroyo. Flocks also may have quenched their thirst at small impoundments around springs or at natural pools carved in the slickrock—some capable of holding hundreds of gallons of rainfall.[45] Over centuries of observing the land as gatherers and hunters, Diné had learned to wring water from stone and glean sustenance for their flocks from stingy hills and desert plains.

Nonetheless, if Diné grazed their stock on these lands year-round, flocks necessarily would have had to remain fairly small.[46] As herd sizes began to grow, fresh grasses, forbs, and browse would have become increasingly hard to find. Goats would have fared especially well in this craggy sagebrush country, and yet they, too, would have stripped the area soon enough. As far as we can tell, of course, herd sizes were indeed small as late as the 1740s, if we can trust the Spanish soldiers' testimonies. But once flocks did begin to grow—as they surely did—Diné herders eventually would have had to search for fresh forage, either by moving out of these canyons seasonally or by moving out altogether.

Sometime in the second half of the eighteenth century, the people abandoned Dinétah. We may never know exactly why. Perhaps they could no longer bear the constant threat of the Utes and Comanches, who increasingly came armed with guns. Perhaps a droughty period in 1752–53 drove families out.[47] And yet it may well be that spectacular success as shepherds spurred them to expand westward toward greener pastures, just as prosperous pastoralists have done the world over. The Diné may have left, in part, because these narrow canyons and mesas could no longer support a burgeoning population of sheep and goats, especially in conjunction with drought. Growing flocks would have soon outstripped the capacity of this land to feed them. In the face of expanding flocks, declining forage, drought, and the continued goad of Ute warfare, this storied homeland might have become downright inhospitable.

Even by the early 1700s, some families—perhaps those with the greatest livestock wealth—had already moved south of Dinétah. Some migrated down Largo Canyon and along Chaco Wash, up to the lower benches along Chacra Mesa, which rises along the western edge of Chaco Canyon. That canyon was once a center of Anasazi civilization and encompasses the incomparable Pueblo Bonito, a sweeping arc of interlocking stone forming hundreds of contiguous apartments, ceremonial kivas, and terraces. Diné eschewed the canyon's western reaches where the ancient ruins stood and lived instead in the eastern portions of the chasm and beyond. Here, fresh forage and relatively abundant waters likely nurtured expanding herds. Grama and galleta grasses covered much of the area, and four-wing saltbush dotted the canyon bottom and its floodplain. Box canyons cast deep shadows that slowed evaporation, and the canyons offered seeps, springs, and easily tapped groundwater. Importantly, a canyon passageway that came to be called "Long Gap" allowed Diné to move their herds to fresh grasslands to the south. Chacra Mesa and Chaco Canyon offered an inviting environment for these nascent pastoralists, and yet they found no peace. Ute raiders continued to cloud the summer horizon. By the 1730s, families here erected fortifications like those they left behind in Dinétah.[48] They could run, but with flocks of sheep, it proved awfully hard to hide.

Others sought refuge in the shadow of the sacred mountain Tsoodził— Mount Taylor—in the San Mateo Mountains. Even as early as 1706, Spanish officials recognized that Cebolleta, a region where a Spanish land grant of

Located in Largo Canyon, this elevated refuge, which archaeologists call Hooded Fireplace, suggests the violence that cast its shadow over Dinétah in the early eighteenth century. Photograph by the author, 1997.

the same name would later be established, just south of Mount Taylor, was on the Navajo frontier; by the 1740s, the locale hosted a Diné population sufficiently large to attract the attention of Franciscan friars, who tried unsuccessfully to establish missions for them.[49] Then came the diaspora. In 1754, New Mexico governor don Thomas Vélez Cachupín reported that most of the Navajos had abandoned their old province and taken shelter from Ute attack in lands far to the south and southwest, as far as the Zuni Mountains.[50] Big Bead Mesa, on an eastern spur of the San Mateo Mountains, became home to one of these new settlements. More than fifty families clustered their hogans on this point of land, blocked off from the rest of the mesa by a twelve-foot wall, complete with loopholes for fighting off enemies.[51]

In expanding south and west, Diné encroached on the people living in the Laguna and Zuni pueblos, overrunning their fields and competing with their sheep, which already grazed these lands. According to Bishop Pedro Tamaron y Romeral, who surveyed the New Mexico missions in 1760, the Zunis had large flocks that they herded across the countryside.[52] And the Lagunas, too, maintained flocks of sheep in the foothills of the San Mateo Mountains.[53] The intrusion of Navajos and their livestock was unwelcome, to say the least.

To the Diné, that mattered little, for the region's ponderosa forests, luxuriant meadows, piñon and juniper woodlands, river valleys, and grasslands proved fabulous for farming, hunting deer, and grazing sheep. Such abundance could be both a blessing and a curse. Before long, Spanish shepherds and cattle ranchers likewise converged on the area around the San Mateo range, securing grants of land from the Spanish Crown, even though they impinged on native corn fields and pastures. Between 1754 and 1770, New Mexico's governors confirmed a dozen grants of land to Spanish ranchers. In 1768, Santiago Durán y Chávez received the right to graze 1,000 sheep, 800 mares, and some mules and cattle in the area, and the following year, Luis Jaramillo also gained grazing rights for 1,000 sheep. These two men were but waves in a flood of Spanish stockowners pouring into the grazing lands around the San Mateo range in the latter half of the eighteenth century. Diné responded in 1774 by launching raids on ranchos and pueblos across the frontier, forcing the settlers to withdraw, if only temporarily.[54] They managed not only to expel the Spaniards but also to appropriate land customarily farmed by the Lagunas. Then in 1800, Governor Fernando de Chacón granted some 200,000 acres of land smack in the middle of Navajo Country to a group of stockowners from Albuquerque, who established the village of Cebolleta.[55] Eventually, Spanish officials acknowledged that Navajos had prior rights to the area and commanded Spanish stockmen to withdraw their flocks, but the proclamation went unheeded.[56]

The encroachment of thousands and thousands of Spanish sheep, and the lure that they held for young Diné men seeking prestige and power, triggered rounds of raiding. In one early episode, Diné raiders allegedly captured three thousand pregnant ewes![57] These assaults crescendoed after 1800, as the press of New Mexican livestock intensified, climaxing in the mid-nineteenth century when New Mexico became United States territory.

The depredation claims against the Navajos, particularly after the 1840s, were certainly exaggerated. Sometimes the raiders were actually Apaches or Utes. At other times, New Mexican herders and stockowners blamed Navajos when they lost their animals to negligence or coyotes, or when the herders themselves stole or sold them. And yet it cannot be denied that groups of young Diné men proved their manly prowess by raiding stock from New Mexicans and nearby pueblos.[58] Half a century of these raids would eventually lead some military officials to characterize Navajos as marauders who acted from "a pure love of rapine and plunder," thereby justifying total war on Navajo Country.⁵⁹ This image of Navajos as wild predators has become such a trope in Southwestern narratives that it has gained an almost mythic quality, mingling in the popular imagination with familiar scenes from Western movies.⁶⁰

And yet the image obscures the complicated motives underlying the attacks. Certainly for those Diné who wanted to acquire their own flocks or rapidly expand those they already possessed, the presence of large Spanish herds may have proved simply irresistible. More importantly, though, raids became the most effective means by which Diné could wrest control of grazing lands. If Spanish settlers and herders felt terrorized by Navajo raiders, it is because Diné sought to terrorize them and drive them back to the Rio Grande. Spanish herds and their shepherds trespassed with impunity, and seizing stock became the one means by which Diné asserted and enforced their claims to pastures.

But it was also in the late eighteenth century that pastoralism—that is, the breeding and herding of domesticated livestock—came to distinguish Navajos just as much as their farming or even their raiding. In 1780, General Teodoro de Croix noted that the Navajos, "although of Apache kinship[,] have a fixed home, sow, raise herds, and weave their blankets and clothes of wool."⁶¹ Likewise, in 1795, before the wave of raids swept across northern New Mexico, Governor Chacón defended Navajos against the charge that they were stealing Spanish stock, writing that, unlike Apaches, the Navajos "do not want for sheep, for those that they possess are innumerable, and their horse herds have increased considerably." In particular, he added, Navajo women had become well known for their weaving skills. "They work their wool with more delicacy and style than Spaniards," he admitted.⁶² The Diné had clearly transformed themselves into weavers and herders.

Perhaps because growing sheep herds required large expanses of forage, Diné spread out across the land within the four sacred mountains in the late eighteenth century. Even by the 1750s, some were grazing beyond the Defiance Plateau as far west as Wide Ruin and Ganado.⁶³ Spanish officials took particular note of the extent of the diaspora. In 1786, Governor don Juan Bautista de Anza reported that Navajos lived not only in the area around the San Mateo Mountains and Cebolleta, but also at Bear Springs (later the site of Fort Wingate, at the foot of the Zuni Mountains), and in the Chuskas and Canyon de Chelly.⁶⁴ A decade later, Lieutenant Colonel don Antonio Cordero specified still more places where Navajos made their homes.⁶⁵

One of the most important of these areas was Canyon de Chelly, which together with Canyon del Muerto forms a deep chasm near the center of Diné Bikéyah. Rio de Chelly and Tsaile Creek, both perennial streams, carved these canyons, whose eroded lower walls soon give way to straight-sided cliffs. Life in these canyons followed the rhythms of the seasons. In summer, green patches of corn, beans, and melons dotted the bottoms, and here and there stood small groves of peach trees, at least some of which were planted by a Hopi clan that for a time took refuge here.[66] Agriculture would always be far more important than livestock in these canyons, but Diné families raised stock here, just the same. In winter, they moved up onto the rim, where shrub-grasslands and piñon-juniper woodlands provided pasture and firewood. Here, stone hogans blended easily with the rimrock, and access to canyon trails afforded a quick retreat in the event of approaching enemies.[67] Or so it seemed, as long as the antagonists were relatively poorly armed Utes.

Unfortunately, the canyons offered little protection against enemies with firearms. In 1805, the people of Canyon de Chelly became the target of an all-out war on Navajos, in retaliation for the previous summer's assault on Cebolleta. Spanish soldiers claimed that more than nine hundred Navajo warriors had stormed that little settlement, a figure that surely was exaggerated. The attack, nonetheless, deeply frightened the villagers, and Governor Chacón resolved to rid himself of the Navajo menace once and for all. The assailants likely were among those who lived around the San Mateo Mountains, where Spanish flocks impinged on Navajo pastures, but Chacón did not stop at establishing a garrison to guard the frontier. Instead, he ordered a two-pronged offensive on all of Navajo Country, dispatching one column to Chaco and a second to canyons de Chelly and del Muerto, where at least some of those in the San Mateo area had fled.[68]

In January 1805, Lieutenant Antonio de Narbona descended into Canyon del Muerto, accompanied by some three hundred troops, a small citizen militia, a company of Opata auxiliaries from Sonora, and Zuni guides. Alerted to the threat by the sound of musket fire, many Diné men, women, and children scrambled to take shelter in a fortified cave high up on the canyon wall. This cave proved inaccessible to Spanish horsemen, but was not out of the reach of their weapons. When the echoes of the fusillade ceased, more than one hundred Diné lay dead, and some thirty more were taken captive.[69] The soldiers celebrated their assault by feasting on 350 Navajo sheep and goats.

The massacre at Canyon del Muerto may well have driven survivors out of the canyons, across Beautiful Valley and toward Black Mesa, which rises high above the surrounding land. From the air, the mesa looks something like a gigantic hand, flexed back with its palm facing upward. At its heel, a 2,000-foot escarpment poses a formidable barrier to intruders approaching from the northeast; its fingers slope down toward the southwest to form the Hopi mesas. Dividing those fingers are the entrenched, intermittent streams known as Moenkopi, Dinnebito, Oraibi, Wepo, and Polacca washes. This rugged mesa made an excellent hideout for refugees from the ill-fated canyons to the east. Since at least the early eighteenth century, Diné men had been coming here seasonally to hunt antelope and deer, and a few Diné may have settled there by 1730. But in the nineteenth century, whole families arrived, trailing their flocks. Shortly after Narbona's assault on Canyon del Muerto, Diné families began establishing homesteads here, and still more families came in the 1820s through the 1860s, a period that witnessed almost relentless military incursions into Canyon de Chelly and the Chuskas.[70]

The mesa was an ideal place to live, in several respects. It stood far from the Spanish settlements, and its sheer cliffs and few approaches discouraged incursions. And yet it was close to the Hopi villages, where the Diné traded wool, pelts, mutton, goat meat, and blankets for peaches, corn, melons, and other produce. High up on Black Mesa, the piñon-juniper woodland helped conceal flocks. Later on, after families returned from Hwéeldi, the people established winter homes along the lower edges of the tree line, where shrub-grasslands intermingled with wooded areas, and they herded their flocks in the open, where grasses mixed with browse.[71] But in those early years, Black Mesa offered concealment.

And yet even in the early nineteenth century, as Diné spread out across the land, they began to move their flocks from one place to another, following ancient transhumant patterns. These seasonal shifts, a practice likely learned from Spanish or Puebloan herders but informed by generations of hunting and gathering, took advantage of each season's bounty and let grazing lands rest.[72] These movements had important ecological purposes. Shifting from piñon-juniper woodlands to shrub-grasslands and highland meadows, Diné could make use of the full variety of resources—grasses, browse, saltbush, water, shelter, firewood—that the land offered, effectively transforming a stingy environment into a land of plenty. Movement across space helped to manage the land by resting

This pictograph chronicles a Ute raid in Canyon del Muerto. Photograph by David Lee Thompson. Courtesy David Thompson.

A pictograph near the entry of Canyon del Muerto chronicles Antonio de Narbona's assault on the Diné. Photograph by James Q. Jacobs. Courtesy James Q. Jacobs.

plants for one or more seasons. At the same time, Diné shaped their land with their flocks, crafting a patchwork of grasses, weeds, shrubs, and trees, laced with stock drives.

Transhumance promoted flexibility in an uncertain environment. At the same time, it reinforced important cultural values. For Diné, movement is the essence of life. Whereas "to be" is the principal verb in English, "to go" is key to the Diné. Ethnographer Gary Witherspoon estimates that the Diné have more than 356,000 distinct conjugations of that verb, and that extraordinary figure does not include "to walk," "to run," and other verbs denoting motion.[73] The Diné world is continually in flux, undergoing repetition, transformation, and cyclical change. Importantly, transhumance reenacted the ritual movements of the Diyin Dine'é from one mountain to the next, the sacred movements that have shaped the land since time out of memory. It reproduced age-old migrations dating to Diné beginnings on the Colorado Plateau. And it brought distant relations together for a few months of each year, reinforcing bonds of kinship, or k'é.

Unfortunately, the genesis of Diné transhumance remains hazy. Perhaps it started with a few families moving seasonally from Dinétah toward Chacra Mesa. We may never know. But by the 1740s, Diné living in the Chacra area were following a seasonal loop, discernible in the archaeological record. By building their winter hogans along the wooded slopes of Chacra Mesa and on benches above the Chaco Canyon floor, they secured easy access both to firewood and hunting grounds above and to winter pastures below. In summer, they moved to lower benches near corn fields.[74] These shifts from canyon to mesa were only a harbinger of the far more substantial migrations that would come to characterize the annual round in search of forage.

Diné families trailed their sheep and goats from place to place, but they were not aimless wanderers. Families returned to the same general area each year to establish their winter homesteads and their summer camps (although in a particularly dry year, they might summer in a different place than in a wetter one). Herding shaped their movements as they searched for forage, but most herders were also farmers, and their corn fields tethered them to the land. As snows melted and the days got longer, Diné men sought out prospective corn fields or replanted lands previously claimed, which generally became the family's first stop on the way to the highlands.[75] These fields were usually fairly close to summer homes, close enough for men to tend them periodically. And in fall, the family returned to the fields for the harvest. So as much as anything, farming patterned transhumance.

Like pastoralists throughout the world, Diné shepherded their flocks in three different patterns across the landscape. One was the local daily movements from the corral to nearby forage. "Our mother used to tell us not to take our sheep in one direction," an old man explained to ethnographer Rosalie Fanale. "You have to take them to the east, take them to the west, to the south and to the north. We've been taught to take our sheep to different directions each day of the week.... That's the way we were taught by our mother—they teach you these things when you are little, how to herd." And he added, "The reason why you can't take sheep in one direction is that you don't want the grass to die.... If you go in one direction pretty soon you will see the trails of the sheep in the grass."[76] Most herders, however, returned home with their flocks during the heat of the day and went back out to pasture late in the afternoon. This practice, and similar repetitive movements to water sources, created denuded "sacrifice" zones around hogans and watering holes.[77]

The second and third types of pastoral mobility involved horizontal moves to distant locations, especially during drought, and seasonal vertical shifts to the highlands. Diné might take their sheep east to the Jemez Mountains, south to Mount Taylor and the Zuni Mountains, west to the foothills of the San Francisco Peaks, or north to the Abajo Mountains of Utah or the San Juan Mountains of Colorado. Their potential grazing lands, in other words, literally took in the entire expanse within the four sacred mountains. Still, the more common seasonal moves went from shrub-grasslands to nearby highland areas, or to places where kinfolk gathered to share good grass and water.[78]

The lush parks of the Chuska range eventually became the backbone of Diné transhumance, although other mountains served people living farther north and west. The ridge rises as much as 8,000 feet above sea level and captures a large volume of rain and snow, which saturates its sandstone cap and recharges the groundwater. Perennial streams, springs, seeps, marshes, and more than one hundred ponds and lakes created a highland oasis. At the highest elevations, sedge-lined meadows carpeted the ground beneath ponderosa pines, Douglas firs, and aspens. Lower down on the slopes, shrub-grasslands mingled with a woodland studded with piñons, junipers, and gambel oak.[79] The Chuskas' rich forage attracted Diné herders each summer, just as the verdant Zuni Mountains did farther south. Indeed, by the 1830s, this long spine through the middle of Diné Bikéyah had apparently become a particularly popular grazing area in summer when the flats turned brown.[80] Diné families made long loops from winter homes in lower elevations to summer camps in the well-watered high country. In so doing, they mapped a pattern that they would trace again and again for generations.

Left Handed's family, for example, made an annual loop in the 1880s from their winter home on Black Mountain to summer pastures, where they joined relatives in an annual rendezvous. Each spring they struck out toward the Carrizo Mountains or Navajo Mountain or the San Juan River. Along the way, they camped at places that often changed from one year to the next—Hill Across, Anything Falls In, Water in Bitter Weeds, Aspens Coming Down, Flowing Through Rocks—wherever there was water and plenty of grass, saltbush, or other feed yet unclaimed.[81] Movement from one place to the next was one way that Diné managed the land. Theoretically, at least, it allowed grazing areas to rest and regenerate. Sheep could be kept in one place for only so long, or their close cropping would deplete the range, forcing families to abandon a camp for several seasons until the grasses regained their vigor.

Scouting for sufficient forage required a practiced eye. At the coming of spring, Left Handed and his father, Old Man Hat, would first watch how the sun's rays struck the slopes of the mountain, guiding them to places where they might find ample fields of tall, ripening grasses and forbs to feed their flocks. They moved frequently in spring, in search of fresh forage and water, before moving on toward their summer camp. Sometimes, too, relatives shared their knowledge of good pastures or playa lakes—ephemeral bodies of water that appeared after rains—that they had seen or had heard of through the grapevine. Except during drought, when any grass, no matter how high, seemed better than nothing, Left Handed and Old Man Hat favored places with a variety of feed, especially tall grasses and salty bushes within grazing distance from water, where they might stop for some period of time before moving on.[82] But by the early twentieth century, drought and a growing population of people and livestock could make tall grasses hard to find.

Since its origins in the early eighteenth century, Diné pastoralism shaped the landscape of Diné Bikéyah. Over the years, Diné developed a distinctive pastoral way of life that distinguished them from their Apache cousins and even, in scale, from the Acomas, the Lagunas, the Zunis, and the Hopis, with whom they jostled. Growing herds on lean lands encouraged Diné to expand their territory and develop an elaborate pattern of transhumance to manage the range.

In the end, transhumance would not be sufficient to conserve the shrub-grasslands of Diné Bikéyah, especially as that land became bounded by a reservation line. The numbers of people grew to perhaps 20,000 by 1900, and flocks proliferated.[83] The richest stockowners appropriated more and more land, but they soon confronted new limits. Hispanic and Anglo stockmen encroached on the margins, making it increasingly difficult to make long-distance moves to favored pastures beyond the reservation. By 1904, when the first range examiner visited Navajo Country, livestock had begun to leave an indelible mark on the earth.

6 · HOOFED LOCUSTS

It was a hot, dusty July afternoon in 1904 when Professor E. O. Wooton set off from Las Cruces, New Mexico, on a fifty-five-day, 1,200-mile expedition through the western and central parts of the territory. In the fourteen years since he had joined the faculty of the New Mexico College of Agriculture and Mechanical Arts, he had established his reputation as the territory's preeminent botanist. Over the course of his career, he would give scientific names to 231 plant species previously unrecorded and write a book, *Flora of New Mexico*, which would remain the definitive work on New Mexican plants through most of the twentieth century. He would become known, too, as New Mexico's foremost expert on range conditions, publishing several influential studies in his capacity as the head botanist with the Agricultural Experiment Station. That expertise came from his careful study of the land, a practical knowledge gleaned from the field trips he took each summer to record and collect plants. By the time he left New Mexico in 1911, he would have added some 35,000 specimens to the college herbarium. But as of 1904, he had yet to venture into the northwestern reaches of the territory. And so, with the exciting prospect of scientific discovery on his mind, he climbed up on his wooden wagon loaded with camping gear, plant presses, blotters, and tin specimen boxes and headed off toward Navajo Country.[1]

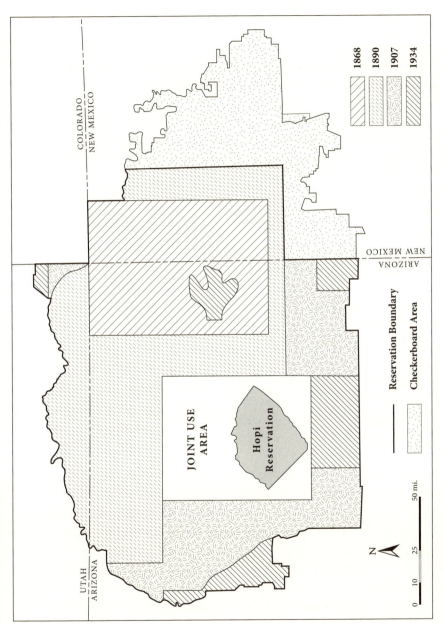

MAP 4 Navajo Reservation

Throughout his journey across western New Mexico, Wooton observed overgrazed rangelands. The problem was not restricted to the Navajo region, by any means. Almost everywhere he went, the range was in bad shape. That condition, no doubt, was due in large part to drought, for Wooton viewed the land in the sixth and final year of the deepest drought that New Mexico had experienced since the famine era of the 1660s.[2] But more than drought had damaged the land. Aside from a few areas of rolling countryside, thickly covered with grass, western New Mexico had been "eaten pretty clean," Wooton noted.[3] The worst area of Navajo Country was actually outside the reservation, around Gallup, in the southern Checkerboard. Here and on the eastern margins of the reservation, sections of public domain—which thousands of Diné occupied at least seasonally—alternated with lands that the federal government had granted to the Atlantic and Pacific Railroad (later the Santa Fe Pacific Railroad) to underwrite railway construction, as well as tracts owned by the New Mexico and Arizona Land Company (a subsidiary of the railroad) and sections set aside to support state institutions and schools, including the state agricultural school where Wooton worked. These lands were contested grazing areas. Anglo and Hispanic ranchers, mostly large-scale operators, leased the railroad- and school-grant sections, which alternated with tracts that would later be allotted to Navajo families, and each group treated the entire area as open, unbounded range.[4] It was here on these heavily grazed, checkerboarded lands that Wooton found the worst conditions. "All this region," he wrote in his journal, "is nearly denuded of grass."[5]

Inside the bounds of the reservation, along a stretch extending from Gallup to Farmington, the range appeared to be in better shape, although here, too, Wooton found disturbing signs. He observed an abundance of native galleta grasses, four-wing saltbush, and shadscale, all offering good grazing or excellent winter browse. And several indigenous plants flourished that were nutritionally inadequate for livestock but a normal part of the landscape, plants like alkali sacaton, Mormon tea, and greasewood. Still, Wooton recorded signs of overuse. It was especially significant, he felt, that blue grama, the most valuable forage grass and one that withstands heavy grazing, had been largely "killed out by sheep." Perhaps just as troubling, weeds grew everywhere. The abundance of weeds, even when native, suggested to Wooton that the Navajo range was overstocked. Cockleburr and bugseed, a plant that he later described as a tumbleweed, were particularly prolific. Golden crownbeard and sunflowers also colored the land with a riot of lovely yellow blossoms, but to Wooton's trained eye, this profusion of native flowers was troubling.[6]

Wooton's observations are important because he offered the first scientific appraisal of the condition of at least part of the Navajo range. To be sure, he studied only one transect of the reservation's biologically diverse landscape. He missed the well-watered and shaded pastures of the mountains and the varied lands lying to the west in Arizona, and it's worth noting that his journey took him through the "rain shadow" of the Chuskas, where a sparser, more arid vegetation grew. And yet his records make clear that by 1904, the eastern Navajo reservation was deteriorating.

A few years later, Herbert Gregory, a professor of geology at Yale, traversed much of Navajo Country, not only the lowlands, but also the plateaus and mountains, and he, too, noted overgrazing. Between 1909 and 1913 (except for one year, when illness forced him home), he spent his summers studying the reservation's geology for the U.S. Geological Survey, in part to identify those places where the Bureau of Indian Affairs might develop water sources for stock. Over the course of those summers—one of the wettest strings of years since the mid-1800s—he found good grasslands in much of the high country and in relatively unpopulated areas and those without much stock-water. Black Mesa, in the western part of the reservation, for example, offered abundant grass of excellent quality. Likewise, Monument Valley had much grass, albeit little water for stock to drink. The most populated areas were another matter. The Black Creek Valley between Fort Defiance and the Chuskas had scant grass remaining, and the adjacent Manuelito Plateau appeared "much overgrazed," including areas of rank weeds, to the exclusion of forage.[7] True, he found many of the plateaus and mountains well supplied with both grass and water. But generally speaking, the well-watered areas of Navajo Country were clearly overstocked.

It was the spectacular success of Diné pastoralism within the increasingly restricted boundaries of their range that led to the environmental decline that Gregory and Wooton reported. After their return from Hwéeldi, the Diné population boomed, and their livestock holdings grew phenomenally from a small foundation herd in the 1870s to three-quarters of a million mature sheep and goats in 1930.[8] That exponential increase conspired with a series of significant climatic events that began with the severe drought of 1899–1904, followed by the string of arroyo-cutting wet years extending through 1920. Diné stockowners had managed to weather the drought, holding onto their flocks as best they could, so that large numbers of animals continued to feed on depleted forage. A number of particularly rich stockowners aggravated declining conditions by appropriating the best lands for themselves and pushing poorer owners onto more marginal tracts. And as Anglo ranchers encroached along the reservation's periphery, the problem intensified. The result was an overgrazed range.

The 1860s are a benchmark for understanding environmental change due to livestock grazing on the Navajo Reservation. For much of that decade, most of the Diné were held captive at Hwéeldi, and relatively few sheep and goats remained on the land. Kit Carson's soldiers and their Ute allies slaughtered most of the Diné flocks or drove them to Fort Sumner.[9] Diné refugees, to be sure, kept some herds hidden in western outposts, and small, scattered bands of wild horses likely roamed remote pockets of the plateau. But in general, few livestock grazed the land for much of the decade.

When the people returned, they came with the intent of rebuilding their herds. Certainly federal authorities hoped that they would do so; the treaty establishing the Navajo Reservation promised a small foundation herd so that the Navajos could support themselves without subsidies, and the Diné worked hard to build their flocks through natural increase.[10] In the first few years, stockowners refrained from eating their ewes or lambs, choosing instead to survive on rations and small game so that their herds would multiply rapidly. The BIA reinforced the effort to build herds by generally prohibiting reservation trading posts from purchasing Navajo livestock, a prohibition that lasted until World War I, and even then only lambs, wethers (castrated males), and old, unproductive ewes—not their breeding stock—could be sold. As a result of this policy, Navajo flocks grew beyond federal officials' wildest dreams. By 1890, the Navajos reportedly had an astonishing 1.6 million sheep and goats.[11]

How is it possible that flocks could have grown so enormously so fast?

Ecologists have developed a theory that they call "ungulate irruption." When wild ungulates (that is, hoofed, herbivorous mammals like sheep) are introduced into a new environment with far more nutrient-rich forage than the animals need, the population increases exponentially until the animals exceed the capacity of the vegetation to sustain them (the so-called carrying capacity). The initial abundance of forage makes this incredible rate of growth possible by keeping death rates among vulnerable lambs low and fertility among ewes high. As the animal population rises and consumes forage, the vegetation begins to decline, both in density and diversity. According to this theory, there is a moment when these reciprocal trajectories actually intersect. For one brief year, the demand by sheep for nutritious food and the supply of forage match. But as the next generation is born, suddenly far too many sheep are searching for even less forage, which is quickly depleted. Before long, the animals begin to starve to death, the ewes become less fruitful, and the population crashes dramatically. Such a crash rarely leads to extinction. Instead, as grazing pressure plummets, plant communities begin to recover, eventually reaching a kind of accommodation, with fewer sheep consuming sparser, shorter, less diverse vegetation. Ecologists have observed this pattern among such wild ungulates as reindeer, mountain goats, and mountain sheep in various environments throughout the world.[12]

According to this classical theory, animal and plant communities will continue to reproduce at this newly established, relatively stable level unless some radical change in environmental conditions creates an extraordinary increase in carrying capacity, triggering the process once again. But even then, the initial irruption will have permanently changed vegetation patterns, dampening subsequent irruptions so that population booms and busts become far less spectacular. These smaller oscillations might be described as a kind of equilibrium that arises even out of seemingly chaotic fluctuations in population.[13]

Ungulate irruption is an exceedingly elegant model, almost breathtaking as theories go. Historian Elinor Melville drew on it for her trailblazing study of grazing and environmental decline in Mexico's Valle del Mezquital. And yet, this theory is far too simple to explain the complex interactions between animals and plants on the southern Colorado Plateau. In the ideal world of theory, we should be able to look at livestock population figures over time and trace an undulating line that looks something like a bell curve gone awry. Such a curve would help us pinpoint the year when Diné flocks exceeded the ability of the land to sustain them and perhaps even infer some notion of the original quality of the vegetation.[14] Unfortunately, the model ignores so much that goes on in the real world that it becomes almost useless for understanding the history of the Diné range.

The story of the rise and fall of sheep populations is not as simple as the model would lead us to believe. For example, the theory assumes a reciprocal relationship between the number of plants and animals: as ungulate populations rise, vegetation declines, and vice versa. But on the southern

Colorado Plateau, this relationship was surely far more complicated. As sheep and horses depleted certain grasses, such as sideoats grama, bush muhly, and Indian ricegrass, other grasses that tolerated or even thrived on grazing, grasses like galleta and sand dropseed, as well as such forbs as globemallow and woolly plantain, would have spread into newly created openings. And as the availability of palatable grasses and forbs diminished, sheep would have shifted their feeding strategy to include shrubby plants like sagebrush. By stimulating increases in grazing-resistant grasses and incorporating woody shrubs into their diet, sheep populations could have continued to grow long after significant changes in plant communities began to take place. And there are other processes that the story of ungulate irruption simply ignores. Periodic drought, heavy snowfall, or unseasonably late frost could abruptly decrease the availability of forage in a given year, regardless of the size of the livestock population. So stock might starve one year, even though the same numbers could have thrived in another year marked by milder weather.[15]

By the same token, the model assumes that the reciprocal relationships between animals and plants are unmediated by humans. Nature simply takes its course. And yet, Diné managed their landscape in myriad ways that influenced livestock populations. Once herds began to grow sufficiently, Diné started consuming sheep and goats. They ate especially large numbers during droughts and at other times when crop failure or rotten caches of corn meant fewer food alternatives. True, they tended to slaughter barren or older animals that had aged beyond their reproductive years, and they especially avoided butchering lambs or kids, thereby enhancing the ability of a given population to reproduce itself.[16] Nonetheless, in consuming stock, they reduced animal populations independent of the availability of forage.[17] At the same time, the handful of commercial stockowners, men like Chee Dodge, who purchased or sold animals to traders off the reservation, meddled with the natural rise and fall of livestock populations. Bear in mind, too, that Diné shepherded their flocks in ways that made it possible for the land to maintain higher population densities than it might have otherwise. When they trailed their sheep and goats to well-watered highlands in summer, they concentrated their stock on relatively lush meadows, while in winter, families spread out across the land, where their sheep could consume brushy browse even when snow covered dry grasses. By the early twentieth century, a few families even raised alfalfa hay for their stock, to supplement wild grasses and browse, or to sell at trading posts.[18] In caring for and consuming flocks, they edited the simplistic story of ungulate irruption in ways that we can never know.

Even if the Diné had done nothing to affect the magnitude of population change, the truth is that we have no idea how many head of stock there were on the Navajo Reservation until the 1930s. We have only a few hard facts. The Diné came back from Hwéeldi with some 4,200 sheep and goats and more than 560 horses in tow. Soon, in 1869, the BIA issued some 14,000 churra sheep and 1,000 goats, in accordance with the treaty that established the reservation, and two years later, the agent at Fort Defiance distributed nearly 9,450 more ewes. The Diné received a final ration of 7,500 sheep in 1878. We might assume, then, that the Diné started off with roughly 36,000 sheep and goats, but these figures offer only partial insight into the size of the herds that initially grazed the reservation. Those people who had managed to elude capture in the 1860s had held onto at least some stock, but there is no way of quantifying how many. Some families, as well, traded surplus annuity goods, blankets, and wild horses for even more sheep, and a handful resorted to theft to augment their herds. On the other side of the balance sheet, in 1874, a blizzard caused heavy stock losses.[19] All of these events affected the potential breeding population of ewes and nanny goats.

Compounding our problem of determining the number of livestock on the range, the reports of Navajo stock numbers after the 1870s are misleading. Keep in mind that the Diné lived in fairly dispersed rural settlements within an area about the size of West Virginia, and until the 1920s, the only way to get around this rugged landscape was on horseback or by foot.[20] It was the rare Indian agent who ventured away from his desk and visited Navajo families at their hogans. Instead, agents generally gathered their information when Navajos came to the agency to obtain rations or special equipment such as wagons, and they tended to extrapolate their observations about large-scale owners to the general population. In many instances, when bureaucrats in Washington asked for facts, agents simply made them up, based on previous reports and their impressions as to whether the number of animals had gone up or down, given the weather. So we must look at livestock figures with skepticism.[21]

Indeed, if we read the agents' reports carefully, we can only conclude that none of them really had any solid information about the number of animals on the range. They offered only guesstimates. Consider for a moment the report by C. E. Vandever, who claimed to have actually visited every part of the reservation during his tenure of nineteen months. In 1889, he estimated that the Navajos had 900,000 sheep and goats, 250,000 horses, and 5,000 head of cattle. Remarkably, the following year there was no change, with the exception of an additional 1,000 beeves and 100 mules.[22] Vandever made it clear that he found it impractical to conduct a census. Still, his otherwise detailed comments about Navajo life might give us the impression that he had unrivaled insight into the numbers of stock.

Until we look at his predecessor's reports.

In 1888, agent S. S. Patterson had reported exceedingly similar figures. Like Vandever, he grumbled that the law requiring an annual census of Indian reservations was ridiculous. "Owing to the nomadic habits of the Navajo Indians and their constant moving about, with their herds and flocks, over a vast territory," Patterson complained, "it is absolutely impossible to obtain a correct census." Instead, he asked around among some of the Navajo men. The result was what he called a "careful estimate": 1.1 million sheep and goats, perhaps 250,000 horses, and about 3,500 cattle. Interestingly, he had arrived at almost identical figures for the two previous years—with minor alterations, perhaps so that they seemed more real (the classic bureaucrats' ploy).[23] The constancy in the number of horses from 1886 through 1890 is especially noteworthy. Since most of these horses were mustangs that ranged away from hogans, there is little chance that this figure was anything more than a wild guess. In fact, the improbable consistency of both Patterson's and Vandever's figures and the admission by almost all the agents that they conducted no counts make it clear that we cannot trust the official estimates, at least not in terms of actual numbers.

Happily for us, federal authorities did make several diligent efforts to enumerate Navajo stock holdings. The first came in 1890, when the federal Census Bureau reported that the Navajos had amassed 1.6 million sheep and goats (a figure that likely included lambs and kids), nearly 119,000 horses, and some 9,000 head of cattle. We must necessarily wonder, again, about the accuracy of that count, considering how thinly the people and their stock spread out over an enormous area and how difficult it was to get to remote places like Navajo Mountain and the Kaibito Plateau. After all, the following year agent David Shipley complained that a complete count would take fifteen men at least three months of work.[24] Unfortunately, fire destroyed the 1890 census schedules, so we have no way of assessing the validity of the data. Still, it bucked the numerical trends that Patterson and Vandever had established.

This stereoscopic postcard, published by the Keystone View Company, shows a Diné man with a flock of sheep in northeastern Arizona, ca. 1880. Notice the mix of black and white sheep. Author's collection.

Perhaps we can rely on the figures that the agency superintendent, Peter Paquette, meticulously collected twenty-five years later, in 1915. By that time, the reservation was divided into several smaller administrative units, and Paquette generally confined his efforts to his own centrally located Navajo Agency, so he had less ground to cover. He also had the assistance of four Navajo men, making it easier to locate and communicate with each and every family. Even though Paquette focused on a limited area—about half of the present reservation—it was the most populous region within Navajo Country and so remains useful for getting some idea of overall livestock ownership. Traveling from hogan to hogan, the superintendent and his assistants enumerated nearly 525,000 sheep and goats, plus almost 29,000 horses, burros, and mules, and about 14,500 head of cattle.[25] Those figures, of course, give us only a partial glimpse of livestock ownership across the Navajo landscape.

Not until 1930, when the BIA began to try to make accurate counts at sheep dipping vats, do we get a good sense of the number of small stock grazing the entire Navajo range. That year, government officials recorded more than three-quarters of a million mature sheep and goats. If anything, that figure was a conservative one. Many people refused to dip their flocks: trailing sheep to the vats and back could be hard on animals, they sometimes died in the noxious solution of nicotine sulphate, and the chemical residues hurt the eyes of the women and girls who carded and spun the wool, among other reasons.[26] Nonetheless, the 1930 count tells us with near certainty that the range supported at least some 575,000 sheep and nearly 187,000 goats, not to mention other domestic herbivores.[27]

Whatever their numbers, it is clear that the exponential growth of Diné livestock coincided with a decline in certain native grasses that livestock prefer and an explosion of prickly grasses and weeds that they tend to avoid. Most scholars have viewed that correlation as cause and effect. And we, too, might leave it at that. Certainly there is evidence to support that conclusion. When Wooton made his journey through the reservation in 1904, he documented an apparent correspondence between overstocking and troubling shifts in vegetation, leaving little doubt that large numbers of horses, sheep, goats, and cattle had devoured much of the range.

Overstocking, however, was not the only reason that Wooton found the land in such sad shape. Climate was also to blame. Deep drought, followed by convective summer storms, had carved arroyos into the land, a process that overgrazing surely accelerated. Those gullies lowered water tables below the reach of many grasses and encouraged the spread of woody plants and weeds with deep taproots. H. F. Robinson, an engineer with the U.S. Forest Service, had seen Polacca Wash—which stretched from Black Mesa southward through the Hopi villages to the Little Colorado River—grow from a shallow depression in the ground into a deep arroyo by the early 1920s.[28] Each year, the gullies increased, carving away the earth. The ironic result: while stock numbers grew ever larger, the range grew smaller and smaller.

Climate and overgrazing also intertwined to restructure the reservation's high-country parklands into a thickly wooded landscape. In the mid-nineteenth century, visitors to the Chuska Mountains and Defiance Plateau had been struck by the open, grassy, parklike forests. Lieutenant James Simpson, the topographer for the Washington expedition, described a Chuska forest of towering ponderosa pines, which were as large as twelve feet in circumference, along with "very pretty wide-spreading oak," indicating an open forest structure.[29] Similarly, in the 1870s, the journalist John Beadle praised the "magnificent forest" on the Defiance Plateau as a "splendid natural park," adding that the pines, "from three inches to two feet in thickness, mingled with a few dwarfish oaks, were scattered in regular proportion," their branches completely excluding the sunshine.[30] Even as late as the 1910s, Herbert Gregory observed that throughout Navajo

Country, the pine trees were "widely spaced" and enclosed "groves of oak and grass-floored parks of singular beauty."[31] This pastoral vision was not mere hyperbole. Scientific analysis of the ages of the trees in the Chuskas confirms that the forest was far less dense than it is today.[32]

The parklike forests that so impressed visitors were largely the product of climatic contingencies and frequent fires. In the arid Southwest, ponderosa pine forests reproduce infrequently. A low-intensity fire or other mechanism must first remove the grasses (which compete with seedlings for moisture) and prepare the seedbed with a surge of nitrogen. It then takes a warm spring to produce a seed crop, followed by sufficient rain in July or August for the seeds to germinate, and then in the next year, an unusually wet spring and summer so that the seedlings survive. Without this sequence of events, southwestern ponderosa pines do not produce new trees, and such a combination happens episodically, in pulses tied to climatic oscillations. Analyses of tree rings not only in the Chuskas but also in northern Arizona's forests, beyond Navajo Country, reveal that relatively few trees propagated during the entire second half of the nineteenth century. Climate was the largest force shaping the Chuska forest, but also important were the low-intensity surface fires, fueled by fine grasses and pine needles, which swept through patches of the Chuskas roughly every three to six years, killing small, weak seedlings, scarring yet sparing mature ponderosas, and maintaining an open mosaic of meadows, glades, and woodlands.[33]

Those fires, too, were strongly influenced by climate. Although Diné may have set some forest fires while hunting deer or clearing agricultural land, intentional fires produced a mere flicker compared to the great number of fires regularly generated by the lightning storms ushering in the annual summer monsoons. The Southwest is more prone to lightning fire than any other region in the country. In the Jemez Mountains, just east of Navajo Country, for example, lightning strikes some 9,000 to 23,000 times per year. Importantly, too, the fluctuations in weather popularly known as El Niño and La Niña, produced by oscillations in atmospheric pressure and Pacific sea surface temperatures, had a marked effect on the region's pattern of fires. In El Niño years, warm sea surface temperatures in the equatorial Pacific bring wet winters and deep snow, while in La Niña years, cooler ocean temperatures mean dry winters. Tree-ring data correlating fire-scars with these climatic oscillations reveal that most fires throughout the region followed dry winters, which turned grasses into fuel.³⁴ La Niña, lightning, and a layer of fine grasses fed the cycle of fire that preserved the open parklands that Euro-Americans so admired.

That cycle of fire ended in the Chuskas about 1830, when Diné livestock apparently began to impact the mountain meadows and glades, cropping the grasses and denuding areas, which then served as fire-breaks, so that surface fires no longer spread through the forest. Livestock grazing thus began to restructure the forest landscape. And yet contrary to popular belief, the elimination of fire itself did not produce a more thickly wooded landscape, at least not right away. Another eighty years or so would come and go before the right climatic conditions—a dry spring followed by a series of wet seasons—brought pulses of new tree growth, not only here but throughout the Colorado Plateau, creating thickets of thin, scraggly trees. These were, in fact, the same events that triggered arroyo-cutting in the lowlands. Overgrazing made possible those thickets of trees, not only by eliminating the low-intensity fires that might have kept seedlings in check but also by reducing competition for moisture from grass and preparing a seedbed through trampling, which churned up the soil, mixing in nitrogen-rich urine and manure.³⁵ At the same time, the browsing of seedlings by goats made the Chuska woodlands somewhat less dense than they might have been otherwise.³⁶ Some might argue that browsing and grazing, in essence, substituted for fire.³⁷ But they proved to be a poor substitute; instead of maintaining a healthy mosaic of trees, glades, and meadows, they mutilated it.

Down in the lowlands, the combination of overgrazing and climatic fluctuations rapidly devastated the range, for this part of the southern Colorado Plateau is a readily erodible landscape. A sandstone foundation, aridity, and the subsequent structure of its vegetation make it easy for wind, water, and gravity to take their toll. For the most part, this cold desert supports bunch grasses. A handful of the most important grasses—blue grama, galleta, and western wheat—form loose mats of stems and roots. Others, like Indian ricegrass, grow in individual, often widely spaced tufts. Since the most useable, or "effective," moisture comes to this region in the form of winter snow, many of these grasses grow rapidly in early spring and finish their growth by July. Over the summer, they cope with aridity by becoming completely dormant.³⁸ The scattered distribution of grasses and shrubs, especially during dormant periods, exposes the earth to the erosive forces of wind and water. That exposure becomes most critical when livestock disturb the living crust of cyanobacteria, lichens, and mosses that stabilize the soil, help fix nitrogen, and enhance the absorption of nutrients. As hooves trample these crusts and overgrazing further diminishes vegetative cover, the high winds that often sweep through Navajo Country begin to blow away the soil.[39]

The effect of livestock on this brittle environment was cumulative and dynamic. Sheep shared the Diné range with goats, horses, and cattle, and each occupied a slightly different ecological niche when forage was lush. (By the same token, when vegetation dwindled, foraging strategies overlapped considerably.) Sheep are opportunistic herbivores. They prefer nutritious but short-lived forbs and young, tender grasses, but as these become scarce, sheep become less choosy, first cropping plants closely, then moving on to shrubs and even trees. In winter, they eat dried grama and wheat grasses, if any are left. When these are consumed or snowfall becomes too deep, sheep readily move on to sagebrush, saltbush, shadscale, and winterfat. In shifting to shrubs, sheep compete with goats, whose sharp rear teeth allow them to thrive not only on the brush that characterizes much of Navajo Country but also on the prickly plants that spread across the land as it became overgrazed. Indeed, one reason that Diné preferred goats in some areas may well have been a response to an overgrazed landscape. At higher elevations, goats like to browse deerbriar, cliffrose, piñon pines, and juniper trees, standing up on their hind legs to reach the lowest branches. Unfortunately, they particularly enjoy bark, which they peel off with their lower incisors, often inflicting serious damage to trees.[40] Mixed flocks of goats and sheep, if not moved frequently, can devour the range.

The damage they inflict is compounded by cows and horses, both of which eat grasses almost exclusively and both of which must range widely to find sufficient forage. Due to anatomical differences, horses and cows can consume much rougher, more mature grasses than sheep or goats do, and they take advantage of alkali sacaton and other grasses that offer the smaller stock relatively little nutrition. Cows—unlike sheep, whose cleft upper lips allow them to graze exceedingly close to the ground—find it difficult to eat short or ground-hugging, decumbent grasses, so they require a much larger forage area. Horses, for their part, have specialized teeth that allow them to eat even the toughest grass. And yet they never evolved the complex digestive systems that permit ruminants like cows and sheep to extract larger amounts of nutrition from plants, so they must cover large areas of land in search of food. Horses, cattle, goats, and sheep each favored different forage and consumed them in distinctive ways, both intensifying and extending the damage.[41]

With hundreds of thousands of head of stock foraging scattered bunch grasses and shrubs, changes in the composition of plant communities were inevitable, but overgrazing means more than mere shifts in vegetation patterns. Traditionally, range managers have defined overgrazing in terms of livestock. According to that measure, overgrazing takes place when nutritious plants decrease and inedible weeds increase in such quantities that animals begin to lose weight, threatening their health and, even more important, their market value.[42] Animal well-being was one of the primary standards that the Soil Conservation Service used in the 1930s, pointing to emaciated horses and scrawny sheep as proof. More recently, range ecologists have defined overgrazing in terms of vegetation, based in part on the theory that a healthy, diverse ecosystem means healthy animals. Severe and frequent grazing while a plant is still growing results in reduced plant productivity and ultimately death. As perennial plants die, the vegetation community becomes increasingly less diverse, weedy, and barren, the ultimate mark of overgrazing.[43]

Overgrazing means more than grazing. It begins when an animal defoliates a healthy, growing plant, removing all of the stem and leaves down to a couple of inches. That in itself may not necessarily cause long-term damage as long as the base of the plant remains. But when an animal bites the plant a second time before it can recover (perhaps because the herd has remained in the same pasture too long or returns too soon, or because another herd moves in), the roots begin to die. Frequent grazing reduces a plant's vigor and will eventually kill it altogether. Although some of the most important grasses in Navajo country reproduce to some extent through spreading rhizomes and tillers, others propagate only or primarily through seeds. If eaten late in the season before having a chance to set seed, those plants may die without having reproduced themselves.[44]

Overgrazing not only kills individual plants, it restructures the vegetation. As some plants die, others that are less palatable, grow more rapidly after defoliation, or sprout earlier in the season gain a competitive advantage and begin to spread. Nature, they say, abhors a vacuum. So some native forage like sand dropseed, galleta, and even blue grama may expand into areas vacated by less resistant grasses. At the same time, less palatable grasses and forbs colonize newly formed openings. Many of these have special defenses against grazing that make them particularly competitive. Some have awns that get into an animal's eyes, nose, or fleece; others are toxic. Sheep tend to avoid those plants, unless they are truly starving, which allows rabbitbrush, snakeweed, sneezeweed, Russian thistle, and locoweed to take hold.[45]

Stripping plants of their leaves is just one way that Diné livestock shaped their environment. In a complex process that remains poorly understood, ungulates affect the flow of nutrients and water through the ecosystem by trampling, urinating, defecating, and consuming the leaves and stems that otherwise litter the ground. It remains uncertain whether these effects, on balance, are beneficial or detrimental to arid ecosystems. Goats, for example, arrest the accumulation of litter underneath shrubs. This layer of decaying leaves, if allowed to fall, assists water infiltration by slowing runoff and keeps the soils cooler by shielding them from the sun. In preventing the build-up of litter, goats inhibit infiltration, widen the extremes of ground temperatures, and make soils more arid.[46] On the other hand, livestock can play a positive role in ecosystem functioning. While decayed litter recycles nitrogen into the soil in pulses brought on by rainfall, this cycle can take a very long time in the arid Southwest. Ruminants like goats and sheep help speed up this process by eating plants, both dead and alive, and releasing and dispersing nitrogen in a more useable form through their urine and manure.[47] Still, while stock may be an important part of the nutrient cycle, when they overgraze the land, they consume more than they give back.

In an arid environment, of course, water is the key resource that limits which lands can be used as pasture, and the scarcity of water in the lowlands of Navajo Country made livestock all the more devastating. Diné herders tended to take their flocks only a few miles away from a spring, tank, pond, playa lake, or arroyo, so that animals concentrated in particularly well-watered areas. (Except in winter, when sheep and goats consumed snow instead and, thus, could spread out more thinly.) Shepherds trailed their flocks back and forth to these watering holes, creating large swaths of trampled plants as stock rushed to take a drink.[48] This kind of trampling inspired the naturalist John Muir, writing in a different context, to grouse that sheep were like "hoofed locusts."[49] Sheep and goats killed willows by eating their bark. And the land around the watering holes quickly became denuded of any vegetation, except Russian thistle and other unpalatable or toxic weeds. Where the water source was a stream or arroyo, the sheep cut deep paths across the banks, creating new gullies.[50]

With hundreds of thousands of stock on the range, the reservation was perhaps bound to become overgrazed, especially in the Checkerboard.[51]

Since time out of memory, these lands had been part of the Diné range. Even after the creation of the reservation, Diné families continued to occupy these borderlands, despite their official designation as public domain, railroad lands, or state lands. Even more shepherds streamed seasonally into the Checkerboard to winter their stock. Unlikely as it seems, even the ancient, stabilized sand dunes north of the Bisti badlands lured shepherds, attracted by abundant stands of Indian ricegrass and by the perennial lake known as Be'ek'id Ahąąh Dikaní (Lakes Joined Together), fringed with cattails, and the numerous playa lakes that formed following heavy rains.[52] Many not only grazed their stock on the Checkerboard, but also established their winter hogans there, with the tacit approval of BIA officials.[53] Indeed, in recognition that the ancestral Navajo lands extended far beyond the original reservation established by treaty, the government expanded the reservation several times between 1878 and 1907, by presidential executive order. Growing opposition from increasingly powerful Euro-American stock growers in New Mexico forced the government to relinquish the westernmost additions between 1908 and 1911, but the Diné who had long made their homes in the area refused to budge.[54]

In a backdoor effort to secure Navajo title to these lands, Anselm Weber, the Father Superior at St. Michael's Mission, and S. F. Stacher, the agency superintendent at Crownpoint, worked tirelessly during the 1910s and 1920s to acquire individual allotments for Navajo families on non-reservation borderlands under the Dawes and Homestead acts. Although the Dawes Act is best known for breaking up reservations into individually owned farmsteads, a fate the Navajos escaped, the act also allowed non-reservation Indians to obtain homesteads. Cato Sells, the commissioner of Indian affairs from 1913 until 1921, creatively interpreted the law to claim allotments for Navajos on the public domain. In fact, he hoped—in vain—to secure for Navajos the control of springs and other watering holes and thereby appropriate all of their traditional range for their exclusive use.[55]

Although some 2,400 Diné had applied for allotments through this initiative, by 1919 only about 600 applications were approved and 100 titles patented (and held in trust by the BIA). Significant obstacles stood in the way. The General Land Office, which administered the allotment of land on the public domain, required allottees to build hogans, erect fences, dam arroyos, or make other "improvements" on each quarter-section claimed, a provision decidedly at odds with grazing. Those areas the Diné *had* improved tended to belong to women, and therein lay a second obstacle. Until 1920, when the regulations were changed, the land office, in its wisdom, rejected applications by married Navajo women because Congress restricted homesteads to "heads of families," which the government gendered male. Officials with the BIA, recognizing that "the wife of a Navajo is really the head of the family," had followed Navajo custom and allotted homesites to women. By rejecting women's applications, the land office deprived many families of their homes. Even after 1920, only a handful of women succeeded in patenting their titles on the Checkerboard.[56] The failure of the government to secure Navajo possession of this land in the first decades of the twentieth century would prove disastrous.

Opposition by more politically powerful, Anglo absentee ranchers, who flooded the area after the discovery of artesian water at the turn of the twentieth century, made it increasingly difficult for Diné to acquire these lands. These ranchers homesteaded the public domain, leased railroad land, school sections, and even Navajo allotments, and dared Navajos to continue grazing the range as they had for generations. As early as 1885, agent John Bowman had warned his superiors that these interlopers refused to recognize Navajo rights of possession. Navajos tended to live at a distance from water, a practice that acknowledged communal rights to this scarce resource. Anglo ranchers, Bowman observed, were seldom willing to recognize that a brush shelter located a mile or so away amounted to a bona fide claim to a desirable spring, even if the Navajo resident drove his sheep there daily.[57]

Problems became especially acute in the areas east of the Zuni Reservation and south of Chaco Canyon, where absentee stockmen wintered at least 100,000 sheep by 1920.[58] To assume control of winter grazing areas, these commercial ranchers fenced entire townships, thirty-six square miles in extent, enclosing not only the lands they themselves owned or leased, but also Navajo allotments—many of them patented—along with major lakes and springs and sections of public domain. Some of these sheep barons allowed Navajos access to their allotments; others completely fenced them out, tore down hogans, shot Navajo livestock, and threatened shepherds, even children, with guns. In one case, a rancher from Albuquerque fenced in at least three entire townships, including nineteen patented Navajo allotments. The worst offenders, no less, were powerful political and business figures. Lieutenant Governor Edward Sargent of Chama, one of New Mexico's largest sheepmen and a part-owner of at least two trading posts catering to Navajos, engrossed nearly seven townships, or more than 161,000 acres, in the eastern Checkerboard, and George Breece of Albuquerque, owner of one of the state's largest lumber companies, monopolized another seven townships, where he ran 15,000 sheep.[59] Traditional Diné pastures became private ranch lands.

As fences went up, Diné found themselves confined to smaller and smaller areas or forced off their land altogether. Casa Mera, a Diné man who had lived since 1872 near Mariano Lake, southwest of Crownpoint, complained that all the fencing made it impossible to move his stock. More than that, the fences confined him as though he himself were sheep. He and his family, he complained, had come to "feel like *we* are in a corral."[60]

Anglo ranchers were not the only ones appropriating the best grazing areas; wealthy Diné stockowners, too, pushed poorer kin and neighbors onto more marginal lands. The growth of large herds in the nineteenth century encouraged wealthy Diné to expand the breadth of their range to encompass large areas. Solidifying their claims to use the land, wealthy families formed marital alliances with other rich stockowners who might otherwise threaten their hold on favored grazing territories. This had a cascading effect. Middling families intermarried to minimize range disputes with neighbors and consolidate their traditional use areas. Poorer families, except when incorporated into wealthier ones, moved to the periphery.[61]

Some scholars argue that this rise of livestock wealth came with the arrival of railroads, trading posts, and a new market orientation.[62] And yet large-scale stock ownership long predated the development of a commercial mentality in Navajo Country. At least as early as 1853, a class of wealthy stockowners emerged among the Diné, according to agent Henry Linn Dodge. He knew the Navajos better than any bilagáana had known them up to that point, for he married a close relative of the Diné headman Zarcillos Largos and lived with his wife near Sheep Springs. Dodge reported that "one hundred men in the tribe own as many as 15,000 horses, and 100,000 head of sheep." Although in the next breath, he added that "the women own all the sheep, and the men dare not sell them without their permission."[63] No matter who owned the flocks, there is no doubt that some Diné were quite wealthy. Even during the turmoil of the 1860s, some managed to hang onto and consolidate wealth. Those who avoided incarceration at Hwéeldi, men like Dághá Sikaad of the Kaibito Plateau and Hashké Neiniih, the renowned hataałii from the Monument Valley area, rounded up the sheep and horses that those less fortunate had left behind.

Building on that foundation, these men shaped the northern frontier into a center of livestock wealth long before the trading posts arrived.[64]

The rise of trading posts, nonetheless, exacerbated this trend, although Diné stockowners would not become fully enmeshed in the market until World War I launched a skyrocketing demand for wool and lambs. Between 1875 and 1882, the arrival of Mormons to the north and the railroad to the south brought the first ripples of commercial activity.[65] At the turn of the twentieth century, about a dozen posts dotted the reservation, mostly at major springs; a few more scattered across the Checkerboard, and a string of stores, strategically located at ferry crossings, stretched along the north bank of the San Juan River. Many traders were also ranchers who grazed their own sheep and cattle on the public domain, or sometimes illicitly on the reservation itself.[66] By 1910, thirty-nine trading posts had opened shop on the reservation, and still more operated along the periphery.[67] In these first decades, most Diné engaged in trading only sporadically to obtain such goods as calico, clothing, crockery, flour, coffee, and sugar, in exchange for surplus wool, textiles, piñon nuts, and buckskins.[68] Trading-post goods largely supplemented a household economy in which families continued to sustain themselves with corn, mutton, goat meat, goat milk, and goat cheese. World War I changed all that. With a high demand for wool for military uniforms and a temporary easing of federal restrictions on the sale of Navajo lambs, traders flooded the reservation or expanded to new locations, doubling the number of posts.[69]

As traders extended their reach, subsistence and middling owners expanded their herds, and the ranks of large-scale owners grew significantly. Even after the war, traders and agency superintendents encouraged Navajos to increase their flocks and market their wool and wether lambs.[70] The data are sketchy for these years, but it appears that Diné stockowners, for the most part, continued to resist the push to become commercial ranchers; a typical sale was for three or four sheep.[71] Still, the sheep dipping records for the Ganado area suggest that in the postwar years many families with subsistence flocks developed more substantial herds, while some in the middling class joined the ranks of the wealthy. Between 1925 and 1927, Yellow Hair's family, for example, expanded its herd from fewer than 400 sheep to nearly 600, and two years later Tom Morgan's flock grew from almost 875 head to more than 1,200.[72] It was not only the lure of the market that promoted large herds; the BIA expressly forbade the sale of female lambs and breeding ewes so that Navajo flocks would continue to grow.[73] And yet, the trading posts did their utmost to encourage Navajos to increase their holdings, enticing them to sell more wool, rugs, and lambs with an array of canned tomatoes and fruit, coffee, velveteen, fancy Pendleton shawls and robes, tools, tack, treadle sewing machines, enamelware, and luxuries like china and porcelain dolls.

Even without incentives at the trading posts, the Diné likely would have increased their herds, for their own growing numbers required more sheep and goats simply to survive. Diné population growth is one of the few success stories in the demographic history of the native peoples of North America. Despite high infant mortality and epidemics of tuberculosis and influenza, between 1868 and 1930 the number of Diné increased nearly fivefold, from roughly 8,000 to 39,000 people, a gain probably attributable to the high-quality protein that a diet rich in mutton, goat meat, and goat milk afforded.[74] If each additional person had owned only twenty-five sheep and goats, Diné herds would have increased by three-quarters of a million head, precisely the total tallied on the reservation in 1930. Subsistence needs alone, then, could account for the increase in herds.

And yet, these animals were not distributed equally among the Diné. In 1915, for instance, roughly 20 percent of the households in the central part of the reservation had no stock except the horses they used for transportation, and some not even that. At the other end of the scale, nearly 5 percent of the enumerated families had livestock holdings of more than 1,000 animals, accounting for 22 percent of the region's livestock wealth. Not all of these large-scale stockowners were commercial operators, however, since nearly 30 percent of them also owned substantial numbers of goats and horses, for which there was little market.[75]

A dozen or so of the richest stockowners, nonetheless, had become fullfledged commercial ranchers by the early twentieth century.[76] Some of them, men like Ben Damon and Robert Martin, got their start as trading post operators. The wealthiest were Chee Dodge and his wife Nánībaa'. Dodge was, admittedly, unusual. He was the former interpreter for the BIA and the government-designated spokesman for the Navajos, initially as the government's appointed "head chief" and later as the first chairman of the Navajo Tribal Council. He likely expanded his herd as manager and part-owner, with Stephen Aldrich, of the Round Rock Trading Post.[77] Unlike most Diné, who might sell five or ten sheep in a year, it was not uncommon for Dodge to sell 1,800 head in one fell swoop.[78] His livestock business was so prosperous that he and Nánībaa', along with his second

Chee Dodge (*center*) chaired the Navajo Tribal Council in 1943, when it repudiated stock reduction. James Stewart sits to the right of Dodge at the table; John Collier sits far right. Photograph by Milton Snow. Records of the BIA, RG75, National Archives at College Park, Md., RG75-CP-Nav-106.

wife (Nánibaa's sister) and children, lived in a substantial stone house at Sonsela Buttes, designed by a German architect from Flagstaff, no less. He also maintained a second ranch at Tanner Springs and drove a fancy automobile. Although (surely with a knowing wink) he owned a Dodge in 1915, within a few years one of his sons was chauffeuring him around in a Buick touring car, outfitted with white sidewall tires and chrome-covered spares mounted on the front fenders. He is likely the man who, according to Superintendent Peter Paquette, had the largest bank account in Gallup, second only to that of the coal companies, and was such an important local businessman that he became one of the bank's directors.[79]

In 1915, Dodge and Nánibaa' together ran about 5,000 head of sheep and goats and more than 1,000 head of cattle across an enormous part of the Diné range.[80] Their flock was so large that they divided it into smaller bands, managed by herders who probably worked for a share of the annual lamb crop. To provide for their huge herds, Dodge and his extended family claimed use rights to an extensive area of land, from west of the Defiance Plateau to the Chuskas and Lukachukais and onto the Checkerboard, where Dodge owned an allotment near Bisti.[81] Náníbaa' even fenced in an especially lush pasture near Tsaile known locally as "the meadow." According to federal officials, Dodge and his family controlled at least 131,000 acres, or 2 percent of the Navajo range.[82] They dominated nearly as much territory as the greediest Anglo stockman.

By the early twentieth century, competition among Diné families for grazing land became fierce. Every community had at least one large-scale stockowner, whose animals jostled against the burgeoning flocks of their neighbors. As those with large herds ranged over greater expanses of land, they pushed poorer herders onto the marginal grasslands of the Checkerboard, already penned up by Anglo and Hispanic ranchers. Complaints filed with the BIA revealed an increasingly crowded landscape. Stockowners on Black Mountain's relatively good grasslands objected to the presence of outsiders from overgrazed regions of the reservation; some years later, Ganado's residents protested the intrusion of shepherds from the mountains—perhaps Black Mountain itself.[83] By the mid-1920s, conflicts like these were reaching flashpoint. Conditions grew especially dire in the most crowded sections, particularly the Checkerboard and the central reservation. When shameless Diné stockowners from those regions moved their flocks to rangelands near Shiprock that had been reserved for winter forage, they provoked a bitter outcry.[84] The central reservation, too, complained of crowding. Nearly three hundred women and men from the Chinle Valley observed that the land was so overstocked that "many of us find it difficult to graze our sheep and cattle properly, and must keep them constantly on the move."[85] Diné stockowners clearly felt desperate as they searched hither and yon for fresh forage.

Missionaries and government officials who genuinely cared about the Navajos' welfare voiced alarm over the condition of the range. Anselm Weber reported in 1911 that Navajo land, "on and off the reservation, is very much overgrazed."[86] Nearly twenty years later, forester William Zeh thought the situation had not improved. At the root of the problem, he wrote, was insufficient water for stock. The scarcity of water led to overgrazing and trampling around washes, ponds, and springs, creating a whole new vegetation zone, a "pure weed range with very little grass remaining."[87] Forester Donald Harbison echoed Zeh's words, writing that "such a severe use has been made of the range that now great areas of formerly beautiful stands of chamis[e] are . . . rapidly being killed out and . . . replaced by useless snakeweed and Russian thistle."[88] The land was going to ruin.

Since 1904, when Wooton made his journey to Navajo Country, range experts had documented the overgrazed condition of large areas of the reservation in increasing detail. Botanists, hydrologists, and foresters agreed that the land was overstocked. Grass was giving way to weeds, denuded areas were spreading around watering holes, soil was eroding away. The Navajos' sheep, goats, horses, and cattle were eating themselves out of house and home. The truth of the matter was considerably more complicated, of course. Climate change helped deplete forage and channel arroyos, and Anglo and Hispanic ranchers increasingly hemmed in the Navajos, intensifying the impact of their sheep. Something had to be done, but what? Some felt that the government should acquire more reservation land; others proposed drilling wells. But there was another idea, as well, one that had first been suggested in the early 1880s, when agent Denis Riordan recommended reducing the number of sheep and goats by one-half or two-thirds. No one had listened to him then. But by the early 1930s, stock reduction seemed like an idea whose time had come.

PART 4 · *Erosion*

7 · MOURNING LIVESTOCK

A sense of urgency filled the air one February morning in 1931 as some seventeen men crowded into a conference room at a Bureau of Indian Affairs office in Albuquerque to discuss the rapidly deteriorating condition of the Navajo range. Herbert Hagerman—the aristocratic scion of a millionaire land speculator and railroad developer, the former governor of New Mexico territory, and now the special commissioner to the Navajos—was already under fire for his conduct in overseeing oil leases up by Shiprock, and he wanted to make sure that his handling of the Navajo range did not become the latest scandal.[1] Top officials within the BIA's southwestern district and other related agencies were present, including Chester Faris, the district supervisor; William Zeh, the chief forester; William Post, the newly appointed irrigation director; and F. L. Schneider of the Bureau of Animal Industry. Joining them were the various superintendents and area specialists who administered Navajo Country.[2]

Over the course of two days, the men discussed a number of ways to improve the Navajo range. Eradicating prairie dogs was high on their list. And more dipping vats, they thought, would help. As it currently stood, as many as ninety thousand sheep and goats at a time trampled across great distances to the vats, then congregated for several days, denuding the land for miles around. One man argued, too, that the agencies could do a better job of teaching Navajos to manage their stock, if only they had more staff.

Another suggested that at least some Navajos might make their living by farming alfalfa for sale to fellow tribesmen. A couple of the men even floated the idea of resettling some Navajo stockowners onto the Pima, Fort Apache, and Colorado River reservations to help relieve overstocking, certain that the Pimas, Apaches, and Mohaves would not mind. As Faris mused, surely the Navajos would be "a good addition to any Indian tribe" in the Southwest.[3]

There were other plans in the works, too. Hagerman informed the group that before too long he expected Congress to consolidate much of the land in the Checkerboard, which would provide Navajos with secure access to the range around their off-reservation allotments. The BIA hoped to negotiate for the exchange or sale of the patchwork of lands owned by the railroad, the states, and private owners. Toward that end, Secretary of the Interior Ray Wilbur had already withdrawn four million acres of public domain from further sale or entry. This proposed extension of the reservation would not provide new lands for grazing, because as many as ten thousand Diné already lived on or drifted their flocks across these ranges. On the contrary, the consolidation of allotments into one large block would actually concentrate Diné into a smaller territory than they historically occupied outside the reservation, and it would allow the railroads and the states to create larger, consolidated tracts of their own on the periphery. In the process, some Diné would have to give up valued allotments in exchange for other, less desirable land. As one woman named Bah, who lived southwest of Chaco Mesa, would later complain, the proposed exchange offered her "nothing but rocks."[4] Still, consolidation would eliminate competition and conflict with Anglo stockmen. It would also give the BIA more control over land use.

One way to achieve better land use, many of the men agreed, would be to develop more sources of stock water. As things stood, scarce water on the shrub-grasslands at lower elevations limited the proper scheduling of seasonal moves from winter to summer pastures. Once snows melted on these winter ranges, the scarcity of water forced families to move up onto the mountains even though grasses had just begun to sprout. If the BIA could develop springs, drill wells, and build stock tanks across the flats, stockowners could not only hold their flocks on the shrub-grasslands a few weeks longer but also more readily move from one pasture to the next, allowing land to rest at key points in the growing season. The irrigation director William Post even suggested that the bureau consider building water tanks on wagons, which could be moved around high desert areas to encourage the Navajos to rotate pastures. (Such a program, he admitted, would first require a system of roads, since most of these areas were served only by trails.) Additional watering holes would also relieve crowding at existing water sources and make it possible to distribute stock more thinly across the land.

Not everyone thought that water would be a panacea. Some of the men warned that creating water sources could do more damage than good. New watering holes might simply open relatively ungrazed areas to intensive use. Hagerman, who was himself a New Mexican rancher, observed that "we have often said the only places left in New Mexico where grass is properly preserved is where no water is available except occasionally where[,] in the winter[,] the ground is covered with deep snow or where water can not be found except in holes during the rainy season."[5] By the same token, Post added, establishing additional watering holes in already crowded places might encourage more families to flock there, creating even greater concentrations than before. Water would benefit the range only when fewer animals grazed the land.

The key to that was stock reduction.

Eliminating worthless horses must be the first step toward better range management, several of the men argued. Horses caused far more damage than sheep because they could travel long distances without water, eating up otherwise untouched grasses along the way. Hagerman noted that the BIA had been working since the early 1920s to reduce the number of horses roaming Navajo Country, despite resistance from Navajo men who valued large herds as a measure of wealth and as a medium of exchange. The horse reduction program, strangely enough, had been aided by the spread of dourine, a sexually transmitted parasite that leads to emaciation, paralysis, and death. The BIA itself inadvertently introduced the disease in the 1910s when it unknowingly bred infected stallions with Navajo ponies in an effort to "improve" the breed.[6] Many of the ponies weakened and died, and many more were rounded up by the Bureau of Animal Industry and sold to a dog-food processing plant in Gallup in an effort to eradicate the parasite. Now there was little surplus, agency superintendents argued, since the estimated forty thousand horses remaining on the reservation amounted to the minimum of four or five ponies that a family needed to take care of their flocks and travel across rough country. And yet, more could be done, the agents thought. A handful of Navajo men—mostly older headmen—still owned enormous herds of one hundred horses or more, and those could be reduced to subsistence size.

But the real problem, as superintendent S. F. Stacher of the Eastern Navajo Agency at Crownpoint put it, was that so many of these horses were absolutely useless, too small and too weak to do much work. A lot of worthless ponies, he thought, could be eliminated quite easily by encouraging owners to slaughter and eat them, since most Navajos considered horseflesh a delicacy. John Hunter, superintendent of the Southern Navajo Agency headquartered at Fort Defiance, suggested that the bureau might also help families get along with fewer horses by replacing scrawny ones with more robust stock. Horses, of course, were only one part of the problem, all agreed. There were simply too many sheep and goats.

As several agents described their efforts to gradually reduce the size of flocks, C. L. Walker of the Western Navajo Agency at Tuba City found he could hold his tongue no longer. "Governor Hagerman," he broke in, "I think, with the present number of sheep . . . the range will grow worse. It can't stand still. A gradual reduction will just enable us to hold the range where it is. The thing to do is to have a *big and sudden cut*." Perhaps, he continued, the bureau might even set a limit on the number of stock each family could hold on the reservation. "The forest division," he pointed out, "saved the livestock industry for the white man by having [the] authority to say you can run only so many head of stock on a given area. I wonder if it has ever been considered giving the Indian Service that authority."[7]

Walker knew, surely, that in 1928 the BIA tried to assess a grazing fee on large flocks of more than 1,000 head of sheep (or their equivalent in horses and cattle), with absolutely no success. Diné customs of individual stock ownership frustrated that effort. As one agent complained, "When you go to collect . . . no single individual owns more than a thousand head because they belong to the son and the daughter and the wife and the son-in-law and the daughter-in-law, and sometimes to wives No. 2 and No. 3, and so, when it is all sifted down, there is nothing to collect." Some Diné, moreover, saw the grazing maximum as an invitation to *build* their individual flocks to the limit, an idea that Edgar B. Meritt, then assistant commissioner of Indian affairs, had inexplicably encouraged just three years earlier.[8] Now, as crisis appeared imminent, it seemed obvious to Superintendent Walker that a sharp reduction in livestock was the only way to save the Navajos from utter ruin.

During a break in the two-day meeting, someone—perhaps Hagerman—must have commented that the Navajos would never stand for the kind of sharp reduction that Walker called for. The next day, Post, who was only recently appointed to his position, asked the others whether it was true that the stockowners would resist. One of the agents replied that he thought there would be little problem, as long as the government raised the market value of sheep through improved breeding. But Hagerman needed reassurance. "There is no doubt in your mind," he asked the six agency heads, that "they will see the necessity of carrying it out?" There was no doubt, they replied, almost to a man.[9] There would be no trouble.

Government officials seriously misjudged the Navajos' likely response to livestock reduction, and that mistake would hold long-lasting implications for the condition of the range. Diné rejected stock reduction and ultimately the entire land management program, for it threatened not only to impoverish them but also to undermine the very foundations of their culture and social relationships. And yet it would be a mistake to assume that all Diné spoke with one voice during this tumultuous period. Many Diné leaders agreed that the land was overgrazed and tried to offer their own observations and solutions. It would also be a mistake to assume that the conservation program's failure was unavoidable considering the cultural differences between Diné stockowners and scientifically trained conservationists. Many things went wrong in the New Deal effort to conserve the land, but none of them were inevitable. All along the way, policymakers saw signposts that could have averted disaster. True, a formidable cultural divide separated the New Dealers and the Diné. But the failure to bridge that gap reflected the conservationists' stubborn unwillingness to listen, as much as it did cultural misunderstanding. Certain that only they knew the answers, policymakers and scientists generally ignored the Navajos' warnings and their suggestions for alternate paths. The more frantically the Navajos signaled, the more determinedly the New Dealers stayed the course.

That said, the impulse to act quickly to save the land—and with it, the people—was not only understandable, but admirable. By the spring of 1931, overgrazing on the Navajo range had grown so acute that it became the focus of a series of Senate hearings conducted as part of a nationwide investigation into the plight of Indian people. Lynn Frazier of North Dakota headed the committee, which included Burton Wheeler of Montana and Elmer Thomas of Oklahoma, along with Henry Ashurst of Arizona and

Sam Bratton of New Mexico as ex officio members. The group gathered information about each of the jurisdictions within Navajo Country by touring the region and holding hearings at Leupp, Winslow, Fort Wingate, Crownpoint, Shiprock, Fort Defiance, Ganado, Keams Canyon, and finally Tuba City. At each of these locations, the senators interviewed a lengthy cast of characters including agency and school officials, traders, Anglo ranchers, Navajos, and anyone else with a complaint or a request regarding the reservation.[10]

Diné flocked to these hearings, and they must have presented quite a spectacle to the men from Washington. Diné men in suits (mostly fairly young men who had attended Indian boarding schools and viewed themselves as progressive leaders) crowded next to others wearing blue jeans and cowboy hats. Older women in striped Pendleton blankets wrapped over brilliantly colored skirts and velvet blouses stood with younger ones in fashionable calico dresses. Adding to the colorful scene were the large pieces of turquoise and silver jewelry—necklaces, bracelets, earrings, concho belts—that wealthy men and women wore to any important gathering. Some of the richest among the Diné joined the throngs, but so too did some of the poorest. A good number of those in the audience came to address the committee themselves. Over the course of eight days, two Diné women and more than sixty Diné men spoke before the senators. Many of these men were recognized leaders who served on the Navajo Tribal Council or as officers in one of the local chapters or livestock associations.[11]

But the star of the show was Senator Burton Wheeler, a man who expressed paternalistic compassion for the Navajos, leavened with condescension. Wheeler dominated the proceedings, exhorting the audience to become more market-minded, chastising agency officials for negligence, demanding that the bureau relieve starvation, expressing his inability to fathom why people would cling to land that offered them only appalling poverty. His concern for Navajo well-being seemed sincere, and yet he had little patience for the things the people came to tell him. As he challenged or dismissed Navajo witnesses, assured them that Congress would set things right, or commended them for being "good Indians," he framed the way in which the senators heard Navajo testimony.

Most of the Diné who spoke sounded two themes: water and land. Uppermost was the need to extend the reservation boundary so that it encompassed all of the region the Diné occupied within the Checkerboard. They did not seek new lands (although they certainly would have welcomed an expanded territory); they simply sought to secure the tracts they already used without legal title on the public domain. That was their moral right, they argued, since their families had grazed those places for generations before the railroads and sheep barons arrived.[12] But they also argued that they could be good stewards of the land only if the government provided them with sufficient pastures.

John Dixon, a Diné man who lived near Shiprock, explained that his people could no longer maintain separate winter and summer ranges, as they had in the past, because they were hemmed in by large-scale ranchers. Those white ranchers, he complained, were able to drive their sheep and cattle over a vast territory, extending from the Colorado mountains in summer to the public lands around the reservation in winter, while his own people were restricted to a much smaller area.[13] How could Diné be good stewards of the land if they could not control its use?

Officials with the Bureau of Indian Affairs confirmed Dixon's story. Montoya Lope, a Diné man who worked as a BIA stockman, complained that Ed Sargent, from Chama, brought forty thousand head of sheep into the Checkerboard each winter, devastating the range and leaving the people who lived there destitute. Another official, James Ashcroft, had observed the same thing for years. He himself had once ranched in the Checkerboard; now he oversaw range issues on Indian allotments around Ramah, where a large band of Navajos lived. Each year, he reported, herders for large cattle and sheep operations drove their stock to the patchwork of lands around the reservation, grazing off the grass and leaving the Navajos "nothing but the wind."[14]

The Diné needed more water, as well as land. Across the desert grasslands, many areas that otherwise offered good grazing could not be used without reliable stock water. One man from Gray Mountain, in the western part of the reservation, expressed the problem succinctly. "Wherever there is [f]eed there is not any water," and "wherever there is water they are short of feed." If the government developed springs and tanks across the grasslands, he told the committee, stock owners could rotate pastures and let land rest and reseed.[15]

The senators listened to this litany of land and water, but remain largely unpersuaded. For them, the problem was clear: the Navajos simply had too many worthless horses and goats (and nearly all of them, it seemed, were worthless). The solution was clear, too: eliminate unmarketable animals to save grasses for sheep. Why, the senators asked, hadn't officials spurred the Navajos toward a more rational, market-oriented approach to sheep ranching? Why had they allowed the Navajos to overrun the reservation with goats and horses? Agency heads replied that ridding the reservation of unmarketable livestock was easier said than done, and they patiently tried to explain. The Navajos were particularly fond of their horses and needed them to travel across nearly roadless terrain, and goats were a dietary mainstay for many. But the senators would hear nothing of it. When one of the agency stockmen described his program to castrate dourine-infected horses after the processing plant in Gallup closed, Senator Bratton demanded to know why the man did not just shoot them. Wheeler joined in with a long tirade, badgering bureau employees to simply kill the horses and goats, substitute more marketable sheep, and be done with it. More water, he agreed, would certainly help, but more land was unlikely. Consequently, he maintained, there was only one real solution to the Navajos' problem: stock reduction.[16]

The Diné who sat through these hearings may have seemed to take in these words with stoic resignation, but in fact a good number understood only a fraction of the proceedings, for most of the testimony was in English. The senators considered their time far too valuable to permit a complete translation of their own words. Fortunately for the audience, nearly half the Diné who testified did so in their native tongue (translated for the benefit of the bilagáana), but that offered listeners a somewhat lopsided sense of what was going on. They heard witness after witness explain to the committee that many people preferred goats, which were hardier and good to eat, making it possible for families to save their sheep, whose wool (especially when woven into blankets) and lambs found a market at the trading post.[17] Of course, the audience also learned what the *senators* said when an interpreter translated for the benefit of a native-speaking witness, so they were privy to some of the talk about eliminating stock. But the committee rendered its harshest criticism of livestock holdings only in untranslated English.

Likewise, most of the acknowledged Diné leaders testified in English. Many of those who crowded into the meeting halls thus could not have known what was said when Chee Dodge and Deshna Clah Cheschillige, chairman of the Navajo Tribal Council, took their turns to speak. Both men seemed to seek some kind of compromise that might placate the senators and encourage them to provide Diné untrammeled access to their traditional range. And so, prodded by the committee, each of the two

Diné leaders Dashne Cheschillige (*far left*), Chee Dodge, Tom Dodge, and Henry Taliman. Photograph by Milton Snow, 1938. Records of the BIA, RG75, National Archives at College Park, Md., RG75-NG, NO-11-97.

leaders contradicted hours of Diné testimony. The men suggested—contrary to all evidence presented so far—that their kinsfolk and neighbors would gladly exchange their goats for sheep and willingly, if reluctantly, give up their surplus horses.[18]

No one could have known it then, but there was someone in the audience who would soon find out the hard way whether Navajos would willingly give up their stock. The slender man, wearing round wire-rimmed glasses and a rumpled suit, had beady brown eyes, a gaunt face, and a pointed chin (much later, some Diné would recall that he looked like a rat or a crow).[19] His name was John Collier. As executive secretary of the American Indian Defense Association, he had saved the day in the winter of 1931–32 when a blizzard killed at least 200,000 sheep and threatened even more. Collier had called for a humanitarian relief effort, deliveries of hay had arrived, and thousands and thousands of sheep and goats had survived.[20] He also had been instrumental in urging the Senate Committee on Indian Affairs to hold these hearings and investigate the conditions under which people throughout Indian Country lived. He testified briefly in support of the Navajos' request for more land, observing that they actually required more than the BIA was letting on if they were to sustain their livestock economy. But for the most part, he simply sat and listened.[21]

Less than two years later, the newly elected President Franklin Roosevelt astounded the BIA's old guard by appointing Collier, longtime critic of the bureau, to the position of commissioner of Indian affairs. Collier promptly turned his attention to the Navajos, whom he particularly admired because they held fast to their traditions. Within weeks of taking office, he launched a program to save the rapidly eroding Navajo Reservation. While he understood that it would be necessary to prove to the Navajos that a conservation program would produce demonstrable results, he also felt confident that they were an intelligent people who would follow a rational course of action, if only they were shown the way.[22]

In the fall of 1933, Collier laid out his plan for saving the land at a special session of the Navajo Tribal Council, which convened in Tuba City. Chairman Tom Dodge, an attorney and the son of the reservation's richest stockowner, began the meeting with the observation that the reservation was "very much over-grazed," and he challenged the council to "take the lead in dealing with this question of erosion. We should not be driven to it by outside people," he emphasized. "We ourselves should take the initiative.... Certainly the conditions will not be improved if we graze our sheep as we have been doing in the past."[23] With this introduction, Collier presented a comprehensive erosion control program that included expanding the reservation boundaries, developing new water sources, demonstrating scientific management practices, and creating a more efficient, centralized administrative structure under a single superintendent. And yet, Collier emphasized, all that effort might be in vain. If the Navajos were going to save their land, they had to reduce their livestock holdings.[24]

Collier stressed that the reduction would be voluntary and temporary. Overall, he said, stockowners needed to eliminate 200,000 head of sheep and keep those numbers down for perhaps three to five years to allow the range to rest and recover. The Federal Emergency Relief Administration would buy up to half that number at market value, which Collier estimated might be as little as $1 per ewe and $2 per wether. And he made it clear that he expected the people to cull their herds, selling the old, toothless "gummers" they no longer wanted and preserving their breeding stock.[25]

Former council chairman Chee Dodge warned Collier that his program would backfire. An old man now, Dodge was widely respected as a Diné leader and commercial stockman, and he had experience and wisdom on his side. He pointed out that culling flocks of old barren animals, instead of selling fertile ewes, would frustrate the effort to slash stock on the reservation. With the breeding herd intact, natural reproduction would result in no net loss. He advised the commissioner instead to buy the best ewes at a fair market price, triple the proposed $1 to $1.50 per head, or be disappointed in the outcome.[26] Dodge may well have been maneuvering for a good price for his own sheep; he was a sharp trader. But history proved him right.

Collier emphasized culling flocks in part, perhaps, because he felt uneasy about how the council might respond to the notion of stock reduction. He hemmed and hawed a bit about the total numbers they would need to eliminate and instead focused on how many sheep the government would buy that year. He also passed quickly over his demand that the Navajos make a sharp and permanent reduction in the number of goats, since there were presently no funds to compensate for goat reduction. Later he would argue that he had been straight with the council from the beginning, and, technically speaking, he was. But in trying to soften the blow, he left the distinct impression that he was asking the Navajos to take drastic measures once and only once.

To help alleviate the economic hardships attendant on stock reduction, Collier pledged to triple Navajo income, in part through wage work on conservation projects. Although it never came close to fulfilling that promise, the Emergency Conservation Work program became extremely popular across the reservation. Between 1933 and 1938, when federal funding plummeted, the ECW drilled wells, erected windmills, built check dams in arroyos, constructed reservoirs, poisoned prairie dogs and weeds, and in the process employed and trained young Navajo men.[27]

Still, ECW wages benefited only a fraction of those in need, which some on the tribal council anticipated from the beginning. At the Tuba City meeting, Jim Shirley, representing the Southern Navajo jurisdiction, was unimpressed by Collier's promise of economic prosperity. An articulate, educated man with a sharp tongue, he first asked bluntly whether government officials should be allowed to do all the talking; so far, the Diné hadn't been able to get a word in edgewise. Then he questioned whether the Diné as a whole would benefit from ECW employment. What about the people who were not young, male, and able-bodied? "How will we work this for the people who are not able to work for wages and are relying for their living on the livestock industry?" he demanded.[28] It was a question that deserved a straight answer.

A. C. Cooley, the bureau's director of extension, had already illustrated the agency's economic projections with a graph that showed income rising as livestock numbers fell. But the colorful chart with its falling blue line, representing livestock, and its rising red and yellow lines, representing income from livestock and federal wages, amounted to wishful thinking. Cooley's forecast of increased livestock income was a long way off—it would come only after the range improved, sheep fattened, and fleeces thickened—and his implication that ECW wages would benefit all those who reduced their flocks was just flat wrong.[29] It was a miscalculation that Collier would come to regret.

Collier stressed that he had the authority to limit grazing with the full force of the law if he so chose, since the Navajo Reservation was federal land administered by the Bureau of Indian Affairs. On other reservations and in the national forests, he noted, "when the Government decides that the land is being overgrazed[,] the Government simply issues regulations and fixes how many head can be grazed[,] and that is the end of it. The Government has the authority to limit the grazing . . . to put the *entire force of the Federal Law* back of its orders."[30] And in case those assembled missed his point, he repeated the statement. Whether the commissioner really intended to threaten the council with the power of the state is unclear, but we can imagine that his words pierced the hearts of the councilmen. After all, the forced march to Hwéeldi remained vivid in living collective memory. Indeed, all evidence suggests that those words framed the council's deliberations not only that day, but throughout Collier's tenure.

Nonetheless, Collier underscored that he had no intention of actually using coercion. Instead, he said he wanted the Navajos to make decisions for themselves, even if that meant they might make mistakes. "As long as I am Commissioner," he proclaimed, "we are not going to use compulsion on the Navajo tribe."[31] The Navajos, he observed, had long been models of self-government and self-reliance, and he had no desire to extinguish those long-standing virtues. It was out of his deep respect for the Navajos, he said, that "although the Government has absolute authority to establish range control on this reservation and to regulate the number of sheep and goats, the Government is not going to exercise that authority." On the contrary, he promised, the government would issue regulations "merely in order to back up what your Tribal Council may decide to do." In uttering these words, Collier was not intentionally duplicitous, although his later actions would certainly make him seem so. Philosophically, he was committed to self-governance, at least in the abstract, and in any event he had no doubt that the Navajos would follow his advice of their own volition. He had every confidence that they would choose to sacrifice their stock without compulsion because, in his mind, it was the reasonable, practical, and right thing to do.[32]

As it turned out, Collier had no need to use force that year. For the most part, Diné stockowners willingly sold their culls to the government, which even purchased old gummers that traders would never buy.[33] In essence, the federal purchases took the place of the fall market for lambs, a market that had dwindled to nothing since the beginning of the Great Depression. In just over a month, government agents removed 86,500 sheep from the reservation, filling holding pens in Gallup and other railroad towns. From there, sheep were shipped by rail to canneries, which packaged the meat for distribution to the needy.[34]

Most of those who sold their stock were needy, too, and became increasingly so. Diné surrendered animals on which they depended for food, and they often came away with little of the financial compensation they had been promised. The government administered the program at least partially through traders, who took the opportunity to retire old debts before crediting in trade any balance to the stockowner or handing over cash.[35] While it may have been only fair for the traders to collect their debts, to the Diné it felt like highway robbery.

Not everyone who gave up their sheep did so all that willingly, either. Frank Lenzie, who supervised reduction, reported that "considerable opposition to the disposition of their stock was voiced by a large number of Indians in all parts of the Navajo country, their feeling being that the delegates did not have the right to obligate them to such a course."[36] One of the bureau's stockmen, Carl Beck, reported that women particularly resented the idea that a handful of men had promised they would sell their sheep. Women owned their own flocks, and no one had the right to tell them what to do with their property. But it was not only women who objected. In some quarters, people complained that they were being reduced to poverty, for tribal council members (many of whom were themselves large stockowners) encouraged everyone to reduce 10 percent of their herds across the board, rather than asking the wealthiest to shoulder the burden.[37]

Still, for the most part, this initial reduction went smoothly, seducing Collier into thinking that Navajos understood the need for the program, or at least readily followed the tribal council's lead. And yet it would have been wise for him to listen more carefully at the Tuba City council meeting. One councilman after another tried to advise him that his broader plan to dramatically decrease herds would never find acceptance among the Diné. Henry Taliman, a delegate from Oak Springs, put it most emphatically. He was a handsome, educated man who favored bow ties and wore a pencil-thin mustache, and he would later become chairman of the tribal council. "Under no consideration," he warned, "will the Navajos favor reducing their livestock." He knew full well that the people back home opposed stock reduction. "They are just so afraid this thing is going to be carried out so they begged me especially not to accept this program."[38] Collier apparently pressured Taliman to change his mind during a closed executive session that evening. No minutes were kept of that discussion, so we have no way of knowing what transpired, but when the council reconvened the next day, Taliman himself presented the resolution calling for cooperation with Collier's program.[39] The commissioner declared victory and went home. Had he instead heeded Taliman's warning, he might have better prepared to avoid all-out war.

The next spring, Collier returned to the reservation, this time demanding that the Navajos eliminate nearly half their goats. The bureau singled out goats largely because they had no market value. Navajos raised them for food, and Collier and his advisors believed that marketable sheep could serve that purpose just as well. Navajos, moreover, tended to run sheep and goats together, using goats to lead the flocks, but because those animals moved more rapidly across the range in search of good browse, conservationists felt that they encouraged unnecessary trampling.[40] Goats, thus, seemed expendable. No one—neither Collier nor the council—knew then that goat reduction would mark a crossroad in the government's effort to conserve the Navajo range.

Indeed, the initial council meeting, held in March 1934 at Fort Defiance, went quite well. Collier and James Stewart, the head of the bureau's land division, presented a plan to purchase and remove 150,000 head of stock from the reservation, including at least 100,000 goats. (Later the two men would quietly revise these figures to 150,000 goats and up to 50,000 ewes.) To prevent the population rebound that occurred following the initial sale of sheep (just as Chee Dodge predicted), the plan also required Navajos to castrate all their billy goats and sell 80 percent of their newborn lambs each year, including all the wethers. No one who gave up their stock would go hungry, Stewart assured the council, because they could find employment on any of a number of erosion-control projects across the reservation.[41]

Henry Taliman (*far left*), Superintendent E. R. Fryer, Howard Gorman, and Commissioner John Collier (*at microphone*), 1938. Photograph by Milton Snow. Records of the BIA, RG75, National Archives at College Park, Md., RG75-Nav-K-9.

Diné observers crowd around the speakers' platform at the meeting of the Navajo Tribal Council held in March 1934 at Fort Defiance, where the council debated the wisdom of the fateful goat reduction program. Photograph by Norman B. Conway. Courtesy Museum of New Mexico, Palace of the Governors (MNM/DCA), 90405.

He and Collier used both a goad and a crook to encourage the council to follow them down this path. Although both men made a show of presenting the plan as a choice for the council to consider and discuss with people back home, they explicitly tied it to programs that they knew the Navajos wanted badly. One was water development. The other was the extension of the reservation into the eastern Checkerboard. If the Navajos expected Congress to appropriate money for water projects and other conservation measures, to the tune of $1.5 million, and if they expected legislative approval of an expanded reservation, Stewart exhorted, they would have to demonstrate that they intended to stop erosion by halving their goat herds.[42]

The councilmen listened with particular interest to the discussion of the prospect of more land. Collier's office had drawn up two congressional bills, one providing for the purchase of lands in Arizona and one for New Mexico. The Arizona Boundary Bill would soon pass handily, thanks to the intervention of Senator Carl Hayden, who secured the cooperation of area ranchers. But as early as the summer of 1933, opposition to the New Mexico Boundary Bill arose in San Juan County, where perhaps half of the New Mexico Checkerboard lay.[43] Stewart, nonetheless, all but promised the Navajo Tribal Council that Congress would expand the reservation boundaries, but he added that the necessary legislation and appropriation of federal funds would be contingent on whether the Navajos adopted the government's entire program for controlling erosion. Otherwise, he admonished, "it would be throwing good money after bad.... We feel sure that if we can go back to Congress and tell them that the Navajo Tribe is behind this soil erosion control, range control, and stock reduction, we will get this additional land, and money to buy that land."[44] Stewart was being honest about the sentiment on Capitol Hill; Congress would never extend the reservation boundaries if erosion continued unabated. But in tying stock reduction to the prospect of more land, his words were also, in essence, extortion.

The health of the land, nonetheless, was most certainly at stake, as Stewart reminded the councilmen. A vote to eliminate goats was a vote to save land from destruction. To clinch the argument, Stewart appealed to the councilmen's sense of responsibility to future generations. "You are looking at the matter through *your* eyes," he pointed out to those who seemed hesitant, "and not through the eyes of your living children and the hundreds of unborn children that will follow.... Do you want to leave land that your children can use and raise sheep on, like you do, or do you want to leave them piles of sand and rocks?"[45]

Several of those on the council echoed Stewart's sobering message. "Our land seems to be very sick," agreed Frank Cadman.[46] Jim Shirley also concurred, although he was in no way enamored with the federal officials who stood before him. He had little patience for the arrogance of college-educated experts, and at Tuba City he had voiced annoyance at those who seemed to think that the Diné were ignorant about the nature of their own grasslands. Now, however, he addressed his fellow councilmen. "There are two sources of life," he reminded them, "the land and the livestock." No one could expect to raise healthy stock on deteriorated range, and thus the Diné should not try to hold onto goats without thinking first about the health of the land. "We have to have the range before we can have livestock[,] and for that reason, . . . the bigger question is the land question. If we have the land, we have everything."[47]

No one on the council disputed that idea, but many worried about the welfare of those who depended on goats. Jacob Morgan—who would soon emerge as the leading voice of the beleaguered smallholder and Collier's nemesis—expressed concern for those with few sheep. "I have been wondering," he remarked, "if it would not be possible in some way to think of these people."[48] Henry Taliman suggested that they table the resolution on goat reduction until they could discuss it with the people back home and then "act upon how the livestock can be reduced to the best satisfaction of the people."[49] Chee Dodge thought that the council could resolve the issue now by sparing those with flocks smaller than 100 head. Collier listened thoughtfully to these concerns (it would be one of the last times he would do so) and responded that it might even be possible to help poorer families by replacing goats with sheep acquired from large stock owners.[50] That way, goats would be eliminated, and yet families would still have enough livestock to live on. Collier's assurances laid the council's fears to rest, and the men unanimously resolved to encourage their people to sell half their goats, with the proviso that the delegates would ask the people back home to "consider the matter and devise ways and means" for carrying out the program.[51]

The council's resolve would not last long. Back home, the men quickly discovered that the people who owned goats had no intention of giving them up without a fight. Both Carl Beck, the BIA stockman, and C. N. Millington, national head of the Indian ECW program, who attended several chapter meetings, noted that women were especially vocal in their criticism of the council's decision to sacrifice their goats.[52] Women owned the vast majority of these animals, and they felt betrayed by the men who had promised to cut their herds. Some women resolved to reduce their flocks in their own way by eating lots of goat meat, and they set about butchering the animals for home consumption.[53] All this talk of selling off their goats left them feeling anxious and powerless.[54]

When the council again convened at Crownpoint and later at Keams Canyon, the mood was tense. Throngs of as many as five or six hundred Diné women and men came to observe, their numbers spilling out under the trees.[55] Large crowds often came to these meetings, but now the council members seemed more keenly aware of the people's interest in the proceedings. The night before the Keams Canyon meeting, the council met with a gathering of angry people, who apparently accused the men of failing to represent them. Some of the women and the older men pleaded with the councilmen, demanding to know how they were to support themselves without their goats. Some were very old, too old to find work on ECW projects, they said. They depended on their goats to feed and clothe themselves. The only area of the reservation that expressly supported the program was the Leupp jurisdiction, in the southwestern corner, where people had few goats but wanted to conserve their admittedly overgrazed range.[56] So as this series of meetings opened, the councilmen did their best to explain to the bureau that few favored goat reduction, and they struggled with officials to find some kind of middle ground.

Albert Sandoval, a representative from the Southern Navajo jurisdiction, hoped to find another solution. Sandoval was an educated man who nonetheless tied his long hair in the traditional hourglass bun and likely wore on this occasion the long turquoise earrings and silver concho belt that signified his wealth. At the Crownpoint meeting, he asked whether it would be possible to reduce the goats by eating them and by selling butchered meat to the reservation schools. He figured that if each family ate six head of goats and sheep per month, over the course of a year the Diné could reduce the entire stock population by almost half, not counting the annual reproduction of lambs and kids. James Stewart (who was then standing in for Collier) replied that such an approach would take too long, and besides normal consumption had never brought a decrease in annual livestock numbers. In one sense, Stewart was right, for Sandoval also objected to the idea of giving up 80 percent of the annual production of lambs. That reproduction, left unchecked, would have certainly negated any effort to reduce herds through mere consumption. But Sandoval stood his ground and requested more time to consider the proper course of action, pointedly calling Stewart's attention to the fact that the council's agreement to reduce goats specified that the people themselves would devise the method for cutting their herds down. It had been one of Collier's concessions to self-government. Sandoval challenged Stewart to keep its word in this matter, and the crowd greeted his defiance with laughter and applause.[57]

The well-respected councilman had already won the audience's favor, but then he demanded to know whether this would be the last time the Diné would be asked to sacrifice their stock. He wanted Stewart's promise: "It is strictly understood that after we fulfill this goat reduction, that no more reduction will be asked?" Stewart replied without hesitation: "Absolutely," except for the annual sale of newborn lambs.[58]

That was a lie, and Stewart knew it. Only the month before, he himself had presided at an executive meeting between Collier and the various agency superintendents, where the officials discussed the long-term stock reduction plan. After the current program for eliminating 150,000 goats, the men planned to make cuts of 125,000 head of livestock in each of the following years, so that an estimated 400,000 fewer animals would graze the reservation.[59] Of course, early on Collier informed the Navajo Tribal Council that the bureau's target was 400,000 animals. But as officials began to sense a growing resistance, they offered only snapshots of what the future held, avoiding panoramic discussions of the long-term implications of their program. In doing so, they managed to win the council's approval for cutting back goats.[60] And yet they also set themselves up for ultimate defeat.

The task of reducing the number of goats fell to William Zeh, whom Collier appointed to head the new Consolidated Navajo Jurisdiction. Zeh was a fitting choice. He had championed the reduction of livestock, especially goats, since 1930, when he first documented the imperiled condition of the Navajo range, and helped develop the conservation program.[61] And yet he understood well that the cultural significance of livestock to the Navajos complicated any prospects for reduction. Only through education would Navajos come to see the value of range conservation, he wrote in 1932; it could not "be crammed down their throats."[62] Education, he believed, slowly but surely yielded results. Progressive stockowners like Deshna Clah Cheschillige, he noted, had become increasingly aware of

MOURNING LIVESTOCK   173

Thousands of goats and sheep await shipment to slaughterhouses at a Gallup railhead, 1934. Photograph probably by Milton Snow. Records of the BIA, RG75, National Archives, Pacific Region, Laguna Niguel, Calif. 75-08-11.

deteriorating range conditions in the Carrizo Mountains and, through their own experiments, observed that such measures as deferred grazing could bring about markedly improved grasses.[63] But by the time Collier became commissioner of Indian affairs, Zeh deemed the deterioration of the range so precipitous that he advised "above all ACTION."[64] Unfortunately for Zeh, goat reduction followed Murphy's Law: What can go wrong *will* go wrong.

Goat reduction proceeded haphazardly, and that disorganization contributed mightily to the trauma and fear that many Diné experienced. As animals filled railroad stockyards, a snag materialized. Zeh had arranged to ship the goats to the Tovrea Packing Company in Phoenix, but the cannery, overwhelmed by an enormous shipment of livestock from drought-stricken Texas, alerted him at the last minute that it could handle only a fraction of the Navajos' goats. Unwilling to delay reduction or hold goats on winter ranges that were needed for sheep, Zeh announced that as much as 70 percent of the stock slated for removal should be "condemned" and slaughtered on the spot. As part of that order, he urged agents to allow stockowners to butcher the animals and take the jerked meat home.[65] That suggestion went unheeded in the western part of the reservation, where more than 7,500 goats and nearly 3,400 sheep—almost 40 percent of the animals purchased—were shot en masse and left to rot.[66] Livestock reduction thus acquired the stigma of brutality. Soon stories that goats at Black Mountain and elsewhere were doused with kerosene and burned alive, sparking resistance from angry stockowners, spread across the reservation.[67]

Rebellion against goat reduction did not arise immediately, and even then, it did not appear everywhere. Some areas implemented the program in more humane ways than others, which substantially lessened the immediate shock of diminished herds. In the northeastern section, Diné families butchered a whopping two-thirds of the targeted animals for home consumption, and in much of the rest of the reservation, they consumed about one-third.[68] Some Diné thus took goat reduction in stride. Tully Lincoln, from Ganado, later recalled the event almost nostalgically. People had so much food at that time, he reminisced, that they "walked in meat."[69]

Outward cooperation, to be sure, did not necessarily signal assent. For many Diné, goat reduction marked the beginning of a long nightmare from which they could never seem to wake up. Martin Johnson and his wife were tending their flock at their hogan near Sanostee when a man rode up and told them they had to sell seventy-five of their goats or go to jail. Fearful, the two traveled to the local trading post as ordered. "There was blood running everywhere in the [trading post] corral as we just stood there and watched," Johnson remembered. "My wife was the one who had raised the sheep and goats in her younger years. She cried about her goats as they were killed."[70] Ałk'inanibaa' Burbank, who lived then around Lukachukai, recalled that an implicit threat of force electrified the reservation. People felt too afraid to object because they remembered well the power of the men in Washington. No one could forget that the last time Diné dared defy federal authority, they were stripped of their homeland.[71] Now, however, they were stripped of their ability to support themselves and their families over the long term. As the aptly named Mrs. White Goat, who relinquished 425 goats she kept near Sweetwater, later complained: "I am crying for my goats because I don't have enough to feed my children."[72] She and others would look back on the era as a time of tears and terror.

In implementing goat reduction, Zeh made two fatal errors. One was to allow agents to leave the emaciated carcasses of hundreds and even thousands of animals to the coyotes and buzzards, coloring memories of stock reduction for generations to come. The other was to wipe out small subsistence herds. That action ignored the express wishes of the Navajo Tribal Council. Recall that in approving the reduction plan, the council exempted the owners of small flocks of sheep mixed with relatively small numbers of goats. It did not exempt those subsistence herders who owned mostly goats, and yet agents were supposed to arrange to replace many of those goats with more marketable sheep. Zeh knew of these provisions. He had stood by quietly as Collier himself endorsed these stipulations to win the council's favor.[73] And yet he had already instructed his agents not to exempt "the small man" (or presumably "the small woman") because that practice would encourage families "to split their herds into a large number of small bands in order to be exempt."[74] It is certainly true that, if given the chance, many Diné would have claimed exemption from goat reduction according to their custom of individual stock ownership. Nonetheless, Zeh's decision to reduce all goat herds across the board and his failure to implement a methodical goat-replacement program had long-term consequences. It impoverished thousands of families and turned them squarely against much of the New Deal conservation program.

Especially in the eastern regions of the Checkerboard, where subsistence shepherds competed for land with large-scale commercial stockmen, goat reduction devastated Diné families. Richard Van Valkenburgh, an anthropologist working for the Soil Conservation Service, conducted a survey of destitute people in the eastern Checkerboard and found them living in utter misery. Their abject poverty was not entirely the product of the stock reduction program, for many were already impoverished by the dawn of the New Deal. Over the previous twenty years, even large stockowners had watched their herds plummet, the result of many economic, environmental, and social factors. Traders outside the reservation, beyond the reach of federal restrictions on the purchase of sheep, had induced customers to sell not only lambs but breeding ewes when prices peaked in the years immediately following the Great War, and Diné had lost even more stock to deep snows in the winters of 1925 and 1932. Some men, too, essentially drank their family's holdings, buying bootlegged whiskey on credit at off-reservation posts. When traders came to confiscate lambs in payment, they cared nothing about whether the indebted men or their wives or children actually owned the stock. By the early 1930s, many families in the eastern Checkerboard subsisted only on goats.[75]

Then came the federal goat round-up. Those who seized the stock later reported that people begged to keep their herds. "If you . . . take all of our goats, what will we live on?" they wailed. When agents rebuffed their protests or promised future deliveries of sheep or allotments of land, goat owners acquiesced, depressed and demoralized. Families whose herds had already dwindled found themselves with as few as thirty or forty head, hardly enough to feed themselves for a single year, and their relatives and neighbors had less and less to share. Even those who had sheep began losing ground, because the loss of their goats forced them to eat their breeding stock. That had the likely consequence of eliminating their ability to obtain credit at trading posts, since traders could no longer count on collecting their debts at the end of the lambing season.[76]

Women, who owned most of the goats, were hit particularly hard. Once their herds dropped below subsistence levels, their families consumed the balance in short order. Many women struggled to survive and support their children by weaving blankets, which they sold to trading posts for as little as six dollars. But with fewer and fewer sheep and goats, it became increasingly difficult to find enough fleece. A few women became so wretchedly poor that they resorted to shearing the pelts they used for bedding to scrape up enough wool.[77] Their squalor, wrote Van Valkenburgh, was "beyond belief."[78]

In retrospect, Collier admitted that he blundered badly in asking families living in the eastern Checkerboard to sell their goats. He not only pauperized the people; ironically he further jeopardized the land. Left with little or no stock, families leased their allotments to Anglo stockmen because it was the only asset they had to obtain food. So for every goat removed, at least one head of sheep or cattle moved in. Tragically, Collier and his staff had anticipated this debacle. The commissioner's right-hand man, James Stewart, had promised the tribal council that the bureau would proceed carefully with the program in this patchwork of land, because he knew well that reducing Navajo goats could simply open up more range to commercial grazing.[79] When asked why he had proceeded with goat purchases in this contested area, Collier had no real answer, apologizing lamely that "the thing rolled forward as a matter of momentum and routine."[80]

As a matter of fact, he had still expected Congress to enact the New Mexico Boundary Bill. That measure would have absorbed into the reservation some 2.2 million acres of Checkerboard land, nearly half of it already allotted to Navajos or otherwise under the control of the BIA, and would have ultimately excluded Anglo and Hispanic ranchers. If the bill had passed, history might have turned out somewhat differently. Instead, the legislation died that session before coming to the floor for a vote. In the fall of 1934, however, Collier had every reason to believe that Congress would vote favorably and soon.[81] Congress thus deserved a good measure of the blame for the condition of the eastern Checkerboard, because it failed to pass the boundary bill. Collier, nonetheless, should not have made promises of land he had no power to deliver.

Aside from the Checkerboard, Collier stubbornly refused to believe that his program impoverished the Navajos. Instead he maintained that stock sales and emergency conservation jobs raised overall income on the reservation.[82] His insistence that incomes went up reveals two misconceptions. First, he ignored the fact that those who suffered the worst reductions, women and older men, were ineligible for the conservation jobs he so proudly touted. Second, and just as important, he seriously miscalculated the value of the goats and sheep that the Navajos lost. Government economists, for example, used a market value of $1 to figure the subsistence "income" gained from goats. But that was far too low. According to Robert Youngblood, an agricultural economist with the U.S. Department of Agriculture, a butchered goat would feed a family of five for a week, plus provide a pelt for bedding or sale.[83] Left alive, it might provide milk and cheese every day. By contrast, the $1 that the government paid to compensate for each goat would purchase four cans of tomatoes, or eight cans of milk, or less than one sack of flour at the trading post.[84] Goats provided feasts; Collier's economics brought famine.

Goat reduction would later be remembered as a turning point in the New Deal program for the Navajo Reservation. Watching their neighbors became beggars, Diné councilmen—even those who lauded Collier's effort to improve the range—were no longer willing to support stock reduction. For Collier, too, it was a pivotal moment, for it led to a major defeat for the Indian Reorganization Act. Popularly known as the Wheeler-Howard Act, that legislation represented the culmination of Collier's struggle to reverse a century of devastating Indian policy and return a large measure of political sovereignty and cultural self-determination to native people. It ended the allotment of Indian lands and provided the framework for self-government and economic progress. Collier hoped to showcase the reorganization act on the Navajo Reservation, home to people who had never really lost their cultural traditions. Instead, it became one more casualty of goat reduction.

In the spirit of the reorganization act's promise of self-determination, Collier provided that each tribe could choose to adopt or reject the measure by referendum.[85] In the aftermath of goat reduction, many Diné came to understand the election as a referendum on stock reduction and on Collier himself. Particularly in the reservation's eastern and northern jurisdictions, where goat reduction was especially devastating, people registered their anger at the ballot box. Upon defeat, Collier recognized that women—those most affected by goat reduction—may well have tipped the balance. Many, he learned, had thought that a vote for the act was a vote for continued stock reduction, and he confided that it was this belief that "undoubtedly controlled the votes of a great many of the older Indians, particularly the women."[86]

Mary Chischillie witnessed the voting process at the Naschitti Trading Post near her homestead. On the day of the referendum in June 1935, word spread that the Diné were to vote on whether they wanted to continue to reduce their herds. If the people chose to keep their sheep, officials at the polling place warned, their flocks would die from starvation. As she later explained to her daughter, Kaibah, Chischillie understood that she was supposed to mark a piece of paper with an "X" or an "O." An "X" signified that she wanted to save her sheep by sacrificing more of the herd; an "O" meant that she would keep her sheep and let them starve to death.[87] Either way, she seemed to lose.

For others, the referendum was simply a vote for or against John Collier. By this time, Jacob Morgan, the self-proclaimed leader of disaffected Diné, had mounted a vociferous campaign against Collier and all he stood for. It was Morgan's harangue that carried the day. John Nez of Tohatchi understood that the people were to mark a cross or a circle, the cross standing for Collier, the circle representing Morgan. As Nez later boasted, in his district "the circle won, the cross got beat."[88] Diné narrowly rejected Collier's Indian Reorganization Act by a vote of 8,197 to 7,679, due to a smashing defeat in the eastern and northern parts of the reservation.[89] The irony of this defeat was lost on Collier. He had hoped that the act would remake the Navajos into models of Indian self-determination. What he failed to understand was that they decided to become just that.

Of course, the vote to *approve* the reorganization act, which carried throughout the rest of the reservation, was also a vote for self-determination. Therein lay even more irony. Theoretically, at least, the act would have empowered the Navajo Tribal Council in ways that might have given it more control over future land management issues. Jim Shirley and more than 230 others likely thought so when in 1936 they petitioned President Roosevelt, Secretary of the Interior Harold Ickes, and Congress to hold a second election to allow the people "to express their real and true convictions," to no avail.[90] It is unclear whether passage of the reorganization act would have actually given the Navajos more control over stock reduction. The act itself expressly confirmed the secretary of the Interior's right to restrict the number of livestock on all Indian reservations.[91] Nonetheless, it seems likely that passage of the act would have given the Diné more rhetorical power to shape the conservation program.

Collier's effort to eliminate half the Navajo goats in a single year struck many Diné like a bullet in the heart. Many would forever remember it as the first volley in a long assault on their ability to feed themselves and their children and on their identity as pastoralists. The tribal council understood well that goat reduction would inflame their people, especially women, and some tried mightily to negotiate a different plan of attack. Their words were not mere subterfuge to avoid stock reduction. Tom Dodge, Jim Shirley, Frank Cadman, and others urged the council to face up to their responsibility for the range; each, in his own way, tried to extend a hand and create a true partnership in keeping with Collier's own rhetoric of self-determination. But Collier and his men were far too certain of themselves to take the offer. With that same sense of certainty, he and the conservationists would attempt to revolutionize Navajo relationships with the land. As the opportunity for annexing the Checkerboard into the reservation slipped beyond their grasp, they would renew their resolve to "improve" livestock, control erosion, and revitalize the range through scientific management.

8 · DRAWING LINES ON A MAP

In the fall of 1934, just as federal agents prepared to seize Navajo goats, the conservationist Robert Marshall cautioned Collier against using force to implement erosion control on the Navajo Reservation. Persuasion, not compulsion, he advised, would be far more effective in the long run. He encouraged Collier, moreover, to study "the thought patterns, the habits, and the ideals of the Navajos and especially . . . the influences which make them happy" through an ethnographic approach involving "years of unaggressive and sympathetic life among the people." Only by comprehending the lives of the Navajos would the Bureau of Indian Affairs develop policies that could conserve Navajo lands while also conserving Navajo life. Since conservationists could not "possibly dodge the far-reaching influence" of any erosion control program on Navajo culture, Marshall warned, "we had better contemplate carefully what effect each policy we adopt is likely to have on the future Navajo civilization."[1]

Marshall was one of Collier's most candid and prescient advisors in the creation of Navajo range policy. Paradoxically a socialist and the wealthy son of a New York constitutional lawyer and civil libertarian, he earned a master's degree in forestry at Harvard and a doctorate in plant physiology at Johns Hopkins University. He also dabbled in sociology and ethnography and had published a study of an Alaskan mining town before Collier appointed him director of the BIA's forestry division in 1933. He held that

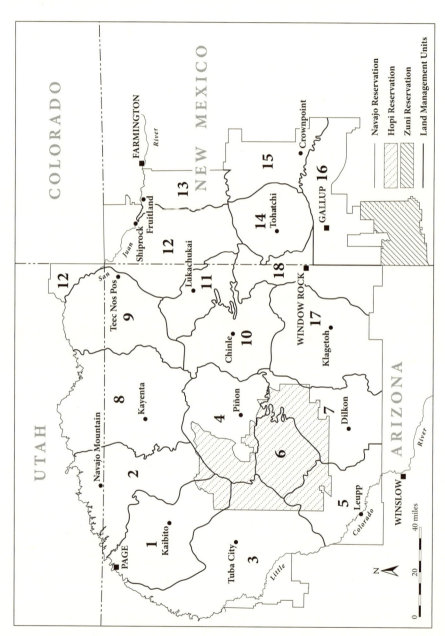

MAP 5 Land Management Units

position until he joined the U.S. Forest Service in 1937. Marshall would later become known as one of the nation's leading proponents of wilderness protection, helping to found the Wilderness Society before succumbing to heart failure in the prime of his life, at age thirty-eight.[2] But in those early days of the New Deal, he devoted most of his attention to the health of forests and grazing lands on the nation's Indian reservations.

Writing to Collier, Marshall argued that hypothetically there were four broad paths that the commissioner could follow, each with a different set of ethical and environmental consequences. Two marked the possible extremes of Indian policy. Collier could continue the long-standing program of trying to turn Indians into white men. Or he could withdraw entirely from protecting or advising the Navajos and "let nature take its course." Either approach, no doubt, would vanquish a valuable civilization. One would make the Navajos "just as ruined as most white men are." The other would allow "the most predatory elements among the whites" to devour the Navajos. Both, Marshall implied, were clearly immoral.

A third path—the one Marshall favored—would give the Navajos complete cultural autonomy and self-determination within the borders of their reservation, while continuing to protect them from the outside world. Under this scheme, federal officials would provide educational programs and technical advice. And yet the Navajos themselves would decide whether to accept or reject that guidance (and the federal subsidies that came with it), without interference. Such an approach would turn Indian policy on its head, Marshall argued. It would promote "Indian initiative with white advice instead of white initiative with Indian advice" and encourage the Navajos to take responsibility for their own future. True, it carried the risk that Navajos might continue to overgraze and erode their rangelands, but as Marshall reminded Collier, "we have insisted dozens of times in the past on some principle in spite of the objections of the Indians[,] who subsequently proved to be right after all."

There was still one more trail that Collier could follow, if he were so inclined. But Marshall did not advise it. The commissioner could act as a kind of enlightened paternalist, one who encouraged the Navajos to preserve their colorful customs—their ceremonies, their hogans, their traditional weavings—yet ruled with an iron fist when it came to important matters like grazing. To make his disdain for this approach clear, Marshall satirized it, noting that Collier would, in essence, say to the Navajos: "'We are a lot more sophisticated and far-seeing than you are.... Of course[,] we don't want to do anything without your advice on the matter and we really are interested in your own thoughts. *We'll even show you what is of value in your own culture.* Nevertheless we won't let you "stew in your own juice." We want you to follow our wisdom voluntarily, but if you persist in not seeing the light, god damn it, we'll make you!'" Marshall counseled Collier against the pernicious path of enlightened despotism, for it smacked of the colonialism that the reformer had spent the last decade criticizing. It coupled "cultural freedom and cultural dictatorship, and there's just no way to reconcile antitheses." It was a slippery slope, Marshall warned. "You can't go swimming without getting wet."[3]

Collier failed to get Marshall's point. He saw no conflict between the ideals of cultural autonomy and self-determination, and governance by what political theorists called indirect rule, an approach perfected by British colonialists in Africa.[4] Chewing on Marshall's advice, the commissioner wrote that perhaps an "administrative power" could best achieve its goal "by indirection," that is, by encouraging Navajo leaders to make the desired decisions, "rather than by mandate." But until the Navajos were better organized and better educated, it would be necessary for federal fathers to provide firm guidance. "We can't ask the tribe to run a race," he responded, "before it has been allowed to use its limbs even to toddle."[5] Collier allowed himself to be seduced by a classic delusion, the belief that paternal coercion might be excused in the name of progressive reform.[6]

Had Collier taken Marshall's advice and empowered the Navajos to craft their own conservation program, perhaps history would have turned out differently. Instead, he and his men unwittingly contributed to the long-term degradation of the land by imposing a rationalized range management program, devised according to a scientific, market-oriented logic that made no sense to most Navajos. The conservationists attempted to make Navajo sheep more marketable by introducing "improved" breeds and new methods of animal husbandry. They opened more rangelands to grazing by providing stock water in "underutilized" areas. And they restricted the movement of flocks to match livestock numbers to the land's so-called carrying capacity. All of these measures, they hoped, would save not only the land but also the livestock economy, though in a much different form based on a masculinized model of ranching. Some initiatives—particularly the development of springs and the drilling of wells—the Diné welcomed. Others left them confused, angry, and rebellious, with long-term consequences for the health of the land.

The year 1936 marked the second phase of the New Deal conservation program: the development and implementation of a comprehensive range management plan that regulated Navajo relationships with their land. That program incited rancor and resistance. It also responded to a new reality: the collapse of the New Mexico Boundary Bill. For three years, Collier had promised the Navajos that if they proved themselves worthy by reducing their stock and improving their range, Congress would expand the reservation to incorporate much of the eastern Checkerboard. But beginning in 1936, Senator Dennis Chavez of New Mexico blocked that expansion.

New Mexico's first native-born Hispanic senator, Chavez rose from poverty to power. Forced to quit school at the age of thirteen to help support his family, he worked for a grocer for five years until he was fired for refusing to deliver food to strikebreakers. That act of defiance signaled the beginning of a long political career. He ascended the ladder of the Democratic Party, first as a Spanish-language interpreter for several statewide political campaigns, next as a clerk in the United States Senate (during which time he earned a law degree, taking night courses at Georgetown University), then as a state legislator, and finally as a congressman. In 1934, he narrowly lost a bitter campaign for the United States Senate to Bronson Cutting, the progressive Republican incumbent.[7] Then in May 1935, an airplane crash took Cutting's life, and Governor Clyde Tingley appointed Chavez to the vacant seat.

Chavez would prove to be a populist New Dealer, supporting especially the rights of Hispanics and the poor. But he would also prove to be equivocal in his dealings with Navajos. True, he helped spearhead the San Juan-Chama Project, which eventually delivered water to the Navajo Indian Irrigation Project before diverting most of it across the Continental Divide to Albuquerque. But he also killed the legislation that would have brought much of their outlying range within the reservation's boundaries and under the BIA's control. He and Collier would soon despise one another. One of Chavez's first acts upon taking office in May 1935 was to intercept the measure, claiming that he needed time to study it.[8] In part, though, he sought to protect the area's Hispanic ranchers who would lose access to the public domain if the government enclosed it for the Navajos. Some of these families had deep roots extending back to settlement under Spanish land grants.[9] By 1936, however, when Collier reintroduced the bill, Chavez became especially allied with large-scale Anglo stockmen and other local interests who were determined to defeat it.[10]

Collier, nonetheless, still believed he would win the battle with Chavez as late as the summer of 1936. In August, Senator Elmer Thomas of Oklahoma convened congressional hearings to consider the bill, traveling to Gallup, Farmington, and Window Rock with a small delegation of the Committee on Indian Affairs. Among the delegates was Chavez, who jabbed at Collier, according to one observer, while a half-dozen Anglo stockmen "fluttered back and forth between their front-row seats and the Senator's place at the hearing table, guiding and directing and prompting him in his questioning and obstructive tactics."[11] Chavez's behavior during the hearings warned of things to come, and yet throughout the proceedings, Collier betrayed a naive faith that the facts would speak for themselves and his logic would prevail.

The commissioner presented a strong case for expanding the reservation. Piling up mounds of research reports before the senators, he argued that the welfare of more than 9,700 Navajos who depended on the meager rangelands of the Checkerboard was far more important than the interests of perhaps three dozen Anglo and Hispanic stockmen who operated on a commercial scale, monopolized the range, and, for the most part, did not actually reside in the area. He brought a score of Navajo witnesses to demonstrate their prior use of the land and the harassment they encountered at the hands of interlopers. And he disproved the allegation by the Association of San Juan County Taxpayers that local and state governments would suffer a significant financial loss if these lands were removed from the tax rolls. Brandishing a stack of statistical data, he revealed that the cost of providing roads, schools, and other infrastructure—costs that the BIA would assume within the expanded reservation boundary—far exceeded the scanty property taxes collected in the area.[12] If political decisions were grounded in facts, Collier surely would have carried the day. Unfortunately, the prize goes to those who tell the most compelling story.

Leading the charge against the boundary bill were commercial stockmen who together controlled much of the eastern Checkerboard. One after another, the sheep baron Edward Sargent, cattlemen I. K. Westbrook and Kelsey Presley, and ranch manager Floyd Lee testified that the Navajo range was not overstocked, but mismanaged.[13] And many of the Navajo witnesses seemed to prove the point. With one or two exceptions, those Navajos who testified displayed no understanding of the practical operation of a commercial livestock business. Floyd Lee blamed the government for this state of affairs, telling the senators that the Navajo Reservation was not overgrazed, but "misgrazed." When Lee spoke, the senators listened. He managed a three-thousand-acre ranch north of Grants for the Fernandez Land and Cattle Company, and was president of the New Mexico Wool Growers Association, a director of the New Mexico Cattle Growers Association, and a member of the New Mexico Senate. Lee argued that plenty of land for the number of livestock was already available on the reservation, conveniently ignoring the fact that more than 10 percent of those lands consisted of geological barrens like the Painted Desert. If the Soil Conservation Service developed new water sources and fenced in pastures for rotational grazing, he contended, the Navajos would need no Checkerboard land for the stock they had.[14] Although Collier's men would dispute Lee's data, they privately agreed that Navajos had mismanaged the range, and they would soon radically reorganize land use.[15]

Lee, however, did more than simply criticize Navajo range management. He claimed that it was *they* who were the interlopers, having moved onto the Checkerboard only after denuding their own range. The documentary record proves otherwise. Diné had grazed the Checkerboard at least seasonally since the eighteenth century, long before Anglo ranchers arrived. But Lee dismissed that history, adding that those Navajos living outside the boundaries of the reservation should move inside and manage their lands more wisely.[16] Lee's story, echoed again and again by the sheep barons and commercial cattlemen, sounded to the ears of the senators like the ring of truth.

Collier misjudged the political power of his adversaries, both off and on the reservation, making it impossible for him to keep the solemn promise he had made to the Navajos to gain control of their Checkerboard lands. Even some Navajos hobbled him. By 1937, Jacob Morgan threw his support behind Chavez, in exchange for the senator's sponsorship of a bill that would have exempted New Mexico's Navajos from the Indian Reorganization Act. Such legislation was unnecessary since the Navajos had already voted to reject the act. But Morgan, believing the IRA would handicap the assimilation of his people into the modern world, rather than empower them, apparently feared that the commissioner would ask the Navajos to reconsider the measure. The Diné leader had not always opposed the boundary bill. In fact, he initially supported it, testifying that it would fulfill a promise of land that government officials made to the Diné in 1886, when several companies of Indian troops, including his father, helped the army fight Apaches.[17] Soon, however, Morgan came to fear that the boundary extension would require an enormous expenditure of tribal funds to buy out private landowners, funds that he felt would be better spent damming the San Juan River for irrigated farming.[18] Morgan thus rallied his followers to protest Collier's entire Navajo New Deal.[19] Collier countered by organizing the Eastern Navajo Boundary Association, nominally headed by Howard Gorman and consisting of off-reservation Navajos, sympathetic traders, supportive Gallup-area merchants, and poor whites wanting to sell their failed Checkerboard farms to the government.[20] The group's efforts proved ineffective in battling Chavez, and by 1939, Collier surrendered.

And yet Collier did not, by any means, give up his effort to control outlying lands completely. As the boundary bill stalled and then died, he and his advisors devised an innovative strategy for governing the area indirectly through the Taylor Grazing Act. Passed in 1934, the act—so far unenforced in the Checkerboard because of Collier's intervention—would regulate the numbers of stock on the public domain by requiring federal permits. Collier long feared that a failed boundary bill would lead to the dispossession of Navajos from the Checkerboard, because the grazing act privileged those landowners who owned or controlled wells, springs, or other permanent water sources and could prove that they already used public lands for grazing. Many Navajos only *occupied* their Checkerboard land, and nearly all their wells and stock tanks were federally owned; consequently, few Navajos could hope to claim a permit, and Anglo ranchers, who used fences to control access to their water, including natural sources, would gain dominion.[21]

As those Checkerboard ranchers began clamoring for the enforcement of the grazing act, in the hope of displacing Navajos, Collier played his trump card. In 1939, he and Secretary of the Interior Harold Ickes created a special grazing district, whose outlines were essentially coterminous with those originally delineated by the boundary bill. The order establishing the district defined Navajos as owners not only of all of their allotments, whether patented or not, but also of all federally developed water; better yet, its rules for granting grazing permits favored subsistence, rather than commercial, ranchers.[22] Overall, the Diné managed to secure their foothold in the district and win most of the permits, judging from the complaints filed by Anglo stockmen.[23] Few Diné recognized the reprieve that Collier's scheme granted those living in the area. Some found the application process for grazing permits strange and confusing, and many rightly feared that the permits presaged renewed stock reduction.[24] Indeed, the Taylor Grazing Act limited the number of sheep that Navajos could legally graze, just as it restricted Hispanic subsistence ranchers in northern New Mexico and small-scale stockowners throughout the West.[25] Yet there is little doubt that without Collier's ingenuity, Anglo stockmen would have used the act to drive Navajos from the Checkerboard entirely.

The special grazing district, nonetheless, was a poor substitute for the boundary bill. A compromise, at best, it did not completely exclude Anglo and Hispanic stockmen and it handed control of the area, in large measure, to the Grazing Service (now the Bureau of Land Management), which cared little about the welfare of impoverished Navajos.[26] Importantly, the BIA could not spend its erosion-control monies in the district, since it lay outside the reservation. Collier, thus, viewed the creation of the district as a bittersweet victory. The reservation had clearly reached its geographical limits; it was no longer politically possible to acquire or control significantly more land. And so, with these limitations in mind, Collier and his men focused anew on a program for rationalized range management on the reservation.

The first initiative, already begun in 1933 at Mexican Springs (now Nakaibito), enclosed large sections of the reservation to demonstrate to Navajos the efficacy of scientific range management. The Soil Conservation Service fenced off eight areas of the reservation, ranging from roughly 5,600 to 43,000 acres in extent, each encompassing an entire watershed. These enclosures, the conservationists were certain, would not only function as scientific laboratories for studying range management but also prove to Navajos that conservative grazing could regenerate grasslands and produce more profitable sheep.[27]

Restoring these grasslands required intensive effort. Under the direction of engineers, Navajo laborers constructed dams, dikes, and water-spreading structures to arrest erosion.[28] They planted willows, cottonwoods, and exotic salt cedar to stabilize stream banks. They reseeded denuded areas with grasses. They destroyed the toxic locoweed and whorled milkweed that invaded overgrazed grasslands. They poisoned prairie dogs with strychnine-laced oats on the grounds that the rodents competed with sheep for forage.[29] SCS employees then stocked enclosures with demonstration flocks, consisting of sheep that Navajo "cooperators" temporarily turned over to federal control in exchange for their share of the lamb crop and the wool clip.[30] They fed the demonstration flocks supplemental hay when forage was scarce. And they created buck pastures for purebred Rambouillet rams, which they used to "improve" Navajo sheep.[31] Aside from the breeding program, such an intensive, costly effort could not possibly be replicated across the reservation.

The SCS, nonetheless, did demonstrate what *could* be accomplished with enough money and conservative stocking at or below the estimated carrying capacity. Mexican Springs and Steamboat, especially, became poster projects for range rehabilitation, producing abundant grasses, robust Rambouillet-hybrid lambs, and heavy fleeces.[32] Some Diné recognized a marked change in forage in the demonstration areas by 1935, a year of increased rainfall.[33] Ned Plummer of Coyote Canyon noticed the difference at nearby Mexican Springs. His elders had told him stories of grasslands that he himself had never seen, ranges they described as carpeted with vigorous and valuable forage, the variety of female and male plants that signified, to Diné, a healthy landscape. Now he could see that those plants were "coming back to his country."[34]

A few Diné like Plummer supported the government's efforts to demonstrate the value of scientific range improvement, but many more chafed at the enclosure of vast swaths of land and their exclusion from traditional grazing areas. Fencing the range became, next to stock reduction itself, the most contested conservation effort, a target for opposition to the Navajo New Deal. Although the government obtained agreements with local chapter officers before wrapping pastures in barbed wire and removing livestock, the local leaders who signed were not necessarily the ones whose use areas became off-limits. In some cases, fences denied Diné access to their hogans, corrals, farms, and wells, sparking bitter animosity. Consider, for example, the story told by Frank Cadman, a tribal councilman from Mexican Springs. "At my hogan, where there used to be lots of hogans," he testified, "there is this fence, and it looks like it holds the spirit of the people who used to live there. . . . The people who used to live there used to be free, just the same as anybody else, but now they have to abide by rules and regulations governing the area."[35] E. R. Fryer, who helped develop the demonstration projects at Mexican Springs and Ganado before becoming the reservation's superintendent, later admitted that "many injustices" arose from the displacement of people like Cadman from their traditional grazing areas.[36]

Even the success of the demonstration areas brought complaints. When erosion control and reseeding generated new vegetation, the marked differences between the areas inside and outside the fences provoked protests. Federal fences likely seemed little different from those that large-scale stockowners, both Anglo and Diné, had long used to appropriate well-watered pastures. Seeing lush vegetation within the demonstration areas, Diné charged that the government had taken from them the best grazing lands.[37] Some protested by sneaking horses and sheep through pasture gates late at night, despite the risk of fines, so that they, too, could benefit from improved ranges.[38] It seemed only fair that their stock should be allowed to graze lands that, by comparison with the depleted areas to which they were restricted, seemed understocked.

Diné denounced many parts of the New Deal conservation program, but their discontent was neither universal nor unbounded. They especially welcomed the development of springs and stock tanks and the erection of windmills.[39] By 1939, the government had drilled numerous artesian wells, dug nearly 290 deep wells topped by windmills, and built approximately 1,800 stock tanks.[40] In making stock water more widely available, the SCS sought to delay the timing of transhumant moves to higher ground after snows melted, open "understocked" ranges to summer grazing and, thereby, spread animals more thinly across the land, and, in general, foster more efficient land use.

More water, however, could be a mixed blessing. When new sources of water beckoned in relatively ungrazed areas, Diné shepherds quite naturally drove their livestock there, leading to the "rapid depletion of the few remaining good patches of range," one SCS official observed.[41] In fact, one of the most overgrazed areas in the westernmost part of the reservation lay in the vicinity of a reservoir constructed in the 1920s. Before the stock tank was built, grama grass thickly blanketed the area; ten years later, only a thin cover of snakeweed remained.[42] These winter ranges appeared "understocked" because they rested in summer when the plants put out seed and reproduced themselves. By encouraging more efficient year-round use of ranges, the New Dealers may well have inadvertently promoted overgrazing, just as Hagerman predicted in 1932. Water development, nonetheless, responded to a long-standing demand and, thus, earned the gratitude of Diné.

Similarly, a program to preserve traditional—albeit genetically "improved"—churra sheep arose in response to entreaties by Diné women. Since the 1880s, agents with the BIA had disparaged Navajo sheep, long-haired churras (often corrupted as "churros"), which the Diné first

After centuries of adaptation to the arid environments of northwestern Iberia and Diné Bikéyah, churra sheep, with their characteristic four horns, were ideally suited to Diné life and the needs of Diné weavers. Their long hair and lanky bodies, though, found few markets. The Soil Conservation Service program therefore targeted them, nearly eradicating the breed.

Photograph by Milton Snow. Records of the BIA, RG75, National Archives at College Park, Md., RG75-Nav-A-11.

At the Sheep Laboratory at Fort Wingate, scientists crossed long-haired churra sheep, visible in the foreground, with short-wool breeds in hopes of creating a hybrid that met the needs of Diné weavers as well as the market. Photograph probably by Milton Snow, 1941. Records of the BIA, RG75, National Archives at College Park, Md., RG75-TLA-19-FRH-34.

acquired from the Spanish and then from the federal government upon their return from Hwéeldi.[43] To bilagáana eyes accustomed to fat merinos or Rambouillets, whose fine white wool brought top dollar in commercial markets, the lanky, hairy, often multicolored churra sheep were "scrubby," "inbred," and "degenerate."[44] One agent, drawing on racist notions of purity, noted in 1886 that "fully one-fourth of the number [are] black and appear to be deteriorating in blood and value."[45] Churras had narrow bodies and produced a lightweight fleece, which lowered their commercial value for mutton and wool. To "improve" the breed, as early as 1903, federal agents introduced "fine blooded" rams, especially Rambouillets, initially with limited success.[46] Rambouillet bucks could not keep up with the long-legged, fast-walking churras and goats, and Diné women found the fine, short-stapled wool, which was both greasy and kinky, unsuitable for spinning and hand-weaving.[47] Nonetheless, by the early 1930s, persistent BIA agents, with the help of reservation traders, had transformed many of the Navajo flocks, except those in the most remote areas, into nappy hybrids with greater commercial value.[48] Then stock reduction targeted the lowly churras, nearly eradicating the breed.[49]

Commercial markets scorned them, but the churras were ideally suited for the environmental conditions of the Colorado Plateau and the cultural needs of the Diné. Native to northwestern Iberia, the churra had already adapted to the severe winters and hot dry summers of that region before its introduction to northern New Spain. By the 1900s, more than two centuries of Diné livestock husbandry and natural selection had produced a particularly hardy variety, which breeders now call the Navajo-Churro. Since sheep can breed throughout the year and the Diné did not separate their rams from their ewes (until federal agents convinced them to do so, largely in the 1930s), many lambs were born in winter. Only the hardiest survived. The churras' long legs, upright carriage, and nearly bare bellies proved advantageous in the scrubby environment. And they could go for days during transhumant moves without access to springs or ponds, absorbing only dew from plants.[50] Churras were so well adapted to arid lands, they seemed native.

They were also well adapted to Diné life. Although commercial buyers considered them scrawny, the extremely light-boned churras produced quantities of milk and naturally lean, mild-tasting mutton, which the Diné relished. Just as important, they produced a fleece that was ideal for hand-weaving. It consisted of an outer protective layer of coarse, hairlike fibers and an inner coat of long, lustrous wool. This straight, long-stapled wool required far less carding than crimpy Rambouillet or merino fleece, was easier to hand spin, offered good tensile strength, and produced durable blankets and rugs. And because Diné women necessarily washed their wool by hand, if at all, it was important that churra fleeces did not come larded with lanolin, so that they did not attract too much dirt and absorbed dyes readily. The wool came in a variety of colors, too, not only white, but also brown and black, which women highly prized for weaving. By the 1920s, however, Rambouillet hybrids dominated many Navajo flocks, and their fine, short-stapled wool produced lumpy rugs of poor quality, frustrating weavers.[51]

When the agricultural economist Robert Youngblood studied the Navajo economy in 1934, women across the reservation complained to him that they found it difficult to feed and clothe their children because they could no longer weave good rugs. During the long winter lull between the lamb and wool markets, women depended on the sales of their textiles to purchase goods at the trading posts. But it was impossible to make a rug worth much money with the wool from Rambouillet hybrids. Red Shirt's Wife, a weaver living near Navajo Mountain, pleaded with Youngblood through an interpreter: "Can't you do something to save our Old Navajo sheep[?] . . . There are only a few left and these will soon be gone, and then we will be able to make only inferior rugs."[52]

Collier responded, at Youngblood's behest, by funding one of the few New Deal projects specifically designed to address the needs of Navajo women. Established on the grounds of Fort Wingate, near Gallup, and directed by the Bureau of Animal Industry, the Southwestern Range and Sheep Breeding Laboratory worked to recover the desirable qualities of the churra, while also making it more marketable. The laboratory began its work in 1936 with a foundation herd of 800 churra ewes and 20 rams, acquired from remote and relatively inaccessible regions of the reservation, such as Navajo Mountain, where "improved breeding" made fewer inroads. By crossbreeding the churras with Corriedales and Romneys, and then reciprocally mating their progeny, animal scientists hoped to create a hybrid that retained the hardiness, the good mothering instincts, the milk, and the coarse long-stapled wool of the old Navajo sheep, yet produced heavier lambs and more mutton. They also hoped to eliminate the hairy outer coat and create greater uniformity in the fiber so that it might find a commercial market.[53]

John Cooper, director of the lab, approached this task with high hopes. He studied high-resolution images of the fibers to understand their physical characteristics and compared that wool to the fibers in more than 160 historic Navajo rugs in museums and private collections. He was also careful to study whether modern Navajo women would find the improved wool satisfactory. Toward that end, he hired Lillian Brown, a Diné weaver, to make rugs with the wools that the lab produced and evaluate their desirability for hand-weaving. Cooper's goal proved elusive. The lab never managed to produce a hybrid sheep whose wool compared favorably with that of the old churras, nor did they succeed in making the sheep more marketable. By 1949, the laboratory gave up. Noting that Navajo women used only 10 percent of the annual wool clip for weaving anyway—a dubious statistic, because, for many, quantities of suitable wool were not available—the scientists refocused their efforts on developing a hardy, short-stapled breed for commercial ranching.[54] It never seems to have occurred to anyone that the Navajos might breed two types of sheep, one for market and one—a pure churra—for weavers.[55]

Looking back on this era, few—if any—Diné recall the New Dealers' efforts to revive weavers' wool and develop water. Those projects quickly faded from memory, overshadowed by stories of families riven by regulations that restricted their relationships to the land. During this phase of the Navajo New Deal, range managers implemented a revolutionary new program devised by William McGinnies. An expert in desert rangelands, McGinnies would later establish the celebrated Office of Arid Lands Studies at the University of Arizona. But he had little understanding of or patience for Navajos, characterizing those who opposed grazing regulations and stock reduction as simply ignorant, blind, lazy, or dishonest.[56] Under his direction, range specialists sought to change traditional practices in livestock husbandry, tie families and flocks to specific tracts, and control their movements across the land. In short, they resolved to remake Navajo pastoralists into modern ranchers.

The problem, as McGinnies and his men saw it, was not grazing *per se*; indeed, sheep grazing was the best use of the land, they thought. The problem was the mode of Navajo livestock husbandry and land use. Navajos encouraged abuse of the range, they maintained. Instead of using salt licks, which officials admitted were prohibitively expensive, Navajos drove their animals periodically to thickets of four-wing saltbush, defoliating large areas of brush and ultimately killing plants. Most seriously, they argued, by using goats to lead the flocks, herding too closely, trailing twice daily to water and feed, traversing the same ground month in and month out, and corralling night after night in the same place, Navajos promoted excessive trampling of the range and denuded areas around hogans, corrals, and water sources.[57]

To ameliorate these problems, range managers prodded Navajos to adopt the herding and husbandry practices used by Anglo and Hispanic ranchers. Some efforts proved relatively successful. At the government's insistence, many, though not all, Diné separated their rams into buck pastures to control breeding and thus delayed lambing season until spring, when nutritious forage sprouted. Other efforts largely failed. Through educational workshops at chapter houses and demonstration projects, extension agents urged Navajos to abandon the practice of sending out flocks with women and children, who returned them twice daily to the home corral. Instead, they encouraged Navajos to band flocks into large communal herds and keep them out on the range around the clock for as long as a month, under the watchful eye of adult male shepherds. "Bedding out," as this practice was known, rotating pastures according to an established schedule, and allowing sheep to spread out over the range would discourage excessive trampling and overgrazing.[58] Over time, range specialists believed, these practices could help restore the grasslands.

Officials recognized it would be difficult to persuade Navajos to adopt these "modern American methods" of range management. The idea of communal herds in itself would arouse opposition, observed one range specialist. Suspicion and distrust would surface whenever individual owners suffered the inevitable loss of sheep to theft, predators, and natural causes, leading to bickering and conflict within families and communities. Banding and bedding out flocks also required, in essence, that women's dominion over their care diminish, creating a new masculinized model of pastoralism. New Deal administrators entertained the idea of erecting portable looms on wagons, so that weavers could follow the herds. But no one seriously suggested that women sleep alone on the range, away from their hogans for weeks at a time, nor did they propose to turn Navajo families into true nomads. In fact, breaking families into two groups—one that herded and one that tended home and hearth—was part of the point, for it would remove children from the range and thereby accomplish two goals at once: place herding in the hands of more responsible adults and free children to attend school.⁵⁹ Modern American range management would foster modern American families.

The Diné roundly rejected these proposed changes to traditional practices, not just because they meddled with gender and generational roles, but because, from their perspective, they made no sense. The Diné world was peopled with spirits, not only Diyin Dine'é, but also malevolent ghosts and skinwalkers, witches disguised in wolf skins. It was under the cover of darkness that these *ch'įįdii* and *yee naaldlooshii* prowled about, so no Diné would willingly risk sleeping by themselves on the range.⁶⁰ Just as ridiculous to Diné was the idea of allowing sheep to scatter across the land, for only close herding kept coyotes at bay.⁶¹ Federal officials harbored no illusions that changing Navajo herding patterns would be easy, and they were right. Two decades after the New Dealers went home, Diné continued to adhere in large measure to their old herding customs.⁶²

While his men struggled to instill new husbandry practices, McGinnies developed a plan to regulate the movements of livestock across the land by drawing lines on a map. Each Navajo family would be assigned to a specific grazing district, beyond which they could not take their flocks without written permission. The boundaries of each of the eighteen "land management units" typically fell along the topographical features enclosing an entire watershed; over the first few years, these lines were redrawn to take in most of the winter and summer ranges used by cooperating groups of families—so-called land use communities—along with the trading posts and dipping vats that those communities frequented.⁶³ Dividing the reservation into smaller units also allowed range examiners to study the flora, fauna, water resources, soils, and erosional conditions in more detail and to estimate the number of animals the range could support.⁶⁴ These eighteen land management units, then, became the foundation for the final round of stock reduction, which would link the maximum allowable numbers of livestock within each district to its estimated carrying capacity.

As a prelude to drawing at least some district boundaries, range examiners, working with Diné assistants, surveyed the seasonal movements of Navajo stockowners. They went from hogan to hogan to ascertain where each family lived in winter and summer, where they dipped their flocks, which trading posts they frequented, and how many livestock they owned.⁶⁵ This was a laudable effort to understand the seasonal movements of flocks and families, and suggested a growing recognition of the importance of comprehending Navajo life. And yet, these snapshots of land use, while seeming to specify the summer and winter ranges of each family, offered somewhat deceptive impressions that failed to capture the actual distribution of Navajos and their herds and the patterns of transhumance traced over the course of a year. The studies led range managers to view Navajo livestock movements as relatively static or as two single points, defined as a summer and a winter range, rather than as a series of stops along a loop.

This misunderstanding arose, in part, because they asked the wrong questions. According to the hataałii Frank Goldtooth, they asked: "'Where is your winter grazing site? Where is your summer grazing site?'" These queries puzzled Goldtooth, because they revealed a misunderstanding about Diné conceptions of land use. While families typically used lands associated with particular matrilineages, "most of the people did not have *grazing sites*," he explained. "They took their sheep wherever they wanted, where there was plenty of water and vegetation."[66] Range examiners elicited information about seasonal hogans and camps but learned little of the actual movements of flocks, which varied according to the availability of forage, browse, and water. As the hataałii Frank Mitchell later recalled, "We never stayed at one place very long; we would spend a few days here and then move on to some other location. That is the way we lived, even in the wintertime; in spite of the cold and the deep snow, we moved even then."[67] The questions range examiners asked also missed the significance of mobility to Diné culture and the importance of long-distance moves to visit relatives and reinforce k'é, the familial obligations of reciprocity and cooperation.

Nonetheless, an examination of the data that the range examiners collected suggests that seasonal patterns of movement no longer rested the range. According to those studies, in the dry western regions especially, people tended to concentrate in winter near a few sources of permanent water. In summer, some families did shift to highland or canyon areas, perhaps believing that the winter range would recuperate before they returned. But oftentimes, as they moved out, another group moved in. Others dispersed but did not scatter; they moved in clusters of families related through women and in summer reunited with still more clusters of kinsfolk, putting enormous grazing pressure on favored places. Many more stayed in the same general area the year round.[68] The sheer numbers of families and flocks within an increasingly constricted Navajo range surely meant that transhumance no longer conserved the range as it once did. It was this unregulated, overlapping use of the range that McGinnies resolved to stop.

With the creation of grazing districts and the regulation of livestock numbers, McGinnies hoped to save the Navajos from what the ecologist Garrett Hardin would later call "the tragedy of the commons." Hardin wrote his famous essay in 1968, but E. O. Wooton articulated the same idea sixty years earlier. Basically, the theory holds that when land is held in common, all of the users share in the loss of forage from overgrazing, while the profits for each animal added to the range accrues to the individual owner. If an individual herder conserves a part of the range, that simply encourages his competitors to bring their stock in to consume the forage. Thus, the only rational action for an individual herdsman is to "put the extra stock on himself." For Wooton, the solution was simple: "Men will make the necessary effort to improve and protect the range only when they are absolutely guaranteed that whatever of benefit may come as the result of their efforts shall become their own gain."[69]

McGinnies certainly subscribed to Wooton's theory. And as he saw it, there were two ways to head off tragedy on the Navajo commons. One was to regulate the numbers of livestock; the other was to create a semblance of private property by dividing open range into districts that would force Navajos to take personal responsibility for their impacts on the land. What he did not understand was that Diné did not hold the land in common; each community of interrelated families held "use rights" to particular areas of land, rights that included the flexibility to visit kinsfolk when conditions warranted. Perhaps that system no longer functioned in this impoverished landscape, especially when a handful of large-scale owners like Chee Dodge appropriated enormous areas. But it is also true that grazing districts could mean less flexibility in managing the range. As rainfall and forage grew scarce at the end of the 1930s, stockowners had no place to go.[70] The logic behind the grazing districts made sense only if conditions improved, or if range managers could respond quickly to deteriorating conditions by removing stock from the reservation, either to slaughterhouses or to grasslands elsewhere.

The news that the Navajo Service planned to partition the reservation into numerous grazing districts provoked a startled outcry. Officials tried to squelch rumors that the government planned to fence in each district, remove the sheep with federal troops if necessary, and band them into community herds.[71] Anticipating trouble, Collier's men gave up nearly all pretense of Navajo self-government and presented the plan to the tribal council in November 1936 as a fait accompli. "We are not asking you to approve the plan of setting up 18 districts," warned James Stewart as councilmen maneuvered against the plan. "Those districts have already been set up and are in operation.... So forget that angle." When delegates observed that transhumant stockowners would have to transgress boundaries in order to move to distant pastures, Superintendent E. R. Fryer made it clear that restricting the movements of those with large flocks was exactly the point. Those who traversed large stretches of land in search of good forage, Fryer charged, were "aggressive individuals," who would now be forced to choose one district; they "would not be permitted to roam over the reservation at will and use range belonging to others."[72] It was not a matter for debate.

Grazing regulations confused, saddened, and angered stockowners, who learned that they could be fined or jailed for taking their flocks across demarcated borders.[73] As one man complained to an investigator with the New Mexico Association on Indian Affairs, "I see grass growing one and [a] half miles from here, but I can't cross that line with my sheep." Another grumbled that he had grazing land in one district (probably with his mother or sister), while his wife's land was in another. "In winter we [live] over here—in summer time we go over there on top [of] that canyon line. They say we can not go over there.... I do not understand about that—why I can not go over there." Still another lamented that he could no longer take his flocks "where my grandma and grandpa went"; he could no longer graze his natal land. For the Diné, these new boundaries meant a loss of freedom.[74]

The Navajo Service did attempt to accommodate those who innocently dipped their sheep while away from home in 1937, when officials assigned stockowners to specific districts. A person who was erroneously assigned to a district while visiting relatives or distant trading posts, or who subsequently married or divorced someone who lived across the border, could change his or her assignment.[75] But in requiring Navajos to come hat in hand for permission to move their flocks, federal authorities made a people who valued their mobility feel frustrated, powerless, and resentful.

Collier and the conservationists imposed a system of rationalized range management that made little sense in this unpredictable arid land. While they believed that such a system emulated the practices of modern American ranchers, they ignored the fact that the Anglo and Hispanic sheepmen who grazed Navajo Country, like Edward Sargent, also trailed their flocks long distances to greener pastures elsewhere. Perhaps if Collier had listened to Robert Marshall and encouraged Navajos themselves to develop a range management system, they might have invented a hybrid, one that integrated the cultural values of mobility, cooperation, and reciprocity with the ecological value of rotating pastures. But aside from confining families within districts, the program for range management was never fully implemented. Along with an assignment to a land management district came a new system of grazing permits that placed an absolute limit on the number of stock each family could own, together with a specific cap on the number of horses. These new limits incited a new wave of resistance from which the conservation program would never fully recover.

9 · MAKING MEMORIES

In the late spring of 1936, as rumors of grazing districts and renewed stock reduction swirled across Diné Bikéyah, newspapers in border towns claimed that Navajo women were threatening revolt. Trouble was brewing on the reservation, the *Gallup Independent* claimed, in the racist language of yellow journalism, "due to the dissatisfaction of the squaws over Collier's policies."[1] Solid evidence of this simmering rebellion is admittedly meager. Very few Navajo women spoke English, and the government officials who created much of the historical record tended to ignore them. But the few clues that do surface here and there are certainly suggestive.[2] Consider the account of a community meeting near Kayenta, where perhaps 250 Diné, nearly all of them men, gathered. Before them stood a woman known as Denehotso Hattie. Although almost blind from trachoma, she was the meeting's "unquestioned, dominating leader," and an "aggressive and vigorous speaker." Pointing her finger at Superintendent Fryer, Hattie denounced the government's plan for range management. She spoke so heatedly and rapidly that Fryer's interpreter, Howard Gorman, could not keep up, or perhaps Gorman was reluctant to translate her invective. Nonetheless, it was clear that the woman did not blame government officials alone. She scolded Diné men, too, pointing at them as they hung their heads.[3] Diné councilmen and community leaders had acquiesced to the wholesale slaughter of stock and the confinement of flocks into grazing districts, bringing poverty and despair to their people. Hattie held them all accountable.

Diné men and women like Denehotso Hattie challenged stock reduction and the government's entire range-management program. Their protests proliferated between 1936 and 1941 as conservationists imposed maximum limits on the numbers of livestock each family could graze; these limits leveled wealth—striking for the first time at the richest stockowners—and targeted horses, the markers of masculine prestige. One might argue that these protests involved relatively few people, who were concentrated within only a few areas and manipulated by a handful of politically motivated men. And yet this resistance movement held a significance far beyond that of the participants themselves, for it tattooed an indelible memory of this era, a collective memory of Collier's conservation program as an economic and environmental injustice.

The man Collier chose to administer this phase of his conservation program was E. Reesman Fryer, whom friends called "Si." Fryer headed a reorganized reservation that combined the former six jurisdictions into one and merged the local operations of the BIA and the SCS into a single, centralized Navajo Service.[4] He was a young ecologist who had grown up in the Mormon community of Mesa, Arizona, before studying fisheries and forestry at the University of Washington. Upon graduation, he supervised a ranch and citrus farm in the Phoenix area, and he and his wife owned a dude ranch in the Sierra Ancha mountains, south of Payson, Arizona, before it went bust in the early days of the Depression. But he was also no stranger to Navajo Country. He had overseen construction of the Mexican Springs Demonstration Project and administered a similar effort at Ganado before becoming director of land management for the Pueblo Indian Agency.[5]

Nonetheless, Fryer was an inauspicious choice to head the Navajo Service. The tall man, with a thatch of curly blond hair, was only thirty-five years old when Collier appointed him, and his youth did not draw the respect that the Diné had bestowed on his older predecessors. He was sympathetic to the Navajos, especially the small-scale stockowners, and he could be restrained in his dealings.[6] Yet with his forceful, combative personality, short temper, blunt language, and stubborn streak, he often struck the Diné as callous and abrasive.[7] He himself admitted that many of the actions blamed on Collier were, in fact, his own decisions.[8] Fryer's temperament was poorly suited for the task of implementing a radical revolution in class hierarchies on the Navajo Reservation.

Nor did he endear himself with the poor. Long after he left Navajo Country, Fryer wrote that he continued to be haunted by a memory of two destitute old women who had walked from some distant corner of the reservation to his office in Window Rock. The only animals they owned, they told him, were two burros, which they used to carry wood and water from a distant windmill to their hogans. Range riders had seized their burros during a roundup of excess horses and marked them for slaughter. The women wept as they begged Fryer to release their pack animals. He sympathized, but he also feared that helping them would bring a deluge of appeals from others and undermine the authority of his subordinates. So he turned them away. "I still recall," Fryer wrote nearly fifty years later, "the weeping of those two nearly ragged old women as they left my office," and he remembered the look on his interpreter's face, "as he scowled at me for my apparent lack of compassion."[9]

Stock reduction shifted into high gear during Fryer's administration. In 1935, range managers estimated that the reservation could carry roughly 560,000 sheep and goats, or their equivalent in cattle and horses. (Since cattle and horses required more forage, each counted as four or five sheep, respectively.) And yet after years of effort to cut the number of stock, more than 918,000 "sheep units" (SU) remained (table 1).[10] The Navajos still needed to bring the stocking pressure down by nearly 40 percent, but this time, under Fryer's leadership, the Navajo Service would take a new approach. Until now, subsistence owners had borne the brunt of stock reduction, and it was clear that they could suffer no more losses. It was time to shift the burden onto the rich.

With this new phase of stock reduction, Fryer and Collier intended to engage in social engineering as much as soil conservation. For some time, Collier's closest advisor, Walter Woehlke, had believed that wealthy stockowners such as Chee Dodge were helping to stir up opposition to stock reduction and grazing districts. The fact that these rich men had often been the commissioner's greatest allies in his earlier battles against Jacob Morgan and other opponents no longer mattered. Wealthy councilmen had formulated the horizontal approach used so far, one that reduced all herds by a flat percentage, so that they got away with simply culling their own flocks while poorer people suffered. As a consequence, Woehlke confided to Collier, "we have been creating a Navajo proletariat.... At the same time we have apparently increased the Navajo aristocracy."[11] To both Collier and Fryer, this concentration of wealth in the hands of the few

TABLE 1 Navajo Livestock Census, Navajo Reservation 1933–44

Year	Sheep	Goats	Horses*	Cattle*	Sheep Units
1933	544,726	164,999	42,000	20,000	999,725
1934	502,619	147,427	40,000	19,000	926,046
1935	548,579	92,222	40,270	19,020	918,231
1936	408,564	65,816	23,545	11,787	639,253
1937	380,528	54,838	40,921	16,977	707,879
1938–39	n.a.	n.a.	n.a.	n.a.	n.a.
1940	356,791	57,113	31,100	13,045	621,584
1941	357,229	52,762	27,539	9,299	584,882
1942	362,157	52,142	27,406	8,060	583,569
1943	337,785	47,431	26,895	8,144	552,267
1944	344,227	41,772	26,246	7,612	547,677

*Note that 1937 was the first year for which the BIA attempted an actual count of horses and cattle through a reservation-wide round-up. All previous figures are guesses.

SOURCE: Committee on Indian Affairs, *Survey of Conditions*, pp. 17978, 17995; Young, *Navajo Yearbook*, 1955, p. 116; Lee Muck, "Survey of the Range Resources and Livestock Economy of the Navajo Nation," 10 Dec. 1947, CCF 301, box 120, Navajo Area Office, RG 75, NARA-PR.

seemed absolutely unfair. They resolved to use stock reduction as a tool to redistribute resources more evenly across the reservation.[12]

To do so, authorities developed a graduated system of wealth based on the sheep dipping records for 1937. For each district, administrators established the "maximum permit number," using a calculation that took into account the number of stock a family could possess if the carrying capacity were divided equally, adjusted by the number of animals that those with even smaller flocks actually owned. Those with fewer animals could keep all of them but acquire no more. Families with more than the maximum had to remove the surplus stock from the reservation either by selling them or (for those few who could afford it, like Chee Dodge) leasing pastures elsewhere.[13]

Consider how this was supposed to work in the southcentral part of the reservation. District 17 offered relatively good forage and could carry about 75,000 SU. According to the dipping records of more than 750 owners, nearly 81,500 sheep and goats, or their equivalent in cattle and horses, grazed the area. Authorities established the district's maximum permit level at 275 SU. That figure included a limit on the number of horses a family could keep, which varied from four to ten, apparently depending on the owners' demonstrated need for work stock and transportation. For example, Yah Bah, whose subsistence flocks consisted of 186 sheep, twenty-four goats, two cattle, and twelve horses, could keep half of her ponies and all of her other stock, and she could even acquire another twenty-seven sheep once her surplus horses were gone, giving her just enough for the average family of seven to live on.[14]

By contrast, a rich woman like Mary Lynch would watch her wealth evaporate. According to the 1937 dipping records, she owned 2,595 sheep, eighty-two cattle, and seventy-seven horses, making her one of the reservation's richest stockowners. To meet the new grazing requirements, she would have to eliminate all but ten of her horses and 90 percent of the rest of her stock. Even if she chose to sell all of her cattle, she could hold onto only 225 sheep.[15] That would be enough for her family to subsist on, perhaps, but it meant that her hard-earned prestige and her legacy to her children would be gone. The grazing permits purposely leveled wealth, bringing all stockowners, including Mary Lynch, down to the class of subsistence herders.

The blow struck even harder in the more arid northwestern reaches of the reservation. Take a wealthy man like Crooked Finger, who in 1937 owned the equivalent of nearly 1,900 sheep, which he wintered on the Kaibito Plateau. The grazing regulations established a limit of only 225 SU in his district, so he could legally keep just over half of his nineteen horses and 175 sheep and goats—even fewer if he decided to hang onto any cattle. On the other hand, his neighbor, Boyd Warner, who had only ninety-three sheep, three goats, and ten horses, could keep all of his sheep and goats and five horses, the maximum number for an average family in his district. He could even acquire another twenty-five sheep once he eliminated his surplus ponies, but he could not further expand the size of his flock, even though it already came in under the cap.[16]

Poorer herders like Warner still suffered disproportionately under this new program. They could increase their flocks only after the number of animals in a given district dropped below carrying capacity *and* wealthy owners decreased their flocks proportionately. Until then, the permits not only leveled wealth; they froze the size of smaller flocks. People like 'Asdzáá Nez, who owned only twenty-one sheep, three goats, and a horse, became permanently destitute, dependent on the kindness of their relatives or the welfare state.[17]

The very idea of leveling wealth on the reservation surely struck many Navajos as an arrogant attack on their prosperity, their notions of prestige, and their customs of reciprocity between richer and poorer kin. Chee Dodge, for one, protested that slashing his herds would further impoverish his already needy neighbors and relatives who depended on his largess. This suggestion that a few wealthy stockowners could support thousands of poor Navajo families struck Collier as preposterous.[18] And yet, eliminating wealth undermined familial systems of support but did not offer the poor any hope for independence. Even the thin middle strata felt the cudgel of stock reduction. Only about five hundred Diné families with flocks larger than what was absolutely necessary for sustenance formed a nascent middling class; yet they, too, saw their legacies vanish. From a purely economic standpoint, demoting all stockowners to subsistence shepherds was cruel and unusual. After all, no one in America, except perhaps Huey Long, had seriously suggested leveling the nation's wealth, even as the republic became mired in its deepest economic depression.[19]

For Collier, however, it was a simple matter of equity. The range belonged equally to all the Navajos, and yet rich owners of as many as three thousand sheep units—he and his colleagues likened them to an oligarchy—monopolized the forage by appropriating the best lands.[20] The ranks of the rich were small. Only about one hundred families across all of Navajo Country had more than a medium-sized flock of five hundred sheep and goats, and a mere twenty stockowners, concentrated in three districts, were truly wealthy, operating on the scale of Anglo and Hispanic commercial ranchers.[21] All in all, 3 percent of the stockowners accounted for 15 percent of the livestock and preempted even more of the range, since they tended to travel long distances between seasonal pastures.[22] Collier found that unconscionable, especially when thousands and thousands of Navajo families owned fewer than one hundred sheep and goats, and thousands more had none at all. The rich and even the middle strata, in his view, were usurping and eroding the range by stocking it far beyond its carrying capacity.

Bringing the number of stock down to the land's carrying capacity required an accurate count of the animals, recorded at dipping vats and branding roundups. This became the official register for a grazing permit system designed to convey or withhold land-use rights forevermore. At the same time, the inventory linked livestock brands to a designated owner, who was also, in essence, "branded." Back in 1927, the BIA registered the

At sheep dips, federal officials recorded a census of livestock holdings, which became the official roster for grazing permits. Photograph by Milton Snow. Courtesy of Fort Lewis College, Center of Southwest Studies, Fryer Papers.

Navajos themselves, assigning each a "census number" linked to a card bearing his or her fingerprints and stamped onto a brass medal suitable for wearing around the neck.[23] This system helped to eliminate the BIA's longstanding problem of identifying Navajos, whose multiplicity of nicknames, kinship names, "schoolboy" names, and often undisclosed "war" or ceremonial names—including the ubiquitous female name "Bah"—led many agents to complain that the Navajos had no names at all.[24] For many agents, the identities of individual Navajos had long seemed indecipherable. Registration made both people and livestock legible.[25]

Navajo Service administrators wanted an authoritative register of ownership because they had long been frustrated with what they saw as Indian chicanery. In the late 1920s, for example, the BIA had imposed a grazing fee on especially large flocks to no avail. Many bureau employees believed that Navajos had circumvented those early grazing regulations by claiming that large herds were in fact clusters of smaller, individually owned flocks of a few hundred head. Those tactics, officials thought, had stymied efforts to levy grazing fees and thereby discourage enormous herds.[26]

In truth, of course, each family member actually *did* own her or his own flock and pooled animals to herd them or take them through the dipping vats. One woman, whom Gladys Reichard called "Dezba," tried to explain Diné conceptions of ownership to a government worker. When Dezba and her family took their sheep to the Ganado vat just before the first stock reduction, an agent told her that, by his count, she had 810 sheep and goats. But Dezba begged to differ. She clarified that they were not all hers: Some belonged to her husband, others to her brother, and still more to her two daughters and her two sons. She herself owned only 125 head. But nothing she said convinced the man, and he walked off in disgust.[27] Government officials, in fact, seemed almost mulishly unwilling to comprehend the complex fabric of the Navajo economy, which wove together communal conceptions of land use and obligations of reciprocity with highly autonomous notions of livestock ownership. That failure to grasp basic property concepts caused a good deal of animosity that might have been avoided.

Instead of crediting actual owners, federal officials assigned possession of an entire family flock to the federally designated "head of household." Generally, that person was a man. Only widowed, divorced, or unmarried women could be registered stockowners.[28] A few married women made it onto the list by taking their sheep and goats through the dipping vats themselves. But their designation did not last long. Take 'Asdzą́ą́ Yazzie, for example. She lost her chance at a permit when her husband amended the record to include his sheep, which had been counted erroneously with someone else's flock. On learning of the error, the district supervisor deleted her from the register and issued a permit in her husband's name.[29] Crediting men with the family flock reflected the patriarchal values of Superintendent Fryer and his colleagues, not the values of the matricentered Diné.[30] In Fryer's eyes, when a man and a woman ran their flocks together, they became a single economic unit, headed by a man. To his credit, the superintendent followed this logic through the twists and turns of Navajo marital relationships. When a couple divorced, the woman reasserted and regained a recognized autonomy. Even polygamous women who lived apart from their husbands in independent households could gain permits for their flocks.[31] And yet, when a woman shared her hearth with a man, or even with her natal family, she lost an important measure of her autonomy: her independent grazing rights.

As word spread that the registration of sheep heralded a new and dramatic program for reducing livestock, many Diné became defiant.

Resistance flared especially in those districts where large numbers of herds exceeded stingy stock limits.[32] In the northern districts, a handful of stockowners were arrested and sentenced to six months in jail for interfering with the roundup of horses and cattle.[33] The most infamous case involved Hastiin Tso, Mister Big Man, the vice president of the Twin Lakes chapter, who refused to take his sheep to the dipping vat for the official count. To make an example of Big Man, Fryer asked the Navajo Tribal Court to issue a warrant for his arrest. As Big Man stopped in Gallup on his way home from a protest meeting, three Navajo policemen attempted to take him into custody. When he resisted arrest, the officers beat him with blackjacks and a pistol. The tribal court dismissed the case against Big Man, in part because the police had been outside their jurisdiction. Ironically, the brutal beating landed the police themselves in the New Mexico penitentiary for a brief time. The story of the attack, nonetheless, lingered in the minds of Diné as a vivid reminder of the power of the state.[34]

Diné also blamed their leaders for failing them. Tall Woman remembered this era with reluctance and regret. Her husband, Frank Mitchell, a renowned hataałii and a tribal councilman, had been one of the leaders, and "he and the other leaders really took the brunt of it," she recalled. "People were very, very angry and they started saying nasty words to all the leaders, blaming them. Even though Frank explained the order came from Washington, for some reason people blamed him. They even threatened to harm him and his children because of it. Those things worried me greatly." Yet Mitchell himself agreed with the conservationists that overgrazing had nearly denuded much of the land. So "he kept telling us he had to do his job; the People were going to have to listen and obey those instructions. He said if they didn't, the reservation would have no future; the land would never recover and everything would come to an end." Even decades later, she added, "People still talk about the stock reduction and the suffering it caused. In our family, we don't talk about it very much because it brings back the hardships it caused for Frank . . . and others who had to enforce those orders. It wasn't right that people blamed them for causing it; the overgrazing did it. But some of the People couldn't understand that, so they blamed all the leaders, from Washington right on down . . . to the headmen in the local areas."[35] Mitchell ruefully remembered those times, too. He himself received a permit for only ten sheep and two horses, and yet his neighbors accused him and the council, "saying that we had urged the government to reduce their livestock and not ours."[36] Only a few strong Diné men could weather the impending storm.

Resistance grew as officials implemented the new grazing program. In early 1938, supervisors of the various grazing districts began issuing official certificates granting grazing rights, printed on special "safety paper" in government green and stamped with a red seal. Many Diné rejected these outright. Some refused to accept their permits; others burned them in campfires. At Sheep Springs, Diné men allegedly threatened the range riders who distributed them, and in the area around Aneth, men assaulted a range rider and destroyed the detested documents. Range riders and the Navajo police were part of the problem. Often their unnecessarily rough treatment of stockowners sparked violence, and Fryer did little to restrain them.[37] The resistance to the distribution of permits continued to reverberate in the collective memory decades later. It signified a time when Diné mustered the courage to defy the government.

Collier and his most trusted advisors, in fact, anticipated this defiance. In 1936, the forester Robert Marshall warned Collier that "many Navajos will probably exert physically violent opposition" to the plan to level herds. Any confiscation of livestock, he cautioned, would likely require the use of armed force, and "some people will probably be killed." The result? "All your enemies will howl like hell and Congress will make a nasty investigation." To discourage violence and avoid inflicting severe hardship, Marshall urged Collier to purchase all excess livestock at far-above-market prices and to do so somewhat gradually over a period of three years. Nonetheless, he prodded the commissioner to begin without delay. Since 1934, when he had first recommended restraint, the land had become increasingly eroded. Immediate action now appeared necessary to save the range from utter ruin. If Collier failed, the reservation would be "wrecked for centuries," the Navajos would become "in effect, landless," and Boulder Dam would be damaged, costing the government millions and millions of dollars. The result? "All your enemies will howl like hell and Congress will make a nasty investigation of why you permitted the Navajos to destroy their own civilization."[38]

Marshall feared violence, but surprisingly few sparks flared, considering how high emotions ran in these years. Indeed, the most common form of protest was the all-American petition drive. At trading posts, chapter houses, day schools, and ceremonial dances, Diné signed petitions denouncing stock reduction, John Collier, and the entire New Deal. As early as 1937, when the official livestock counts began, men and women—thousands of people altogether—gathered at chapter houses to register their dissent. Most could not write, so they marked these petitions with their thumbprints, which since the early 1900s had replaced the traditional "X" for signing important documents.

We have little to tell us about these protest meetings, but the thumbprints themselves are suggestive. At each chapter house or trading post, more than 40 percent of those who came to convey their displeasure were women. We can imagine these women in their colorful Pendleton blankets as they waited patiently to make their mark. They likely gossiped with one another and discussed the troubles they had feeding themselves and their children ever since John Collier demanded that they give up their goats. At one chapter house, Bah stood with twelve other women, among them Rachel Tsosie, 'Asdzą́ą́ Łtsoii, and Yił Deezbaa'. John W. Goat was next, but then came five more women eager to make their feelings known. This scenario repeated itself again and again as women and men waited their turn to stick their thumbs onto the black pad of ink and express their anger.[39]

Morgan helped organize at least some of these campaigns, apparently in concert with Senator Dennis Chavez, so Fryer and others with the Navajo Service dismissed the petitions out of hand as a political vendetta against Collier and no more. Fryer believed that the Navajos had no idea of what they were signing and that the petitions represented the sentiments of "not more than twenty-four people."[40] It is true that Morgan clearly influenced and perhaps orchestrated these meetings. Yet it was a mistake to disregard the Diné as mere dupes in a political struggle. Several of the preambles to these petitions specified that the people gathered specifically to voice their objections to stock reduction. And in a few locations, women and men offered personal notes attesting to their heartfelt refusal to allow the government to "execute" their horses or take more of their stock. Even though people may have signed after listening to a rousing diatribe against Collier and his New Deal program, their sentiments were no less sincere.

Amidst these protests, in January 1938, the tribal council, pressured by Collier, endorsed the plan to impose grazing limits and remove excess livestock from the reservation. Collier made it clear that the council really had no choice. The secretary of the Interior had issued special grazing regulations for the Navajo Reservation in June 1937. If the Navajos failed to remove

Petitions like this one testify to Diné women's protests against stock reduction. "Bah," found as part of many of the names shown here, means "warrior woman." Courtesy University of New Mexico, Center for Southwest Research, Chavez Papers.

surplus livestock as mandated under those regulations, the BIA would begin enforcing its General Grazing Regulations, adopted long ago for Indian reservations nationwide. Those rules, Collier told the council, would allow each person to run only twelve sheep for free; for additional stock, the bureau would charge a grazing fee. Fryer then explained how the grazing limits would work under the proposed regulations, using an example from a district with relatively high permit levels (and erroneous figures, at that). He stressed that only a fraction of the people—mostly rich stockowners—would be affected at all. The average family need not worry.[41]

When the actual limits became known, Diné were stunned. In District 14, a heavily overgrazed area near the eastern Checkerboard, a family could own no more than 61 SU, including their horses, each of which counted as five units. About one-third of the population, some with as few as thirty-eight sheep and goats, would be forced to reduce their flocks if they kept one horse for each family member. Such low limits were not all that unusual. Three other districts allowed fewer than 90 SU; even the most generous permits, in Districts 3 and 5, authorized only 280. These limits, of course, reflected the amount of available forage and the population of stockowning families. They were low largely because overgrazing had severely damaged easily erodible land or because the soils made grasses lean already. But the low limits came as a staggering shock, nonetheless. Councilman Scott Preston wrote Congressman John Murdock, of Arizona, that the grazing limit in his district was devastating, even though, at 280 SU, it was the highest on the reservation. If a family kept five horses and one cow, that left only 251 sheep, which he argued was "not sufficient for even the bare existence of a moderate size Navajo family without additional income." In principle, Preston agreed with grazing regulations, but families had to be able to eat. How could the Navajos abide a policy that impoverished them?[42]

Diné did not take the impending reduction of their sheep lightly. A delegation from Oljato, Navajo Mountain, and Kayenta raised money to go to Washington, D.C., where they arranged an audience with Eleanor Roosevelt, whom they begged to intervene. One of the delegates, 'Asdzą́ą́ Nez, explained to Roosevelt through an interpreter: "Our sheep are our children, our life and our food." Because of stock reduction, she added, the Diyin Dine'é would send no more rain.[43] Back home on the reservation, when range riders approached John Nez from the Black Mesa area, he reportedly exclaimed, "If you take my sheep you kill me. So kill me now. Let's fight right here and decide this thing."[44] Fryer later claimed that, aside from horses, no one was ever forced to reduce their sheep.[45] The testimony of the Diné tells us otherwise.

Hoping to dampen the expected outcry against renewed reduction, Fryer first targeted horses. Some Diné, especially men, still possessed astonishing numbers of ponies. One man, Arthur Chester, claimed 134 mustangs, and nearly three dozen families kept herds of 30 or more. And those were only the horses people claimed. Still more ran wild through the remote reaches of the reservation. Such numbers struck Fryer as utterly ridiculous. No family, he argued, needed more than a few horses for transportation and farmwork; the rest were "unproductive" and, therefore, worthless.[46]

He and his men, it must be noted, seriously miscalculated the number of necessary horses. Few Diné had automobiles or trucks, so they depended on these animals for travel across rough terrain and as beasts of burden. In placing strict limits on the number a family could own, officials often

Starving horses offered proof of a significantly overgrazed range and became targets of the stock reduction program, leading to defiance and violence in some reservation districts. Photograph by Milton Snow. Records of the BIA, RG75, National Archives at College Park, Md., RG75-NN-5-2.

failed to provide each person with a pony to ride and made no provision for a young man to take his own steed with him when he married.[47] Nor did they consider the important cultural value of horses. For Diné men, large herds signified masculinity and manly prowess. Young men, moreover, gave horses to their brides' families as wedding gifts, representing their future prosperity.

To Fryer and the conservationists, however, those meanings were immaterial. Each horse consumed enough forage for five sheep; if the Navajos just sold their excess ponies, Fryer told the tribal council, there would be little need to eliminate other "productive" livestock. Or so he thought. Truth be told, many horses were so starved that they were nothing but skin and bones.[48] Slaughter may well have been mercy.

Nonetheless, Collier—recalling the goat-reduction debacle—counseled caution as Fryer moved to enforce the limits on horses. A badly implemented program could create a backlash and "handicap a hundred other things," he warned, adding that if large numbers of Navajos resisted, it would be impossible to enforce the regulations, and the conservation program would fail. He thus urged Fryer to cultivate cooperation.[49] Heeding Collier's wise counsel, Fryer initially encouraged Navajos to sell their

MAKING MEMORIES   215

surplus horses voluntarily. He even managed to convince one man—owner of the reservation's third-largest horse herd and, allegedly, the "toughest opponent" of stock reduction—to sell more than fifty horses, in hopes that others would follow his example. But when buyers offered only three dollars, or less, per head, Navajo horsemen balked, parting only with their "cripples and scare-crows."[50]

Frustrated by failure, Fryer decided to replace the carrot with the stick. He would haul into court a handful of those who flouted the grazing regulations and make examples of them. Victory in the courts, he argued, would affirm the authority of the BIA to enforce its grazing regulations and quell calls to resist.[51] Between 1938 and 1941, the government prosecuted at least nineteen cases for grazing violations, involving some thirty-nine men and women. (Although married women were not counted as the owners of record, the government held them equally accountable for excess stock.) Fryer first chose a dozen leading stockowners in three Arizona grazing districts, embracing the Kaibito Plateau, Tuba City, and the Leupp Extension, where resistance had become widespread.[52] Range riders issued grazing permits and, less than a week later, returned with notices ordering permit holders to remove excess horses within ten days.[53] As anticipated—indeed hoped—the bewildered owners refused, and the bureau filed formal complaints in United States District Court.

William Brophy, who drew up the complaints, had little doubt that the courts would uphold Collier's authority. An attorney from Albuquerque, Brophy would later succeed Collier as commissioner of Indian affairs and establish the Indian Land Claims Commission. As he understood the law, the Navajos possessed only the right to occupy the reservation, which was owned by the United States and under the regulatory authority of the secretary of the Interior. Secretary Ickes's signature alone gave the Navajo Grazing Regulations the force of law, but they gained legal vigor, he added, by virtue of the Navajo Tribal Council's stamp of approval. Those who grazed more stock than their permits specified thus engaged in unauthorized use of tribal lands and were guilty of trespass.[54] By this reasoning, each of the Navajo defendants found themselves charged with trespassing on their own land.

On May 13, 1939, the court for the District of Arizona issued a summary judgment in favor of the secretary of the Interior's authority to regulate grazing rights and ordered the defendants to remove their excess horses within thirty days.[55] Fryer followed that decision with the roundup of thousands and thousands of generally emaciated horses across the western part of the reservation. Most were transported to processing plants and turned into dog chow, chicken feed, and glue.[56] But hundreds died of starvation along the way to shipping points or were shot while making a break from the herd. Dead horses lined the trails to the railheads, and the putrid stench of their rotting carcasses permeated the air. This specter, like the wanton slaughter of goats, etched deeply into Diné memory. Indeed, for many, these scenes of dying horses writhing on the ground reprised that earlier round of horse reduction aimed at eradicating dourine in the 1920s. In their stories of this era, the killing of horses formed the leitmotif of livestock reduction.[57]

Fryer next turned his attention to the northern districts. He and his men threatened legal action against dozens of people in Districts 9 and 12, aiming especially at agitators who spoke out against stock reduction or disrupted public meetings. Collier questioned the wisdom of continued legal action, so Brophy wisely dropped a number of the charges for insufficient evidence. But Fryer remained determined to use the courts to browbeat rabble-rousers into submission. Among his targets was Jake Yellowman. He had prevented a range rider from distributing permits and done his utmost to discredit federal authority, but he was by no means a major stockowner. His fourteen horses did exceed the ten-horse limit, but his (or his wife's) small flock of perhaps 112 sheep barely kept the family fed. Kit Seally, a well-known hataałii and tribal councilman with a middling flock of perhaps 450 sheep, was a more suitable target, for he owned a large herd of thirty-three horses. But Seally's more egregious crime, as Fryer made clear, was his leadership in a new organization known as the Navajo Rights Association.[58]

Formed in 1940, the Navajo Rights Association led the resistance against stock reduction through the rest of the decade. It was, for the most part, a moderate group, aside from its adamant opposition to stock reduction and its outspoken position against Fryer's campaign to threaten those who protested with jail. Its spokesman was Deshna Clah Cheschillige, of Shiprock, a former tribal council chairman. In the early 1930s, government officials held him up as an example of a progressive stockman who carefully managed his range through deferred grazing. An intelligent, educated man and a gifted orator, Cheschillige emerged as the voice of disaffected Diné during the 1940s, replacing Jacob Morgan in that capacity. Morgan made an about-face shortly after his own election to the chairmanship of the council in 1938 and generally worked closely with Fryer thereafter.⁵⁹ Cheschillige, too, made an about-face. Once a supporter of the federal conservation program, he became a vociferous critic.

Cheschillige opposed Collier's program to level livestock wealth. Fryer labeled him an opportunist and lumped him with large-scale stockowners, like Chee Dodge, who also became active with the Navajo Rights Association. But Fryer exaggerated.⁶⁰ Cheschillige was not rich—not on Chee Dodge's scale—although his family was certainly well-to-do, with around four hundred sheep and some thirty cattle. Like many Diné, Cheschillige believed that his livestock wealth came with hard work and ceremonial knowledge. He began each day singing prayers to his sheep and horses. "We pray to get rich . . . and have more stock," he once observed. "We don't pray that we might lose our stock and be poor the rest of our lives."⁶¹ Indeed, it seemed as though the government was intent on making him poor. Grazing permits in his district allowed a maximum of only 83 su, only a few dozen more than a typical family would eat in a single year.⁶² Understandably, Cheschillige refused to exchange prosperity for privation without a fight.

As Fryer turned his sights on the northern districts, he found that what the physicists say is true: for every action, there is an equal and opposite reaction. It began, perhaps, at Shiprock, a stronghold for defiant stockowners. In January 1940, as many as five hundred men and women attended a meeting to voice their opposition to horse reduction, and meetings in other parts of District 12 attracted hundreds more. The situation became so heated that Kitty Blackhorse, an opposition leader charged with grazing violations by the Navajo Tribal Court, disrupted the court's proceedings, intimidated the judges, and scrapped with the police before going into hiding. By summer 1941, the air sizzled with tension. A group of fifteen men attacked two range riders and released a herd of captured horses from a holding pen. Within weeks, as government officials issued trespass notices, the people around Aneth, Monument Valley, and Navajo Mountain—the descendants of Hashké Neiniih and Whiteman Killer—threatened armed resistance.⁶³ It seemed that the northern Navajo Reservation was about to explode.

Fryer proceeded to Navajo Mountain, intent on impressing the rebels with the full power of the state. He brought with him a Captain Johnson from Fort Wingate for the "psychological effect an officer's uniform might have." Fryer warned the forty or so men and women who gathered that day that continued refusal to turn over their excess horses would give him "no alternative but to enforce the grazing regulations with the use of police power." In case those listening did not understand the superintendent's threat, the uniformed captain made it plain that they would be sorry if he brought troops in, for the "troops would no doubt shoot any horses that they couldn't round up."[64] Those words surely angered his listeners, but they also, no doubt, chilled them down to their toes. When the army last marched through Diné Bikéyah and herded people off to Hwéeldi, Navajo Mountain had been a refuge. It seemed a refuge no more.

Fryer assured Collier that he really had no intention of calling in troops; nonetheless, his saber rattling proved effective. A few days later, the Navajo Mountain rebels brought in their horses for branding. This scene repeated itself in Shiprock and Teec Nos Pos. Fryer and his men threatened belligerents with jail, then made peace by promising leniency in exchange for cooperation.[65] In each case, this tactic brought grudging compliance, although the Navajo Rights Association continued to try to stir up crowds. As a measure of Fryer's victory, in early fall, the anthropologist Solon Kimball reported that even the holdouts at Navajo Mountain now accepted stock reduction and pledged to "go along with the government."[66] Kimball confused coercion with cooperation. Nonetheless, the strength of the resistance was broken.

The uprising in the northern districts troubled Collier, who finally began to doubt Fryer's leadership. In fall 1941, he asked William Zeh and Frank Lenzie, both veterans of the goat reduction debacle, to make an independent investigation of Navajo opinion in hopes of finding an alternative to Fryer's high-handed approach. "I have an instinct," he confided, "that were I able to go out there for a period of weeks" and live among the Navajos, "I might discover some possible improvement—something which would save the range and yet be less implacable, less emotionally hard on the Navajos than the existent plan." The bitter battles against the grazing permits made him realize, apparently for the first time, that "a violation of deep sentiments may be taking place." He at long last acknowledged that, with limited flocks, Navajo families could no longer pass sheep on to daughters and sons without risking their own survival. And so he asked Zeh and Lenzie whether they might devise a new permit system that would "take into account the Navajo tradition of descent, and the ambitions of the coming-of-age group."[67] At long last, Collier seemed to grasp that the Navajos might have legitimate reasons for resisting stock reduction.

A cascade of events in 1941 brought a period of calm to the reservation. Light snow and abundant yet gentle rainfall came, producing exceptionally rich forage, better than anyone had seen in a long, long time. This gave Collier the cover he needed to relax regulations, create more flexibility for expanding families, and thereby quiet the opposition.[68] With Collier's encouragement, the Navajo Tribal Council passed a resolution to issue special temporary permits that year, allowing qualified stockowners who had not yet reduced their flocks to retain up to 350 head.[69] To qualify, an owner had to brand his or her horses and dispose of all stock exceeding the new limit, not only horses, but also sheep and goats. These special permits, in effect, rewarded people with relatively middling herds who had yet to comply fully with grazing regulations. Those with fewer than 350 SU but more than allowed on their existing permit got special permits for the number they owned, and no more. At the same time, a person with more than 350 SU had to make an immediate reduction to take advantage of the special permit, or the old grazing rules would be enforced.[70]

The announcement of these relaxed restrictions relieved much of the tension on the reservation, and most of the larger stockowners slowly complied with their permits. Some took the opportunity to sell stock on the booming livestock market occasioned by the buildup to war. Others distributed some of their sheep to poorer relatives with room on their permits. Still others leased grazing land off the reservation.[71] A tribal enterprise, the Many Farms Cannery, purchased thousands and thousands of sheep and goats, which Diné women then turned into canned stew.[72] Voluntary livestock sales during the war, compulsion to comply with the new grazing permits (which officials called "adjustment," in a move away from the despised term "reduction"), and the consumption of mutton by families brought a continual decline in the numbers of livestock grazing the range. By 1944, in all but six districts where resistance to reduction remained strong, the numbers of livestock were down to the calculated carrying capacity. Two years later, overall stock numbers dropped well below the official capacity, to fewer than 450,140 SU, and the range—at least in some areas—appeared to be recovering.[73]

Or so it seemed. In 1948, a range examiner reported that the reservation's carrying capacity had continued to decline, even as livestock reduction impoverished Navajos. The tall grasses in 1941 and 1942 had encouraged an optimism that the crisis had passed, that the range was finally recuperating. On the contrary, a new range survey, though limited in scope, suggested that the carrying capacity had declined by 30 percent in ten years, to just over 359,000 SU.⁷⁴ The structure of plant communities, continually shifting in response to rain and drought, grazing pressure, dropping water tables, changes in nutrient levels and soil conditions, invasive vegetation, and other ecological variables, apparently crossed a threshold from which the land never recovered.⁷⁵

Nonetheless, America's entry into World War II marked the beginning of the end of stock reduction and any meaningful regulation of grazing on the Navajo Reservation. Frustrated that Fryer had bungled the horse reduction program, Collier took advantage of the national emergency after the bombing of Pearl Harbor and released him to oversee the organization of Japanese relocation camps. James Stewart, who took Fryer's place, continued to vigorously enforce grazing permits in overstocked districts. Around Teec Nos Pos, violent resistance occurred in two or more separate incidents in 1945, in which angry stockowners, including at least one woman, bound and beat government officials. Yet Stewart also proved more flexible than Fryer. The special limit of 350 SU was to have been only a temporary eight-month reprieve, after which the maximum number was to drop to 300. But to preserve the overall spirit of cooperation that had ensued since issuing these permits, Stewart extended them for another year.⁷⁶

The summer of 1943 opened a new chapter in range management on the Navajo Reservation. That spring, Stewart had issued instructions to begin enforcing the regular permits in all but six districts. The tribal council, chaired by Chee Dodge, countered by passing a series of resolutions that essentially repudiated stock reduction and much of the conservation program. It voted to extend the special permits indefinitely, allow small-scale owners to exceed their permits, and open demonstration areas to unrestricted grazing.⁷⁷ One Diné woman was so moved by the council's courage that she asked to speak before the vote. Congratulating the delegates, she exulted, "I have always wanted our Navajo people to come together and unite[,] and today I believe they have done so."⁷⁸ When Collier took office, the Diné lacked a strong political organization; now they proved united against New Deal conservation. The council's resolutions, however, did not signal immediate victory. At Stewart's urging, Collier vetoed this legislation, and the superintendent continued to enforce the more restrictive permits throughout most of the reservation.⁷⁹ But Collier did not have the last word.

In September of that year, Felix Cohen, the associate solicitor at the Department of the Interior, issued an opinion on the legality of the continued enforcement of grazing limits, in light of the council's actions. A proponent of native sovereignty, Cohen soon became widely recognized as the leading authority on Indian law. The Navajo grazing regulations, he argued, rested on the consent of the council, which had in essence withdrawn that consent. The BIA could continue to discourage large herds under the General Grazing Regulations, which pertained to all Indian reservations. But, in his opinion, the bureau had lost its authority to prevent Navajos with few or no sheep from building their flocks, as long as they did not exceed their fair share of carrying capacity. Four years later, Lee Muck, the assistant to the secretary of the Interior in charge of land utilization, declared that stocking limits that froze small flocks and kept families in perpetual poverty were immoral and of doubtful legality. On his recommendation, the new Interior secretary Julius Krug terminated the stock reduction program and even initiated a restocking policy.[80]

By the late 1940s, the tribal council felt emboldened to take charge of grazing management and, in a series of resolutions, effectively suspended stock limits, which the BIA thus stopped enforcing.[81] Soon, in 1947, BIA personnel questioned the legality of conferring grazing rights only to men, so the agency quietly began to follow Navajo custom and allow women to hold permits in their own name, making their de facto ownership more secure.[82] The council passed its own rules in 1956 and established local grazing committees to administer the conservation program.[83] Under tribal administration, stock numbers began to climb slowly, although they never approach those of the early 1930s (table 2).

Diné defiance brought an end to stock reduction and the enforcement of grazing restrictions. The resistance included not only famous leaders such as Jacob Morgan and Deshna Clah Cheschillige, but also the countless women and men who stood in line to express their thoughts with their thumbs. This rebellion against Collier's conservation program would live on in collective memory. As grandmothers and grandfathers passed down their stories to their grandchildren, few would recall Collier's work to lay the foundation for native nationalism, preserve religious freedom, protect allottees on the Checkerboard, or even open up wells. Instead, they would reflect on the days when they had lots of sheep and curse Collier for destroying their pastoral way of life.

TABLE 2 Navajo Livestock Census, Navajo Reservation 1945–54

Year	Sheep	Goats	Horses	Cattle	Sheep Units
1945	284,224	32,597	26,155	7,391	477,160
1946	257,286	29,202	26,506	7,500	449,018
1947–50	n.a.	n.a.	n.a.	n.a.	n.a.
1951	234,619	39,014	27,439	9,205	447,648
1952	220,476	41,997	27,802	8,847	436,871
1953	233,109	45,196	27,309	9,997	454,838
1954	252,261	52,678	26,972	11,149	484,395

SOURCE: Muck Report; Young, *Navajo Yearbook*, 1961, p. 167.

Listen to the words of one woman who "wept bitterly" as she spilled her heart to sociologist Floyd Pollock in 1940:

> The last eight years we have seen nothing but trouble.... We have six children and can barely get enough for them to eat, and we are better off than many.... Eight years ago we had our sheep and were so happy and we knew we could give our children what they needed. Collier is at the bottom of all our trouble. Many of us are now paupers.... This may sound awful for me to say, but I really hate John Collier.... When I think of what he has done to us, I realize that I could even kill him myself just like I could kill a mad dog. I don't like to feel about anyone the way I feel toward John Collier, but he has ruined our home, our lives, and our children, and I will hate him until the day I die.[84]

Collier promised the Navajos self-determination, but instead he hobbled them, economically and emotionally. Certainly, he had the best of intentions when he launched his most ambitious New Deal program. Since the early 1900s, men such as Anselm Weber and William Zeh, both of whom cared deeply about the welfare of the Navajos, had expressed growing concern about the condition of the range. Now, at last, the election of Franklin Roosevelt brought about a happy convergence: a compassionate, conservation-minded commissioner of Indian affairs, a new, energetic Soil Conservation Service, and enough New Deal funding to make a difference. Livestock, drought, and arroyo-cutting rains gnawed the land. As Collier grasped this serious threat, he felt an almost messianic impulse to act quickly before the area became another Dust Bowl. Adding to his sense of urgency was the sudden availability of federal conservation funds, which he rightly feared might soon evaporate.[85] Collier intended to save Navajo life, both literally and culturally, by saving Navajo land. And yet, as the old adage goes, the road to hell is paved with good intentions.

The suspension of grazing regulations and the assumption of responsibility for range management by the Navajo Tribal Council coincided with one of the worst droughts since the 1500s. Between 1951 and 1959, Navajo Country and much of the nation saw little rain, far less than in the 1930s.[86] Unfortunately for the land, the numbers of sheep, goats, and especially cattle crept up, while drought-stricken forage died out.[87] In 1957, herds once again surpassed the "official" carrying capacity of the range (a standard that was, according to range specialists, too high), and they continued to grow.

By then, few Diné families supported themselves with sheep or goats. Even by the mid-1940s, only about five hundred families had even subsistence or middling flocks of 150–300 sheep; a couple dozen had more. The vast majority of those with permits—about four thousand families—had fewer than fifty sheep. Another twenty-five hundred had none at all. Many Diné, to be sure, worked hard to rebuild their flocks, holding back their productive ewes and lambs from slaughter or sale, just as they had after their return from Hwéeldi.[88] Others looked to the future with despair. According to councilman Tseche Notah, the people felt bewildered, panicky, and disheartened. "Many of the people have lost their ambition and pride," he confided in 1940. "Every day I hear people say, 'What's the use? What's the use of trying to do anything?'"[89]

Some sought solace for their despondence and destitution by turning to drink, others to faith. Especially in border towns and in communities along the reservation's margins, drunkenness became a scourge, bringing with it a high incidence of violence and neglect.[90] At the same time, the temperance-oriented Native American Church, often labeled the Peyote Religion for its sacramental use of the spineless cactus buttons, gained a large following, especially in eastern districts hit hard by stock reduction. In the 1950s, about half of the people in two eastern districts followed this syncretic faith, which wove Christianity with native rituals.[91] Participation in the Native American Church and other Christian sects did not necessarily mean abandoning traditional beliefs and ceremonies.[92] And yet some Diné feared that continued erosion signaled that the people were forgetting the proper way to perform their rituals, that they were forgetting how to sing the songs that could restore hózhǫ́.[93]

For a brief time, World War II brought respite from the suffering of stock reduction. Hundreds of Diné men and women, including the celebrated Code Talkers, joined the armed forces. Hundreds more found employment at the Fort Wingate Ordnance Depot near Gallup and at the Navajo Ordnance Depot near Flagstaff, and thousands left the reservation to work in defense-related industries in Phoenix, Albuquerque, Denver, and Los Angeles.[94] Whether serving in uniform or on the factory floor, these workers sent most of their wages home, helping their families to make a living. Many received a bitter homecoming. They returned only to find that while they were off winning the war, their permits had been canceled and their flocks reduced to nothing.[95]

Poverty became pervasive after the war. Per capita income for the Diné was only $82 per year; the average American made fourteen times more. Most of that income came from wages and payments to war veterans, accounting for nearly 70 percent of the total. Sales of livestock, wool, and weavings amounted to only 26 percent. These figures, to be sure, ignore the mutton, goat meat, beef, goat milk, and wool that people consumed at home, but families with fewer than one hundred sheep had to be frugal or risk literally eating up their flocks. Many became increasingly dependent on goods they bought on credit at the trading post. According to the anthropologist William Adams, traders nurtured Navajo dependency. Adams should know. He grew up on the reservation during the 1930s and studied the workings of trading posts while briefly running one at Shonto in the mid-1950s. He observed that after the war, traders extended credit in anticipation of not only future lamb and wool sales but also future payroll, unemployment, and welfare checks, which they cashed only after deducting their due. Since merchants also functioned as the local postmasters, some held back checks until their predictable value and the payee's credit account matched.[96] Many families, thus, became trapped in a cycle of debt.

Those who did find wage-earning employment were generally men, who emerged as a new Navajo working class. Some herded stock for local Hispanic and Mormon ranchers. Others cobbled together seasonal jobs harvesting and packing beets, cotton, carrots, and other crops in Arizona, Colorado, California, and Utah. They worked for the railroads, maintaining tracks. They labored in coal mines and, later, uranium mines, both on and off the reservation. In later years, some even obtained well-paid, union jobs at the coal-fired generating stations built on the reservation near Page, Arizona, and Shiprock, New Mexico. It would seem that the entry of these men into distant capitalist markets would pull their communities apart. And yet, familial and ritual obligations continually drew the men back home. As the historian Colleen O'Neill observes, they insisted on "working the Navajo way." Echoing the mobility of seasonal transhumance between summer and winter ranges, they divided their time between distant jobs and sojourns home to shear sheep, chop wood, plant and harvest corn, attend rodeos and ceremonies, and in myriad ways participate in the lives of their families and communities.[97]

Men's paychecks often gave them increased power over household decision-making, especially in families without sheep, where women suddenly found themselves economically dependent on men. Following Diné custom, earnings remained the sole property of the worker, to keep or share as he or she saw fit. Most men, to be sure, worked hard to support and care for their families. But some women now bristled at having to ask their husbands for money.[98] It hurt their self-esteem and made them feel vulnerable. As one woman complained to the ethnographer Laila Shukry, "You know, when we had lots of sheep, we don't care when the husband go away and don't send no money. We butcher sheep and sell lamb. We make rugs and have money that way." But because of stock reduction, "we don't have no sheeps now."[99] And too many men squandered their paychecks in bars or on cars, rather than bringing their hard-earned cash home. This was particularly true on the periphery of the reservation, in border towns, where young couples moved away from their extended families to enter the wage economy, and in Fruitland, a BIA experiment in irrigated farming, where insufficient acreage forced most of the men to work for wages in Farmington, Shiprock, and elsewhere. Even when families continued to raise stock, the balance seemed to shift. Between the mid-1950s and the 1970s, the number of cattle nearly quadrupled, while the number of sheep and goats inched up by only 12 percent.[100] Since men owned most (though not all) of the cattle, their livestock wealth increased, while that of women stagnated.

And yet, the story of Diné women does not fit the expected declension narrative. They did not "lose status," as some would have it.[101] In the heart of Diné Bikéyah, women retained their influential position within communities that remained largely matricentered. With men often away at distant jobs, wives, mothers, daughters, and sisters held their families and communities together, caring for their children and elderly parents, herding flocks, tending farms, and weaving for the trading post.[102] Even when men were at home, women retained a good measure of autonomy, as long as they kept at least a small flock of sheep or goats. The family matriarch continued to organize the daily herding. And weavers continued to make the difference between want and plenty, just as they had in the old livestock economy, because they could trade their textiles for groceries year-round, even when men's seasonal work slacked off.[103]

Nonetheless, dwindling flocks diminished women's claims to land, and conflicts between neighbors and kin escalated. Grazing regulations encouraged people to hoard access to specific ranges and water sources. Whereas Diné once shared their matrilineal lands with visiting kin during times of need, now they treated them as trespassers.[104] This was particularly true in the Checkerboard, where stockowners fenced lands and paid grazing fees under the Taylor Grazing Act.[105] Even on the reservation, observed George Blueeyes, a hataałii from Rock Point, people started shouting "'This is my land!! Not yours!! Go away, back where you came from!!!' Everybody began to say that."[106] Quarrels over land divided families, friends, and neighbors, aggravated by accusations that grazing committee members favored their own kinsfolk in settling land-use disputes.[107]

Grazing regulations and stock reduction wreaked havoc throughout Diné Bikéyah. They rapidly transformed Diné life, much as the Dawes Act transformed the lives of native peoples elsewhere in the early twentieth century. Stock reduction subverted the acclaimed self-sufficiency of the Diné, destroying their pride and their sense of security. And yet it failed to resuscitate the range.

EPILOGUE

A View from the Defiance Plateau

In the summer of 1997, I returned to the luminous red rock mesas and canyons of the Navajo Nation. As I headed toward Window Rock in the dead of night, flashes of lightning streaked across the sky, and a torrential downpour, *níłtsą́ bikąʼ*, made for a nerve-wracking drive. That summer received gloriously plentiful rainfall—the most on record, the local newspaper exaggerated.[1] When I set out the next morning, I could not believe my eyes. What a difference rain can make! Where in the previous drought year I had seen only naked ground, now verdant grasses grew thigh-high. Indeed, for the first time in my experience in Navajo Country, I viewed a pastoral scene, in all its connotations. Indian ricegrass, especially, but also western wheat and galleta waved in the breeze; even blue grama had begun to inch its way across the land. For a brief moment, it seemed that perhaps last year's dull, dead landscape could simply be blamed on drought, just as many Navajos had claimed.

But a closer look revealed troubling signs that all was not well. On the Defiance Plateau, the grasses spread out thinly under the trees, and much of it was closely clipped already. Even more disquieting, snakeweed, three-awn grass, cheatgrass, and Russian thistle—all of which spread with overgrazing—dominated vast areas of the Navajo range.[2] Their verdure carpeted the land, but tricked the eye. In fact, the abundant vegetation, more than the denuded ground I had seen before, proved just how much livestock had hammered the land.

Clearly, the New Deal program to save a rapidly eroding land through stock reduction and scientific range management had failed. Its focus on soil conservation regardless of the human cost left the once independent Diné impoverished and dependent on trading-post credit, federal largess, and whatever wage work they could find. At the same time, erosion continued largely unabated. Torrential rains churned silt through networks of arroyos and down through the watershed of the Colorado River. Grasses thinned, and aggressive, noxious plants spread like, well, weeds. With greater aridity came a whole new ecosystem of plants that tolerated hotter, drier soils.[3]

Compounding these problems were other changes. Stockowners no longer managed their herds as they once did. District boundaries, coupled with the construction of permanent cinder-block houses, discouraged families from moving their flocks as frequently or as far as they did before.[4] Worse yet, as children went off to school and no longer served as herders, some families ceased to tend to their flocks at all and let them run loose. Others replaced sheep with cattle, which they allowed to range freely. As traditional livestock husbandry broke down, overgrazing intensified.[5] But the Navajos were not the only ones at fault. In the 1950s, BIA conservationists ripped out large sections of sagebrush under the mistaken assumption that the brush had replaced former grasslands. They sowed grass seed in these areas, too, but unaccompanied by rain, their folly, at least in some areas, exposed newly naked ground to the summer sun and howling winds.[6]

Bare ground all across the reservation opened the door to the highly adaptable Eurasian colonizer, downy brome, which probably hitched a ride to the Colorado Plateau in bags of agricultural seed. Easily identifiable by its reddish-purple color, this invader vanquishes native grasses. Its winning strategy is its contrary growth cycle. When natives go dormant in fall, downy brome germinates; it grows throughout winter and produces abundant seed in spring. Then, just as native seedlings begin to sprout, the intruder's extensive, well-developed root system steals their water (hence its nickname, cheatgrass). The deathblow comes, ironically, when cheatgrass dies in mid-summer. It burns readily, but unlike the natives, which perish, it thrives on flames, spreading ever more rapidly and fueling new cycles of fire that eventually consume all other grasses, forbs, and shrubs.[7]

Although cheatgrass first appeared on the Colorado Plateau in the 1920s, it apparently did not colonize the reservation until, perhaps, the late 1950s, for none of the New Deal range examiners ever recorded it in their inventories. By the 1980s, it dominated some areas of Navajo Country.[8]

No doubt, the land was in terrible shape when the New Dealers arrived, but it's important to remember that the Navajos were not the only ones who overgrazed the western range. Some of the most ravaged rangelands lay well outside Navajo Country. Euro-American cattlemen and sheepmen, the West's preeminent pastoralists, had overgrazed more than two-thirds of the public domain and half of their privately owned ranch lands by the 1930s.[9] Cheatgrass colonized this trampled terrain so rapidly, the conservationist Aldo Leopold once observed, that "one simply woke up one fine spring to find the range dominated by a new weed."[10] Today, cheatgrass carpets more than 100 million acres of the Intermountain West, a testament to widespread overgrazing. It's not that the region is simply unsuitable for livestock. Examples of well-managed ranches rich in biodiversity and replete with tall, vigorous grasses can be found throughout the arid West. And yet much of the West's public lands have been laid waste without any help from Navajos.[11]

It's also important to note that the Diné were enormously successful pastoralists for quite some time. Over three generations, between 1870 and 1930, the number of sheep and goats exploded from more than thirty-six thousand to roughly three-quarters of a million. Such fecundity, even if supplemented by purchase or theft, attests to the long-term availability of abundant grasses and browse. Diné found fresh forage by expanding across a vast part of the Colorado Plateau and by managing the range with transhumance. A diet rich in animal protein, moreover, may well have fed the astonishing fivefold increase in the Diné population over the same period, one of the great demographic success stories in the otherwise dismal history of Native America.

That very success, unfortunately, led to overgrazing. While the human and sheep populations increased exponentially during the half century after the return from Hwéeldi, the available range grew steadily smaller, penned in on all sides by Anglo and Hispanic ranchers. Competition from outsiders eroded and eliminated access to the lush grasses around the Little Colorado River, the San Francisco Peaks, and the Zuni Mountains, as well as seasonal grazing areas in southern Utah and much of the southern and eastern Checkerboard. Swelling flocks on shrinking ranges coincided with a period of climate change in the early twentieth century: severe drought followed by pounding thunderstorms. The result was devastating. Collier and the conservationists rightly believed that the number of stock had to be adjusted to the declining forage, or the land would grow increasingly barren.

And yet the scientists and technicians who came to the Navajo Reservation mistakenly understood range conservation as merely an ecological issue involving animals and land. They viewed the problem, in essence, as a mathematical calculation. A sharp and rapid decrease in the numbers of sheep, goats, and horses would trigger an increase in plants, restoring equilibrium. Once conservationists brought land and animals back into balance and instituted scientific herding practices, the range would heal itself, although, as they believed, it might take as many as fifty years.[12]

But it was not so simple as that. The conservationists never quite grasped the human dimensions of their ecological project. To the extent that they thought about the "human problem," they viewed it as chiefly economic. Stock reduction meant that Navajo shepherds would need to learn to support themselves with far fewer sheep, so New Deal programs focused on developing more efficient, market-oriented ranchers, cast in a masculinized Western mold. Modern ranching methods and improved livestock breeds promised to increase the marketability of lambs, put more meat on the bones of full-grown sheep, raise the quality and productivity of wool, and thereby increase the income derived from each "animal unit."[13] Those who could no longer make a living as ranchers, so the New Dealers thought, might be directed toward some other pursuit, such as irrigated farming or wage work beyond the reservation.

This purely economic picture of pastoralism ignored the myriad ways in which livestock intertwined with nearly every aspect of Diné culture. Since time out of memory, Diné had viewed domestic stock, especially sheep, as essential to their identity as a people. Sheep, goats, and horses were Changing Woman's most precious gift to the Diné. They offered sustenance and a medium of exchange. More than that, they promoted prestige and social stratification, helped integrate kin through networks of obligation and reciprocity, and amplified women's autonomy and authority within matricentered communities. Livestock formed the warp upon which the Diné wove their cultural fabric.

John Collier only belatedly, and imperfectly, comprehended the meanings livestock held for Diné, and he never fully fathomed long-established

John Collier (*standing, far right*) speaks at a Navajo Tribal Council meeting in July 1943, with Paul Jones (*center*), interpreting. Photograph probably by Milton Snow. Records of the BIA, RG75, National Archives at College Park, Md., RG75-CP-Nav-109.

patterns of stock ownership, blinded in part by a masculinized notion of ranching. It is not trivial that he and the conservationists always spoke of the Navajo pastoralist using the male pronoun; stockowners were sheep-*men*, even though the commissioner was well aware that Navajo women owned their own sizeable herds. By controlling their means of production and having unmediated access to matrilineal grazing land, women enjoyed economic autonomy and stood at the center of a distinctive social landscape in which their opinions mattered. When conservationists imposed measures to reduce stock without even consulting these women, they provoked a resistance that would, in the long run, lay waste to the land.

 Ignoring women was a major mistake, but that wasn't Collier's only blunder. Hubris led the romantic reformer to think he knew Navajos far better than he did. He admired their cultural traditions and their artistry. He appreciated their ceremonial practices and their spiritual life, at least in the abstract. But he never comprehended their cultural conceptions of nature, which struck him and his colleagues as quaint folklore. Modern ecological science alone understood the workings of nature and it alone could heal the deteriorating range. Collier had little doubt that the Navajos, whom he considered intelligent and adaptive, would soon grasp the wisdom of the conservation program, or at least follow his lead, and voluntarily, if reluctantly, reduce their herds. When they refused, he blamed a changing cast of male political adversaries and dug in his heels.

Collier's authoritarian approach to stock reduction reinforced among the Diné a deep distrust of the federal government that continues to reverberate today. Those who lived through those years recall the coercive power of the state, and they do so with a profound sense of betrayal. For decades, the government had encouraged the Navajos to build their flocks, and then that very same government perversely punished them for their success. Many likened the experience to their parents' and grandparents' captivity at Hwéeldi. Those two electrifying events, even now, mark the long chronology of Diné history, much as the Civil War, the Great Depression, and World War II mark the history of the United States. In Diné stories, both were attempts at cultural genocide.

The story of stock reduction is a tragedy of classical proportions. But was it inevitable? Looking back, some conservationists held that stock reduction was necessary, and that the cultural turmoil was unfortunate, yet unavoidable. E. R. Fryer maintained that the cultural chasm extending between ecologists and "primitive," prescientific Navajos proved virtually impossible to bridge. Taking a somewhat different view, the ethnographer Edward Spicer, who analyzed the program in a textbook on applied anthropology in 1952, concluded that language barriers, the pressure to act quickly while conservation funds were available, the absence of a Navajo tradition of representative government, and the reluctance of administrators to tap into grassroots systems of leadership made conflict all but inevitable.[14] This theme of inevitability has pervaded most scholarly analyses of stock reduction.

Other observers were not so sure. In the years immediately after Collier was ousted in 1945, most of those who weighed in sharply criticized government coercion as counterproductive. Elizabeth Clark, who investigated reservation conditions for the Home Missions Council of North America, pointed out that conservationists in other parts of the country had been forced to win the cooperation of ranchers and farmers to regulate grazing and control erosion. But, of course, those men were independent, white citizens. On the Navajo Reservation, federal authorities acted dictatorially *because they could*, which naturally provoked resistance.[15] Lee

Muck, with the Department of the Interior, placed the blame squarely on Fryer for imperiously implementing an unreasonable—and in his view, unlawful—permit system. "A policy of sympathetic cooperation," rather than force, he believed, would have been far more effective.[16] The ethnographer Solon Kimball agreed. Fryer's unilateral administration, he wrote, subverted the professed goal of self-government. As an employee of the Navajo Service, Kimball had proposed an alternative approach—creating cooperative conservation plans in concert with the leaders of local communities—that Fryer scuttled. Such a program of *"joint responsibility and participation,"* Kimball argued, would have met less resistance, and importantly, would have allowed Navajos to learn from their mistakes.[17]

A truly cooperative conservation program would not have been easily achieved, Kimball admitted. The obstacles were not, as Fryer thought, Navajo "primitiveness," obstinacy, or malevolence, or even differences in language. The problem was a fundamental "conceptual contrast," which made agreement between Navajos and New Dealers nearly impossible. The federal conservation program had been rooted in experimental science and law, while the Navajos' response had been rooted in the "obligations between generations," that is, the duty of parents to give each of their children a foundation flock, and the "sanctions deeply embedded in a spiritualized universe." In this analysis, Kimball echoed Fryer, and yet he did not believe the chasm was unbridgeable. Negotiating a middle course between these two different cultural ways of knowing was complicated by asymmetrical power. "There was no apparent common meeting ground," Kimball reflected, "except that of political maneuvering in a game in which the government seemed to hold the winning hand and to call the play."[18]

In his memoirs, Collier, too, looked back on that era with a critical eye. He did not engage in self-flagellation, but he did reproach himself for failing to uphold the ideals he professed. To be sure, he could not bring himself to own up to all his sins. He rationalized that he had only carried out the Navajo Tribal Council's resolutions, denying the facts that he had coerced the councilmen to approve *his* policies and that he rarely took their advice. Nonetheless, he conceded that his decision to work through the council, rather than through local communities, may have been a profound error. He might have taken a slower approach, as some on his staff urged him to do, educating local groups through discussion and demonstration, and vesting responsibility for developing and implementing conservation plans in local headmen and hataałii. He had rejected that path as impractical. But now, with the wisdom of hindsight, he realized the gravity of his mistake. Working with local land-use communities, he reflected, the Navajo Service "might have remade itself into an anthropologically realistic, democratic, and grass-rooted co-partnership with the Navajos." His dismissal of that approach, he now knew, coupled with the sometimes authoritarian ethos of his administrators, whose air of scientific superiority nettled Navajos, cost the government and the Navajos dearly.[19]

Most important, Collier now admitted that his program had focused too much on soil and not enough on Navajos. He grievously erred, he now believed, in his failure to fully address the broader cultural, spiritual, and psychological dimensions of Navajo pastoralism. He had not then understood that science and technology were only a small part of the conservation equation. Most important were the people involved, and yet the BIA had been, and remained, he wrote, oblivious to the organization of Navajo society and the "Navajo mind." Perhaps he would have failed to gain the trust and cooperation of the Navajos in any event. But the truth was, he confessed, he had never really tried.[20]

Even if Collier *had* tried, conserving the Navajo range while preserving Navajo life was a particularly thorny problem with no simple solution. Navajos did not own an extravagant number of sheep and goats, considering the number of mouths to feed. As the number of families rose from perhaps 2,000 to 10,000 between 1870 and 1930, the number of livestock necessarily had to increase just to sustain them. In fact, if all of the families with livestock in 1937 maintained small flocks of 125 animals, just enough for survival, they would have had 867,000 sheep and goats, about 100,000 more than they actually owned when Collier arrived. So, putting aside, for the moment, the inequities between rich and poor, neither the size of Navajo flocks nor the total number of animals was unreasonable, given the population. Nor was the problem really the fault of the rich. If every prosperous stockowner enumerated in 1937 had eliminated all but 500 sheep and goats (or their equivalent in horses and cattle)—that is, if everyone retained only a middling flock—the result would have been about 38,000 fewer animals, a fraction of the 200,000 the conservationists thought they needed to remove from the reservation. The real issue, as historian Richard White has pointed out, was not too much stock, but too little land for a growing population of small-scale pastoralists. Nor were there any real economic alternatives, other than oil-drilling and mining, which in turn created a constellation of new, sometimes deadly, environmental consequences.[21] Even if, say, farming had been a viable economic alternative, the cultural value of sheep, goats, and horses would have made stock reduction challenging.

Navajo intransigence made it all the more difficult. Understandably, most refused to accept poverty and cultural privation as the price of erosion control. But many Navajos spent the 1930s in deep denial, refusing even to acknowledge that the land was eroding, the grasses thinning, the weeds invading, and the arroyos deepening. Certainly not all refused to see. A number of Diné leaders—Jim Shirley, Tom Dodge, Robert Martin, Sam Ahkeah—admitted at one time or another that overgrazing was obvious.[22] Grey Eyes, a Diné man from around Rough Rock, told Kimball that "we call the earth our mother and we have never taken care of her. Look how raggedy she has become. . . . Look at the grass which has been almost destroyed by our sheep, horses and cattle."[23] His observation, however, was the exception. And the first step to solving a problem is admitting you have one.

Many Diné concluded that stock reduction itself devastated the range. According to traditional Diné epistemology, thought and speech create physical reality; thus, the constant talk of desolate lands, the conflicts over livestock, and the disputes about ranges produced the disharmony and disorder known as hóchxǫ́, which manifested itself in increased aridity and unabated erosion. Blessingway, moreover, teaches that horses and sheep created the vegetated landscape, so some Diné maintain that the removal of stock itself depleted the grasslands. Still others hold that the cruel and wasteful slaughter of goats and horses angered the Diyin Diné'é. And so the rain disappeared and the land was laid waste.[24]

Some skeptics might argue that Navajo epistemology and spiritual beliefs lay at the root of their troubles. Just as the biblical scripture giving man "dominion over the fish of the seas, over the birds of the sky, and over every living thing that moves on the earth" encourages some Christian believers to rapaciously exploit natural resources, so too—as this argument goes—did Navajos allow themselves to overgraze, convinced that the presence of sheep, in itself, would vivify vegetation.[25] And just as the Southern Cheyennes overhunted bison, secure in their belief that infinite numbers of the large herbivores would emerge supernaturally each spring from the ground of the Llano Estacado, so too did the Navajos have faith they could renew the earth through ceremony.[26] Certainly, many Navajos believe in the power of ceremony alone to restore hózhǫ́. Nonetheless, I am not convinced that faith precluded pragmatic problem-solving. Hataałii Frank Mitchell, a man who spent his entire adult life as a Blessingway singer, recognized that the land was overgrazed and consented to serve on his local grazing committee, despite the animosity of his neighbors.[27] If Mitchell could simultaneously believe in the efficacy of Blessingway and the responsibility of Diné to revitalize their range through stock reduction, it seems unlikely that traditional spiritual teachings stood in the way of good stewardship. Indeed, as Milford Muskett, a Diné scholar of environmental ethics, has pointed out, the central message of Blessingway is to treat the earth with humility and respect and to maintain a relationship with nature that exemplifies hózhǫ́.[28] Whether people act according to their beliefs is a different story.

To the extent that Navajo faith in ceremony complicated conservation efforts, so too did New Deal belief in the doctrine of carrying capacity. Ideally, carrying capacity refers to the number of animals the land will support without permanent injury in the worst year, a principle that ecologists refer to as "Liebig's law of the minimum."[29] In reality, William McGinnies, who oversaw the range management program, based his estimate of carrying capacity on an "average" year. That meant that an especially dry year would surely result in overgrazing, even if the number of stock matched the official "carrying capacity." And he was optimistic in more ways than one. His calculations included areas without stock water, under the assumption that many more wells would be drilled and stock tanks added than funds allowed. Thus, the so-called carrying capacity was somewhat wishful thinking.[30] He also tended to act as though it were a stable number, even though he knew full well that the capacity in a given year fluctuates with dynamic changes in climate, forage, and soil quality.[31] The effects of these assumptions became clear during the deep drought of the 1950s, when "understocked" areas declined drastically, perhaps permanently.[32] McGinnies did not make these mistakes out of stupidity, but out of his desire to minimize the adverse effects of stock reduction, from both a political and a humanitarian perspective.

The number of animals the range will actually carry, as McGinnies knew, is not simply a mathematical formula; it depends on how animals are managed. The official carrying capacity assumed not only an optimum distribution of stock tanks, but also scientific management, especially rotational grazing and deferred grazing in spring, when new growth could lure shepherds to higher elevations before grasses were sufficiently tall.[33]

The SCS intended to teach Navajos the virtues of these practices through its demonstration areas. But it failed to recognize that people learn best by doing, through a direct and personal relationship with the land. The agency hired young Navajo men as herders, but it excluded the families who once used these ranges, allowing them inside only during special "demonstration days."[34] People could see vigorous grasses growing inside the fence, but they had no practical way of knowing how those results were achieved. It seemed as though the rain somehow favored those areas, as one Diné man remarked. Instead of recognizing this comment as a sign of their own poor pedagogy, McGinnies and Fryer viewed it as an amusing example of Navajo "primitiveness."[35] Perhaps direct participation in the demonstration areas, as at Steamboat—which, for a while, achieved greater success—would have taught more Navajos the advantages and methods of scientific range management.[36]

At the same time, if the conservationists had walked the land with Navajos, the native people might have taught the conservationists a thing or two about the range. As Kimball observed in his brief work with the people of Black Mesa, the Navajos had an intimate knowledge of the local vegetation, the terrain, and the actions of water, soil, and sun that "could only come from those who were long-time residents."[37] Perhaps the Diné would have explained how they managed their flocks, taking them in different directions each day. Together with the conservationists, they might have figured out a hybrid approach, one that drew on both native and scientific ways of rotating pastures. Perhaps, too, the Diné would have convinced the conservationists of the value of more flexible transhumance, a contingent mobility allowing families to take advantage of greener pastures where their kinsfolk lived, rather than trapping them within their land management districts, no matter what the conditions. The Diné knew a great deal about the southern Colorado Plateau that the conservationists might have profited from. At the same time, policymakers might have helped craft a creative solution that actually made sense to the Diné, one that was grounded in Diné values and ways of knowing.

Just as mistakes were lamentable, so too were the missed opportunities. In meeting after meeting, Navajo councilmen pondered the problem of conserving their land, often offering solutions. Rarely did Collier or his staff pay attention. We cannot help but wonder whether Collier might have found a more culturally acceptable solution to his environmental problem if he had really listened to the men as they struggled to figure out how to reduce stock without engendering the wrath of the women and men back home. What if Collier had followed his own instincts and created a truly collaborative program?

Not all of the Navajos' ideas were necessarily good ones, it's true. In one of the earliest meetings between Collier and the tribal council, Naalnishí, from around Leupp, suggested that there was no need to aggressively reduce stock. "Nature does it," he observed. "Severe winter weather reduces our sheep." The blizzard of 1931–32, for example, eliminated an estimated two hundred thousand sheep, including three hundred of Naalnishí's own flock.[38] In some places, half of the animals died.[39] And drought, too, culled flocks. "It is the course of nature," noted tribal chairman Sam Ahkeah in 1951.[40] Why not simply let it run its course? It sounds simple enough. When population exceeds resources, the population crashes, restoring nature's balance. That was the traditional way, and no doubt, in the absence of government intervention, livestock would have suffered massive starvation and dehydration during the 1930s, reducing herds considerably. But starvation is an especially cruel way to reduce flocks. Surely there was a more humane approach.

Recall Albert Sandoval's suggestion. His community proposed to reduce their herds through home consumption, an idea that officials dismissed out of hand as too slow. And yet, his scheme might have helped. Suppose that each family had simply consumed roughly forty sheep and goats per year and then sold 80 percent of the annual reproduction of lambs and kids, the latter a provision of the stock reduction plan that the SCS never implemented.[41] Within just four short years, the number of livestock would have declined well below the promulgated carrying capacity, without any reduction in cattle or horses.[42] In other words, the conservationists would have met their goal only one year later than their own timetable demanded—and eight years before they achieved it—without the wanton slaughter of goats and the marketing of mature herds. Admittedly, convincing stock owners to sell 80 percent of their annual "lamb crop" would not have been easy (and, in fact, Sandoval objected to mandatory sales), especially as the size of herds began to plummet. Lambs held special value for Diné. Each represented many future offspring, and parents typically gave lambs to their children as foundation herds. Lambs meant legacy, and a program to sell off most of them each year would surely have met resistance. But it could not possibly have been as traumatic as the program Collier implemented.

To be sure, Sandoval's idea would not have worked on its own. There were simply too many small-scale owners already scraping too close to the bone. At some point, they would have begun to scrimp and save, and the stock numbers would have rebounded. Part of the problem was the inequality of livestock wealth. Only about 60 percent of the stockowners had flocks numbering more than one hundred animals. If those families, alone, had been asked to bear the burden, as Chee Dodge originally suggested to protect the poor from pauperism, they would have had to voluntarily impoverish themselves to reach the so-called carrying capacity. That was unlikely. Consumption and commerce was not the panacea that Sandoval suggested. But it might have helped.

There were other possibilities for consuming herds. Conservationists might have encouraged, rather than disparaged, the Blessingway and Enemyway ceremonies that Diné frantically conducted throughout the New Deal era as they tried to counteract the disharmony and disorder of stock reduction and restore hózhǫ́ to the range. Setting aside, for the moment, the spiritual meaning they held for Diné, ceremonies would have created opportunities to eat large numbers of stock, for such events always occasioned feasts, often provided by wealthier families. Great feasts across the reservation might have changed the whole tone of stock reduction. Instead of remembering the era as one of loss, perhaps, in the words of Tully Lincoln, Diné would have recalled it as a time when the people "walked in meat."

And what about the ceremonies themselves? Solon Kimball mused in retrospect that the conservationists might have framed a program around the fundamental Diné belief in hózhǫ́, a concept not all that unlike the scientific notion of equilibrium.[43] I don't mean to suggest that the New Dealers should have simply draped scientific concepts in Navajo metaphysics. Not at all. I mean that working closely with Navajos like Frank Mitchell, they might have discovered common ground, or perhaps a middle ground, a place to rethink range rehabilitation in terms of restoring hózhǫ́. Finding common ground, of course, would have required the conservationists to set aside the notion that Western science offers all the answers, indeed the only answers, to ecological problems. And that would have been, perhaps, too much to expect. But all systems of knowledge seek to explain the same physical reality of the nonhuman world, and it is simply hubris to believe that only Western science comprehends the workings of nature. As the biologist and cultural theorist Donna Haraway has remarked, nature does not speak through scientists, like a ventriloquist, unmediated by culture. Western science, like Diné metaphysics, is a product of culture.[44] If we acknowledge that fact, we must also acknowledge that other ways of knowing nature can offer valuable wisdom.

For example, Diné perceived the "discordant harmony of nature," to borrow the ecologist Daniel Botkin's phrase, something that scientists are just now beginning to grasp. They knew that hózhǫ́ and hóchxǫ́, order and chaos, were both inherent to the natural world.[45] No doubt, their spiritual metaphors did not fully comprehend the complexities of nature any more than the New Dealer's mechanistic metaphors did. Both imagined an idealized nature, and both sought to control it, one through technology, the other through ceremony. Both believed in a kind of homeostasis. But unlike the conservationists, who thought that nature remained static in the absence of human disturbance, the Diné fathomed the flukiness of the natural world.

If the New Dealers could not give credence to Navajo metaphysics, they might have at least given their own ideas more careful consideration. Collier, for example, might have taken Robert Marshall's suggestion and paid Navajos far above market price for their sheep, goats, and horses. Or he might have paid Navajos not to graze, just as the Department of Agriculture paid white farmers not to grow cotton or hogs during the Depression.[46] Neither of these approaches alone would have brought herds down to a sustainable size, for as even Fryer admitted, livestock meant far more to Diné than money. But some stockowners surely would have sold a portion of their flocks if the price had been right, just as they did in 1933. Collier's advisors also suggested the possibility of removing stock from the reservation to graze on greener pastures. Late in the game, for example, Fryer encouraged large-scale owners to lease off-reservation land. That idea came up early on; had it been pursued with federal funds, tens of thousands of animals might have been removed posthaste. Others suggested purchasing state-owned sections in the lush Zuni Mountains, and the Babbitt Brothers' ranching operation offered to sell some of their prime ranges for the Navajos' use.[47] Both of these areas were part of the historic Diné range. They might have become the equivalent of modern-day "grass banks," places where livestock can graze temporarily while the grasses back home rest and recover.[48] Grass banks are a late-twentieth-century idea, but they were not out of the realm of imagination in the 1930s. None of these ideas were pursued, in part, because of their cost, and yet the price of restoring the damage done—in the tens of millions of dollars—continued to climb.

Conserving the Navajo range while preserving Navajo life was a complex problem, and no single solution could have averted economic and cultural impoverishment altogether. And yet the most important step was never taken, as Collier himself admitted. Had the New Dealers treated the Navajos as equal partners, they may well have created a culturally and economically acceptable plan. Had they collaborated with local land-use communities of women and men, they may have come to understand and address the legitimate concerns of the people most affected. A collaboration with Navajos, of course, would have led to the same result as long as Collier treated it as yet another exercise in indirect rule, yet another way to "persuade" the Navajos to follow his course of action.[49] Collier and his men would have had to learn the value of real consensus decision-making, something he endorsed but never embraced.[50] The Diné themselves had a long tradition of consensus decision-making, but the New Dealers showed little patience for it. It took too long, especially because every speech had to be translated into Navajo or English. More than that, it would have meant deviating from the predetermined course of action. True consensus requires people to listen thoughtfully to one another and develop creative solutions that address all concerns and fears. As it was, Collier and his men—so certain that only they knew the answers—viewed Navajo counsel as only a means to ratify and legitimate decisions they had already made.

The New Deal conservation program could not possibly have worked as long as policymakers ignored the values and ideas of the Navajo people. When conservationists high-handedly imposed measures that were profoundly antithetical to Diné culture, they helped begin the process of their program's unraveling. That is perhaps the central lesson of this episode in environmental history. In our quest to restore ecological diversity and conserve land, we cannot ignore the people who make their living from it. We cannot rob them of their right to make a living. And for Navajos, "making a living" meant more than making money; it meant being fully engaged in the spiritual, familial, and social relations that maintain hózhǫ́, all of which intertwined with livestock.[51]

We might make this argument solely on the grounds of environmental justice. In their crusade to save the land, federal agencies rendered the Navajos nearly powerless over their lives. Notice how the Navajo story differs from that of Anglo ranchers, who reluctantly came under the Taylor

Grazing Act during the same period. Under that act, those ranchers gained a powerful voice in the administration of public lands, which they themselves managed, and thus controlled, through local committees. By contrast, federal conservationists managed every aspect of the Navajo range program. The resulting economic and cultural impacts of stock reduction and the restrictions on mobility proved reprehensible, a shock from which the Navajos are only now beginning to recover.

The New Deal program teaches us that we must be mindful of people and their values not only from a humanitarian perspective but also from an ecological one. If we want to protect the land, we must consider carefully those who use it. When New Deal conservationists dismissed Navajo cultural traditions and values, they made a grievous mistake. For when the next administration turned the range management program over to the Navajos, they relinquished the reins to people for whom conservation had come to seem anathema. Even today, memories of stock reduction complicate efforts to conserve the range. A Diné man who works for the Navajo Department of Forestry told the ethnogeographer Patrick Pynes that most people now will not "touch grazing issues on the reservation with a ten foot pole."[52] The program that might have been a means to restore hózhǫ́ came to be viewed as the origin of a seemingly perpetual state of hóxchǫ́.

Diné memories preserve a history of stock reduction that continues to shape life and land. In the early 1980s, Charlie Łtsoii, a hataałii from Kayenta, recalled the struggles and sorrows of the New Deal era. In so doing, he articulated a collective memory of terror, betrayal, loss, and grief that continues to resonate throughout Diné Bikéyah. "I took my sheep all the way down to a place called Teeł Chʼínítʼiʼ, Cat Tails Come Out, and hid them," he told his visitor. "All the horses and goats and many sheep around here were killed. Their bones still lie around. We live among their bones." And then he added: "When they reduced the stock, many men, women, boys and girls died. They died of what we call *chʼééná*, which is sadness for something that will never come back."[53]

Slim Woman, by then quite elderly, confessed to the ethnographer Charlotte Frisbie that her sheep, though long gone, were never far from her mind. "When I go to sleep I dream about herding the sheep," she said. "I know as I get older I'll do what others have done. I'll start imagining all of that in my mind even during the day. People do that when they get real old. They talk about the sheep day and night, all the time." Older women often became addled and spent their days talking to their sheep and worrying about their welfare. "It's like they forget everything else except the sheep. That's because that's all we were raised with, that's all we did—take care of the sheep."[54]

Today, Diné gather each year to celebrate a modest program to return churra sheep to the red rock mesas and canyons of the Navajo Nation. "Sheep Is Life" proclaims the gathering—part festival, part Extension Service workshop, part rural county fair. People come from all across the reservation to think about acquiring a flock of the old breed, which produces the lanky wool women prefer for weaving. They come to see the sheep that their grandmothers once called their own. They come to see the sheep that once made them proud and prosperous. The people cluster to watch the animals parading before the competition judges, and you can see it in their eyes, you can see them imagining their grandmothers' land blanketed with bleating sheep. As they look out over the land of their imagination, they recall the stories of tall grasses blowing in the breeze, of ranges and valleys covered with beautiful flowers. And they continue to dream about sheep.

NOTES

ABBREVIATIONS

ADL	Arizona Collection, Arizona Department of Library, Archives, and Public Records, Phoenix
AHF	Arizona Historical Foundation, Arizona State University, Tempe
AHS	Arizona Historical Society Archives, Tucson
ASM	Arizona State Museum Archives, Tucson
ASU	Department of Archives and Manuscripts, Hayden Library, Arizona State University, Tempe
BIA	Bureau of Indian Affairs
CCF	Central Classified Files
COIA	Commissioner of Indian Affairs
CSUF	Oral History Program, California State University, Fullerton
DF	Decimal Files
FGD	Forestry and Grazing Division, Phoenix Area Office
FLC-CSSL	Center of Southwest Studies Library, Fort Lewis College, Durango, Colorado
FLC-CSSSC	Center of Southwest Studies, Special Collections, Fort Lewis College, Durango, Colorado
HTP	Hubbell Trading Post National Monument, Ganado, Arizona
LR	Letters Received
MANM	Mexican Archives of New Mexico
MIAC-LA	Laboratory of Anthropology Archives, Museum of Indian Arts and Culture, Santa Fe, New Mexico
MNA	Museum of Northern Arizona, Flagstaff

NA	National Archives, Washington, D.C.
NA-CP	National Archives, Still Pictures Unit, College Park, Maryland.
NARA-PR	National Archives and Records Administration, Pacific Region, Laguna Niguel, California
NARA-RMR	National Archives and Records Administration, Rocky Mountain Region, Denver, Colorado
NAU	Special Collections, Cline Library, Northern Arizona University, Flagstaff
NMSRCA	New Mexico State Records Center and Archives, Santa Fe
NMSU	Rio Grande Historical Collections, Branson Library, New Mexico State University, Las Cruces
NNRMC	Navajo Nation Records Management Center, Window Rock, Arizona
NOHT	Navajo Oral Histories, American Indian Oral History Transcriptions
OIA	Office of Indian Affairs
RG	Record Group
SANM	Spanish Archives of New Mexico
SCS	Soil Conservation Service
UA	Special Collections, University of Arizona Library, Tucson
UNM	Center for Southwest Research, Zimmerman Library, University of New Mexico, Albuquerque
WMAI	Wheelwright Museum of the American Indian, Santa Fe, New Mexico

PREFACE

1. I am not the first to make this observation; see William M. Denevan, "Livestock Numbers in Nineteenth-Century New Mexico, and the Problem of Gullying in the Southwest," *Annals* (Association of American Geographers) 57 (1967): 691–763; Richard White, *The Roots of Dependency: Subsistence, Environment, and Social Change among the Choctaws, Pawnees, and Navajos* (1983), 229.

2. Influential in shaping my approach were Donald Worster's *Dust Bowl: The Southern Plains in the 1930s* (1979); William deBuys's *Enchantment and Exploitation: The Life and Hard Times of a New Mexico Mountain Range* (1985); and Nancy Langston's *Forest Dreams, Forest Nightmares: The Paradox of Old Growth in the Inland West* (1995).

3. Donald L. Parman, *The Navajos and the New Deal* (1976), ch. 12.

4. White, *Roots of Dependency*, 310–14.

5. Ruth Roessel and Broderick H. Johnson, eds., *Navajo Livestock Reduction: A National Disgrace* (1974); the editors summarize the book's themes in the foreword and on p. 224.

6. Virginia J. Scharff, "Man and Nature! Sex Secrets of Environmental History," in *Seeing Nature Through Gender* (2003), 16.

7. Carolyn Merchant blazed the path with *The Death of Nature: Women, Economy, and the Scientific Revolution* (1980) and *Ecological Revolutions: Nature, Gender, and Science in New England* (1989), as did Vera Norwood in *Made from This Earth: American Women and Nature* (1993). But also consult Virginia J. Scharff's critique: "Are Earth Girls Easy? Ecofeminism, Women's History, and Environmental History," *Journal of Women's History* 7 (1995): 164–75. More recent, exciting scholarship on women, gender, and environmental history is introduced in the collection of essays edited by Scharff, *Seeing Nature through Gender*. Also see Susan R. Schrepfer's *Nature's Altars: Mountains, Gender, and American Environmentalism* (2005). A fairly well-established literature focuses on women's leadership in the public health and environmental justice movements, from the Progressive Era to the present. See, for example, Suellen Hoy, *Chasing Dirt: The American Pursuit of Cleanliness* (1995), Linda Lear, *Rachel Carson: Witness for Nature* (1997), and Rachel Stein, ed., *New Perspectives on Environmental Justice: Gender, Sexuality, and Activism* (2004). Particularly influential on how I approached the history of Navajo women was Theda Perdue's *Cherokee Women: Gender and Culture Change, 1700–1835* (1998).

8. Peter Iverson, *The Navajo Nation* (1981), xxvi.

9. See Jennifer Nez Denetdale, *Reclaiming Diné History: The Legacies of Navajo Chief Manuelito and Juanita* (2007); Kathy M'Closkey, *Swept under the Rug: A Hidden History of Navajo Weaving* (2002); and Colleen O'Neill, *Working the Navajo Way: Labor and Culture in the Twentieth Century* (2005).

10. For a provocative examination of a number of these struggles, consult Stein, ed., *New Perspectives on Environmental Justice*. Also see Robert J. Brulle, *Agency, Democracy, and Nature: The U.S. Environmental Movement from a Critical Theory Perspective* (2000), 207–21.

11. For example, between 1910 and 1933, the Blackfeet lost their right to hunt in Glacier National Park, the Timbisha Shoshones became squatters on their own land with the designation of Death Valley as a national monument, and the Spanish land grant communities of northern New Mexico lost their communal lands to the Carson National Forest. Although not framed in these terms, deBuys's *Enchantment and Exploitation*, Louis S. Warren's *The Hunter's Game: Poachers and Conservationists in Twentieth-Century America* (1997), Mark David Spence's *Dispossessing the Wilderness: Indian Removal and the Making of the National Parks* (1999), and Philip Burnham's *Indian Country, God's Country: Native Americans and the National Parks* (2000) illustrate the history of "environmental injustice." More recent scholars have reframed this history of dispossession; see, for example, Laura Pulido, *Environmentalism and Economic Justice: Two Chicano Struggles in the Southwest* (1996), and Diane-Michele Prindeville, "The Role of Gender, Race/Ethnicity, and Class in Activists' Perceptions of Environmental Justice," in *New Perspectives on Environmental Justice*, ed. Rachel Stein (2004).

12. Dorceta E. Taylor, "Environmentalism and the Politics of Inclusion," in *Confronting Environmental Racism: Voices from the Grassroots*, ed. Robert D. Bullard (1993), 57.

13. Debra L. Donahue, *The Western Range Revisited: Removing Livestock from Public Lands to Conserve Native Biodiversity* (1999), 115.

PROLOGUE: A VIEW FROM SHEEP SPRINGS

1. The botanical names are *Artemisia tridentata* (sagebrush) and *Gutierrezia sarothrae* (snakeweed).

2. The basic guide to the geography of Navajo Country is James M. Goodman, *The Navajo Atlas: Environments, Resources, People, and History of the Diné Bikeyah* (1982).

3. Consult Neil E. West, ed. *Ecosystems of the World*, vol. 5, *Temperate Deserts and Semi-Deserts* (1983), ch. 12; William A. Dick-Peddie, *New Mexico Vegetation: Past, Present, and Future* (1993), chs. 7 and 8; and Raymond M. Turner, "Great Basin Desert Scrub," in *Biotic Communities of the American Southwest—United States and Mexico*, ed. David E. Brown (1982), 145–55. The botanical terms for the plants mentioned are *Pinus ponderosa* (ponderosa pine), *Pinus edulis* (piñon), *Juniperus* spp. (juniper), *Atriplex canescens* (four-wing saltbush), *Atriplex confertifolia* (shadscale), and *Sarcobatus vermiculatus* (greasewood).

4. The bureau has been designated over the years as the Indian Service, the Office of Indian Affairs, and now the Bureau of Indian Affairs. For simplicity, I use the agency's current name throughout this book.

5. White, *Roots of Dependency*.

6. Marley Shebala, "Council Asking for Livestock Adjustment," *Navajo Times*, 13 June 1996.

7. "Just How Dry Is the Rez?" *Navajo Times*, 9 May 1996; Bill Donovan, "1996 Top Story Is One That Never Ran," *Navajo Times*, 31 Dec. 1996. That year, Tuba City experienced its worst drought since 1900, according to precipitation data recorded at weather stations across the Navajo Nation. For many areas, however, 1989 continues to hold the record for least precipitation (as of 2005). Still, 1996 may well have witnessed the worse drought since the 1950s, which remains a record-setting decade throughout much of Navajo Country. Unfortunately, the available data list only the extremes. Precipitation data for many points on the Navajo Nation and in its vicinity are available from the Western Regional Climate Center, published at http://www.wrcc.dri.edu/summary/Climsmaz.html. My thanks to Ron Towner for pointing me toward this source.

8. Bill Donovan, "Tribe's 40-Year-Old Grazing Regs May Finally Be Changed," *Navajo Times*, 28 Feb. 1996.

9. Idem, "Tour Allows Hard Look at Land Situation," *Navajo Times*, 23 May 1996.

10. Shebala, "Council Asking for Adjustment"; Bill Donovan, "Ranchers Taking Hale's Advice, Reducing Herds by the Hundreds," *Navajo Times*, 27 June 1996; *Declaring a State of Emergency on the Navajo Nation Due to Drought Conditions on the Navajo Nation Caused by a Lack of Moisture*, CJN-48-96, 6 June 1996, Navajo Nation Council Minutes, NNRMC; Navajo Nation Department of Agriculture, Grazing Management Office, "Navajo Nation Water Resources Management: Grazing Acres and Livestock Count" (St. Michaels, Ariz., n.d.).

11. Letter to the editor from Nelson Roanhorse, "Keep Politics Out of Rangeland," *Navajo Times*, 6 June 1996; Shebala, "Council Asking for Adjustment"; letter to the editor from Lawrence Ruzow, "The Unmentionable," *Navajo Times*, 13 June 1996.

12. Elizabeth Manning, "Drought Has Navajos Discussing a Taboo Subject—Range Reform," *High Country News*, 5 Aug. 1996.

13. Bill Donovan, "BIA Willing If Nation Helps," *Navajo Times*, 27 June 1996. On "political suicide," see Donovan, "Tribe's Grazing Regs May Be Changed"; idem, "Tour Allows Hard Look."

14. *Navajo Times*, 13 June 1996. John "Collie" is the name many Diné use when referring to Collier.

15. My thinking on this subject has been clarified by James C. Scott's insightful *Seeing Like a State: How Certain Schemes to Improve the Human Condition Have Failed* (1998).

16. Donovan, "Ranchers Taking Hale's Advice."

17. Ernest Nelson, interview in Roessel and Johnson, *Navajo Livestock Reduction*, 159.

18. See, for example, the interview with Fred Descheene in Roessel and Johnson, *Navajo Livestock Reduction*, 189–96.

19. My understanding of the phenomenon of collective memory and the relationship between history and memory owes a debt to David W. Blight, *Beyond the Battlefield: Race, Memory, and the American Civil War* (2002); Edward S. Casey, *Remembering: A Phenomenological Study* (1987); Paul Connerton, *How Societies Remember* (1989); Kenneth E. Foote, *Shadowed Ground: America's Landscapes of Violence and Tragedy* (1997); Pierre Nora, *Realms of Memory: Rethinking the French Past*, trans. by Arthur Goldhammer (1996); Jan Vansina, *Oral Tradition as History* (1985), ch. 6; Richard White, *Remembering Ahanagran: Storytelling in a Family's Past* (1998); and Nancy Wood, *Vectors of Memory: Legacies of Trauma in Postwar Europe* (1999).

20. Pat Sheen, interview in Roessel and Johnson, *Navajo Livestock Reduction*, 168. Oral history interviews are full of stories of piles of sheep, goat, and horse bones, particularly in the area around Navajo Mountain and Kayenta. See the interviews in Dean Sundberg and Fern Charley, eds., *Navajo Stock Reduction Interviews*, 1–2, CSUF.

21. See, for example, interviews with Buck Austin, Tacheadeny Tso Begay, and Billy Bryant in Roessel and Johnson, *Navajo Livestock Reduction*, 17–22, 109–13, 140.

22. Robert S. McPherson, "Navajo Livestock Reduction in Southeastern Utah, 1933–46: History Repeats Itself," *American Indian Quarterly* 22 (1998): 10.

23. Ruth Roessel and Broderick Johnson preserved this social memory and made it explicit in their collection of oral histories, compiled under the politically charged title *Navajo Livestock Reduction: A National Disgrace*. Although the book actually reveals a variety of viewpoints, including recollections of an eroded range and the memories of Diné range riders, the pathos of most of the stories and the illustrations depicting violence and grim scenes of animals burned alive overshadow the multiple perspectives that the book and the larger historical record offer.

24. Lee Muck, "Survey of the Range Resources and Livestock Economy of the Navajo Indian Reservation," Exhibits B and E, CCF 301—Lee Muck, box 120, Navajo Area Office, Records of the BIA, RG75, NARA-PR. Because of their greater forage requirements, horses count as five "sheep units" and cattle count as four.

25. I am indebted to Bill deBuys and Kris Havstad for pointing this out. For an explanation of the threshold concept, consult Tamzen K. Stringham, William C. Krueger, and Patrick L. Shaver, "State and Transition Modeling: An Ecological Process Approach," *Journal of Range Management* 56 (2003): 106–13; and Brandon T. Bestelmeyer et al., "Development and Use of State-and-Transition Models for Rangelands," ibid.: 114–26.

26. My thinking about competing cultural understandings of nature and the hubris that often underlies the decisions made by federal policymakers is indebted to Nancy Langston, *Forest Dreams, Forest Nightmares: The Paradox of Old Growth in the Inland West* (1995).

27. Daniel B. Botkin, *Discordant Harmonies: A New Ecology for the Twenty-first Century* (1990), offers an excellent overview of the history of ecological thought, as well as an explanation of newer, more complex ecological models; see especially ch. 10. Also consult James Gleick, *Chaos: Making a New Science* (1987), and Stephen Jay Gould, *Wonderful Life: The Burgess Shale and the Nature of History* (1989).

28. Scott, in *Seeing Like a State*, offers numerous examples of this syndrome; I am indebted to him for crystallizing my thinking on this score.

1 COUNTING SHEEP

1. Howard Gorman, interview in Roessel and Johnson, *Navajo Livestock Reduction*, 46. On his role as Fryer's assistant, see E. Reeseman Fryer, "Erosion, Poverty and Dependency: Memoir of My Time in Navajo Service, 1933–1942" (manuscript, 1986), 34, FLC-CSSL.

2. Billy Bryant, interview in Roessel and Johnson, *Navajo Livestock Reduction*, 141.

3. U.S. Congress, Senate, Committee on Indian Affairs, *Survey of Conditions of the Indians of the United States*, pt. 34, *Navajo Boundary and Pueblos in New Mexico* (1937), pp. 17806, 17988 (hereinafter cited as Committee on Indian Affairs, *Survey of Conditions*, pt. no.).

4. Billy Bryant, interview in Roessel and Johnson, *Navajo Livestock Reduction*, 141.

5. Sarah Begay, interview, 20 June 1974, pp. 8–9, in Sundberg and Charley, *Navajo Stock Reduction Interviews*, CSUF.

6. Howard Gorman, interview in Roessel and Johnson, *Navajo Livestock Reduction*, 47.

7. Hasteen Klah, *Navajo Creation Myth: The Story of the Emergence*, recorded by Mary C. Wheelwright (1942), 123–24. Diyin Diné'é is often glossed as "Holy People," but John Farella argues that such a translation is incorrect. See *The Main Stalk: A Synthesis of Navajo Philosophy* (1984), 23.

8. Many Diné attribute prolonged drought to stock reduction. See the interviews with Hoske Yeba Doyah, John Tom, Ernest Nelson, and Curly Mustache in Roessel and Johnson, *Navajo Livestock Reduction*, 146, 150, 159, 172.

9. Interview in Roessel and Johnson, *Navajo Livestock Reduction*, 47.

10. The following synopsis of Collier's life is drawn from Lawrence C. Kelly's excellent biography, *The Assault on Assimilation: John Collier and the Origins of Indian Policy Reform* (1983). Also consult Flannery Burke, *From Greenwich Village to Taos: Primitivism and Place at Mabel Dodge Luhan's* (2008), ch. 2.

11. *Cherokee Nation v. Georgia*, 30 U.S. Reports 1 (18 March 1831).

12. U.S. Congress, Senate, Select Committee to Examine into the Condition of the Sioux and Crow Indians, *Report on the Condition of Indian Tribes in Montana and Dakota* (1884), 81.

13. The classic account of malfeasance in the wake of the Dawes Act is Angie Debo, *And Still the Waters Run: The Betrayal of the Five Civilized Tribes* (1940; reprint, 1984).

14. Peter Iverson offers an excellent synthesis of this period in *Diné: A History of the Navajos* (2002), ch. 2. Lawrence Kelly offers the classic narrative, along with extractions from the historical record, in *Navajo Roundup: Selected Correspondence of Kit Carson's Expedition against the Navajo, 1863–1865* (1970). For the Diné viewpoint, see Ruth Roessel, ed., *Navajo Stories of the Long Walk Period* (1973).

15. Collier, "The Fate of the Navajos: What Will Oil Money Do to the Greatest of Indian Tribes?" *Sunset Magazine*, Jan. 1924, 11. For insight into the romantic reformers of the 1920s and 1930s, consult Sherry L. Smith, *Reimagining Indians: Native Americans through Anglo Eyes, 1880–1940* (2000), pt. 3.

16. The classic account of Collier's years as commissioner of Indian affairs is Graham D. Taylor, *The New Deal and American Indian Tribalism: The Administration of the Indian Reorganization Act, 1934–45* (1980); see especially ch. 4. Also consult Parman, *Navajos and the New Deal*, ch. 2.

17. "John Collier Becomes Commissioner of Indian Affairs," 21 April 1933, envelope 4, box 1, Reference File of Commissioner John Collier, Records of the Commissioner of Indian Affairs (hereinafter Collier's Reference File), RG 75, NA.

18. Collier, "A Birdseye View of Indian Policy, Historic and Contemporary," 30 Dec. 1935, p. 13, Policy Statement—Indian Service file, box 2, Office Files of Assistant Commissioner John H. Province, 1946–50, RG 75, NA.

19. H. H. Bennett et al., "Report of the Conservation Advisory Committee for the Navajo Reservation," pp. 1–5, CCF 31777-1935-344, Navajo Agency, RG 75, NA; White, *Roots of Dependency*, 252.

20. Minutes of the Eleventh Annual Session of the Navajo Tribal Council, Fort Wingate, New Mexico, 7–8 July 1933, pp. 13–19, and Minutes of the Meeting of the Navajo Tribal Council, Keams Canyon, Ariz., 10–12 July 1934, p. 80, both in NNRMC; the quote is from the latter.

Richard White, in *Roots of Dependency*, 252, argues that Boulder Dam served as the catalyst for stock reduction, since federal officials had observed overgrazing for decades but failed to address the problem until it threatened the dam and the region's economic development. I disagree. The catalyst for stock reduction was Collier's appointment as commissioner and the availability of funding through New Deal programs. For the first time, a commissioner of Indian affairs cared deeply about the ultimate survival of the Navajos. The Dust Bowl and the development of the Soil Conservation Service, furthermore, brought greater attention to the problem of erosion during the New Deal years. And finally, the availability of New Deal funding made it possible to implement an already contemplated plan that formerly had been deemed too expensive. It is true that Collier brought up the threat to Boulder Dam at his second meeting with the Navajo Tribal Council in the fall of 1933, and he frequently cited that threat as a rationale for stock reduction. And yet he had expressed grave concern about overgrazing on the reservation years before his tenure as commissioner of Indian affairs, with no mention of the proposed dam. Collier likely used the dam as leverage to obtain the massive funding he needed for the reservation's erosion-control program. That does not mean that he implemented stock reduction primarily to protect the Los Angeles water and power supply. For Collier's mention of Boulder Dam, see, for example, Minutes of the Special Session of the Navajo Tribal Council, Tuba City, Ariz., 30–31 Oct. and 1 Nov. 1933, p. 18, CCF 00-1933-054, General Services; and Collier to Administrator of Public Works, July 1933, CCF 27066-1937-021.5, Navajo, both in RG 75, NA. For his early concern about overgrazing, see Collier, "Fate of the Navajos," 13, and "Navajo Land Needs—Crisis and Touchstone," *American Indian Life*, American Indian Defense Association Bulletin no. 18 (July 1931), 5. For discussions of the financial constraints to massive stock reduction before Collier took office, see E. A. Johnson to COIA, 21 Jan. 1933, CCF 301.14, box 166, FGD, RG 75, NARA-PR.

21. Forester William H. Zeh made the first detailed report on Navajo range conditions in *General Report Covering the Grazing Situation on the Navajo Indian Reservation*, reprinted in Committee on Indian Affairs, *Survey of Conditions*, pt. 18, *Navajos in Arizona and New Mexico* (1932), pp. 9121–32. His findings were confirmed by the Bennett Report, pp. 3–5.

22. For a good administrative history of Collier's program on the Navajo Reservation, consult Parman, *Navajos and the New Deal*. David F. Aberle provides a useful chronology of livestock reduction in *The Peyote Religion among the Navaho* (1991), 58–59, 75; and Carl Beck, acting chief for extension on the Navajo Reservation, offers a summary and generally candid critique of this first phase in his "History of Stock Reduction Program on Navajo Reservation," printed in Committee on Indian Affairs, *Survey of Conditions*, pt. 34, pp. 17985–89. My overview of the program also draws extensively on White, *Roots of Dependency*, chs. 12 and 13.

23. Committee on Indian Affairs, *Survey of Conditions*, pt. 34, pp. 17537, 17806, 17995. These figures include the Eastern Agency, which covered the Checkerboard. Later government figures include only mature sheep and goats, because they counted only mature animals against the carrying capacity of the range. The number of mature animals on the reservation proper in 1933 was 709,725, with an additional 177,900 on the Checkerboard. Livestock numbers in this chapter are rounded to the nearest 100.

24. Robert V. Boyle, "Range Management Policy Statement," 8 July 1935, p. 6, folder 33, box 7, SCS Records, UNM.

25. Committee on Indian Affairs, *Survey of Conditions*, pt. 34, p. 17806. These figures include the Checkerboard.

26. William H. Zeh to Navajo Superintendents, 6 Oct. 1934; Zeh to Collier, 10 Oct. 1934; Frank B. Lenzie to Zeh, 19 Oct. 1934; Lenzie, Hugh Harvey, and Forrest M. Parker to Collier, 30 Jan. 1935, all in CCF 301 Livestock Reduction Program file, Navajo Area Office, RG 75, NARA-PR.

27. Committee on Indian Affairs, *Survey of Conditions*, pt. 34, p. 17988.

28. Ernest Nelson, interview in Roessel and Johnson, *Navajo Livestock Reduction*, 155.

29. Committee on Indian Affairs, *Survey of Conditions*, pt. 18, pp. 9120–21, 9247–48, 9556–57, 9559; ibid., pt. 34, pp. 17784.

30. Ibid., pt. 34, pp. 17806, 17978–79. These figures include the Hopi Reservation and the Eastern Agency. The reduction numbers that appear in the published chart are in error. The reported numbers of livestock remaining on the reservation, moreover, exclude lambs and kids. Between November 1933 and November 1935, the government purchased 268,900 sheep and goats from Navajos living on the reservation proper (plus 46,900 on the Checkerboard). That figure does not include livestock that the people consumed, sold to the BIA to feed school children, or bartered with traders over the normal course of the years; nor does it

include those that died due to natural causes, drought, and the like. The difference between the number of livestock purchased and the drop in actual population represents a substantial rebound in the numbers of mature sheep (the number of lambs and, especially, goats did, in fact, drop).

31. Fryer, "Erosion, Poverty and Dependency," 10, FLC-CSSL.

32. Parman offers the most thorough account of this political battle in *Navajos and the New Deal*; also consult Lawrence C. Kelly, *The Navajo Indians and Federal Indian Policy, 1900–1935* (1968), chs. 9, 11, and epilogue; and White, *Roots of Dependency*, chs. 12 and 13.

33. Iverson, *Diné*, 120–21, 138.

34. SCS, "Annual Report, Navajo District, for the Year Ending June 30, 1936," plate 7, folder 56, box 7, SCS Records, UNM; Committee on Indian Affairs, *Survey of Conditions*, pt. 34, p. 17989; Proceedings of the Meetings of the Navajo Tribal Council and the Executive Committee, Window Rock, Ariz., 17–20 Jan. 1938, pp. 93–94, ADL; U.S. Department of the Interior, Office of Indian Affairs, "Grazing Regulations for the Navajo and Hopi Reservations," 2 June 1937, folder 12, box 6, Berard Haile Papers, UA; also consult "Regulations Governing Grazing and Stock Adjustments to the Carrying Capacity of the Range for the Navajo and Hopi Reservations," 11 Dec. 1936, CCF 62000-1935-301, pt. 1, Navajo, and [Walter] Woehlke, Memorandum on Navajo Problem, 27 March 1935, file 1-13, box 11, Office Files of Commissioner John Collier, Collier's Navajo Documents (hereinafter Collier's Navajo Documents), both in RG 75, NA.

35. Woehlke to Collier, 13 Dec. 1937, CCF 301 (2 of 2), box 119, Navajo Area Office, RG 75, NARA-PR; Tribal Council Minutes, Jan. 1938, pp. 94–95, 99–100, ADL.

36. See the oral histories in Roessel and Johnson, *Navajo Livestock Reduction*, and voluminous petitions in folders 31 and 33, box 80; folders 6, 10–12, and 21, box 81; and folders 9–10, box 82, all in Dennis Chavez Papers, UNM.

37. Parman, *Navajos and the New Deal*, 69–76.

38. White, *Roots of Dependency*, 313.

39. Consult Donald L. Fixico, *The American Indian Mind in a Linear World: American Indian Studies and Traditional Knowledge* (2003), ch. 3.

2 RANGE WARS

1. Frank Goldtooth, interview in Roessel and Johnson, *Navajo Livestock Reduction*, 105.

2. Ibid., 98–107; the quote is from p. 106.

3. John H. Provinse, "Physical Condition of the Reservation," script for KTGM radio broadcast, Window Rock, 18 Oct. 1938, pp. 1 and 4, folder 20, box 1, Thomas Dodge Collection, ASU. Provinse later became assistant commissioner of Indian affairs.

4. My argument here echoes that of Solon T. Kimball, one of the anthropologists eventually employed to assist the conservationists; see "Land Use Management: The Navajo Reservation," in *The Uses of Anthropology*, ed. Walter Goldschmidt (1979), 63–65.

5. For an analysis of the social construction of grasslands ecology, see Ronald C. Tobey, *Saving the Prairies: The Life Cycle of the Founding School of American Plant Ecology, 1895–1955* (1981).

6. U.S. Department of the Interior, Commissioner of Indian Affairs (henceforth COIA), *Annual Report, 1883* (1883–84), 122.

7. For evidence of trading restrictions, see Samuel E. Day, Jr., "Grazing Report for the Month of October, Zuni National Forest, District 1 and 2," 1 Nov. 1909, folder 3, box 3, series 3, Day Family Collection, NAU; F. H. Abbott to J. L. Hubbell, 18 Dec. 1909, Indians 1909 file, box 43, and C. L. Walker to Lorenzo Hubbell, 13 Sept. 1932, Indians 1932–33 file, box 44, both in Hubbell Trading Post Papers, UA. My examination of trading post records uncovered no purchases of Diné livestock, except a lone sale by Chee Dodge, before 1909; prior to that time, Diné stockowners traded wool, pelts, and blankets. For reports of poor range conditions, see, for example, COIA, *Annual Report, 1893* (1893), 109.

8. William H. Zeh to J. P. Kinney, 19 May 1932, CCF 301.14, Range Management, Navajo, Prior to June 1, 1941, box 166, FGD, RG75, NARA-PR.

9. Zeh, "General Report," 9123–27, 9131. For information on Zeh's survey, see Zeh to Kinney, 22 Sept. 1930, Zeh Correspondence file, 1929–1930, box 148, FGD, RG75, NARA-PR.

10. See, for example, J. W. Toumey, "Overstocking the Range," *Arizona Agricultural Experiment Station Bulletin No. 2* (1891); E. O. Wooton, *The Range Problem in New Mexico* (1908), 19–23; and J. J. Thornber, *The Grazing Ranges of Arizona* (1910), 335–40.

11. Joe A. Stout, Jr., "Cattlemen, Conservationists, and the Taylor Grazing Act," *New Mexico Historical Review* 44 (1970): 311–32; U.S. Department of Agriculture (henceforth USDA), *The Western Range: A Great but Neglected Natural Resource* (1936).

12. The best history of the Dust Bowl is Donald Worster, *Dust Bowl* (1979); also see R. Douglas Hurt, *The Dust Bowl: An Agricultural and Social History* (1981). Brian Q. Cannon's *Remaking the Agrarian Dream: New Deal Rural Resettlement in the Mountain West* (1996) provides a useful study of the Resettlement Administration.

13. [H. H. Bennett], "Report to the Navajo Council by Conservation Advisory Committee for the Navajo Reservation," 1933, pp. 1–2, folder 3, box 18, and W. G. McGinnies, "The Problem of Soil Erosion on the Navajo Indian Reservation and Methods Being Used for Its Solution," 1936, pp. 2–4, folder 11, box 8, both in SCS Records, UNM; and Collier to [Harold Ickes], July 1933, CCF 27066-1937-021.5, Navajo Agency, RG 75, NA.

14. Henry G. Knight to [Henry Wallace], 9 June 1933, CCF 19414-1933-344, Civilian Conservation Corps–Indian Division (CCC-ID), RG 75, NA.

15. Wellington Brink, *Big Hugh: The Father of Soil Conservation* (1951), 22, 27, 48, 84; Hugh Hammond Bennett, *Elements of Soil Conservation* (1955), iv, vi. Also consult Donald Worster, "A Sense of the Soil," in *The Wealth of Nature: Environmental History and the Ecological Imagination* (1993), 71–75, and Sandra S. Batie, "Soil Conservation in the 1980s: A Historical Perspective," *Agricultural History* 59 (1985): 107–23.

16. Hugh Hammond Bennett, *Our American Land: The Story of Its Abuse and Its Conservation* (1948), 6.

17. Bennett, "Report to the Navajo Council," 2–4. The botanical names for these plants are: *Bouteloua gracilis* (blue grama), *Hilaria jamesii* (galleta grass), and *Gutierrezia sarothrae* (snakeweed). By "chamiso," Bennett likely meant four-wing saltbush (*Atriplex canescens*), highly valued as sheep forage. Throughout this book, my information on plant characteristics is based on: William A. Dick-Peddie, *New Mexico Vegetation: Past, Present, and Future* (1993); William W. Dunmire and Gail D. Tierney, *Wild Plants and Native Peoples of the Four Corners* (1997); Francis H. Elmore, *Shrubs and Trees of the Southwest Uplands* (1976); Robert R. Humphrey, *Arizona Range Grasses: Their Description, Forage Value, and Management* (1970); "Living from Livestock" (n.d.); James Stubbendieck, Stephan L. Hatch, and Charles H. Butterfield, *North American Range Plants* (1981); and Tom D. Whitson et al., eds., *Weeds of the West* (1996).

18. Bennett, "Report to the Navajo Council," 5; E. R. Fryer, interview by Donald Parman, 21 July 1970, p. 19, Interview no. 890, reel 4, American Indian Oral History Transcriptions: Navajo (hereinafter NOHT), UNM. This idea did not originate with Bennett. In early 1933, E. A. Johnson, a range specialist and silviculturist with the BIA's forestry division, recommended a demonstration project at Mexican Springs. See Johnson to [J. P.] Kinney, 6 March 1933, file 301.14, box 166, FGD, RG 75, NARA-PR.

19. Gifford Pinchot, *Breaking New Ground* (1998), 281–87, 306–9; the quote is from p. 261. Although generally attributed to Pinchot himself, the maxim originated with Secretary of Agriculture James Wilson. Wallace Stegner discusses the creation and professionalization of government scientific agencies in *Beyond the Hundredth Meridian: John Wesley Powell and the Second Opening of the West* (1954). Also consult Batie, "Soil Conservation," 112–13; Samuel Hays, *Conservation and the Gospel of Efficiency: The Progressive Conservation Movement, 1890–1920* (1959), 267; and Langston, *Forest Dreams*, 98–99.

20. McGinnies, "Problem of Soil Erosion," p. 5; Hugh G. Calkins and F. D. Matthews, "Report on Proposed Erosion Control Methods, Navajo Reservation," 18 Jan. 1935, pp. 5–8, folder 37, box 7, SCS Records, UNM.

21. Some version of this story appears in many of the Soil Conservation Service's reports. See, for example, McGinnies, "Problem of Soil Erosion," pp. 1–2;

and Charles W. Collier, "Soil Conservation in the Navajo Country," *Soil Conservation* (SCS) 1 (October 1935): 1–2.

22. For a more complete discussion of the ecological effects of overgrazing, see chapter 6.

23. William Cronon, "A Place for Stories: Nature, History, and Narrative," *Journal of American History* 78 (1992): 1347–76, offers a perceptive analysis of the implications of the different ways we tell stories. Diana K. Davis analyzes a strikingly similar story in "Potential Forests: Degradation Narratives, Science, and Environmental Policy in Protectorate Morocco, 1912–1956," *Environmental History* 10 (2005): 211–38.

24. Frederic E. Clements, "Nature and Structure of the Climax," in *Foundations of Ecology: Classic Papers with Commentaries*, ed. Leslie A. Real and James H. Brown (1991), 59–97; Clements, "Plant Indicators," "Climaxes, Succession and Conservation," and "The Relict Method in Dynamic Ecology," all in *Dynamics of Vegetation: Selections from the Writings of Frederic E. Clements*, ed. B. W. Allred and Edith S. Clements (1949), 91, 96, 189, 204, 206. Also see Clements, "The Origin of the Desert Climax and Climate," in *Essays in Geobotany, in Honor of William Albert Setchell*, ed. T. H. Goodspeed (1936), 87–140. For background on Clements and his influence on soil conservationists, consult Donald Worster, *Nature's Economy: A History of Ecological Ideas* (1994), ch. 11; Tobey, *Saving the Prairies*, especially chs. 4 and 7; Nathan F. Sayer, "Recognizing History in Range Ecology: 100 Years of Science and Management on the Santa Rita Experimental Range," in *Santa Rita Experimental Range: 100 Years (1903-2003) of Accomplishments and Contributions*, comp. Mitchel P. McClaran, Peter F. Ffolliott, and Carleton B. Edminster (2003), especially 5–7; and Tony L. Burgess, "Desert Grassland, Mixed Shrub Savanna, Shrub Steppe, or Semidesert Scrub? The Dilemma of Coexisting Growth Forms," in *The Desert Grassland*, ed. Mitchel P. McClaran and Thomas R. Van Devender (1995), 51–56. Burgess's essay concerns the Sonoran and Chihuahuan deserts, but his observations regarding Clements's influence on soil conservationists are applicable here as well. Jason G. Hamilton's essay, "Changing Perceptions of Pre-European Grasslands in California," *Madroño* 44 (1997): 311–33, offers a penetrating evaluation of the assumptions underlying Clements's ideas in a different ecological context. For the Soil Conservation Service's expression of equilibrium theory in Navajo Country, see "Land Management in the Navajo Area," [draft of pamphlet, c. 1937], CCF 300, box 117, Navajo Area Office, RG75, NARA-PR.

25. James H. Simpson, *Navaho Expedition: Journal of a Military Reconnaissance from Santa Fe, New Mexico, to the Navaho Country Made in 1849 by Lieutenant James H. Simpson*, ed. Frank McNitt (2003), 73–75, 105; the quote is from p. 75.

26. Provinse, "Physical Condition," pp. 4–5.

27. Simpson, *Navaho Expedition*, 70; emphasis in original. Simpson's description of a wasteland was likely exaggerated; a New Jersey native, Simpson loathed

the southwestern landscape. Nonetheless, below the highlands and beyond riparian areas, Washington's troops found scant forage.

28. In 1851, Private Josiah Rice, then under Colonel Edwin Sumner's command, found good grazing primarily at springs, along creeks, and at Cañon Bonito, which the army promptly appropriated for Fort Defiance; the rest of the landscape bore scant grass. See Josiah M. Rice, *A Cannoneer in Navajo Country: Journal of Private Josiah M. Rice, 1851* (1970), 55–79.

29. A. W. Whipple reported similarly verdant conditions in 1853, an especially wet year. See A. W. Whipple, *A Pathfinder in the Southwest: The Itinerary of Lieutenant A. W. Whipple during His Explorations for a Railway Route from Fort Smith to Los Angeles in the Years 1853 and 1854*, ed. Grant Foreman (1941), 148–53.

30. During his journey between August 15, when he left Albuquerque, and September 9, when he skirted the southwestern corner of the reservation, Beale recorded rain—some of it heavy or day-long—on nine days. One reason for Beale's lush riparian landscape was the presence of beavers. On his trip in 1857, Beale had noted "beaver... in large numbers." The following year, when he returned to supervise construction of the wagon road, Beale brought with him two Native Americans—known as "the Delaware" and Little Axe—to hunt and trap. Over the course of nine days along the southern edge of the Navajo Reservation, the two men trapped fourteen beavers. Little did Beale realize that beaver dams along the Little Colorado River slowed the flow of the stream, trapped nutrient-rich sediments, fostered the growth of bank-stabilizing plants, and created the wetlands, ponds, and meadows that fed and watered his horses. Whether the demise of the ecosystem that beavers constructed was due to overgrazing and the consequent loss of habitat or overtrapping of beavers is still a matter of debate. See U. S. Congress, House, *Wagon Road from Fort Defiance to the Colorado River*, by Edward F. Beale (1858), 33–48; U.S. Congress, House, *Wagon Road—Fort Smith to Colorado River*, by Edward F. Beale (1860), 41–43; Robert W. Adler, *Restoring Colorado River Ecosystems: A Troubled Sense of Immensity* (2007), 73–75; Robert J. Naiman, Carol A. Johnston, and James C. Kelley, "Alteration of North American Streams by Beaver," *Bioscience* 38 (1988): 753–62.

31. H. C. Lockett and Milton Snow, *Along the Beale Trail: A Photographic Account of Wasted Range Land* (1939), 2–3, 12–19, 48–49. According to Beale, the dimensions at Jacob's Well were one-quarter mile in circumference and one hundred yards deep, which is what Lockett published; I've used the numbers provided by May Humphreys Stacy, who accompanied Beale and measured the dimensions with a chain. See Lewis Burt Lesley, ed., *Uncle Sam's Camels: The Journal of May Humphreys Stacey, Supplemented by the Report of Edward Fitzgerald Beale* (1929), 90.

32. U.S. Congress, *Wagon Road from Fort Defiance*; the quote is from p. 40. The botanical name for greasewood is *Sarcobatus vermiculatus*.

33. Compare U.S. Congress, *Wagon Road from Fort Defiance*, 34–35, with Lockett and Snow, *Along the Beal Trail*, 6–7. Beale was quite specific that the meadow

"very much resembling the blue grass of Jamaica" was at Agua Azure (Blue Water) and that he was some five miles distant from the base of the Zuni Mountains. It is impossible to say with certainty where Beale camped, however, because he split from his party, detouring to Fort Defiance, via Blue Water, while the rest of his men headed south to Zuni. The published chart of the expedition's itinerary, which provides the latitude and longitude of each camp, follows the main party, not Beale's diversion. (For a narrative describing the larger party's journey, see Lesley, *Uncle Sam's Camels*). Snow took his photograph a half mile north of South Chavez, New Mexico, several miles distant from the area Beale described and in a considerably different terrain. (Caption for photograph Window-11, folder 4, box 1, RG75-FC, NA-CP.) The author located the area where Snow snapped his photograph in 2007; it bears no geographical resemblance to the description of Beale's camp.

Even if Snow took the photo where Beale camped, it's worth noting that in 1892, the Zuni Mountains Cattle Company started operations at the newly established village of Bluewater. Moreover, by the late 1880s, nearby San Rafael was a major Hispanic center for sheep raising, and the Arizona Cattle Company, the Cebola Cattle Company, and the Acoma Land and Cattle Company operated in the area. More importantly, the place where Snow actually took his photograph was the domain of the New Mexico and Arizona Land Company, which leased grazing lands to non-Navajos. Navajos clearly were not the only source of grazing pressure in the area. See Neil C. Mangum, "In the Land of Frozen Fires—A History of Human Occupation in El Malpais Country," in *Natural History of El Malpais National Monument*, comp. Ken Mabery (1997), 173–82; land use map, Pueblo Bonito Agency folder, box 142-2 075-03-078, Papers of Herbert J. Hagerman, RG 75, NARA-PR.

Bluewater Creek was dammed in 1927 to create a reservoir, and the original soils and vegetation were removed in the process. Farther upstream, the creek remains carpeted with luxuriant grass even today.

34. U.S. Congress, Senate, *Report upon the Colorado River of the West*, by Joseph C. Ives (1861), 117, 128. Similarly, John Beadle ventured off the beaten path in the 1870s and described a "generally barren" country. See John H. Beadle, *Undeveloped West; or, Five Years in the Territories* (1873), 566.

35. Passing references to the long-standing history of overgrazing since the late nineteenth century can be found in Calkins and Matthews, "Report on Proposed Erosion Control Methods," p. 3, and "Justification of Present Plan of District Range Control," Collier's Navajo Documents, 49-54, box 11, RG75, NA.

36. For a perceptive discussion of the value and limitations of these "proxy" data for historical studies, consult Thomas W. Swetnam, Craig D. Allen, and Julio L. Betancourt, "Applied Historical Ecology: Using the Past to Manage for the Future," *Ecological Applications* 9 (1999): 1189–1206. For a basic primer in dendroclimatology, see Paul R. Sheppard et al., "The Climate of the US Southwest," *Climate Research* 21 (2002): Appendix 1.

37. Throughout this book, my information on rainfall and drought comes from an analysis of E. R. Cook et al., "Long-Term Aridity Changes in the Western United States," *Science* 306 (2004): 1015–18, published in www.ncdc.noaa.gov/paleo/pdsidata.html, and Fenbiao Ni et al., "Cool-Season Precipitation in the Southwestern USA since 1000: Comparison of Linear and Nonlinear Techniques for Reconstruction," *International Journal of Climatology* 22 (2002): 1645–62, published in www.ncdc.noaa.gov/paleo/pubs/ni2002/. Supplementing this information is Sheppard, "Climate of the US Southwest," 228–31.

38. My discussion of the patterns of Indian agents' observations is based on COIA, *Annual Reports* for 1881–82 (p. 195), 1882–83 (p. 188), 1887 (p. 171), 1888 (p. 190), 1893 (p. 109), 1895 (p. 118), 1896 (p. 112), 1897 (p. 106), 1899 (pp. 156–57), 1900 (p. 191–2), 1901 (p. 180), 1903 (p. 125), 1905 (p. 167). Their subjective observations are largely corroborated by the tree-ring data, except that 1896 was a drought year. See Ni, "Cool-Season Precipitation," and Cook, "Long-Term Aridity." Also consult Herbert E. Gregory, *The Navajo Country: A Geographic and Hydrographic Reconnaissance of Parts of Arizona, New Mexico, and Utah* (1916), 51; Robert C. Balling, Jr., and Stephen G. Wells, "Historical Rainfall Patterns and Arroyo Activity within the Zuni River Drainage Basin, New Mexico," *Annals* (Association of American Geographers) 80 (1990): 613–14.

39. COIA, *Annual Report, 1893*, 109.

40. COIA, *Annual Report, 1903*, 125.

41. Simpson, *Navaho Expedition*, 105–6; Herbert E. Gregory, *Geology of the Navajo Country: A Reconnaissance of Parts of Arizona, New Mexico, and Utah* (1917), 130–31; USDA, *Western Range*, 119, 308–12.

42. Calkins and Matthews, "Report on Proposed Erosion Control Methods," pp. 4–5, UNM. Also see, for example, H. F. Johnson and Lucian A. Hill, "Work Report, Soil and Erosion Survey, Land Management Unit No. 4," 1936, pp. 17–18, folder 32, box 8; and Lewis K. Armstrong and Ray H. Kerr, "Work Report, Soil and Erosion Survey, Land Management Unit No. 18," 1936, p. 6, folder 63, box 7, both in SCS Records, UNM. C. Warren Thornthwaite, C. F. Stewart Sharpe, and Earl F. Dosch offer an excellent discussion of channel-cutting in *Climate and Accelerated Erosion in the Arid and Semi-Arid Southwest with Special Reference to the Polacca Wash Drainage Basin, Arizona* (1942), 95–99. For a discussion of the effects of arroyos on plants, see Kirk Bryan, "Change in Plant Associations by Change in Ground Water Level," *Ecology* 9 (1928): 474–78.

43. Gregory, *Geology of Navajo Country*, 131–32; Kirk Bryan, "Recent Deposits of Chaco Canyon, New Mexico, in Relation to the Life of the Pre-Historic Peoples of Pueblo Bonito," *Journal of the Washington Academy of Sciences* 16 (4 February 1926): 75–76; Bryan, "Date of Channel Trenching (Arroyo Cutting) in the Arid Southwest," *Science* 62 (1925): 338–44; Bryan, "Erosion in the Valleys of the Southwest," *New Mexico Quarterly* 10 (1940): 227–32. John T. Hack, a student of Bryan's

who would become an influential geomorphologist, found ancient arroyos, as well, in the Jeddito Valley; see his "The Late Quaternary History of Several Valleys of Northern Arizona: A Preliminary Announcement," *Museum Notes* (Museum of Northern Arizona) 11 (May 1939): 67–73. Bryan's findings were later confirmed by geographer Stephen A. Hall, "Late Quaternary Sedimentation and Paleoecologic History of Chaco Canyon, New Mexico," *Geological Society of America Bulletin* 88 (1977): 1593–1618. It's worth noting that a new episode of downcutting took place in the 1950s, even though all grazing had been excluded for several years and the wash stabilized with check-dams, trees, and shrubs; see Yi-Fu Tuan, "New Mexican Gullies: A Critical Review and Some Recent Observations," *Annals* (Association of American Geographers) 56 (1966): 591.

44. Woehlke to Collier, 8 Sept. 1939 and 26 Sept. 1939, frames 600 and 604, reel 18, John Collier Papers.

45. For a biography, see John R. Mather and Marie Sanderson, *The Genius of C. Warren Thornthwaite, Climatologist-Geographer* (1996).

46. C. Warren Thornthwaite, C. F. Stewart Sharpe, and Earl F. Dosch, "Climate of the Southwest in Relation to Accelerated Erosion," *Soil Conservation* (SCS) 6 (1941): 300–301; Thornthwaite, Sharpe, and Dosch, *Climate and Accelerated Erosion*, 123–24; the quote is from p. 123. Initially, Thornthwaite believed that Bryan mistook natural layering for ancient arroyos at Chaco; at Polacca Wash, he argued, layers formed as heavy rains lengthened the gullies upstream and deposited sediment downstream, creating a pattern of successive filling and cutting similar to that at Chaco.

47. Thornthwaite, Sharpe, and Dosch, "Climate of the Southwest," 298; also see Thornthwaite, Sharpe, and Dosch, *Climate and Accelerated Erosion*, 123–24.

48. William L. Graf offers an excellent history of the study of arroyo development in "The Arroyo Problem—Palaeohydrology and Palaeohydraulics in the Short Term," in *Background to Palaeohydrology: A Perspective*, ed. K. J. Gregory (1983), 279–302. The literature on southwestern arroyos is vast. Particularly useful is Denevan, "Livestock Numbers," 691–763; Richard Hereford and Robert H. Webb, "Historic Variation of Warm-Season Rainfall, Southern Colorado Plateau, Southwestern U.S.A.," *Climatic Change* 22 (1992): 239–56; and Luna B. Leopold, "Rainfall Frequency: An Aspect of Climatic Variation," *Transactions* (American Geophysical Union) 32 (1951): 347, 350–51, who argues persuasively that, in examining average annual rainfall and failing to disaggregate the data to examine statistical differences, Thornthwaite overlooked significant changes in seasonal rainfall. Also consult William L. Graf, "Fluvial Erosion and Federal Public Policy in the Navajo Nation," *Physical Geography* 7 (1986): 97–115; Ronald U. Cooke and Richard W. Reeves, *Arroyos and Environmental Change in the American Southwest* (1976), 1–15; Balling and Wells, "Historical Rainfall Patterns," 603–17; Tuan, "New Mexican Gullies," 573–79. Also useful is Thomas R. Van Devender, "Desert

Grassland History: Changing Climates, Evolution, Biogeography, and Community Dynamics," in *The Desert Grassland*, ed. Mitchel P. McClaran and Thomas R. Van Devender (1995), 92–93. For a countervailing argument regarding environmental changes in southeastern Arizona, however, see Conrad Joseph Bahre, *A Legacy of Change: Historic Human Impact on Vegetation of the Arizona Borderlands* (1991), especially ch. 5.

49. L. D. McFadden and J. R. McAuliffe, "Lithologically Influenced Geomorphic Responses to Holocene Climatic Changes in the Southern Colorado Plateau, Arizona: A Soil-Geomorphic and Ecologic Perspective," *Geomorphology* 19 (1997): 303–332, and J. R. McAuliffe, Louis A. Scuderi, and Leslie D. McFadden, "Tree-Ring Record of Hillslope Erosion and Valley Floor Dynamics: Landscape Responses to Climate Variation during the Last 400 Yr in the Colorado Plateau, Northeastern Arizona," *Global and Planetary Change* 50 (2006): 184–201. I thank Brandon Bestelmeyer for bringing this work to my attention and Les McFadden for discussing his findings with me.

50. Western Regional Climate Center, precipitation tables for Chaco Canyon, Crownpoint, Farmington 3NE, and Shiprock; Sheppard et al., "Climate of the US Southwest," 229–30. Fort Defiance and Kayenta also recorded especially dry growing seasons in the 1930s.

51. USDA, *Western Range*, 146–47.

52. John T. Hack, "Dunes of the Western Navajo Country," *Geographical Review* 31 (1941): 243–45, 256–57, 262–63; D. G. Anderson, "Range Management Branch Report, Land Management Unit No. 3," Jan. 1938, p. 11, vol. 7, box 1; and Anderson, "Range Management Report, Land Management Unit No. 1," May 1937, pp. 6–7, vol. 3, both in SCS Collection, UA. The botanical name for rabbitbrush is *Chrysothamnus nauseosa*.

53. Hack, "Dunes," 240, 243–45, 251, 253, 259.

54. Leopold offers an autobiographical sketch in "Geomorphology: A Sliver Off the Corpus of Science," *Annual Review of Earth and Planetary Sciences* 32 (2004): 1–12.

55. Luna B. Leopold, "Vegetation of Southwestern Watersheds in the Nineteenth Century," *Geographical Review* 41 (1951): 295.

56. Constance I. Millar and Wallace B. Woolfenden, "The Role of Climate Change in Interpreting Historical Variability," *Ecological Applications* 9 (1999): 1207–16.

57. For information on demonstration areas, see, for example, Robert V. Boyle, "Range Management Plan, Ganado Demonstration Area," 1 Aug. 1935, folder 32, box 7, SCS Records, UNM; John G. Hunter to Zeh, 26 June 1934, CCF 21341-1933-344, vol. 2, CCC-ID, General Records, Southern Navajo, RG75, NA; and "Steamboat Demonstration Area," folder 20, box 82, Chavez Papers, UNM.

58. Collier to H. H. Bennett, 20 Dec. 1935, CCF 31777-1935-344, Cooperative Plan for Soil Conservation with the Department of Agriculture, RG75, NA.

59. Lawrence C. Kelly, "Anthropology in the Soil Conservation Service," *Agricultural History* 59 (1985): 140.

60. Ibid.; Kelly, "Anthropology and Anthropologists in the Indian New Deal," *Journal of the History of the Behavioral Sciences* 16 (1980): 14; "Sociological Survey of the Navajo Reservation: A Statement of Procedure," Regional Conservation Bulletin no. 32, Conservation Economics Series no. 5, May 1936, p. 8, folder 18, box 8, SCS Records, UNM.

61. Kimball, "Land Use Management," 65–66, 69–70; "Sociological Survey Procedure," p. 15; BIA, Division of Socio-Economic Surveys, *Statistical Summary: Human Dependency Survey, Navajo Reservation and Grazing District 7*, 1940, box 10, SCS Records, UNM; Emma Reh, "Navajo Consumption Habits (for District 1)," draft report, 24 Oct. 1939, Navajo Consumption Habits folder, box 32, SCS Records, NMSU.

62. Kelly, "Anthropology in the Soil Conservation Service," 141; Kelly, "Anthropology and Anthropologists," 16; Marvin Harris, *The Rise of Anthropological Theory: A History of Theories of Culture* (1968), 526–27; Kimball, "Land Use Management," 66–67. Provinse would eventually become commissioner of Indian affairs.

63. Solon T. Kimball and John H. Provinse, "Navajo Social Organization in Land Use Planning," *Applied Anthropology* 1 (1942): 18–25; [Solon T. Kimball], "Research and Concept Formation in Community Study," in *Culture and Community*, ed. Conrad M. Arensberg and Solon T. Kimball (1965), 49–59; Solon T. Kimball, "Land Use Management," 67, 73–75. Clyde Kluckhohn and Dorothea Leighton would later coin the term "outfit" for this social grouping.

64. "Working Agreement," "Range Management Plan," and "Amendment No. 3 to Working Agreement No. IS/5-016," all relative to cooperative erosion control work on lands traditionally used by the Natani Tsani Indian Operating Group in Land Management District no. 4, Amendment no. 3—Agreement no. IS/5-016 file, box 176, Phoenix Area Office, Branch of Soil Conservation, RG 75, NARA-PR.

65. Kimball, "Land Use Management," 72–75; the quote is from p. 72.

66. Ibid., 64.

67. Parman, *Navajos and the New Deal*, 160–66, 211–13. Oliver La Farge, president of the National Association on Indian Affairs, recommended Reichard to Collier, so Collier himself was certainly aware of her presence and expertise. See Oliver La Farge to Collier, 2 Feb. 1934 and 11 April 1934, and Collier to La Farge, 13 April 1934, frames 66 and 83–84, reel 15, Collier Papers.

68. Kimball, "Land Use Management," 64. Emphasis in the original.

69. The bibliography of Haile's recordings of Navajo ceremonies, including Blessingway, Moving Up Way, Flintway, and Enemyway, is quite lengthy; for his research into Navajo customs, see box 5 of the Berard Haile Papers, UA. For background on Haile, see Murray Bodo, ed., *Tales of an Endishodi: Father Berard Haile and the Navajos, 1900–1961* (1998), xix–xxv. Donald Parman, in *Navajos and the New Deal*, 160, states that Haile received a Ph.D. from the University of Chicago, but

his sources erred; Haile's doctorate in letters came from St. Bonaventure College. He was briefly at the University of Chicago, where he served as a research associate of Edward Sapir, the noted Athabaskan linguist. Kimball and Provinse's disdain for "romantic" information on religion and mythology can be gleaned from John H. Provinse, "The Work of the Human Surveys Branch," p. 53, in H. C. Lockett, ed., "Proceedings of the First Navajo Service Land Management Conference, 2–6 March 1937, Flagstaff, Arizona," Navajo Service School Bulletin no. 1, UNM.

70. For a history of anthropological thought, see Harris, *Rise of Anthropological Theory*.

71. For an excellent discussion of the multiple ways in which gender biases limited the acceptance of Reichard's work among male colleagues, see Louise Lamphere, "Gladys Reichard among the Navajo," in *Hidden Scholars: Women Anthropologists and the Native American Southwest*, ed. Nancy J. Parezo (1993), 157–81. Also consult Parezo's critique of professional boundary-drawing in "Anthropology: The Welcoming Science," 3–27, contained in the same volume, and William H. Lyon, "Gladys Reichard at the Frontiers of Navaho Culture," *American Indian Quarterly* 13 (1989): 137–63.

72. By contrast, Leland Wyman, another noted scholar of Navajo ceremonies, showed high regard for and friendship with Reichard. Professional rivalry partly governed the relationships among Haile, Kluckhohn, and Reichard, who was thin-skinned and yet could be scathing in her criticism of others, such as Mary Wheelwright, whom she considered a charlatan. Clyde [Kluckhohn] to Gladys [Reichard], 12 Nov. 1943, and Lee [Wyman] to [Reichard], 2 April 1947, both in folder 2, Gladys Reichard Collection, MNA; Parman, *Navajos and the New Deal*, 211.

73. The political economist James Scott perceptively explores the contours of indigenous, practical knowledge, which he calls *mētis*. According to Scott, *mētis* can be acquired only through practice and "represents a wide array of practical skills and acquired intelligence in responding to a constantly changing natural and human environment." See *Seeing Like a State*, 311–41; the quote is from p. 313.

74. Alan Wilson and Gene Dennison, *Navajo Place Names: An Observer's Guide* (1995). Throughout this book, I use this guide as my reference for place names. For a similar, yet more thorough, analysis of Western Apache epistemology, consult Keith H. Basso, *Wisdom Sits in Places: Landscape and Language among the Western Apache* (1996).

75. Washington Matthews, "Navajo Names for Plants," *American Naturalist* 20 (1886): 767–77; and Matthews, "Natural Naturalists," manuscript read before the Philosophical Society of Washington, 25 Oct. 1884, in *Washington Matthews: Studies of Navajo Culture, 1880–1894*, ed. Katherine Spencer Halpern and Susan Brown McGreevy (1997), 193–201.

76. A number of scholars have maintained that an understanding of belief systems is crucial to the study of the environmental history of Native Americans.

See, for example, Richard White's masterful essay, "The Cultural Landscape of the Pawnees," *Great Plains Quarterly* 2 (1982): 31–40; Dan Flores, "Bison Ecology and Bison Diplomacy: The Southern Plains from 1800 to 1850," in *A Sense of the American West: An Anthology of Environmental History*, ed. James E. Sherow (1998), 65–90; and Paul Hirt, "The Transformation of a Landscape: Culture and Ecology in Southeastern Arizona," *Environmental Review* 13 (1989): 169–72.

77. Slim Curley, Version I, in Leland C. Wyman, *Blessingway* (1970), 245–46.

78. Kay Bennett, *Kaibah: Recollection of a Navajo Girlhood* (1964), 240–41; Walter Dyk, *Son of Old Man Hat: A Navaho Autobiography* (1938; reprint, 1966), 104–13, 129–31, 153–58, 173–78; COIA, *Annual Report* for 1893 (p. 109), 1895 (p. 118), and 1900 (p. 192).

79. Franc Johnson Newcomb, *Hosteen Klah: Navaho Medicine Man and Sand Painter* (1964), 11–12. I am indebted to David Brugge for bringing this point to my attention.

80. My rather cursory discussion of hóchxǫ́, hózhǫ́, thought, and creation draws heavily on the masterful work of Gary Witherspoon, *Language and Art in the Navajo Universe* (1977), p. 9 and ch. 1, which explicates these concepts in far greater depth and complexity. My discussion of hózhǫ́ and hóchxǫ́ is also informed by Milford B. Muskett, "Identity, *Hózhǫ́*, Change, and Land: Navajo Environmental Perspectives" (2003), 136–37, 159–60. The role that thought, speech, and—by extension—breath play in creating reality can be seen throughout Blessingway, but consult especially Frank Mitchell, Version II, in Wyman, *Blessingway*, 354–55. My explanation of Diné metaphysics is also indebted to the wisdom of James C. Faris in "Taking Navajo Truths Seriously: The Consequences of the Accretions of Disbelief," in *Papers from the Third, Fourth, and Sixth Navajo Studies Conferences*, ed. June-el Piper (1993), 181–86.

81. Songs for increasing livestock are included in Slim Curley, Version I, in Wyman, *Blessingway*, 248–64.

82. Dyk, *Son of Old Man Hat*, 257. References to songs can be found throughout this autobiography of Left Handed; see especially pp. 33, 76–78. Also consult Walter Dyk and Ruth Dyk, *Left Handed: A Navajo Autobiography* (1980), 287–88, 450.

83. See, for example, Henry Zah, interview in Roessel and Johnson, *Navajo Livestock Reduction*, 122.

84. W. G. McGinnies, "The Agricultural and Range Resources of the Navajo Reservation in Relation to the Subsistence Needs of the Navajo Indians," 12 May 1936, pp. 2–3, folder 11, box 8, SCS, UNM.

85. Don Watson, "Navahos Pray for the Good of the World," *Mesa Verde Notes* 7, no. 1 (1937): 16–18. Emphasis mine.

86. Ason Attakai, interview in Roessel and Johnson, *Livestock Reduction*, 129.

87. Fred Descheene, interview in Roessel and Johnson, *Livestock Reduction*, 194.

88. See, for example, John Arthur and wife, interview, 5 July 1953, folder 135, box 5, Collier and Ross field notes, Dorothea C. and Alexander H. Leighton

Collection, NAU. This viewpoint is a constant refrain in the interviews published by Roessel and Johnson in *Navajo Livestock Reduction*; see especially pp. 131, 146, 150, and 172.

89. Nancy Shoemaker, *American Indian Population Recovery in the Twentieth Century* (1999), 33. On the frustrating problems with obtaining reliable population figures, see especially Denis Foster Johnston, *An Analysis of Sources of Information on the Population of the Navaho* (1966), 68–111; thanks to David Brugge for bringing this work to my attention. My figure on the magnitude of the increase in Navajo stock is necessarily hypothetical. It assumes that there were approximately 50,000 sheep and goats by the early 1870s, including the number belonging to those who never went to the Bosque Redondo; that number is no more than a guess (see ch. 6). The figure for 1930 includes lambs and kids.

90. Dyk, *Son of Old Man Hat*, 129–143; Petition to President from Chin Lee Valley, [ca. 1924?], box 30, folder 6, Franciscan Papers, UA.

91. Ernest Nelson, interview in Roessel and Johnson, *Navajo Livestock Reduction*, 159.

92. The botanical names for these plants are: *Amaranthaceae* spp. (pigweed) and *Astralagus* and *Oxytropis* spp. (locoweed).

93. Clyde Kluckhohn and Dorothea Leighton, *The Navaho* (1946), 30–31.

94. The botanical name for the common sunflower is *Helianthus annuus*. Throughout this book, my ethnobotany reference is Dunmire and Tierney, *Wild Plants*; however, the most thorough reference is Francis H. Elmore's *Ethnobotany of the Navajo* (1943).

3   WITH OUR SHEEP WE WERE CREATED

1. Buck Austin, interview in Robert W. Young and William Morgan, comps., *Navajo Historical Selections* (1954), 62. Hastiin Tó Łtsoii, a member of the Tó Dích'íí'nii (Bitter Water) clan, was also known as Buck Austin. Before stock reduction, he owned 600 sheep, and his wife owned 200 more.

2. Howard Gorman, interview by Dan Tyler, 25 Oct. 1968, p. 10, Interview no. 533, reel 4, NOHT.

3. Patrick Hogan, "Dinetah: A Reevaluation of Pre-Revolt Navajo Occupation in Northwest New Mexico," *Journal of Anthropological Research* 45 (1989): 54–55; Paul F. Reed and Lori Stephens Reed, "Reexamining Gobernador Polychrome: Toward a New Understanding of the Early Navajo Chronological Sequence in Northwestern New Mexico," in *The Archaeology of Navajo Origins*, ed. Ronald H. Towner (1996), 85–86. The date that the Diné entered Diné Bikéyah remains controversial (see ch. 5). The Diné themselves maintain that their presence dates much further back.

4. My understanding of the formation of cultural and ethnic identity has been informed by Benedict Anderson, *Imagined Communities: Reflections on the Origin*

and Spread of Nationalism (1991); Homi K. Bhabha, *The Location of Culture* (1994); John L. and Jean Comaroff, "The Madman and the Migrant: Work and Labor in the Historical Consciousness of a South African People," *American Ethnologist* 14 (1987): 191–209; Patricia Galloway, *Choctaw Genesis, 1500–1700* (1997); Néstor García Canclini, *Hybrid Cultures: Strategies for Entering and Leaving Modernity*, trans. Christopher L. Chiappari and Silvia L. Lopez (1995); Nancie L. Gonzalez, *Sojourners of the Caribbean: Ethnogenesis and Ethnohistory of the Garifuna* (1988); Patricia C. Albers, "Changing Patterns of Ethnicity in the Northern Plains, 1780–1870," 90–118, and Nancy P. Hickerson, "Ethnogenesis in the South Plains: Jumano to Kiowa?" 70–89, both in *History, Power, and Identity: Ethnogenesis in the Americas, 1492–1992*, ed. John D. Hill (1996); Michael Holquist, *Dialogism: Bakhtin and His World* (1990); David Rich Lewis, *Neither Wolf nor Dog: American Indians, Environment, and Agrarian Change* (1994); Eugeen E. Roosens, *Creating Ethnicity: The Process of Ethnogenesis* (1989); Renato Rosaldo, *Culture and Truth: The Remaking of Social Analysis* (1993).

5. River Junction Curly, Version III, in Wyman, *Blessingway*, 622–34. Compare this rendition with those in the same volume by Slim Curly in 1932 and Frank Mitchell in 1930, pp. 245–46 and 421–26. These two accounts of Blessingway attribute the creation of sheep and horses to First Man or to Changing Woman alone. In all versions, however, the creation of livestock preceded that of the Diné. Also constant is the symbolic reference to four years. To Diné, the number four signifies, among other things, the passage of time necessary for significant events to take place.

6. Diné use the phrases "it is said" and "they say" to denote historical narratives that carry the authority of tradition. I use the phrase in keeping with that custom.

7. My understanding of Navajo cosmology as expressed throughout this chapter draws on the work of Witherspoon, *Language and Art*; Farella, *Main Stalk*; James C. Faris, *The Nightway: A History and a History of Documentation of a Navajo Ceremonial* (1990); Jerrold E. Levy, *In the Beginning: The Navajo Genesis* (1998); and to a lesser extent, Gladys A. Reichard, *Navaho Religion: A Study of Symbolism* (1963). For a very clear and concise summary of Diné ceremonialism, consult Klara Bonsack Kelley and Harris Francis, *Navajo Sacred Places* (1994), 19–25. Clifford Geertz provided theoretical guidance with *The Interpretation of Cultures* (1973).

8. Other historians have written about the very events recounted here without probing metaphysics, and I believe their interpretations suffered as a result. Compare, for example, Chee Dodge's testimony before the U.S. Senate in support of extending the boundary of the Navajo Reservation to encompass the birthplace of Changing Woman (Committee on Indian Affairs, *Survey of Conditions*, pt. 34, pp. 17905–6) and Parman's characterization of that testimony as "meandering badly" in *Navajos and the New Deal*, 150.

9. My thinking on this subject has profited from John and Jean Comaroff, *Ethnography and the Historical Imagination* (1992); Vansina, *Oral Tradition*; and Angela Cavender Wilson, "Power of the Spoken Word: Native Oral Traditions in American Indian History," in *Rethinking American Indian History*, ed. Donald L. Fixico (1997); and from conversations with Phil Deloria, Milford Muskett, and Jacki Thompson Rand. For background on the practice of ceremonials, see Witherspoon, *Language and Art*, 25.

10. See note 4 (Anderson, etc.). I am also indebted to conversations with John Nieto-Phillips.

11. Iverson points this out in *Diné*, 64–65.

12. Albert B. Lord, *The Singer of Tales* (1960; reprint, 1965), especially chs. 3 and 5; Vansina, *Oral Tradition*, particularly chs. 1 and 6.

13. Lord, *Singer of Tales*, 4–5, 13, 43–44, 99–101; Vansina, *Oral Tradition*, 41–42. I do not mean to imply that singers of traditional stories compose "original" songs. As Lord argues, the singer conceives of the song as a set of themes, some of which are expressed and others omitted, in response to the needs of the particular performance. From the singer's viewpoint, the song has not changed as long as the essence of the story remains. Faris (*Nightway*, 103–4) argues that this flexibility in ceremonial practice accounts, in part, for what some have erroneously characterized as different "versions" of Diné ceremonies. For insight into the ways in which Blessingway singers themselves understand their work, consult Frank Mitchell, *Navajo Blessingway Singer: The Autobiography of Frank Mitchell, 1881–1967*, ed. Charlotte J. Frisbie and David P. McAllester (1978), ch. 8.

14. Vansina, *Oral Tradition*, 42–43, 53–54, 161.

15. Ibid., 19–24, 167–78.

16. Note, however, that wild mountain sheep are central to one of the most important healing ceremonies, the Nightway. See Washington Matthews, *The Night Chant, a Navaho Ceremony* (1902).

17. [W. W. Hill], "From Hill's Final Report on the Navajo," 1–2, Navajo 1940 file, box 12, Collier's Office Files, RG 75, NA; emphasis mine. On the history of the pernicious effect of the "cultural borrowers" concept, see Erika Marie Bsumek, "The Navajos as Borrowers: Stewart Culin and the Genesis of an Ethnographic Theory," *New Mexico Historical Review* 79 (2004): 319–51.

18. Eric Hobsbawm and Terence Ranger, eds., *The Invention of Tradition* (1983), 1–12. Levy (*In the Beginning*, ch. 6) argues that the Diné developed a complex religion amalgamating Puebloan and Apachean (or Athabaskan) beliefs into a spiritual system uniquely their own. He does *not*, however, suggest (as some Southwesterners have) that Diné borrowed from Puebloan traditions in order to establish hegemony. It is important to note, too, that historically the Diné did not claim to be the original inhabitants of Diné Bikéyah. According to Tall Chanter's story of origins, not only were the ancient Puebloan people, or Anasazi, present

in the underworld, where they taught agriculture to the Diyin Diné'é; they were already present in Chaco Canyon when the Diné migrated to the land within the four sacred mountains. See Washington Matthews, *Navaho Legends* (1897; reprint, 1994), 68, 81.

19. That does not mean these theories have no value. I've used them both, to some degree, to help me understand how livestock came to be closely intertwined within Diné culture.

20. The quoted phrase comes from Vansina, *Oral Tradition*, 160.

21. See Faris, *Nightway*, 21–31. Also consult Trudy Griffin-Pierce, *Earth Is My Mother, Sky Is My Father: Space, Time, and Astronomy in Navajo Sandpainting* (1992): 102–3.

22. According to Matthews, the narrative stories associated with rituals were widely known; it was the rituals themselves and the more esoteric parts of the myths that the hataałii retained as secret knowledge (Faris, *Nightway*, 30). Matthews's observation is born out by the large number of people who incorporate these stories into their oral histories. See NOHT, especially reels 1–3 and 6. Also consult Connerton, *How Societies Remember*, 53–54.

In 1954, the Navajo Tribal Council, while acknowledging that there was no "official" Blessingway chant—that the story differed from one hataałii, from one clan, and from one locale to the next—formally approved the publication of these three tellings of the ceremony so that they would be preserved for future generations. See minutes of Navajo Tribal Council meeting, 1–4 March 1954, Window Rock, 41–61, 66–75, NNRMC. Unfortunately, no earlier record of Blessingway exists.

Nightway, first recorded by Washington Matthews in 1902, also offers an important clue regarding the antiquity of sheep (albeit wild sheep) in Diné thought. In that ceremony, bighorn sheep give Nightway to the Dreamer. However, I have elected not to elaborate that story because Nightway is not a widely published oral tradition and its ceremonial content is both closely held and sacred (Faris, *Nightway*, 31).

23. This origin story comes from Haneełnéhee, Moving Up Way. I base the following summary on Tall Chanter's account in Matthews, *Navaho Legends*, 63–159. Paul G. Zolbrod, who created an annotated version of Matthews's translation, augmented by other versions and recast in poetic form under the title *Diné Bahane': The Navajo Creation Story* (1984), also informs my understanding of the story. But also consult Frank Goldtooth's account, as told by Stanley A. Fishler, *In the Beginning: A Navaho Creation Myth* (1953). Different versions of the story recount varying numbers of underworlds, ranging from three (with emergence into the Fourth World) to eleven (with emergence into the Twelfth).

Matthews identifies Tall Chanter as his informant in *Navaho Legends*, 29, 50–51. (Levy, *In the Beginning*, 42, erroneously attributes the story to Old Torlino, a Blessingway singer, but Old Torlino provided the alternative rendition, labeled "Version A.") Tall Chanter, of the Táchii'nii (Red-Running-Into-Water-People) clan, came from around Nutria, near the Zuni Mountains, where Fort Wingate, New Mexico, was located; this must have been his wife's home, since his father, Gishin, a member of the Tó Dích'íi'nii clan, came from around Rainbow Bridge. Tall Chanter collaborated with Matthews to the extent that he made a trip to Washington, D.C., where he helped check Matthews's field notes. (Faris provides the clan in *Nightway*, 82; information on his home comes from Matthews.)

Matthews, although officially an army surgeon, became an ethnographer while working among the Hidatsas at Fort Berthold in the Dakota Territory. The Bureau of American Ethnology arranged his army assignment at Fort Wingate so that he could make the first serious ethnographic study of Navajos during two tours of duty, 1880–84 and 1890–94. His interpreters were Ben Damon, who was educated at Carlyle, and Chee Dodge. See Matthews to Pliny Goddard, 26 Dec. 1903, Washington Matthews Papers, frame 536, reel 1, WMAI. For background on Matthews, consult Katherine Spencer Halpern and Susan Brown McGreevy, eds., *Washington Matthews: Studies of Navajo Culture, 1880–1894* (1997), especially the essay by Charlotte Frisbie: "Washington Matthews' Contribution to the Study of Navajo Ceremonialism and Mythology."

24. Matthews, *Navaho Legends*, 63, 65. Except when quoted, these stories reflect my own paraphrasing of Tall Chanter's lengthy oral tradition, vastly simplified to omit many of the details but capture the essence of the creation narrative.

Robert Young, in *The Role of the Navajo in the Southwestern Drama* (1968), 2, and Rex Lee Jim, in "Navajo," *Encyclopedia of North American Indians*, ed. Frederick E. Hoxie (1996), 442, have proposed that the story of emergence through the underworlds offers a metaphorical account of migration from Canada to the Southwest. For a provocative explication of the ways in which Native American origin stories may relate the early history of migrations, see Roger Echo Hawk, "Kara Katit Pakutu: Exploring the Origins of Native America in Anthropology and Oral Traditions" (1994).

25. There is some disagreement over the identity of the eastern and northern mountains. Some accounts identify Tsisnaajinii as Redondo (a.k.a. Pelado) Peak, in the Jemez Mountains, and Dibé Ntsaa as the San Juan Mountains of Colorado. Like many scholars, I follow the geography adopted by the Navajo Tribal Council; see record of the Navajo Tribal Council, 29 Jan. 1974, 292–93, NNRMC, and Wyman, *Blessingway*, 16–20. But consult Frederick W. Sleight, "Navajo Traditional Geography Studies, Part One," folder 14, box 44, Franciscan Papers, UA, for an argument that Tsisnaajinii is actually Redondo Peak.

26. Traditionally, Diné believe that wind "gives life, thought, speech, and the power of motion to all living things." See James Kale McNeley, *Holy Wind in Navajo Philosophy* (1981) (the quote is from p. 1); Witherspoon, *Language and Art*, 54.

27. Note that in all three published accounts of Blessingway and in the chronicles of origins told by Hosteen Klah and Gishin Biye', Changing Woman creates

mortals from her epidermis. Sandoval, by contrast, provides both of these descriptions of the creation of the Earth Surface People. See Wyman, *Blessingway*, 239–40, 447–48, 633; Klah, *Navajo Creation Myth*, 114–15; Aileen O'Bryan [ed.], *The Dîné: Origin Myths of the Navaho Indians* [as told by Sandoval] (1956), 102–3, 166–67; and Berard Haile, *The Upward Moving and Emergence Way: The Gishin Biye' Version*, ed. Karl W. Luckert (1981), 162.

28. Wyman, *Blessingway*, 30–32, 47–48, 65, passim; Ruth Roessel, *Women in Navajo Society* (1981), 72–73; Reichard, *Navaho Religion*, xxxvi, 540–41, 576, 582. Additional members of the "corn pantheon" include White Corn Talking God, Yellow Corn Calling God, Varicolored Corn Girl, Black Corn Boy, Blue Corn Boy, Round Corn Girl, Round Corn Boy, Pollen Girl, and Pollen Boy.

29. Matthews, *Navaho Legends*, 111–14.

30. My thinking here was inspired by Thongchai Winichakul, "Siam Mapped: The Making of Thai Nationhood," *Ecologist* 26 (1996): 215–21.

31. Manuelito made a similar statement when he initially refused to go to Hwéeldi. For Barboncito's speech, see "Proceedings of a Council between the United States and the Navajo Tribe," 28 May 1868, *Native American Legal Materials Collection*, Title 4323 (1968), 2. Jesus Arviso, a Mexican captive who grew up among the Diné, translated Barboncito's entreaty. Manuelito's statement is quoted in Kelly, *Navajo Roundup*, 165.

32. See, for example, Garrick Bailey and Roberta Glenn Bailey, *A History of the Navajos: The Reservation Years* (1986), 10. For a detailed account of the closing of the Bosque Redondo, see Gerald Thompson, *The Army and the Navajo: The Bosque Redondo Reservation Experiment, 1863–68* (1976), ch. 9.

33. Matthews, *Navaho Legends*, 82–87; the quotes are from 83, 86–87. In another version of this episode, which Sandoval told to O'Bryan (*Dîné*, 62) in 1928, there is no mention of domesticated livestock. According to Levy (*In the Beginning*, 101–3), the Be'gochídí—associated with the creation and control of animals—comes from Apachean traditions.

34. Faris (*Nightway*, 82–91) has created the most complete apprenticeship genealogy for hataałii. Although it focuses on Night Chant singers, it includes three of the Blessingway singers—Tall Chanter, Hosteen Klah, and Slim Curley—whose traditions are related in this chapter.

35. I am indebted to Levy, *In the Beginning*, 3, 6, 18, and to Faris, *Nightway*, 103–5, for these insights.

36. According to Faris, both men were sons of Gishin (Mr. Cane) and both presumably apprenticed to their father, making the differences (Tall Chanter compresses twelve worlds into five) and general similarities between the two versions especially interesting. Cane Man's Son, an Evilway singer, first told his story to Alexander Stephen in 1885, but that narrative breaks off in mid-telling. See A. M. Stephen, "Navajo Origin Legend," *Journal of American Folklore* 43 (1965): 88–104.

37. Haile, *Upward Moving and Emergence Way*, 162–67.

38. Ibid., 188–89. Also consult O'Bryan, *Dîne*, 81.

39. Haile's informants were Slim Curly, of Crystal, who was a member of the Tsi'naajinii clan (Black Streak Wood People), and Frank Mitchell and River Junction Curly, both of whom lived around Chinle and were members of the Tó 'Aheedlíinii (Water-Flows-Together) clan.

40. River Junction Curly, Version III, in Wyman, *Blessingway*, 622–23.

41. Oftentimes, however, the colors are given as white, blue, yellow, and black.

42. River Junction Curly, Version III, in Wyman, *Blessingway*, 623–28, 572–73 (the quote is from p. 628); Matthews, *Navaho Legends*, 131.

43. I draw this composite narrative from the stories told by Slim Curly, Frank Mitchell, and River Junction Curly, in Wyman, *Blessingway*, 239–40, 327–33, 447–48, 633–34. The reference to livestock in this story comes from Slim Curly; Mitchell does not mention livestock, and River Junction Curly's account was cut short by Berard Haile. Slim Curly's story is similar to that of Klah, *Navajo Creation Myth*, 123–24.

Although Tall Chanter specified that the Diné were made from ears of corn, most published accounts say Changing Woman created mortals from her skin. Still other chronicles of origin, like that related by Sandoval, include both stories without any sense of contradiction. Similarly, the Bible offers more than one story of human creation. I am indebted to Levy (*In the Beginning*, 14–15) for reminding me of this.

44. Slim Curly, Version I, in Wyman, *Blessingway*, 244–64.

45. "Proceedings of a Council," 2.

4 A WOMAN'S PLACE

1. Kay Bennett, *Kaibah: Recollection of a Navajo Girlhood* (1964), 68, 185–86, 204. This fictionalized autobiography—written from her mother's viewpoint—recounts Kaibah's family's daily life from 1928 through 1935. Kaibah left the reservation in 1935 to live with a missionary and his wife in Los Angeles. She later married a bilagáana engineer, Russell Bennett, and made her home in Gallup. In 1990, toward the end of her life, Kay Curley Bennett became the first woman to run for the presidency of the Navajo Nation. See her obituary, *Albuquerque Journal*, 15 Nov. 1997, B-8. In my telling of her story, I have restored the actual names and places, where known.

2. Bennett, *Kaibah*, 73. Similarly, Old Mexican's mother gave him a kid when he was only five. See Walter Dyk, *A Navaho Autobiography* (1947), 17–18.

3. Bennett, *Kaibah*, 174–75.

4. My perspective throughout this chapter is indebted to the work of David Aberle, Louise Lamphere, Gary Witherspoon, Mary Shepardson, and Gladys

Reichard. Also important is Jerrold E. Levy, Eric B. Henderson, and Tracy J. Andrews, "The Effects of Regional Variation and Temporal Change on Matrilineal Elements of Navajo Social Organization," *Journal of Anthropological Research* 45 (1989): 351–77. Ruth Roessel's *Women in Navajo Society* initially stimulated my thinking.

To my knowledge, Louise Lamphere coined the term "matricentric" in *To Run after Them: Cultural and Social Bases of Cooperation in a Navajo Community* (1977), 70. "Matricentered" captures a way of organizing and thinking about the world that means far more than the commonly used phrases "matrilocal" and "matrilineal."

5. George, interview with James Downs, folder A-524, James F. Downs Collection, ASM; Tracy Joan Andrews, "Descent, Land Use and Inheritance: Navajo Land Tenure Patterns in Canyon de Chelly and Canyon del Muerto" (1985), 23–24; Denetdale, *Reclaiming Diné History*, 156–57.

6. I borrow my definition of power from Klein and Ackerman, who understand it as a process, not a status. Power, they write, "is an active reality that is being created and redefined through individual life stages and through societal history." Power is not restricted to a formal political structure, but can be found "as profoundly within the family as it is in the community council." See Laura F. Klein and Lillian A. Ackerman, eds., *Women and Power in Native North America* (1995), 12, 231–38. Carolyn Garrett Pool has argued that power is necessarily intertwined with the ownership and control of productive resources; see "Reservation Policy and the Economic Position of Wichita Women," *Great Plains Quarterly* 8 (1988): 158. Also consult Louise Lamphere, "Strategies, Cooperation, and Conflict among Women in Domestic Groups," in *Women, Culture, and Society*, ed. Michelle Zimbalist Rosaldo and Louise Lamphere (1974), 97–112, and Joan Wallach Scott, *Gender and the Politics of History* (1988). I am also indebted to conversations with Linda Gordon regarding women, power, and personal politics.

7. Joan Bamberger disputes the myth of "mother-rule" in "The Myth of Matriarchy: Why Men Rule in Primitive Society," in *Women, Culture, and Society*, ed. Rosaldo and Lamphere, 263–80. On romantic feminism, which is apparent in the work of some female ethnographers who studied the Navajos, see Margaret D. Jacobs, *Engendered Encounters: Feminism and Pueblo Culture, 1879–1934* (1999), especially chs. 1 and 3. Some scholars have accused Gladys Reichard of viewing Navajos through a feminist lens; see Deborah Gordon, "Among Women: Gender and Ethnographic Authority of the Southwest, 1930–1980," in *Hidden Scholars: Women Anthropologists and the Native American Southwest*, ed. Nancy J. Parezo (1993), 129–45. But also read Louise Lamphere's critique in that same volume: "Gladys Reichard," 170. According to my own reading of Reichard, while she sometimes romanticized aspects of Navajo life, she described them with more nuance than her critics give her credit; moreover, her observations were confirmed by Clyde Kluckhohn,

who had no feminist agenda. On the issue of dominance in Diné society, consult Louise Lamphere, "Historical and Regional Variability in Navajo Women's Roles," *Journal of Anthropological Research* 45 (1989): 431.

8. E. R. Fryer, "Navajo Social Organization and Land Use Adjustment," *Scientific Monthly* 55 (1942): 410, 411; emphasis added. Fryer's report closely paraphrases (sometimes almost verbatim) a professional journal article written by ethnographers Kimball and Provinse, although they were a bit more restrained in their choice of words. See Kimball and Provinse, "Navajo Social Organization," 18–25.

9. David F. Aberle, "The Navajo," in *Matrilineal Kinship*, ed. David M. Schneider and Kathleen Gough (1961), 144.

10. This pattern is apparent throughout Dyk, *Son of Old Man Hat*.

11. Kluckhohn and Leighton, *Navaho*, 55, 69–71; Malcolm Carr Collier, *Local Organization among the Navaho* (1966), 37–39, 62–63. Malcolm Collier (John Collier's daughter-in-law, who became a noted ethnographer) did her fieldwork in 1938 and 1939; Kluckhohn and Leighton conducted their field work in the years 1942 through 1944.

12. Kluckhohn and Leighton, *Navaho*, 55.

13. Historians have made this same point about other Native American groups; see Jacobs, *Engendered Encounters*, 6, and Perdue, *Cherokee Women*, 13. For an overview of the theory of complementarity and its salience in native North America, see Klein and Ackerman, *Women and Power*, especially pp. 245–47, and the essay in that volume by Lillian Ackerman, "Complementary but Equal: Gender Status in the Plateau," 75–100.

14. Among the many scholars of Diné thought, Witherspoon offers the most cogent analysis of gender in *Language and Art*, 140–44, and I am indebted to his insights. For examples of gendered conceptions, see that volume, p. 42; Wyman, *Blessingway*, 131–33, 203, 344–45, 396–97, 477, 607; Matthews, *Navaho Legends*, 114; Young and Morgan, *Analytical Lexicon*, 990; and Mary Shepardson, "The Gender Status of Navajo Women," in *Women and Power*, ed. Klein and Ackerman (1995), 167. Recall, too, that the entire pantheon of Diyin Dine'é assume the form of complementary pairs: White Corn Boy and Yellow Corn Girl, Pollen Girl and Pollen Boy, and so forth. These particular pairs mimic sexual divisions, but not all of the supernatural pairs do. For example, Water Woman is paired with Mountain Woman, but the latter is gendered male. According to the hataałii Frank Mitchell, Water Woman is in charge of all the waters collected on the ground, including lakes, streams, and springs, whereas Mountain Woman is in charge of game.

15. Some scholars have glossed "nádleeh" as hermaphrodite or transvestite; see, for example, W. W. Hill, in "The Status of the Hermaphrodite and Transvestite in Navaho Culture," *American Anthropologist* 37 (1935): 273–79. However, it is unclear whether there was a biological dimension to this gender identity; the

only attributes described were behavioral. (In the Diné language, "nádleeh" literally means "he repeatedly becomes or changes.") Diné did not view nádleeh in wholly positive terms; in some ceremonies, they are associated with death, incest, infertility, or witchcraft (Levy, *In the Beginning*, 208–17). Similar figures were common in other Native American societies. Traditionally scholars have labeled them *berdache*; more recently, some have called them "two spirit people." See Beatrice Medicine, "Gender," in *Encyclopedia of North American Indians*, ed. Hoxie (1996), 216–17, and Charles Callender and Lee M. Kochems, "The North American Berdache," *Current Anthropology* 24 (1983): 443–56. For a Diné scholar's contemporary perspective, consult Wesley Thomas, "Navajo Cultural Constructions of Gender and Sexuality," in *Two-Spirit People: Native American Gender Identity, Sexuality, and Spirituality*, ed. Sue-Ellen Jacobs, Wesley Thomas, and Sabine Lang (1997), 156–73.

16. For a good understanding of women's work, see Mitchell, *Tall Woman*, especially pp. 32–46, 205, 240–41. Gertrude Honaghani, a Diné girl at St. Michael Indian School, located on the reservation, likewise provides a good description in "The Navajo Woman and Her Home," *Franciscan Missions of the Southwest* 9 (1921): 35–36. Also consult Charlotte J. Frisbie, "Traditional Navajo Women: Ethnographic and Life History Portrayals," *American Indian Quarterly* 6 (1982), 13; Gladys Reichard, *Social Life of the Navajo Indians* (1928; reprint, 1969), 52; and Kluckhohn and Leighton, *Navaho*, 50–51. For a discussion of farming practices, see W. W. Hill, *The Agricultural and Hunting Methods of the Navaho Indians* (1938), 28–42. The absence of a strict sexual division of labor is clear in the life history of Left Handed (Dyk and Dyk, *Left Handed*).

17. Mitchell, *Tall Woman*, 296–97.

18. The classic analysis of the doctrine of separate spheres is Nancy F. Cott, *The Bonds of Womanhood: "Woman's Sphere" in New England, 1780–1835* (1997).

19. I base much of the following discussion of clans on Gary Witherspoon, *Navajo Kinship and Marriage* (1975), especially ch. 5; Aberle, "Navajo," 108–13; Joann Carol Fenton, "A Cultural Analysis of Navajo Family and Clan" (1974); and Shepardson, "Gender Status." There is no agreement on which four clans were first. Tall Chanter provides an account of clan formation in Matthews, *Navaho Legends*, 138–59. But also consult the stories told by Slim Curly and Frank Mitchell, Versions I and II, in Wyman, *Blessingway*, 327–33, 458–59.

20. Lansing B. Bloom, "Bourke on the Southwest," *New Mexico Historical Review* 11 (1936): 220–22. In his diary, Bourke identifies his informant simply as "Chi," but since Chee Dodge was the interpreter for the Indian agency, I have inferred that the informant was Dodge. The actual number of clans in the 1880s is unclear. Washington Matthews listed forty-seven clans, including one omitted from Dodge's roster (the Many Goats clan), which clearly existed in the Black Mesa area, according to Left Handed's life histories. These discrepancies may simply be the result of differences in personal knowledge. Chee Dodge and Matthews's informant, Tall Chanter,

were from the eastern part of the reservation, around Fort Defiance and Fort Wingate; they may have been unaware of some distant clans. Today more than sixty are recognized; some of these may have been added since the 1880s. See Matthews, *Navajo Legends*, 29–31; Reichard, *Social Life*, 11–13; and Young and Morgan, *Analytical Lexicon*, 1090.

21. *t'áálá'í sáanii sidziinígíí nanadaazdeelii'ii*. See Fenton, "Cultural Analysis," 54.

22. Wilson and Dennison, *Navajo Place Names*, 60; Kelley and Francis, *Navajo Sacred Places*, 166.

23. Note, however, that recognizing the clan one is "born for" is not the same as linking oneself to a patrilineal chain. Those who are "born for" their father's clan do not gain membership in that clan, and their children do not become members. See Levy, Henderson, and Andrews, "Effects of Regional Variation," 353, and Witherspoon, *Navajo Kinship*, 42.

24. Dyk and Dyk, *Left Handed*, xxi. This practice was documented repeatedly from the 1920s through the 1940s; see, for example, Kluckhohn and Leighton, *Navaho*, 64.

25. The issue of exogamy is complicated by the fact that different Diné communities defined different types of clan relationships as incestuous. Furthermore, Diné also recognized especially close relationships between certain clans, which also invoked exogamy. I have omitted any discussion of clan groups, however, both for simplicity's sake and because the Diné themselves disagree about the composition of those groups. See Witherspoon, *Navajo Kinship*, ch. 5.

26. Dyk, *Son of Old Man Hat*, 38–39. In the mid-1920s, Reichard observed a similar encounter between her interpreter Swett Billagodi of Tuba City, with whom she was traveling, and a stranger who was a member of Billagodi's father's clan. See *Social Life*, 34.

27. Diné family members have lived in clusters since at least the sixteenth century, according to archaeological evidence, and yet they have no special terminology for these clusters, although Diné living around Window Rock in the 1950s and 1960s referred to them in English as "homesites," according to ethnohistorian David Brugge (personal communication, 2005). Most ethnographers use the term "camp," but this seems to connote a temporary quality that is not quite accurate for the more permanent winter residence. I have chosen to use the term "homestead" for the winter home, because of its connotation of a collection of buildings and land, reserving "camp" for the more ephemeral summer residence. Louise Lamphere discusses the absence of special terminology in *To Run after Them*, 82.

28. Mitchell, *Tall Woman*, 71, 46.

29. Bloom, "Bourke on the Southwest," 228.

30. I draw this summary from my reanalysis of the data that Malcolm Carr Collier collected on the Navajo Mountain Community in 1938, presented in *Local Organization*, 91–93. Also consult Klara B. Kelley, *Navajo Land Use: An Ethnoarchaeo-*

logical Study (1986), 48, whose late-1970s study of a portion of the Checkerboard between Window Rock, Arizona, and Gallup, New Mexico, included a reconstruction of land tenure patterns since 1915. My analysis of these patterns follows Aberle, "A Century of Navajo Kinship Change," *Canadian Journal of Anthropology*: 2 (1981): 27.

31. Lamphere, although discussing a later period, describes this fission and growth process in *To Run after Them*, 76–78. A scholarly debate has arisen in recent decades, with some ethnographers arguing that their colleagues have overstated the matrilocal organization of Navajo society. They cite not only modern patterns of living but also changes dating back to the 1860s, bringing into question my picture of a matricentered way of life. A close analysis of the historical and ethnographic evidence, however, suggests that while pronounced deviations from the matrilocal ideal emerged during periods of upheaval, as the aftershocks died down, families again settled into old familiar patterns that continued into the 1930s.

32. For a more in-depth discussion, see chapter 5. Classic accounts of the cycles of raids and reprisals between Navajos and their enemies are provided by Frank McNitt, *Navajo Wars: Military Campaigns, Slave Raids, and Reprisals* (1990), and Frank D. Reeve, "Seventeenth Century Navaho-Spanish Relations," *New Mexico Historical Review* 32 (1957): 36–52. David Brugge offers the most detailed description of Navajo captivity in *Navajos in the Catholic Church Records, 1694–1875* (1968), especially chs. 4 and 5. For a more personal account of the Ute-Mexican slave trade in Diné women, see Notah Draper, interview in Roessel, *Navajo Stories of the Long Walk*, 226–27.

33. Yasdesbah Silversmith and Casamire Baca, interviews in Roessel, *Navajo Stories of the Long Walk*, 118, 139. For Slim Woman's story, see Newcomb, *Hosteen Klah*, 49; similarly, see Mitchell, *Tall Woman*, 4–6.

34. Kelly, *Navajo Roundup*, 17–19, 30, 38–39, 98; Roessel, *Navajo Stories of the Long Walk*; also see excerpts in Correll, *Through White Men's Eyes*, vol. 3, pp. 340, 413, 456; vol. 4, pp. 44–46; and vol. 5, pp. 104–5, 136, 325–27. For background on the use of Black Mesa as a refuge during the Fearing Time, consult Thomas R. Rocek, "Navajo Cultural History," in *Excavations on Black Mesa, 1982: A Descriptive Report*, ed. Deborah L. Nichols and F. E. Smiley (1984), 413–14.

35. Bailey and Bailey, *History of the Navajos*, 26–27. My reconstruction of this process of reconnecting family to land comes from reading between the lines of the histories of western communities; see especially Collier, *Local Organization*, 97–101.

36. Eric Bruce Henderson, "Wealth, Status and Change among the Kaibeto Plateau Navajo" (1985), 22; Levy, Henderson, and Andrews, "Effects of Regional Variation," 359–64.

37. Whiteman Killer's family maintains that he acquired grazing rights from a Paiute man in exchange for horses, but the Paiutes dispute that claim. (See Collier, *Local Organization*, 18–19.) It's worth noting, though, that archaeological evidence indicates that Diné families may have built hogans here as early as the

mid-nineteenth century. As to Whiteman Killer's provocative name, he acquired it after killing a Mormon man, Lot Smith, in self-defense during a dispute after his sheep strayed into Smith's pasture. For the full story, see Mary Shepardson and Blodwen Hammond, *The Navajo Mountain Community: Social Organization and Kinship Terminology* (1970), 32–33, 41–42.

38. This summary is based on my analysis of Collier's data in *Local Organization* (15–16, 22–27, 87–93), supplemented by information on the same families in Shepardson and Hammond, *Navajo Mountain Community*, table B. My interpretation differs from that of Collier (and later of Shepardson and Hammond), who sees a mix of matrilocal and patrilocal residential choices. Instead, I follow Aberle's lead in "Navajo," where he coined the term "virimatrilocality" to refer to a practice in which some sons choose to live with their mothers. We see evidence of this choice in Dyk and Dyk, *Left Handed*, in which Abaa's son and only child, Left Handed, repeatedly expresses his desire to remain with his widowed mother after his marriage. At Navajo Mountain, two of the women who moved into their husbands' households no longer had living parents. In other situations, plural marriages may have created labor shortages that kept some sons home.

Salt Woman is a pseudonym, based on Diné naming practices, for a woman whose name may be lost to the historical record. She was a member of the Salt Clan and may have been Mabel Onesalt, but the historical record is unclear.

39. Collier, *Local Organization*, 46–65, 97–108.

40. Shepardson, "Gender Status," 160; David Aberle, "Navajo Coresidential Kin Groups and Lineages," *Journal of Anthropological Research* 37 (1981): 2. The one exception to this rule of which I'm aware involved Chee Dodge, the wealthiest man among the Diné. After one of Dodge's wives, Kee'hanaban, left him, he took her baby girl into his own household; that child became the renowned Diné leader, Annie Wauneka. See Carolyn Niethammer, *I'll Go and Do More: Annie Dodge Wauneka, Navajo Leader and Activist* (2001), 22.

41. Fenton, "Cultural Analysis," 5; Shepardson and Hammond, *Navajo Mountain Community*, 50 and 124. Presumably this potential vulnerability was at least one factor in the tendency for two or three clans within one community to intermarry, because men (like women) could then easily maintain familial relationships and would remain within their natal community in the event of divorce.

42. For discussions of Diné marriages, see Witherspoon, *Navajo Kinship*, chs. 3 and 13; Reichard, *Social Life*, ch. 6; and Lamphere, *To Run after Them*, 76–78. Technically, the mother-in-law taboo prevented him only from *looking* at his mother-in-law; he could, however, talk to her. This taboo was just beginning to dissolve in the 1930s, according to Reichard.

43. The following discussion summarizes the events described in Dyk and Dyk, *Left Handed*, ch. 12. According to his version of events, Left Handed was actually visiting his surrogate father Slim Man. But his wife's suspicions may well have

been warranted, since Left Handed had several affairs during his marriage. As the old adage goes, there are three sides to every divorce story: his, hers, and the truth. Unfortunately, we have only Left Handed's account.

44. Dyk and Dyk, *Left Handed*, 217.

45. Ibid., 168–71, 244–45, 559–63.

46. Reichard, *Social Life*, 91; Berard Haile, *Property Concepts of the Navajo Indians* (1949; reprint, 1968), 3–4, 18–19, 42; Klara Kelley, "Navajo Political Economy before Fort Sumner," in *The Versatility of Kinship: Essays Presented to Harry W. Basehart*, ed. Linda S. Cordell and Stephen Beckerman (1980), 12; Henderson, "Wealth, Status and Change," 106. Note that although Haile did not publish his pamphlet until 1949, he wrote it in 1929, and thus it reflects his observations of property concepts on the eve of the New Deal.

47. Kluckhohn and Leighton, *Navaho*, 59–60; Shepardson, "Gender Status," 160; Kelley, *Navajo Land Use*, 48–52; Denetdale, *Reclaiming Diné History*, 156–57, 161. For example, Fred Tsosi Chis Chiliazzi [*sic*] supported the extension of the reservation boundary "because of my grandmother and others who have occupied this land" (Committee on Indian Affairs, *Survey of Conditions*, pt. 34, p. 17794).

48. Reichard, *Social Life*, 51; *Dezba: Woman of the Desert* (1939), 10–12.

49. U.S. Congress, House, "House Resolution 3476 to Promote the Rehabilitation of the Navajo and Hopi Tribes of Indians, Hearings before the Committee on Public Lands" (hereinafter, Committee on Public Lands, Rehabilitation Hearings), p. 124, folders 1 and 2, box 13, subject files, Navajo Area Office, RG 75, NARA-PR. In the record, Deeshchii'nii's name is spelled Descheene.

50. For Paquette's background, see his obituary, *Banner-Journal* (Black River Falls, Wisc.), 20 Sept. 1938. I thank Joan Jensen for sharing this and other material on the Paquettes.

51. Peter Paquette, "Census of the Navajo Reservation under Jurisdiction of Peter Paquette, Superintendent, Year 1915," Indian Census Rolls, 1885–1940 (Navajo), frame 20, reel 273, RG 75. (Hereinafter simply 1915 Navajo Census, frame no.)

52. Haile, *Property Concepts*, 19; Reichard, *Social Life*, 51–53, 89.

53. 1915 Navajo Census, frames 76, 251. Paquette spelled her name as Yeadebah.

54. At least as early as 1918, New Mexico required all sheep in or shipped through the state to be dipped; see "Sheep Dipping Is Properly Defined by Our State Board," *Evening Herald* (Albuquerque), 20 March 1918, attached to J.C. Logan to S. F. Stacher, 25 April 1918, Letters to and from the Superintendent, 1918, box 3, Eastern Navajo Agency, RG 75, NARA-PR. Until about 1930, however, compliance differed from one area of the reservation to another; see, for example, H. J. Hagerman, "Report . . . for the Fiscal Year Ending June 30, 1924," 28 July 1924, Papers of Herbert J. Hagerman, box 2, folder: Commissioner, July–Dec. 1924, RG 75, NARA-PR.

55. See, for example, the dipping records for Tsaile and Ganado in 2.1.C Dipping Records, box 10, subject files of Supt. August F. Duclos (hereinafter Duclos

Files), and CCF 537 Cattle and Sheep Dip, 1926–1930, box 151, both in Navajo Area Office, RG 75, NARA-PR.

56. Greasewood account books, 1932–34 and 1933, items 7A and 8, box 437, and Black Mountain sheep journal, 1937, box 320, both in Hubbell Papers, UA; books 7 and 9, Hubbell Collection, AHF. Hubbell spelled Yazzie's name as Nahki Yazzie.

57. Committee on Indian Affairs, *Survey of Conditions*, pt. 18, p. 9222.

58. Mitchell, *Tall Woman*, 58–59, 193, 472 (n. 6); Dyk and Dyk, *Left Handed*, 15–16. On the relationship between rumors of witchcraft and social control, see Kluckhohn and Leighton, *Navaho*, 177–81, and Richard Hobson, *Navaho Acquisitive Values* (1954; reprint, 1973), 17–20.

59. Witherspoon, *Language and Art*, 84–85, 105; Henderson, "Wealth, Status and Change," 107; Kluckhohn and Leighton, *Navaho*, 161–63, 222; Billy Bryant, interview in Roessel and Johnson, *Navajo Livestock Reduction*, 141. Also consult Dyk and Dyk, *Left Handed*, 14–16, 222–23.

60. Emma Reh, "Navajo Consumption Habits for District 1" (draft), 24 Oct. 1939, p. 27, Navajo Consumption Habits file, box 32, SCS Records, NMSU.

61. 1915 Navajo Census, frames 60, 238. 'Asdzą́ą́ Yazzie (spelled in the census as "Ason Yazzie") was also listed in the census as Bitsiyalnatsaye. Actual ownership of this flock may have been divided among her family, including her sixteen-year-old granddaughter and two younger grandsons.

62. Dyk and Dyk, *Left Handed*, 266–67, 287–88. Hashké Neiniih's name has been spelled a number of ways in the literature; I follow Young and Morgan, *Analytical Lexicon*. It means "he distributed them with angry insistence," referring to his insistence on giving away breeding stock to those who returned from Hwéeldi.

63. 1915 Navajo Census, frame 249. Because federal agents destroyed many horses in the 1920s in a successful effort to rid the reservation of dourine, a sexually transmitted parasite, it is necessary to look to data in earlier years to get an accurate sense of the size of men's horse herds.

64. LaVerne Harrell Clark, *They Sang for Horses: The Impact of the Horse on Navajo and Apache Folklore* (2001). Also see Honaghani, "Navajo Woman," 36; Dyk and Dyk, *Left Handed*, especially 56–57, 450–51.

65. According to ethnographer Gary Witherspoon (*Language and Art*, 91–94), the term *shimá*—literally "my mother"—was also used to refer to the earth, the sheep herd, and other life-giving things, such as the corn field and the mountain soil bundle. Many Diné, in discussing stock reduction, referred to sheep as "my mother."

66. Jonathan Letherman, "Sketch of the Navajo Tribe of Indians, Territory of New Mexico," *Tenth Annual Report of the Board of Regents of the Smithsonian Institution* (1856), 294. For similar early observations, see A. M. Stephen, "Notes about the Navajoes," *Canadian Indian* 1 (Oct. 1890): 16; Cosmos Mindeleff, "Navajo Houses,"

in Smithsonian Institution, Bureau of American Ethnology, *Seventeenth Annual Report of the Bureau of American Ethnology, 1895–1896*, pt. 2 (1898), 485. The wife of the Diné leader Narbona and 'Asdzáá̧ Tł'ógi, better known as Juanita, the wife of Chief Manuelito, were both known for their oratory. Both women traveled with delegations to Washington, D.C., and participated in official peace councils. See Denetdale, *Reclaiming Diné History*, 149–50.

67. Reichard, *Social Life*, 52. Also consult her "Household" typescript in folder 41, Reichard Collection, MNA.

68. The classic history of the trading posts is Frank McNitt, *The Indian Traders* (1989). Willow Roberts Powers offers an excellent recent study: *Navajo Trading: The End of an Era* (2001).

69. Henderson, "Wealth, Status and Change," 46.

70. Joan M. Jensen, *Promise to the Land: Essays on Rural Women* (1991), 13–14.

71. For information on the rise of weaving for trade in the 1890s, see M'Closkey, *Swept under the Rug*, 41, and Powers, *Navajo Trading*, 63–70. For an early, albeit racist, discussion of the weavers' work, consult L[eopold] O[stermann], "The Navajo Indian Blanket," *Franciscan Missions of the Southwest* 6 (1918): 1–14. For a good picture of the labor women devoted to weaving, consult Mitchell, *Tall Woman*, 47–48, 240.

72. Daniel S. Matson and Albert H. Schroeder, eds. and trans., "Cordero's Description of the Apache—1796," *New Mexico Historical Review* 32 (1957): 356.

73. Josiah Gregg, *Commerce of the Prairies*, ed. Max L. Moorhead (1844; reprint, 1954), 199. For a more detailed early description, consult Beadle, *Undeveloped West*, 518–19; also see COIA, *Annual Report, 1876*, 513.

74. M'Closkey, in *Swept under the Rug*, documents the exploitation of weavers by traders and the appropriation of their designs by commercial woolen mills. E. H. Plummer condemned that exploitation in a letter to John Walker, 24 Oct. 1894, folder 9, Plummer Papers, NMSRCA. Also consult Peter Hubbard, interview by David M. Brugge, 23 Jan. 1972, pp. 45–48, Oral History Files, HTP.

75. M'Closkey, *Swept under the Rug*, chs. 7 and 8.

76. Roseann Sandoval Willink and Paul G. Zolbrod, *Weaving a World: Textiles and the Navajo Way of Seeing* (1996). The prayer is from p. 8; I have placed the prayer in stanzas and capitalized the first word of each line.

77. M'Closkey, *Swept under the Rug*, 97. The archaeological record also provides insight into the trade goods that Diné families acquired. See, for example, Terry del Bene and Dabney Ford, eds., *Archaeological Excavations in Blocks VI and VII, N.I.I.P.* (1983), 67, 69, 88, 145, 147, and 185.

78. Most of the extant records for trading posts cover the late 1930s through the 1950s, after stock reduction diminished the amount of wool available for weaving. Nonetheless, a sense of the relative value of blankets before the 1930s can be gleaned from the records of C. N. Cotton's Round Rock Trading Post (Crum and Cotton Ledger, 1915–16, box 2, George Babbitt Collection, NAU); the Hubbell

Trading Post's operations on the Navajo and Hopi reservations (Lorenzo Hubbell to E. K. Miller, 24 May 1926, Hubbell Papers File, HTP); and trading posts' sales in the Northern Navajo jurisdiction (Traders' Record of Livestock Products, attached to Sophus Jensen and George Hedden to E. H. Hammond, 14 May 1931, Northern Navajo Agency file, box 7, Correspondence of Agency Superintendents, 1929–32, Navajo Area Office, RG 75, NARA-PR). The actual relationship of blanket sales to wool and sheep differed by year and area.

79. "Statements from Traders on the Navajo Reservation," attached to Herbert King, Jr., to William H. Zeh, 1 April 1935, 533 Sheep 1924–38, box 151, Navajo Area Office, RG 75, NARA-PR.

80. Proceedings of the Meeting of the Executive Committee of the Navajo Tribal Council, Window Rock, 2–3 May 1938, p. 17, ADL.

81. Colleen O'Neill makes this point with her interview with Margaret Kee, from St. Michaels, whom she quotes in *Working the Navajo Way*, 38.

5 HERDING SHEEP

1. Mitchell, *Tall Woman*, 27.

2. Lynn R. Bailey's *If You Take My Sheep: The Evolution and Conflicts of Navajo Pastoralism, 1630–1868* (1980) originally stimulated my thinking about the origins of Diné pastoralism.

3. In the 1580s, Diego Pérez de Luxán used the terms "Querechos" or "Corechos" interchangeably with "Chichimecos." See "Diego Pérez de Luxán's Account of the Antonio de Espejo Expedition into New Mexico, 1582," in *The Rediscovery of New Mexico, 1580–1594*, ed. George P. Hammond and Agapito Rey (1966), 182, 189. For a more general discussion of the use of "Chichimeca" as a generic term for nomadic peoples in northern Mexico, consult Thomas D. Hall, *Social Change in the Southwest, 1350–1880* (1989), 63–65. My critical stance toward the traditional ways in which historians have interpreted the historical record is shared by Klara B. Kelley and Peter M. Whiteley in *Navajoland: Family Settlement and Land Use* (1989), ch. 2.

4. I am not the first scholar to make this observation. See Ronald H. Towner and Jeffrey S. Dean, "Questions and Problems in Pre-Fort Sumner Navajo Archaeology," in *The Archaeology of Navajo Origins*, ed. Ronald H. Towner (1996), 4. The classic accounts of warfare between the Spanish and Navajos are McNitt, *Navajo Wars*; Reeve, "Seventeenth-Century Relations"; and Reeve, "Navaho-Spanish Wars, 1680–1720," *New Mexico Historical Review* 33 (1958): 204–31. Also see Elizabeth A. H. John, *Storms Brewed in Other Men's Worlds: The Confrontation of Indians, Spanish, and French in the Southwest, 1540–1795* (1996). While Spanish and Puebloan captives most certainly observed their Navajo captors up close, no detailed account of captivity has surfaced in the historical record.

5. Steadman Upham points out that archaeologists have ignored less sexy Anasazi sites as well, in "Archaeological Visibility and the Underclass of Southwestern Prehistory," *American Antiquity* 53 (1988): 245–61. The relative randomness of archaeological discoveries stems, in part, from their funding sources. Most archaeological investigations in the Southwest are salvage operations paid for by federal agencies and by energy companies, building contractors, and others using government subsidies or requiring federal permits for their mines, transmission lines, roads, logging operations, or other land-disturbing activities. Under the terms of the American Antiquities Act and the National Historic Preservation Act, these corporations and agencies must determine whether significant archaeological resources will be adversely affected. If so, they must "mitigate" those effects, which generally involves excavating those sites that may yield substantial information about the past. On the Navajo Reservation and its environs, archaeologists have extensively investigated Black Mesa for the Peabody Coal Company and Gallegos Mesa for the Navajo Indian Irrigation Project, thereby enriching our understanding of the Diné past. Additionally, concerted efforts by the U.S. Bureau of Land Management and the Navajo Nation Historic Preservation Department have deepened our knowledge of early eighteenth-century Diné history. At the same time, large expanses of the Navajo Reservation and its surrounding lands remain largely unexplored archaeologically, their stories untold.

6. I do not mean to imply that dendrochronology, or tree-ring dating, is never accurate; far from it. In those instances where multiple logs with their final rings intact yield tightly clustered dates, we can assume that the end of the tree's life represents the cutting date and that the logs were used soon after they were cut. Archaeologists have obtained many such clusters of cutting dates from sites in Dinétah, providing firm data on the construction of masonry pueblitos, including the season when the timber was cut. Outside of Dinétah, however, most Navajo sites have yielded problematic evidence. Throughout my own analysis in this chapter, I have taken a conservative path, trusting only clusters of tree-ring dates that specialists have determined to be cutting dates. For discussions of the problems with radiocarbon and tree-ring dating techniques, consult especially Gary M. Brown, "Old Wood and Early Navajo: A Chronometric Analysis of the Dinétah Phase," in *Diné Bikéyah: Papers in Honor of David M. Brugge*, ed. Meliha S. Duran and David T. Kirkpatrick (1998). Also see Jerry Fetterman, "Radiocarbon and Tree-Ring Dating at Early Navajo Sites: Examples from the Aztec Area," in *The Archaeology of Navajo Origins*, ed. Ronald H. Towner (1996), 71–78; Gary M. Brown and Patricia M. Hancock, "The Dinetah Phase in the La Plata Valley," in *Cultural Diversity and Adaptation: The Archaic, Anasazi, and Navajo Occupation of the Upper San Juan Basin*, ed. Lori Stephens Reed and Paul F. Reed (1992), 85–89; Meade F. Kemrer, "An Appraisal of the Piedra Lumbre Phase in North Central New Mexico," in *History and Ethnohistory along the Rio Chama*, by Frank J. Wozniak, Meade F.

Kemrer, and Charles M. Carrillo (1992), 69–88; and Hogan, "Dinetah," 61–63. But also consult Kemrer, "The Dynamics of Western Navajo Settlement, A.D. 1750–1900: An Archaeological and Dendrochronological Analysis" (1974), 49–65, and Ronald H. Towner and Byron P. Johnson, *The San Rafael Canyon Survey: Reconstructing Eighteenth Century Navajo Population Dynamics in the Dinétah* (1996), 9–10, 29–34, 47–52, where the authors offer a sophisticated analysis of tree-ring data. For an alternative perspective, see Klara Kelley and Harris Francis, "Anthropological Tradition versus Navajo Tradition in Early-Navajo History," in *Diné Bíkéyah*, ed. Duran and Kirkpatrick (1998), 143–55. In *Defending the Dinétah: Pueblitos in the Ancestral Navajo Homeland* (2003), 212, Towner discusses the archaeological biases toward dating pueblitos while neglecting less impressive hogans, which perhaps distorts our understanding of the antiquity of hogans.

7. Curtis F. Schaafsma, "Ethnic Identity and Protohistoric Archaeological Sites in Northwestern New Mexico: Implications for Reconstructions of Navajo and Ute History"; Gary M. Brown, "The Protohistoric Transition in the Northern San Juan Region"; and David M. Brugge, "Navajo Archaeology: A Promising Past," all in *The Archaeology of Navajo Origins*, ed. Ronald H. Towner (1996), 19–69, 257–60. Also see Kemrer, "Appraisal of Piedra Lumbre Phase," 100–101, and Gary M. Brown et al., *Archaeological Data Recovery at San Juan Coal Company's La Plata Mine, San Juan County, New Mexico* (1991), 64–65.

8. Morris E. Opler offers a similar argument in "The Apachean Culture Pattern and Its Origins," in *Handbook of North American Indians*, vol. 10, *Southwest*, ed. Alfonso Ortiz (1983), 381.

9. Wyman, *Blessingway*, 239–40, 327–33, 447–48, 633–34.

10. See, for example, Schaafsma, "Ethnic Identity," 44. The archaeologist David Wilcox has posited a widely accepted hypothesis that Diné entered the Southwest via the High Plains of Texas after Francisco Vásquez de Coronado made his famous quest for Cíbola. I find Wilcox's argument ultimately unpersuasive. He depends largely on negative archaeological evidence, a groundless interpretation of the identity of the "Querechos" whom Coronado saw on his journey to Quivira, and a good deal of speculation. See Wilcox, "The Entry of the Athabaskans into the American Southwest: The Problem Today," in *The Protohistoric Period in the North American Southwest, A.D. 1450–1700*, ed. David Wilcox and W. Bruce Masse (1981), 213–56. But also consult David M. Brugge's "Comments on Athabaskans and Sumas" in the same volume, pp. 291–320. J. Loring Haskell offers a competing but equally speculative and even more problematic theory in *Southern Athapaskan Migration, A.D. 200–1750* (1987). Ronald F. Towner summarizes and critiques the dominant migration hypothesis and offers his own in *Defending the Dinétah*, 194–216.

11. George P. Hammond and Agapito Rey, eds., "Don Juan de Oñate to the Viceroy of New Spain, March 2, 1599," in *Don Juan de Oñate, Colonizer of New*

Mexico, 1595–1628 (1953), 485. My understanding of the Spanish period draws heavily on David J. Weber's extraordinary synthesis and interpretation, *The Spanish Frontier in North America* (1992); see especially chs. 2, 3, and 5.

12. Brown et al., *Archaeological Data*, 729–31; Brown, "Protohistoric Transition," 56, 63, 66–67; Fetterman, "Radiocarbon and Tree-Ring Dating," 80–82; Alan D. Reed and Jonathan C. Horn, "Early Navajo Occupation of the American Southwest: Reexamination of the Dinetah Phase," *Kiva* 55 (1990): 283–300; Brown and Hancock, "Dinetah Phase," 71–75, 85–89. The La Plata Mine sites remain the subject of lively debate among archaeologists. Some scholars argue that Navajos lived in the La Plata Valley as early as 1350, based on radiocarbon dating. However, those dates may have been produced by old construction wood that predated the actual occupation of the site. The 1500–1600 dates come from the charred remains of juniper berries that clung to the boughs used in hogan construction and are, thus, more reliable. I have elected to follow this more conservative interpretation but fully expect that future investigations will push Diné presence in the area back even further. Other archaeologists argue that these are not Diné sites at all, that they are Ute. However, their reasoning is unpersuasive, since it relies on evidence dating two centuries after the fact. See Schaafsma, "Ethnic Identity," but also consult Brugge, "Navajo Archaeology," 258–59.

13. *Documentos para servir a la historia del Nuevo Mexico, 1538–1778* (1962), 194–95. Historians generally have incorrectly given the date of Zárate Salmerón's publication as 1626, following the lead of Charles F. Lummis, who published the first English translation in the 1899 and 1900 volumes of *The Land of Sunshine*. However, Alicia Ronstadt Milich points out that the priest could not have written it before 1627. See Gerónimo de Zárate Salmerón, *Relaciones*, trans. Alicia Ronstadt Milich (1966), 16–17, 93–94. For general information on Zárate Salmerón, consult Joe S. Sando, "Jemez Pueblo," in *Handbook of North American Indians*, vol. 9, *Southwest*, 418.

The archaeologist Curtis F. Schaafsma maintains that a series of sites along the Chama around the present-day Abiquiu Reservoir are the Navajo sites to which Zárate Salmerón referred. These date from about 1650 to 1710 and consist of scattered clusters of rectangular and circular stone dwellings, similar to those found in the canyons of Dinétah, along with stone corrals and lamb pens. If so, these sites represent the earliest evidence of Diné pastoralism. Other archaeologists argue that these sites are Tewa sheep herders' camps, an interpretation supported largely by the abundance of Tewa and Peñasco pottery. Schaafsma demonstrates, however, that there is no historical evidence that the Tewas settled this far up the Chama. It is unlikely that a Tewa settlement here would have escaped Spanish hegemony, and the structures seem too substantial for a seasonal camp. Unfortunately, the documentary evidence that this was home to Diné pastoralists is only circumstantial, and distinctive Diné cultural traits such as forked-stick hogans (found in association with similar masonry structures in the Dinétah area), sweat lodges, and Diné pottery are absent. The Navajos to whom Zárate Salmerón referred may have lived farther up the Chama, closer to the San Juan River. Nonetheless, it is worth noting that by the mid-1690s, when don Diego de Vargas reconquered the pueblos, at least some "Navajo Apaches" neighbored the Jemez and Cochiti pueblos. Moreover, in 1714, when Roque Madrid carried out one of a series of assaults on Dinétah, he traveled up the Chama Valley by way of the Piedra Lumbre, where he attacked some Navajos in "torreones," or fortresses; Spanish maps of the late 1770s locate the Piedra Lumbre near Abiquiu. Additional archaeological investigations in the Abiquiu area and along the Chama may help resolve this debate. See Schaafsma, *Apaches de Navajo: Seventeenth-Century Navajos in the Chama Valley of New Mexico* (2002); Schaafsma, *The Cerrito Site (AR-4): A Piedra Lumbre Phase Settlement at Abiquiu Reservoir* (1979); Schaafsma, *Archaeological Survey of Maximum Pool and Navajo Excavations at Abiquiu Reservoir, Rio Arriba County, New Mexico* (1976). But also consult Frank J. Wozniak, "Ethnohistory of the Abiquiu Reservoir Area," in *History and Ethnohistory along the Rio Chama*, by Frank J. Wozniak, Meade F. Kemrer, and Charles M. Carillo (1992), and Kemrer, "Appraisal of Piedra Lumbre Phase," 101–7. For information on the proximity of the Navajos to the Abiquiu area, see Diego de Vargas, *Blood on the Boulders: The Journals of Don Diego de Vargas, New Mexico, 1694–97*, ed. John L. Kessell, Rick Hendricks, and Meredith D. Dodge (1998), 67, and Rick Hendricks and John P. Wilson, trans. and eds., *The Navajos in 1705: Roque Madrid's Campaign Journal* (1996), 99.

14. "Athabaskan" refers to a family of related languages, much as German and English are related. The languages of the Navajos and other Apachean groups (with the exception of the Kiowa Apaches) are so close that they are mutually intelligible. Thanks to Scott Rushforth for clarifying this issue.

15. Benavides, *Memorial of 1630*, trans. Peter P. Forrestal (1954). For a facsimile of the original Spanish edition, see *The Memorial of Fray Alonso de Benavides, 1630*, trans. Mrs. Edward E. Ayer, ed. Frederick Webb Hodge and Charles Fletcher Lummis (1916), 137–38. Although some scholars, following the lead of the archaeologist Edgar Lee Hewett, suggest that "Navajú" referred to a particular locale, John P. Harrington, the linguist and specialist in Tewa geographical terminology, maintained that "Nabajú" referred more generally to arroyos with cultivated fields. The anthropologist Edward H. Spicer later observed that modern Tewa speakers construed the meaning of the word as "to take from fields." Nonetheless, the Spanish certainly understood their Jemez informants (who were themselves Towa, not Tewa, speakers) to mean that the Nabajú were farmers. See Harrington, "Southern Peripheral Athapaskawan Origins, Divisions, and Migrations," in *Essays in Historical Anthropology of North America* (1940), 518, and Spicer, *Cycles of Conquest: The Impact of Spain, Mexico, and the United States on the Indians of the Southwest, 1533–1960* (1986), 211.

16. Benavides, *Fray Alonso Benavides' Revised Memorial of 1634*, trans. and ed. Frederick Webb Hodge, George P. Hammond, and Agapito Rey (1945), 85; S. Ly-

man Tyler and H. Darrel Taylor, "The Report of Fray Alonso de Posada in Relation to Quivira and Teguayo," *New Mexico Historical Review* 33 (1958): 304. It is unclear just how many Diné lived along the San Juan River; Benavides's information was secondhand, and his estimate of thirty thousand warriors was most certainly hyperbole. Archaeologists examining the Navajo Reservoir area discovered 140 sites dating from approximately 1700 to 1750, a period when population in the area boomed. This figure does not include the pueblitos found in the Gobernador area, and the archaeologists also likely overlooked some sites during this hasty salvage project, which focused on the Anasazi. See James Schoenwetter and Frank W. Eddy, *Alluvial and Palynological Reconstruction of Environments, Navajo Reservoir District* (1964), 22; Frank W. Eddy, *Prehistory in the Navajo Reservoir District, Northwestern New Mexico*, pt. 2 (1966), 505–15.

17. Polly Schaafsma, *Rock Art in the Navajo Reservoir District* (1971), 37, 39, 60; James M. Copeland, "Navajo Hero Twin Ceremonial Art in Dinetah," in *Diné Bíkéyah: Papers in Honor of David M. Brugge*, ed. Meliha S. Duran and David T. Kirkpatrick, 57–68; River Junction Curly, Version III, in Wyman, *Blessingway*, 624; Floyd Laughter, interview in Karl W. Luckert, *Navajo Mountain and Rainbow Bridge Religion* (1977), 44.

18. As part of his diligent effort to retrace Roque Madrid's military route, the archaeologist John P. Wilson identified the mountain ridge extending from Dulce to Llaves, New Mexico, where it merges with an even higher corderilla, as the most likely meaning of the enigmatic location known as Casa Fuerte. I have followed his lead here. Wilson notes that this long, steep ridge is broken by only five easily guarded passes, making it such a natural line of defense that the Spanish called it impregnable. See Hendricks and Wilson, *Navajos in 1705*, 68.

19. James F. Brooks offers a provocative interpretation of the contradictions of conflict, captivity, and consanguinity in *Captives and Cousins: Slavery, Kinship, and Community in the Southwest Borderlands* (2002).

20. Perhaps the best explication of intra-Navajo factionalism is offered by McNitt in *Navajo Wars*. Pueblo factionalism played a role as well; consult David M. Brugge, "Pueblo Factionalism and External Relations," *Ethnohistory* 16 (1969): 191–200. A number of historians have written on the rise of Navajo political identity, each locating that moment of genesis at a different moment in time. See Thompson, *Army and the Navajo*, 164; Parman, *Navajos and the New Deal*, ch. 12; and Iverson, *Navajo Nation*.

21. John O. Baxter, *Las Carneradas: Sheep Trade in New Mexico, 1700–1860* (1987). For evidence of the diaspora to the "Navajo Province," see the statement by Indian prisoners from two different pueblos to Governor Diego de Vargas, along with Roque Madrid to Vargas, 11 Nov. 1696; Vargas to the Conde de Moctezuma, 28 Nov. 1696; and Baltasar de Tovar's report, 6 March 1697, all in Vargas, *Blood on the Boulders*, vol. 2, pp. 842, 1003, 1059, 1064, 1102–3. The evidence of trade with

Navajos, much of it illicit, is sparse, but see Brooks, *Captives and Cousins*, 202, and David M. Brugge, "Eighteenth-Century Fugitives from New Mexico among the Navajos," in *Papers from the Third, Fourth, and Sixth Navajo Studies Conferences*, comp. Alexandra Roberts and Jenevieve Smith (1993), 281.

22. My understanding of raiding owes much to McNitt, *Navajo Wars*, especially ch. 1, and Reeve, "Navaho-Spanish Wars."

23. "Documents concerning . . . an Expedition against the Apaches, June [16]–July, 1669," incomplete document found by France V. Scholes, courtesy of Marc Simmons; [Francisco de Ayeta], Petition, 10 May 1679, in *Historical Documents Relating to New Mexico, Nueva Vizcaya, and Approaches Thereto, to 1773*, vol. 3, ed. and trans. Charles W. Hackett (1937), 302.

24. Reeve, "Seventeenth Century Navaho-Spanish Relations," 49–50; Hendricks and Wilson, *Navajos in 1705*, 137–38, n. 2; Schoenwetter and Eddy, *Alluvial and Palynological Reconstruction*, 120–24.

25. Hendricks and Wilson, *Navajos in 1705*, xvi, 1, 3–4, 13–14, 19, 24–33, 93, 112–18. In relating the account that follows, I have relied on Hendricks and Wilson's translation of the journal.

26. My thinking on this subject has benefited from Kelley, *Navajo Land Use*, 16.

27. Hendricks and Wilson, *Navajos in 1705*, 25–26. Alfonzo Rael de Aguilar noted that when he accompanied a second expedition in 1714, he observed that the Navajos dwelled on the tops of these mesas. See testimonies sent by Governor Codallos y Rabal to the Viceroy, *New Mexico Originals*, microfilm reel 3, Bancroft Library, University of California, Berkeley; and W. W. Hill, trans. and ed., "Some Navaho Culture Changes during Two Centuries (Including Testimonials Sent by Governor Codallos y Rabal to the Viceroy in the Year 1745)," in *Essays in Historical Anthropology of North America* (1940), 411. Hill's translations are sometimes imprecise; I am grateful to Rick Hendricks for correcting and verifying them. For background on the Codallos y Rabal hearing, see Brugge, "Eighteenth-Century Fugitives," 279.

28. Antonio de Ulibarrí, Statement, *New Mexico Originals*; Hill, "Some Navaho Culture Changes," 408–9. The term used throughout the Codallos y Rabal hearing was *ganado menor*, meaning small stock such as sheep and goats; the context makes it clear that sheep are specified, but it is likely that goats were present too, in keeping with the Spanish practice of mixed flocks.

29. Alfonzo Rael de Aguilar, Statement, *New Mexico Originals*; Hill, "Some Navaho Culture Changes," 411.

30. Francisco Cuervo y Valdez, "Report . . . 18 Aug. 1706," in *Historical Documents Relating to New Mexico*, 381–82; Cuervo to the Duque of Albuquerque, 23 June 1706, courtesy of David Brugge; translation courtesy of Rick Hendricks.

31. McNitt, *Navajo Wars*, 23.

32. Hendricks and Wilson, *Navajo in 1705*, 6–7, 116; Antonio Martín and Alfonzo Rael de Aguilar, Statements, *New Mexico Originals*; Hill, "Navaho Culture

Changes," 41, 404, 411; Towner, *Defending the Dinétah*, 137. The best study of early Ute history is found in Ned Blackhawk, *Violence over the Land: Indians and Empires in the Early American West* (2006); also consult Virginia McConnell Simmons, *The Ute Indians of Utah, Colorado, and New Mexico* (2000), 32–33.

33. Patrick Hogan offers a fascinating (and sobering) discussion of how conjecture can become accepted "fact" through scholarly misinterpretation and repetition in "Navajo-Pueblo Interaction during the Gobernador Phase," in *Rethinking Navajo Pueblitos* (1991), 1–22. Also consult A. V. Kidder, "Ruins of the Historic Period in the Upper San Juan Valley, New Mexico," *American Anthropologist* 22 (1920): 327–29.

Malcolm F. Farmer first suggested that Navajos themselves built the defensive structures at Dinétah in "Navaho Archaeology of Upper Blanco and Largo Canyons, Northern New Mexico," *American Antiquity* 8 (1942): 69. For current scholarship, consult Towner, *Defending the Dinétah*, 29–46, 203–4; Towner, "The Pueblito Phenomenon: A New Perspective on Post-Revolt Navajo Culture," in *Archaeology of Navajo Origins*, 162–66, 168; Ronald H. Towner and Jeffrey S. Dean, "LA 2298: The Oldest Pueblito Revisited," *Kiva* 57 (1992): 315–29; Margaret A. Powers and Byron P. Johnson, *Defensive Sites of Dinetah* (1987), 27–28; Michael P. Marshall, "The Pueblito as a Site Complex: Archeological Investigations in the Dinetah District; The 1989–1990 BLM Pueblito Survey," in *Rethinking Navajo Pueblitos*, ch. 5; Marshall, *A Chapter in Early Navajo History: Late Gobernador Phase Pueblito Sites of the Dinetah District* (1995), 8, 60–69; and Brugge, "Navajo Archaeology," 262.

34. Report by Diego de Vargas et al., and Vargas to the Conde de Galve, 1 Sept. 1694, in Vargas, *Blood on the Boulders*, 324–27, 358–77.

35. Despite a growing consensus that Tapacito Pueblito is a uniquely Puebloan site in Dinétah, dissenters remain. Most scholars concur that the building was constructed in the fall of 1694, shortly after the July conquest of Jemez, based on numerous intact tree-ring samples. Nonetheless, the archaeologist John Wilson (whose work ironically helped confirm the 1694 date) disputes this finding. Wilson argues that Tapacito Pueblito did not yet exist in 1705, because Madrid and his men did not take notice of it. I find this negative evidence unpersuasive. See John P. Wilson and A. H. Warren, "LA 2298: The Earliest Pueblito?" *Awanyu* 2 (1974): 8–26; Hendricks and Wilson, *Navajo in 1705*, 85–86; Towner and Dean, "LA 2298."

Some archaeologists point to Tapacito Pueblito as evidence disproving the notion of a *large* Puebloan influx into Dinétah. This building stands out from most of the other structures in the area, which were erected decades later. The well-regarded ethnohistorian and anthropologist David Brugge, by contrast, remains a stalwart proponent of the "pueblo refugee hypothesis." In light of recent scholarship, he concedes that the so-called pueblitos were built largely by Diné, and yet he continues to hold that they hosted a fairly good-sized population of Puebloan people, who taught them religious stories, weaving, herding techniques, and other cultural knowledge, thereby engendering the hybrid Athabaskan-Puebloan-Hispanic culture that we recognize as "Navajo." He points out that the Puebloan influx did not necessarily come solely in the aftermath of the Spanish Reconquest. Some people may have fled to Dinétah well after the Reconquest period or joined the Diné as captives. Circumstantial evidence, especially the presence of Puebloan elements in Diné ceremonies, lends credence to Brugge's hypothesis. Moreover, the rise of pastoralism, which required considerable knowledge of sheep husbandry and the practice of transhumance, also suggests the presence of Puebloan women, who learned their techniques from the Spanish (Brugge, personal communication). I remain unconvinced, however, that the sharing of ideas was necessarily the result of a large in-migration of Puebloan refugees. There were many other opportunities for Diné to appropriate useful knowledge: when Diné captured Puebloan peoples; when occasional intermarriage forged bonds of kinship; when trading excursions brought Diné to the pueblos, where they could make friends, observe, and learn. Moreover, Diné could have learned to care for sheep while serving as slaves in Spanish households, from which they later escaped. Conversations with Patrick Hogan and Jim Copeland helped to confirm and clarify my thinking on this subject; also consult Hogan, "Navajo-Pueblo Interaction," 16–22, and Brooks, *Captives and Cousins*, 95–97.

36. Hendricks and Wilson, *Navajo in 1705*, 20; Towner, "Pueblito Phenomenon," 168.

37. For a discussion of captives among the Navajos, see Brooks, *Captives and Cousins*, 241–50; however, most of the evidence of Puebloan captives among the Navajos comes a century later. It is worth noting, too, that many Navajos were held as captives in Spanish and, later, Mexican settlements. As late as 1872, the agent at Fort Defiance reported that during a two-month period, "about one hundred women and children returned to this reservation from the Mexican settlements, and still there are complaints received at this agency almost every day from relatives of others, who say they are kept by the citizens against their will." See COIA, *Annual Report, 1872*, House Ex. Doc. 1, SS 1560 (1872–73), 688.

38. In this discussion, I am indebted to the generosity of Doug Dykeman and Jeff Wharton, of the Navajo Nation Archeology Department in Farmington, and especially to Jim Copeland, of the U.S. Bureau of Land Management, all three of whom guided me in experiencing a number of these defensive structures firsthand. My grasp of the geography of these sites also draws heavily on Powers and Johnson, *Defensive Sites*, ch. 2; Marshall, "Pueblito"; and Marshall, *Chapter in Early Navajo History*, ch. 2. Also consult Roy L. Carlson, *Eighteenth Century Navajo Fortresses of the Gobernador District* (1965), 2, 100–101.

39. Marshall, "Pueblito," ch. 8, 237–44; Marshall, *Early Navajo History*, 17–28; Powers and Johnson, *Defensive Sites of Dinetah*, 61–65; LouAnn Jacobson, Stephen Fosberg, and Robert Bewley, "Navajo Defensive Systems in the Eighteenth Cen-

tury," in *Cultural Diversity and Adaptation: The Archaic, Anasazi, and Navajo Occupation of the Upper San Juan Basin*, ed. Lori Stephens Reed and Paul F. Reed, 110. On the contemporaneity of the hogans and pueblos, see Towner and Johnson, *San Rafael Canyon Survey*, 23–33.

40. Farmer, "Navaho Archaeology," 66; Jacobson, Fosberg, and Bewley, "Navajo Defensive Systems," 130–36; Powers and Johnson, *Defensive Sites*, 9 (also refer to the individual site descriptions contained in this report).

41. In addition to the historical record, which documents the destruction of Diné corn fields, the archaeological evidence of maize agriculture is abundant, including carbonized corn kernels, corn petroglyphs, and the manos and metates that women used to grind corn into meal. Evidence of bean cultivation, mentioned by five Spanish soldiers in their testimony before Codallos y Rabal in 1743, is also substantiated at Split Rock Pueblito in Largo Canyon. Abundant evidence of deer hunting and limited evidence of gathering is also present in the archaeological record. Consult statements by Antonio Montoya, Antonio Martín, Alfonzo Rael de Aguilar, Juan Vigil, and Antonio Tafoya, in *New Mexico Originals*; Hill, "Navajo Culture Changes," 400, 404, 410–12; Powers and Johnson, *Defensive Sites*, 16–17, 19, 43, 52, 56, 90; Marshall, *Chapter in Early Navajo History*, 133, 161–86, 213–17; and Marshall, "Pueblito," 246–47.

42. Powers and Johnson, *Defensive Sites*, 12, 21; Marshall, "Pueblito," 15, 16, 39, 83, 120, 249–50, 281; Marshall, *Chapter in Early Navajo History*, 145, 217–19; Eddy, *Prehistory in the Navajo Reservoir District*, pt. 2, p. 510; Dorothy L. Keur, "A Chapter in Navaho-Pueblo Relations," *American Antiquity* 10 (1944): 81; Carlson, *Eighteenth Century Navajo Fortresses*, 36, 38, 42, 102, 113. For an example of the use of natural enclosures in the nineteenth century, see Dyk and Dyk, *Left Handed*, 4–6.

Marshall has documented corrals or lamb pens as evidence of livestock husbandry, but other archaeologists question his interpretations, maintaining that his evidence comes from a later period. Peggy Gaudy, an archaeologist with the Bureau of Land Management, however, has documented one corral that included Gobernador polychrome pottery from this early era and notes that the dead wood used in structures like corrals is extremely prone to deterioration and difficult to identify and date. (Jim Copeland, personal communication; Peggy Gaudy, personal communication; Michael Marshall, personal communication.)

43. Frank D. Reeve, "The Navaho-Spanish Peace: 1720s–1770s," *New Mexico Historical Review* 34 (1959): 11–12. I am grateful to David Brugge for bringing the peaceful nature of this encounter to my attention.

44. Antonio Montoya, Juan Tafoya, and Manuel Saenz de Garvisu, Statements, *New Mexico Originals*, translation courtesy of Rick Hendricks. Also see Hill, "Navajo Culture Changes," 400, 404, and 407. Nearly all of those who visited Casa Fuerte in 1743 reported that Navajo women wove mantas, the woolen blankets used as currency and tribute throughout northern New Spain.

45. Marshall, "Pueblito," 16, 88, 109, 183, 211. My description draws on Marshall's site descriptions and my own observations in the area.

46. Whether Diné lived in the area only seasonally or year-round is unclear. In those few instances in which archaeologists have reported the construction season, building activities occurred in summer; likewise, the Spaniards' recorded observations of Casa Fuerte took place in the summer and early fall. It is entirely possible that the residents of these canyons lived elsewhere in winter and migrated here seasonally. Consult Towner, *Defending the Dinétah*, 56, 74–75, 210–11; John Loring Haskell, "The Navajo in the Eighteenth Century: An Investigation Involving Anthropological Archaeology in the San Juan Basin, Northwestern New Mexico" (1975), 161, 176.

47. Juan Joseph Lobato to Governor don Thomas Vélez Cachupín, 17 Aug. 1752, quoted in Alfred Barnaby Thomas, *The Plains Indians and New Mexico, 1751–1778: A Collection of Documents Illustrative of the History of the Eastern Frontier of New Mexico* (1940), 117; Bentura, Statement to Governor Joachín Codallos y Rabal, 20 July 1748, SANM, frames 827–34, reel 8. The incentives for out-migration were likely multiple. Musket parts found at Frances Canyon Pueblito, along with musket balls and their impact marks at Shaft House in Largo Canyon, hint at why the Diné may have left. Drought, too, may have played a part, although scholars disagree on this issue. Some have attributed out-migration to drought in 1748, others to a more extended drought beginning in 1752. A Kiowa man named Bentura, who had lived a year and a half among Navajos, reported that a 1748 drought brought crop failure to Navajo Country; hence, some archaeologists have suggested that this event encouraged families to abandon the area. The archaeologist Ronald Towner, however, points out that the following year, 1749, was a rather wet one and that Diné were perfectly capable of weathering one bad year. Moreover, Diné built new pueblitos and added onto old ones after that drought. A six-year droughty period after 1752, however, appears to coincide with a precipitous drop in construction in Dinétah in the 1750s. Perhaps a combination of drought and overgrazing so depleted forage that only a few families could hold on. See Towner, *Defending the Dinétah*, 158–61, 183–85; Jacobson, Fosberg, and Bewley, "Navajo Defense Systems," 122; Marshall, *Chapter in Early Navajo History*, 25, 45–47; Brugge, "Eighteenth-Century Fugitives," 280; Brugge, "The Navajo Exodus" (1972); Reeve, "Navaho-Spanish Peace," 20–21. For tree-ring data on the 1748 and 1752–57 droughts, see Cook, "Long-Term Aridity."

48. The following discussion of Diné movement into the Chaco area draws largely on David M. Brugge, *Tsegai: An Archeological Ethnohistory of the Chaco Region* (1986), 5–10, 14–24, 77–84, and Alden C. Hayes, David M. Brugge, and W. James Judge, *Archeological Surveys of Chaco Canyon, New Mexico* (1981), 36–37, 69–71, 99–100. Also consult R. Gwinn Vivian, "The Navajo Archaeology of the Chacra Mesa" (1960).

49. Cuervo to the Duque of Albuquerque, 23 June 1706. Frank McNitt discusses the Navajos of Cebolleta at length in *Navajo Wars*, ch. 2. Also consult Reeve, "Navaho-Spanish Peace," 17–29.

50. Instruction of don Thomas Vélez Cachupín, 12 Aug. 1754, in Thomas, *Plains Indians and New Mexico*, 138.

51. Dorothy Louise Keur, *Big Bead Mesa: An Archaeological Study of Navaho Acculturation, 1745–1812* (1941). Keur found some fifty hogan sites, but subsequent investigations have located many more (David Brugge, personal communication).

52. Pedro Tamaron y Romeral, *Bishop Tamaron's Visitation of New Mexico, 1760*, ed. Eleanor B. Adams (1954), 68. Also consult T. J. Ferguson and E. Richard Hart, *A Zuni Atlas* (1985), maps 12, 13, 14, and 15.

53. The written record on Navajo-Laguna interactions in the eighteenth century is scant; for a summary, see Myra Ellen Jenkins and Ward Alan Minge, eds., "Navajo Activities Affecting the Acoma-Laguna Area, 1746–1910," in *Navajo Indians II* (1974).

54. James Brooks offers a most compelling interpretation of conflicts between the Spanish settlers and the Cebolleta Navajos, who eventually became known to other Diné as Diné Ana'aii (Enemy Navajos), in *Captives and Cousins*, 103–16. Also consult McNitt, *Navajo Wars*, 29; Frank D. Reeve, "Navaho-Spanish Peace," 29–38; Reeve, "Navaho-Spanish Diplomacy, 1770–1790," *New Mexico Historical Review* 35 (1960): 206–10.

55. "Town of Cebolleta Grant, Surveyor General Report No. 46," frames 936–72, reel 1, Surveyor General Records and the Records of the Court of Private Claims, SANM, series 1.

56. Fernando de Chacón to Nemecio Salcedo, Diary of Events, 10 May 1804, frames 275–79, reel 15; Investigation of Complaints, 25 May–9 July 1808, frames 488–99, reel 16; Josef Mariano de la Peña, Orders to Withdraw Livestock from Navajo Frontier, 18 Nov. 1818, frames 447–48, reel 19, all in SANM. For English synopses of these documents, see Correll, *Through White Men's Eyes*, 98, 108, 116–17.

57. Chacón to Salcedo, Diary of Events, 10 May 1804.

58. Correll, *Through White Men's Eyes*, vols. 1–3, provides an illuminating overview of the cycle of depredation and retaliation in the Spanish, Mexican, and American periods. For accounts of the first wave of raids in the nineteenth century, see, for example, Chacón to Salcedo, Diary of Events, 16 May 1804; Blas Antonio Chávez to Francisco Sarracino, 6 Feb. 1834, MANM, frames 215–16, reel 18; English synopses appear in Correll, *Through White Men's Eyes*, vol. 1, 98, 152. One revealing episode of raiding during the 1850s is documented in a series of letters: H. L. Dodge to W. H. Davis, 19 April 1856, and Dodge to D. Meriwether, 16 May 1856, frames 205–6 and 276–77, reel 548, LR, Office of Indian Affairs, New Mexico Superintendency, 1856–1857, M234; H. L. Kendrick to W. A. Nichols, 21 April 1856, 2 June 1856, and 13 June 1856, frames 818–20, 830–32, 836–39, reel 5, LR, Headquarters Department of New Mexico, 1854–1865, M1120, all in RG 75, NA. Complaints

about New Mexican herders impinging on Navajo flocks are recorded in Kendrick to Meriwether, 10 Feb. 1854 and 13 May 1854, frames 815–16 and 828–30, reel 3, LR, M1120, RG 75, NA. For comments on how at least some thefts were exaggerated or inaccurately blamed on Navajos, see Meriwether to G. W. Manypenny, 30 June 1856; W. F. M. Arny to S. B. Waltrous, 11 Oct. 1861; and J. L. Collins to Waltrous, 26 Oct. 1861, frames 286–88, reel 548, and frames 474–75 and 476–83, reel 550, LR, M234, RG 75, NA.

59. See, for example, James S. Calhoun to William Medill, 1 Oct. 1849, in Calhoun, *The Official Correspondence of James S. Calhoun*, ed. Annie Louise Abel (1915), 32.

60. See, for example, Marc Simmons, *New Mexico: An Interpretive History* (1988), 82.

61. Teodoro de Croix to Joseph de Gálvez, 23 Feb. 1780, in Alfred Barnaby Thomas, trans. and ed., *Forgotten Frontiers: A Study of the Spanish Indian Policy of Don Juan Bauista de Anza, Governor of New Mexico, 1777–1787* (1932), 144.

62. Chacón to Pedro de Nava, 15 July 1795, frames 735–36, reel 13, SANM; translation courtesy of Rick Hendricks.

63. Dennis Gilpin, "Early Navajo Occupation West of the Chuska Mountains," in *The Archaeology of Navajo Origins*, ed. Ronald H. Towner (1998), 179–83; Bryant Bannister, John W. Hannah, William J. Robinson, *Tree-Ring Dates from Arizona K, Puerco-Wide Ruin-Ganado Area* (1966), 24; Karin L. Jones, *Excavation of the Sand Dune Site at Hubbell Trading Post National Historic Site* (1988), courtesy of Harley Shaw. See Donald E. Worcester, "The Navaho during the Spanish Regime in New Mexico," *New Mexico Historical Review* 26 (April 1951): 107, for evidence of Navajos venturing as far west as Havasupai Country in 1686.

64. "An Account of the Events concerning the Dissolution of the Gila-Navajo Alliance, 1785–1786," in Thomas, *Forgotten Frontiers*, 350. Anza's "Hozo" is a misspelling of "Oso," Spanish for bear, referring to the Diné name for Bear Springs, Shash Bitoo'. My thanks to David Brugge for clarifying this point. Although Anza may have written the first descriptive reference to Canyon de Chelly, don Bernardo de Miera y Pacheco depicted it even earlier, in 1778. On a map of the "Provincia de Nabajoo," Miera drew "Sierra de Chegui" as a noteworthy locale between the Chuskas and the Hopi mesas. However, his map did not indicate that any Spaniards confirmed the presence of Navajos in these canyons. The map appears in Silvestre Vélez de Escalante, *The Domínguez-Escalante Journal: Their Expedition through Colorado, Utah, Arizona, and New Mexico in 1776*, trans. Angelico Chavez and ed. Ted J. Warner (1995).

65. Matson and Schroeder, "Cordero," 356. That translation is based on a transcript of Cordera's field report, incorporated into Manuel Orozoco y Berra's geography, written in 1864. Like so much in the Spanish record, these references give us only sketchy ideas about the spread of Diné across the southern Colorado Plateau.

As to the Chuskas, a letter from Chacón to Nava (18 Nov. 1799, frame 462, reel 14, SANM) confirms that Navajos were using the ridge (referred to as Sierra de Navajó), at least intermittently, by the turn of the century.

66. Stephen C. Jett, ed., "The Destruction of Navajo Orchards in 1864: Captain John Thompson's Report," *Arizona and the West* 16 (1974): 369.

67. My discussion of canyons de Chelly and del Muerto draws on Pamela C. Magers, "Navajo Settlement in Canyon del Muerto," in *The Canyon del Muerto Survey Project: Anasazi and Navajo Archeology in Northeastern Arizona*, by Patricia L. Fall, James A. McDonald, and Pamela C. Magers (1981). I am indebted to Scott Travis for the insights he provided on the history of the Diné in this canyon during an extraordinary tour in 1996.

68. McNitt, *Navajo Wars*, 39–44. Among those taken captive was Segundo, a Diné leader from the San Mateo area who sought peace with the Spanish and was not among the raiders; he apparently sought refuge in Canyon del Muerto.

69. My account of this event draws on McNitt, *Navajo Wars*, 39–44; David Brugge's translation of Narbona's report in that volume, appendix A; and a Diné oral tradition reported in Magers, "Navajo Settlement in Canyon del Muerto," 57–58.

70. Kemrer offers a generally persuasive analysis of the waves of early settlement on Black Mesa in "Dynamics of Western Navajo," 62, 77–78, 127–28, 133–36. Also see Rocek, "Navajo Cultural History," 413–14. For reports on military incursions made between 1823 and 1860, see David M. Brugge, ed., "Vizcarra's Navajo Campaign of 1823," *Arizona and the West* 6 (1964): 223–44; Simpson, *Navaho Expedition*; Rice, *Cannoneer*; J. G. Walker and O. L. Shepherd, *The Navajo Reconnaissance: A Military Exploration of the Navajo Country in 1859*, ed. L. R. Bailey (1964); Max L. Heyman, Jr., "On the Navaho Trail: The Campaign of 1860–61," *New Mexico Historical Review* 26 (1951): 44–63.

I draw my image of Black Mesa from Shirley Powell and George J. Gumerman, *People of the Mesa: The Archaeology of Black Mesa, Arizona* (1987), 6–8.

71. Correll, *Through White Men's Eyes*, vol. 1, 294; Deborah L. Nichols and F. E. Smiley, eds., *Excavations on Black Mesa, 1982: A Descriptive Report* (1984), 443–45, 469–72; Andrew L. Christenson and William J. Parry, *Excavations on Black Mesa, 1983: A Descriptive Report* (1985), 274, 277–78; Kemrer, "Dynamics of Western Navajo," 144–47.

72. For the history of a much more complex transhumance in Spain, organized by stockowners' associations, see E. H. Carrier, *Water and Grass: A Study in the Pastoral Economy of Southern Europe* (1932; reprint, 1980), chs. 10 and 11.

73. Witherspoon, *Language and Art*, 21, 48–49; Patrick Gordon Pynes, "Erosion, Extraction, and Reciprocation: An Ethno/Environmental History of the Navajo Nation's Ponderosa Pine Forests" (2000), 165.

74. Brugge, *Tsegai*, 15–24, 77–84, and Hayes, Brugge, and Judge, *Archeological Surveys of Chaco Canyon*, 36–37, 69–71, 99–100.

75. See, for example, Dyk, *Son of Old Man Hat*, 178–79.

76. Rosalie Angelina Fanale, "Navajo Land and Land Management: A Century of Change" (1982), 103. Richard P. Tucker offers a discussion of similar patterns in "The Evolution of Transhumant Grazing in the Punjab Himalaya," *Mountain Research and Development* 6 (1986): 17–28.

77. James F. Downs, *Animal Husbandry in Navajo Culture and Society* (1964), 32–35. According to Downs, sheep refused to graze in the heat and would bunch together to shade their eyes from the sun. On cool days, shepherds kept the flocks out all day.

78. These moves are common for pastoralists; see Carrier, *Water and Grass*, 5. For examples of Navajo movements, see Pynes, "Erosion, Extraction, Reciprocation," 174, and Fanale, "Navajo Land and Land Management," 111–17.

79. Linda Popelish and Russell T. Fehr, *Archaeological Investigations in the Northern Chuska Mountains: The N-13 Road Survey at Red Rock and Lukachukai, Navajo Nation* (1983), 9, 13–21. The botanical names for these trees are *Pinus ponderosa* (ponderosa), *Pseudotsuga menziesii* (Douglas fir), *Populus tremuloides* (quaking aspen), *Pinus edulis* (piñon), *Juniperus monosperma* (one-seed juniper), and *Quercus gambelii* (Gambel oak).

80. The popularity of the Chuskas for grazing can be inferred from the fire-scar record. As increasing numbers of livestock eliminated the grasses that provided fuels for surface fires, the frequency of fire plummeted about 1830. See Melissa Savage and Thomas W. Swetnam, "Early 19th-Century Fire Decline Following Sheep Pasturing in a Navajo Ponderosa Pine Forest," *Ecology* 71 (1990): 2374–78.

81. Dyk, *Son of Old Man Hat*, provides detailed accounts of one family's seasonal movements. Also consult Stephen C. Jett, "Navajo Seasonal Migration Patterns," *Kiva* 44 (1978): 65–75.

82. Dyk, *Son of Old Man Hat*, 104–13, 129–32, 178–79, 225.

83. Shoemaker, *American Indian Population*, 34.

6 HOOFED LOCUSTS

1. Background on Wooton and his expedition comes from Kelly W. Allred, "Elmer Ottis Wooton and the Botanizing of New Mexico," *Systematic Botany* 15 (1990): 700–719, and Allred, "The Trail of E. O. Wooton," *New Mexico Resources* 9 (1993): 3–18. Also consult E. O. Wooton to W. J. Spillman, 17 Sept. 1904, Letterbook, pp. 417–18, box 5, Elmer Ottis Wooton Papers, NMSU. I am indebted to Bill deBuys for bringing the Wooton expedition and collection to my attention.

2. All climate data in this chapter come from my analysis of Cook, "Long-Term Aridity," and Ni, "Cool-Season Precipitation."

3. See, for example, Wooton's 1904 Field Journal entries for 14, 18, and 26 July 1904, box 6, Wooton Papers, NMSU.

4. For a good discussion of the creation of the Checkerboard, see Kelly, *Navajo Indians*, 16–25. Also consult Sanford A. Mosk, *Land Tenure Problems in the Santa Fe Railroad Grant Area* (1944), 11–20, 36–37. On the use of these areas by non-Navajo sheep men, see, for example, A. Eichwald to COIA, 29 Oct. 1908, CFF 73488-1908-301, Navajo Agency, RG 75, NA.

5. Wooton's 1904 Field Journal, 1 Aug. 1904, Wooton Papers, NMSU. Similarly, Wooton found the areas around the Mormon settlements in the San Juan River valley near Fruitland to be a bit weedier than the reservation itself.

6. For Wooton's trek through the reservation, see his 1904 Field Journal, 3–5 Aug. 1904, Wooton Papers, NMSU. The botanical names for these plants are: *Hilaria jamesii* (galleta grass), *Atriplex canescens* (four-wing saltbush), *Atriplex confertifolia* (shadscale), *Sporobolus airoides* (alkali sacaton), *Ephedra trifurca* (Mormon tea), *Sarcobatus vermiculatus* (greasewood or chico), *Bouteloua gracilis* (blue grama), which Wooton refers to in his journal as *Bouteloua oligostachye*, *Xanthium strumarium* (cockleburr), *Corispermum americanum* (bugseed), and *Verbesina encelioides* (golden crownbeard). For the common names of the plants mentioned throughout this discussion of Wooton's field trip, I have relied on E. O. Wooton and Paul C. Standley, *Flora of New Mexico*, vol. 19 (1915). Also see the references cited in chapter 2, n. 17 of this book. My thanks to Kelly Allred for helping me understand Wooton's findings and for clarifying key points about the plants I discuss here.

7. Gregory, *Navajo Country*, 26, 33, 41, 48.

8. Robert Young, comp., *The Navajo Yearbook of Planning in Action* (1955), 113; Committee on Indian Affairs, *Survey of Conditions*, pt. 34, p. 17979. I use Young's figures, taken from "old BIA records," instead of the dipping records published in 1937, because he counts mature sheep and goats, omitting lambs and kids, in keeping with the practice of counting only mature animals when determining carrying capacity.

9. Kelly, *Navajo Roundup*, 31–32, 38–40, 98–101.

10. John O. Baxter, "Restocking the Navajo Reservation after Bosque Redondo," *New Mexico Historical Review* 58 (1983): 325; "Treaty between the United States of America and the Navajo Tribe of Indians," concluded 1 June 1868, *Native American Legal Materials Collection*, Title 4321, p. 7.

11. COIA, *Annual Report, 1870* (p. 612) and *Annual Report, 1891* (p. 309); William H. Harrison to COIA, 11 Sept. 1907, CCF 76859-07-916, Navajo, RG 75, NA; *Felix S. Cohen's Handbook of Federal Indian Law* ([1971]), 204–5; Howard Gorman, interview in Roessel, *Navajo Stories of the Long Walk*, 40. Exceptions were made to this pre-WWI ban. In 1890, agent C. E. Vandever reported the sale of 12,000 sheep; in 1893, sheep sales were permitted to offset crop failures; and in 1909 the BIA allowed at least some traders to purchase sheep and goats, mostly wethers, from the Navajos. See COIA, *Annual Report, 1890* (p. 162) and *Annual Report, 1893* (p. 109); F. H. Abbott to

J. L. Hubbell, 18 Dec. 1909, box 43, Indians 1909 file, Hubbell Papers, UA; Livestock Book, Sept. 1909, p. 1, box 2, Babbitt and Roberts Trading Post Records, UNM.

12. Elinor G. K. Melville, *A Plague of Sheep: Environmental Consequences of the Conquest of Mexico* (1994), 6–7, 47–55; Graeme Caughley, "Wildlife Management and the Dynamics of Ungulate Populations," *Applied Biology* 1 (1976): 196–98; Caughley, "What Is This Thing Called Carrying Capacity?" in *North American Elk: Ecology, Behavior, and Management*, ed. Mark S. Boyce and Larry D. Hayden-Wing (1980), 2–8; N. Leader-Williams, *Reindeer on South Georgia: The Ecology of an Introduced Population* (1988), esp. 19–21; Valerius Geist, *Mountain Sheep: A Study in Behavior and Evolution* ([1971]), 289–90.

13. Ungulate irruption is a classic example of chaos theory. See Gleick, *Chaos*, 3–8, 62–64.

14. Melville, *Plague of Sheep*; see especially chs. 2 and 4. Also consult the thoughtful critique offered by Andrew Sluyter, "From Archive to Map to Pastoral Landscape: A Spatial Perspective on the Livestock Ecology of Sixteenth-Century New Spain," *Environmental History* 3 (1998): 508–28.

15. My understanding of the complexities of population dynamics has been informed by Anthony R. Ives, "Population Ecology: The Waxing and Waning of Populations," in *Ecology*, ed. Stanley I. Dodson et al. (1998), 236–64, and conversations with Ives and Nancy Langston. Also see John MacNab, "Carrying Capacity and Related Slippery Shibboleths," *Wildlife Society Bulletin* 13 (1985): 405. The botanical names for the plants named here are *Bouteloua curtipendula* (sideoats grama), *Muhlenbergia porteri* (bush muhly), *Oryzopsis hymenoides* (Indian ricegrass), *Hilaria jamesii* (galleta), *Sporobolus cryptandrus* (sand dropseed), *Sphaeralcea* spp. (globemallow), and *Plantago patagonica* (woolly plantain).

16. See, for example, COIA, *Annual Report, 1895*.

17. The same drought conditions that depleted corn crops generally also meant less forage, so declines in forage could coincide with declines in stock population as a result of slaughter. That correlation, however, is indirect. Even if the Diné chose to slaughter stock in response to decreased forage, such a mediated response is not the type of direct cause and effect articulated by ungulate irruption theory.

18. See, for example, Mitchell, *Tall Woman*, 55, 249; Dyk, *Navaho Autobiography*, 85.

19. Baxter, "Restocking," 331–34, 338–39; Bailey and Bailey, *History of the Navajos*, 38–40; Howard Gorman, Teddy Draper, Akinabh Burbank, and Tezbah Mitchell, interviews in Roessel, *Navajo Stories of the Long Walk*, 41, 51, 134, 252; COIA, *Annual Report, 1874* (1874–75), 372. The numbers given here are rounded off and slightly inflated. The first lot of stock consisted of 13,700 ewes, 300 rams, 900 nanny goats, and 100 billies. However, some 250 head of stock were stolen or accidentally killed by overcrowding before they were issued. See COIA, *Annual Report, 1870*, 612.

20. The initial reservation was much smaller—a little less than the size of New Jersey—but since subsequent expansions of the reservation boundaries merely took in areas where Diné already lived, I have used the larger size here.

21. For insight into the methods agents used to arrive at their population and livestock estimates, see COIA, *Annual Report* for 1870 (pp. 612, 616–17), 1872 (p. 688), 1877 (p. 555), 1879 (pp. 221–22), 1883 (pp. 120–21), 1888 (p. 189), and 1889 (p. 256).

22. COIA, *Annual Report, 1889* (p. 256) and *Annual Report, 1890* (pp. 161–62).

23. COIA, *Annual Report* for 1886 (p. 42), 1887 (p. 171), and 1888 (pp. 189–90).

24. COIA, *Annual Report, 1891* (p. 309) and *Annual Report, 1892* (p. 208). The Census Bureau surveyed Indian reservations for the first time in 1890. For a brief discussion, consult Shoemaker, *American Indian Population*, 106.

25. 1915 Navajo Census. I have recalculated the sums that Paquette reported to correct his addition errors. His figures were likely approximations, since most of the enumerations are given in multiples of ten.

26. See, for example, "Testimony of Indians from San Juan Agency in Red Rock Vat Trouble," 5 Sept. 1925, file 8, box 30, Franciscan Papers, UA; [S. F.] Stacher to Gentlemen, 9 Dec. 1925, file 2.1.c Dipping Operations, box 10, Duclos Files, and E. R. Fryer to M. J. Bedwell, 6 July 1940, CCF 301 (1 of 2), box 119, Navajo Area Office, both in RG 75, NARA-PR; and Committee on Indian Affairs, *Survey of Conditions*, pt. 18, p. 9006–7.

27. Young, *Navajo Yearbook*, 113. This number differs from that reported by Zeh in chapter 2 because he included lambs and kids. Conservationists counted only mature sheep and goats against carrying capacity, and I follow their lead throughout the rest of this book.

28. Robinson's observations were recorded in Scott, "Report on the Navajo Indians," p. 18, Board of Indian Commissioners Special Reports, RG 75, NA.

29. Simpson, *Navaho Expedition*, 73. For a primer on reading the forest landscape, see P. L. Marks and Sana Gardescu, "Inferring Forest Stand History from Observational Field Evidence," in *The Historical Ecology Handbook: A Restorationist's Guide to Reference Ecosystems*, ed. Dave Egan and Evelyn A. Howell (2001); Vinson Brown's classic *Reading the Woods: Seeing More in Nature's Familiar Faces* (1969), especially ch. 6, is also useful.

30. Beadle, *Undeveloped West*, 547–48. For a similar comment on the Zuni Mountains, see J. T. Rothrock, "Preliminary Botanical Report," in *Annual Report upon the Geographical Exploration and Surveys West of the One Hundredth Meridian*, by George M. Wheeler (1875), 120.

31. Gregory, *Geology of the Navajo Country*, 14.

32. Melissa Savage, "Structural Dynamics of a Southwestern Pine Forest under Chronic Human Influence," *Annals* (Association of American Geographers) 8 (1991): 274–77. Throughout this discussion, I have also drawn on the detailed

research report in Savage's dissertation, "Structural Dynamics of a Pine Forest in the American Southwest under Chronic Human Disturbance" (1989).

33. Charles F. Cooper, "Changes in Vegetation, Structure, and Growth of South-Western Pine Forests since White Settlement," *Ecological Monographs* 30 (1960): 133–34, 136, 151–52, 157–58; Alan S. White, "Presettlement Regeneration Patterns in a Southwestern Ponderosa Pine Stand," *Ecology* 66 (1985): 591–93; Melissa Savage, Peter M. Brown, and Johannes Feddema, "The Role of Climate in a Pine Forest Regeneration Pulse in the Southwestern United States," *Ecoscience* 3 (1996): 311–12; Michael H. Madany and Neil E. West, "Livestock Grazing–Fire Regime Interactions within Montane Forests of Zion National Park, Utah," *Ecology* 64 (1983): 661–67; Savage, "Structural Dynamics of a Southwestern Pine Forest," 274–75; Savage and Swetnam, "Early 19th-Century Fire Decline," 2376.

34. Consult Craig D. Allen, "Lots of Lightning and Plenty of People: An Ecological History of Fire in the Upland Southwest," in *Fire, Native Peoples, and the Natural Landscape*, ed. Thomas R. Vale (2002), 143–93; Thomas W. Swetnam and Christopher H. Baisan, "Historical Fire Regime Patterns in the Southwestern United States since A.D. 1700," in *Fire Effects in Southwestern Forests: Proceedings of the Second La Mesa Fire Symposium, Los Alamos, New Mexico, March 29–31, 1994*, ed. Craig D. Allen (1996), 11–32; and Thomas W. Swetnam and Julio L. Betancourt, "Fire-Southern Oscillation Relations in the Southwestern United States," *Science* 249 (1990): 1017–20.

Some historians have argued that fires lit by Native Americans to herd game and regenerate grasses shaped the pre-conquest landscape throughout North America, including the American Southwest. See, for example, Stephen J. Pyne, *Fire in America: A Cultural History of Wildland and Rural Fire* (1982; reprint, 1997), 514–29. There is little documentation, however, of deliberate fires set by Diné, aside from camp fires; that evidence comes from Hill, *Agricultural and Hunting Methods*, 97, and Gary Paul Nabhan, Marcelle Coder, and Susan J. Smith, *Woodlands in Crisis: A Legacy of Lost Biodiversity on the Colorado Plateau* (2004), 64. Fire-scar evidence regarding the synchronicity of fire and drought and the seasonality of fire, along with the incredible number of lightning strikes, have led most southwestern fire ecologists to conclude that lightning can account for the vast majority of fires before 1900.

35. Savage and Swetnam, "Early 19th-Century Fire Decline," 2375–77; Savage, "Structural Dynamics of a Southwestern Pine Forest," 283–86. On the well-documented relationship between overgrazing and the cessation of natural fire regimes, consult Ramzi Touchan, Thomas W. Swetnam, and Henri D. Grissino-Mayer, "Effects of Livestock Grazing on Pre-Settlement Fire Regimes in New Mexico," in *Proceedings: Symposium on Fire in Wilderness and Park Management, March 30–April 1, 1993, Missoula, Montana*, ed. James K. Brown et al. (1995); and Henri D. Grissino-Mayer and Thomas W. Swetnam, "Multi-Century History of Wildfire in the Ponderosa Pine Forests of El Malpais National Monument," in

Natural History of El Malpais National Monument, comp. Ken Mabery (1997), 167–68. On the equally well-documented region-wide pulse of regeneration, consult Cooper, "Changes in Vegetation," 157–58; and Savage, Brown, and Feddema, "Role of Climate," 312, 315–16.

36. In the 1920s and 1930s, conservationists complained that goats and sheep damaged new production in the Zuni and Chuska mountains through browsing and trampling. See K. C. Kartchner to Stacher, 14 Aug. 1922, file F, box 13, Eastern Navajo Agency, RG 75, NARA-PR; and Navajo Service, "Land Management Unit 18, Integrated Report," 1936, p. 49, file 9, box 8, SCS Records, UNM.

37. See, for example, Savage, "Structural Dynamics of a Southwestern Pine Forest," 283.

38. Much of my discussion of the shrub-grasslands comes from West, *Temperate Deserts*, especially ch. 12, supplemented by Dick-Peddie, *New Mexico Vegetation*, chs. 7 and 8. I am also indebted to the discussion of bunch grasses offered by Langston in *Forest Dreams*, 202–4, augmented by D. D. Briske, "Developmental Morphology and Physiology of Grasses," in *Grazing Management: An Ecological Perspective*, ed. Rodney K. Heitschmidt and Jerry W. Stuth (1991), 85–108. The botanical names for these grasses are *Bouteloua gracilis* (blue grama), *Hilaria jamesii* (galleta), *Agropyron smithii* (western wheatgrass), and *Oryzopsis hymenoides* (Indian ricegrass).

39. Jack D. Brotherson, Samuel R. Rushforth, and Jeffrey R. Johansen, "Effects of Long-Term Grazing on Cryptogam Crust Cover in Navajo National Monument, Ariz.," *Journal of Range Management* 36 (September 1983): 579–81; Renee J. Beymer and Jeffrey M. Klopatek, "Effects of Grazing on Cryptogamic Crusts in Pinyon-Juniper Woodlands in Grand Canyon National Park," *American Midland Naturalist* 127 (1992): 139–48; Jayne Belnap and Dale A. Gillette, "Vulnerability of Desert Biological Soil Crusts to Wind Erosion: The Influences of Crust Development, Soil Texture, and Disturbance," *Journal of Arid Environments* 39 (1998): 133–42; Kimball T. Harper and Jayne Belnap, "The Influence of Biological Soil Crusts on Mineral Uptake by Associated Vascular Plants," *Journal of Arid Environments* 47 (2001): 347–57.

40. C. V. Hulet, G. Alexander, and E. S. E. Hafez, "The Behavior of Sheep," in *The Behavior of Domestic Animals*, ed. E. S. E. Hafez, 3rd ed. (1975), 250–53; Ulrich Jaudas, *The New Goat Handbook*, trans. Elizabeth D. Crawford (1989), 31, 34, 37–38. For useful background on goats, consult Dan Scurlock, "A Poor Man's Cow: The Goat in New Mexico and the Southwest," *New Mexico Historical Review* 73 (1998): 7–24. The botanical names for these plants are *Artemisia* spp. (sagebrush), *Atriplex* spp. (saltbush and shadscale), *Ceratoides lanata* (winterfat), *Ceanothus fendleri* (deerbriar), and *Cowania mexicana* (cliffrose).

41. E. S. E. Hafez and M. F. Bouissou, "The Behavior of Cattle," in *The Behavior of Domestic Animals*, ed. E. S. E. Hafez (1975), 203–13; Jerry W. Stuth, "Foraging

Behavior," and J. E. Huston and W. E. Pinchak, "Range Animal Nutrition," both in *Grazing Management: An Ecological Perspective*, ed. Rodney K. Heitschmidt and Stuth (1991); "Living from Livestock," 29.

42. Allen D. Wilson and Neil D. MacLeod, "Overgrazing: Present or Absent," *Journal of Range Management* 44 (1991): 475, 481; D. D. Briske and R. K. Heitschmidt, "An Ecological Perspective," in *Grazing Management: An Ecological Perspective*, ed. Heitschmidt and Jerry W. Stuth (1991), 22.

43. Allan Savory, *Holistic Resource Management* (1988), 152–54, 511; Thomas L. Fleischner, "Ecological Costs of Livestock Grazing in Western North America," *Conservation Biology* 8 (1994): 631. Also see MacNab, "Carrying Capacity," 403–10.

44. Savory, *Holistic Resource Management*, especially ch. 19; Briske, "Developmental Morphology"; Harold E. Heady and R. Dennis Child, *Rangeland Ecology and Management* (1994), chs. 2 and 3; R. M. Moore and E. F. Biddiscombe, "The Effects of Grazing on Grasslands," in *Grasses and Grasslands*, ed. C. Barnard (1964), 221, 225–26. For a clearly written primer on vegetation change due to grazing, consult Thomas R. Vale, *Plants and People: Vegetation Change in North America* (1982), 24–28.

45. Briske, "Developmental Morphology," 94–96, 102–6. Botanical names for increasers are *Chrysothamnus nauseosus* (rabbitbrush), *Gutierrezia sarothrae* (snakeweed), *Helenium hoopesii* (sneezeweed), *Salsola iberica* (Russian thistle), and *Astragalus* spp. (locoweed).

46. Kieth Severson and Leonard F. Debano, "Influence of Spanish Goats on Vegetation and Soils in Arizona Chaparral," *Journal of Range Management* 44 (1991): 117.

47. N. E. West and John Skukiņš, eds., *Nitrogen in Desert Ecosystems* (1978), ch. 17; W. G. Whitford, "Decomposition and Nutrient Cycling in Deserts," in *Pattern and Process in Desert Ecosystems* (1986), ch. 5.

48. Zeh, *General Report Covering the Grazing Situation on the Navajo Indian Reservation*, reprinted in Committee on Indian Affairs, *Survey of Conditions*, pt. 18, *Navajos in Arizona and New Mexico* (1932), p. 9125.

49. Muir, *The Mountains of California*, orig. pub. 1894; reprinted in *John Muir: Nature Writings*, ed. William Cronon (1997), 387.

50. Dyk, *Navaho Autobiography*, 58; Zeh, *General Report*, 9126; [D. E. Harbison], "Working Plan Report of the Grazing Resources and Activities of the Southern Navajo Indian Reservation, Arizona and New Mexico," 24 Dec. 1930, p. 9200, in Committee on Indian Affairs, *Survey of Conditions*, pt. 18.

Making paths toward water is a general sheep trait. See Hulet, Alexander, and Hafez, "Behavior of Sheep," 256.

51. COIA, *Annual Report, 1885* (1885–86), 381.

52. Fred Nials, "Geology and Geomorphology," and Garrick A. Bailey and Roberta Glenn Bailey, "Ethnohistory," both in *Prehistory and History of the Ojo Amarillo: Archaeological Investigation of Block II, Navajo Indian Irrigation Project, San*

Juan County, New Mexico, ed. David T. Kirkpatrick, vol. 4 (1980), 1210–22, 1465, 1467; Bailey and Bailey, *Historic Navajo Occupation of the Northern Chaco Plateau* (1982), 21, 26, 41, 45. Be'ek'id Ahąąh Dikaní, which disappeared in the 1930s, was once deeper than a horse's back and edged with aquatic vegetation. For a description of the development of playa lakes on the flats around Kayenta, see Dyk, *Navaho Autobiography*, 32.

53. COIA, *Annual Report, 1890*, 164–65 and *Annual Report, 1892*, 208–9; COIA, *Report on the Situation among the Navajo Indians in New Mexico and Arizona* (1891–92); W. A. Jones to Secretary of the Interior, 13 Nov. 1901, file 204, box 6, Records of the Arizona State Land Department, Archives Division, ADL. Iverson perceptively explains the resettlement of Diné homelands in *Diné*, 66–69.

54. Kelly, *Navajo Indians*, 17–27.

55. Ibid., 23–24, and n. 12; 24 *U.S. Statutes at Large*, 388–91. For a discussion of Weber's generally unsung efforts, see Iverson, *Diné*, 104–6. The idea of acquiring legal rights to checkerboarded lands through the Homestead Act goes back to the 1880s. See COIA, *Annual Report, 1881–82*, 196.

56. A. W. Simington to Cato Sells, 18 Dec. 1919, CCF 65898-1918-304, Pueblo Bonito Agency, RG 75, NA; Sells to [Alexander] Vogelsang, 27 Dec. 1919, and Sells to Anselm Weber, 14 Feb. 1920, both in file 3, box 27, Franciscan Papers, UA; the quote is from the letter of 27 Dec. 1919. For evidence of the difficulty women faced in patenting their allotments, see Navajo Allotment Book, 1913–31, file 12, box 29, Franciscan Papers, UA, and the allotment records published in Bailey and Bailey, *Historic Navajo Occupation*, 628–55.

57. Kelly, *Navajo Indians*, 23; COIA, *Annual Report, 1885*, 381.

58. R. J. Bauman to COIA, 9 Feb. 1918, file 3, box 27, Franciscan Papers, UA; Hugh L. Scott, "Report on the Navajo Indians of Arizona and New Mexico," pp. 3–8, 11 Oct. 1921, vol. 4, box 2, entry 1388, Records of the Board of Indian Commissioners, Special Reports, RG 75, NA; [Stacher] to Homer Powers, 24 March 1920, Hagerman file 2, box 13, Eastern Navajo Agency, RG 75, NARA-PR.

59. Anselm Weber, *The Navajo Indians: A Statement of Facts* (1914), 23; Minutes of a Hearing with Attsidi Nez et al., before E. B. Meritt, 10 Jan. 1917, CCF 3546-1917-056, Navajo Agency, RG 75, NA; Committee on Indian Affairs, *Survey of Conditions*, pt. 34, pp. 18022–23; Fred Tsosi Chis Chiliazzi, testimony in Committee on Indian Affairs, *Survey of Conditions*, pt. 34, pp. 17787–89; Mosk, *Land Tenure Problems*, 34–35; Klara B. Kelley, "Ethnoarchaeology of Navajo Trading Posts," *Kiva* 51 (1985): 24–25. Also see the following in RG75, NARA-PR: Petition from Navajos from Seven Lakes and Pueblo Alto to H. J. Hagerman, n.d. (Hagerman file 1), box 13; H. J. Hagerman, Memorandum on Crown Point Exchanges, 12 Oct. 1923, and Minutes of a Meeting with Gen. Hugh L. Scott, 2 Sept. 1921 (both in Hagerman file 2), box 13; and E. B. Meritt to Clay Tallman, 17 Dec. 1920 (Hagerman file 3), box 14, all in the records of the Eastern Navajo Agency; Hagerman to Charles H. Burke, 23 June

1927 (Burke file 1), box 1; Stacher to COIA, 25 Jan. 1926 (Pueblo Bonito Agency file), box 4; and land use map (Pueblo Bonito Agency file), box 142-2 075-03-078, all in the Hagerman Papers.

60. Minutes of a Meeting with Gen. Hugh L. Scott, 2 Sept. 1921, Hagerman file 2, box 13, Eastern Navajo Agency, NARA-PR. Emphasis mine.

61. This process is evident on the Kaibito Plateau; see Levy, Henderson, and Andrews, "Effects of Regional Variation," 361, 369–70.

62. See, for example, Frederick Fay York, "Capitalist Development and Land in Northeastern Navajo Country, 1880s to 1980s" (1990), and Lawrence David Weiss, *The Development of Capitalism in the Navajo Nation: A Political-Economic History* (1984).

63. Correll, *Through White Men's Eyes*, vol. 1, 377. Unfortunately, Dodge left no ethnographic record; he sent only a few letters to his superiors and failed to write the usual daily or weekly reports. For background on Dodge, see Frank McNitt's epilogue to Simpson, *Navaho Expedition*, 181–211.

64. J. Lee Correll, "Navajo Frontiers in Utah and Troublous Times in Monument Valley," *Utah Historical Quarterly* 39 (1971): 149–51; Robert S. McPherson, *The Northern Navajo Frontier, 1860–1900: Expansion through Adversity* (1988), 9–10. For the fascinating history of Hashké Neiniih, see McNitt, *Indian Traders*, ch. 13.

65. The first traders—ex-soldiers and sutlers—set up shop soon after the reservation was established, but their reach was minimal. The percentage of Mormon traders, especially in the Northern Navajo Jurisdiction, was quite large; see [Hagerman] to Charles H. Burke, 13 June 1927, Burke file no. 1, box 1, Hagerman Papers, RG 75, NARA-PR. Also see William Y. Adams, *Shonto: A Study of the Role of the Trader in a Modern Navajo Community* (1963), 151, and McPherson, *Northern Navajo Frontier*, 64–65.

66. William H. Harrison to COIA, 22 May 1908, CCF 76859-07-916, Navajo, RG 75, NA; Committee on Indian Affairs, *Survey of Conditions*, pt. 34, p. 17550; Fred Yazzie, interview in Samuel Moon, *Tall Sheep: Harry Goulding, Monument Valley Trader* (1992), 84–85; Kelley, "Ethnoarchaeology of Navajo Trading Posts," 24–26, 30.

67. The literature on trading posts, much of it memoir, is vast. The best overview is Powers, *Navajo Trading*. Also useful are the classic McNitt, *Indian Traders*; Elizabeth Compton Hegemann, *Navaho Trading Days* (1963); Adams, *Shonto*; Kelley, "Ethnoarchaeology of Navajo Trading Posts," 19–37; Willow Roberts, *Stokes Carson: Twentieth-Century Trading on the Navajo Reservation* (1987); Moon, *Tall Sheep*; Sallie Wagner, *Wide Ruins: Memories from a Navajo Trading Post* (1997); and M'Closkey, *Swept under the Rug*.

68. For example, Left Handed's two-volume life history, which recalls his daily life in the 1880s in numbing detail, includes only a few encounters with trading posts, probably because none were sufficiently close to his home at Black Mountain. See Dyk, *Son of Old Man Hat*, 105, 120; and Dyk and Dyk, *Left Handed*,

370–71, 400. Similarly, see Dyk, *Navaho Autobiography*, 37–38, 75, and Mitchell, *Tall Woman*, 30. For a glimpse of the goods available at trading posts in these first decades, see the ledgers in file 16, box 1, series 4, Day Collection, and vol. 1, box 1, series 1, Raymond Blair Collection, both at NAU.

69. For insight into lamb and wool sales during the war, see the Crum and Cotton Ledger, 1915–25, box 2, George Babbitt Collection, NAU. Also consult Powers, *Navajo Trading*, 57.

70. Evan W. Estep to Farmers, Traders and Indians, San Juan Reservation, 2 April 1923, file F no. 2, box 13, Eastern Navajo Agency; A. H. Kneale to C. E. Faris, 11 Jan. 1927, San Juan Jurisdiction file no. 1, box 4, and Kneale to Hagerman, 14 Jan. 1925, San Juan Jurisdiction file no. 2, box 5, both in Hagerman Papers; and Livestock file, CCF 510.191-531, box 150, Navajo Area Office, all in RG 75, NARA-PR.

71. Sheep book, Aug. 1922, box 1, Babbitt and Roberts Trading Post, UNM.

72. Ownership data for the period before 1930 are scanty. The best set of records I unearthed covers two years at the Ganado vat. A complete record exists for 1927, but the record for 1925 appears incomplete, making comparisons risky. Nonetheless, if we assume that the weekly records in August 1925 were representative, those stockowners with subsistence herds of 300 head or fewer declined from 40 to 32 percent of the stockholder population between 1925 and 1927; those with middling herds of 301–500 head declined from 26 to 22 percent; those with substantial herds of 501–1000 head grew from 26 to 31 percent; and those with large-scale herds of 1001 or more grew from 9 to 14 percent. See Dipping Operations file, box 10, Duclos Files, and List of Sheep Dipped at Ganado Sheep Dip, 1927, CCF 537, box 151, both in Navajo Area Office, RG 75, NARA-PR.

73. Generally speaking, the Bureau of Indian Affairs limited sales to culls and wethers. See, for example, C. L. Walker to All Bonded Traders, Western Navajo Agency, 31 Aug. 1927, Indians 1927 file, and John G. Hunter to Orvill L. Hathorne and Roman Hubbell, 23 July 1930, Indians 1930–31 file, both in box 44, Hubbell Papers, UA. But also see traders' reports of livestock sales in 1927, including lambs, in CCF 530 Livestock, 1926–1936, box 150, Navajo Area Office, NARA-PR; some specified wether lambs, but the sex was not always recorded.

74. John H. Provinse to Carl Taylor, 10 Dec. 1938 (attachment), Navajo Population and Census file, box 32, SCS Records, NMSU. For information on disease among the Navajos, see Robert A. Trennert, *White Man's Medicine: Government Doctors and the Navajo, 1863–1955* (1998), 96–100, 122–27.

75. 1915 Navajo Census, frames 245–71; Robert McPherson, "Ricos and Pobres: Wealth Distribution on the Navajo Reservation in 1915," *New Mexico Historical Review* 60 (1985): 415–34.

76. Dane Coolidge and Mary Roberts Coolidge, *The Navajo Indians* (1930), 66.

77. Carolyn Niethammer offers perhaps the most complete biography in *I'll Go and Do More*, ch. 1. Also consult McNitt's brief biography in his epilogue to

Simpson, *Navaho Expedition*, 182, n. 20; Parman, *Navajos and the New Deal*, 18; and McNitt, *Indian Traders*, 279.

78. An analysis of the sheep accounts for the Greasewood Trading Post in 1933 reveals that most people sold one to five sheep. Of 133 sellers, only 11 sold more than twenty sheep; the largest sale was for 100 head. Since this record (the earliest detailed account of sales that I uncovered) included the first round of stock reduction, it probably overstates annual sales in the pre-reduction era. See Greasewood Accounts, 1933, Items 2 and 8, box 437, Hubbell Papers, UA. For an example of Dodge's sales, see Bill of Sale, Henry Dodge to Charles L. Day and D. H. Mitchell, 26 Feb. 1906, file 43, box 1, series 4, Day Collection, NAU; also see Committee on Indian Affairs, *Survey of Conditions*, pt. 34, p. 17905.

79. 1915 Navajo Census, frames 16 and 22; Peter Paquette to COIA, 13 Nov. 1914, CCF 125342-1914-916, Navajo, RG 75, NA; Hagerman to Burke, 20 Nov. 1923, Burke file, box 1, Hagerman Papers, RG 75, NARA-PR; Parman, *Navajos and the New Deal*, 18; Niethammer, *I'll Go and Do More*, 21.

80. 1915 Navajo Census, frames 77 and 241. Some observers have asserted that Chee Dodge was sole owner of this vast herd, but he himself testified that his wife owned half. See Committee on Indian Affairs, *Survey of Conditions*, pt. 18, p. 9222.

81. Tom Allen, interview by Daniel Tyler, 1 Oct. 1968, p. 11, Interview no. 534, reel 6, NOHT; Kelley and Whiteley, *Navajoland*, 83. On Dodge's use of herders, see George Blueeyes, interview in *Between Sacred Mountains: Navajo Stories and Lessons from the Land* (1982), 160. The use of herders by the wealthiest stockowners goes back to at least the nineteenth century, though the documentation is scanty. Oftentimes herders were poorer family members, for whom herding offered a way to acquire their own stock; working as a herder, however, could also mean dependency. For a brief discussion of this practice, see Henderson, "Wealth, Status and Change," 107. Also see Newcomb, *Hosteen Klah*, 8–9.

82. W. G. McGinnies to [John Collier], 8 May 1936, and [Lyle Young], memorandum re. Dodge holdings in Tsaile Butte area, 31 July 1936, both in Decimal File (henceforth DF) 150 Senate Info, box 18, Navajo Service, RG 75, NARA-RMR.

83. Weber to C. F. Hauke, 29 April 1911, file 2, and Paquette to Sells, 7 Feb. 1918, file 3, both in box 27, Franciscan Papers, UA.

84. Kneale to COIA, 7 Dec. 1926, San Juan Jurisdiction file 1, box 4, Hagerman Papers, RG 75, NARA-PR.

85. Petition to President from Chin Lee Valley, [ca. 1924?], box 30, file 6, Franciscan Papers, UA.

86. Weber to Hauke, 29 April 1911, file 2, box 27, Franciscan Papers, UA.

87. Zeh, *General Report*, 9123–26; the quote is from page 9123.

88. Harbison, "Working Plan Report of the Grazing Resources and Activities of the Southern Navajo Indian Reservation, Arizona and New Mexico," in Committee on Indian Affairs, *Survey of Conditions*, pt. 18, p. 9200.

7 MOURNING LIVESTOCK

1. Kathleen P. Chamberlain, *Under Sacred Ground: A History of Navajo Oil, 1922–1982* (2000), ch. 4; Kenneth R. Philp, *John Collier's Crusade for Indian Reform, 1920–1954* (1977), 103–10.

2. This discussion is based on a transcript of the conference, held 19–20 February 1931 and published in Committee on Indian Affairs, *Survey of Conditions*, pt. 18, pp. 9268–93.

3. Committee on Indian Affairs, *Survey of Conditions*, pt. 18, p. 9281. Indeed, between 1945 and 1951, the BIA relocated 148 Navajo and Hopi families to the Colorado River Indian Reservation north of Yuma, Arizona, but in 1952, the Mohaves and Chemehuevis—fearing that they would be outnumbered—voted to halt continued colonization. See Bernard L. Fontana, "The Hopi-Navajo Colony on the Lower Colorado River: A Problem in Ethnohistorical Interpretation," *Ethnohistory* 10 (1963): 162–82.

4. Memorandum of Meeting of the Whitehorse Chapter House, 19 April 1932, Land file, box 96, Subject Files, Eastern Navajo Agency, RG 75, NARA-PR. The reluctance of Diné to relinquish allotments was understandable. Between 1921 and 1933, 113 Diné relinquished allotments, amounting to more than 235,000 acres, for the purpose of consolidating Indian and railroad lands, but the government returned them to the public domain instead of holding them in trust or offering the Navajos lieu allotments. See John Collier to [Harold Ickes], 11 July 1939, CCF 60179-1939-013, Navajo, RG 75, NA.

5. Transcript of 1931 conference, in Committee on Indian Affairs, *Survey of Conditions*, pt. 18, p. 9270.

6. Otis B. Goodall, "Report of an Inspection of the Navajo Schools and Agency, Arizona, 29 Aug. to 13 Sept. 1915," p. 21, CCF 101160-1915-910, Navajo Agency, RG 75, NA.

7. Transcript of 1931 conference, in Committee on Indian Affairs, *Survey of Conditions*, pt. 18, p. 9280; emphasis mine.

8. Minutes of the General Navajo Tribal Council, Leupp, Ariz., 13 Nov. 1928, pp. 32–43, CCF 20204-1930-054, and Minutes of the Eighth Annual Session of the Navajo Tribal Council, Fort Wingate, 7–8 July 1930, pp. 39–41, CCF 24619-1930-054, both in General Services, RG 75, NA; the quote is from the latter.

9. Transcript of 1931 conference, in Committee on Indian Affairs, *Survey of Conditions*, pt. 18, pp. 9292–93. E. H. Hammond of the Northern Navajo jurisdiction spoke seldom during the meeting and remained silent during this discussion.

10. The following discussion is based on a close reading of the entire hearing record in Committee on Indian Affairs, *Survey of Conditions*, pt. 18, with the exception of the hearings at two Hopi villages, Toreva and Oraibi.

11. My snapshot of the audience comes from snatches of evidence in Committee on Indian Affairs, *Survey of Conditions*, pt. 18, especially pp. 8937, 9023, 9829–30, photographs of similar types of events in the 1930s, and Arthur Hubbard, Sr., interview by David Brugge, 1 Dec. 1971, pp. 5–6, Interview no. 10, Oral History Files, HTP.

12. See, for example, Committee on Indian Affairs, *Survey of Conditions*, pt. 18, p. 9223.

13. Ibid., 9829. For a list of the Anglo stockholders in the Checkerboard, see E. R. Fryer to [Collier], 26 Oct. 1938 (attachment), CCF 67379-1938-301, Navajo, RG75, NA.

14. Committee on Indian Affairs, *Survey of Conditions*, pt. 18, pp. 9707, 9572; the quote is from the latter. (Lope's first name was misspelled as Montoy in the hearing record.) Even today, the most abused lands on the northern Chaco Plateau once belonged to Anglo ranchers. See, for example, del Bene and Ford, *Archaeological Excavations*, ch. 10.

15. Committee on Indian Affairs, *Survey of Conditions*, pt. 18, p. 9488.

16. Ibid., 9736–39; also see pp. 9119, 9829.

17. Ibid., 9247–48, 9685–88.

18. Ibid., 9225, 9783.

19. Parman, *Navajos and the New Deal*, 40; John Nez, interview by Tom Ration, Feb. 1969, p. 14, Interview 343, reel 2; Ben Morris, interview by Ration, April 1969, p. 6, Interview 415, reel 3; Gorman interview, p. 3, side 2, Interview 533, reel 4, all in NOHT. The hearing record erroneously states Collier's affiliation with the Indian Rights Association, a group whose conservative, assimilationist policies he had long opposed.

20. Collier, "What Has Hagerman Done for the Navajos in Their Great Storm Disaster?" frame 543, reel 7, Collier Papers; Randolph C. Downes, "Navajo Report" (Draft), box 46, Statistics Division, RG 75, NA.

21. Committee on Indian Affairs, *Survey of Conditions*, pt. 18, p. 9650.

22. Collier to Administrator of Public Works, July 1933, pp. 3–4, CCF 27066-1937-021.5, Navajo, RG 75, NA; Tribal Council Minutes, Oct.–Nov. 1933, pp. 37–38, NA. On the controversy surrounding Collier's appointment, see Philp, *John Collier's Crusade*, 115–17.

23. Reprinted in Peter Iverson, ed., *"For Our Navajo People": Diné Letters, Speeches and Petitions, 1900–1960* (2002), 168.

24. Tribal Council Minutes, Oct.–Nov. 1933, p. 36, NA.

25. Ibid., 36–37, 62–63, 94. Collier's written instructions, contrary to his public statements, advised agents not to accept gummers, but they did nonetheless. See Collier to S. F. Stacher, 14 Nov. 1933, DF 150 Senate Info., box 18, Navajo Service, RG 75, NARA-RMR; Frank B. Lenzie to [Collier], 3 April 1934, CCF 301.14, box 166, FGD, RG 75, NARA-PR.

26. Tribal Council Minutes, Oct.–Nov. 1933, p. 94, NA.

27. Ibid., 37–38. For a brief description of the ECW program on the Navajo Reservation, see Parman, *Navajos and the New Deal*, 32–35, 185–86. The Emergency Conservation Work program was later known as the Civilian Conservation Corps (CCC), but I have elected to use the name commonly employed on the Navajo Reservation.

28. Tribal Council Minutes, Oct.–Nov. 1933, p. 44, NA.

29. Ibid., 38–39.

30. Ibid., 37; my emphasis.

31. Ibid.

32. Ibid., 38.

33. Minutes of the Special Session of the Navajo Tribal Council, Crownpoint, 9–11 April 1934, pp. 61–62, NNRMC; Lenzie to [Collier], 3 April 1934, file 301.14, box 166, CCF 1927–52, FGD, RG 75, NARA-PR. But also consult Edward T. Hall, *West of the Thirties: Discoveries among the Navajo and Hopi* (1994), 128–29, 135–37.

34. Committee on Indian Affairs, *Survey of Conditions*, pt. 34, p. 17806; Parman, *Navajos and the New Deal*, 48–49.

35. Tribal Council Minutes, July 1934, p. 74, NNRMC.

36. Lenzie to [Collier], 3 April 1934, file 301.14, Range Management-Navajo-Prior to June 1, 1941, box 166, FGD, RG 75, NARA-PR.

37. Beck, "History of Stock Reduction," in Committee on Indian Affairs, *Survey of Conditions*, pt. 34, p. 17987; Minutes of a Meeting of the Navajo Tribal Council, Fort Defiance, 27 Jan 1934, p. 23, CCF 21341-1933-344, vol. 1, CCC-ID, Southern Navajo, RG 75, NA.

38. Tribal Council Minutes, Oct.–Nov. 1933, pp. 46–47, NA; also see Nal Nishi's testimony, p. 44.

39. When Jacob Morgan challenged him to explain his reversal, Taliman claimed that further contemplation of Cooley's economic projections changed his mind. See Tribal Council Minutes, Oct.–Nov. 1933, pp. 62, 66, NA; Parman, *Navajos and the New Deal*, 45.

40. Committee on Indian Affairs, *Survey of Conditions*, pt. 34, p. 17801; McGinnies, "Agricultural and Range Resources," pp. 3, 14, UNM. Contrary to the conservationists' opinion, Navajos would argue that goats kept sheep herds active, ensuring that sheep did not stay in the same place too long. See Downs, *Animal Husbandry*, 31.

41. Minutes of the Special Session of the Navajo Tribal Council, Fort Defiance, 12–13 March 1934, pp. 23, 43, NNRMC. Collier was using the figure of 150,000 goats by the end of that meeting, and four months later, he added a provision for the government to buy ewes from those Navajos who chose to sell them. See Tribal Council Minutes, July 1934, p. 64, NNRMC.

42. Tribal Council Minutes, 12–13 March 1934, pp. 22–23, 27.

43. Parman, *Navajos and the New Deal*, ch. 6, offers an excellent discussion of the New Mexico Boundary Bill. For opposition in San Juan County, see the following in NMSRCA: Minutes of Association of San Juan Co. Taxpayers, 5 Aug. 1933; Resolution of the Board of County Commissioners of San Juan County, 7 Aug. 1933; H. B. Sammons to Arthur Seligman, 14 Sept. 1933; William Butler to Seligman, 21 Aug. 1933, all in Special Issues file, Arthur Seligman Papers; and Clarence Iden to A. W. Hockenhull, 8 Nov. 1933, Special Reports and Issues file, Andrew H. Hockenhull Papers.

44. Tribal Council Minutes, March 1934, p. 22, NNRMC.

45. Ibid., 27–28, 43; the quote is from page 43 (emphasis mine).

46. Ibid., 44.

47. Tribal Council Minutes, Oct.–Nov. 1933, pp. 43–44, NA; ibid., March 1934, pp. 44–45, NNRMC; the quote is from the latter. For Shirley's opinion of pointy-headed experts, see his letter in Committee on Indian Affairs, *Survey of Conditions*, pt. 34, pp. 18017–19.

48. Tribal Council Minutes, March 1934, p. 47, NA.

49. Ibid., 45.

50. Ibid., 48–49.

51. Ibid., 51–52.

52. Tribal Council Minutes, April 1934, pp. 64–65, NNRMC; Beck, "History of Stock Reduction," in Committee on Indian Affairs, *Survey of Conditions*, pt. 34, p. 17988; C. N. Millington to [Collier], 22 May 1934, CCF 21341-1933-344, vol. 2, CCC-ID, General Records, Southern Navajo, RG 75, NA. Aside from passing comments on women's reactions, there is a paucity of evidence regarding the substance of the response, probably because few Diné women spoke English and none of those recording observations spoke the Diné language.

53. Meeting of Superintendents, Keams Canyon, 9 July 1934, p. 4, 301 Livestock Reduction Program file, box 120, Navajo Area Office, RG 75, NARA-PR.

54. New Mexico Association on Indian Affairs, *Urgent Navajo Problems* (Santa Fe, 1940), 8, in Information Concerning Navajo file, box 22, Subject Files, Navajo Area Office, RG 75, NARA-PR.

55. For descriptions of the large crowds at Crownpoint and Tuba City, see Ben Morris, interview by Tom Ration, April 1969, pp. 6, 12, tape 2, Interview 415, reel 3, NOHT.

56. Tribal Council Minutes, July 1934, pp. 66, 79, and Tribal Council Minutes, April 1934, p. 59, both in NNRMC; Minutes of a Meeting Held at Leupp, 7 April 1934, Dodge Papers, ASU.

57. Tribal Council Minutes, April 1934, pp. 59, 63–64, NNRMC. The description of Sandoval is based on coverage of a 1928 council meeting in the *Los Angeles Times*, 6 Sept. 1929, sec. 1, p. 10.

58. Tribal Council Minutes, April 1934, pp. 58–59.

59. Notes on a Meeting of John Collier, Commissioner, with Superintendents and Representative Employees of the Navajo Agencies, 10 March 1934, Dodge Papers, ASU.

60. Tribal Council Minutes, July 1934, pp. 85–86, NNRMC.

61. Zeh to [J. P.] Kinney, 6 Dec. 1930, William H. Zeh Correspondence (1929–1930) file, box 148; and Zeh to Collier, 5 June 1933, 301.14 Range Management—Navajo (pre-1941) file, box 166, FGD, RG 75, NARA-PR.

62. [Zeh] to Kinney, 7 April 1932, and Zeh to T. C. Spaulding, 18 June 1932, both in William H. Zeh Correspondence (1932) file, box 148, FGD, RG 75, NARA-PR.

63. Zeh to Kinney, 10 July 1932, Zeh Correspondence (1932) file, box 148, FGD, RG 75, NARA-PR.

64. Zeh to Collier, 5 June 1933, 301.14 Range Management, Navajo (pre-1941) file, box 166, FGD, RG 75, NARA-PR.

65. Zeh to Navajo Superintendents, 6 Oct. 1934; G. J. Baber to Zeh, 12 Oct. 1934; Lenzie to Zeh, 19 Oct. 1934; Zeh to A. C. Cooley, 19 Nov. 1934; and Lenzie, Hugh Harvey, and Forrest M. Parker to [Collier], 30 Jan. 1935, all in 301 Livestock Reduction Program file, box 120, Navajo Area Office, RG 75, NARA-PR. Also see Zeh to Tom Dodge, 16 Oct. 1934, file 9, box 1, Dodge Collection, ASU.

66. Lenzie, Harvey, and Parker to [Collier], 30 Jan. 1935, p. 5, 301 Livestock Reduction Program file, box 120, Navajo Area Office, RG 75, NARA-PR. Also see Beck, "History of Stock Reduction," in Committee on Indian Affairs, *Survey of Conditions*, pt. 34, p. 17988, and the recollection of Lamar Bedoni, of Navajo Mountain, in Moon, *Tall Sheep*, 94–95. Parman offers an insightful discussion of these events in *Navajos and the New Deal*, 62–65.

67. See, for example, Billy Bryant, Curly Mustache, and Fred Descheene, interviews in Roessel and Johnson, *Navajo Livestock Reduction*, 141, 172, and 190; Katherine Quimayousie, interview by David Brugge, 10 May 1973, p. 36, and Ben Wilson, interview by Vernon Morgan, n.d., p. 2, both in Oral History Files, HTP.

68. Lenzie, Harvey, and Parker to [Collier], 30 Jan. 1935, pp. 5–8, 301 Livestock Reduction Program file, box 120, Navajo Area Office, RG 75, NARA-PR.

69. Tully Lincoln, interview by John D. Sylvester and David M. Brugge, 14 Sept. 1970, pp. 43–44, Interview no. 646, American Indian Oral History Project, University of Utah, and Quimayousie, interview by Brugge, 10 May 1973, pp. 36–37, both in Oral History Files, HTP. Quimayousie noted that some traders also purchased butchered meat at above-market prices for sale at trading posts. See interview with Chee Carrol in Roessel and Johnson, *Navajo Livestock Reduction*, 152, for a similar account; Carrol lived west of Chinle.

70. Martin Johnson, interview in Roessel and Johnson, *Navajo Livestock Reduction*, 94.

71. Akinabh Burbank, interview in Roessel and Johnson, *Navajo Livestock Reduction*, 124–26.

72. Quoted from a sheaf of letters written in January 1938, p. 2, file 17, box 81, Chavez Papers, UNM. Similar stories appear in interviews conducted 13 July 1972 with Nedra Tódích'íi'nii (p. 5), and Kitty At'íinii (p. 4), in Sundberg and Charley, *Navajo Stock Reduction Interviews*, CSUF.

73. Tribal Council Minutes, March 1934, p. 51, and ibid., July 1934, pp. 71–73, both in NNRMC.

74. Zeh, Memorandum Covering Goat Reduction on the Navajo, 5 July 1934, DF 150 Senate Info, box 18, Navajo Service, RG 75, NARA-RMR.

75. Committee on Indian Affairs, *Survey of Conditions*, pt. 34, pp. 17756, 18004–5; ibid., pt. 18, pp. 9580–81, 9685.

76. Ibid., pp. 17753–54, 17758–62, 17784–85, 17789, 17790–93.

77. Ibid., 17758–60, 17768–70, 17813. Also see Elizabeth Pablo to [S. F. Stacher], 27 Feb. 1933, No. 5 Wingate Valley file, box 99, Eastern Navajo Agency Subject Files, ca. 1935–1939, RG75, NARA-PR.

78. Committee on Indian Affairs, *Survey of Conditions*, pt. 34, p. 17758.

79. Ibid., 17754–56, 17801; Tribal Council Minutes, July 1934, p. 70, NNMRC.

80. Committee on Indian Affairs, *Survey of Conditions*, pt. 34, p. 17801.

81. Ibid., 17973. At the 1936 senate hearing, Collier blamed himself, saying that he knew that the boundary bill might not pass at all when he issued orders to reduce the goats. But his chronology was confused on this point. In his apology, he repeatedly stated that goat reduction took place in the fall of 1935 (after Chavez's appointment to the senate), when it actually happened a year earlier. For Collier's erroneous statement, see p. 17801.

82. Committee on Indian Affairs, *Survey of Conditions*, pt. 34, pp. 17448, 17542–43, 17578; Collier to Chee Dodge, 8 Sept. 1938, CCF 62000-1935-301, pt. 6, RG 75, NA.

83. W[alter] Woehlke, Memorandum on Navajo Problem, 27 March 1935, file 1–13, box 11, Collier's Navajo Documents, RG 75, NA.

84. B. Youngblood, "Navajo Trading," in Committee on Indian Affairs, *Survey of Conditions*, pt. 34, p. 18069. I have calculated these equivalences using the average price for trading-post goods in 1934.

85. See Parman, *Navajos and the New Deal*, ch. 3, for a detailed discussion of the referendum on the Wheeler-Howard Act.

86. Collier to C. N. Faris, 17 June 1935, frame 315, reel 13, Collier Papers.

87. This vignette comes from Bennett, *Kaibah*, ch. 29. On the conflation of the IRA and stock reduction, also consult Roman Hubbell to Collier, 16 June 1936, frame 440, reel 14, Collier Papers.

88. John Nez, interview by Tom Ration, Feb. 1969, pp. 5–6, Interview no. 344, reel 2, NOHT.

89. For a thorough treatment of Morgan's anti-Collier campaign, consult Parman, *Navajos and the New Deal*; the statistic is from page 76.

90. See petition published in Committee on Indian Affairs, *Survey of Conditions*, pt. 34, pp. 18035–36.

91. "Wheeler-Howard Act," *Public Acts of the Seventy-Third Congress, Second Session, 1934*, ch. 576, in *Indian Affairs: Laws and Treaties*, vol. 5, comp. and ed. Charles J. Kappler (1941).

8 DRAWING LINES ON A MAP

1. The following discussion and the quotations come from Robert Marshall, "You Can't Go Swimming without Getting Wet," [ca. Sept. 1934], frames 1200–1201, reel 15, Collier Papers.

2. For a succinct discussion of Marshall's philosophy and career, see Paul Sutter, *Driven Wild: How the Fight against Automobiles Launched the Modern Wilderness Movement* (2002).

3. I have regularized the punctuation in this paragraph and corrected typographic errors. I also use italics where Marshall used quotation marks for emphasis.

4. Collier referred to "indirect administration" in his first press release as commissioner. See "John Collier Becomes Commissioner of Indian Affairs," 21 April 1933, envelope 4, box 1, Collier's Reference File, RG 75, NA. Also consult John Collier, *From Every Zenith* (1963), 345–46; and Bill Cooke, "A New Continuity with Colonial Administration: Participation in Development Management," *Third World Quarterly* 24 (2003): 47–61. Thanks to Peter Edward for bringing Cooke's research on Collier and colonialism to my attention and to Cooke for his email discussion with me.

5. John Collier, "You Can't Go Swimming without Getting Wet," frame 1202, reel 15, Collier Papers. For additional evidence of Collier's conscious adoption of "indirect rule," see Collier to E. R. Fryer, 7 Aug. 1937, Morgan-Palmer file, box 10, Collier's Office Files, RG 75, NA.

6. Scott, *Seeing Like a State*, ch. 3.

7. For background on Chavez, see Maria E. Montoya, "Dennis Chavez and the Making of Modern New Mexico," in *New Mexico Lives: Profiles and Historical Stories*, ed. Richard W. Etulain (2002), 242–64; Rose Diaz, "El Senador, Dennis Chavez: New Mexico Native Son, American Senior Statesman, 1888–1962" (2006), ch. 5; and Parman, *Navajos and the New Deal*, 142–43. For background on Cutting, see Richard Lowitt, *Bronson M. Cutting, Progressive Politician* (1992).

8. Some observers have maintained that Chavez despised Collier and Harold Ickes for backing the reelection of Cutting, whose support for the boundary bill had seemingly assured its passage, and that he blocked the bill simply to settle the

score. See Parman, *Navajos and the New Deal*, 143–44; Parman's interview with Fryer, pp. 16–17, reel 4, NOHT.

9. Dennis Chavez to M. L. Woodard, 14 July 1941, CCF 37010-1935-916 pt. 4, box 177, Navajo, RG 75, NA.

10. For a thorough discussion of the defeat of the New Mexico Boundary Bill, consult Parman, *Navajos and the New Deal*, ch. 6. Also see Fryer interview, 15–17. Opponents included the Association of San Juan County Taxpayers, the San Juan County Board of Supervisors, and the odd coalition of Jacob Morgan and Paul Palmer, a Mormon real estate speculator from Farmington who feigned concern for Navajos while pursuing his own vested interests.

11. [Allan Harper], memorandum attached to Collier's letter to R. H. Hanna, 7 Sept. 1937, frame 1027, reel 13, Collier Papers.

12. Committee on Indian Affairs, *Survey of Conditions*, pt. 34, pp. 17543, 17550, 17620–21, 17626–53, 18149. Also consult Fryer to [Collier], 26 Oct. 1938, CCF 67379-1938-301, Navajo, RG 75, NA. Collier gives the number of commercial stockmen as fifteen to twenty-five, but my compilation of tax rolls included in Collier's reports indicates perhaps thirty-five. (This figure is uncertain, because livestock data are not provided for McKinley and Sandoval counties; however, several known commercial operators from those areas are listed.) Also, approximately eighty Anglo and Hispanic families farmed and kept small subsistence herds in the area. Most of the Anglos had arrived fairly recently, during a wetter period; as dust storms rolled across the land, many now welcomed the opportunity to sell their land back to the government. See, for example, John L. Ballard to Chavez, 12 May 1936, file 27, box 80, Chavez Papers, UNM.

13. "Cattle Men Attack Extension," *Gallup Independent*, 7 Feb. 1936; Edward Sargent to Chavez, 22 Feb. 1937, file 27, box 80, Chavez Papers, UNM.

14. For statistics on badlands, see Committee on Indian Affairs, *Survey of Conditions*, pt. 34, p. 17613.

15. W. G. McGinnies, Discussion of statement made by Floyd Lee at senate hearings, DF 170, box 24, Navajo Service, RG 75, NARA-RMR.

16. Committee on Indian Affairs, *Survey of Conditions*, pt. 34, pp. 17677–82. Also see I. K. Westbrook's written statement, p. 17694, and Westbrook to Chavez, 6 June 1936, folder 27, box 80, Chavez Papers, UNM.

17. Committee on Indian Affairs, *Survey of Conditions*, pt. 34, pp. 17477–78. The fear that Collier would ask Navajos to reconsider the IRA was reasonable, considering that some Navajos had petitioned to revote on the issue.

18. Fryer to Collier, 10 Feb. 1937, Morgan-Palmer file, box 10, Collier's Office Files, RG 75, NA.

19. Reams of petitions may be found in boxes 80–82, Chavez Papers, UNM.

20. Howard Gorman to Chavez, 25 Feb. 1938, file 17, box 81, Chavez Papers, UNM; Parman, *Navajos and the New Deal*, 153.

21. *Taylor Grazing Act*, 43 U.S. Code 315, ch. 8A (1946 ed.); Hugh Calkins, "Effect of Taylor Act on Indians in the Eastern Navajo Area," Special Grazing District, Navajo Proposal file, box 14, Collier's Office Files, RG 75, NA.

22. "Modification and Order Establishing Grazing District No. 7 in the State of New Mexico," 1 Sept. 1939, CCF 60179-1939-013, Navajo, RG 75, NA. That this was a scheme to circumvent Chavez's moves to block the boundary bill is evident in Fryer to [Walter] Woehlke, 24 Aug. 1937; Woehlke to Fryer, 26 Aug. 1937; Collier to Harold Holman and Hugh Calkins, 31 Aug. 1938 (unsent), all in Special Grazing District, Navajo Proposal file, box 14, Collier's Office Files, RG 75, NA, and Harold Ickes to Chavez, 17 June 1940, CCF 301 (file 2), box 119, Navajo Area Office, RG 75, NARA-PR.

23. For protests against the favor given Navajos, see Ickes to A. T. Hannett, 16 April 1942; "Chairman of District Grazing Board No. 7 Resigns Protesting Navajos Given Unfair Advantage over Whites," *New Mexico Stockman*, April 1942; and Collier to [Oscar Chapman], 5 Aug. 1942. All are in CCF 42327-1934-301, Navajo, NA

24. See, for example, petition from Pueblo Pintado and White Horse Lake chapters, [ca. 1945], CCF 301 Grazing District 7, box 119, Navajo Area Office, RG 75, NARA-PR (courtesy of Peter Iverson).

25. For an overview of a subject that deserves more study, consult Stout, "Cattlemen." Hispanic ranchers were hit even harder by the U.S. Forest Service, which in the 1930s began enforcing livestock limits on lands that for centuries had been communal grazing areas within Spanish land grants. For a sense of the effect of the Taylor Grazing Act and the Forest Service on Hispanic subsistence ranchers, consult the voluminous correspondence and petitions in file 117, box 91, and files 55 and 56, box 92, both in Chavez Papers, UNM, and the petition from residents of the Espirito Santos Grant, Special Reports file, Clyde Tingley Papers, NMSRCA. William deBuys's *Enchantment and Exploitation* offers an excellent study of the dispossession of the land grantees from their communal forests.

26. Conflict between the Grazing Service and the BIA over the administration of the district is evident in Fryer to H. W. Naylor, 27 May 1941, and J. M. Stewart to [Collier], 19 May 1942, both in CCF 42327-1934-301, Navajo, RG 75, NA.

27. SCS, *Annual Report, Navajo District, 1936*, p. 38, file 56, box 7, and SCS, *Annual Report, Navajo District, Region 8, 1937*, p. 15, file 37, box 8, both in SCS Records, UNM; Hugh G. Calkins and D. S. Hubbell, "A Range Conservation Demonstration in the Land of the Navajos," *Soil Conservation* (SCS) 6 (September 1940): 65. For more information on the scientific studies undertaken at the demonstration areas, see Parman, *Navajos and the New Deal*, 83–88. In addition to creating range demonstration projects, the SCS also developed agricultural demonstration projects. For the perspective of those who managed these areas, see E. R. Smith, interview by Donald Parman, 24 June 1970, Interview no. 642, reel 6, NOHT.

28. F. D. Matthews, "Engineering Phases of Work on S.E.S. Navajo Project," 2 Feb. 1935, file 26, box 7, SCS Records, UNM.

29. For summaries of the various projects to reshape the vegetation, see the annual reports of the scs, especially those for 1935–1937, boxes 7 and 8, scs Records, UNM. On prairie dog eradication, see E. D. Eaton to J. G. Hamilton, 26 June 1935, CCF 57055-1936-933, Navajo, RG 75, NA.

Range ecologists now disagree as to whether prairie dogs harm or help ecosystems. Some ecologists argue that prairie dogs are a keystone species that aerates the soil and stimulates nutrient cycling, thereby producing more succulent and nutritious grasses. Prairie dogs also create habitat for other species, such as burrowing owls, and provide food for coyotes. Others suggest that prairie dogs may be a symptom, rather than a cause, of degraded rangelands. See Brian Miller, Gerardo Ceballos, and Richard Reading, "The Prairie Dog and Biotic Diversity," *Conservation Biology* 8 (1994): 677–81; but also consult Paul Stapp, "A Reevaluation of the Role of Prairie Dogs in Great Plains Grasslands," *Conservation Biology* 12 (1998): 1253–59, and Steve Archer and Fred E. Smeins, "Ecosystem-Level Processes," in *Grazing Management: An Ecological Perspective*, ed. Rodney K. Heitschmidt and Jerry W. Stuth (1991), 115–16.

Collier questioned the wisdom of the effort to eradicate prairie dogs, arguing that "I know perfectly well that nature never works in terms of going all this way or all that way, and that complete extermination is apt to upset the balance of nature fully as much as complete protection." If the government eliminated the rodents, he noted, the coyotes who preyed on them would likely kill more sheep. His unease with the eradication program led to studies of the effects of prairie dogs on desert grasslands. See Collier to Marshall, 28 Sept. 1936, frame 1232, reel 15, Collier Papers. Also see Ernest G. Holt to Collier, 6 May 1937; Collier to Fryer, 13 May 1937 (the source of the quote); Fryer to [Collier], 2 Feb. 1939; and Working Agreement between the scs and the BIA Relative to Cooperative Prairie Dog Field Test, no. IS/5-0136, all in CCF 26350-1937-933, Navajo, RG 75, NA.

30. For examples of the cooperative agreements between Diné stockowners and the scs, see Cooperative Range Management Agreement files, box 147, Phoenix Area Office, Branch of Soil Conservation, RG 75, NA.

31. SCS, *Annual Report, 1935*, pp. 166–67, UNM.

32. "The Government and the Navajo: 1936 to 1940" (draft), 26 March 1941, folder 15, box 5, E. Reesman Fryer Papers, FLC-CSSSC.

33. Although 1934 was a drought year, rainfall in the Checkerboard was average or above average in 1935. For precipitation records, see Ni, "Cool-Season Precipitation," and Cook, "Long-Term Aridity."

34. "Report of Meeting of Representatives of Five Chapters . . . Held in the Office of Superintendent C. E. Faris," 29 Oct. 1935, p. 11, DF 157 Reports of Meetings no. 2, box 21, Navajo Service, RG 75, NARA-RMR. Also consult the testimony of Benny Tohe in Committee on Indian Affairs, *Survey of Conditions*, pt. 34, p. 17908. For a different viewpoint, see the testimony of Frank Cadman, ibid., p. 17958.

35. Committee on Indian Affairs, *Survey of Conditions*, pt. 34, p. 17959. Complaints were made against buck pastures, as well as demonstration areas. Some alleged that range riders brandished rifles when land users challenged them. See statements by Navajos in attachment to minutes of a meeting at the Piñon Trading Post, 25 Aug. 1937, file 15, box 81, Chavez Papers, UNM.

36. Fryer interview, pp. 19–20, NOHT.

37. Notes of meeting in Indian Club Room, Santa Fe, 7–8 Dec. 1939, p. 2, CCF 53240-1939-720, RG 75, NA.

38. Committee on Indian Affairs, *Survey of Conditions*, pt. 34, pp. 17958–61.

39. See, for example, Salina Chapter to Collier, 16 June 1934, CCF 21341-1933-344, vol. 2, CCC-ID, Southern Navajo, RG 75, NA; John Curley to William H. Zeh, 10 Jan. 1935, 301 Grazing Permits Returned (file 2), Navajo Area Office, RG 75, NARA-PR; Lukachukai Chapter minutes, file 51, box 2, series 3, Day Collection, NAU.

40. Thomas Jesse Jones et al., *The Navajo Indian Problem* (1939), 16.

41. McGinnies, Discussion of statement by Floyd Lee, NARA-RMR.

42. Anderson, "Land Planning Report, LMU 3," pp. 80–81, UNM.

43. Baxter, *Las Carneradas*, 20; Baxter, "Restocking," 332.

44. COIA, *Annual Report, 1883*, p. 122; COIA, *Annual Report, 1884* (1884–85), 134; COIA, *Annual Report, 1905*; William H. Harrison to COIA, 11 Sept. 1907, CCF 76859-07-917, Navajo, RG 75, NA.

45. COIA, *Annual Report, 1886*, p. 42.

46. Dyk, *Navaho Autobiography*, 1947; Roberts, *Stokes Carson*, 53; W[illiam] H. Harrison to COIA, 28 Jan. 1907, CCF 76859-07-916, Navajo, RG 75, NA.

47. R. S. Connell to COIA, 29 March 1907, CCF 76859-07-917, Navajo, RG 75, NA.

48. See, for example, *Annual Report, Southern Navajo Jurisdiction, 1931*, p. 13, Fort Defiance-Southern Navajo file, box 8, Correspondence of Agency Superintendents, 1929–32, Navajo Area Office, RG 75, NARA-PR; Jewel McGee, interview in Powers, *Navajo Trading*, 19–20.

49. Frank B. Lenzie to [Collier], 3 April 1934, file 301.14, Range Management-Navajo, box 166, FGD, and "Land Management in the Navajo Area" (draft), pp. 21–22, CCF 300, box 117, Navajo Area Office, both in RG 75, NARA-PR. But also see D. G. Anderson, "Range Management Branch Report, Land Management Unit 2," Nov. 1937, pp. 28–29, file 17, box 9, SCS Records, UNM.

50. Cecil T. Blunn, "Characteristics and Production of Old-Type Navajo Sheep," pp. 2, 9, CCF 37010-1935-916, pt. 4, Navajo, RG 75, NA; Baxter, *Las Carneradas*, 20.

51. James O. Grandstaff, "Wool Characteristics in Relation to Navajo Weaving," pp. 4–5, CCF 37010-1935-916, pt. 4, Navajo, RG 75, NA; George M. Sidwell, Jack L. Ruttle, and Earl E. Ray, *Improvement of Navajo Sheep* (1970), 2, 4; M'Closkey, *Swept under the Rug*, 43. On the value of black sheep, see Dyk and Dyk, *Left Handed*, 465; Dyk, *Navaho Autobiography*, 17; Mitchell, *Tall Woman*, 169; and Adams, *Shonto*, 120.

52. B. Youngblood to Collier, 10 Jan. 1942, 37010-1935-916, pt. 4, Navajo, RG 75, NA. Also see statement by Chester Tso, attached to minutes of meeting with head men in Palmer's office, 27 Jan. 1938, DF 171 Senate Bill 2597, box 24, Navajo Service, RG 75, NARA-RMR.

53. Sidwell, Ruttle, and Ray, *Improvement of Navajo Sheep*, 2, 4, 6. Initially, the scientists also conducted experimental crossbreeding with Rambouillet rams, but soon discontinued that program, since the wool proved unsuitable. See Minutes of the Committee on Planning and Organizing the Southwestern Range and Sheep Breeding Laboratory, 23 Nov. 1938, CCF 37010-1935-916, pt. 1A, Navajo, RG 75, NA.

54. Sidwell, Ruttle, and Ray, *Improvement of Navajo Sheep*, 6, 9–10; Grandstaff, "Wool Characteristics," pp. 10–11, NA; "Report of Conditions and Activities, Southwestern Range and Sheep Breeding Laboratory," March–April 1937, pp. 4–5, CCF 37010-1935-916, pt. 2, Navajo, RG 75, NA.

55. Since the 1970s, the Navajo Sheep Project, the Navajo-Churro Sheep Association, and Los Ganados del Valle have worked to revitalize the breed, whose weaving qualities have been rediscovered by Diné weavers. Diné celebrate and promote the Navajo-Churro at an annual "Sheep Is Life" fair on the Navajo Nation. See www.navajo-churrosheep.com.

56. W. G. McGinnies, "Stock Reduction and Range Management," pp. 11–13, in H. C. Lockett, "Proceedings of the First Navajo Service Land Management Conference, 2-6 March 1937, Flagstaff, Arizona," UNM.

57. Anderson, "Range Management Report, Land Management Unit No. 3," March 1937, p. 24, vol. 7, box 1, SCS Collection, UA; McKinney, "Range Management Report, LMU 4," pp. 13, 19–22; "Land Management in the Navajo Area," pp. 24–28, NARA-PR.

58. Downs, *Animal Husbandry*, 35; Boyle, "Range Management Policy," pp. 11–13, 29, UNM; SCS, "Range Management Plan, Ganado Demonstration Area," 1 Aug. 1935, pp. 6, 8, folder 32, box 7, SCS Records, UNM.

59. "Land Management in the Navajo Area," pp. 28–30, and E. A. Johnson to [J. P.] Kinney, 6 March 1933, 301.14 Range Management-Navajo, box 166, FGD, RG 75, both in NARA-PR.

60. Fryer, "Erosion, Poverty and Dependency," 9, FLC-CSSL; Kluckhohn and Leighton, *Navaho*, 127–28; Farella, *Main Stalk*, 28. For women, there was the added specter of rape. Accounts of women raped on the range appear occasionally in the historical record. See, for example, Mitchell, *Tall Woman*, 407, n. 10; Mitchell, *Navajo Blessingway Singer*, 98; and Collier, *Local Organization*, 59.

61. Boyle, "Range Management Policy," 22, UNM; Hoke Denetsosie, interview in Broderick H. Johnson, ed., *Stories of Traditional Navajo Life and Culture* (1977), 74.

62. Studies of Navajo herding on both the eastern and western sides of the reservation revealed cultural continuity on this score. See Downs, *Animal Husbandry*, 32–34; Lamphere, *To Run after Them*, 111–15.

63. See, for example, J. T. Rigden, "Range Management Branch Report, Land Management Unit 10," Jan. 1937, pp. 1–3, CCF 59055-1936-344, General Records, CCC-ID, and Holman to Fryer, 26 Oct. 1938, CCF 62000-1935-301, pt. 2, Navajo, both in RG 75, NA. Harold Ickes established the authority for these grazing districts in special "Regulations Affecting the Carrying Capacity and Management of the Navajo Range," 6 Nov. 1935, CCF 62000-1935-301, pt. 1, Navajo, RG 75, NA.

64. The SCS produced voluminous reports (not all of them extant) for each land management unit, covering a range of topics: reconnaissance surveys, soils, wildlife biology, forestry, land planning, range management, watershed planning, agronomy, engineering, and sociology, as well as integrated reports. The largest collection of these reports, though incomplete, is at SCS Records, UNM; copies of some reports may also be found in SCS Collection, UA; SCS Records, NMSU; and records of the CCC-ID, RG 75, NA.

65. These procedures were followed in at least some western districts. I did not unearth these studies for most districts, but the record is incomplete. Albert Sombrero, "Present Livestock Movement on District No. 3," attached to Anderson, "Range Management Report, LMU 3," UA; [idem], appendix to Anderson, "Range Management Report, LMU 2," UNM; W. R. McKinney and J. Russell, "Livestock Movements," attached to McKinney, "Range Management Branch Report, Land Management Unit No. 4," Dec. 1936, file 65, box 7, SCS Records, UNM.

66. Frank Goldtooth, interview in Roessel and Johnson, *Navajo Livestock Reduction*, 101, 103. The emphasis is mine.

67. Mitchell, *Navajo Blessingway Singer*, 31. An especially thorough portrait of Navajo livestock movements in the late nineteenth century emerges from a close reading of Dyk and Dyk, *Left Handed*.

68. This discussion is based on Collier, *Local Organization*, 15–16 and 55–56, and the following reports at UNM: Anderson, "Land Planning Report, LMU 3," p. 37; Anderson, "Range Management Report, LMU 2," p. 28; and an analysis of data gathered by Alberto Sombrero, published in an appendix to Anderson's report for LMU 2. For a Diné perspective, see Mitchell, *Navajo Blessingway Singer*, 28.

69. Garrett Hardin, "The Tragedy of the Commons," *Science* 162 (1968): 1243–48; Wooton, *Range Problem*, 28, 31–32. The quotes are from the latter. For an insightful analysis of the complex history of the commons, see Arthur F. McEvoy, *The Fisherman's Problem: Ecology and Law in the California Fisheries, 1850–1980* (1986).

70. Holman to Karl Foster, 11 July 1939, DF 300.10 Permits, box 1, 8NS-75-92-092, Range Unit Case Files, 1949–1961, Navajo Service, RG 75, NARA-RMR. All evidence from tree-ring data shows a decline in rainfall in the last years of the 1930s. See Cook, "Long-Term Aridity"; Ni, "Cool-Season Precipitation"; and Henri Grissino-Mayer, "A 2129-Year Reconstruction of Precipitation for Northwestern New Mexico, USA," in *Tree Rings, Environment and Humanity*, ed. J. S. Dean, D. M. Meko, and

T. W. Swetnam (1996), accessed through http://www.ncdc.noaa.gov/paleo/drought/drght_grissno.html.

71. Minutes of a meeting, 16 Jan. 1936, DF 157, Reports of Meetings file 2, Navajo Service, RG 75, NARA-RMR. There is no evidence that the government planned to fence each district, which would have been prohibitively expensive, or to use armed force to remove stock. However, proposals to band flocks into community herds appeared in many planning documents; federal denials on this point were disingenuous.

72. Minutes of the Navajo Tribal Council, Window Rock, 24 Nov. 1936, [unpaginated], Dodge Papers, ASU.

73. Russell Bradley to Fryer, 2 March 1939, CCF 300 Lands, box 118, Navajo Area Office, RG 75, NARA-PR.

74. New Mexico Association on Indian Affairs, *Urgent Navajo Problems: Observations and Recommendations* (1940), 11.

75. Holman to Unit Supervisors, 8 Oct. 1937, Permits and Contracts file, box 97, Eastern Navajo Agency, RG 75, NARA-PR. For example, see E. G. Jonas to Powers, Sept. 1940, Indian Livestock file, box 10, Subject Files of Fred G. Maxwell (hereinafter Maxwell files), Chinle Subagency, RG 75, NARA-PR. Despite efforts to correct erroneous assignments, some stockowners lost their rights to their home pastures. Consider the unusual story of Dibé Łizhiní Yazzie (Little Black Sheep), who lived in District 10. He was visiting his sister in District 5, as he did every spring, when he dipped his sheep in 1937. The location of the 1937 sheep dipping became the reference point for assignment to districts, so he was assigned to that of his sister. When he applied to have his permit transferred to his home district, his council delegate refused to approve it. We can only guess at the intragroup conflict revealed by the delegate's disapproval. See C. H. Powers to Willard Brimhall, 15 July 1940, CCF 301 Grazing Matters file 2, box 120, Navajo Area Office, RG 75, NARA-PR.

9 MAKING MEMORIES

1. "Fryer Denies Navajo Revolt Report," *Gallup Independent*, 7 May 1936; also see C. P. Giragi, "Collier Bubble at Bursting Point," *Winslow Mail*, 8 May 1936.

2. Periodically, tribal council men would indicate that anxious and angry women had spurred them to speak out against stock reduction or grazing regulations. See, for example, Deeshchii'nii's testimony before Congress in Committee on Public Lands, Rehabilitation Hearings, p. 124, NARA-PR.

3. Fryer, "Erosion, Poverty and Dependency," 35.

4. "Unified Navajo Program," 10 April 1936, CCF 9054-1936-341, pt. A, Navajo, RG 75, NA; "Clarifying Statement of Policy and Procedure for the Navajo Service," n.d., Navajo Population and Census folder, box 32, SCS Records, NMSU. Chester Faris served as the first superintendent of the reorganized reservation, but his op-

position to stock reduction and attacks on his leadership by some of Collier's closest advisors cut short his administration. See Parman, *Navajos and the New Deal*, 104–6; [Ward] Shepard to John [Collier], 11 Jan. 1936, file 28–48, box 11, Collier's Navajo Documents, RG 75, NA; Walter V. Woehlke to [Collier], 15 Jan. 1936, frame 396, reel 18, Collier Papers.

5. Fryer interview, p. 1, reel 4, NOHT; Fryer, "Erosion, Poverty and Dependency," 2–5, FLC-CSSL; Fryer resume, file 3, box 1, Fryer Papers, FLC-CSSSC.

6. See, for example, Fryer to Collier, 29 June 1938, CCF 62000-35-301, pt. 1, Navajo, RG 75, NA. When Navajos attacked a range rider around Aneth, Fryer recommended talking to the perpetrators, rather than punishing them.

7. Donald Parman, who developed a friendship with Fryer over the course of writing his book, provides a snapshot of the superintendent's demeanor in *Navajos and the New Deal*, 107–9. For a sense of the perceptions of the Diné, see Gorman, interview in Roessel and Johnson, *Navajo Livestock Reduction*, 52; and interviews with Navajos in District 9, CCF 301 Northern Navajo Grazing Trespass, Branding File 1, box 119, Navajo Area Office, RG 75, NARA-PR.

8. Fryer, "Erosion, Poverty and Dependency," 33, FLC-CSSL.

9. Ibid., 31.

10. "Annual Report, Navajo District, for the Year Ending June 30, 1936," p. 12, file 56, box 7, SCS Records, UNM. The carrying capacity was later revised to 512,922, to eliminate the Hopi Reservation (District 6) from the calculation.

11. Woehlke, Memorandum on Navajo Problem, 27 March 1935, file 1-13, box 11, Collier's Navajo Documents, RG 75, NA.

12. Lockett, "Proceedings," 101–2, UNM.

13. Office of Indian Affairs, "Grazing Regulations," 2 June 1937, UA; Tribal Council Minutes, Jan. 1938, pp. 92–94, ADL; Collier to Chee Dodge, 8 Sept. 1938, CCF 62000-1935-301, pt. 6, RG 75, NA.

14. "Annual Report, 1936," table 1, SCS Records, UNM; "Livestock Census, Maximum Limit and Permit Compilation, District 17," 15 Feb. 1940, CCF 62000-1935-301, pt. 4A, Navajo, RG 75, NA. These figures are based on the 1937 record. For insight into how the Navajo Service determined the number of permitted horses, see the notes for District 3, beginning with the Bodaway Subunit, in DF 850.3 Hearings, box 1, 8NS-75-92-092, Range Unit Case Files, 1949–1961, Navajo Service, RG 75, NARA-RMR.

On average family size, see "Statistical Summary, Human Dependency Survey, Navajo Reservation, 1940," Oct. 1941, table 1, box 10, SCS Records, UNM. According to the economist Robert Youngblood's analysis, the average family consumed fifty sheep and goats per year; a subsistence flock required at least twenty-five animals per family member. See Woehlke, Memorandum on Navajo Problem, 27 March 1935, file 1-13, box 11, Collier's Navajo Documents, RG 75, NA.

15. "Livestock Census, District 17," NA.

16. "Livestock Census, Maximum Limit, and Permit Compilation, District 1," CCF 62000-1935-301, pt. 4A, Navajo, RG75, NA; OIA, "Grazing Regulations," 2 June 1937, UA. The figures for Crooked Finger, taken from the 1937 dipping record, differ from those that Fryer misreported at the January 1938 council meeting and those in Anderson, "Range Management Report, LMU 1," UA; the reason for these disparities is unknown.

17. "Livestock Census, District 17," NA.

18. Dodge to Collier, 30 Aug. 1938, and Collier to Dodge, 8 Sept. 1938, both in CCF 62000-1935-301, pt. 6, RG 75, NA.

19. William E. Leuchtenburg offers an analysis of some of the leading figures on the left in his classic study of New Deal politics, *Franklin D. Roosevelt and the New Deal* (1963), ch. 5.

20. Collier, "Use of Authority to Establish Range Control on the Navajo Reservation," 5 Oct. 1936, CCF 62000-135-301, pt. 1, Navajo, and "The Monopoly of Tribal Resources," file 49-54, box 11, Collier's Navajo Documents, both in RG 75, NA. The author of the second memo, with its purple prose referring to the "czarist fashion" of the rich, was likely Walter Woehlke.

21. Calculated from "Livestock Census, Maximum Limit and Permit Compilation," recorded in 1937, for LMUs 1–5, 7–15, and 17–18, CCF 62000-1935-301, pt. 4A, Navajo, RG 75, NA. The data for the Hopi Reservation (LMU 6) and the area around Zuni (LMU 16) were not included in this record. I have defined those with more than 1,000 SU as truly "wealthy." Fewer than seventy stockowners possessed fairly large herds of 550–999 SU. Collier misapprehended the extent of wealth on the reservation, believing that more than 200 families had more than 500 sheep, or their equivalent in cattle and horses.

22. Committee on Indian Affairs, *Survey of Conditions*, pt. 34, pp. 17467–68, 17839–40, 17843; W. G. McGinnies to [Collier], 8 May 1936, DF 150 Senate Info, box 18, Navajo Service, RG 75, NARA-RMR.

23. H. J. Hagerman discusses this program in his letter to Charles H. Burke, 13 July 1927, Charles Burke file, 1927 (1 of 2), box 1, Hagerman Papers, RG 75, NARA-PR. For examples of the census cards, complete with fingerprints and medals, see Census Cards, box 181, Navajo Area Office, RG 75, NARA-PR.

24. COIA, *Annual Report, 1870*, 616; COIA, *Annual Report, 1880* (1880–81), 254; Ed Ford to H. E. Holman, 3 Nov. 1939, Ed Ford file, box 95, Eastern Navajo Agency Subject Files, and E. R. Fryer, Superintendent's Circular no. 41-52, 007 Personal files—circulars, box 13, Chinle Subagency, both in RG 75, NARA-PR. For a cogent discussion of Navajo naming practices, consult Kluckhohn and Leighton, *Navaho*, 66–68.

25. As James Scott brilliantly illuminates, nation-states have a long history of making people "legible" through the creation of permanent last names, population registers, and other records, so that they can monitor, tax, and conscript them; consult *Seeing Like a State*, 2–3, 64–65.

26. Committee on Indian Affairs, *Survey of Conditions*, pt. 18, pp. 9201, 9209; E. R. Fryer, "Why the Government Is Trying Navajo Grazing Cases in the Federal Courts," 8 Feb. 1941, p. 8, Navajo Stock Reduction file no. 1, box 13, Collier's Office File, RG 75, NA.

27. Reichard, *Dezba*, 11–13. Although Reichard represented her book as a fictionalized story with composite characters, she also insisted that she "used no incidents or details which are not true" (p. vi). Indeed, Dezba appears to be based largely on Maria Antonia, whose family she studied in *Spider Woman: A Story of Navajo Weavers and Chanters* (1934). Maria Antonia's husband, Miguelito, was a well known hataałii.

28. OIA, "Grazing Regulations," 2–3, UA; "Livestock Census, District 17," NA. Nothing in the grazing regulations actually defined heads of households as male, but it is clear that officials with the Navajo Service defined them so; see, for example, J. M. Stewart to Office of Indian Affairs, 20 Dec. 1946, CCF 301.1 Grazing Permits, box 157, FGD, RG 75, NARA-PR.

29. Similarly, officials canceled the permit of a woman (probably a widow) known as Yellow Hair's Wife when they discovered that she was living with David Begody, who was issued a permit presumably for their combined flock. See C. H. Powers to Willard Brimhall, 26 Aug. 1940, DF 300.10 Permits, and the untitled notes on permits in District 3, DF 850.3 Hearings, both in box 1, 8NS-75-92-092, Range Unit Case Files, 1949–1961, Navajo Service, RG 75, NARA-RMR. Also consult "Livestock Census, District 10," NA.

30. In designating men as head of household, Fryer and Collier followed a path laid out by earlier policymakers with the BIA, who, as a rule, endeavored to transform native women from agricultural producers and hide processors into good American housewives. Collier challenged the principle of cultural assimilation that governed Indian affairs, but he never questioned its patriarchal underpinnings.

31. Guy Sheets to Powers, 25 Nov. 1940; E. G. Stocks to Fryer, 27 Jan. 1941 (two letters); Sheets to Fryer, 28 Jan. 1941; Fryer, Memorandum for files, 22 May 1941, all in CCF 301 Grazing Permits Returned (1 of 2), box 119, Navajo Area Office, RG 75, NARA-PR.

32. Eric Henderson, "Navajo Livestock Wealth and the Effects of the Stock Reduction Program of the 1930s," *Journal of Anthropological Research* 45 (1989): 393. More than half of those who exceeded their permits lived in districts 4, 8, 9, 12, and 14, all of which became centers of resistance. Three of these had extremely low maximum permits, ranging from 61 to 83 SU. Calculated from "Livestock Census" for districts 1–5, 7–15, 17–18, NA.

33. Lamar Bedoni, interview, 30 June 1972, pp. 1–2, in Sundberg and Charley, *Navajo Stock Reduction Interviews*, CSUF; Narrative Report, May 1941, CCF 13321-1936-032, Eastern District, RG 75, NA.

34. David W. Carmody to Dennis Chavez, 6 Aug. 1937, file 31, box 80; D. W. Roberts to Chavez, 12 Aug. 1937, file 15, and Statement of Bob Lee, file 21, both in box 81, all in Chavez Papers, UNM; William A. Brophy to Collier, 29 Nov. 1937, CCF 62000-1935-301, pt. 1, Navajo, RG 75, NA. Also consult Fryer to Collier, 7 Aug. 1937, Morgan-Palmer file, Collier's Office Files, box 10, RG 75, NA; Parman, *Navajos and the New Deal*, 179–80.

35. Mitchell, *Tall Woman*, 211–12.

36. Mitchell, *Navajo Blessingway Singer*, 259.

37. Frank Goldtooth and Billy Bryant, interviews in Roessel and Johnson, *Navajo Livestock Reduction*, 103, 140; Rudolph Zweifel, statement, n.d., CCF 301 Grazing Permits Returned (1 of 2), box 119, and Hearing concerning Toadcheni Tso [*sic*], Julius Bainbridge, Chee Wilson, and John Balony, 30 March 1938, and William W. McClellan, Jr., to Holman, 5 April 1938, both in CCF 301 Grazing Matters (1 of 2), box 120, all in Navajo Area Office, RG 75, NARA-PR; Fryer to Collier, 29 June 1938, CCF 62000-1935-301, pt. 1, Navajo, and William Zimmerman, Jr., to Carl A. Hatch, 14 Oct. 1941, Navajo Stock Reduction file no. 2, box 13, Collier's Office Files, both in RG 75, NA.

38. Marshall to Collier, 22 May 1936, file 28-48, box 11, Collier's Navajo Documents, RG 75, NA.

39. The Chavez Papers are filled with these petitions, spanning a long period from 1937 through the early 1940s. See especially boxes 81 and 82, UNM. My specific discussion here draws on petitions from Rock Dale [*sic*], Rock Point, Twin Lakes, St. Michaels, Hunters Point, and Red Rock, as well as two collections of more personal expressions, one from Sweetwater and one that begins with a note from Tom Harvey and Pauline and Sarah Barton, location unknown. The names used in this description were written phonetically by the person who labeled the thumbprints; I have regularized the spelling here.

40. Fryer interview, p. 35, NOHT.

41. OIA, "Grazing Regulations," Haile Papers, UA; Tribal Council Minutes, Jan. 1938, pp. 78–88, 93–94, ADL.

42. Preston to Murdock, 14 Feb. 1940, file 33, box 620, Carl T. Hayden Papers, ASU. Also consult Minutes of Meeting Held at Shiprock, 5 March 1938, pp. 6–7, J. C. Morgan Activities re. Stock Reduction file, box 10, Collier's Office Files, RG 75, NA. Preston actually stated erroneously that his permit allowed 282 SU; I have used the official federal figure in my discussion.

43. Quoted in Roberts, *Stokes Carson*, 108–9. Also see Pearl Phillips, interview in Sundberg and Charley, *Navajo Stock Reduction Interviews*, CSUF.

44. Quoted in Downs, *Animal Husbandry*, 20. Downs glosses the man's name as Tall John.

45. Fryer, "Erosion, Poverty and Dependency," FLC-CSSL.

46. See "Livestock Census" for LMUs 1–3, 7–12, 14, and 17–18, NA; Tribal Council Minutes, Jan. 1938, pp. 94, 100, ADL.

47. Tribal Council Minutes, Jan. 1938, pp. 121–22, ADL. For example, John Salt's extended family, consisting of five households, had thirty-one members, but only twenty-five horses between them. Some of these household members were likely children, but they would need their own horses as they got older. See Supplemental Census Rolls, Northern Navajo Agency, box 183, Navajo Area Office, RG 75, NARA-PR.

48. Tribal Council Minutes, Jan. 1938, pp. 94, 99–100, ADL; John C. McPhee, "Narrative Report of Progress on the Navajo Reservation during the Month of November 1937," p. 3, box 48, Statistics Division, RG 75, NA. Also consult the photographs in CCF 48, box 21, Navajo Area Office, RG 75, NARA-PR.

49. Collier to Fryer, 7 Aug. 1937, Morgan-Palmer file, box 10, Collier's Office Files, RG 75, NA. Also consult the draft of this letter, dated 6 Aug. 1937, and E. Shevky and Woehlke to Collier, 7 Aug. 1937, both in the same file.

50. McPhee, "Narrative Report, November 1937," pp. 1–4, Reports and Other Records, 1933–48, box 48, Statistics Division, RG 75, NA; Woehlke to Collier, 13 Dec. 1937, CCF 301 (2 of 2), box 119, Navajo Area Office, RG 75, NARA-PR. Hastiin Yázhí Jesus's relative worth comes from "Livestock Census, LMU 14," NA; only Arthur Chester and Mary Lynch, both in LMU 17, had more, according to official counts.

51. John H. Provinse, Memorandum for Files, 13 June 1938, Navajo Court Cases file, box 32, SCS Records, NMSU; Collier to [E. K.] Burlew, 24 June 1938, Navajo Grazing file, box 12, and E. R. Fryer, "Why the Government Is Trying Grazing Cases," 8 Feb. 1941, p. 10, Navajo Stock Reduction file no. 1, box 13, both in Collier's Office Files, RG 75, NA; Fryer, "Erosion, Poverty and Dependency," 62, FLC-CSSL.

52. Copies of the first twelve complaints, filed in 1938 in federal court for the District of Arizona, charging trespass in grazing districts 1, 3, and 5, may be found in: CCF 62000-1935-301, pt. 1, Navajo, RG 75, NA; Navajo Court Cases file, box 32, SCS Records, NMSU; and folder 13, box 30, Franciscan Papers, UA. Subsequent court filings, filed in 1940 in the districts of Utah and Arizona, charging trespass in grazing districts 9 and 12, are located in CCF 62000-1935-301, pts. 2 and 3, Navajo, RG 75, NA. Records for cases filed in 1941 in the District of Utah, for trespass in District 9, are in file 117, box 5, Richard Van Valkenburgh Papers, AHS.

53. See, for example, Notice of Trespass issued to Hosteen Soni, 14 April 1938, and U.S. v. Hosteen Soni and Asdzan Nez Soni, E-205 (1938), both in Navajo Court Cases file, box 32, SCS Records, NMSU.

54. "Memorandum of Law on Cases Filed in the United States District Court...," CCF 62000-1935-301, pt. 3, Navajo, RG 75, NA. By the time the initial cases went to court in 1939, Brophy had received a temporary appointment to the

University of Colorado law school and turned his cases over to William Barker, who presented the oral arguments. Brophy, however, developed the legal strategy, along with Norman Littell, assistant attorney general for lands, and he oversaw all the subsequent cases.

55. U.S. v. Hosteen Tso and Chery Bumah Tso, E-204 (1939), CCF 62000-1935-301, pt. 2, Navajo, RG 75, NA. This decision was affirmed by the court for the District of Utah in U.S. v. Beletso et al. See "Transcript of Oral Decision of Court," 14 Feb. 1941, and "Findings of Fact and Conclusions of Law," both in file 117, box 5, Van Valkenburgh Papers, AHS, and Fryer to Collier, 18 Feb. 1941, CCF 62000-1936-301, pt. 4, Navajo, RG 75, NA.

56. Press release, 9 June 1939, Navajo 1939 file, box 12, Collier's Office Files, RG 75, NA.

57. Kenneth Allen, "Road to Hibbard, Ariz., Is Strewn with Dead Horses," *Albuquerque Tribune*, 14 Aug. 1939; Fryer to C. D. McCauley, 3 Aug. 1939, DF 155 Complaints 1939 no. 1, Navajo Service, RG 75, NARA-RMR; Fred Descheene, interview in Roessel and Johnson, *Navajo Livestock Reduction*, 192. Many of those interviewed in this compilation conflated the killing of dourine-infected horses with New Deal–era horse reduction. See, for example, the interviews with Eli Gorman, Mose Denejolie, Ason Attaki, Deneh L. Bitsilly, and Pete Sheen, pp. 24, 96–97, 127–28, 131, 162.

58. From RG 75, NA: Collier to Brophy, 20 May 1940, Navajo Grazing file, box 12, and Fryer to Collier, 10 June 1941, Navajo Stock Reduction file no. 1, box 13, both in Collier's Office Files; Brophy to Fryer, 23 July 1940, Fryer to Collier, 3 Nov. 1940, U.S. v. Jake Yellowman and Lucy Yellowman, [28 Aug. 1940], "Findings of Fact and Conclusions of Law," and U.S. v. Kit Seally and Bahih Seally, [28 Aug. 1940], "Findings of Fact and Conclusions of Law," all in CCF 62000-1935-301, pt. 3, Navajo. From RG 75, NARA-RMR: Powers, Memorandum to File, 6 June 1941, DF 175 Special Investigation Case no. 1, box 26, and Zweifel to Stewart, 7 Dec. 1942, DF 325.9 Trespass, box 1, 8NS-75-92-092, Range Unit Case Files, 1949–1961, both in Navajo Service records. From RG 75, NARA-PR: Zweifel, undated report on meeting at Sweetwater, CCF 301 Grazing Permits Returned file, box 119, and Holman to Fryer, 21 March 1940, CCF 301 Northern Navajo Grazing Trespass (2 of 2), box 120, both in Navajo Area Office records. The numbers of sheep are estimates, since Yellowman and Kit Seally may have owned a few head of cattle, as they did in 1937.

59. Cheschillige to Chavez, 8 Dec. 1940, folder 16, box 6, Chavez Papers, UNM; Cheschillige's stockowner status comes from "Livestock Census, District 9," NA. Parman provides a brief biographical sketch of Cheschillige in *Navajos and the New Deal*, 40, and a detailed discussion of Morgan's change of heart in chapter 10.

60. Fryer to Collier, 3 Feb. 1941, CCF 301 Northern Navajo Grazing Trespass, box 119, Navajo Area Office, RG 75, NA; Fryer to Collier, 10 June 1941, Navajo Stock Reduction file no. 1, box 13, Collier's Office Files, RG 75, NA.

61. Proceedings of the Meeting of the Navajo Tribal Council, Window Rock, 7–8 Nov. 1938, p. 14, ADL.

62. "Livestock Census, District 9," NA.

63. From RG 75, NA: McClellan to Fryer, 17 Jan. 1940, McClellan to Fryer, 26 Jan. 1940, and [Allan Harper?], "Memorandum re: Navajo 'Uprising' at Shiprock," 24 Feb. 1940, all in CCF 301 Northern Navajo Grazing Trespass (2 of 2), box 120, Navajo Area Office; Lucy W. Adams to Collier, 21 July 1941, H. M. Critchfield to Collier, 28 July 1941, Fryer to Collier, 31 July 1941, all in Navajo Stock Reduction file no. 1, box 13, Collier's Office Files. From RG 75, NARA-RMR: Powers to Fryer, 1 July 1941, DF 400.2 Livestock—Indians, box 1, 8NS-75-92-092, Range Unit Case Files, 1949–1961, Navajo Service.

64. Fryer to Collier, 12 Aug. 1941, CCF 62000-1935-301, pt. 4, Navajo, RG 75, NA.

65. Ibid.; Fryer to Collier, 6 Aug. 1941, CCF 62000-1935-301, pt. 4, Navajo, RG 75, NA; Powers to Fryer, 25 Aug 1941, CCF 301 (1 of 2), box 119, Navajo Area Office, RG 75, NARA-PR.

66. Kimball to [Collier?], 26 Sept. 1941, CCF 301.14 Navajo, box 166, FGD, RG 75, NARA-PR.

67. Collier to [William] Zeh and [Frank] Lenzie, 12 Sept. 1941, CCF 301.14 Navajo, box 166, FGD, RG 75, NARA-PR; Woehlke to Collier, 12 Sept. 1941, Navajo Stock Reduction file no. 2, box 13, Collier's Office Files, RG 75, NA.

68. Woehlke to Collier, 1 Feb. 1941, and Zeh et al. to Collier, 9 Oct. 1941, CCF 62000-1935-301, pt. 4, Navajo; Ward Shepard to Collier, 12 Sept. 1941, Navajo Stock Reduction file no. 2, box 13, Collier's Office Files; and Narrative Report, Sept. 1941, CCF 13321-1936-032, Eastern District, all in RG 75, NA; Lorenzo Hubbell to Collier, 12 Sept. 1941, CCF 301.14 Navajo, box 166, FGD, RG 75, NARA-PR.

69. For the debate on this resolution, see Proceedings of the Meeting of the Navajo Tribal Council, Window Rock, 7–11 April 1941, NNRMC. Shrewdly, Collier made it appear that Tribal Chairman Jacob Morgan and Howard Gorman, the vice chairman, instigated the higher permit levels, but they did so at Woehlke and Fryer's suggestion. See Woehlke to Collier, 1 Feb. 1941, and Morgan and Gorman, Memorandum for the Commissioner, 25 Feb. 1941, both in CCF 62000-1935-301, pt. 4, Navajo, RG 75, NA.

70. Collier, order regarding temporary special permits, 8 April 1941, Range Management Grazing Regulations file, box 97, Subject Files, Eastern Navajo Agency, RG 75, NARA-PR. Those with special permits for fewer than 350 SU could not increase their flocks beyond that limit; even if they remained under the larger cap, they were charged with trespass. See, for example, the documents pertaining to Billy Black Horse in CCF 62000-1935-301, pt. 6, Navajo, RG 75, NA. David Aberle (*Peyote Religion*, 67) and Richard White (*Roots of Dependency*, 308) assert that these more liberal permits were available only in five districts, but they err on that point. Special permits were available in all districts until 1943, when they

were restricted to districts 4, 8, 9, 12, 14, and the portion of 15 that lay inside the reservation. See Memorandum from Powers to All District Supervisors, 14 July 1941, Range Management Grazing Regulations file, box 97, Subject Files, Eastern Navajo Agency, RG 75, NARA-PR; and Stewart, Memorandum to All Supervisors (Superintendent[']s Circular no. 43-56), 28 May 1943, folder 5, box 32, Franciscan Papers, UA.

71. Kimball to Fryer, 25 Sept. 1941, CCF 301.14 Navajo, box 166, FGD, RG 75, NARA-PR; Fryer to Collier, 19 Nov. 1941, Navajo Stock Reduction file no. 2, box 13, Collier's Office Files, and Narrative Report, Feb. 1944, CCF 13321-1936-032, Eastern District, both in RG 75, NA.

72. For a personal recollection of the Many Farms Cannery Project, see Ned Campbell's narrative, folder 2, box 25, Fryer Papers, FLC-CSSSC.

73. From RG 75, NA: Stewart, Superintendent[']s Circular no. 42-49, 21 Aug. 1942, Stewart to Woehlke, 5 Feb. 1944, and Woehlke to Edwin C. Johnson, 9 Feb. 1944, all in CCF 62000-1935-301, pt. 6, Navajo; Narrative Reports for Aug. 1945 and Sept. 1945, CCF 13321-1936-032, Eastern District. From RG 75, NARA-PR: 1946 Summary of Livestock Situation, 31 Dec. 1946, CCF 301 Lee Muck, box 120, Navajo Area Office.

74. Millin to Bitney, 30 Jan. 1948, CCF 301.4 Carrying Capacity, Navajo Agency, box 171; Carl D. Rawie, Joseph V. Chiarella, and Richard B. Millin, "Utilization Check Report, Navajo Indian Reservation, 1947–1948," p. 7, and "Summary of Utilization Surveys" table, CCF 301.1 Utilization Checks-Navajo, box 164, all in FGD, RG 75, NARA-PR. This survey could not possibly have been comprehensive, but it indicates a decline in the study areas.

75. On thresholds, see Stringham, Krueger, and Shaver, "State and Transition Modeling," and Bestelmeyer et al., "Development and Use of State-and-Transition Models."

76. Collier to Zeh and Lenzie, 12 Sept. 1941, CCF 301.14 Navajo, box 166, FGD, RG 75, NARA-PR; Tribal Council Minutes, April 1941, p. 20, NNRMC; Parman, *Navajos and the New Deal*, 283 (n. 37), 286; Aberle, *Peyote Religion*, 83. Capiton Benally and Tacheadeny Tso Begay, interviews in Roessel and Johnson, *Navajo Livestock Reduction*, 33–35, 110–13, describe their participation in the beatings of district supervisor Rudolph Zweifel and range rider Rod Palmer; also see Nedra Tó Díchʼííʼnii, interview in Moon, *Tall Sheep*, 93.

77. Stewart, Memorandum to All Supervisors (Superintendent[']s Circular no. 43-56), 28 May 1943, folder 5, box 32, Franciscan Papers, UA; Minutes of the Navajo Tribal Council, Window Rock, 9–11 July 1943, pp. 38–39, 63, 72, 98, 103, ADL.

78. Tribal Council Minutes, July 1943, pp. 36–37, ADL.

79. Stewart to Collier, 19 July 1943; W. Barton Greenwood to Dodge, 30 July 1943; Harold L. Ickes to Dodge, 30 Oct. 1943; Stewart to Woehlke, 2 May 1944, all in CCF 62000-1935-301, pt. 6, Navajo, RG 75, NA; Dodge to Members of the Na-

vajo Tribal Council, 28 March 1944, Circulars file, box 7, Maxwell files, RG 75, NARA-PR.

80. Collier, *From Every Zenith*, 173; Cohen, Memorandum for the Solicitor, 24 Sept. 1943, and Cohen to Mr. Flanery, 22 Feb. 1944, both in CCF 62000-1935-301, pt. 6, Navajo, RG 75, NA; Lee Muck, "Survey of the Range Resources and Livestock Economy of the Navajo Nation," 10 Dec. 1947, and Krug to Acting COIA, 26 Jan. 1948, both in CCF 301 Lee Muck, box 120, Navajo Area Office, RG 75, NARA-PR.

81. Minutes of the Navajo Tribal Council, Window Rock, 10–13 July 1945, p. 239, and Proceedings of the Meeting of the Navajo Tribal Council, Window Rock, 18–21 Feb. 1947, pp. 80–81, and 18–23 March 1948, p. 17, all in NNRMC; Allan G. Harper to Dillon S. Myer, 16 July 1952, Proposed Grazing Regulations file (1 of 2), FRC 72969, 075-57A-0065, Division of Resources, Navajo Area Office, RG 75, NARA-PR.

82. H. A. Mathiesen to Woehlke, 18 March 1947, CCF 301.1 Grazing Permits-Navajo Service, box 157, FGD, RG 75, NA. In a grazing-permit case involving Ethyl Herring, the Diné wife of an Anglo trader, Mathiesen noted that Herring met the legal definition of "head of household" and expressed concern that denying a permit on the basis of sex could result in a lawsuit that might undo the entire permit system.

83. White, *Roots of Dependency*, 309–10.

84. Quoted in Floyd Allen Pollock, *A Navajo Confrontation and Crisis* (1989), 96–97.

85. Tribal Council Minutes, July 1933, p. 19, and July 1934, p. 80, both NNRMC; Collier, *From Every Zenith*, 219–20.

86. Ni, "Cool-Season Precipitation"; Cook, "Long-Term Aridity."

87. Economic Analysis and Consulting, "Navajo Livestock Numbers, 1868–1975," 10 Jan. 1985, folder 2, box 25, Fryer Papers, FLC-CSSSC; Young, *Navajo Yearbook* (1955), 117; Young, *Navajo Yearbook* (1961), 163, 167.

88. Muck, "Survey of the Range Resources," 12, NARA-PR; Tribal Council Minutes, April 1941, p. 30, NNRMC; Adams, *Shonto*, 46–47, 118.

89. Quoted in Pollock, *Navajo Confrontation and Crisis*, 94.

90. The descriptions of dysfunctional behavior at Ramah are particularly disturbing. See, for example, [Dorothea] C. Leighton, notes kept while giving psychological tests to Navajo children around Ramah, 1942, pp. 78, 84, 95, 129–31, courtesy of Louise Lamphere; entry for Rosie Eriacho file, 1 Feb. 1952, Dorothy Henio file, 11 July and 8 Aug. 1950, Frank Navajo file, 23–24 Aug. 1949, Ramah Research Files, MIAC-LA.

91. Aberle, *Peyote Religion*, 109–10; Parman, *Navajos and the New Deal*, 257–60. The Native American Church has its origins among the Kiowas and Comanches of Oklahoma. For a good overview of its history and practice, consult Omer C. Stewart, *Peyote Religion: A History* (1987).

92. Continued practice of ceremonies is evident in community studies conducted in the 1960s. See, for example, Lamphere, *To Run after Them*, ch. 8.

93. Kluckhohn and Leighton, *Navaho*, 228.

94. O'Neill, *Working the Navajo Way*, 86; Iverson, *Diné*, 182–88.

95. Many letters from men in the armed services and from returned veterans complaining that their flocks were reduced or their grazing permits terminated while they were away at war are contained in CCF 301.4 Carrying Capacity-Navajo Agency, box 116, FGD, RG 75, NARA-PR, and in CCF 62000-1935-301, pt. 6, RG 75, NA. The termination of permits for those working off the reservation for at least one year was standard policy. See comments on draft revisions to the Navajo grazing regulations, 22 Aug. 1942, p. 10, CCF 62000-1935-301, pt. 5, Navajo, RG 75, NA, and Stewart, Memorandum to All Supervisors (Superintendent[']s Circular no. 43-56), file 5, box 32, Franciscan Papers, UA.

96. "Statistical Summary, Human Dependency Survey, Navajo Reservation, 1940," Oct. 1941, tables 3, 22, and 23, box 10, SCS Records, UNM; Elizabeth P. Clark, "Report on the Navajo," 1946, pp. 8, 16, Ephemera Collection, ASU; U.S. Department of Commerce, Bureau of the Census, *Statistical Abstract of the United States, 1947* (1947), 272; Adams, *Shonto*, 188–90. In 1940, annual home consumption of sheep and goats plummeted to only three animals per capita, on average.

97. Lamphere, "Historical and Regional Variability," 436; O'Neill, *Working the Navajo Way*, offers an excellent analysis of Navajo wage-workers in the postwar years.

98. Laila Shukry Hamamsy, "The Role of Women in a Changing Navaho Society," *American Anthropologist* 59 (1957): 106; O'Neill, *Working the Navajo Way*, 78, 102.

99. Quote from Shukry's field notes in Lamphere, "Historical and Regional Variability," 442. After she married, Laila Shukry published under her married name, Hamamsy, and later el-Hamamsy.

100. O'Neill, *Working the Navajo Way*, 78–79; Lamphere, "Historical and Regional Variability," 447, 450; Hamamsy, "Role of Women," 106–7; Economic Analysis and Consulting, "Navajo Livestock Numbers," Fryer Papers, FLC-CSSSC.

101. See, for example, Hamamsy, "Role of Women," 111.

102. Lamphere, "Historical and Regional Variability," 437, 439, 445. This same pattern among Hispanos is evident in Sarah Deutsch, *No Separate Refuge: Culture, Class, and Gender on an Anglo-Hispanic Frontier in the American Southwest, 1880–1940* (1987).

103. Lula Stanley, interview, 20 June 1974, p. 5, in Sundberg and Charley, *Navajo Stock Reduction Interviews*, CSUF; James F. Downs, *The Navajo* (1972), 35; Lamphere, *To Run after Them*, 114; O'Neill, *Working the Navajo Way*, 57, 71–73.

104. Minutes of a meeting re. Tully Bia and Harry Price, 17 June 1940, CCF 64 Councils, Acts of Tribal Meetings file, box 13, Chinle Subagency, and Minutes of District 18 Navajo Tribal Delegates Meeting, Fort Defiance, 6 Sept. 1951, CCF 60 Tribal Relations file (folder 2), box 37, Navajo Area Office, both RG 75, NARA-PR.

105. Fanale, "Navajo Land and Land Management," 282–84.
106. George Blueeyes, interview in *Between Sacred Mountains*, 160.
107. Meeting with Mr. Morelock and delegation from Nazlini community..., 12 Jan. 1956, DF 301 District Grazing Committee-General file, box 9, 8NS-75-92-092, Range Unit Case Files, 1949–1961, Navajo Service, RG 75, NARA-RMR.

EPILOGUE

1. Only in Gallup did 1997 set the record. Throughout the rest of Navajo Country, precipitation records were established primarily in the 1940s and 1960s. See Western Regional Climate Center, precipitation tables.
2. The botanical name for three-awn grass is *Aristida longiseta*.
3. Muck, "Survey of the Range Resources," 31, NARA-PR. Range reports in the 1950s describe severely eroded conditions, which were certainly exacerbated by drought. See, for example, Don W. Clark and Paul A. Krause, reports of range utilization on the Navajo Indian Reservation for both 1952 and 1953, Range Utilization Report file, box FRC 72969, 075-57A-0065, Division of Resources, Navajo Area Office, RG 75, NARA-PR.
4. Fanale, "Navajo Land and Land Management," 283–85.
5. This scenario draws on conversations with Virginia Yazzie-Ashley, U.S. Forest Service, as well as Judy Willeto and Casey Begay, both then with the Navajo Nation Grazing Management Office, all in June 1997.
6. "Long-Range Program Plans, Branch of Soil and Moisture Conservation, Fiscal Year 1953," and Memorandum to Director re. Branch of Soil Conservation meeting with Tribal Resources Committee, 30 July 1954, both in Soil and Moisture Conservation file (1 of 2), box FRC 72969, 075-57A-0065, Division of Resources, Navajo Area Office, RG 75, NARA-PR; Collier, *From Every Zenith*, 256. Thanks also to Rick Tafoya and a comment by an anonymous Diné man at a public lecture at New Mexico State University, Oct. 2003.
7. William L. Halvorson and Patricia Guertin, "Factsheet for *Bromus tectorum*" (2003), 7–11, 18–20, http://sdrsnet.srnr.arizona.edu/data/sdrs/ww/docs/bromtect.pdf. The classic account of the invasion of European weeds is Alfred W. Crosby, *Ecological Imperialism: The Biological Expansion of Europe, 900–1900* (1986), ch. 7. But predating Crosby's book by more than half a century is the extraordinary study of plant invasions by Herbert Guthrie-Smith, *Tutira: The Story of a New Zealand Sheep Station* (1921; reprint, 1999); see especially ch. 27.
8. *Between Sacred Mountains*, 118. The absence of *Bromus tectorum* from range inventories in the 1930s is not likely due to botanical ignorance on the part of the technicians, for the plant is mentioned in the "Instructions for Range Surveys," adopted by the BIA and the SCS on 24 April 1937; see CCF 62000-1935-301, pt. 3, Navajo, RG 75, NA. Even through 1953, the last year for which I collected range

inventories, downy brome was not mentioned by name, though it could have been among the nameless unpalatable annuals that were supplanting native forage.

9. USDA, *Western Range*, 3–7, 135. Overgrazing may have even contributed to the Dust Bowl on the southern plains. Although Worster, in *Dust Bowl*, attributes the calamity to capitalist-driven, large-scale wheat production, Geoff Cunfer's recent study, *On the Great Plains: Agriculture and Environment* (2005), maintains that 70 percent of the southern plains remained in pasture. Cunfer discounts overgrazing, but his data suggest that overstocking during drought may have helped expose the soil to wind erosion.

10. Aldo Leopold, *A Sand County Almanac, and Sketches Here and There* (1949; reprint 1987), 155.

11. Halvorson and Guertin, "Fact Sheet for *Bromus tectorum*," 11; Donahue, *Western Range Revisited*, 120–21.

12. W. G. McGinnies, Discussion of Statement by Floyd Lee, NARA-RMR.

13. McGinnies, "Statement of the Present Plan of Land Management on the Navajo Reservation," 11 June 1936, p. 2, file 28–48, Collier's Navajo Documents, RG 75, NA.

14. Fryer interview, p. 40, NOHT; Edward H. Spicer, "Sheepmen and Technicians: A Program of Soil Conservation on the Navajo Indian Reservation," in *Human Problems in Technological Change: A Casebook* (1952), 185–205.

15. Clark, "Report on the Navajo," 21, ASU.

16. Muck, "Survey of the Range Resources," 16–17, NARA-PR; the quote is from page 20.

17. Solon T. Kimball, "Future Problems in Navajo Administration," 1949, p. 3, Navajo Pamphlets, Bulletins, and Sketches file, box 12, Walter O. Olson Subject Files, Navajo Area Office, RG 75, NARA-PR. The emphasis is Kimball's.

18. Kimball, "Land Use Management," 63–64.

19. John Collier, *On the Gleaming Way: Navajos, Eastern Pueblos, Zunis, Hopis, Apaches, and Their Land; and Their Meanings to the World*, 2nd ed. (1949; reprint, 1962), 65–67; Collier, *From Every Zenith*, 240–43, 252–53 (the long quote is from p. 219); Collier, "Comment," in *Human Problems in Technological Change: A Casebook*, ed. Edward H. Spicer (1952), 205. Fryer, too, rationalized that he had done nothing that was not "approved" and "sanctioned" by the council; see Fryer interview, p. 4, NOHT.

20. The quote is from Collier, *From Every Zenith*, 219; also see Collier, "Comment," 205, 207.

21. White, *Roots of Dependency*, 311. The decline of pastoralism and rise of deadly economies took place throughout northern New Mexico. For a discussion of the repercussions, see Prindeville, "Role of Gender."

22. Tribal Council Minutes, March 1934, pp. 44–45, NNRMC; Robert Martin to Collier, 11 March 1940, CCF 53240-1939-720, Navajo, and Sam Ahkeah to Dennis

Chavez, 18 June 1941, Navajo Stock Reduction file no. 1, Collier's Office Files, both in RG 75, NA.

23. Quoted in Kimball to John H. Provinse, 7 March 1938, J. C. Morgan Activities re. Stock Reduction file, box 10, Collier's Office Files, RG 75, NA. A small number of Diné wrote government officials in support of one or more aspects of stock reduction, each time connecting depleted grasslands to overgrazing. See, for example, Adolph Maloney to Fryer, 9 Aug. 1937, CCF 002.1 Administration file, box 1, Navajo Area Office, RG 75, NARA-PR; Robert Martin to Collier, 11 March 1940, CCF 53240-1939-720, Navajo, RG 75, NA.

24. Nedra Tó Dích'íi'nii and Tallas Holiday, interviews in Moon, *Tall Sheep*, 93–94, 98–99; interviews with Hite Chee, 20 July 1974, p. 13, and Sarah Begay, p. 11, in Sundberg and Charley, *Navajo Stock Reduction Interviews*, CSUF; Fanale, "Navajo Land and Land Management," 318.

25. For an analysis of the environmental views of some fundamentalist Christians, see Glenn Scherer, "The Godly Must Be Crazy," *Grist Magazine*, 27 Oct. 2004, http://www.grist.org/news/maindish/2004/10/27/scherer-christian/index.html. The quotation from Genesis 1:28 comes from the *World English Bible*.

26. For the story of the bison-hunting Cheyennes, see Flores, "Bison Ecology," 485.

27. Mitchell, *Navajo Blessingway Singer*, 259, 316; Mitchell, *Tall Woman*, 211–12.

28. Muskett, "Identity, *Hózhǫ́*, Change, and Land," 136–37.

29. Walter P. Taylor, "Significance of Extreme or Intermittent Conditions in Distribution of Species and Management of Natural Resources, with a Restatement of Liebig's Law of Minimum," *Ecology* 15 (1934): 378. Oddly, Arthur W. Sampson, whose *Livestock Husbandry on Range and Pasture* (1928) was the authority for McGinnies and other range ecologists during the New Deal, relegated his discussion of carrying capacity to a footnote. He defined carrying capacity as "the number of acres required to support an 'animal unit' *amply* for a given period without permanent injury to the forage crop" (p. 16; my emphasis). I am indebted to Harley Shaw for discussions on this issue.

30. McGinnies, "Stock Reduction and Range Management," pp. 15–16, in "Proceedings," ed. Lockett, UNM; Fryer to Collier, 20 April 1938, Navajo-General file, box 12, Collier's Office Files, RG 75, NA. For a sharp critique of McGinnies's approach, see Rawie, Chiarella, and Millin, "Utilization Check Report, 1947–1948," NARA-PR.

31. Edward N. Hardies, "Studies in Adjusting the Number of Livestock to a Fluctuating Range Forage Supply" (draft), CCF 301.4 Range Surveys, FGD, RG 75, NARA-PR; McGinnies, Discussion of Statement by Floyd Lee, NARA-RMR. For procedures on determining carrying capacity, consult "Instructions for Range Surveys," 24 April 1937, CCF 62000-1935-301, pt. 3, Navajo, RG 75, NA.

The erroneous notion of a fixed "carrying capacity" led Lee Muck, an experienced forester, to declare in 1948 that the reservation was understocked by 100,000 SU, stimulating political pressure to rebuild flocks. Muck, "Survey of the Range Resources," 7–8; also see the response by District Forester Bitney to [Richard] Millin, 30 Jan. 1948, CCF 301.4 Carrying Capacity, Box 171, FGD, RG 75, both in NARA-PR.

32. Clark and Krause, "Report of 1953 Range Utilization on the Navajo Indian Reservation," Range Utilization Report file, box FRC 72969, 075-57A-0065, Division of Resources, Navajo Area Office, RG 75, NARA-PR.

33. McGinnies, Discussion of statement by Floyd Lee, p. [2], NARA-RMR. For a discussion of the science on deferred grazing, see Sampson, *Livestock Husbandry*, 77–81.

34. "Agreement between the Soil Erosion Service-Experiment Station and the People of the Five Chapters for the Mexican Springs Area," 20 March 1934, folder 9, box 1, Dodge Collection, ASU, provides information on hiring herders. Also consult Parman, *Navajos and the New Deal*, 88–89.

35. Fryer interview, p. 46, NOHT.

36. "Steamboat Demonstration Area," p. 3, folder 20, box 82, Chavez Papers, UNM; Downes, "Navajo Report," p. 32, NA.

37. Kimball, "Land Use Management," 72.

38. Tribal Council Minutes, Oct.–Nov. 1933, p. 44, NA; Naalnishí's name (meaning "worker"), is spelled Nal Nishi in the record. In 1949, Deeshchii'nii, echoing Naalnishí's statement, described deep snows at Black Mesa that took many sheep and prompted an emergency relief program by the Red Cross to airlift hay to save herds. These snows blanketed the western part of the reservation, resulting in a loss of half of that year's lambs. See Committee on Public Lands, Rehabilitation Hearings, pp. 123–24, NARA-PR; BIA, "Summary of Navajo Developments," 8 April 1949, folder 28, box 82, Chavez Papers, UNM; American National Red Cross, "Report of Relief Activities of the American National Red Cross on the Navajo and Hopi Indian Reservations in Arizona during the Spring of 1949," 14 July 1949, folder 29, box 55, Hayden Papers, ASU.

39. Roberts, *Stokes Carson*, 83–84.

40. Minutes of a meeting of the Advisory Committee, 2–6 April 1951, box 43, CCF 64, Navajo Area Office, RG 75, NARA-PR.

41. The assumption of forty animals consumed by each family is conservative, based on the average reported consumption in the Tsaile and Chinle areas; in the latter community, agriculture, not livestock, was more important. (Consult "Report of Sociological Survey" for LMU 11-Tsaile, p. 5, Aug. 1936, folder 28, box 8, and for LMU 10-Chinle, p. 8, Jan. 1937, folder 10, box 9, both in SCS Records, UNM.) Economist Robert Youngblood reported that the average family consumed fifty sheep and goats annually (see ch. 9, n. 14). Albert Sandoval suggested a consumption rate of seventy-two head per family.

42. This calculation also assumes no increase in the number of horses and cattle. My calculation is based on consumption by the 4,669 owners of sheep and goats (that is, permit holders) in 1941, the only year for which specific data are available. It assumes an annual lamb crop of 54 percent and an annual kid crop of 59 percent, the average reported in the revised livestock data attached to J. G. Hamilton to [Collier], 30 Jan. 1936, CCF 13395-1936-031, Navajo, RG 75, NA. Moreover, it assumes that 97 percent of the sheep and goats that the Navajos retained were ewes and nannies, and that the ratio of sheep to goats remained constant.

43. Kimball, "Land Use Management," 65.

44. Donna J. Haraway, "Universal Donors in a Vampire Culture: It's All in the Family; Biological Kinship Categories in the Twentieth-Century United States," in *Uncommon Ground: Toward Reinventing Nature*, ed. William Cronon (1995), 323.

45. Botkin, *Discordant Harmonies*, 127. I thank Art McEvoy and Sherry Smith for bringing this to my attention.

46. Howard Gorman makes this point in his interview in Roessel and Johnson, *Navajo Livestock Reduction*, 71–72.

47. Fryer interview, p. 28, NOHT; Fryer to [Collier], 3 April 1940, CCF 62000-1935-301, pt. 2, Navajo, and Ward Shepard to [Collier], 12 Sept. 1941, Navajo Stock Reduction file no. 2, box 13, Collier's Office Files, both in RG 75, NA; C. J. Babbitt to Carl Hayden, 4 March 1937, file 277, box 11, Babbitt Brothers Trading Company Collection, NAU. This land offered by Babbitt Brothers was in addition to the lands along the Little Colorado River that the company had already sold, adding to the Leupp Extension.

48. Model grass banks in New Mexico are operated by the Malpai Borderlands Group and the Quivera Coalition. For information, see http://www.malpaiborderlandsgroup.org/gb.asp, http://quiviracoalition.org/Rowe_Mesa_Grassbank/index.html, and http://www.conservationfund.org/node/474.

49. For a trenchant, yet not altogether satisfying, critique of participatory development projects, see Bill Cooke and Uma Kothari, *Participation: The New Tyranny?* (2001). Thanks to Peter Edward for bringing this work to my attention.

50. Collier, *From Every Zenith*, 232–33.

51. O'Neill, in *Working the Navajo Way*, 133–34, articulates this idea beautifully.

52. Pynes, "Erosion, Extraction, and Reciprocation," 172.

53. Interview with Charlie Yellow, quoted in *Between Sacred Mountains*, 173.

54. Quoted in Mitchell, *Tall Woman*, 394, n. 15.

GLOSSARY

'asdzą́ą́. Woman.

Baa'. Warrior woman; often spelled Bah.

bilagáana. White people; white person.

ch'į́įdii. Malevolent spirits of the dead.

Diné. The People; Navajos.

Diné Bikéyah. Navajo Country, defined by the four sacred mountains.

Dinétah. The historic Navajo homeland in the general area of Navajo Dam and Gobernador Canyon.

Diyin Dine'é. Holy People; supernaturals.

hastiin. An honorific for an older man; "mister."

hataałii. Ceremonial healer and keeper of ceremonies, history, and oral traditions; singer; chanter; medicine man.

hóchxǫ́. Spiritual disorder.

hogan. An earthen house traditionally used by Diné and important to ceremonial practice; different forms include the conical forked-pole hogan, the corbeled-log hogan, the stone hogan, and the palisaded hogan. Also spelled hooghan.

hózhǫ́. The central concept in Diné philosophy, referring to balance, beauty, harmony, health, and other positive qualities.

Hwéeldi. The location at Fort Sumner, New Mexico, where the Diné were interned from 1863 until 1868; Bosque Redondo.

k'é. The ideal for Diné social relationships; expresses kinship and embodies a code of conduct among kin that includes compassion, cooperation, generosity, harmony, helpfulness, kindness, love, respect, solidarity, and physical and emotional sustenance.

nádleeh. A third gender that embodies masculine and feminine qualities in a single whole (complementarity); literally, "he repeatedly becomes or changes."

níłtsą́ bi'áád. Female rain; gentle rain shower.

níłtsą́ biką́. Male rain; violent torrential downpour; cloudburst.

są'a naagháii bik'eh hózhǫ́. The central concept of Navajo philosophy, often conveyed simply as "hózhǫ́"; usually glossed as "long life and happiness."

shimá. My mother.

tó. Water.

yee naaldlooshii. Werewolf, or skinwalker; a witch disguised in a wolf's skin.

PLANTS

Common Name	Botanical Name	Navajo Name
alkali sacaton	*Sporobolus airoides*	tł'oh dahakałii
aspen	*Populus tremuloides*	t'iisbáí
blue grama	*Bouteloua gracilis*	tł'oh nástasí
bugseed	*Corispermum americanum*	unknown
bush muhly	*Muhlenbergia porteri*	unknown
cheatgrass	See downy brome	
cliffrose	*Cowania mexicana*	'awééts'áál
cockleburr	*Xanthium strumarium*	unknown
deerbriar	*Ceanothus fendleri*	bįįhdą́ą́'
Douglas fir	*Pseudotsuga menziesii*	ch'o deenínii
downy brome	*Bromus tectorum*	shį́ yináldzidí
four-wing saltbush	*Atriplex canescens*	díwózhiiłbéí
galleta	*Hilaria jamesii*	tł'oh dich'ízhí
Gambel oak	*Quercus gambelii*	tchétc'ilńtł'ízíh*
globemallow	*Sphaeralcea cuspidata*	'azee'ntł'iníłibáhígíí
golden crownbeard	*Verbesina encelioides*	ntígíliinłtchiníh*
greasewood	*Sarcobatus vermiculatus*	díwózhii
Indian ricegrass	*Oryzopsis hymenoides*	nididlídii
juniper	*Juniperus* spp.	gad
locoweed	*Astragalus* and *Oxytropis* spp.	łįį' bináá' ííłdįįhi
Mormon tea	*Ephedra trifurca*	tł'oh azihii

Common Name	Botanical Name	Navajo Name
pigweed	*Amaranthaceae* spp.	tł'ohdeeí hoshí
piñon	*Pinus edulis*	deestsiin
Ponderosa pine	*Pinus ponderosa*	ńdíshchíí'
rabbitbrush	*Chrysothamnus* spp.	k'iiłtsoii
Russian thistle	*Salsola iberica*	ch'il deenínii
sagebrush	*Artemisia tridentata*	ts'ah
sand dropseed	*Sporobolus cryptandrus*	tł'ohtsohzhóó'
shadscale	*Atriplex confertifolia*	tá'ak'óojteenínih*
sideoats grama	*Bouteloua curtipendula*	unknown
snakeweed	*Gutierrezia sarothrae*	ch'il dilyésii
sneezeweed	*Helenium hoopesii*	ne'éctjaa' yil khee'éh*
sunflower	*Helianthus annuus*	ndíyíliitsoh
three-awn grass	*Aristida longiseta*	dlǫ́ǫ́' bibé'ézhóó'
western wheatgrass	*Agropyron smithii*	tłoolé
winterfat	*Ceratoides lanata*	gahtsodą́ą́'
woolly plantain	*Plantago patagonica*	'azee'it'eł

*The orthography used here is from Francis Elmore's *Ethnobotany of the Navajo* (1943). All other plant names use the orthography adopted by Young and Morgan, *Analytical Lexicon of Navajo* (1992).

BIBLIOGRAPHY

MANUSCRIPT COLLECTIONS

Arizona State Land Department Records (RG 59). Archives Division. Arizona Department of Library, Archives, and Public Records. Phoenix.

Babbitt Brothers Trading Company Collection (MS 83). Special Collections. Cline Library. Northern Arizona University. Flagstaff.

Babbitt, George, Collection (MS 44). Special Collections. Cline Library. Northern Arizona University. Flagstaff.

Babbitt and Roberts Trading Post Records (MSS 435). Center for Southwest Research. Zimmerman Library. University of New Mexico. Albuquerque.

Blair, Raymond, Collection (MS 303). Special Collections. Cline Library. Northern Arizona University. Flagstaff.

Chavez, Dennis, Papers (MSS 394). Center for Southwest Research. Zimmerman Library. University of New Mexico. Albuquerque.

Collier, John, Papers. Microfilm. Yale University. New Haven, Conn.

Day Family Collection (MS 89). Special Collections. Cline Library. Northern Arizona University. Flagstaff.

Dodge, Thomas, Collection (MSS 33). Department of Archives and Manuscripts. Hayden Library. Arizona State University. Tempe.

Downs, James F., Collection. Archives. Arizona State Museum. Tucson.

Franciscan Papers (AZ 500). Special Collections. University of Arizona. Tucson.

Fryer, E. Reeseman. "Erosion, Poverty and Dependency: Memoir of My Time in Navajo Service, 1933–1942." Unpublished manuscript, 1986. Center of Southwest Studies Library. Fort Lewis College. Durango, Colo.

Fryer, E. Reesman, Papers (M179). Special Collections. Center of Southwest Studies. Fort Lewis College. Durango, Colo.

Haile, Berard, Papers (AZ 132). Special Collections. University of Arizona. Tucson.

Hayden, Carl T., Papers (MSS 1). Department of Archives and Manuscripts. Hayden Library. Arizona State University. Tempe.

Hockenhull, Andrew H., Papers (1959-103). New Mexico State Records Center and Archives. Santa Fe.

Hubbell Collection (MSS 100). Arizona Historical Foundation. Hayden Library. Arizona State University. Tempe.

Hubbell Trading Post Miscellaneous Files. Library. Hubbell Trading Post National Monument. Ganado, Ariz.

Hubbell Trading Post Oral History Files. Hubbell Trading Post National Monument. Ganado, Ariz.

Hubbell Trading Post Papers (AZ 375). Special Collections. University of Arizona. Tucson.

Indian Census Rolls, 1885–1940: Navajo. Microfilm. National Archives. Washington, D.C.

Leighton, Dorothea C. and Alexander H., Collection (MS 216). Special Collections. Cline Library. Northern Arizona University. Flagstaff.

Letters Received by Headquarters Department of New Mexico, 1854–1865. Microfilm (M1120). National Archives. Washington, D.C.

Letters Received by the Office of Indian Affairs, New Mexico Superintendency. Microfilm (M234). National Archives. Washington, D.C.

Lockett, H. C., ed. "Proceedings of the First Navajo Service Land Management Conference, 2–6 March 1937, Flagstaff, Arizona." Navajo Service School Bulletin no. 1. Center for Southwest Research. Zimmerman Library. University of New Mexico. Albuquerque.

Matthews, Washington, Papers. Microfilm. Wheelwright Museum of the American Indian. Santa Fe, N. Mex.

Mexican Archives of New Mexico, 1821–1846. Microfilm. New Mexico State Records Center and Archives. Santa Fe.

Navajo Oral Histories. American Indian Oral History Transcriptions. Microfilm. Center for Southwest Research. Zimmerman Library. University of New Mexico. Albuquerque.

Navajo Tribal Council Minutes. Arizona Collection. Arizona Department of Library, Archives, and Public Records. Phoenix.

Navajo Tribal Council Minutes. Navajo Nation Records Management Center. Window Rock, Ariz.

Plummer, E. H., Papers (1965-001). New Mexico State Records Center and Archives. Santa Fe.

Ramah Research Files. Archives. Laboratory of Anthropology. Museum of Indian Arts and Culture. Santa Fe, N.Mex.

Reichard, Gladys, Collection. Museum of Northern Arizona. Flagstaff.

Seligman, Arthur, Papers (1959-102). New Mexico State Records Center and Archives. Santa Fe.

Spanish Archives of New Mexico, 1621–1821. Microfilm. New Mexico State Records Center and Archives. Santa Fe.

Sundberg, Dean, and Fern Charley, eds. *Navajo Stock Reduction Interviews*. Microfilm. Oral History Program. California State University. Fullerton.

Surveyor General Records and the Records of the Court of Private Claims. Spanish Archives of New Mexico, series 1. Microfilm. New Mexico State Records Center and Archives. Santa Fe.

Testimonies Sent by Governor Codallos y Rabal to the Viceroy. *New Mexico Originals*. Microfilm. Bancroft Library. University of California. Berkeley.

Tingley, Clyde, Papers (1959-104). New Mexico State Records Center and Archives. Santa Fe.

U.S. Bureau of Indian Affairs Records (RG 75). National Archives. Washington, D.C.

U.S. Bureau of Indian Affairs Records (RG 75). National Archives, Pacific Region. Laguna Niguel, Calif.

U.S. Bureau of Indian Affairs Records (RG 75). National Archives, Rocky Mountain Region. Denver, Colo.

U.S. Bureau of Indian Affairs Records (RG 75). National Archives, Still Pictures Unit. College Park, Md.

U.S. Soil Conservation Service Collection (AZ 124). Special Collections. University of Arizona. Tucson.

U.S. Soil Conservation Service Records (MSS 289). Center for Southwest Research. Zimmerman Library. University of New Mexico. Albuquerque.

U.S. Soil Conservation Service Records (MS 190). Rio Grande Historical Collections. Branson Library. New Mexico State University. Las Cruces.

Van Valkenburgh, Richard, Papers (MS 831). Archives. Arizona Historical Society. Tucson.

Wooton, Elmer Ottis, Papers (MS 334). Rio Grande Historical Collections. Branson Library. New Mexico State University. Las Cruces.

BOOKS, ARTICLES, AND REPORTS

Aberle, David F. "A Century of Navajo Kinship Change." *Canadian Journal of Anthropology* 2 (Spring 1981): 21–36.

———. "The Navajo." In *Matrilineal Kinship*, edited by David M. Schneider and Kathleen Gough. Berkeley: University of California Press, 1961.

———. "Navajo Coresidential Kin Groups and Lineages." *Journal of Anthropological Research* 37 (Spring 1981): 1–7.

———. *The Peyote Religion among the Navaho*. 2nd ed. Norman: University of Oklahoma Press, 1991.

Ackerman, Lillian. "Complementary but Equal: Gender Status in the Plateau." In *Women and Power in Native North America*, edited by Laura F. Klein and Lillian A. Ackerman. Norman: University of Oklahoma Press, 1995.

Adams, Eleanor B., ed. and trans. *Bishop Tamaron's Visitation of New Mexico, 1760*. Publications in History 15. Albuquerque: Historical Society of New Mexico, 1954.

Adams, William Y. *Shonto: A Study of the Role of the Trader in a Modern Navajo Community*. Bureau of American Ethnology Bulletin 188. Washington, D.C.: Government Printing Office, 1963.

Adler, Robert W. *Restoring Colorado River Ecosystems: A Troubled Sense of Immensity*. Washington, D.C.: Island Press, 2007.

Albers, Patricia C. "Changing Patterns of Ethnicity in the Northern Plains, 1780–1870." In *History, Power, and Identity: Ethnogenesis in the Americas, 1492–1992*, edited by John D. Hill. Iowa City: University of Iowa Press, 1996.

Allen, Craig D. "Lots of Lightning and Plenty of People: An Ecological History of Fire in the Upland Southwest." In *Fire, Native Peoples, and the Natural Landscape*, edited by Thomas R. Vale. Washington, D.C.: Island Press, 2002.

Allred, Kelly W. "Elmer Ottis Wooton and the Botanizing of New Mexico." *Systematic Botany* 15 (1990): 700–719.

———. "The Trail of E. O. Wooton." *New Mexico Resources* (New Mexico State University, College of Agriculture and Home Economics) 9 (1993): 3–18.

Anderson, Benedict. *Imagined Communities: Reflections on the Origin and Spread of Nationalism*. Rev. ed. London: Verso, 1991.

Andrews, Tracy Joan. "Descent, Land Use and Inheritance: Navajo Land Tenure Patterns in Canyon de Chelly and Canyon del Muerto." Ph.D. diss., University of Arizona, 1985.

Archer, Steve, and Fred E. Smeins. "Ecosystem-Level Processes." In *Grazing Management: An Ecological Perspective*, edited by Rodney K. Heitschmidt and Jerry W. Stuth. Portland, Ore.: Timber Press, 1991.

[Ayeta, Francisco de]. Petition, 10 May 1679. In *Historical Documents Relating to New Mexico, Nueva Vizcaya, and Approaches Thereto, to 1773*. Vol. 3. Edited and translated by Charles Wilson Hackett. Washington, D.C.: Carnegie Institution of Washington, 1937.

Bahre, Conrad Joseph. *A Legacy of Change: Historic Human Impact on Vegetation of the Arizona Borderlands*. Tucson: University of Arizona, 1991.

Bailey, Garrick A., and Roberta Glenn Bailey. "Ethnohistory." In *Prehistory and History of the Ojo Amarillo: Archaeological Investigation of Block II, Navajo Indian*

Irrigation Project, San Juan County, New Mexico, edited by David T. Kirkpatrick. Vol. 4. Las Cruces: New Mexico State University, Department of Sociology and Anthropology, 1980.

———. *Historic Navajo Occupation of the Northern Chaco Plateau*. Tulsa, Okla.: University of Tulsa, Faculty of Anthropology, 1982.

———. *A History of the Navajos: The Reservation Years*. Santa Fe, N.Mex.: School of American Research, 1986.

Bailey, Lynn R. *If You Take My Sheep: The Evolution and Conflicts of Navajo Pastoralism, 1630–1868*. Pasadena, Calif.: Westernlore Publications, 1980.

Balling, Robert C., Jr., and Stephen G. Wells. "Historical Rainfall Patterns and Arroyo Activity within the Zuni River Drainage Basin, New Mexico." *Annals* (Association of American Geographers) 80 (1990): 603–17.

Bamberger, Joan. "The Myth of Matriarchy: Why Men Rule in Primitive Society." In *Women, Culture, and Society*, edited by Michelle Zimbalist Rosaldo and Louise Lamphere. Stanford, Calif.: Stanford University Press, 1974.

Bannister, Bryant, John W. Hannah, and William J. Robinson. *Tree-Ring Dates from Arizona K, Puerco-Wide Ruin-Ganado Area*. Tucson: Laboratory of Tree-Ring Research, 1966.

Basso, Keith H. *Wisdom Sits in Places: Landscape and Language among the Western Apache*. Albuquerque: University of New Mexico Press, 1996.

Batie, Sandra S. "Soil Conservation in the 1980s: A Historical Perspective." *Agricultural History* 59 (1985): 107–23.

Baxter, John O. *Las Carneradas: Sheep Trade in New Mexico, 1700–1860*. Albuquerque: University of New Mexico Press, 1987.

———. "Restocking the Navajo Reservation after Bosque Redondo." *New Mexico Historical Review* 58 (1983): 325–45.

Beadle, John H. *Undeveloped West; or, Five Years in the Territories*. Philadelphia: National Publishing, 1873.

Belnap, Jayne, and Dale A. Gillette. "Vulnerability of Desert Biological Soil Crusts to Wind Erosion: The Influences of Crust Development, Soil Texture, and Disturbance." *Journal of Arid Environments* 39 (1998): 133–42.

Benavides, Alonso de. *Fray Alonso Benavides' Revised Memorial of 1634*. Translated and edited by Frederick Webb Hodge, George P. Hammond, and Agapito Rey. Albuquerque: University of New Mexico Press, 1945.

———. *Memorial of 1630*. Translated by Peter P. Forrestal. Washington, D.C.: Academy of American Franciscan History, 1954.

———. *The Memorial of Fray Alonso de Benavides, 1630*. Translated by Mrs. Edward E. Ayer, edited by Frederick Webb Hodge and Charles Fletcher Lummis. Chicago: Edward E. Ayer, 1916.

Bennett, Hugh Hammond. *Elements of Soil Conservation*. 2nd ed. New York: McGraw-Hill, 1955.

———. *Our American Land: The Story of Its Abuse and Its Conservation*. Miscellaneous Publication no. 596, Soil Conservation Service. Rev. ed. Washington, D.C.: Government Printing Office, 1948.

Bennett, Kay. *Kaibah: Recollection of a Navajo Girlhood*. Los Angeles: Westernlore Press, 1964.

Bestelmeyer, Brandon T., et al. "Development and Use of State-and-Transition Models for Rangelands." *Journal of Range Management* 56 (March 2003): 114–26.

Between Sacred Mountains: Navajo Stories and Lessons from the Land. Tucson: University of Arizona Press, 1982.

Beymer, Renee J., and Jeffrey M. Klopatek. "Effects of Grazing on Cryptogamic Crusts in Pinyon-Juniper Woodlands in Grand Canyon National Park." *American Midland Naturalist* 127 (1992): 139–48.

Bhabha, Homi K. *The Location of Culture*. London: Routledge, 1994.

Blackhawk, Ned. *Violence over the Land: Indians and Empires in the Early American West*. Cambridge, Mass.: Harvard University Press, 2006.

Blight, David W. *Beyond the Battlefield: Race, Memory, and the American Civil War*. Amherst: University of Massachusetts Press, 2002.

Bloom, Lansing B. "Bourke on the Southwest." *New Mexico Historical Review* 11 (1936): 77–122, 217–282.

Bodo, Murray, ed. *Tales of an Endishodi: Father Berard Haile and the Navajos, 1900–1961*. Albuquerque: University of New Mexico Press, 1998.

Botkin, Daniel B. *Discordant Harmonies: A New Ecology for the Twenty-first Century*. New York: Oxford University Press, 1990.

Boyce, George A. *When Navajos Had Too Many Sheep: The 1940s*. San Francisco: Indian Historian Press, 1974.

Brink, Wellington. *Big Hugh: The Father of Soil Conservation*. New York: MacMillan, 1951.

Briske, D. D. "Developmental Morphology and Physiology of Grasses." In *Grazing Management: An Ecological Perspective*, edited by Rodney K. Heitschmidt and Jerry W. Stuth. Portland, Ore.: Timber Press, 1991.

Briske, D. D., and R. K. Heitschmidt. "An Ecological Perspective." In *Grazing Management: An Ecological Perspective*, edited by Rodney K. Heitschmidt and Jerry W. Stuth. Portland, Ore.: Timber Press, 1991.

Brooks, James F. *Captives and Cousins: Slavery, Kinship, and Community in the Southwest Borderlands*. Chapel Hill: University of North Carolina Press, 2002.

Brotherson, Jack D., Samuel R. Rushforth, and Jeffrey R. Johansen. "Effects of Long-Term Grazing on Cryptogam Crust Cover in Navajo National Monument, Ariz." *Journal of Range Management* 36 (September 1983): 579–81.

Brown, Gary M. "Old Wood and Early Navajo: A Chronometric Analysis of the Dinétah Phase." In *Diné Bíkéyah: Papers in Honor of David M. Brugge*, edited by Meliha S. Duran and David T. Kirkpatrick. Albuquerque: Archaeological Society of New Mexico, 1998.

———. "The Protohistoric Transition in the Northern San Juan Region." In *The Archaeology of Navajo Origins*, edited by Ronald H. Towner. Salt Lake City: University of Utah Press, 1996.

Brown, Gary M., et al. *Archaeological Data Recovery at San Juan Coal Company's La Plata Mine, San Juan County, New Mexico*. Albuquerque, N.Mex.: Mariah Associates, 1991.

Brown, Gary M., and Patricia M. Hancock. "The Dinetah Phase in the La Plata Valley." In *Cultural Diversity and Adaptation: The Archaic, Anasazi, and Navajo Occupation of the Upper San Juan Basin*, edited by Lori Stephens Reed and Paul F. Reed. Santa Fe: Bureau of Land Management, New Mexico State Office, 1992.

Brown, Vinson. *Reading the Woods: Seeing More in Nature's Familiar Faces*. Harrisburg, Pa.: Stackpole Books, 1969.

Brugge, David M. "Comments on Athabaskans and Sumas." In *The Protohistoric Period in the North American Southwest, A.D. 1450–1700*, edited by David Wilcox and W. Bruce Masse. Anthropological Research Papers, no. 24. Tempe: Arizona State University, 1981.

———. "Eighteenth-Century Fugitives from New Mexico among the Navajos." In *Papers from the Third, Fourth, and Sixth Navajo Studies Conferences*, compiled by Alexandra Roberts and Jenevieve Smith. Window Rock, Ariz.: Navajo Nation Historic Preservation Department, 1993.

———. "Navajo Archaeology: A Promising Past." In *The Archaeology of Navajo Origins*, edited by Ronald H. Towner. Salt Lake City: University of Utah Press, 1996.

———. "The Navajo Exodus." Archaeological Society of New Mexico, Supplement no. 5. Las Cruces: Archaeological Society of New Mexico, 1972.

———. *Navajos in the Catholic Church Records, 1694–1875*. Window Rock, Ariz.: Navajo Parks and Recreation Department, 1968.

———. "Pueblo Factionalism and External Relations." *Ethnohistory* 16 (1969): 191–200.

———. *Tsegai: An Archeological Ethnohistory of the Chaco Region*. Publications in Archeology 18C, Chaco Canyon Studies. Washington, D.C.: National Park Service, 1986.

———, ed. "Vizcarra's Navajo Campaign of 1823." *Arizona and the West* 6 (1964): 223–44.

Brulle, Robert J. *Agency, Democracy, and Nature: The U.S. Environmental Movement from a Critical Theory Perspective*. Cambridge, Mass.: MIT Press, 2000.

Bryan, Kirk. "Change in Plant Associations by Change in Ground Water Level." *Ecology* 9 (1928): 474–78.

———. "Date of Channel Trenching (Arroyo Cutting) in the Arid Southwest." *Science* 62 (1925): 338–44.

———. "Erosion in the Valleys of the Southwest." *New Mexico Quarterly* 10 (1940): 227–32.

———. "Recent Deposits of Chaco Canyon, New Mexico, in Relation to the Life of the Pre-Historic Peoples of Pueblo Bonito." *Journal of the Washington Academy of Sciences* 16 (4 February 1926): 75–76.

Bsumek, Erika Marie. "The Navajos as Borrowers: Stewart Culin and the Genesis of an Ethnographic Theory." *New Mexico Historical Review* 79 (2004): 319–51.

Burgess, Tony L. "Desert Grassland, Mixed Shrub Savanna, Shrub Steppe, or Semidesert Scrub? The Dilemma of Coexisting Growth Forms." In *The Desert Grassland*, edited by Mitchel P. McClaran and Thomas R. Van Devender. Tucson: University of Arizona Press, 1995.

Burke, Flannery. *From Greenwich Village to Taos: Primitivism and Place at Mabel Dodge Luhan's*. Lawrence: University of Kansas Press, 2008.

Burnham, Philip. *Indian Country, God's Country: Native Americans and the National Parks*. Washington, D.C.: Island Press, 2000.

Calhoun, James S. *The Official Correspondence of James S. Calhoun*. Edited by Annie Louise Abel. Washington, D.C.: Government Printing Office, 1915.

Calkins, Hugh G., and D. S. Hubbell. "A Range Conservation Demonstration in the Land of the Navajos." *Soil Conservation* (SCS) 6 (September 1940): 64–67.

Callender, Charles, and Lee M. Kochems. "The North American Berdache." *Current Anthropology* 24 (August–October 1983): 443–56.

Cannon, Brian Q. *Remaking the Agrarian Dream: New Deal Rural Resettlement in the Mountain West*. Albuquerque: University of New Mexico Press, 1996.

Carlson, Roy L. *Eighteenth Century Navajo Fortresses of the Gobernador District*. University of Colorado Studies, Series in Anthropology, no. 10. Boulder: University of Colorado Press, 1965.

Carrier, E. H. *Water and Grass: A Study in the Pastoral Economy of Southern Europe*. 1932. Reprint, London: Christophers, 1980.

Casey, Edward S. *Remembering: A Phenomenological Study*. 2nd ed. Bloomington: Indiana University Press, 1987.

Caughley, Graeme. "What Is This Thing Called Carrying Capacity?" In *North American Elk: Ecology, Behavior, and Management*, edited by Mark S. Boyce and Larry D. Hayden-Wing. Laramie: University of Wyoming, 1980.

———. "Wildlife Management and the Dynamics of Ungulate Populations." *Applied Biology* 1 (1976): 183–246.

Chamberlain, Kathleen P. *Under Sacred Ground: A History of Navajo Oil, 1922–1982*. Albuquerque: University of New Mexico Press, 2000.

Christenson, Andrew L., and William J. Parry. *Excavations on Black Mesa, 1983: A Descriptive Report*. [Carbondale]: Southern Illinois University at Carbondale, Center for Archaeological Investigations, 1985.

Clark, LaVerne Harrell. *They Sang for Horses: The Impact of the Horse on Navajo and Apache Folklore*. Rev. ed. Boulder: University of Colorado Press, 2001.

Clements, Frederic E. "Climaxes, Succession and Conservation." In *Dynamics of Vegetation: Selections from the Writings of Frederic E. Clements*, edited by B. W. Allred and Edith S. Clements. New York: H. W. Wilson, 1949.

———. "Nature and Structure of the Climax." In *Foundations of Ecology: Classic Papers with Commentaries*, edited by Leslie A. Real and James H. Brown. Chicago: University of Chicago Press, 1991. First published in *Journal of Ecology* 24 (1936): 252–84.

———. "The Origin of the Desert Climax and Climate." In *Essays in Geobotany, in Honor of William Albert Setchell*, edited by T. H. Goodspeed. Berkeley: University of California Press, 1936.

———. "Plant Indicators." In *Dynamics of Vegetation: Selections from the Writings of Frederic E. Clements*, edited by B. W. Allred and Edith S. Clements. New York: H. W. Wilson, 1949. First published in Frederic E. Clements, *Plant Succession and Indicators*. New York: H. W. Wilson, 1928.

———. "The Relict Method in Dynamic Ecology." In *Dynamics of Vegetation: Selections from the Writings of Frederic E. Clements*, edited by B. W. Allred and Edith S. Clements. New York: H. W. Wilson, 1949. First published in *Journal of Ecology* 22 (1934): 39–68.

Cohen, Felix S. *Felix S. Cohen's Handbook of Federal Indian Law*. Albuquerque: University of New Mexico Press, [1971].

Collier, Charles W. "Soil Conservation in the Navajo Country." *Soil Conservation* (SCS) 1 (October 1935): 1–4.

Collier, John. "Comment." In *Human Problems in Technological Change: A Casebook*, edited by Edward H. Spicer. New York: John Wiley & Sons, Science Editions, 1952.

———. "The Fate of the Navajos: What Will Oil Money Do to the Greatest of Indian Tribes?" *Sunset Magazine*, January 1924.

———. *From Every Zenith*. Denver: Sage Books, 1963.

———. *On the Gleaming Way: Navajos, Eastern Pueblos, Zunis, Hopis, Apaches, and Their Land; and Their Meanings to the World*. 2nd ed. 1949. Reprint, Denver: Sage Books, 1962.

Collier, Malcolm Carr. *Local Organization among the Navaho*. New Haven, Conn.: Human Relations Area Files, 1966.

Comaroff, John L., and Jean Comaroff. *Ethnography and the Historical Imagination*. Boulder, Colo.: Westview Press, 1992.

———. "The Madman and the Migrant: Work and Labor in the Historical Consciousness of a South African People." *American Ethnologist* 14 (1987): 191–209.

Connerton, Paul. *How Societies Remember*. Cambridge: Cambridge University Press, 1989.

Cook, E. R., et al. "Long-Term Aridity Changes in the Western United States." *Science* 306 (2004): 1015–18. www.ncdc.noaa.gov/paleo/pdsi.html.

Cooke, Bill. "A New Continuity with Colonial Administration: Participation in Development Management." *Third World Quarterly* 24 (2003): 47–61.

Cooke, Bill, and Uma Kothari. *Participation: The New Tyranny?* London: Zed Books, 2001.

Cooke, Ronald U., and Richard W. Reeves. *Arroyos and Environmental Change in the American South-West*. Oxford: Clarendon Press, 1976.

Coolidge, Dane, and Mary Roberts Coolidge. *The Navajo Indians*. Boston: Houghton Mifflin, 1930.

Cooper, Charles F. "Changes in Vegetation, Structure, and Growth of South-Western Pine Forests since White Settlement." *Ecological Monographs* 30 (1960): 129–64.

Copeland, James M. "Navajo Hero Twin Ceremonial Art in Dinetah." In *Diné Bíkéyah: Papers in Honor of David M. Brugge*, edited by Meliha S. Duran and David T. Kirkpatrick. Albuquerque: Archaeological Society of New Mexico, 1998.

Correll, J. Lee. "Navajo Frontiers in Utah and Troublous Times in Monument Valley." *Utah Historical Quarterly* 39 (1971): 143–61.

———. *Through White Men's Eyes: A Contribution to Navajo History; A Chronological Record of the Navajo People from Earliest Times to the Treaty of June 1, 1868*. Vols. 1–6. Window Rock, Ariz.: Navajo Heritage Center, 1979.

Cott, Nancy F. *The Bonds of Womanhood: "Woman's Sphere" in New England, 1780–1835*. 2nd ed. New Haven, Conn.: Yale University Press, 1997.

Cronon, William. "A Place for Stories: Nature, History, and Narrative." *Journal of American History* 78 (March 1992): 1347–76.

Crosby, Alfred W. *Ecological Imperialism: The Biological Expansion of Europe, 900–1900*. Cambridge: Cambridge University Press, 1986.

Cuervo y Valdez, Francisco. "Report of Francisco Cuervo y Valdez, 18 Aug. 1706." In *Historical Documents Relating to New Mexico, Nueva Vizcaya, and Approaches Thereto, to 1773*. Vol. 3. Edited and translated by Charles Wilson Hackett. Washington, D.C.: Carnegie Institution of Washington, 1937.

Cunfer, Geoff. *On the Great Plains: Agriculture and Environment*. College Station: Texas A & M University Press, 2005.

Davis, Diana K. "Potential Forests: Degradation Narratives, Science, and Environmental Policy in Protectorate Morocco, 1912–1956." *Environmental History* 10 (2005): 211–38.

Debo, Angie. *And Still the Waters Run: The Betrayal of the Five Civilized Tribes*. 1940. Reprint, Norman: University of Oklahoma Press, 1984.

deBuys, William. *Enchantment and Exploitation: The Life and Hard Times of a New Mexico Mountain Range*. Albuquerque: University of New Mexico Press, 1985.

del Bene, Terry, and Dabney Ford, eds. *Archaeological Excavations in Blocks VI and VII, N.I.I.P., San Juan County, New Mexico.* Navajo Nation Papers in Anthropology, no. 13. Farmington, N.Mex.: Navajo Indian Irrigation Project, 1983.

Denetdale, Jennifer Nez. *Reclaiming Diné History: The Legacies of Navajo Chief Manuelito and Juanita.* Tucson: University of Arizona Press, 2007.

Denevan, William M. "Livestock Numbers in Nineteenth-Century New Mexico, and the Problem of Gullying in the Southwest." *Annals* (Association of American Geographers) 57 (December 1967): 691–763.

Deutsch, Sarah. *No Separate Refuge: Culture, Class, and Gender on an Anglo-Hispanic Frontier in the American Southwest, 1880–1940.* New York: Oxford University Press, 1987.

Diaz, Rose. "El Senador, Dennis Chavez: New Mexico Native Son, American Senior Statesman, 1888–1962." Ph.D. diss., Arizona State University, 2006.

Dick-Peddie, William A. *New Mexico Vegetation: Past, Present, and Future.* Albuquerque: University of New Mexico Press, 1993.

Documentos para servir a la historia del Nuevo Mexico, 1538–1778. Coleccion chimalistac de libros y documentos acerca de la Nueva España, 13. Madrid: Ediciones Jose Porrua Turanzas, 1962.

Donahue, Debra L. *The Western Range Revisited: Removing Livestock from Public Lands to Conserve Native Biodiversity.* Norman: University of Oklahoma Press, 1999.

Downs, James F. *Animal Husbandry in Navajo Culture and Society.* University of California Publications in Anthropology 1. Berkeley: University of California Press, 1964.

———. *The Navajo.* New York: Holt, Rinehart and Winston, 1972.

Dunmire, William W., and Gail D. Tierney. *Wild Plants and Native Peoples of the Four Corners.* Santa Fe: Museum of New Mexico Press, 1997.

Dyk, Walter. *A Navaho Autobiography.* Viking Fund Publications in Anthropology, no. 8. New York: Viking Fund, 1947.

———. *Son of Old Man Hat: A Navaho Autobiography.* 1938. Reprint, Lincoln: University of Nebraska Press, 1966.

Dyk, Walter, and Ruth Dyk. *Left Handed: A Navajo Autobiography.* New York: Columbia University Press, 1980.

Echo Hawk, Roger. "Kara Katit Pakutu: Exploring the Origins of Native America in Anthropology and Oral Traditions." M.A. thesis, University of Colorado, 1994.

Eddy, Frank W. *Prehistory in the Navajo Reservoir District, Northwestern New Mexico*, part 2. Museum of New Mexico Papers in Anthropology, no. 15. Santa Fe: Museum of New Mexico Press, 1966.

Elmore, Francis H. *Ethnobotany of the Navajo.* University of New Mexico and School of American Research Bulletin, vol. 1, no. 7. Albuquerque: University of New Mexico, 1943.

———. *Shrubs and Trees of the Southwest Uplands*. Tucson: Southwest Parks and Monuments Association, 1976.

Engles, Mary Tate, ed. *Tales from Wide Ruins: Jean and Bill Cousins, Traders*. Lubbock: Texas Tech University Press, 1996.

Fanale, Rosalie Angelina. "Navajo Land and Land Management: A Century of Change." Ph.D. diss., Catholic University of America, 1982.

Farella, John R. *The Main Stalk: A Synthesis of Navajo Philosophy*. Tucson: University of Arizona Press, 1984.

Faris, James C. *The Nightway: A History and a History of Documentation of a Navajo Ceremonial*. Albuquerque: University of New Mexico Press, 1990.

———. "Taking Navajo Truths Seriously: The Consequences of the Accretions of Disbelief." In *Papers from the Third, Fourth, and Sixth Navajo Studies Conferences*, edited by June-el Piper. Window Rock, Ariz.: Navajo Nation Historic Preservation Department, 1993.

Farmer, Malcolm. "Navaho Archaeology of Upper Blanco and Largo Canyons, Northern New Mexico." *American Antiquity* 8 (1942): 65–79.

Fenton, Joann Carol. "A Cultural Analysis of Navajo Family and Clan." Ph.D. diss., Northwestern University, 1974.

Ferguson, T. J., and E. Richard Hart. *A Zuni Atlas*. Norman: University of Oklahoma Press, 1985.

Fetterman, Jerry. "Radiocarbon and Tree-Ring Dating at Early Navajo Sites: Examples from the Aztec Area." In *The Archaeology of Navajo Origins*, edited by Ronald H. Towner. Salt Lake City: University of Utah Press, 1996.

Fishler, Stanley A. *In the Beginning: A Navaho Creation Myth*. University of Utah Anthropological Papers, no. 13. Salt Lake City: University of Utah Press, 1953.

Fixico, Donald L. *The American Indian Mind in a Linear World: American Indian Studies and Traditional Knowledge*. New York: Routledge, 2003.

Fleischner, Thomas L. "Ecological Costs of Livestock Grazing in Western North America." *Conservation Biology* 8 (September 1994): 629–44.

Flores, Dan. "Bison Ecology and Bison Diplomacy: The Southern Plains from 1800 to 1850." In *A Sense of the American West: An Anthology of Environmental History*, edited by James E. Sherow. Albuquerque: University of New Mexico Press, 1998.

Fontana, Bernard L. "The Hopi-Navajo Colony on the Lower Colorado River: A Problem in Ethnohistorical Interpretation." *Ethnohistory* 10 (1963): 162–82.

Foote, Kenneth E. *Shadowed Ground: America's Landscapes of Violence and Tragedy*. Austin: University of Texas Press, 1997.

Forman, Richard T. T., and Michel Godron. *Landscape Ecology*. New York: John Wiley, 1986.

Frisbie, Charlotte J. "Traditional Navajo Women: Ethnographic and Life History Portrayals." *American Indian Quarterly* 6 (1982): 11–33.

———. "Washington Matthews' Contribution to the Study of Navajo Ceremonialism and Mythology." In *Washington Matthews: Studies of Navajo Culture, 1880–1894*, edited by Katherine Spencer Halpern and Susan Brown McGreevy. Albuquerque: University of New Mexico Press, 1997.

Fryer, E. R. "Navajo Social Organization and Land Use Adjustment." *Scientific Monthly* 55 (1942): 408–22.

Galloway, Patricia. *Choctaw Genesis, 1500–1700*. Lincoln: University of Nebraska Press, 1997.

García Canclini, Néstor. *Hybrid Cultures: Strategies for Entering and Leaving Modernity*. Translated by Christopher L. Chiappari and Silvia L. Lopez. Minneapolis: University of Minnesota Press, 1995.

Geertz, Clifford. *The Interpretation of Cultures*. New York: Basic Books, 1973.

Geist, Valerius. *Mountain Sheep: A Study in Behavior and Evolution*. Chicago: University of Chicago Press, [1971].

Gilpin, Dennis. "Early Navajo Occupation West of the Chuska Mountains." In *The Archaeology of Navajo Origins*, edited by Ronald H. Towner. Salt Lake City: University of Utah Press, 1996.

———. "Patterns and Processes of Material Culture Change, Gallegos Mesa, 1907–1950." In *Cultural Resource Investigations on Gallegos Mesa: Excavations in Blocks VIII and IX, and Testing Operations in Blocks X and XI, Navajo Indian Irrigation Project, San Juan County, New Mexico*, edited by Lawrence E. Vogler, Dennis Gilpin, and Joseph K. Anderson. Vol. 3. Navajo Nation Papers in Anthropology, no. 24. Farmington, N.Mex.: Navajo Nation, Branch of Cultural Resources, 1983.

Gilpin, Dennis, Lawrence E. Vogler, and Joseph K. Anderson, eds. *Archaeological Survey and Excavation on Blocks I, X, and XI, Navajo Indian Irrigation Project, San Juan County, New Mexico*. Vol. 1. Navajo Nation Papers in Anthropology, no. 25. Window Rock, Ariz.: Navajo Nation, Branch of Cultural Resources, 1984.

Gleick, James. *Chaos: Making a New Science*. New York: Viking, 1987.

Gonzalez, Nancie L. *Sojourners of the Caribbean: Ethnogenesis and Ethnohistory of the Garifuna*. Urbana: University of Illinois Press, 1988.

Goodman, James M. *The Navajo Atlas: Environments, Resources, People, and History of the Diné Bikeyah*. Norman: University of Oklahoma Press, 1982.

Gordon, Deborah. "Among Women: Gender and Ethnographic Authority of the Southwest, 1930–1980." In *Hidden Scholars: Women Anthropologists and the Native American Southwest*, edited by Nancy J. Parezo. Albuquerque: University of New Mexico Press, 1993.

Gould, Stephen Jay. *Wonderful Life: The Burgess Shale and the Nature of History*. New York: W. W. Norton, 1989.

Graf, William L. "The Arroyo Problem—Palaeohydrology and Palaeohydraulics in the Short Term." In *Background to Palaeohydrology: A Perspective*, edited by K. J. Gregory. Chichester, Eng.: John Wiley and Sons, 1983.

———. "Fluvial Erosion and Federal Public Policy in the Navajo Nation." *Physical Geography* 7 (1986): 97–115.

Gregg, Josiah. *Commerce of the Prairies*. 1844. Reprint, edited by Max L. Moorhead. Norman: University of Oklahoma Press, 1954.

Gregory, Herbert E. *Geology of the Navajo Country: A Reconnaissance of Parts of Arizona, New Mexico, and Utah*. U.S. Geological Survey, Professional Paper 93. Washington, D.C.: Government Printing Office, 1917.

———. *The Navajo Country: A Geographic and Hydrographic Reconnaissance of Parts of Arizona, New Mexico, and Utah*. U.S. Geological Survey, Water-Supply Paper 380. Washington, D.C.: Government Printing Office, 1916.

Griffin-Pierce, Trudy. *Earth Is My Mother, Sky Is My Father: Space, Time, and Astronomy in Navajo Sandpainting*. Albuquerque: University of New Mexico Press, 1992.

Grissino-Mayer, Henri. "A 2129-Year Reconstruction of Precipitation for Northwestern New Mexico, USA." In *Tree Rings, Environment and Humanity*, edited by J. S. Dean, D. M. Meko, and T. W. Swetnam. Tucson, Ariz.: Radiocarbon, 1996. Accessed through http://www.ncdc.noaa.gov/paleo/drought/drght_grissno.html.

Grissino-Mayer, Henri D., and Thomas W. Swetnam. "Multi-Century History of Wildfire in the Ponderosa Pine Forests of El Malpais National Monument." In *Natural History of El Malpais National Monument*, compiled by Ken Mabery. Bulletin 156. Socorro: New Mexico Bureau of Mines and Mineral Resources, 1997.

Guthrie-Smith, Herbert. *Tutira: The Story of a New Zealand Sheep Station*. 1921. Reprint, Seattle: University of Washington Press, 1999.

Hack, John T. "Dunes of the Western Navajo Country." *Geographical Review* 31 (1941): 240–63.

———. "The Late Quaternary History of Several Valleys of Northern Arizona: A Preliminary Announcement." *Museum Notes* (Museum of Northern Arizona) 11 (May 1939): 67–73.

Hafez, E. S. E., and M. F. Bouissou. "The Behavior of Cattle." In *The Behavior of Domestic Animals*, edited by E. S. E. Hafez. Baltimore: Williams and Wilkins, 1975.

Haile, Berard. *Property Concepts of the Navajo Indians*. Catholic University of America Anthropological Series, no. 17. 1949. Reprint, St. Michaels, Ariz.: St. Michael's Press, 1968.

———. *The Upward Moving and Emergence Way: The Gishin Biyé Version*. Edited by Karl W. Luckert. Lincoln: University of Nebraska Press, 1981.

Hall, Edward T. *West of the Thirties: Discoveries among the Navajo and Hopi*. New York: Doubleday, 1994.

Hall, Stephen A. "Late Quaternary Sedimentation and Paleoecologic History of Chaco Canyon, New Mexico." *Geological Society of America Bulletin* 88 (1977): 1593–1618.

Hall, Thomas D. *Social Change in the Southwest, 1350–1880*. Lawrence: University Press of Kansas, 1989.

Halpern, Katherine Spencer, and Susan Brown McGreevy, eds. *Washington Matthews: Studies of Navajo Culture, 1880–1894*. Albuquerque: University of New Mexico Press, 1997.

Halvorson, William L., and Patricia Guertin. "Factsheet for *Bromus tectorum*." U.S. Geological Survey, Weeds in the West Project, 31 Dec. 2003. http://sdrsnet.srnr.arizona.edu/data/sdrs/ww/docs/bromtect.pdf.

Hamamsy, Laila Shukry. "The Role of Women in a Changing Navaho Society." *American Anthropologist* 59 (1957): 101–11.

Hamilton, Jason G. "Changing Perceptions of Pre-European Grasslands in California." *Madroño* 44 (1997): 311–33.

Hammond, George P., and Agapito Rey, eds. *Don Juan de Oñate, Colonizer of New Mexico, 1595–1628*. Coronado Cuarto Centennial Publications, 1540–1940, vol. 5. Albuquerque: University of New Mexico Press, 1953.

Haraway, Donna J. "Universal Donors in a Vampire Culture: It's All in the Family; Biological Kinship Categories in the Twentieth-Century United States." In *Uncommon Ground: Toward Reinventing Nature*, edited by William Cronon. New York: W. W. Norton, 1995.

Hardin, Garrett. "The Tragedy of the Commons." *Science* 162 (1968): 1243–48.

Harper, Kimball T., and Jayne Belnap. "The Influence of Biological Soil Crusts on Mineral Uptake by Associated Vascular Plants." *Journal of Arid Environments* 47 (2001): 347–57.

Harrington, John P. "Southern Peripheral Athapaskawan Origins, Divisions, and Migrations." In *Essays in Historical Anthropology of North America*. Smithsonian Miscellaneous Collections, vol. 100. Washington, D.C.: Smithsonian Institution, 1940.

Harris, Marvin. *The Rise of Anthropological Theory: A History of Theories of Culture*. New York: Thomas Y. Crowell, 1968.

Haskell, John Loring. "The Navajo in the Eighteenth Century: An Investigation Involving Anthropological Archaeology in the San Juan Basin, Northwestern New Mexico." Ph.D. diss., Washington State University, 1975.

———. *Southern Athapaskan Migration, A.D. 200–1750*. Tsaile, Ariz.: Navajo Community College Press, 1987.

Hayes, Alden C., David M. Brugge, and W. James Judge. *Archeological Surveys of Chaco Canyon, New Mexico*. Publications in Archeology 18A, Chaco Canyon Studies. Washington, D.C.: National Park Service, 1981.

Hays, Samuel. *Conservation and the Gospel of Efficiency: The Progressive Conservation Movement, 1890–1920*. Cambridge, Mass.: Harvard University Press, 1959.

Heady, Harold E., and R. Dennis Child. *Rangeland Ecology and Management*. Boulder, Colo.: Westview Press, 1994.

Hegemann, Elizabeth Compton. *Navaho Trading Days*. Albuquerque: University of New Mexico Press, 1963.

Henderson, Eric Bruce. "Navajo Livestock Wealth and the Effects of the Stock Reduction Program of the 1930s." *Journal of Anthropological Research* 45 (1989): 379–403.

———. "Wealth, Status and Change among the Kaibeto Plateau Navajo." Ph.D. diss., University of Arizona, 1985.

Hendricks, Rick, and John P. Wilson, eds. and trans. *The Navajos in 1705: Roque Madrid's Campaign Journal*. Albuquerque: University of New Mexico Press, 1996.

Hereford, Richard, and Robert H. Webb. "Historic Variation of Warm-Season Rainfall, Southern Colorado Plateau, Southwestern U.S.A." *Climatic Change* 22 (1992): 239–56.

Heyman, Max L., Jr. "On the Navaho Trail: The Campaign of 1860–61." *New Mexico Historical Review* 26 (1951): 44–63.

Hickerson, Nancy P. "Ethnogenesis in the South Plains: Jumano to Kiowa?" In *History, Power, and Identity: Ethnogenesis in the Americas, 1492–1992*, edited by John D. Hill. Iowa City: University of Iowa Press, 1996.

Hill, W. W. *The Agricultural and Hunting Methods of the Navaho Indians*. Yale University Publications in Anthropology, no. 18. New Haven, Conn.: Yale University Press, 1938.

———, trans. and ed. "Some Navaho Culture Changes during Two Centuries (Including Testimonials Sent by Governor Codallos y Rabal to the Viceroy in the Year 1745)." In *Essays in Historical Anthropology of North America*. Smithsonian Miscellaneous Collections, vol. 100. Washington, D.C.: Smithsonian Institution, 1940.

———. "The Status of the Hermaphrodite and Transvestite in Navaho Culture." *American Anthropologist* 37 (April–June 1935): 273–79.

Hirt, Paul. "The Transformation of a Landscape: Culture and Ecology in Southeastern Arizona." *Environmental Review* 13 (1989): 167–89.

Hobsbawm, Eric, and Terence Ranger, eds. *The Invention of Tradition*. Cambridge: Cambridge University Press, 1983.

Hobson, Richard. *Navaho Acquisitive Values*. Papers of the Peabody Museum of American Archaeology and Ethnology, Harvard University, vol. 42, no. 3. 1954. Reprint, Millwood, N.Y.: Kraus Reprint, 1973.

Hogan, Patrick. "Dinetah: A Reevaluation of Pre-Revolt Navajo Occupation in Northwest New Mexico." *Journal of Anthropological Research* 45 (Spring 1989): 53–66.

———. "Navajo-Pueblo Interaction during the Gobernador Phase." In *Rethinking Navajo Pueblitos*. Albuquerque, N.Mex.: Bureau of Land Management, Farmington Resource Area, 1991.

Holquist, Michael. *Dialogism: Bakhtin and His World*. London: Routledge, 1990.

Honaghani, Gertrude. "The Navajo Woman and Her Home." *Franciscan Missions of the Southwest* 9 (1921): 35–36.

Hoy, Suellen. *Chasing Dirt: The American Pursuit of Cleanliness*. New York: Oxford University Press, 1995.

Hulet, C. V., G. Alexander, and E. S. E. Hafez. "The Behavior of Sheep." In *The Behavior of Domestic Animals*, edited by E. S. E. Hafez. 3rd ed. Baltimore: Williams and Wilkins, 1975.

Humphrey, Robert R. *Arizona Range Grasses: Their Description, Forage Value, and Management*. Rev. ed. Tucson: University of Arizona Press, 1970.

Hurt, R. Douglas. *The Dust Bowl: An Agricultural and Social History*. Chicago: Nelson-Hall, 1981.

Huston, J. E., and W. E. Pinchak. "Range Animal Nutrition." In *Grazing Management: An Ecological Perspective*, edited by Rodney K. Heitschmidt and Jerry W. Stuth. Portland, Ore.: Timber Press, 1991.

Iverson, Peter. *Diné: A History of the Navajos*. Albuquerque: University of New Mexico Press, 2002.

———, ed. *"For Our Navajo People": Diné Letters, Speeches and Petitions, 1900–1960*. Albuquerque: University of New Mexico Press, 2002.

———. *The Navajo Nation*. Westport, Conn.: Greenwood Press, 1981.

Ives, Anthony R. "Population Ecology: The Waxing and Waning of Populations." In *Ecology*, edited by Stanley I. Dodson et al. New York: Oxford University Press, 1998.

Jacobs, Margaret D. *Engendered Encounters: Feminism and Pueblo Culture, 1879–1934*. Lincoln: University of Nebraska Press, 1999.

Jacobson, LouAnn, Stephen Fosberg, and Robert Bewley. "Navajo Defensive Systems in the Eighteenth Century." In *Cultural Diversity and Adaptation: The Archaic, Anasazi, and Navajo Occupation of the Upper San Juan Basin*, edited by Lori Stephens Reed and Paul F. Reed. Santa Fe: Bureau of Land Management, New Mexico State Office, 1992.

Jaudas, Ulrich. *The New Goat Handbook*. Translated by Elizabeth D. Crawford. New York: Barron's, 1989.

Jenkins, Myra Ellen, and Ward Alan Minge, eds. "Navajo Activities Affecting the Acoma-Laguna Area, 1746–1910." In *Navajo Indians II*. New York: Garland, 1974.

Jensen, Joan M. *Promise to the Land: Essays on Rural Women*. Albuquerque: University of New Mexico Press, 1991.

Jett, Stephen C., ed. "The Destruction of Navajo Orchards in 1864: Captain John Thompson's Report." *Arizona and the West* 16 (1974): 365–78.

———. "The Navajo in the American Southwest." In *To Build in a New Land: Ethnic Landscapes in North America*, edited by Allen G. Noble. Baltimore: Johns Hopkins University Press, 1992.

———. "Navajo Seasonal Migration Patterns." *Kiva* 44 (1978): 65–75.

Jim, Rex Lee. "Navajo." In *Encyclopedia of North American Indians*, edited by Frederick E. Hoxie. Boston: Houghton Mifflin Co., 1996.

John, Elizabeth A. H. *Storms Brewed in Other Men's Worlds: The Confrontation of Indians, Spanish, and French in the Southwest, 1540–1795*. 2nd ed. Norman: University of Oklahoma Press, 1996.

Johnson, Broderick H., ed. *Stories of Traditional Navajo Life and Culture*. Tsaile, Ariz.: Navajo Community College Press, 1977.

Johnston, Denis Foster. *An Analysis of Sources of Information on the Population of the Navaho*. Bureau of American Ethnology Bulletin 197. Washington, D.C.: Government Printing Office, 1966.

Jones, Karin L. *Excavation of the Sand Dune Site at Hubbell Trading Post National Historic Site*. Santa Fe, N.Mex.: Southwest Archaeological Consultants, 1988.

Jones, Thomas Jesse, et al. *The Navajo Indian Problem*. New York: Phelps-Stokes Fund, 1939.

Kelley, Klara B. "Ethnoarchaeology of Navajo Trading Posts." *Kiva* 51 (1985): 19–37.

———. *Navajo Land Use: An Ethnoarchaeological Study*. Orlando, Fla.: Academic Press, 1986.

———. "Navajo Political Economy before Fort Sumner." In *The Versatility of Kinship: Essays Presented to Harry W. Basehart*, edited by Linda S. Cordell and Stephen Beckerman. New York: Academic Press, 1980.

Kelley, Klara Bonsack, and Harris Francis. "Anthropological Tradition versus Navajo Tradition in Early-Navajo History." In *Diné Bíkéyah: Papers in Honor of David M. Brugge*, edited by Meliha S. Duran and David T. Kirkpatrick. Albuquerque: Archaeological Society of New Mexico, 1998.

———. *Navajo Sacred Places*. Bloomington: Indiana University Press, 1994.

Kelley, Klara B., and Peter M. Whiteley. *Navajoland: Family Settlement and Land Use*. Tsaile, Ariz.: Navajo Community College Press, 1989.

Kelly, Lawrence C. "Anthropology and Anthropologists in the Indian New Deal." *Journal of the History of the Behavioral Sciences* 16 (1980): 6–24.

———. "Anthropology in the Soil Conservation Service." *Agricultural History* 59 (1985): 136–47.

———. *The Assault on Assimilation: John Collier and the Origins of Indian Policy Reform*. Albuquerque: University of New Mexico Press, 1983.

———. *The Navajo Indians and Federal Indian Policy, 1900–1935*. Tucson: University of Arizona Press, 1968.

———, ed. *Navajo Roundup: Selected Correspondence of Kit Carson's Expedition against the Navajo, 1863–1865*. Boulder, Colo.: Pruett Publishing Co., 1970.

Kemrer, Meade F. "An Appraisal of the Piedra Lumbre Phase in North Central New Mexico." In *History and Ethnohistory along the Rio Chama*, by Frank J.

Wozniak, Meade F. Kemrer, and Charles M. Carrillo. Albuquerque, N.Mex.: U.S. Army Corps of Engineers, 1992.

———. "The Dynamics of Western Navajo Settlement, A.D. 1750–1900: An Archaeological and Dendrochronological Analysis." Ph.D. diss., University of Arizona, 1974.

Keur, Dorothy Louise. *Big Bead Mesa: An Archaeological Study of Navaho Acculturation, 1745–1812*. Memoirs of the Society for American Archaeology, no. 1. Menasha, Wisc.: Society for American Archaeology, 1941.

———. "A Chapter in Navaho-Pueblo Relations." *American Antiquity* 10 (1944): 75–86.

Kidder, A. V. "Ruins of the Historic Period in the Upper San Juan Valley, New Mexico." *American Anthropologist* 22 (1920): 322–29.

Kimball, Solon T. "Land Use Management: The Navajo Reservation." In *The Uses of Anthropology*, edited by Walter Goldschmidt. Special publication of the American Anthropological Association, no. 11. Washington, D.C.: American Anthropological Association, 1979.

———. "Research and Concept Formation in Community Study." In *Culture and Community*, edited by Conrad M. Arensberg and Solon T. Kimball. New York: Harcourt, Brace, 1965.

Kimball, Solon T., and John H. Provinse. "Navajo Social Organization in Land Use Planning." *Applied Anthropology* 1 (1942): 18–25.

Kirkpatrick, David T., ed. *Prehistory and History of the Ojo Amarillo: Archaeological Investigations of Block II, Navajo Indian Irrigation Project, San Juan County, New Mexico*. Vol. 1–5. Las Cruces: New Mexico State University, Department of Sociology and Anthropology, 1980.

Klah, Hasteen. *Navajo Creation Myth: The Story of the Emergence*. Recorded by Mary C. Wheelwright. Navajo Religion Series, vol. 1. Santa Fe, N. Mex.: Museum of Navajo Ceremonial Art, 1942.

Klein, Laura F., and Lillian A. Ackerman, eds. *Women and Power in Native North America*. Norman: University of Oklahoma Press, 1995.

Kluckhohn, Clyde, and Dorothea Leighton. *The Navaho*. Cambridge, Mass.: Harvard University Press, 1946.

Lamphere, Louise. "Gladys Reichard among the Navajo." In *Hidden Scholars: Women Anthropologists and the Native American Southwest*, edited by Nancy J. Parezo. Albuquerque: University of New Mexico Press, 1993.

———. "Historical and Regional Variability in Navajo Women's Roles." *Journal of Anthropological Research* 45 (1989): 431–56.

———. "Strategies, Cooperation, and Conflict among Women in Domestic Groups." In *Women, Culture, and Society*, edited by Michelle Zimbalist Rosaldo and Louise Lamphere. Stanford, Calif.: Stanford University Press, 1974.

———. *To Run after Them: Cultural and Social Bases of Cooperation in a Navajo Community*. Tucson: University of Arizona Press, 1977.

Langston, Nancy. *Forest Dreams, Forest Nightmares: The Paradox of Old Growth in the Inland West*. Seattle: University of Washington Press, 1995.

Leader-Williams, N. *Reindeer on South Georgia: The Ecology of an Introduced Population*. Cambridge: Cambridge University Press, 1988.

Lear, Linda. *Rachel Carson: Witness for Nature*. New York: Henry Holt, 1997.

Leopold, Aldo. *A Sand County Almanac, and Sketches Here and There*. Special commemorative ed. New York: Oxford University Press, 1987.

Leopold, Luna B. "Geomorphology: A Sliver Off the Corpus of Science." *Annual Review of Earth and Planetary Sciences* 32 (May 2004):1–12.

———. "Rainfall Frequency: An Aspect of Climatic Variation." *Transactions* (American Geophysical Union) 32 (1951): 347–57.

———. "Vegetation of Southwestern Watersheds in the Nineteenth Century." *Geographical Review* 41 (1951): 295–316.

Lesley, Lewis Burt, ed. *Uncle Sam's Camels: The Journal of May Humphreys Stacey, Supplemented by the Report of Edward Fitzgerald Beale*. Cambridge, Mass.: Harvard University Press, 1929.

Letherman, Jonathan. "Sketch of the Navajo Tribe of Indians, Territory of New Mexico." In *Tenth Annual Report of the Board of Regents of the Smithsonian Institution*. Washington, D.C.: A. O. P. Nicholson, 1856.

Leuchtenburg, William E. *Franklin D. Roosevelt and the New Deal*. New York: Harper Torchbooks, 1963.

Levy, Jerrold E. *In the Beginning: The Navajo Genesis*. Berkeley: University of California Press, 1998.

Levy, Jerrold E., Eric B. Henderson, and Tracy J. Andrews. "The Effects of Regional Variation and Temporal Change on Matrilineal Elements of Navajo Social Organization." *Journal of Anthropological Research* 45 (1989): 351–77.

Lewis, David Rich. *Neither Wolf nor Dog: American Indians, Environment, and Agrarian Change*. New York: Oxford University Press, 1994.

"Living from Livestock." Photocopied handbook, courtesy of Ralph Goh. St. Michaels, Ariz.: Natural Resources Conservation Service, n.d.

Lockett, H. C., and Milton Snow. *Along the Beale Trail: A Photographic Account of Wasted Range Land*. Lawrence, Kans.: U.S. Office of Indian Affairs, 1939.

Lord, Albert B. *The Singer of Tales*. 1960. Reprint, New York: Atheneum, 1965.

Lowitt, Richard. *Bronson M. Cutting, Progressive Politician*. Albuquerque: University of New Mexico Press, 1992.

Luckert, Karl W. *Navajo Mountain and Rainbow Bridge Religion*. Flagstaff: Museum of Northern Arizona, 1977.

Lyon, William H. "Gladys Reichard at the Frontiers of Navaho Culture." *American Indian Quarterly* 13 (1989): 137–63.

MacNab, John. "Carrying Capacity and Related Slippery Shibboleths." *Wildlife Society Bulletin* 13 (1985): 403–10.

Madany, Michael H., and Neil E. West. "Livestock Grazing–Fire Regime Interactions within Montane Forests of Zion National Park, Utah." *Ecology* 64 (1983): 661–67.

Magers, Pamela C. "Navajo Settlement in Canyon del Muerto." In *The Canyon del Muerto Survey Project: Anasazi and Navajo Archaeology in Northeastern Arizona*, by Patricia L. Fall, James A. McDonald, and Pamela C. Magers. Publications in Anthropology, no. 15. Tucson, Ariz.: Western Archeological Center, 1981.

Mangum, Neil C. "In the Land of Frozen Fires—A History of Human Occupation in El Malpais Country." In *Natural History of El Malpais National Monument*, compiled by Ken Mabery. Bulletin 156. Sorocco: New Mexico Bureau of Mines and Mineral Resources, 1997.

Marks, P. L., and Sana Gardescu. "Inferring Forest Stand History from Observational Field Evidence." In *The Historical Ecology Handbook: A Restorationist's Guide to Reference Ecosystems*, edited by Dave Egan and Evelyn A. Howell. Washington, D.C.: Island Press, 2001.

Marshall, Michael P. *A Chapter in Early Navajo History: Late Gobernador Phase Pueblito Sites of the Dinetah District*. Albuquerque: University of New Mexico, Office of Contract Archeology, 1995.

———. "The Pueblito as a Site Complex: Archeological Investigations in the Dinetah District; The 1989–1990 BLM Pueblito Survey." In *Rethinking Navajo Pueblitos*. Farmington, N.Mex.: Bureau of Land Management, 1991.

Mather, John R., and Marie Sanderson. *The Genius of C. Warren Thornthwaite, Climatologist-Geographer*. Norman: University of Oklahoma Press, 1996.

Matson, Daniel S., and Albert H. Schroeder, eds. and trans. "Cordero's Descriptions of the Apache—1796." *New Mexico Historical Review* 32 (1957): 335–56.

Matthews, Washington. "Natural Naturalists." Unpublished manuscript read before the Philosophical Society of Washington, 25 October 1884. In *Washington Matthews: Studies of Navajo Culture, 1880–1894*, edited by Katherine Spencer Halpern and Susan Brown McGreevy. Albuquerque: University of New Mexico Press, 1997.

———, ed. and trans. *Navaho Legends*. 1897. Reprint, Salt Lake City: University of Utah Press, 1994.

———. "Navajo Names for Plants." *American Naturalist* 20 (September 1886): 767–77.

———. *The Night Chant, a Navaho Ceremony*. Memoirs of the American Museum of Natural History, vol. 6. New York: American Museum of Natural History, 1902.

McAuliffe, J. R., Louis A. Scuderi, and Leslie D. McFadden. "Tree-Ring Record of Hillslope Erosion and Valley Floor Dynamics: Landscape Responses to Climate Variation during the Last 400 Yr in the Colorado Plateau, Northeastern Arizona." *Global and Planetary Change* 50 (2006): 184–201.

McEvoy, Arthur F. *The Fisherman's Problem: Ecology and Law in the California Fisheries, 1850–1980*. Cambridge: Cambridge University Press, 1986.

McFadden, L. D., and J. R. McAuliffe. "Lithologically Influenced Geomorphic Responses to Holocene Climatic Changes in the Southern Colorado Plateau, Arizona: A Soil-Geomorphic and Ecologic Perspective." *Geomorphology* 19 (1997): 303–32.

M'Closkey, Kathy. *Swept under the Rug: A Hidden History of Navajo Weaving*. Albuquerque: University of New Mexico Press, 2002.

McNeley, James Kale. *Holy Wind in Navajo Philosophy*. Tucson: University of Arizona Press, 1981.

McNitt, Frank. *The Indian Traders*. Rev. ed. Norman: University of Oklahoma Press, 1989.

———. *Navajo Wars: Military Campaigns, Slave Raids, and Reprisals*. Rev. ed. Albuquerque: University of New Mexico Press, 1990.

McPherson, Robert S. "Navajo Livestock Reduction in Southeastern Utah, 1933–46: History Repeats Itself." *American Indian Quarterly* 22 (1998): 1–18.

———. *The Northern Navajo Frontier, 1860–1900: Expansion through Adversity*. Albuquerque: University of New Mexico Press, 1988.

———. "Ricos and Pobres: Wealth Distribution on the Navajo Reservation in 1915." *New Mexico Historical Review* 60 (1985): 415–34.

Medicine, Beatrice. "Gender." In *Encyclopedia of North American Indians*, edited by Frederick E. Hoxie. Boston: Houghton Mifflin Co., 1996.

Melville, Elinor G. K. *A Plague of Sheep: Environmental Consequences of the Conquest of Mexico*. Cambridge: Cambridge University Press, 1994.

Merchant, Carolyn. *The Death of Nature: Women, Economy, and the Scientific Revolution*. San Francisco: Harper and Row, 1980.

———. *Ecological Revolutions: Nature, Gender, and Science in New England*. Chapel Hill: University of North Carolina Press, 1989.

Millar, Constance I., and Wallace B. Woolfenden. "The Role of Climate Change in Interpreting Historical Variability." *Ecological Applications* 9 (1999): 1207–16.

Miller, Brian, Gerardo Ceballos, and Richard Reading. "The Prairie Dog and Biotic Diversity." *Conservation Biology* 8 (1994): 677–81.

Mindeleff, Cosmos. "Navajo Houses." In *Seventeenth Annual Report of the Bureau of American Ethnology, 1895–1896*. Pt. 2. Smithsonian Institution, Bureau of American Ethnology. Washington, D. C.: Government Printing Office, 1898, pp. 469–517.

Mitchell, Frank. *Navajo Blessingway Singer: The Autobiography of Frank Mitchell, 1881–1967*. Edited by Charlotte J. Frisbie and David P. McAllester. Tucson: University of Arizona Press, 1978.

Mitchell, Rose. *Tall Woman: The Life Story of Rose Mitchell, a Navajo Woman, c. 1874–1977*. Edited by Charlotte J. Frisbie. Albuquerque: University of New Mexico Press, 2001.

Montoya, Maria. "Dennis Chavez and the Making of Modern New Mexico." In *New Mexico Lives: Profiles and Historical Stories*, edited by Richard W. Etulain. Albuquerque: University of New Mexico Press, 2002.

Moon, Samuel. *Tall Sheep: Harry Goulding, Monument Valley Trader*. Norman: University of Oklahoma Press, 1992.

Moore, R. M., and E. F. Biddiscombe. "The Effects of Grazing on Grasslands." In *Grasses and Grasslands*, edited by C. Barnard. London: Macmillan, 1964.

Mosk, Sanford A. *Land Tenure Problems in the Santa Fe Railroad Grant Area*. Berkeley: University of California Press, 1944.

Muir, John. *The Mountains of California*. 1894. Reprinted in *John Muir: Nature Writings*, edited by William Cronon. New York: Library of America, 1997.

Muskett, Milford B. "Identity, *Hózhó*, Change, and Land: Navajo Environmental Perspectives." Ph.D. diss., University of Wisconsin–Madison, 2003.

Nabhan, Gary Paul, Marcelle Coder, and Susan J. Smith. *Woodlands in Crisis: A Legacy of Lost Biodiversity on the Colorado Plateau*. [Flagstaff, Ariz.]: Bilby Research Center, 2004.

Naiman, Robert J., Carol A. Johnston, and James C. Kelley. "Alteration of North American Streams by Beaver." *Bioscience* 38 (1988): 753–62.

"Navajo Land Needs—Crisis and Touchstone." *American Indian Life* (American Indian Defense Association Bulletin) 18 (July 1931): 3–10.

Navajo Nation Department of Agriculture. Grazing Management Office. "Navajo Nation Water Resources Management: Grazing Acres and Livestock Count." St. Michaels, Ariz., n.d.

Newcomb, Franc Johnson. *Hosteen Klah: Navaho Medicine Man and Sand Painter*. Norman: University of Oklahoma Press, 1964.

New Mexico Association on Indian Affairs. *Urgent Navajo Problems: Observations and Recommendations*. Santa Fe: New Mexico Association on Indian Affairs, 1940.

Ni, Fenbiao, et al. "Cool-Season Precipitation in the Southwestern USA since 1000: Comparison of Linear and Nonlinear Techniques for Reconstruction." *International Journal of Climatology* 22 (2002): 1645–62. www.ncdc.noaa.gov/paleo/pubs/ni2002/.

Nials, Fred. "Geology and Geomorphology." In *Prehistory of the Ojo Amarillo: Archaeological Investigation of Block II, Navajo Indian Irrigation Project, San Juan County, New Mexico*, edited by David T. Kirkpatrick. Vol. 4. Las Cruces: New Mexico State University, Department of Sociology and Anthropology, 1980.

Nichols, Deborah L., and F. E. Smiley, eds. *Excavations on Black Mesa, 1982: A Descriptive Report*. Research Paper no. 39. Carbondale: Southern Illinois University, Center for Archaeological Investigation, 1984.

Niethammer, Carolyn. *I'll Go and Do More: Annie Dodge Wauneka, Navajo Leader and Activist*. Lincoln: University of Nebraska Press, 2001.

Nora, Pierre. *Realms of Memory: Rethinking the French Past*. Translated by Arthur Goldhammer. New York: Columbia University Press, 1996.

Norwood, Vera. *Made from This Earth: American Women and Nature*. Chapel Hill: University of North Carolina Press, 1993.

O'Bryan, Aileen, [ed.]. *The Dîné: Origin Myths of the Navaho Indians* [as told by Sandoval]. Smithsonian Institution, Bureau of American Ethnology Bulletin 163. Washington, D.C.: Government Printing Office, 1956.

O'Neill, Colleen. *Working the Navajo Way: Labor and Culture in the Twentieth Century*. Lawrence: University of Kansas Press, 2005.

Opler, Morris E. "The Apachean Culture Pattern and Its Origins." In *Handbook of North American Indians*. Vol. 10. *Southwest*, edited by Alfonso Ortiz. Washington, D.C.: Smithsonian Institution, 1983.

O[stermann], L[eopold]. "The Navajo Indian Blanket." *Franciscan Missions of the Southwest* 6 (1918): 1–14.

Parezo, Nancy J. "Anthropology: The Welcoming Science." In *Hidden Scholars: Women Anthropologists and the Native American Southwest*. Albuquerque: University of New Mexico Press, 1993.

Parman, Donald L. *The Navajos and the New Deal*. New Haven, Conn.: Yale University Press, 1976.

Perdue, Theda. *Cherokee Women: Gender and Culture Change, 1700–1835*. Lincoln: University of Nebraska Press, 1998.

Pérez de Luxán, Diego. "Diego Pérez de Luxán's Account of the Antonio de Espejo Expedition into New Mexico, 1582." In *The Rediscovery of New Mexico, 1580–1594*, edited by George P. Hammond and Agapito Rey. Albuquerque: University of New Mexico Press, 1966.

Philp, Kenneth R. *John Collier's Crusade for Indian Reform, 1920–1954*. Tucson: University of Arizona Press, 1977.

Pinchot, Gifford. *Breaking New Ground*. Commemorative ed. Washington, D. C.: Island Press, 1998.

Pollock, Floyd Allen. *A Navajo Confrontation and Crisis*. Tsaile, Ariz.: Navajo Community College Press, 1984.

Pool, Carolyn Garrett. "Reservation Policy and the Economic Position of Wichita Women." *Great Plains Quarterly* 8 (Summer 1988): 158–71.

Popelish, Linda, and Russell T. Fehr. *Archaeological Investigations in the Northern Chuska Mountains: The N-13 Road Survey at Red Rock and Lukachukai, Navajo Nation*. Navajo Nation Papers in Anthropology 18. Window Rock, Ariz.: Navajo Nation Cultural Resources Management Program, 1983.

Powell, Shirley, and George J. Gumerman. *People of the Mesa: The Archaeology of Black Mesa, Arizona*. Tucson, Ariz.: Southwest Parks and Monuments Association, 1987.

Powers, Margaret A., and Byron P. Johnson. *Defensive Sites of Dinetah.* Cultural Resources Series no. 2. Albuquerque, N.Mex.: Bureau of Land Management, Albuquerque District, 1987.

Powers, Willow Roberts. *Navajo Trading: The End of an Era.* Albuquerque: University of New Mexico Press, 2001.

Prindeville, Diane-Michele. "The Role of Gender, Race/Ethnicity, and Class in Activists' Perceptions of Environmental Justice." In *New Perspectives on Environmental Justice: Gender, Sexuality, and Activism*, edited by Rachel Stein. New Brunswick, N.J.: Rutgers University Press, 2004.

"Proceedings of a Council between the United States and the Navajo Tribe, 28 May 1868." *Native American Legal Materials Collection*, Title 4323. Flagstaff, Ariz.: K. C. Publications, 1968.

Pulido, Laura. *Environmentalism and Economic Justice: Two Chicano Struggles in the Southwest.* Tucson: University of Arizona Press, 1996.

Pyne, Stephen J. *Fire in America: A Cultural History of Wildland and Rural Fire.* Princeton, N.J.: Princeton University Press, 1982; Seattle: University of Washington Press, 1997.

Pynes, Patrick Gordon. "Erosion, Extraction, and Reciprocation: An Ethno/Environmental History of the Navajo Nation's Ponderosa Pine Forests." Ph.D. diss., University of New Mexico, 2000.

Reed, Alan D., and Jonathan C. Horn. "Early Navajo Occupation of the American Southwest: Reexamination of the Dinetah Phase." *Kiva* 55 (1990): 283–300.

Reed, Lori Stephens, and Paul F. Reed, eds. *Cultural Diversity and Adaptation: The Archaic, Anasazi, and Navajo Occupation of the Upper San Juan Basin.* Santa Fe: Bureau of Land Management, New Mexico State Office, 1992.

Reed, Paul F., and Lori Stephens Reed. "Reexamining Gobernador Polychrome: Toward a New Understanding of the Early Navajo Chronological Sequence in Northwestern New Mexico." In *The Archaeology of Navajo Origins*, edited by Ronald H. Towner. Salt Lake City: University of Utah Press, 1996.

Reeve, Frank D. "Navaho-Spanish Diplomacy, 1770–1790." *New Mexico Historical Review* 35 (1960): 206–10.

———. "The Navaho-Spanish Peace: 1720s–1770s." *New Mexico Historical Review* 34 (1959): 9–40.

———. "Navaho-Spanish Wars, 1680–1720." *New Mexico Historical Review* 33 (1958): 204–31.

———. "Seventeenth Century Navaho-Spanish Relations." *New Mexico Historical Review* 32 (1957): 36–52.

Reichard, Gladys A. *Dezba: Woman of the Desert.* New York: J. J. Augustin, 1939.

———. *Navaho Religion: A Study of Symbolism.* Princeton, N.J.: Princeton University Press, 1963.

———. *Social Life of the Navajo Indians*. 1928. Reprint, New York: AMS Press, 1969.

———. *Spider Woman: A Story of Navajo Weavers and Chanters*. New York: MacMillan, 1934.

Rice, Josiah M. *A Cannoneer in Navajo Country: Journal of Private Josiah M. Rice, 1851*. Edited by Richard H. Dillon. Denver: Old West, 1970.

Roberts, Willow. *Stokes Carson: Twentieth-Century Trading on the Navajo Reservation*. Albuquerque: University of New Mexico Press, 1987.

Rocek, Thomas R. "Navajo Cultural History." In *Excavations on Black Mesa, 1982: A Descriptive Report*, edited by Deborah L. Nichols and F. E. Smiley. Research Paper no. 39. Carbondale: Southern Illinois University, Center for Archaeological Investigation, 1984.

Roessel, Ruth, ed. *Navajo Stories of the Long Walk Period*. Tsaile, Ariz.: Navajo Community College Press, 1973.

———. *Women in Navajo Society*. Rough Rock, Ariz.: Rough Rock Demonstration School, Navajo Resource Center, 1981.

Roessel, Ruth, and Broderick H. Johnson, eds. *Navajo Livestock Reduction: A National Disgrace*. Chinle, Ariz.: Navajo Community College Press, 1974.

Roosens, Eugeen E. *Creating Ethnicity: The Process of Ethnogenesis*. Frontiers of Anthropology, vol. 5. Newbury Park, Calif.: Sage Publications, 1989.

Rosaldo, Michelle Zimbalist, and Louise Lamphere, eds. *Women, Culture, and Society*. Stanford, Calif.: Stanford University Press, 1974.

Rosaldo, Renato. *Culture and Truth: The Remaking of Social Analysis*. Boston: Beacon Press, 1993.

Rothrock, J. T. "Preliminary Botanical Report." In *Annual Report upon the Geographical Exploration and Surveys West of the One Hundredth Meredian*, by George M. Wheeler. Washington, D.C.: Government Printing Office, 1875.

Sampson, Arthur W. *Livestock Husbandry on Range and Pasture*. New York: John Wiley and Sons, 1928.

Sando, Joe S. "Jemez Pueblo." In *Handbook of North American Indians*. Vol. 9. *Southwest*, edited by Alfonso Ortiz. Washington, D.C.: Smithsonian Institution, 1979.

Savage, Melissa. "Structural Dynamics of a Pine Forest in the American Southwest under Chronic Human Disturbance." Ph.D. diss., University of Colorado, 1989.

———. "Structural Dynamics of a Southwestern Pine Forest under Chronic Human Influence." *Annals of the Association of American Geographers* 8 (1991): 271–89.

Savage, Melissa, Peter M. Brown, and Johannes Feddema. "The Role of Climate in a Pine Forest Regeneration Pulse in the Southwestern United States." *Ecoscience* 3 (1996): 310–18.

Savage, Melissa, and Thomas W. Swetnam. "Early 19th-Century Fire Decline Following Sheep Pasturing in a Navajo Ponderosa Pine Forest." *Ecology* 71 (1990): 2374–78.

Savory, Allan. *Holistic Resource Management*. Washington, D.C.: Island Press, 1988.

Sayer, Nathan F. "Recognizing History in Range Ecology: 100 Years of Science and Management on the Santa Rita Experimental Range." In *Santa Rita Experimental Range: 100 Years (1903–2003) of Accomplishments and Contributions*, compiled by Mitchel P. McClaran, Peter F. Ffolliott, and Carleton B. Edminster, Tucson, 30 Oct.–1 Nov. 2003. USDA Forest Service Proceedings RMRS-P-30. Ogden, Utah: U.S. Department of Agriculture, 2003.

Schaafsma, Curtis F. *Apaches de Navajo: Seventeenth-Century Navajos in the Chama Valley of New Mexico*. Salt Lake City: University of Utah Press, 2002.

———. *Archaeological Survey of Maximum Pool and Navajo Excavations at Abiquiu Reservoir, Rio Arriba County, New Mexico*. Santa Fe, N.Mex.: School of American Research, 1976.

———. *The Cerrito Site (AR-4): A Piedra Lumbre Phase Settlement at Abiquiu Reservoir*. Santa Fe, N.Mex.: School of American Research, 1979.

———. "Ethnic Identity and Protohistoric Archaeological Sites in Northwestern New Mexico: Implications for Reconstructions of Navajo and Ute History." In *The Archaeology of Navajo Origins*, edited by Ronald H. Towner. Salt Lake City: University of Utah Press, 1996.

Schaafsma, Polly. *Rock Art in the Navajo Reservoir District*. Papers in Anthropology, no. 7. Santa Fe: Museum of New Mexico Press, 1971.

Scharff, Virginia J. "Are Earth Girls Easy? Ecofeminism, Women's History, and Environmental History." *Journal of Women's History* 7 (1995): 164–75.

———. "Man and Nature! Sex Secrets of Environmental History." In *Seeing Nature through Gender*. Lawrence: University of Kansas Press, 2003.

———, ed. *Seeing Nature through Gender*. Lawrence: University of Kansas Press, 2003.

Scherer, Glenn. "The Godly Must Be Crazy." *Grist Magazine*, 27 November 2004. http:///www.grist.org/news/maindish/2004/10/27/scherer-christian/index.html.

Schoenwetter, James, and Frank W. Eddy. *Alluvial and Palynological Reconstruction of Environments, Navajo Reservoir District*. Museum of New Mexico Papers in Anthropology, no. 13. Santa Fe: Museum of New Mexico Press, 1964.

Schrepfer, Susan R. *Nature's Altars: Mountains, Gender, and American Environmentalism*. Lawrence: University of Kansas Press, 2005.

Scott, James C. *Seeing Like a State: How Certain Schemes to Improve the Human Condition Have Failed*. New Haven, Conn.: Yale University Press, 1998.

Scott, Joan Wallach. *Gender and the Politics of History*. New York: Columbia University Press, 1988.

Scurlock, Dan. "A Poor Man's Cow: The Goat in New Mexico and the Southwest." *New Mexico Historical Review* 73 (1998): 7–24.

Severson, Kieth, and Leonard F. Debano. "Influence of Spanish Goats on Vegetation and Soils in Arizona Chaparral." *Journal of Range Management* 44 (1991): 111–17.

Shepardson, Mary. "The Gender Status of Navajo Women." In *Women and Power in Native North America*, edited by Laura F. Klein and Lillian A. Ackerman. Norman: University of Oklahoma Press, 1995.

Shepardson, Mary, and Blodwen Hammond. *The Navajo Mountain Community: Social Organization and Kinship Terminology*. Berkeley: University of California Press, 1970.

Sheppard, Paul R., et al. "The Climate of the US Southwest." *Climate Research* 21 (2002): 219–38.

Shoemaker, Nancy. *American Indian Population Recovery in the Twentieth Century*. Albuquerque: University of New Mexico Press, 1999.

Sidwell, George M., Jack L. Ruttle, and Earl E. Ray. *Improvement of Navajo Sheep*. Agricultural Experiment Station Research Report 172. Las Cruces: New Mexico State University, Agricultural Experiment Station, 1970.

Simmons, Marc. *New Mexico: An Interpretive History*. Albuquerque: University of New Mexico Press, 1988.

Simmons, Virginia McConnell. *The Ute Indians of Utah, Colorado, and New Mexico*. Boulder: University Press of Colorado, 2000.

Simpson, James H. *Navaho Expedition: Journal of a Military Reconnaissance from Santa Fe, New Mexico, to the Navaho Country Made in 1849 by Lieutenant James H. Simpson*. Edited by Frank McNitt. Norman: University of Oklahoma Press, 2003.

Sluyter, Andrew. "From Archive to Map to Pastoral Landscape: A Spatial Perspective on the Livestock Ecology of Sixteenth-Century New Spain." *Environmental History* 3 (1998): 508–528.

Smith, Sherry L. *Reimagining Indians: Native Americans through Anglo Eyes, 1880–1940*. New York: Oxford University Press, 2000.

Spence, Mark David. *Dispossessing the Wilderness: Indian Removal and the Making of the National Parks*. New York: Oxford, 1999.

Spicer, Edward H. *Cycles of Conquest: The Impact of Spain, Mexico, and the United States on the Indians of the Southwest, 1533–1960*. Tucson: University of Arizona Press, 1986.

———. "Sheepmen and Technicians: A Program of Soil Conservation on the Navajo Indian Reservation." In *Human Problems in Technological Change: A Casebook*. New York: John Wiley & Sons, 1952.

Stapp, Paul. "A Reevaluation of the Role of Prairie Dogs in Great Plains Grasslands." *Conservation Biology* 12 (1998): 1253–59.

Stegner, Wallace. *Beyond the Hundredth Meridian: John Wesley Powell and the Second Opening of the West*. New York: Penguin Books, 1954.

Stein, Rachel, ed. *New Perspectives on Environmental Justice: Gender, Sexuality, and Activism*. New Brunswick, N.J.: Rutgers University Press, 2004.

Stephen, A. M. "Navajo Origin Legend." *Journal of American Folklore* 43 (1965): 88–104.

———. "Notes about the Navajoes." *Canadian Indian* 1 (October 1890): 15–16.

Stewart, Omer C. *Peyote Religion: A History*. Norman: University of Oklahoma Press, 1987.

Stout, Joe A. "Cattlemen, Conservationists, and the Taylor Grazing Act." *New Mexico Historical Review* 44 (1970): 311–32.

Stringham, Tamzen K., William C. Krueger, and Patrick L. Shaver. "State and Transition Modeling: An Ecological Process Approach." *Journal of Range Management* 56 (March 2003): 106–13.

Stubbendieck, James, Stephan L. Hatch, and Charles H. Butterfield. *North American Range Plants*. Lincoln: University of Nebraska, 1981.

Stuth, Jerry W. "Foraging Behavior." In *Grazing Management: An Ecological Perspective*, edited by Rodney K. Heitschmidt and Jerry W. Stuth. Portland, Ore.: Timber Press, 1991.

Sutter, Paul. *Driven Wild: How the Fight against Automobiles Launched the Modern Wilderness Movement*. Seattle: University of Washington Press, 2002.

Swetnam, Thomas W., Craig D. Allen, and Julio L. Betancourt. "Applied Historical Ecology: Using the Past to Manage for the Future." *Ecological Applications* 9 (1999): 1189–1206.

Swetnam, Thomas W., and Christopher H. Baisan. "Historical Fire Regime Patterns in the Southwestern United States since A.D. 1700." In *Fire Effects in Southwestern Forests: Proceedings of the Second La Mesa Fire Symposium, Los Alamos, New Mexico, March 29–31, 1994*, edited by Craig D. Allen. Fort Collins, Colo.: U.S. Forest Service, 1996.

Swetnam, Thomas W., and Julio L. Betancourt. "Fire-Southern Oscillation Relations in the Southwestern United States." *Science* 249 (1990): 1017–20.

Tamaron y Romeral, Pedro. *Bishop Tamaron's Visitation of New Mexico, 1760*. Edited by Eleanor B. Adams. Historical Society of New Mexico Publications in History, vol. 15. Albuquerque: Historical Society of New Mexico, 1954.

Taylor, Dorceta E. "Environmentalism and the Politics of Inclusion." In *Confronting Environmental Racism: Voices from the Grassroots*, edited by Robert D. Bullard. Boston: South End Press, 1993.

Taylor, Graham D. *The New Deal and American Indian Tribalism: The Administration of the Indian Reorganization Act, 1934–45*. Lincoln: University of Nebraska Press, 1980.

Taylor, Walter P. "Significance of Extreme or Intermittent Conditions in Distribution of Species and Management of Natural Resources, with a Restatement of Liebig's Law of Minimum." *Ecology* 15 (1934): 374–79.

Thomas, Alfred Barnaby, trans. and ed. *Forgotten Frontiers: A Study of the Spanish Indian Policy of Don Juan Bauista de Anza, Governor of New Mexico, 1777–1787*. Norman: University of Oklahoma Press, 1932.

———. *The Plains Indians and New Mexico, 1751–1778: A Collection of Documents Illustrative of the History of the Eastern Frontier of New Mexico*. Coronado Cuarto

Centennial Publications, vol. 11. Albuquerque: University of New Mexico Press, 1940.

Thomas, Wesley. "Navajo Cultural Constructions of Gender and Sexuality." In *Two-Spirit People: Native American Gender Identity, Sexuality, and Spirituality*, edited by Sue-Ellen Jacobs, Wesley Thomas, and Sabine Lang. Urbana: University of Illinois Press, 1997.

Thompson, Gerald. *The Army and the Navajo: The Bosque Redondo Reservation Experiment, 1863–68*. Tucson: University of Arizona Press, 1976.

Thornber, J. J. *The Grazing Ranges of Arizona*. Bulletin no. 65. Tucson: University of Arizona, Agricultural Experiment Station, 1910.

Thornthwaite, C. Warren, C. F. Stewart Sharpe, and Earl F. Dosch. *Climate and Accelerated Erosion in the Arid and Semi-Arid Southwest with Special Reference to the Polacca Wash Drainage Basin, Arizona*. Technical Bulletin no. 808. Washington, D.C.: U.S. Department of Agriculture, 1942.

———. "Climate of the Southwest in Relation to Accelerated Erosion." *Soil Conservation* (SCS) 6 (1941): 298–302ff.

Tobey, Ronald C. *Saving the Prairies: The Life Cycle of the Founding School of American Plant Ecology, 1895–1955*. Berkeley: University of California Press, 1981.

Touchan, Ramzi, Thomas W. Swetnam, and Henri D. Grissino-Mayer. "Effects of Livestock Grazing on Pre-Settlement Fire Regimes in New Mexico." In *Proceedings: Symposium on Fire in Wilderness and Park Management, March 30–April 1, 1993, Missoula, Montana*, edited by James K. Brown et al. General Technical Report INT-GTR-320. Ogden, Utah: U.S. Forest Service, 1995.

Toumey, J. W. "Overstocking the Range." *Arizona Agricultural Experiment Station Bulletin No. 2*. Tucson: Citizen, 1891.

Towner, Ronald H., ed. *The Archaeology of Navajo Origins*. Salt Lake City: University of Utah Press, 1996.

———. *Defending the Dinétah: Pueblitos in the Ancestral Navajo Homeland*. Salt Lake City: University of Utah Press, 2003.

———. "The Pueblito Phenomenon: A New Perspective on Post-Revolt Navajo Culture." In *The Archaeology of Navajo Origins*. Salt Lake City: University of Utah Press, 1996.

Towner, Ronald H., and Jeffrey S. Dean. "LA 2298: The Oldest Pueblito Revisited." *Kiva* 57 (1992): 315–329.

———. "Questions and Problems in Pre-Fort Sumner Navajo Archaeology." In *The Archaeology of Navajo Origins*, edited by Ronald H. Towner. Salt Lake City: University of Utah Press, 1996.

Towner, Ronald H., and Byron P. Johnson. *The San Rafael Canyon Survey: Reconstructing Eighteenth Century Navajo Population Dynamics in the Dinétah*. Farmington, N.Mex.: Western Cultural Resource Management, 1996.

"Treaty between the United States of America and the Navajo Tribe of Indians," concluded 1 June 1868. *Native American Legal Materials Collection*, Title 4321. Microform. Honolulu: Law Library Microform Consortium, 1990.

Trennert, Robert A. *White Man's Medicine: Government Doctors and the Navajo, 1863-1955*. Albuquerque: University of New Mexico Press, 1998.

Tuan, Yi-Fu. "New Mexican Gullies: A Critical Review and Some Recent Observations." *Annals* (Association of American Geographers) 56 (1966): 573-97.

Tucker, Richard P. "The Evolution of Transhumant Grazing in the Punjab Himalaya." *Mountain Research and Development* 6 (1986): 17-28.

Turner, Raymond M. "Great Basin Desert Scrub." In *Biotic Communities of the American Southwest—United States and Mexico*, edited by David E. Brown. Tucson: University of Arizona, Boyce Thompson Southwestern Arboretum, 1982.

Tyler, S. Lyman, and H. Darrel Taylor. "The Report of Fray Alonso de Posada in Relation to Quivira and Teguayo." *New Mexico Historical Review* 33 (1958): 285-314.

Upham, Steadman. "Archaeological Visibility and the Underclass of Southwestern Prehistory." *American Antiquity* 53 (1988): 245-61.

U.S. Congress. House. *Wagon Road—Fort Smith to Colorado River*, by Edward F. Beale. Executive Document 42. Serial Set 1048. 36th Congress, 1st Session, 1860.

———. *Wagon Road from Fort Defiance to the Colorado River*, by Edward F. Beale. Executive Document 124. Serial Set 959. 35th Congress, 1st Session, 1858.

U.S. Congress. Senate. *Report upon the Colorado River of the West*, by Joseph C. Ives. Ex. Doc. 36th Congress, 1st Session, 1861.

U.S. Congress. Senate. Committee on Indian Affairs. *Survey of Conditions of the Indians of the United States*. Hearings before a Subcommittee. Pt. 18. *Navajos in Arizona and New Mexico*. 71st Congress, 3rd Session, 1932.

———. *Survey of Conditions of the Indians of the United States*. Hearings before a Subcommittee. Pt. 34. *Navajo Boundary and Pueblos in New Mexico*. 75th Congress, 1st Session, 1937.

U.S. Congress. Senate. Select Committee to Examine into the Condition of the Sioux and Crow Indians. *Report on the Condition of Indian Tribes in Montana and Dakota*. Senate Report 283. Serial Set 2174. 48th Congress, 1st Session, 1884.

U.S. Department of Agriculture. *The Western Range: A Great but Neglected Natural Resource*. Senate Document 199. 74th Congress, 2nd Session. Washington, D.C.: Government Printing Office, 1936.

U.S. Department of Commerce. Bureau of the Census. *Statistical Abstract of the United States, 1947*. Washington, D.C.: Government Printing Office, 1947.

U.S. Department of the Interior. Commissioner of Indian Affairs. *Annual Report, 1870*. House Executive Document 1. Serial Set 1449. 41st Congress, 3rd Session, 1870-71.

———. *Annual Report, 1872*. House Executive Document 1. Serial Set 1560. 42nd Congress, 3rd Session, 1872-73.

———. *Annual Report, 1874*. House Executive Document 1. Serial Set 1639. 43rd Congress, 2nd Session, 1874-75.

———. *Annual Report, 1876*. House Executive Document 1. Serial Set 1749. 44th Congress, 2nd Session, 1876-77.

———. *Annual Report, 1877*. House Executive Document 1. Serial Set 1801. 45th Congress, 2nd Session, 1877-78.

———. *Annual Report, 1879*. House Executive Document 1. Serial Set 1910. 46th Congress, 2nd Session, 1879-80.

———. *Annual Report, 1880*. House Executive Document 1. Serial Set 1959. 46th Congress, 3rd Session, 1880-81.

———. *Annual Report, 1881-82*. House Executive Document 1. Serial Set 2018. 47th Congress, 1st Session, 1881-82.

———. *Annual Report, 1882-83*. House Executive Document 1. Serial Set 2100. 47th Congress, 2nd Session, 1882-83.

———. *Annual Report, 1883*. House Executive Document 1. Serial Set 2191. 48th Congress, 1st Session, 1883-84.

———. *Annual Report, 1884*. House Executive Document 1. Serial Set 2287. 48th Congress, 2nd Session, 1884-85.

———. *Annual Report, 1885*. Executive Document 1. Serial Set 2379. 49th Congress, 1st Session, 1885-1886.

———. *Annual Report, 1886*. House Executive Document 1. Serial Set 2467. 49th Congress, 2nd Session, 1886-87.

———. *Annual Report, 1887*. Washington, D.C.: Government Printing Office, 1887.

———. *Annual Report, 1888*. Washington, D.C.: Government Printing Office, 1888.

———. *Annual Report, 1889*. House Executive Document 1. Serial Set 2725. 51st Congress, 1st Session, 1889-90.

———. *Annual Report, 1890*. Washington, D.C.: Government Printing Office, 1890.

———. *Annual Report, 1891*. Washington, D.C.: Government Printing Office, 1891.

———. *Annual Report, 1893*. Washington, D.C.: Government Printing Office, 1893.

———. *Annual Report, 1895*. Washington, D.C.: Government Printing Office, 1895.

———. *Annual Report, 1896*. Washington, D.C.: Government Printing Office, 1897.

———. *Annual Report, 1897.* Washington, D.C.: Government Printing Office, 1897.

———. *Annual Report, 1899.* Washington, D.C.: Government Printing Office, 1899.

———. *Annual Report, 1900.* Washington, D.C.: Government Printing Office, 1900.

———. *Annual Report, 1901.* Washington, D.C.: Government Printing Office, 1901.

———. *Annual Report, 1903.* Washington, D.C.: Government Printing Office, 1903.

———. *Annual Report, 1905.* Washington, D.C.: Government Printing Office, 1905.

Vale, Thomas R. *Plants and People: Vegetation Change in North America.* Washington, D.C.: Association of American Geographers, 1982.

Van Devender, Thomas R. "Desert Grassland History: Changing Climates, Evolution, Biogeography, and Community Dynamics." In *The Desert Grassland*, edited by Mitchel P. McClaran and Thomas R. Van Devender. Tucson: University of Arizona Press, 1995.

Vansina, Jan. *Oral Tradition as History.* Madison: University of Wisconsin Press, 1985.

Vargas, Diego de. *Blood on the Boulders: The Journals of Don Diego de Vargas, New Mexico, 1694–97*, edited by John L. Kessell, Rick Hendricks, and Meredith D. Dodge. Albuquerque: University of New Mexico Press, 1998.

Vélez de Escalante, Silvestre. *The Domínguez-Escalante Journal: Their Expedition through Colorado, Utah, Arizona, and New Mexico in 1776.* Translated by Angelico Chavez, edited by Ted J. Warner. Salt Lake City: University of Utah Press, 1995.

Vivian, R. Gwinn. "The Navajo Archaeology of the Chacra Mesa." M.A. thesis, University of New Mexico, 1960.

Vogler, Lawrence E., ed. *Human Adaptation and Cultural Change: The Archaeology of Block III, N. I. I. P.* Vol. 1–4. Navajo Nation Papers in Anthropology, no. 15. Window Rock, Ariz.: Navajo Nation Cultural Resource Management Program, 1983. Courtesy of New Mexico Laboratory of Anthropology.

Vogler, Lawrence E., Kristin Langenfeld, and Dennis Gilpin. *Dáá'ák'eh Nitsaa: An Overview of the Cultural Resources of the Navajo Indian Irrigation Project, Northwestern New Mexico.* Navajo Nation Papers in Anthropology, no. 29. Window Rock, Ariz.: Navajo Nation Archaeology Department, 1993.

Wagner, Sallie. *Wide Ruins: Memories from a Navajo Trading Post.* Albuquerque: University of New Mexico Press, 1997.

Walker, J. G., and O. L. Shepherd. *The Navajo Reconnaissance: A Military Exploration of the Navajo Country in 1859.* Edited by L. R. Bailey. Los Angeles: Westernlore Press, 1964.

Warren, Louis S. *The Hunter's Game: Poachers and Conservationists in Twentieth-Century America*. New Haven, Conn.: Yale University Press, 1997.

Watson, Don. "Navahos Pray for the Good of the World." *Mesa Verde Notes* 7, no. 1 (1937): 16–18.

Weber, Anselm. *The Navajo Indians: A Statement of Facts*. St. Michaels, Ariz.: n.p., 1914.

Weber, David J. *The Spanish Frontier in North America*. New Haven, Conn.: Yale University Press, 1992.

Weiss, Lawrence David. *The Development of Capitalism in the Navajo Nation: A Political-Economic History*. Minneapolis: MEP Publications, 1984.

West, Neil E., ed. *Ecosystems of the World*. Vol. 5. *Temperate Deserts and Semi-Deserts*. Amsterdam: Elsevier Scientific, 1983.

West, N. E., and John Skukiņš, eds. *Nitrogen in Desert Ecosystems*. Stroudsburg, Pa.: Dowden, Hutchinson and Ross, 1978.

Western Regional Climate Center. General Climate Summary Tables: Precipitation. http:www.wrcc.dri.edu/summary/Climsmaz.html.

"Wheeler-Howard Act," *Public Acts of the Seventy-Third Congress, Second Session, 1934*. Chapter 576. In *Indian Affairs: Laws and Treaties*, vol. 5, compiled and edited by Charles J. Kappler. Washington, D.C.: Government Printing Office, 1941. Available at http://digital.library.okstate.edu/kappler/index.htm.

Whipple, A. W. *A Pathfinder in the Southwest: The Itinerary of Lieutenant A. W. Whipple during His Explorations for a Railway Route from Fort Smith to Los Angeles in the Years 1853 and 1854*. Edited by Grant Foreman. Norman: University of Oklahoma Press, 1941.

White, Alan S. "Presettlement Regeneration Patterns in a Southwestern Ponderosa Pine Stand." *Ecology* 66 (1985): 589–94.

White, Richard. "The Cultural Landscape of the Pawnees." *Great Plains Quarterly* 2 (1982): 31–40.

———. *Remembering Ahanagran: Storytelling in a Family's Past*. New York: Hill and Wang, 1998.

———. *The Roots of Dependency: Subsistence, Environment, and Social Change among the Choctaws, Pawnees, and Navajos*. Lincoln: University of Nebraska Press, 1983.

Whitford, W. G. "Decomposition and Nutrient Cycling in Deserts." In *Pattern and Process in Desert Ecosystems*. Albuquerque: University of New Mexico Press, 1986.

Whitson, Tom D., et al., eds. *Weeds of the West*. 5th ed. Newark, Calif.: Western Society of Weed Science, 1996.

Wilcox, David. "The Entry of the Athabaskans into the American Southwest: The Problem Today." In *The Protohistoric Period in the North American Southwest, A.D. 1450–1700*, edited by David Wilcox and W. Bruce Masse. Anthropological Research Papers, no. 24. Tempe: Arizona State University, 1981.

Willink, Roseann Sandoval, and Paul G. Zolbrod. *Weaving a World: Textiles and the Navajo Way of Seeing*. Santa Fe: Museum of New Mexico Press, 1996.

Wilson, Alan, and Gene Dennison. *Navajo Place Names: An Observer's Guide*. Guilford, Conn.: Jeffrey Norton, 1995.

Wilson, Allen D., and Neil D. MacLeod. "Overgrazing: Present or Absent." *Journal of Range Management* 44 (1991): 475–82.

Wilson, Angela Cavender. "Power of the Spoken Word: Native Oral Traditions in American Indian History." In *Rethinking American Indian History*, edited by Donald L. Fixico. Albuquerque: University of New Mexico Press, 1997.

Wilson, John P., and A. H. Warren. "LA 2298: The Earliest Pueblito?" *Awanyu* 2 (1974): 8–26.

Winichakul, Thongchai. "Siam Mapped: The Making of Thai Nationhood." *Ecologist* 26 (1996): 215–21.

Witherspoon, Gary. *Language and Art in the Navajo Universe*. Ann Arbor: University of Michigan Press, 1977.

———. *Navajo Kinship and Marriage*. Chicago: University of Chicago Press, 1975.

Wood, Nancy. *Vectors of Memory: Legacies of Trauma in Postwar Europe*. Oxford: Berg, 1999.

Wooton, E. O. *The Range Problem in New Mexico*. Bulletin no. 66, Agricultural Experiment Station, New Mexico College of Agriculture and Mechanical Arts. Albuquerque: Albuquerque Morning Journal, 1908.

Wooton, E. O., and Paul C. Standley. *Flora of New Mexico*. Contributions from the United States National Herbarium (U.S. National Museum), vol. 19. Washington, D.C.: Government Printing Office, 1915.

Worcester, Donald E. "The Navaho during the Spanish Regime in New Mexico." *New Mexico Historical Review* 26 (April 1951): 101–27.

Worster, Donald. *Dust Bowl: The Southern Plains in the 1930s*. Oxford: Oxford University Press, 1979.

———. *Nature's Economy: A History of Ecological Ideas*. 2nd ed. Cambridge: Cambridge University Press, 1994.

———. "A Sense of the Soil." In *The Wealth of Nature: Environmental History and the Ecological Imagination*. Oxford: Oxford University Press, 1993.

Wozniak, Frank J. "Ethnohistory of the Abiquiu Reservoir Area." In *History and Ethnohistory along the Rio Chama*, by Frank J. Wozniak, Meade F. Kemrer, and Charles M. Carillo. Albuquerque, N.Mex.: U.S. Army Corps of Engineers, 1992.

Wyman, Leland C. *Blessingway*. Tucson: University of Arizona Press, 1970.

York, Frederick Fay. "Capitalist Development and Land in Northeastern Navajo Country, 1880s to 1980s." Ph.D. diss., State University of New York, Binghamton, 1990.

Young, Robert, compiler. *The Navajo Yearbook of Planning in Action*. Window Rock, Ariz.: Navajo Agency, 1955.

———. *The Navajo Yearbook of Planning in Action*. Window Rock, Ariz.: Navajo Agency, 1961.

———. *The Role of the Navajo in the Southwestern Drama*. Gallup, N.Mex.: Gallup Independent, 1968.

Young, Robert W., and William Morgan, compilers. *Navajo Historical Selections*. Phoenix: Bureau of Indian Affairs, 1954.

Young, Robert W., and William Morgan, Sr. *Analytical Lexicon of Navajo*. Albuquerque: University of New Mexico Press, 1992.

Zárate Salmerón, Gerónimo de. *Relaciones*. Translated by Charles F. Lummis in "Pioneers of the Far West: The Earliest History of California, New Mexico, Etc., from Documents Never Before Published in English." *Land of Sunshine* 11 (1899) and 12 (1900).

———. *Relaciones*. Translated by Alicia Ronstadt Milich. Albuquerque, N.Mex.: Horn and Wallace, 1966.

Zolbrod, Paul G. *Diné Bahane': The Navajo Creation Story*. Albuquerque: University of New Mexico Press, 1984.

INDEX

Abaa', 87–88
Acoma Land and Cattle Company, 259*n*33
Acoma pueblo, 111
Adams, William, 225
agriculture, 121, 226, 269*n*18, 291*n*41; alfalfa, 156; corn, 124–25. *See also* corn; Diné
Ahasteen, Jack, 7
Ahkeah, Sam, 236, 239
Aldrich, Stephen, 148
allotments. *See* Checkerboard
Along the Beale Trail, 39, 41–42
Alvarez Castrillón, Antonio, 111
Anasazi, 45, 71, 74, 107, 117, 268–69*n*18
Aneth, Utah, 218
anthropologists: on cultural traditions, 69; during New Deal era, 50–53, 75, 90; on Navajo poverty, 176; on practical information, 50, 52; on women, 83, 94, 99. *See also* ethnographic research
anthropology: professionalization of, 52–53

Anza, Juan Bautista de, 120
Apaches, 119
archaeological methods, 107–8, 283*n*5, 283*n*6
Arizona Boundary Bill, 170
Arizona Cattle Company, 259*n*33
arroyos, 41–42; arroyo cutting, 37, 40, 47, 138, 261*n*43; and climate change, 44–46, 47, 261*n*46
'Asdzą́ą́ 'Adika'í (Gambler Woman), 57
'Asdzą́ą́ Łtsoii, 212
'Asdzą́ą́ Nez (Tall Woman, aka Rose Mitchell, of Chinle), 86, 88, 105, 210
'Asdzą́ą́ Nez (Tall Woman, of Ganado), 206
'Asdzą́ą́ Nez (Tall Woman, of Oljato vic.), 214
'Asdzą́ą́ Tł'ógi (Juanita), 281*n*66
'Asdzą́ą́ Tsosie (Slim Woman, Narbona's granddaughter), 89
'Asdzą́ą́ Tsosie (Slim Woman, of Chinle), 243–44
'Asdzą́ą́ Yazzie (Little Woman, of Chinle vic.), 209

'Asdzą́ą́ Yazzie (Little Woman, of Red Willow Wash), 97
Ashcroft, James, 161
Ashurst, Henry, 159
Association of San Juan County Taxpayers, 186, 314*n*10
Atchison, Topeka and Santa Fe Railroad. *See* Atlantic and Pacific Railroad
Athabaskan, 286*n*14
Atlantic and Pacific Railroad, 99, 130, 147
Ayeta, Fr. Francisco de, 111

Babbitt Brothers, 241
Bah (of Chaco Mesa vic.), 156
Bah (of Rock Dale), 212
Barboncito, 73, 78
Barker, William, 326*n*54
Bautista de Anza, Juan, 120
Beadle, John, 138, 259*n*34
Beale, Edward, 39, 41–42, 258*n*30, 258–59*n*33
beavers, 258*n*30
Beck, Carl, 25–26, 167, 171–72
Be'ek'id Ahą́ąh Dikaní (Lakes Joined Together), 144, 303*n*52
Béésh Biwoo'í (Frank Goldtooth), 31–32, 198
Begay, Casey, 5
Begay, Sarah, 18
Benavides, Fr. Alonso de, 109
Bennett, Hugh Hammond, 35–36
Bennett, Kay (Kaibah), 79–80, 272*n*1
berdache. *See* nádleeh
Big Bead Mesa, 118
Black Creek Valley, 131
Blackgoat, Jim, 95
Blackhorse, Kitty, 218
Black Mesa, 51–52, 90, 122, 131
Black Mountain, 90, 150, 175

Black Whiskers, 96
Blanca Peak (Tsisnaajinii), 71
Blessingway, 54, 56, 64, 70, 75, 237, 269*n*22; and creation of Diné, 64–65, 76; and livestock origins, 54, 64–65, 68–69, 75–77
Blueeyes, George, 227
Bluewater Creek, 40, 42, 259*n*33
Boas, Franz, 53
Bosque Redondo. *See* Hwéeldi
Botkin, Daniel, 241
Boulder Dam, 24, 211, 252*n*20
Bourke, John Gregory, 88
Bratton, Sam, 160, 162
Breece, George, 146
Brophy, William, 216, 217, 325–26*n*54
Brown, Lillian, 195
Bryan, Kirk, 45–46
Bryant, Billy, 17–18
Burbank, Ałk'inanibaa', 175
Bureau of Animal Industry, U.S. Department of Agriculture, 157, 194–95
Bureau of Biological Survey, U.S. Department of Agriculture, 36
Bureau of Indian Affairs, U.S. Department of Interior, 22; and allotments on Checkerboard, 144–45; and dourine introduction, 157; and general grazing regulations, 158, 166, 180, 208, 213, 222; Indian agents' reports on Navajo livestock, 135–36; Indian policy (pre-1933), 21, 323*n*30; Indian policy under New Deal, 24, 183–84; legal authority for livestock reduction, 166, 216, 222; and livestock adjustment (1996), 6; livestock policy (pre-1933), 22, 33, 132, 147, 158, 297*n*11; on Navajo families, 196–97; and Navajo grazing regulations, 28–29, 212–14, 216, 220, 221–22; and

Navajo legibility, 207–8; programs and policies re. women, 145, 191, 194, 209, 222; range management meeting (1931), 155–59. *See also* Collier, John; Fryer, E. Reeseman; grazing permits; Indian Reorganization Act; livestock reduction; Navajo Service; Soil Conservation Service

Bureau of Land Management, U.S. Department of Interior, 189

Cadman, Frank, 171, 190
Cane Man's Son (Gishin Biye'), 74–75, 271n36
Cañoncito Bonito, 44
Canyon de Chelly, 38, 121, 122
Canyon del Muerto, 121, 122
captives, 89, 110, 111, 113, 114, 121, 290n37
Carrizo Mountains, 174
carrying capacity, 132, 197, 237, 333n29, 334n31; calculation of, 36, 237, 253n23; historical changes in, 39; of Navajo Reservation, 28, 204, 205–6, 220–21, 321n10; and overstocking, 34, 224
Carson, Christopher (Kit), 73, 90, 132
Casa Fuerte. *See* Dinétah
Casa Mera, 146
Cebola Cattle Company, 259n33
Cebolleta, 117–18, 119, 121
census of 1915, 95, 137. *See also* Diné
ceremonies, 65, 67, 74, 268n13; during 1930s, 56; and feasts, 97, 240; power of, 55–56, 236. *See also* Blessingway; creation stories; hataałii; Moving Up Way; oral traditions; rituals
Chaco Canyon, 45, 46, 117, 124
Chacón, Fernando de, 119, 120, 121
Chacra Mesa, 124
Changing Woman, 71, 72, 77, 86, 110; and creation of Diné, 64–65, 75, 76; and creation of livestock, 54, 64–65, 76; and Diné Bikéyah, 73; and migration of Diné, 76–77, 108; and symbolic relationship with women, 86, 98–99. *See also* Diyin Dine'é

chaos theory, 241
chapters (units of government), 31, 83, 172, 190, 196, 211–12
Chavez, Dennis, 185–86, 187, 212, 313–14n8
Checkerboard, 3; allotments on, 144–45, 177, 188; appropriation of land by Euro-American ranchers, 145–46, 177, 188; competition among Diné, 94, 149–50, 227; consolidation of allotments, 156, 307n4; and Euro-American farmers, 314n12; executive order lands, 20, 144; and goat reduction, 176–77; Grazing District No. 7, 188–89; land tenure, 130, 144–46, 156, 160–61, 185, 186, 187, 188; map of, 12–13; poverty on, 176–77, 178; range conditions, 42, 130. *See also* Eastern Navajo Boundary Association; Euro-American ranchers; land tenure; New Mexico Boundary Bill; Taylor Grazing Act
Cheyenne, Southern, 236
Chinle Valley, 150
Chischillie, Mary, 79, 179
Chuska Mountains, 38–39, 125–26, 138–39, 140
Civilian Conservation Corps. *See* Soil Conservation Service: Emergency Conservation Work
Clah Cheschillige, Deshna, 162–63, 173–74, 217–18
clans, 87, 275–76n20, 276n23; function of, 64, 87–88; origin of, 72, 75, 86–87
Clark, Elizabeth, 233
Clements, Frederic, 38

climate: blizzards, 163, 239, 334n38; climate change, 43–44, 45–47, 131, 138; effects on forests, 139–40; El Niño Southern Oscillation, 139–40; historical records of, 43–44, 45; lightning strikes, 139, 300n34. *See also* drought
Coal Mine Mesa, 18
Codallos y Rabal, Joachín, 116
Cohen, Felix, 222
Collier, John, 20–21, 22, 163, 233, 327n69; acknowledges mistakes, 177, 219, 234–35, 312n81; Diné attitudes toward, 6, 19–20, 163, 223; and E. Reeseman Fryer, 215, 219, 221; on economic leveling, 204–5, 207; and ethnographic studies, 49–50, 181, 263n67; ideas about native peoples, 21, 22, 23–24; ideas about Navajos, 22–23, 24, 29–30, 164, 166–67, 219; as Indian policy reformer, 20, 21, 23–24, 29, 163, 178; and indirect rule, 166, 183–84; on livestock reduction program, 164–66, 168, 171, 215, 220; on Navajo erosion problem, 24, 35, 164, 252n20; and Navajo self-determination, 166, 173, 179, 183–84, 199–200; and Navajo Tribal Council, 26, 28, 164–66, 167–68, 171; and New Mexico Boundary Bill, 26, 28, 185, 186–89; paternalism of, 23–24, 183–84; and power relations, 166, 212–13, 233; and prosecutions for grazing violations, 217; and women, 180, 194, 223. *See also* Bureau of Indian Affairs; ethnographic research; Indian Reorganization Act; livestock reduction
Colorado Plateau, 38, 45, 140, 230
Colorado River, 24, 37
Comanches, 113, 117
commercial stockowners. *See* livestock ownership
commons, tragedy of the, 199

Cook, E. R., 43
Cooley, A. C., 165–66
Cooper, John, 195
Cordero, Antonio, 120
corn: in creation stories, 68, 71, 72; and cultural identity, 64, 72
Covered Spring, 18
creation stories, 68–70, 84, 268n18; and birth of Diné, 64–65, 272n43; and livestock, 54, 63, 64–65, 68–69; and migration to Southwest, 270n24. *See also* Blessingway; ceremonies; Moving Up Way; oral traditions
Croix, Teodoro de, 120
Crooked Finger, 206
Cuervo y Valdez, Francisco, 112
cultural identity, 66. *See also* Diné
cultural traditions, 66–67, 69, 77
culture, xix. *See also* Diné
Curley, Robert, 102
Cutting, Bronson, 185

Dághá Sikaad, 90–91, 146
Damon, Ben, 148, 270n23
Dawes Severalty Act of 1887, 21, 144
Deeshchii'nii, Fred, 57, 94
Defiance Plateau, 138, 228
demonstration projects. *See* soil conservation program
dendroclimatology. *See* tree-ring data
Denehotso Hattie, 202–3
Denetdale, Jennifer Nez, xviii
Department of Agriculture, U.S., 241. *See also* Bureau of Animal Industry; Forest Service
Dezba, 209
Dibé Łizhiní Yazzie (Little Black Sheep), 320n75
Diné: alcoholism among, 176, 224; and class stratification, 96–97, 146–48, 204, 207, 322n21; cultural identity, 64,

380 INDEX

72, 73, 77–78; ethnogenesis of, 63–64, 65, 70, 72, 77–78, 110; as farmers, 109, 111–12, 286n15; geographical expansion of, 117–19, 120, 122, 125; as hunters and gatherers, 109; as imagined community, 64, 87; independence of, 22; legibility of, 207–8; and malevolent spirits, 197; metaphysics, 55–56, 236; migration to Colorado Plateau, 69, 76–77, 108, 268–69n18, 270n24, 284n10, 285n12; naming practices, 208; and Native American Church, 224; as pastoralists, 112–13, 115–17, 120, 285–86n13, 291n42; political leadership, 83, 94; population increase, 58, 148, 230, 235; as raiders, 110–11, 119–20; and reciprocity, 96–97; at Senate hearings, 160, 162, 172; settlement patterns, 90–92, 122, 276n27. *See also* clans; economy; matricentered society; matrilocality; Navajos; women

Diné Bikéyah, 64, 125; and cultural identity, 72–74, 78; map of (ca. 1500–1860), 104; sacred mountains of, 71; and symbolic relationship with sheep, 75–76. *See also* Colorado Plateau; Navajo Country; Navajo Reservation

Dinétah, 71, 109–10, 111–17, 292n47; map of, 104

Dixon, John, 161

Diyin Dine'é, 18–19, 55, 68, 74, 124; Banded Rock Boy, 56; Be'gochídí, 74, 75, 271n33; Calling God, 71; and creation of Diné, 71–72; and creation of livestock, 75, 76; Diné references to, 56, 73, 86, 214, 267n8; First Man, 71; First Woman, 71; Hero Twins, 72–73, 75–76, 98, 110; Mirage Man, 64, 76; Mirage People, 71; Monster Slayer, 75–76; Sun (the diety), 64, 72–73, 75, 76, 98; Talking God, 71–72; Wind (the diety), 72, 73, 270n26. *See also* Changing Woman

Dodge, Chee, 87, 148–50, 162–63, 221, 270n23, 275–76n20, 278n40; as commercial stockowner, 134, 148–50; and livestock ownership, 96; on livestock reduction, 164–65, 171, 207; and opposition to livestock reduction, 218

Dodge, Mabel (Luhan), 20–21

Dodge, Tom, 164, 236

Domínguez de Mendoza, Juan, 111

drought: of 1750s, 117, 292n47; of 1899–1904, 130, 131–32; of 1930s, 47; 1951–59, 47, 224, 237; of 1996, 4–5; of 2002–03, 9; Diné perceptions of, 47, 55; Diné response to, 55, 56, 58; historical patterns of, 43–44, 46. *See also* climate

Durán y Chávez, Santiago, 119

Dust Bowl, 34

Eastern Navajo Boundary Association, 188

ecology: equilibrium theory, 38, 240; of grasslands, 140–41; Liebig's law of the minimum, 237; thresholds, 221, 237; ungulate irruption theory, 132–35, 298n17. *See also* science

economy, 22, 235–36; conservation jobs, 165–66, 168, 172, 178; government valuation of livestock, 178; market economy, rise of, 147; post–World War II, 224, 225–27; poverty, 167, 176–77, 178, 225; pre-market orientation, 146–47; wage work, 165–66, 168, 178, 225–26; and World War I, 99, 147, 176; and World War II, 225. *See also* agriculture; trading posts; weaving

Emergency Conservation Work program. *See* Soil Conservation Service
environmental justice movement, xviii–xix
environmental racism, xviii, 247*n*11
equilibrium theory. *See* ecology
erosion, 24; causes of, 19, 45–47, 57, 131–32; geological, 45, 47–48; observations of, 32, 34, 35; process of, 37, 46–47, 48, 140–41, 229. *See also* arroyos; climate; overgrazing
ethnogenesis. *See* Diné
ethnographic research, 50–53, 90, 181, 197–98. *See also* anthropologists
ethnographic theory, 51, 53
Euro-American ranchers: on Checkerboard, 145–46, 147, 161, 185, 186, 259*n*33, 314*n*12; competition with Diné, 58, 119, 147, 230; impact on land, 42, 130, 161, 259*n*33; Spanish, 119
explorers' accounts, 38–39, 41–42, 49, 138

Fanale, Rosalie, 125
Faris, Chester, 155, 156, 320–21*n*4
Fearing Time, 73, 89–90
Federal Emergency Relief Administration, 164
fencing, 187, 190–91; of demonstration projects, 189, 199; by Diné stockowners, 150, 227; by Euro-American ranchers, 145–46, 188
fire, 139–40, 300*n*34
forests: changes in structure, 140; and climate, 139–40; descriptions of (pre-1933), 138–39; and fire, 139–40; reproduction in, 139–40
Forest Service, U.S. Department of Agriculture, 158, 315*n*25
Fort Defiance, 90

fortresses, 113, 114–15, 117, 118
Fort Sumner. *See* Hwéeldi
Fort Wingate, 90, 194
Fort Wingate Ordnance Depot, 225
Frazier, Lynn, 159
Frisbie, Charlotte, 243
Fruitland, New Mexico, 226
Fryer, E. Reeseman, 28, 190, 203–4, 221; acknowledges mistakes, 190, 204; enforces grazing regulations, 210, 216, 217, 218–19; and gender assumptions, 82, 209; and horse reduction, 215–17; ideas about Navajos, 233, 238; on Navajo horses, 214, 215; and Navajo resistance, 202, 212, 218–19, 321*n*6; and power relations, 234; and range management, 241; on transhumance, 200

Ganado, Arizona, 17, 42, 147, 150
gender: bias, 53; and complementarity, 84–86, 274*n*14; Diné understandings of, 84; government assumptions about, 50–51, 82, 94–96, 145, 209, 232, 323*n*30; and labor, 85–86; and livestock ownership, 97–99; male roles, 82–83. *See also* masculinity; women
General Allotment Act of 1887, 21, 144
General Land Office, 144–45
Gishin Biye' (Cane Man's Son), 74–75, 271*n*36
Goat, John W., 212
goat reduction, 25–26, 168, 173–77; and the Indian Reorganization Act, 178–79; memories of, 8–9, 18, 175, 178, 180; proposed, 168, 170. *See also* livestock reduction
goats, 141; conservationists' objections to, 168; value of, 26, 162, 178, 309*n*40. *See also* livestock
Gobernador Knob (Ch'óol'í'í), 71, 110

Goldtooth, Frank (Béésh Biwoo'í), 31–32, 198
Gorman, Howard, 17, 188, 202, 327n69; on livestock origins, 63; on livestock reduction, 17, 19–20; on value of livestock, 18
Grand Canyon, 90
grass banks, 241
grasses: alkali sacaton (*Sporobolus airoides*), 130, 141; blue grama (*Bouteloua gracilis*), 42, 130, 140, 141, 142, 191; bunch grasses, 45, 48, 140; bush muhly (*Muhlenbergia porteri*), 134; downy brome (*Bromus tectorum*, aka cheatgrass), 228, 229–30; galleta (*Hilaria jamesii*), 35, 130, 134, 140, 142; growth patterns, 140; Indian ricegrass (*Oryzopsis hymenoides*), 134, 140, 144; sand dropseed (*Sporobolus cryptandrus*), 134, 142; sideoats grama (*Bouteloua curtipendul*), 134; three-awn grass (*Aristida longiseta*), 228; western wheat (*Agropyron smithii*), 140, 141. *See also* vegetation; weeds
Gray Mountain, 90
grazing: conflicts over, in American West, xix; effects on ecosystems, 140–43; and landscape change, 134. *See also* overgrazing
grazing districts. *See* Checkerboard; land management units
grazing permits, 29, 205, 207, 211, 218, 330n95; compliance with (in 1996), 5; destruction of, 9, 211; enforcement of, 216, 217, 218–19; sheep units, 204; special permits, 220, 221; and trespass, 216; and women, 209, 222, 329n82. *See also* livestock reduction
grazing regulations. *See* Bureau of Indian Affairs

Grazing Service, U.S. Department of Interior, 189
Gregg, Josiah, 100
Gregory, Herbert, 45, 131, 138–39
Grey Eyes, 236

Hack, John Tilton, 48
Hagerman, Herbert, 155, 156, 157, 159
Haile, Fr. Berard, 52, 53, 75, 263–64n69
Hale, Albert, 5
Haraway, Donna, 240–41
Harbison, Donald, 150
Hardin, Garrett, 199
Hashké Neiniih, 97, 146, 218, 280n62
Hastiin Tó Łtsoii (Mr. Yellow Water), 63
Hastiin Tso (Mister Big Man), 210
hataałii, 56, 65, 97; and oral traditions, 68, 69, 70, 74, 268n13. *See also* creation stories
Hataałii Nez (Tall Chanter), 71, 74, 269–70n23, 271n36, 275–76n20
Hayden, Carl, 170
Hayzlett, G. W., 44
Herring, Ethyl, 329n82
Hill, W. W., 69
Hobsbawm, Eric, 69, 70
hóchx̨ǫ́, 19, 55, 57
Holy People. *See* Diyin Dine'é
Homestead Act, 144
Hoover Dam. *See* Boulder Dam
Hopi, 121
Hopi mesas, 122
horse reduction, 29, 214–17; and dourine eradication, 157, 162; enforcement of, 216–17, 218–19; maximum allowance, 206; memories of, 8, 217, 326n57; proposed, 157–58
horses, 141; cultural value of, 98, 214–15; numbers of, 97, 157–58
hózhǫ́, 19, 33, 55, 237, 240

Hubbell, Lorenzo, 96
Hubbell, Roman, 96
Hubbell Trading Post, 17, 96. *See also* trading posts
human dependency survey, 50–51. *See also* ethnographic research
Hunter, John, 158
Hwéeldi, 21–22, 73–74, 90; as environmental benchmark, 132; and refugees in western outposts, 90–92, 132, 146–47; and tradition, 67

Ickes, Harold, 188
Indian policy. *See* Bureau of Indian Affairs
Indian Reorganization Act, 23, 24, 26, 178–80, 187; referendum on, 179–80
Iverson, Peter, xviii
Ives, Joseph, 42

Jacob's Well, 41, 258*n*31
Jaramillo, Luis, 119
Jemez Mountains, 139
Jemez pueblo, 111, 112, 113–14
Joe, Ivan, 5–6
Johnson, Broderick, xvii
Johnson, Captain, 218–19
Johnson, Martin, 175
Jones Canyon, 26
Jornada Experimental Range, 47
Juanita ('Asdzą́ą́ Tł'ógi), 281*n*66

Kaibah (Kay Bennett), 79–80, 272*n*1
Kaibito Plateau, 90, 91
Kayenta, 9, 18, 202
k'é, 97, 124
Kee, Margaret, 102
Kimball, Solon, 51–52, 219, 234, 240
Klagetoh, 92
Kluckhohn, Clyde, 53, 83
Krug, Julius, 222

La Farge, Oliver, 263*n*67
Laguna pueblo, 118, 119
land management units (aka grazing districts), 197, 199–200, 229; assignment to, 200, 320*n*75; Diné complaints about, 200; map, 182; rationale for, 199. *See also* Bureau of Indian Affairs; range management
landscape: ancient, 45, 47–48; Diné perceptions of, 31–32, 54, 57–59, 75–76, 190; Diné vs. scientific perceptions of, 31–32; scientific assumptions about, 41–42; scientific perceptions of, 38–39, 44–45, 49. *See also* vegetation change
land tenure, 149–50, 199, 207, 216; conflicts over, 120, 132, 227; and matrilocality, 80, 94. *See also* Checkerboard
land use community, 51, 197, 234–35
land use rights. *See* land tenure
La Plata Valley, 109, 285*n*12
Lee, Floyd, 186–87
Left Handed, 56, 87–88, 93–94, 126
Lenzie, Frank, 167, 219
Leopold, Aldo, 230
Leopold, Luna, 48–49
Letherman, Jonathan, 99
Liebig's law of the minimum, 237
Lincoln, Tully, 175
Littell, Norman, 326*n*54
Little Colorado River, 24
livestock: cattle, 141, 226, 229; cultural value of, 18–19, 97–99, 102, 218, 239; Diné management of, 134; government issue of, 135; feeding strategies, 141; husbandry, 143, 155, 196, 229; raids, 89, 110–11, 119–20; songs for, 56, 77, 98, 218. *See also* creation stories; goats; grazing; horses; pastoralism; sheep; transhumance

livestock, origin of: in creation stories, 54, 63, 64, 74, 75–77; introduction by Spanish, 63, 111, 193

livestock ownership, 79–80, 97, 158, 208–9; and class stratification, 96, 204–7, 322*n*21; commercial stockowners, 91, 94, 99, 134, 148; and grazing permits, 209; large-scale herds, 146–48, 207, 220, 305*n*72; post–World War II, 226; subsistence flocks, 321*n*14; unequal distribution of, 148, 240; and women, 79–80, 81, 94–96, 146, 209

livestock population: (1868–79), 135; (1880–1929), 132, 136–37; (1930–44), 25, 137–38, 204, 205, 220, 253*n*23; (1945–54), 223; census of, 95–96, 205, 223; growth of herds, 58, 131, 132, 147–48, 222, 235; sheep units, 204; uncertainty of, pre-1930, 135–37; ungulate irruption theory, 132–35

livestock reduction, 24–25, 173, 235, 239, 253–54*n*30; (1933–34), 25–26, 164–68; (1935), 26; (1937–41), 28–29, 197, 212–17, 218–19; (1941–43), 220, 221; 1996, 4, 5; conflicts over, among Diné, 167, 171–72, 202–3, 210–11; economic effects of, 4, 167, 176–77; and economic leveling, 28–29, 204–7; enforcement of, 210; proposed, 33, 157–59, 161–62, 164–66, 211. *See also* goat reduction; grazing permits; horse reduction

local knowledge, 51, 53–54, 58–59, 125, 126, 264*n*73

Lockett, H. Claiborn, 39, 41, 41–42

Logan, John, 21

Long, Huey, 207

Long Walk, 22, 73

Lope, Montoya, 161

Lord, Albert, 67

Łtsoii, Charlie, 243

Luhan, Mabel Dodge. *See* Dodge, Mabel

Lynch, Mary, 206

Madrid, Roque, 111–12, 113

Manuelito, 271*n*31

Manuelito Plateau, 131

Manuelito Valley, 40

Many Farms Cannery, 220

maps, 12–13, 62, 104, 129, 182

Marshall, John, 21

Marshall, Robert, 181, 183–84, 211

Martin, Robert, 148, 236

masculinity: and horses, 97–98, 157–58, 214–15; and livestock reduction, 9, 18; and raiding, 119. *See also* gender

matriarchy, 82

matricentered society, 80, 82, 86–89, 91–94, 226–27, 273*n*4; post-Hwéeldi, 90–92; and women's power, 83, 94. *See also* women

matrilineal kinship, 82

matrilocality, 80, 82–83, 88–89, 94, 277*n*31, 278*n*38; post-Hwéeldi, 91–92. *See also* matricentered society

Matthews, Washington, 71, 270*n*23

McGinnies, William, 56, 195, 197, 199, 237, 238

M'Closkey, Kathy, xviii

McPherson, Robert, 9

medicine men. *See* hataałii

Melville, Elinor, 133

memories: collective, xvii, 6, 7, 195, 210, 233, 243; of goat reduction, 8–9, 18, 175, 178; of horse reduction, 8, 217, 326*n*57; of Hwéeldi, 22; of landscapes, 31–32, 57, 58–59; narrative tropes of, 9; places of, 8–9, 18, 26, 110, 243; of resistance, 9, 29, 179, 211, 222; of sheep, 243–44; of terror and violence, 8, 9, 17–18, 175, 210, 243. *See also* oral traditions

memory: individual vs. collective, 8; political use of, 250n23
Meritt, Edgar B., 158
métis. *See* local knowledge
Mexicans, 89
Mexican Springs Demonstration Project, 35, 189, 190
Millington, C. N., 171–72
Mitchell, Frank, 86, 198, 210–11, 237
Mitchell, Rose ('Asdzą́ą́ Nez, Tall Woman), 86, 88, 105, 210
mobility, 109, 124, 226; in creation stories, 68, 73, 76; and cultural identity, 64, 73. *See also* transhumance
Montoya, Antonio, 116
Monument Valley, 131, 218
Morgan, Jacob, 28, 29, 187–88, 314n10, 327n69; elected as tribal council chairman, 217–18; on livestock reduction, 171; opposition to Collier, 28, 179, 212
Morgan, Tom, 147
Mount Hesperus (Dibé Ntsaa), 71
Mount Taylor (Tsoodził), 71, 117
Moving Up Way, 71–75
Muck, Lee, 222, 233–34, 334n31
Muir, John, 143
Muskett, Milford, 237

Naakaii Yazzie, 96
Naalnishí, 239
Naat'áanii Sání (Old Leader, of Black Mesa), 51–52
nádleeh, 84, 274–75n15
Náníbaa', 96, 148–50
Narbona (Diné leader), 55, 89
Narbona, Antonio de, 121, 123
Narrow Canyon, 18
Native American Church, 224
nature: Diné understandings of, 19, 54–57, 84, 236, 239; scientific vs. Diné understandings of, 32–33, 56–57, 59, 234, 240–41. *See also* ecology; science
Navajo-Churro sheep. *See* sheep
Navajo Country, 3; map of, 12–13; pre-1933 descriptions of, 38–39, 41–42, 44, 49, 138–39, 150. *See also* Diné Bikéyah; range conditions
Navajo Indian Irrigation Project, 185
Navajo Mountain community, Utah, 25–26, 90, 91–92, 218
Navajo Nation Council, 4, 5, 6. *See also* Navajo Tribal Council
Navajo Ordnance Depot, 225
Navajo Reservation, 3; evolution of, 129; executive order lands, 20, 144; map of, 129; proposed expansion of, 26, 28, 156, 170, 177–78, 185–88. *See also* Bureau of Indian Affairs; Checkerboard
Navajo Rights Association, 217–18, 219
Navajos: in the archaeological record, 107–9, 113–15, 283n5, 285n12, 285–86n13, 287n16, 291n41; in early Spanish records, 106–7, 108, 109, 111–12, 117–18, 120, 286n13; in eighteenth century, 111–20; resettlement program, 156, 307n3. *See also* Diné
Navajo Service, 203, 235. *See also* Bureau of Indian Affairs; Soil Conservation Service
Navajo Times, 6, 7
Navajo Tribal Council, 26, 27, 83, 169, 232; approves goat reduction, 171; endorses grazing regulations, 212, 216; endorses special permits, 220; and land management units, 200; on livestock reduction, 164–65, 167–68, 171, 172–73, 239; and power relations, 166; repudiates livestock reduction program, 221, 222; takes charge of grazing program, 222; and women's suffrage, 101–2

Navajo Tribal Court, 210, 218
Ńdíshchíí' (Pine Tree), 91
Nelson, Ernest, 26, 58–59
New Mexico and Arizona Land Company, 130, 259*n*33
New Mexico Boundary Bill, 28, 170, 177–78, 185–88; opposition to, 170, 186–88, 314*n*10
Nez, John (of Black Mesa), 214
Nez, John (of Tohatchi), 179
Nightway, 269*n*22
Notah, Tseche, 224

Old Man Hat, 56, 87, 126
Oñate, Juan de, 63, 108
O'Neill, Colleen, xviii, 226
Oraibi Wash, 51
oral traditions, 69–70, 74; dynamism of, 67–68, 74, 268*n*13; as history, 70. *See also* creation stories
origin story. *See* Blessingway; creation stories; Moving Up Way
outfit. *See* land use community
overgrazing, 5, 142–43, 196; Diné response to, 58; effects of, 24, 37, 47, 59, 125, 140–41; and fire frequency, 140; in forests, 140; indicators of, 35, 44–45, 48, 130–31, 142–43, 228–29; in New Mexico, 130; observations of (pre-1933), 33–34, 130–31, 138, 191; perceptions of, by Diné, 58–59, 150, 171, 172, 210, 236; perceptions of, by soil conservationists, 35, 38–39, 41–47, 150; in western U.S., 230, 332*n*9. *See also* carrying capacity; grazing; range conditions

Paiutes, 91
Palmer, Paul, 314*n*10
Paquette, Peter, 95, 137
Parman, Donald, xvi–xvii, 29
pastoralism: beginnings of, 105, 112–13, 115–17, 120, 285–86*n*13, 291*n*42; success of, 131, 230
Patterson, S. S., 136
peyotism. *See* Native American Church
Picuris pueblo, 112
Pinchot, Gifford, 36
place names, 54
plants. *See* grasses; vegetation; weeds
Plummer, E. H., 44
Polacca Wash, 138
Pollock, Floyd, 223
Post, William, 155, 156–57, 159
power relations, 80–81, 273*n*6; and Anglo-American ranchers, 233, 242–43; and Collier, 166, 181, 183–84, 233; and federal authority, 210, 212–13, 216, 218–19, 233–35; and memories of Hwéeldi, 22; and women, 81–82, 83–84, 99, 226–27
prairie dogs, 155, 316*n*29
Presley, Kelsey, 186
Preston, Scott, 214
Province, John, 32, 51–52
pueblitos. *See* fortresses
Puebloan people: encroachment of Diné on, 118, 119; relationships with Diné, 110, 113–14, 121; and warfare, 89, 110, 111–12, 121
Puebloan people, ancient. *See* Anasazi
Pueblo Bonito, 45
Pueblo Colorado Wash, 42
pueblo refugees, 111, 113–14, 289–90*n*35
Pueblo Revolt, 111
Pynes, Patrick, 243

Radcliffe-Brown, A. R., 51, 53
Rael de Aguilar, Alfonzo, 112
raiding, 110–11, 119–20
railroad. *See* Atlantic and Pacific Railroad

Rainbow Plateau, 91
Ramah, New Mexico, 161
range conditions, 35, 220–21; pre-1933, 33–34, 38, 42, 44, 130–31; scientific assumptions about, 38–39, 41–43, 44–49; in western U.S., 34, 44. *See also* Navajo Country; overgrazing
range management: cooperative conservation plans, 51–52, 234; demonstration projects, 34, 49, 189–91; grass banks, 241; to modernize ranching, 196–97, 200–201; plans, 51–52; scientific, 35–36, 195–99, 237–38; traditional, 125, 126, 195–96, 197, 198–99. *See also* land management units; soil conservation program; transhumance
Ranger, Terence, 69, 70
range riders, 211, 216, 217, 218, 317n35
range studies. *See* Soil Conservation Service
Red Shirt's Wife, 194
Reichard, Gladys, 52–53, 87, 94, 99, 264n72, 273n7
religious beliefs, 54–56, 236–37. *See also* ceremonies; creation stories
resistance movement, 29, 167–68, 203, 209–12, 218–19; and fencing, 190–91; and goat reduction, 175, 179; and Navajo Rights Association, 217–18; petition drives, 211–12, 213; and violence, 211, 218, 221; and women, 167, 171–72, 179, 202–3, 212, 214, 221. *See also* memories
Rice, Josiah, 258n28
Rio de Los Piños, 110
Rio Grande, 73
Riordan, Denis, 33
rituals, 65, 73, 76, 124, 269n22; livestock songs, 56, 77, 98, 218. *See also* ceremonies

River Junction Curley (Curly Tó 'Aheedlíinii), 64, 75
Robinson, H. F., 138
Roessel, Ruth, xvii
Roosevelt, Eleanor, 214

sacred mountains, 125, 270n25; in creation stories, 68, 71, 76; and cultural identity, 64; map of, 62
Saenz de Garvisu, Manuel, 116
Salt, John, 325n47
Sampson, Arthur W., 333n29
sand dunes, 47–48
Sandoval, Albert, 172–73, 239
San Francisco Peaks (Dook'o'oosłííd), 71
San Ildefonso pueblo, 111
San Juan-Chama Project, 185
San Juan County Board of Supervisors, 314n10
San Juan pueblo, 111, 112
San Juan River, 24, 73, 110, 188
San Juan River valley, 109, 111
San Mateo Mountains, 118, 119
Santa Clara pueblo, 111
Santa Fe Pacific Railroad. *See* Atlantic and Pacific Railroad
Sargent, Edward, 145–46, 161, 186, 201
Schaafsma, Curtis F., 285–86n13
Scharff, Virginia, xvii
Schneider, F. L., 155
science: as social construction, 33, 36, 231, 240–41. *See also* ecology; nature; Soil Conservation Service; stories, narration of
scientific debates, 45–46, 47–49, 52–53
Seally, Kit, 217
Sells, Cato, 144
Senate, Committee on Indian Affairs: hearings, 159–63, 186–87
Sheen, Pete, 8–9

sheep, 141; churras, 191–95, 318n55; and cultural identity, 64, 75–78, 269n22; improved-breeding program, 189–90, 191–95. *See also* livestock

sheep dipping, 95–96, 137–38, 208; and assignment to land management units, 200; and erosion, 155; and grazing permits, 205, 207

Sheep Is Life, 244

sheep reduction. *See* livestock reduction

sheep units, 204

Sherman, William Tecumseh, 73

Shevky, Eshref, 50–51

Shipley, David, 136

Shiprock, 219

Shirley, Jim, 165, 171, 236

Shonto Trading Post, 225

shrub grasslands, 3

Shukry, Laila, 226

Simpson, James, 38–39, 44, 138

Slim Judge, 96

Slim Man, 97

Snow, Milton, 39, 41, 42, 43, 259n33

soil conservation program, 229, 231; demonstration projects, 35, 49, 189–91, 196, 238; Diné opposition to, 190–91, 197; Diné support for, 190; failure of, xv, 7–8, 9–11, 229; limitations on Checkerboard, 189; proposed, 164. *See also* land management units; livestock reduction; overgrazing; range management

Soil Conservation Service, 35; Emergency Conservation Work program, 35–36, 165–66, 168, 189; on Navajo erosion problem, 34–35; perceptions of overgrazing, 35, 142; range studies, 35–36, 49, 197–98, 220–21. *See also* Navajo Service; soil conservation program

Soil Erosion Service. *See* Soil Conservation Service

Son of Old Man Hat. *See* Left Handed

Southwestern Range and Sheep Breeding Laboratory, 194–95

Spanish: *entrada*, 108; introduction of livestock, 63, 111; land grants, 119, 315n25; observations of Navajos, 109, 111–12, 116, 118, 120; observations of unknown natives, 106–7, 108; and warfare, 89, 111–12, 121

Spanish Reconquest, 113

Spicer, Edward, 233

Stacher, S. F., 144, 158

Steamboat Demonstration Project, 190

Stewart, James: and goat reduction, 172–73, 177; and grazing regulations, 221; on land management units, 200; on soil conservation program, 168, 170–71

stories, narration of, 32–33, 36–38, 41–43, 46, 53, 57, 59. *See also* oral traditions

Tafoya, Juan, 116

Tafoya, Rick, 5

Taliman, Henry, 168, 171

Tall Chanter (Hataałii Nez), 71, 74, 269–70n23, 271n36, 275–76n20

Tall Woman ('Asdzą́ą́ Nez, aka Rose Mitchell, of Chinle), 86, 88, 105, 210

Tamaron y Romeral, Pedro, 118

Taos pueblo, 112

Taylor, Dorceta, xix

Taylor Grazing Act, 34, 188–89, 227, 233, 242–43

Teec Nos Pos, 219, 221

Teeł Ch'ínít'i' (Cat Tails Come Out), 243

Tesuque pueblo, 112

Thomas, Elmer, 159, 186

Thornthwaite, C. Warren, 45–46, 47, 261n46

INDEX 389

Tingley, Clyde, 185
Tovrea Packing Company, 174
trading posts, 99, 100, 101, 146, 147–48; and Diné poverty, 176–77, 225; and livestock policy (pre-1933), 132; and livestock reduction program, 167; and ranching, 145, 147, 148; records of, 96
traditions. *See* cultural traditions; oral traditions
transhumance, 31–32, 58, 105, 197–99, 230; beginnings of, 122, 124–26; and cultural identity, 64; government views of, 156, 200; value of, 106, 134. *See also* mobility
Treaty of 1868, 22, 132, 135
tree-ring data, 43, 46–47, 139, 283*n*6
Tsosie, Rachel, 212

Ulibarí, Antonio de, 112
ungulate irruption theory. *See* ecology
usufruct rights. *See* land tenure
Utes, 108, 113, 119; and the Carson campaign, 90, 132; and warfare, 89, 117, 118, *123*

Vandever, C. E., 135–36
Vansina, Jan, 67
Van Valkenburgh, Richard, 176, 177
vegetation, 54; cliffrose (*Cowania mexicana*), 141; deerbriar (*Ceanothus fendleri*), 141; forbs, 10; four-wing saltbush (*Atriplex canescens*), 4, 75, 130, 141, 195; greasewood (*Sarcobatus vermiculatus*), 4, 6, 57, 59, 130; juniper (*Juniperus* spp.), 35, 141; Mormon tea (*Ephedra trifurca*), 75, 130; piñon (*Pinus edulis*), 141; ponderosa pines (*Pinus ponderosa*), 43, 138–39, 140; rabbitbrush (*Chrysothamnus nauseosa*), 48, 59, 143; sagebrush (*Artemisia tridentata*), 4, 35, 38, 39, 75, 134, 141; shadscale (*Atriplex confertifolia*), 4, 130, 141; winterfat (*Ceratoides lanata*), 141. *See also* ecology; grasses; weeds
vegetation change, 134, 138, 140, 142–43, 221, 229–30
Vélez Cachupín, Thomas, 118

Walker, C. L., 158
warfare: with pueblos, 89, 110, 111–12; with Spanish, 89, 111–12, 113, 120, 121; with Utes and Comanches, 113, 117
Warner, Boyd, 206
water, development of, 156–57, 161, 170, 191
weaving, 99–100, 193–95; problems with short-staple wool, 194; symbolic meanings of, 100–101. *See also* women
Weber, Anselm, 144, 150, 223
weeds: bugseed (*Corispermum americanum*), 130; cockleburr (*Xanthium strumarium*), 130; globemallow (*Sphaeralcea cuspidata*), 134; golden crownbeard (*Verbesina encelioides*), 130; as indicators of overgrazing, 130–31, 228, 229–30; locoweed (*Astragalus* and *Oxytropis* spp.), 59, 143; medicinal value of, 59; pigweed (*Amaranthaceae* sp.), 59; Russian thistle (*Salsola iberica*), 143, 150, 228; snakeweed (*Gutierrezia sarothrae*), 35, 41, 59, 143, 150, 191, 228; sneezeweed (*Helenium hoopesii*), 143; sunflowers (*Helianthus annuus*), 57, 59, 130; woolly plantain (*Plantago patagonica*), 134. *See also* overgrazing; range conditions; vegetation change
Westbrook, I. K., 186
Wheeler, Burton, 159, 160, 162
Wheeler-Howard Act. *See* Indian Reorganization Act

Whipple, A. W., 258*n*29
White, Richard, xvii, 29, 235, 252*n*20
White Goat, Mrs., 175
Whiteman Killer, 91, 218
Wide Belt Mesa, 75
Wilbur, Ray, 156
Wilcox, David, 284*n*10
Witherspoon, Gary, 124
Woehlke, Walter, 45, 204
women: and allotments on Checkerboard, 144–45; attitudes toward Collier, 223; and autonomy, 79–80, 82, 94, 167, 209, 226–27; and cultural traditions, 67; and divorce, 92–93; and economy, 81–82, 99–101; and grazing permits, 209, 222; and land tenure, 80, 94, 144–45; and livestock ownership, 94–96, 97, 146, 209; and livestock reduction, 9, 18, 175, 177, 179, 202–3, 204; and power, 80–81, 83–84, 99, 226–27; and range management, 196; and rape, 318*n*60; and suffrage, 101–2; and symbolic relationship with livestock, 18, 98–99, 102, 280*n*65; and symbolic relationship with earth, 54, 236, 280*n*65; as weavers, 99–100, 112, 115, 120, 177, 194, 227. *See also* clans; gender; matricentered society; matrilocality; resistance movement; weaving
Wooton, E. O., 128, 130–31, 138, 199

Yaa Diibaa', 95
Yah Bah, 206
Yellow Hair, 147
Yellowman, Jake, 217
Yił Deezbaa', 212
Youngblood, Robert, 178, 194

Zárate Salmeron, Fr. Gerónimo de, 109
Zeh, William, 155, 219, 223; and conservation program, 173–74; erosion study, 34, 150; and goat reduction, 25, 173–76
Zuni Mountains, 42, 125
Zuni Mountains Cattle Company, 259*n*33
Zuni pueblo, 118, 121

WEYERHAEUSER ENVIRONMENTAL BOOKS

The Natural History of Puget Sound Country by Arthur R. Kruckeberg

Forest Dreams, Forest Nightmares: The Paradox of Old Growth in the Inland West by Nancy Langston

Landscapes of Promise: The Oregon Story, 1800–1940 by William G. Robbins

The Dawn of Conservation Diplomacy: U.S.-Canadian Wildlife Protection Treaties in the Progressive Era by Kurkpatrick Dorsey

Irrigated Eden: The Making of an Agricultural Landscape in the American West by Mark Fiege

Making Salmon: An Environmental History of the Northwest Fisheries Crisis by Joseph E. Taylor III

George Perkins Marsh, Prophet of Conservation by David Lowenthal

Driven Wild: How the Fight against Automobiles Launched the Modern Wilderness Movement by Paul S. Sutter

The Rhine: An Eco-Biography, 1815–2000 by Mark Cioc

Where Land and Water Meet: A Western Landscape Transformed by Nancy Langston

The Nature of Gold: An Environmental History of the Alaska/Yukon Gold Rush by Kathryn Morse

Faith in Nature: Environmentalism as Religious Quest by Thomas R. Dunlap

Landscapes of Conflict: The Oregon Story, 1940–2000 by William G. Robbins

The Lost Wolves of Japan by Brett L. Walker

Wilderness Forever: Howard Zahniser and the Path to the Wilderness Act by Mark Harvey

On the Road Again: Montana's Changing Landscape by William Wyckoff

Public Power, Private Dams: The Hells Canyon High Dam Controversy by Karl Boyd Brooks

Windshield Wilderness: Cars, Roads, and Nature in Washington's National Parks by David Louter

Native Seattle: Histories from the Crossing-Over Place by Coll Thrush

The Country in the City: The Greening of the San Francisco Bay Area by Richard A. Walker

Drawing Lines in the Forest: Creating Wilderness Areas in the Pacific Northwest by Kevin R. Marsh

Plowed Under: Agriculture and Environment in the Palouse
   by Andrew P. Duffin
Making Mountains: New York City and the Catskills by David Stradling
The Fishermen's Frontier: People and Salmon in Southeast Alaska
   by David F. Arnold
Shaping the Shoreline: Fisheries and Tourism on the Monterey Coast
   by Connie Y. Chiang
Dreaming of Sheep in Navajo Country by Marsha Weisiger

WEYERHAEUSER ENVIRONMENTAL CLASSICS

The Great Columbia Plain: A Historical Geography, 1805–1910
   by D. W. Meinig
*Mountain Gloom and Mountain Glory: The Development of the Aesthetics
   of the Infinite* by Marjorie Hope Nicolson
Tutira: The Story of a New Zealand Sheep Station by Herbert Guthrie-Smith
*A Symbol of Wilderness: Echo Park and the American Conservation
   Movement* by Mark Harvey
Man and Nature: Or, Physical Geography as Modified by Human Action
   by George Perkins Marsh; edited and annotated by David Lowenthal
Conservation in the Progressive Era: Classic Texts edited by David Stradling
DDT, Silent Spring, and the Rise of Environmentalism: Classic Texts
   edited by Thomas R. Dunlap

CYCLE OF FIRE BY STEPHEN J. PYNE

Fire: A Brief History
World Fire: The Culture of Fire on Earth
*Vestal Fire: An Environmental History, Told through Fire,
   of Europe and Europe's Encounter with the World*
Fire in America: A Cultural History of Wildland and Rural Fire
Burning Bush: A Fire History of Australia
The Ice: A Journey to Antarctica

MARSHA WEISIGER, associate professor of history at New Mexico State University, is the author of *Land of Plenty: Oklahomans in the Cotton Fields of Arizona, 1933–1942*. She received the Angie Debo Prize in the History of the American Southwest and was a finalist for the Oklahoma Book Award, Oklahoma Center for the Book, 1996.